1983 SUPPLEMENT

Cases and Materials on

CONSTITUTIONAL LAW

Tenth Edition

Cases and Materials on

INDIVIDUAL RIGHTS IN CONSTITUTIONAL LAW

Third Edition

By
GERALD GUNTHER
William Nelson Cromwell Professor of Law,
Stanford University

1983 SUPPLEMENT
By
GERALD GUNTHER
and
FREDERICK SCHAUER
Cutler Professor of Law
College of William and Mary

Mineola, New York
THE FOUNDATION PRESS, INC.
1983

PREFACE

This Supplement covers the major constitutional developments since July 1980, when the principal casebooks went to press. It includes full treatment through the Supreme Court session that ended on July 6, 1983. As usual, the Supplement traces developments in Congress as well as on the Court. July 6, 1983 is also the cut-off date for congressional action, although that date is in a sense arbitrary in a way that the last day of a Supreme Court Term is not.

In indicating the places in the casebooks at which these supplementary materials are to be inserted, the following abbreviations are used:

10th ED.—Cases and Materials on Constitutional Law (Tenth Edition)

IND. RTS.—Cases and Materials on Individual Rights in Constitutional Law (Third Edition)

The addition of a new name on this Supplement should be no cause for alarm. Although it would be neither possible nor desirable to keep my own perspectives, biases, and foibles from influencing my contribution, there has been no change in the basic approach to the organization or to individual materials. In order that blame may properly be allocated, however, it should be mentioned that additions to and changes from the previous Supplement have all been made by the undersigned.

I want to thank three extremely able student assistants, Cary Dier, Bob Muilenberg, and Tim Shelly, all students at the Marshall-Wythe School of Law, College of William and Mary, for taking on the challenging and the tedious with equal diligence and enthusiasm. I have also benefited greatly from working on this Supplement in the company of colleagues who were a constant source of discussion, advice, inspiration, and, perhaps most importantly, diversion. Finally, I owe special thanks to the Justices of the Supreme Court, whose willingness to decide many of this Term's important cases early in the session gave unwitting and sorely needed help to a neophyte Supplement-writer.

FREDERICK SCHAUER

Williamsburg, Virginia
July, 1983

*

TABLE OF CONTENTS

Numbers on the left indicate where the new materials fit into the casebooks.
Cases and legislative materials set out at length are in **bold face**.

CHAPTER 6. INTERGOVERNMENTAL IMMUNITIES AND INTERSTATE RELATIONSHIPS

CHAPTER 7. SEPARATION OF POWERS

CHAPTER 11.   THE POST–CIVIL WAR AMENDMENTS
AND CIVIL RIGHTS LEGISLATION

TABLE OF CONTENTS

CHAPTER 12. FREEDOM OF EXPRESSION: BASIC THEMES

CHAPTER 13.   FREEDOM OF EXPRESSION:
ADDITIONAL PROBLEMS

CHAPTER 14.   THE CONSTITUTION AND RELIGION

CHAPTER 15. PROPER CONDITIONS FOR CONSTITUTIONAL ADJUDICATION

APPENDIX A.   TABLE OF JUSTICES

APPENDIX B.   THE U. S. CONSTITUTION

*

TABLE OF CASES

(Cases set out at length are in italic type. All other cases are in roman type. References are to pages.)

*

1983 SUPPLEMENT

Cases and Materials on
CONSTITUTIONAL LAW
Tenth Edition

Cases and Materials on
INDIVIDUAL RIGHTS IN CONSTITUTIONAL LAW
Third Edition

*

Chapter 1

THE NATURE AND SOURCES OF THE
SUPREME COURT'S AUTHORITY

10th ED. and IND. RTS., p. 57
Add to footnote † :

Senator Helms' prediction proved correct: the Helms Amendment to strip the federal courts of jurisdiction in school prayer cases died in the House when the 96th Congress adjourned in 1980. But the jurisdiction-stripping drive reemerged with added momentum in the 97th Congress in 1981 and 1982, as the next addition indicates.

10th ED. and IND. RTS., p. 57
Add after Note 4e:

f. *Efforts to curb the Supreme Court's appellate jurisdiction, 1981–83.* In the 97th Congress which convened in 1981, proposals to eliminate the Supreme Court's appellate jurisdiction in specified categories of cases attracted more attention than they had in years. By late May of 1981, for example, 23 court-curbing proposals had been introduced in the House and 4 in the Senate. Senator Hatch's Subcommittee on the Constitution of the Senate Judiciary Committee held extensive hearings on the constitutionality and desirability of the proposals. The proposals would have eliminated the court's appellate jurisdiction in a number of controversial areas, including busing, abortion, and school prayers. At the Subcommittee hearings, there were witnesses strongly supporting or opposing the proposals. But a number of legal scholars testified that such legislation, while constitutional, would be unwise. Professor Paul Bator, for example, stated that, while Congress probably had the "raw power" to limit appellate jurisdiction, "the argument that it would violate the spirit of the [Constitution] to do so seems to me to be extremely powerful." See generally 39 Cong. Quar.Weekly Report 947 (May 30, 1981).

Nothing came of these proposals in 1981, but debate about efforts to curb the Court's appellate jurisdiction surfaced with renewal intensity in 1982. Most attention was focused on Senator Helms' efforts to deal with the school prayer issue by stripping the Supreme Court and the lower federal courts of jurisdiction relating to "voluntary prayers in public schools and public buildings." The Reagan Administration responded at last to the controversy about the legitimacy of the jurisdiction-stripping device when Attorney General William French Smith sent a letter to Senator Strom Thurmond, Chairman of the Senate Judiciary Committee, on May 6, 1982. With respect to the Supreme Court's appellate jurisdiction, the Attorney General concluded that Congress may not, "consistent with the Constitution, make 'exceptions' to Supreme Court jurisdiction which would intrude upon the core functions of the Supreme Court as an independent and equal branch in our system of separation of powers." With respect to lower court jurisdiction, however, he concluded that "Congress may, within constraints imposed by provisions of the Constitution other than Article III, limit the jurisdiction or remedial authority of the inferior federal courts." *

Senator Helms' efforts to strip the Supreme Court and the lower federal courts of jurisdiction to hear "voluntary" school prayer cases failed in the 97th Congress. Late in the summer of 1982, Senators Baucus, Packwood, and Weicker led a small group in the Senate who successfully filibustered against a school prayer amendment that Senator Helms sought to attach to a measure raising the public debt ceiling. A Helms motion to invoke cloture (thus limiting debate) was rejected 53–45, and a subsequent motion to strip the school prayer amendment from the debt ceiling bill was approved 79–16. Opponents of the school prayer legislation focused the Senate debate on its constitutionality and potential effect on the judicial system. Addressing the latter point, Senator Baucus argued that stripping the Supreme Court of jurisdiction to hear a particular class of constitutional cases would inevitably result in the same provision of the Constitution meaning something different in each of the fifty states. Constitutional guarantees would be truncated and weakened and the federal system damaged. See Cong.Rec. S 11610–11620 (daily ed. Sept. 16, 1982) (statement of Sen. Baucus).

Senator Helm's proposal to strip the Supreme Court and the lower Federal courts of school prayer jurisdiction has been re-introduced in the 98th Congress. Versions of his proposal have been referred to the House and Senate Judiciary Committees. There is no significant momentum behind these proposals in the 98th Congress, however, largely because many school prayer supporters have shifted their efforts to the attempt to amend the Constitution to permit voluntary school prayers. See the addition to 10th Ed., p. 1560; Ind.Rts., p. 1180. It is thus quite unlikely that either committee or the full House or Senate will act favorably on the jurisdiction-stripping proposals. No other proposals that would strip the Supreme Court of appellate jurisdiction are currently pending in the 98th Congress.

10th ED. and IND. RTS., p. 60

Add to first paragraph of Note 2:

Note the comments on congressional power to curtail lower federal court jurisdiction in Justice Stewart's majority opinion in Allen v. McCurry, 449 U.S. 90 (1980). The case involved the applicability of collateral estoppel principles to a state prisoner's Civil Rights Act suit. Although the case dealt mainly with 42 U.S.C. § 1983, Justice Stewart also rejected the lower courts' reliance on an alleged "generally framed principle that every person asserting a federal right is entitled to one unencumbered opportunity to litigate that right in a federal district court, regardless of the legal posture in which the federal claim arises." He commented that "the authority for this principle is difficult to discern. It cannot lie in the Constitution, which makes no such

---

* With respect to the problem of curbing lower federal court jurisdiction, the Attorney General referred to his letter of the same date to Chairman Peter Rodino of the House Judiciary Committee regarding S. 951, Senator Johnston's anti-busing proposal, the "Neighborhood School Act of 1982" (approved by the Senate in March 1982). See the additional notes on that letter to Rodino and on S. 951 below, additions to 10th Ed. and Ind. Rts., p. 60, and to 10th Ed., p. 774; Ind.Rts., p. 394.

guarantee, but leaves the scope of the jurisdiction of the federal district courts to the wisdom of Congress." He added: "The only other conceivable basis for finding a universal right to litigate a federal claim in a federal district court is hardly a legal basis at all, but rather a general distrust of the capacity of the state courts to render correct decisions on constitutional issues." He repudiated that contention by relying on earlier decisions that had reaffirmed "the constitutional obligation of the state courts to uphold federal law" and had expressed "confidence in their ability to do so."

10th ED. and IND. RTS., p. 60
Add to the text:

3. *Congressional proposals to curtail lower court jurisdiction, 1981–83:*
a. *The proposed "Human Life Statute".* In 1981, Senator Helms and Congressman Hyde introduced proposals to enact a so-called "Human Life Statute." (the Helms-Hyde bill, S. 158, H.R. 900, 97th Cong., 1st Sess.). Sec. 1 of the bill (printed and discussed below, addition to 10th Ed., p. 1099; Ind.Rts., p. 719) sought to invoke congressional power to implement or modify the Fourteenth Amendment by asserting a finding that there is "a significant likelihood that actual human life exists from conception." The apparent purpose of the bill was to authorize broader state control of abortions and in effect eliminate the restrictions imposed by Roe v. Wade, the 1973 abortion decision.

In addition to that substantive provision, the Helms-Hyde bill also included a jurisdictional section. Sec. 2 stated: "Notwithstanding any other provision of law, no inferior federal court ordained and established by Congress under article III of the Constitution of the United States shall have jurisdiction to issue any restraining order, temporary or permanent injunction, or declaratory judgment in any case involving or arising from any state law or municipal ordinance that (1) protects the rights of human persons between conception and birth, or (2) prohibits, limits, or regulates (a) the performance of abortions, or (b) the provision at public expense of funds, facilities, personnel, or other assistance for the performance of abortions."

On July 9, 1981, Senator East's Subcommittee on the Separation of Powers of the Senate Judiciary Committee approved an amended version of S. 158 by a 3–2 vote. However, further Senate action on the proposal was postponed—in part because one of the Senators in the majority, Senator Hatch, expressed reservations about the bill's constitutionality and indicated that he favored limiting abortions via the constitutional amendment, not the legislative, route. Senator Hatch later introduced an anti-abortion amendment, which was approved by the Senate Judiciary Committee in March 1982, but before the full Senate was to vote on it late in the summer of 1982 Senator Hatch withdrew the amendment. (See addition to 10th Ed., p. 1099; Ind.Rts., p. 719.) The Senate Judiciary Committee took no further action on the Helms-Hyde proposal before the 97th Congress adjourned.

The Helms-Hyde proposal has been re-introduced in the 98th Congress as S. 26, which has been placed on the Senate calendar and awaits floor action. Is § 2 of the Helms-Hyde proposal, the jurisdictional provision, constitutional?   (Note that this provision does *not* curtail Supreme Court appellate jurisdiction—unlike Senator Helms' bill on school prayers (casebook, p. 56), which sought to abolish Supreme Court as well as lower federal court jurisdiction.)

    b. *Anti-busing proposals.* In March 1982, the Senate adopted a proposal by Senator Johnston of Louisiana to curb busing—the Neighborhood School Act of 1982. (See the additional discussion of this act—§ 2 of S. 951—in the addition to 10th Ed., p. 774; Ind.Rts., p. 394.). The proposal would have allowed federal judges to order busing only in narrowly described circumstances. Senator Johnston partly relied on congressional power regarding lower federal court jurisdiction under Art. III, § 1. The House failed to act on the measure before the 97th Congress adjourned and so the proposal did not become law, but consider the opposing views set forth below on the legitimacy of this claim of congressional power under Art. III, § 1.

    Attorney General Smith expressed the position of the Reagan Administration in a letter to Congressman Peter Rodino on May 6, 1982. Having already expressed a very narrow view of congressional power to curb Supreme Court jurisdiction (see addition to 10th Ed. and Ind.Rts., p. 57, above), the Attorney General endorsed the constitutionality of the Art. III-based anti-busing provisions of S. 951. He noted that the bill did "not withdraw jurisdiction from the Supreme Court or limit the jurisdiction of the federal courts to decide a class of cases." Rather, the effect related "only to one aspect of the remedial power of the inferior federal courts—not unlike the Norris-LaGuardia Act, enacted in 1932." In his discussion of Art. III, he argued that the bill had only a "limited effect on the courts' remedial power" and that it seemed "a necessary inference" from the Framer's decision to leave the creation of inferior federal courts to the discretion of Congress "that, once created, the scope of the courts' jurisdiction was also discretionary." Nor did he think that any Fifth Amendment limitations would curb that exercise of Art. III, § 1 power, since the provisions "neither create a racial classification nor evidence a discriminatory purpose." (Compare the Court's subsequent decision on *state* efforts to restrict busing, noted below, addition to 10th Ed., p. 773; Ind.Rts., p. 393.) As noted below (addition to 10th Ed., p. 774; Ind.Rts., p. 394), the Attorney General also suggested that the provision might be justified under § 5 of the Fourteenth Amendment.

    While agreeing that efforts to restrict lower court actions stand on a different constitutional footing than efforts to restrict the Supreme Court, Senator Thomas Eagleton has otherwise taken issue with Attorney General Smith's opinion. He argues that the practical and legal *adequacy* of the remaining remedies is crucial to the constitutional validity of the congressional restrictions on court-ordered busing. In those cases where busing is the only practical remedy, its denial "would be invalid either as an impermissible congressional interference with the essentials of the independent judicial function or as a violation of the provisions of the Constitution outside of the Article III power (e.g., Due Process), which constrain legislative action, the statute provides that "[r]easonable exemptions to the provisions of

Won . . . But Will We Survive the War?," 39 J.Mo.Bar. 113, 119 (1983) (footnotes omitted).

S. 139, a bill "to provide for civil rights in public schools," is pending in the 98th Congress. It prohibits any lower federal court from ordering the assignment or transportation to any school, or the exclusion therefrom, of any student on the basis of race, color, or national origin. S. 139 partly relies on congressional power under Art. III, § 1. Is the proposal constitutional under Attorney General Smith's analysis? Under Senator Eagleton's?

10th ED. and IND. RTS., p. 66
Add to footnote ** :

An unusual approach to Supreme Court review of state court judgments on federal issues was advocated in Justice Stevens' dissent in Minnesota v. Clover Leaf Creamery Co., 449 U.S. 456 (1981). The case involved an equal protection challenge to a Minnesota environmental law which banned the sale of milk in plastic nonreturnable containers, but permitted such sale in other nonreturnable containers such as paperboard cartons. In sustaining the challengers' claim, the state courts reexamined the conflicting empirical data before the legislature and concluded that the law was not rationally related to the State's purposes. The Court reversed, finding that the state courts had exercised unduly intrusive scrutiny of legislative judgments.

But Justice Stevens argued in dissent that federal review of the case should have been confined to a determination of whether the state courts had articulated the proper federal equal protection standard (which, in his view, they had). He contended that regulation of the relationship between the state courts and the state legislature was beyond federal judicial authority. In his view, the Court lacked power to assert that "it is not the function of a *state court* to substitute its evaluation of legislative facts for that of a state legislature."

Justice Stevens emphasized that "the allocation of functions within the structure of a state government [is] a matter for the State to determine. I know of nothing in the Federal Constitution that prohibits a State from giving lawmaking power to its courts. Nor is there anything in the Federal Constitution that prevents a state court from reviewing factual determinations made by a state legislature or any other state agency. [The] functions that a state court shall perform within the structure of state government are unquestionably matters of state law. [The] factual conclusions drawn by the Minnesota courts concerning the deliberations of the Minnesota Legislature are entitled to just as much deference as if they had been drafted by the State Legislature itself and incorporated in a preamble to the state statute. The State of Minnesota has told us in unambiguous language that this statute is not rationally related to any environmental objective; it seems to me to be a matter of indifference, for purposes of applying the Federal Equal Protection Clause, whether that message to us from the State of Minnesota is conveyed by the State Supreme Court, or by the State Legislature itself."

Justice Brennan's majority opinion vehemently rejected Justice Stevens' approach: "[His] argument, though novel, is without merit. A state court may, of course, apply a more stringent standard of review as a matter of state law under the State's equivalent to the Equal Protection or Due Process Clauses. [But] when a state court reviews state legislation challenged as violative of the Fourteenth Amendment, it is not free to impose greater restrictions as a matter of federal constitutional law than this Court has imposed. Oregon v. Hass, 420 U.S. 714 (1975). The standard of review under Equal Protection rationality analysis—without regard to which branch of the state government has made the legislative judgment—is governed by federal constitutional law, and a state court's application of that standard is fully reviewable in this Court." [See also the additional notes on this case below (additions to 10th Ed., p. 704; Ind.Rts., p. 324, and to 10th Ed., p. 339).]

10th ED. and IND. RTS., p. 70
Add as footnote to Note 1b:

As the Court's workload continues to increase (4,456 cases disposed of in the October 1981 Term), so too has the number of summary dispositions increased. It is not surprising, therefore, that the Court has reemphasized that summary dispositions are to be given only very limited weight. See Anderson v. Celebrezze, 460 U.S. —— (1983), quoted below on this point, addition to 10th Ed., p. 1673 ; Ind.Rts., p. 1293.

10th ED. and IND. RTS., p. 72
Add as footnote at end of Note 2b:

Opinions dissenting from denials of certiorari are of course common, but Justice Stevens has recently written several opinions *justifying* the denial of certiorari. See Castorr v. Brundage, 459 U.S. —— (1982) (Opinion of Stevens, J., respecting the denial of certiorari); McCray v. New York, 461 U.S. —— (1983) (same). In McCray the issue was the constitutionality of permitting prosecutors to use their peremptory challenges to exclude members of a particular racial group from a jury. Justice Stevens, joined by Justices Blackmun and Powell, felt that "it is a sound exercise of discretion for the Court to allow the various States to serve as laboratories in which the issue receives further study before it is addressed by this Court."

10th ED. and IND. RTS., p. 76
Add before "Transitional Note":

4. *Self-help by the Court.* The Court's concern about its caseload continued to grow in 1983, and it took new steps to reduce the size of its docket by discouraging frivolous litigation. In an unprecedented action the Court invoked Supreme Court Rule 49.2 to award to the respondents in Tatum v. Regents of Nebraska-Lincoln, 462 U.S. —— (1983), $500.00 to be paid by the petitioner as "appropriate damages" for filing a "frivolous" petition for certiorari. Earlier in the Term the Court had unanimously denied three separate motions for leave to proceed in forma pauperis, thus refusing to waive the appropriate filing fees. Chief Justice Burger had urged that Rule 49.2 sanctions be imposed in two of those cases, and Justices Rehnquist and O'Connor would have imposed the sanctions in all three. And in In re Bose, 462 U.S. —— (1983), Chief Justice Burger again took a stand against frivolous appeals by dissenting from an attorney's admission to the Supreme Court Bar. The Chief Justice noted that the attorney's confessed purpose in seeking admission was to relitigate an action the lower court had already determined to be unreasonable and vexatious. The Chief Justice feared that the attorney's admission would "implicitly bless" such litigation and dilute the value of imposing sanctions "against counsel whose record manifests unprofessional conduct. [This Court is not the place for] laundering a judicial reprimand."

Chapter 3

THE COMMERCE POWER

10th ED., p. 195
Add after National League of Cities:

HODEL v. VIRGINIA SURFACE MIN. & RECL. ASS'N

452 U.S. 264, 101 S.Ct. 2352, 69 L.Ed.2d 1 (1981).

Justice MARSHALL delivered the opinion of the Court.

These cases arise out of a pre-enforcement challenge to the constitutionality of the Surface Mining Control and Reclamation Act of 1977. [The

District Court] declared several central provisions of the Act unconstitutional. [In] these appeals, we consider whether Congress, in adopting the Act, exceeded its powers under the Commerce Clause of the Constitution, or transgressed affirmative limitations on the exercise of that power contained in the Fifth and Tenth Amendments. We conclude that in the context of a facial challenge, the Surface Mining Act does not suffer from any of these alleged constitutional defects, and we uphold the Act as constitutional.

I. A. The Surface Mining Act is a comprehensive statute designed to "establish a nationwide program to protect society and the environment from the adverse effects of surface coal mining operations." [T]he Secretary of the Interior [is] charged with primary responsibility for administering and implementing the Act. [Section 501] establishes a two-stage program for the regulation of surface coal mining, an initial, or interim regulatory phase, and a subsequent, permanent phase. The interim program mandates immediate promulgation and federal enforcement of some of the Act's environmental protection performance standards, complemented by continuing state regulation. Under the permanent phase, a regulatory program is to be adopted for each State, mandating compliance with the full panoply of federal performance standards, with enforcement responsibility lying with either the State or Federal Government.

Section 501(a) directs the Secretary to promulgate regulations establishing an interim regulatory program during which mine operators will be required to comply with some of the Act's performance standards. [Included] among those selected standards are requirements governing: (a) restoration of land after mining to its prior condition; (b) restoration of land to its approximate original contour; (c) segregation and preservation of topsoil; (d) minimization of disturbance to the hydrologic balance; (e) construction of coal mine waste piles used as dams and embankments; (f) revegetation of mined areas; and (g) soil disposal.

The Secretary is responsible for enforcing the interim regulatory program. A federal enforcement and inspection program is to be established for each State, and is to remain in effect until a permanent regulatory program is implemented in the State. [The] States are [not] required to enforce the

7

interim regulatory standards and, until the permanent phase of the program, the Secretary may not cede the Federal Government's independent enforcement role to States that wish to conduct their own regulatory programs.

Section 501(b) directs the Secretary to promulgate regulations establishing a permanent regulatory program incorporating all the Act's performance standards. [T]hese regulations do not become effective in a particular State until either a permanent state program, submitted and approved in accordance with § 503 of the Act, or a permanent federal program for the State, adopted in accordance with § 504, is implemented.

Under § 503, any State wishing to assume permanent regulatory authority over the surface coal mining operations on "non-Federal lands" within its borders must submit a proposed permanent program to the Secretary for his approval. The proposed program must demonstrate that the state legislature has enacted laws implementing the environmental protection standards established by the Act and accompanying regulations, and that the State has the administrative and technical ability to enforce these standards. The Secretary must approve or disapprove each such proposed program in accordance with time schedules and procedures established by [the Act].[1] In addition, the Secretary must develop and implement a federal permanent program for each State that fails to submit or enforce a satisfactory state program. In such situations, the Secretary constitutes the regulatory authority administering the Act within that State and continues as such unless and until a "state program" is approved.* . . .

B. [This] challenge [was] directed at the sections of the Act establishing the interim regulatory program. [The] District Court [held] several central provisions of the Act unconstitutional. The court rejected plaintiffs' Commerce Clause, equal protection, and substantive due process challenges to the Act. The court held, however that the Act " 'operates to displace the States' freedom to structure integral operations in numerous areas of traditional functions,' and, therefore, is in contravention of the Tenth Amendment." [Quoting National League of Cities.] The court also ruled that various provisions of the Act effect an uncompensated taking of private property [and] agreed with plaintiffs' due process challenges to some of the Act's enforcement provisions. . . .

1. [With] the exception of Alaska, Georgia, and Washington, all States in which surface mining is either conducted or is expected to be conducted submitted proposed state programs to the Secretary by March 3, 1980. The Secretary has made his initial decisions on these programs. Three programs were approved, eight were approved on condition that the States agree to some modifications, 10 were approved in part and disapproved in part, and three were disapproved because the state legislatures had failed to enact the necessary implementing statutes. Virginia's program was among those approved in part and dis-

approved in part. [A] State may revise a plan that has been disapproved in whole or in part and resubmit it to the Secretary within 60 days of his initial decision. [Footnote by Justice Marshall.]

* Contrast the scheme in this case (direct federal enforcement if a State does not adopt an approved plan) with that in EPA v. Brown [footnote *, 10th Ed., p. 195] (States *compelled* to enforce federal standards if they do not adopt an approved plan of their own). (Compare the 1982 decision in FERC v. Mississippi, which follows.)

II. [A]ppellees [plaintiffs] argue [that] the Act's principal goal is regulating the use of private lands within the borders of the States and not, as the District Court found, regulating the interstate commerce effects of surface coal mining. Consequently, [they] contend that the ultimate issue presented is "whether land *as such* is subject to regulation under the Commerce Clause, i.e., whether land can be regarded as being 'in commerce.' " In urging us to answer "no" to this question, appellees emphasize that the Court has recognized that land-use regulation is within the inherent police powers of the States.

[We] do not accept either appellees' framing of the question or the answer they would have us supply. The task of a court that is asked to determine whether a particular exercise of congressional power is valid under the Commerce Clause is relatively narrow. The court must defer to a congressional finding that a regulated activity affects interstate commerce, if there is any rational basis for such a finding. This established, the only remaining question for judicial inquiry is whether "the means chosen by [Congress] is reasonably adapted to the end permitted by the Constitution." [Heart of Atlanta Motel.] See [Darby; Katzenbach v. McClung]. The judicial task is at an end once the court determines that Congress acted rationally in adopting a particular regulatory scheme.

Judicial review in this area is influenced above all by the fact that the Commerce Clause is a grant of plenary authority to Congress. See [e.g., National League of Cities; Jones & Laughlin; Gibbons v. Ogden; Perez v. United States]. [When] Congress has determined that an activity affects interstate commerce, the courts need inquire only whether the finding is rational. Here, the District Court properly deferred to Congress' express findings, set out in the Act itself, about the effects of surface coal mining on interstate commerce. Section 101(c) recites the congressional finding that "many surface mining operations result in disturbances of surface areas that burden and adversely affect commerce and the public welfare by destroying or diminishing the utility of land for commercial, industrial, residential, recreational, agricultural, and forestry purposes, by causing erosion and landslides, by contributing to floods, by polluting the water, by destroying fish and wildlife habitats, by impairing natural beauty, by damaging the property of citizens, by creating hazards dangerous to life and property, by degrading the quality of life in local communities, and by counteracting governmental programs and efforts to conserve soil, water, and other natural resources."

The legislative record provides ample support for these statutory findings. The Surface Mining Act became law only after 6 years of the most thorough legislative consideration. Committees of both Houses of Congress held extended hearings during which vast amounts of testimony and documentary evidence about the effects of surface mining on our Nation's environment and economy were brought to Congress' attention. Both Committees made detailed findings about these effects and the urgent need for federal legislation to address the problem. [The] Committees also explained that inadequacies in existing state laws and the need for uniform minimum nationwide standards made federal regulations imperative. In light of the evidence available to Congress and the detailed consideration that the legislation received, we cannot say that Congress did not have a rational basis for concluding that surface coal mining has substantial effects on interstate commerce. [Appellees'] contention is that the "rational basis" test should not apply in this case because the Act regulates land use, a local activity not affecting interstate commerce. But even assuming that appellees correctly characterize the land use regulated by the Act as a "local" activity, their argument is unpersuasive.

The denomination of an activity as a "local" or "intrastate" activity does not resolve the question whether Congress may regulate it under the Commerce Clause. [T]he commerce power "extends to those activities intrastate which so affect interstate commerce, or the exertion of the power of Congress over it, as to make regulation of them appropriate means to the attainment of a legitimate end, the effective execution of the granted power to regulate interstate commerce." United States v. Wrightwood Dairy Co. See Fry v. United States; Jones & Laughlin. This Court has long held that Congress may regulate the conditions under which goods shipped in interstate commerce are produced where the "local" activity of producing these goods itself affects interstate commerce. See, e.g., [Darby; Wickard v. Filburn]. Appellees do not dispute that coal is a commodity that moves in interstate commerce. Here, Congress rationally determined that regulation of surface coal mining is necessary to protect interstate commerce from adverse effects that may result from that activity. This congressional finding is sufficient to sustain the Act as a valid exercise of Congress' power under the Commerce Clause.

Moreover, the Act responds to a congressional finding that nationwide "surface mining and reclamation standards are essential in order to insure that competition in interstate commerce among sellers of coal produced in different States will not be used to undermine the ability of the several States to improve and maintain adequate standards on coal mining operations within their borders." The prevention of this sort of destructive interstate competition is a traditional role for congressional action under the Commerce Clause. [See Darby.] Finally, we agree with the lower federal courts that have uniformly found the power conferred by the Commerce Clause broad enough to permit congressional regulation of activities causing air or water pollution, or other environmental hazards that may have effects in more than one State. [Appellees'] essential challenge to the means selected by the Act is that they are redundant or unnecessary. Appellees contend that a variety of federal statutes such as the Clean Air Act, the Flood Control Act, and the Clean Water Act adequately address the federal interest in controlling the environmental effects of surface coal mining without need to resort to the land use regulation scheme of the Surface Mining Act. The short answer to this argument is that the effectiveness of existing laws in dealing with a problem identified by Congress is ordinarily a matter committed to legislative judgment. Congress considered the effectiveness of existing legislation and concluded that additional measures were necessary to deal with the interstate commerce effects of surface coal mining. [W]e agree with the court below that the Act's regulatory scheme is reasonably related to the goals Congress sought to accomplish. . . .

III. The District Court invalidated §§ 515(d) and (e) of the Act, which prescribe performance standards for surface coal mining on "steep-slopes",[2] on the ground that they violate a constitutional limitation on the commerce power imposed by the Tenth Amendment. These provisions require "steep-slope" operators: (i) to reclaim the mined area by completely covering the highwall and returning the site to its "approximate original contour"; (ii) to refrain from dumping spoil material on the downslope below the bench or mining cut; and (iii) to refrain from disturbing land above the highwall unless permitted to do so by the regulatory authority. . . .

The District Court's ruling relied heavily on our decision in National League of Cities. [A]lthough the court acknowledged that the Act "ultimately affects the coal mine operator," it concluded that the Act contravenes the Tenth Amendment because it interferes with the States' "traditional governmental function" of regulating land use. The court held, that, as applied to Virginia, the Act's steep-slope provisions impermissibly constrict the State's ability to make "essential decisions."[3] The court found the Act accomplishes this result "through forced relinquishment of state control of land use planning; through loss of state control of its economy; and through economic harm, from expenditure of state funds to implement the act and from destruction of the taxing power of certain counties, cities, and towns." The court therefore permanently enjoined enforcement of [the steep-slope standards].

[I]n order to succeed, a claim that congressional commerce power legislation is invalid under the reasoning of National League of Cities must satisfy *each* of three requirements. First, there must be a showing that the challenged statute regulates the "States as States." Second, the federal regulation must address matters that are indisputably "attributes of state sovereignty." And third, it must be apparent that the States' compliance with the federal law would directly impair their ability "to structure integral operations in areas of traditional functions."[4] When the Surface Mining Act is examined in light of these principles, it is clear that appellees' Tenth Amendment challenge must fail because the first of the three requirements is not satisfied. The District Court's holding to the contrary rests on an unwarranted extension of the decision in National League of Cities.

[T]he steep-slope provisions [govern] only the activities of coal mine operators who are private individuals and businesses. Moreover, the States

2. Section 515(d)(4) defines a "steep slope" as "any slope above 20 degrees or such lesser slope as may be defined by the regulatory authority after consideration of soil, climate, and other characteristics of a region or State." [Footnote by Justice Marshall.]

3. The court reasoned that although the Act allows a State to elect to have its own regulatory program, the "choice that is purportedly given is no choice at all" because the state program must comply with federally pre-scribed standards. [Footnote by Justice Marshall.]

4. Demonstrating that these three requirements are met does not, however, guarantee that a Tenth Amendment challenge to congressional commerce power action will succeed. There are situations in which the nature of the federal interest advanced may be such that it justifies State submission. See Fry v. United States, reaffirmed in National League of Cities v. Usery. See also id. (Blackmun, J., concurring). [Footnote by Justice Marshall.]

are not compelled to enforce the steep-slope standards, to expend any state funds, or to participate in the federal regulatory program in any manner whatsoever. If a State does not wish to submit a proposed permanent program that complies with the Act and implementing regulations, the full regulatory burden will be borne by the Federal Government. Thus, there can be no suggestion that the Act commandeers the legislative processes of the States by directly compelling them to enact and enforce a federal regulatory program. [EPA v. Brown (see footnote * above) and related cases.] The most that can be said is that the Surface Mining Act establishes a program of cooperative federalism that allows the States, within limits established by federal minimum standards, to enact and administer their own regulatory programs, structured to meet their own particular needs. In this respect, the Act resembles a number of other federal statutes that have survived Tenth Amendment challenges in the lower federal courts.[5]

Appellees argue, however, that the threat of federal usurpation of their regulatory roles coerces the States into enforcing the Surface Mining Act. Appellees also contend that the Act directly regulates the States as States because it establishes mandatory minimum federal standards. In essence, appellees urge us to join the District Court in looking beyond the activities actually regulated by the Act to its conceivable effects on the States' freedom to make decisions in areas of "integral governmental functions." And appellees emphasize, as did the court below, that the Act interferes with the States' ability to exercise their police powers by regulating land use.

Appellees' claims accurately characterize the Act insofar as it prescribes federal minimum standards governing surface coal mining, which a State may either implement itself or else yield to a federally administered regulatory program. To object to this scheme, however, appellees must assume that the Tenth Amendment limits congressional power to pre-empt or displace state regulation of private activities affecting interstate commerce. This assumption is incorrect.

A wealth of precedent attests to congressional authority to displace or pre-empt state laws regulating private activity affecting interstate commerce when these laws conflict with federal law. Moreover, it is clear that the Commerce Clause empowers Congress to prohibit all—and not just inconsistent—state regulation of such activities. Although such congressional enactments obviously curtail or prohibit the States' prerogatives to make legislative choices respecting subjects the States may consider important, the Supremacy Clause permits no other result. . . .

Thus, Congress could constitutionally have enacted a statute prohibiting any state regulation of surface coal mining. We fail to see why the Surface Mining Act should become constitutionally suspect simply because Congress chose to allow the States a regulatory role. [N]othing in National League of

5. See, e.g., United States v. Helsley, 615 F.2d 784 (CA9 1979) (upholding the Airborne Hunting Act); Friends of the Earth, Inc. v. Carey, 552 F.2d 25, 36–39 (CA2), cert. denied, 434 U.S. 902 (1977) (upholding the Clean Air Act); Sierra Club v. EPA, cert. denied, 430 U.S. 959 (1977) (upholding the Clean Water Act). [Footnote by Justice Marshall.]

Cities suggests that the Tenth Amendment shields the States from pre-emptive federal regulation of *private* activities affecting interstate commerce. To the contrary, National League of Cities explicitly reaffirmed the teaching of earlier cases that Congress may, in regulating private activities pursuant to the commerce power, "pre-empt express state-law determinations contrary to the result which has commended itself to the collective wisdom of Congress."

[This] conclusion applies regardless of whether the federal legislation displaces laws enacted under the States' "police powers." The Court long ago rejected the suggestion that Congress invades areas reserved to the States by the Tenth Amendment simply because it exercises its authority under the Commerce Clause in a manner that displaces the States' exercise of their police powers. See [e.g., Hoke v. United States; Darby]. [This] Court has upheld as constitutional any number of federal statutes enacted under the commerce power that pre-empt particular exercises of state police power. It would therefore be a radical departure from long-established precedent for this Court to hold that the Tenth Amendment prohibits Congress from displacing state police power laws regulating private activity. Nothing in National League of Cities compels or even hints at such a departure.[6] In sum, appellees' Tenth Amendment challenge to the Surface Mining Act must fail because here, in contrast to the situation in National League of Cities, the statute at issue regulates only "individuals and businesses necessarily subject to the dual sovereignty of the government of the Nation and the State in which they reside."[7] Accordingly, we turn to the District Court's ruling that the Act contravenes other constitutional limits on congressional action. [Justice Marshall overturned those lower court holdings as well. The ruling that the Act violated the Just Compensation Clause of the Fifth Amendment was set aside because it "suffer[ed] from a fatal deficiency: neither appellees nor the court identified any property in which appellees have an interest that has allegedly been taken by operation of the Act." The rulings that the Act violated procedural due process guarantees in several respects were also set aside, in part on the merits, in part on the ground that the challenge was premature.]

---

6. The remaining justification asserted by the District Court for its Tenth Amendment ruling [is] that the steep-slope mining requirements will harm Virginia's economy and destroy the taxing power of some towns and counties in the Commonwealth. In this regard, the court may have been influenced by the discussion in National League of Cities about the likely effects of the challenged regulations on the finances of State and local governments. But as the Court made clear, the determinative factor in that case was the nature of the federal action, not the ultimate economic impact on the States. Moreover, even if it is true that the Act's requirements will have a measurable impact on Virginia's economy, this kind of effect, standing alone, is insufficient to establish a violation of the Tenth Amendment. . . . [Footnote by Justice Marshall.]

7. We have assumed that the District Court correctly held that land use regulation is an "integral governmental function" as that term was used in National League of Cities. Our resolution of the Tenth Amendment challenge to the Act makes it unnecessary for us to decide whether this is actually the case. [Footnote by Justice Marshall. Compare the 1982 decision in United Transportation Union v. Long Island R. Co., which follows.]

[Rulings of unconstitutionality reversed.] [8]

Justice REHNQUIST, concurring in the judgment.

It is illuminating for purposes of reflection, if not for argument, to note that one of the greatest "fictions" of our federal system is that the Congress exercises only those powers delegated to it, while the remainder are reserved to the States or to the people. The manner in which this Court has construed the Commerce Clause amply illustrates the extent of this fiction. Although it is clear that the people, through the States, *delegated* authority to Congress to "regulate Commerce [among] the several states," one could easily get the sense from this Court's opinions that the federal system exists only at the sufferance of Congress.

As interpreted by the Court, Congress' power under the Commerce Clause is broad indeed. [Justice Rehnquist discussed Darby, the Shreveport Rate Case, Jones & Laughlin, Wickard v. Filburn, and Perez v. United States.] [Despite] the holdings of these cases, and the broad dicta often contained therein, there *are* constitutional limits on the power of Congress to regulate pursuant to the Commerce Clause. As Chief Justice Hughes explained: "Undoubtedly the scope of this power must be considered in light of our dual system of government and may not be extended so as to embrace effects on interstate commerce so indirect and remote that to embrace them, in view of our complex society, would effectually obliterate the distinction between what is national and what is local and create a completely centralized government." [Jones & Laughlin.] [Justice Rehnquist also quoted from Justice Cardozo's separate opinions in the Schechter and Carter cases.]

Thus it would be a mistake to conclude that Congress' power to regulate pursuant to the Commerce Clause is unlimited. Some activities may be so private or local in nature that they simply may not be *in* commerce. Nor is it sufficient that the person or activity reached have *some* nexus with interstate commerce. Our cases have consistently held that the regulated activity must have a *substantial* effect on interstate commerce. E.g., [Jones & Laughlin]. Moreover, simply because Congress may conclude that a particular activity substantially affects interstate commerce does not necessarily make it so.

8. In a concurring notation, Chief Justice BURGER stated: "I agree largely with what Justice Rehnquist has said about the 'fictions' concerning delegation, and the gradual case by case expansion of the reach of the Commerce Clause. I agree fully with his view that we often seem to forget [the] doctrine that laws enacted by Congress under the Commerce Clause must be based on a *substantial* effect on interstate commerce. However, I join the Court's opinion because in it the Court acknowledges and reaffirms that doctrine."

In another concurrence, Justice POWELL stated: "The Surface Mining Act mandates an extraordinarily intrusive program of federal regulation and control of land use and land reclamation, activities normally left to state and local governments. But the decisions of this Court over many years make clear that, under the Commerce Clause, Congress has the power to enact this legislation. The Act could affect seriously the owners and lessees of the land and coal in the seven westernmost counties of Virginia. [I] agree with the Court [that] it is premature to consider in this case questions under the Compensation Clause. [But the] 'taking' issue remains available to, and may be litigated by, any owner or lessee whose property interest is adversely affected by the enforcement of the Act. [I] agree with the Court that we cannot say that the Act is facially invalid, and I therefore join its opinion."

Congress' findings must be supported by a "rational basis" and are reviewable by the courts. Cf. Perez v. United States (Stewart, J., dissenting).[1] In short, unlike the reserved police powers of the States, which are plenary unless challenged as violating some specific provision of the Constitution, the connection with interstate commerce is itself a jurisdictional prerequisite for any substantive legislation by Congress under the Commerce Clause.

In many ways, the Court's opinions in these cases are consistent with that approach. In both the Virginia and Indiana cases,† the Court exhaustively analyzes Congress' articulated justifications for the exercise of its power under the Commerce Clause and concludes that Congress' detailed factual findings as to the effect of surface mining on interstate commerce are sufficient to justify the exercise of that power. Though there can be no doubt that Congress in regulating surface mining has stretched its authority to the "nth degree," our prior precedents compel me to agree with the Court's conclusion. I therefore concur in the judgments of the Court.

There is, however, a troublesome difference between what the Court does and what it says. In both cases, the Court asserts that regulation will be upheld if Congress had a rational basis for finding that the regulated activity affects interstate commerce. The Court takes this statement of the proper "test" from Heart of Atlanta Motel. In my view, the Court misstates the test. As noted above, it has long been established that the commerce power does not reach activity which merely "affects" interstate commerce. There must instead be a showing that regulated activity has a *substantial effect* on that commerce. See [e.g., Jones & Laughlin; Shreveport Rate Case; Wickard v. Filburn]. As recently as Maryland v. Wirtz, Justice Harlan stressed that "Neither here nor in Wickard has the Court declared that Congress may use a relatively trivial impact on commerce as an excuse for broad general regulation of state or private activities." Even in [Heart of Atlanta Motel], in the paragraph just prior to the passage relied on by the Court here, the Court emphasized that Congress had the power to regulate local activities "which might have a substantial and harmful effect upon that commerce." Though I believe the Court errs in its statement of the "test," it may be that I read too much into the Court's choice of language. In the Virginia case, for example, it does mention at one point that Congress did have a "rational basis for concluding that surface coal mining has substantial effects on interstate commerce."

In sum, my difficulty with some of the recent Commerce Clause jurisprudence is that the Court often seems to forget that legislation enacted by Congress is subject to two different kinds of challenge, while that enacted by the States is subject to only one kind of challenge. Neither Congress nor the States may act in a manner prohibited by any provision of the Constitution.

1. Of course, once the power of Congress to regulate is established, the Court will rarely question the manner in which that power is exercised. Within its sphere, of authority, the power of Congress is broad and should only rarely be the subject of judicial invalidation. The question here, in contrast, is whether Congress even has the authority to act. [Footnote by Justice Rehnquist.]

† The Indiana case, a companion case to the one from Virginia, is noted immediately below.

But Congress must bear an additional burden: if challenged as to its authority to act pursuant to the Commerce Clause, Congress must show that its regulatory activity has a substantial effect on interstate commerce. It is my uncertainty as to whether the Court intends to broaden, by some of its language, this test that leads me to concur only in the judgments.

———

HODEL v. INDIANA, 452 U.S. 314 (1981), a companion case to the Virginia Surface Mining case, above, also involved a number of constitutional challenges to the Surface Mining Act. The Court pursued an analysis similar to that in the Virginia case and reached the same result: Justice Marshall, in an opinion considerably briefer than his Virginia one, rejected all of the challengers' pre-enforcement claims.

The major targets of the Indiana attack were the "prime farmland" provisions of the Act. These provisions apply to land that qualifies as prime farmland and has historically been used for growing crops. Surface coal mining on such lands is permitted only if the mine operator can meet certain conditions. For example, the operator must demonstrate its "technological capability to restore such mined area, within a reasonable time, to equivalent or higher levels of yield as nonmined prime farmland in the surrounding area under equivalent levels of management."

The District Court found the "prime farmland" provisions to be beyond the Commerce Power, since they were "directed at facets of surface coal mining which have no substantial and adverse effect on interstate commerce." The court relied on statistics in an Interagency Report.[1] The Report stated that the prime farmland acreage disturbed annually by surface mining amounts to only .006% of the total prime farmland acreage in the country. Statistics such as this persuaded the court that surface coal mining on prime farmland has only "an infinitesimal effect or trivial impact on interstate commerce."

Justice MARSHALL rejected the District Court's approach. He noted that the Report had not examined the full impact of surface mining on interstate commerce in agricultural commodities and added: "More important, the court below incorrectly assumed that the relevant inquiry under the rational basis test is the volume of commerce actually affected by the regulated activity. [The] pertinent inquiry [is] not how much commerce is involved but whether Congress could rationally conclude that the regulated activity affects interstate commerce. [W]e have little difficulty in concluding that the congressional finding in this case satisfies the rational basis test. [The legislative record] mandates the conclusion that Congress had a rational basis for finding that surface coal mining on prime farmland affects interstate commerce in agricultural products. [The] court below improperly substituted its judgment for the congressional determination."

Justice Marshall also disagreed with the District Court's conclusion that the challenged provisions are "not reasonably related to the legitimate goal of protecting interstate commerce from adverse effects attributable to surface

1. Report of the Interagency Task Force on the Issue of a Moratorium or a Ban on Mining in Prime Agricultural Lands (1977).

coal mining." He stated: "The [District Court] incorrectly assumed that the Act's goals are limited to preventing air and water pollution. As we noted in [Virginia Surface Mining], Congress was also concerned about preserving the productive capacity of mined lands and protecting the public from health and safety hazards that may result from surface coal mining. All the provisions invalidated by the court below are reasonably calculated to further these legitimate goals."

More generally, Justice Marshall restated his view of proper Commerce Clause analysis as follows: "A court may invalidate legislation enacted under the Commerce Clause only if it is clear that there is no rational basis for a congressional finding that the regulated activity affects interstate commerce, or that there is no reasonable connection between the regulatory means selected and the asserted ends. We are not convinced that the District Court had reliable grounds to reach either conclusion in this case." [2]

Justice Marshall devoted only two paragraphs to setting aside the lower court's invalidation of the challenged provisions on Tenth Amendment grounds. Much like the lower court in the Virginia case, the District Court in Indiana had ruled that the real purpose and effect of the Act was land use regulation—in the court's view, a traditional state governmental function. Justice Marshall relied on his opinion in the Virginia case to reverse this ruling. He concluded: "This Court's decision in National League of Cities simply is not applicable to this case." [3]

UNITED TRANSPORTATION UNION v. LONG ISLAND R. CO., 455 U.S. 678 (1982), decided a year after the Hodel cases, once again rejected an effort to strike down a federal law on the basis of National League of Cities. The Court unanimously upheld the application of the Railway Labor Act to the state-owned Long Island Rail Road, a railroad primarily engaged in the passenger business. A federal appellate court had held that the Act could not constitutionally be applied because New York's operation of the railroad was an integral function of state government. Relying on National

---

2. The challengers also argued that a number of the provisions of the Act "cannot be shown to be related to the congressional goal of preventing adverse effects on interstate commerce." Justice Marshall gave short shrift to this argument, disposing of it in a footnote: "This claim, even if correct, is beside the point. A complex regulatory program, such as established by the Act, can survive a Commerce Clause challenge without a showing that every single facet of the program is independently and directly related to a valid congressional goal. It is enough that the challenged provisions are an integral part of the regulatory program and that the regulatory scheme when considered as a whole satisfies this test. See [Heart of At-

lanta Motel; Katzenbach v. McClung]. Cf. Perez v. United States; Wickard v. Filburn; United States v. Darby."

3. Justice Marshall also rejected the challengers' equal protection, substantive due process, Compensation Clause, and procedural due process claims. He primarily relied on his opinion in the Virginia case. For his formulation of the equal protection standard, see the excerpt printed below (addition to 10th Ed., p. 704; Ind.Rts., p. 324).

The separate statements by Chief Justice Burger and by Justice Rehnquist in the Virginia case applied to the Indiana decision as well.

League of Cities, the Court of Appeals had used a balancing approach and found that the State's interest in controlling the operation of its railroad outweighed the federal interest in having the Act applied.

Chief Justice BURGER found that nothing in the Tenth Amendment or its elaborations in National League of Cities and the Hodel cases barred the application of the Act to the railroad. He concluded: "Federal regulation of state-owned railroads simply does not impair a State's ability to function as a State." Drawing on the three-pronged test articulated in the first Hodel case for evaluating National League of Cities claims, he focused on the third prong, which asks whether "the States' compliance with the federal law would directly impair their ability 'to structure integral operations in areas of traditional functions.' " [1] In this case, he insisted, there was simply no interference with "traditional state functions."

The Chief Justice pointed out that National League of Cities itself had acknowledged the valid application of federal laws to state-owned railroads, as in the 1936 ruling in United States v. California. (See 10th Ed., p. 190.) He insisted that the precedents made it clear "that operation of a railroad engaged in interstate commerce is not an integral part of traditional state activities generally immune from federal regulation under National League of Cities." He was not persuaded by the lower court's attempt to distinguish the earlier cases on the ground that they involved freight rather than passenger carriers: "Operation of passenger railroads, no less than operation of freight railroads, has traditionally been a function of private industry, not state or local governments." The modern phenomenon of state acquisitions of formerly private railroads did not "alter the historical reality that the operation of railroads is not among the functions *traditionally* performed by state and local governments."

Chief Justice Burger insisted that the Court was "not merely following dicta [in National League of Cities] or looking only to the past to determine what is 'traditional.' " He claimed that the Court's emphasis on the "traditional" "was not meant to impose a static historical view of state functions generally immune from federal regulation." Instead, the "traditional" criterion was designed to further the central inquiry "into whether the federal regulation affects basic State prerogatives in such a way as would be likely to hamper the state government's ability to fulfill its role in the Union and endanger its 'separate and independent existence.' " Under this approach, quite apart from the precedents, no Tenth Amendment immunity was appropriate here.

Consider whether the Chief Justice's "explanation" of his allegedly fluid notion of the "traditional" is persuasive. He stated: "Just as the Federal Government cannot usurp traditional state functions, there is no justification

1. Despite his reliance on the reasonably clear-cut three-pronged test, the Chief Justice suggested that a balancing analysis could be superimposed on those three criteria. He stated that, "[e]ven if these three requirements are met, the federal statute is not automatically unconstitutional under the Tenth Amendment. The federal interest may still be so great as to 'justif[y] State submission.' " See footnote [5] to Hodel v. Virginia Surface Min. & Recl. Ass'n., above. Compare footnote [2] in Justice O'Connor's dissent in FERC v. Mississippi, which follows.

for a rule which would allow the States, *by acquiring functions previously performed by the private sector,* to erode federal authority in areas [such as railroads] traditionally subject to federal statutory regulation." (Emphasis added.) He added: "Moreover, the Federal Government has determined that a uniform regulatory scheme is necessary to the operation of the national rail system. [In] addition, a State acquiring a railroad does so knowing that the railroad is subject to this longstanding and comprehensive scheme of federal regulation of its operations and its labor relations." New York had known of and accepted federal regulation when it acquired the Long Island Rail Road in 1966. It had not raised a Tenth Amendment defense until 13 years later—i. e., three years after the National League of Cities decision. The State's failure to press its claim expeditiously reinforced the Court's view that the Act was not "likely to impair the State's ability to fulfill its role in the Union." [2]

FERC v. MISSISSIPPI

456 U.S. 742, 102 S.Ct. 2126, 72 L.Ed.2d 532 (1982).

Justice BLACKMUN delivered the opinion of the Court.

In this case, appellees successfully challenged the constitutionality of Titles I and III, and of § 210 of Title II, of the Public Utility Regulatory Policies Act of 1978 (PURPA or Act). We conclude that appellees' challenge lacks merit and we reverse the judgment below.

I. [The] Act was part of a package of legislation designed to combat the nationwide energy crisis. [In 1978], the generation of electricity consumed more than 25% of all energy resources used in the United States. Approximately one-third of the electricity in this country was generated through use of oil and natural gas. [In] part because of their reliance on oil and gas, electricity utilities were plagued with increasing costs and decreasing efficiency in the use of their generating capacities; each of these factors had an adverse effect on rates to consumers and on the economy as a whole. Congress accordingly determined that conservation by electricity utilities of oil and natural gas was essential to the success of any effort to lessen the country's dependence on foreign oil, to avoid a repetition of the shortage of natural gas that had been experienced in 1977, and to control consumer costs.

---

2. Note also Jefferson County Pharmaceutical Ass'n, Inc. v. Abbott Laboratories, 460 U.S. —— (1983), holding that the Robinson-Patman Act prohibits price discrimination by states as well as by private industry. Justice Powell's majority opinion quickly disposed of the Tenth Amendment claim before turning to the statutory issue. "It is too late in the day to suggest that Congress cannot regulate States under its Commerce Clause powers when they are engaged in proprietary activities. If the Tenth Amendment protects certain state purchases from the Act's limitations, such as for consumption in traditional governmental functions, those purchases must be protected on a case-by-case basis." The Court held that neither the Tenth Amendment nor the Robinson-Patman Act itself exempts from the Act purchases by state and local government hospitals for resale in competition with private retail pharmacies.

A.   Titles I and III.   PURPA's Titles I and III, which relate to regulatory policies for electricity and gas utilities, respectively, [are] designed to encourage the adoption of certain retail regulatory practices.   The Titles share three goals: (1) to encourage "conservation of energy supplied [by] utilities"; (2) to encourage "the optimization of the efficiency of use of facilities and resources" by utilities; and (3) to encourage "equitable rates [to] consumers."   To achieve these goals, Titles I and III direct state utility regulatory commissions and nonregulated utilities to "consider" the adoption and implementation of specific "rate design" and regulatory standards.

Section 111(d) of the Act requires each state regulatory authority and nonregulated utility to consider the use of six different approaches to structuring rates.[1]   [The] Act directed each state authority and nonregulated utility to consider these factors not later than two years after PURPA's enactment, that is, by November 8, 1980, and provided that the authority or utility by November 8, 1981, was to have made a decision whether to adopt the standards.   The statute does not provide penalties for failure to meet these deadlines; the state authority or nonregulated utility is merely directed to consider the standards at the first rate proceeding initiated by the authority after November 9, 1980.   Section 113 [requires] each state regulatory authority and nonregulated utility to consider the adoption of a second set of standards relating to the terms and conditions of electricity service.[2]   [Finally, § 114] directs each state authority and nonregulated utility to consider promulgation of "lifeline rates"—that is, lower rates for service that meets the essential needs of residential consumers—if such rates have not been adopted by November 1980.

Titles I and III also prescribe certain procedures to be followed by the state regulatory authority and the nonregulated utility when considering the proposed standards.   Each standard is to be examined at a public hearing after notice, and a written statement of reasons must be made available to the public if the standards are not adopted.   "Any person" may bring an action in state court to enforce the obligation to hold a hearing and make determinations on the PURPA standards.   [Titles I and III] also set forth certain reporting requirements.   [E.g., within] one year of PURPA's enactment, and annually thereafter for 10 years, each state regulatory authority and nonregulated utility is to report to the Secretary [of Energy] "respecting its consideration of the standards established."

Despite the extent and detail of the federal proposals, however, no state authority or nonregulated utility is required to adopt or implement the speci-

---

1.   The six approaches are: (1) promulgation, for each class of electricity consumers, of rates that, "to the maximum extent practicable," would "reflect the costs [of] service to such class"; (2) elimination of declining block rates; (3) adoption of time-of-day rates; (4) promulgation of seasonal rates; (5) adoption of interruptible rates; and (6) use of load management techniques.

2.   These standards are: (1) prohibition of master-metering in new buildings; (2) restrictions on the use of automatic adjustment clauses; (3) disclosure to consumers of information regarding rate schedules; (4) promulgation of procedural requirements relating to termination of service; and (5) prohibition of the recovery of advertising costs from consumers.

fied rate design or regulatory standards. Thus, [several sections] provide: "Nothing in this subsection prohibits any State regulatory authority or [non-regulated] utility from making any determination that it is not appropriate to [implement or adopt] any such standard, pursuant to its authority under otherwise applicable State law." Similarly, [other provisions] make it clear that any state regulatory authority or nonregulated utility may adopt regulations or rates that are "different from any standard established by this [subchapter or chapter]."

B.   Section 210.   Section 210 of PURPA's Title II seeks to encourage the development of cogeneration and small power production facilities.[3] Congress believed that increased use of these sources of energy would reduce the demand for traditional fossil fuels. But it also felt that two problems impeded the development of nontraditional generating facilities: (1) traditional electricity utilities were reluctant to purchase power from, and to sell power to, the nontraditional facilities, and (2) the regulation of these alternative energy sources by state and federal utility authorities imposed financial burdens upon the nontraditional facilities and thus discouraged their development.

In order to overcome the first of these perceived problems, § 210(a) directs FERC [Federal Energy Regulatory Commission], in consultation with state regulatory authorities, to promulgate "such rules as it determines necessary to encourage cogeneration and small power production," including rules requiring utilities to offer to sell electricity to, and purchase electricity from, qualifying cogeneration and small power production facilities. Section 210(f) requires each state regulatory authority and nonregulated utility to implement FERC's rules. And § 210(h) authorizes FERC to enforce this requirement in federal court against any state authority or nonregulated utility; if FERC fails to act after request, any qualifying utility may bring suit. To solve the second problem perceived by Congress, § 210(e) directs FERC to prescribe rules exempting the favored cogeneration and small power facilities from certain state and federal laws governing electricity utilities. . . .[4]

II.   [T]he State of Mississippi and the Mississippi Public Service Commission, appellees here, filed this action in the United States District Court against FERC and the Secretary of Energy, seeking a declaratory judgment that PURPA's Titles I and III and § 210 are unconstitutional. Appellees maintained that PURPA was beyond the scope of congressional power under

---

3.   A "cogeneration facility" is one that produces both electric energy and steam or some other form of useful energy, such as heat. A "small power production facility" is one that has a production capacity of no more than 80 megawatts and uses biomass, waste, or renewable resources (such as wind, water, or solar energy) to produce electric power. [Footnote by Justice Blackmun.]

4.   Congress recognized that a State's compliance with the requirements of PURPA would involve the expenditure of funds. Accordingly, it authorized the Secretary of Energy to make grants to state regulatory authorities to assist them in carrying out the provisions of Titles I and III, including the reporting requirements, and the provisions of § 210. For each of the fiscal years 1979 and 1980, Congress authorized for appropriation up to $40 million to help state regulatory authorities defray the costs of complying with PURPA. [Footnote by Justice Blackmun.]

the Commerce Clause and that it constituted an invasion of state sovereignty in violation of the Tenth Amendment.

[The District Court [held] that in enacting PURPA Congress had exceeded its powers under the Commerce Clause. The court observed that the Mississippi Public Service Commission by state statute possessed the "power and authority to regulate and control intrastate activities and policies of all utilities operating within the sovereign state of Mississippi." Relying on Carter v. Carter Coal Co. [1936; 10th Ed., p. 146], the court stated: "There is literally nothing in the Commerce Clause of the Constitution which authorizes or justifies the federal government in taking over the regulation and control of public utilities. These public utilities were actually unknown at the writing of the Constitution." Indeed, in the court's view, the legislation "does not even attempt to regulate commerce among the several states but it is a clear usurpation of power and authority which the United States simply does not have under the Commerce Clause of the Constitution."

Relying on [National League of Cities], the court also concluded that PURPA trenches on state sovereignty.[5] It therefore pronounced the statutory provisions void because "they constitute a direct intrusion on integral and traditional functions of the State of Mississippi." For reasons it did not explain, the court also relied on the guarantee of a republican form of government and on the Supremacy Clause. . . .

III.   The Commerce Clause. We readily conclude that the District Court's analysis [is] without merit so far as [it] concern[s] the Commerce Clause. To say that nothing in the Commerce Clause justifies federal regulation of even the intrastate operations of public utilities misapprehends the proper role of the courts in assessing the validity of federal legislation promulgated under one of Congress' plenary powers. The applicable standard was reiterated just last Term in Hodel v. Indiana. [Appellees] nevertheless assert that PURPA is facially unconstitutional because it does not regulate "commerce"; instead, it is said, the Act directs the nonconsenting State to regulate in accordance with federal procedures. This, appellees continue, is beyond Congress' power: "In exercising the authority conferred by this clause of the Constitution, Congress is powerless to regulate anything which is not commerce, as it is powerless to do anything about commerce which is not regulation." Carter v. Carter Coal Co. The "governance of commerce" by the State is to be distinguished from commerce itself, for regulation of the former is said to be outside the plenary power of Congress.[6] It is further argued that the proper test is not whether the regulated activity merely "affects" interstate commerce but, instead, whether it has "a substantial effect" on such commerce, citing Justice Rehnquist's opinion concurring in the judgment in the Hodel cases. PURPA, appellees maintain, does not meet this standard.

5.   "The sovereign state of Mississippi is not a robot, or lackey which may be shuttled back and forth to suit the whim and caprice of the federal government."   [Footnote by Justice Blackmun, quoting the District Court opinion.]

6.   For this proposition, appellees rely on Brown v. EPA, 521 F.2d 827, 839 (CA9 1975), vacated and remanded, 431 U.S. 99 (1977), and District of Columbia v. Train, 521 F.2d 971, 992 (1975), vacated and remanded sub nom. EPA v. Brown, 431 U.S. 99 (1977). [Footnote by Justice Blackmun.] [See footnote *, 10th Ed., p. 195.]

The difficulty with these arguments is that they disregard entirely the specific congressional finding, in § 2 of the Act, that the regulated activities have an immediate effect on interstate commerce. Congress there determined that "the protection of the public health, safety, and welfare, the preservation of national security, and the proper exercise of congressional authority under the Constitution to regulate interstate commerce require," among other things, a program for increased conservation of electric energy, increased efficiency in the use of facilities and resources by electricity utilities, and equitable retail rates for electricity consumers, as well as a program to improve the wholesale distribution of electric energy, and a program for the conservation of natural gas while ensuring that rates to gas consumers are equitable. The findings, thus, are clear and specific.

The Court heretofore has indicated that federal regulation of intrastate power transmission may be proper because of the interstate nature of the generation and supply of electric power. Our inquiry, then, is whether the congressional findings have a rational basis. [The Hodel cases.] The legislative history provides a simple answer: there is ample support for Congress' conclusions. The hearings were extensive. [Congress] concluded that the energy problem was nationwide in scope, and that [recent] developments demonstrated the need to establish federal standards regarding retail sales of electricity, as well as federal attempts to encourage conservation and more efficient use of scarce energy resources. Congress also determined that the development of cogeneration and small power production facilities would conserve energy. The evidence before Congress showed the potential contribution of these sources of energy: it was estimated that if proper incentives were provided, industrial cogeneration alone could account for 7%–10% of the Nation's electrical generating capacity by 1987.

We agree with appellants that it is difficult to conceive of a more basic element of interstate commerce than electric energy, a product used in virtually every home and every commercial or manufacturing facility. No State relies solely on its own resources in this respect. Indeed, the utilities involved in this very case [sell] their retail customers power that is generated in part beyond Mississippi's borders, and offer reciprocal services to utilities in other States. The intrastate activities of these utilities, although regulated by the Mississippi Public Service Commission, bring them within the reach of Congress' power over interstate commerce.[7]

Even if appellees were correct in suggesting that PURPA will not significantly improve the Nation's energy situation, the congressional findings compel the conclusion that " 'the means chosen by [Congress are] reasonably adapted to the end permitted by the Constitution'." It is not for us to say

---

7. PURPA could be upheld even if some of its provisions were not directly related to the purpose of fostering interstate commerce: "A complex regulatory program [can] survive a Commerce Clause challenge without a showing that every single facet of the program is independently and directly related to a valid congressional goal. It is enough that the challenged provisions are an integral part of the regulatory program and that the regulatory scheme when considered as a whole satisfies this test." Hodel v. Indiana. [Footnote by Justice Blackmun.]

whether the means chosen by Congress represent the wisest choice. It is sufficient that Congress was not irrational in concluding that limited federal regulation of retail sales of electricity and natural gas, and of relationships between cogenerators and electric utilities, was essential to protect interstate commerce. That is enough to place the challenged portions of PURPA within Congress' power under the Commerce Clause.[8] Because PURPA's provisions concern private nonregulated utilities as well as state commissions, the statute necessarily is valid at least insofar as it regulates private parties.

IV.   The Tenth Amendment.   Unlike the Commerce Clause question, the Tenth Amendment issue presented here is somewhat novel. This case obviously is related to [National League of Cities] insofar as both concern principles of state sovereignty. But there is a significant difference as well. National League of Cities, like Fry v. United States, presented a problem the Court often confronts: the extent to which state sovereignty shields the States from generally applicable federal regulations. In PURPA, in contrast, the Federal Government attempts to use state regulatory machinery to advance federal goals. To an extent, this presents an issue of first impression.

PURPA, for all its complexity, contains essentially three requirements: (1) § 210 has the States enforce standards promulgated by FERC; (2) Titles I and III direct the States to consider specified rate-making standards; and (3) those Titles impose certain procedures on state commissions. We consider these three requirements in turn:

A.   Section 210.   On its face, this appears to be the most intrusive of PURPA's provisions. The question of its constitutionality, however, is the easiest to resolve. Insofar as § 210 authorizes FERC to exempt qualified power facilities from "State laws and regulations," it does nothing more than pre-empt conflicting state enactments in the traditional way. Clearly, Congress can pre-empt the States completely in the regulation of retail sales by electricity and gas utilities and in the regulation of transactions between such utilities and cogenerators. The propriety of this type of regulation—so long as it is a valid exercise of the commerce power—was made clear in National League of Cities, and was reaffirmed in [Hodel v. Virginia Surface Mining]: the Federal Government may displace state regulation even though this serves to "curtail or prohibit the States' prerogatives to make legislative choices respecting subjects the States may consider important."

Section 210's requirement that "each State regulatory authority shall, after notice and opportunity for public hearing, *implement* such rule [for] each electric utility for which it has ratemaking authority" (emphasis added) is more troublesome. The statute's substantive provisions require electricity utilities to purchase electricity from, and to sell it to, qualifying cogenerator and small power production facilities. Yet FERC has declared that state commissions may implement this by, among other things, "an undertaking to resolve disputes between qualifying facilities and electric utilities arising under [PURPA]." In essence, then, the statute and the implementing regula-

---

8.   This is not to say the Congress can regulate in an area that is only tangentially related to interstate commerce. See Maryland v. Wirtz. That obviously is not the case here. [Footnote by Justice Blackmun.]

tions simply require the Mississippi authorities to adjudicate disputes arising under the statute. Dispute resolution of this kind is the very type of activity customarily engaged in by the Mississippi Public Service Commission.

Testa v. Katt [1947; 10th Ed., p. 373] is instructive and controlling on this point. There, the Emergency Price Control Act [of 1942] created a treble damages remedy, and gave jurisdiction over claims under the Act to state as well as federal courts. The courts of Rhode Island refused to entertain such claims, although they heard analogous state causes of action. This Court upheld the federal program. It observed that state courts have a unique role in enforcing the body of federal law, and that the Rhode Island courts had "jurisdiction adequate and appropriate under established local law to adjudicate this action." Thus the state courts were directed to heed the constitutional command that "the policy of the federal Act is the prevailing policy in every state," " 'and should be respected accordingly in the courts of the State.' "

So it is here. The Mississippi Commission has jurisdiction to entertain claims analogous to those granted by PURPA, and it can satisfy § 210's requirements simply by opening its doors to claimants. That the Commission has administrative as well as judicial duties is of no significance. Any other conclusion would allow the States to disregard both the pre-eminent position held by federal law throughout the Nation, cf. Martin v. Hunter's Lessee, and the congressional determination that the federal rights granted by PURPA can appropriately be enforced through state adjudicatory machinery. Such an approach, Testa emphasized, "flies in the face of the fact that the States of the Union constitute a nation" and "disregards the purpose and effect of Article VI of the Constitution."

B. *Mandatory Consideration of Standards.* We acknowledge that "the authority to make [fundamental] decisions" is perhaps the quintessential attribute of sovereignty. See National League of Cities. Indeed, having the power to make decisions and to set policy is what gives the State its sovereign nature. It would follow that the ability of a state legislative (or, as here, administrative) body [to] consider and promulgate regulations of its choosing must be central to a State's role in the federal system. Indeed, the nineteenth century view, expressed in a well known slavery case, was that Congress "has no power to impose upon a State officer, as such, any duty whatever, and compel him to perform it." Kentucky v. Dennison [1861; 10th Ed., p. 379.]

Recent cases, however, demonstrate that this rigid and isolated statement from Kentucky v. Dennison—which suggests that the States and the Federal Government in all circumstances must be viewed as co-equal sovereigns—is not representative of the law today.[9] While this Court never has sanctioned

9. Justice O'Connor reviews the constitutional history at some length, ultimately deriving the proposition that the Framers intended to deny the Federal Government the authority to exercise "military or legislative power over state governments," *instead* "allow[ing] Congress to pass laws direct- ly affecting individuals." If Justice O'Connor means this rhetorical assertion to be taken literally, it is demonstrably incorrect. See, e.g., Transportation Union v. Long Island R. Co.; Fry v. United States. [Footnote by Justice Blackmun.]

explicitly a federal command to the States to promulgate and enforce laws and regulations, cf. EPA v. Brown, there are instances where the Court has upheld federal statutory structures that in effect directed state decision-makers to take or to refrain from taking certain actions. [E.g., Fry v. United States.] [And] certainly Testa v. Katt reveals that the Federal Government has some power to enlist a branch of state government—there the judiciary—to further federal ends.[10]   In doing so, Testa clearly cut back on both the quoted language and the analysis of the Dennison case of the preceding century.

Whatever all this may forebode for the future, or for the scope of federal authority in the event of a crisis of national proportions, it plainly is not necessary for the Court in this case to make a definitive choice between competing views of federal power to compel state regulatory activity. Titles I and III of PURPA require only *consideration* of federal standards. And if a State has no utilities commission, or simply stops regulating in the field, it need not even entertain the federal proposals. As we have noted, the commerce power permits Congress to pre-empt the States entirely in the regulation of private utilities. In a sense, then, this case is only one step beyond Hodel v. Virginia Surface Min. & Recl. Assn. There, the Federal Government could have pre-empted all surface mining regulations; instead, it allowed the States to enter the field if they promulgated regulations consistent with federal standards. In the Court's view, this raised no Tenth Amendment problem.

Similarly here, Congress could have pre-empted the field, at least insofar as private rather than state activity is concerned; PURPA should not be invalid simply because, out of deference to state authority, Congress adopted a less intrusive scheme and allowed the States to continue regulating in the area on

---

10.   Justice O'Connor's partial dissent finds each of these cases inapposite. Yet the purported distinctions are little more than exercises in the art of ipse dixit. Thus she suggests that Testa v. Katt provides no support for the imposition of federal responsibilities on state legislatures, because "the requirement that [state courts] evenhandedly adjudicate state and federal claims falling within their jurisdiction does not infringe any sovereign authority to set an agenda." Yet the courts have always been recognized as a co-equal part of the State's sovereign decision-making apparatus and it seems evident that requiring state tribunals to entertain federal claims interferes, at least to a degree, with the State's sovereign prerogatives as well as with the amount of time that state courts may devote to adjudicating state claims. Conversely, it is difficult to perceive any fundamental distinction between the state legislature's power to establish limits on the jurisdiction of state courts, and its prerogative to set rate-making criteria for use by quasi-legislative utilities commissions. Justice O'Connor fails to explain, however, why this does not implicate her concern that "[w]hile engaged [in] congressionally mandated tasks, state utility commissions are less able to pursue local proposals."

The partial dissent finds Fry v. United States inapposite because the wage freeze there at issue "displaced no state choices as to how governmental operations should be structured. [Instead], it merely required that the wage scales and employment relationships which the States themselves had chosen be maintained." It seems absurd to suggest, however, that a federal veto of the States' chosen method of structuring their employment relationships is less intrusive in any realistic sense than are PURPA's mandatory consideration provisions. . . . [Footnote by Justice Blackmun.]

the condition that they *consider* the suggested federal standards.[11]   While the condition here is affirmative in nature—that is, it directs the States to entertain proposals—nothing in this Court's cases suggests that the nature of the condition makes it a constitutionally improper one.   There is nothing in PURPA "directly compelling" the States to enact a legislative program.   In short, because the two challenged Titles simply condition continued state involvement in a pre-emptible area on the consideration of federal proposals, they do not threaten the States' "separate and independent existence," and do not impair the ability of the States "to function effectively in a federal system."   To the contrary, they offer the States a vehicle for remaining active in an area of overriding concern.

We recognize, of course, that the choice put to the States—that of either abandoning regulation of the field altogether or considering the federal standards—may be a difficult one.   And that is particularly true when Congress, as is the case here, has failed to provide an alternative regulatory mechanism to police the area in the event of state default.   Yet in other contexts the Court has recognized that valid federal enactments may have an effect on state policy—and may, indeed, be designed to induce state action in areas that otherwise would be beyond Congress' regulatory authority.   Thus in Oklahoma v. Civil Service Comm'n [1947; 10th Ed., p. 237], the Court upheld Congress' power to attach conditions to grants-in-aid received by the States, although the condition under attack involved an activity that "the United States is not concerned with, and has no power to regulate."   [Thus] it cannot be constitutionally determinative that the federal regulation is likely to move the States to act in a given way, or even to "coerc[e] the States" into assuming a regulatory role by affecting their "freedom to make decisions in areas of "integral governmental functions.' "   [Virginia Surface Mining.]

Equally as important, it has always been the law that state legislative and judicial decisionmakers must give preclusive effect to federal enactments concerning nongovernmental activity, no matter what the strength of the competing local interests.   This requirement follows from the nature of governmental regulation of private activity.   "[I]ndividual businesses necessarily [are] subject to the dual sovereignty of the government of the Nation and the State in which they reside" [National League of Cities];   when regulations promulgated by the sovereigns conflict, federal law necessarily controls.   This is true though Congress exercises its authority "in a manner that displaces the States' exercise of their police powers" [Virginia Surface Mining] or in such a way as to "curtail or prohibit the States' prerogatives to make legislative

---

11.   It seems evident that Congress intended to defer to state prerogatives —and expertise—in declining to pre-empt the utilities field entirely.   Justice O'Connor's partial dissent's response to this is peculiar.   On the one hand, she suggests that the States might prefer that Congress simply pre-empt the field, since that "would leave them free to exercise their power in other areas."   Yet Justice O'Connor elsewhere acknowledges the importance of utilities regulation to the States, and emphasizes that local experimentation and self-determination are essential aspects of the federal system.   PURPA, of course, *permits* the States to play a continued role in the utilities field, and gives full force to the States' ultimate policy choices.   Certainly, it is a curious type of federalism that encourages Congress to pre-empt a field entirely, when its preference is to let the States retain the primary regulatory role.   [Footnote by Justice Blackmun.]

choices respecting subjects the States may consider important" [Id.]—or, to put it still more plainly, in a manner that is "extraordinarily intrusive." Id. (Powell, J., concurring). Thus it may be unlikely that the States will or easily can abandon regulation of public utilities to avoid PURPA's requirements. But this does not change the constitutional analysis: as in [Virginia Surface Mining], "[t]he most that can be said is that [the] Act establishes a program of cooperative federalism that allows the States, within limits established by federal minimum standards, to enact and administer their own regulatory programs, structured to meet their own particular needs." [12]

To be sure, PURPA gives virtually any affected person the right to compel consideration of the statutory standards through judicial action. We fail to see, however, that this places any particularly onerous burden on the State. [It] is hardly clear [that] PURPA's standing and appeal provisions grant any rights beyond those presently accorded by Mississippi law, and appellees point to no specific provision of the Act expanding on the State's existing, liberal approach to public participation in ratemaking.[13] In this light, we

12. Justice O'Connor's partial dissent suggests that our analysis is an "absurdity" and variously accuses us of "conscript[ing] state utility commissions into the national bureaucratic army," of transforming state legislative bodies into "field offices of the national bureaucracy," of approving the "dismemberment of state government," of making state agencies "bureaucratic puppets of the Federal Government," and—most colorfully— of permitting "Congress to kidnap state utility commissions." While these rhetorical devices make for absorbing reading, they unfortunately are substituted for useful constitutional analysis. For while Justice O'Connor articulates a view of state sovereignty that is almost mystical, she entirely fails to address our central point.

The partial dissent does not quarrel with the propositions that Congress may pre-empt the States in the regulation of private conduct, that Congress may condition the validity of State enactments in a pre-emptible area on their conformity with federal law, and that Congress may attempt to "coerce" the States into enacting nationally desirable legislation. Given this, the partial dissent fails to identify precisely what is "absurd" about a scheme that gives the States a choice between regulating in conformity with federal requirements, or abandoning regulation in a given field. Though the partial dissent finds [Virginia Surface Mining] inapposite, in our view the parallel is striking: there, the States were directed to legislate consistently with congressional enact-

ments, or not at all; here, the States are asked to regulate in conformity with federal requirements, or not at all. While it is true that PURPA conditions continued state regulatory activity on the performance of certain affirmative tasks, the partial dissent nowhere explains why—so long as the field is pre-emptible—the nature of the condition is relevant. And while PURPA's requirements in practice may be more intrusive and more difficult for the States to avoid than was the legislation at issue in [Virginia Surface Mining], Justice O'Connor herself acknowledges that an "evaluation of intrusiveness [is] simply irrelevant to the constitutional inquiry." Similarly, the difference between PURPA and the Surface Mining Control and Reclamation Act of 1977 identified by the partial dissent cannot be that only the former affects a "traditional function of state government," for regulation of land use is perhaps the quintessential state activity. In short, while the area of state action potentially foreclosed by PURPA may be broader than was the case in [Virginia Surface Mining], the partial dissent has pointed to no constitutionally significant theoretical distinction between the two statutory schemes. [Footnote by Justice Blackmun.]

13. We believe that this seemingly precise parallel between state and federal procedures suffices to overcome Justice Powell's objections to PURPA, at *least* where, as here, the statute is subjected to a facial attack. [Footnote by Justice Blackmun.]

again find the principle of Testa v. Katt controlling: the State is asked only to make its administrative tribunals available for the vindication of federal as well as state-created rights. PURPA, of course, establishes as federal policy the requirement that state commissions consider various ratemaking standards, and it gives individuals a right to enforce that policy; once it is established that the requirement is constitutionally supportable, "the obligation of states to enforce these federal laws is not lessened by reason of the form in which they are cast or the remedy which they provide." Testa v. Katt.

In short, Titles I and III do not involve the compelled exercise of Mississippi's sovereign powers. And, equally important, they do not set a mandatory agenda to be considered in all events by state legislative or administrative decisionmakers. As we read them, Titles I and III simply establish requirements for continued state activity in an otherwise pre-emptible field.[14] Whatever the constitutional problems associated with more intrusive federal programs, the "mandatory consideration" provisions of Titles I and III must be validated under the principle of [Virginia Surface Mining].[15]

C. The Procedural Requirements. Titles I and III also require state commissions to follow certain notice and comment procedures when acting on the proposed federal standards. In a way, these appear more intrusive than the "consideration" provisions; while the latter are essentially hortatory, the procedural provisions obviously are prescriptive. [Appellants] argue that the procedural requirements simply establish minimum due process standards, something Mississippi appears already to provide, and therefore may be upheld as an exercise of Congress' Fourteenth Amendment powers. We need not go that far, however, for we uphold the procedural requirements under the same analysis employed above in connection with the "consideration" provisions. If Congress can require a state administrative body to consider proposed regulations as a condition to its continued involvement in a pre-empti-

---

14. Justice O'Connor's partial dissent accuses us of undervaluing National League of Cities, and maintains that our analysis permits Congress to "dictate the agendas and meeting places of state legislatures." These apocalyptic observations, while striking, are overstated and patently inaccurate. We hold only that Congress may impose conditions on the State's regulation of private conduct in a pre-emptible area. This does not foreclose a Tenth Amendment challenge to federal interference with the State's ability "to structure employer-employee relationships" while providing "those governmental services which [its] citizens require," as was the case in National League of Cities. It does not suggest that the Federal Government may impose conditions on state activities in fields that are not pre-emptible, or that are solely of intrastate concern. And it does not purport to authorize the imposition of general affirmative obligations on the States. [Footnote by Justice Blackmun.]

15. As we note above, PURPA imposes certain reporting requirements on state commissions. But because these attach only if the State chooses to continue its regulatory efforts in the field, we find them supportable for the reasons addressed in connection with the other provisions of Titles I and III. Appellees nevertheless suggest that PURPA's requirements must fall because compliance will impose financial burdens on the States. We are unconvinced: in a Tenth Amendment challenge to congressional activity, "the determinative factor [is] the nature of the federal action, not the ultimate economic impact on the States." [Virginia Surface Mining.] In any event, Congress has taken steps to reduce or eliminate the economic burden of compliance. See n. [4], supra. [Footnote by Justice Blackmun.]

ble field—and we hold today that it can—there is nothing unconstitutional about Congress' requiring certain procedural minima as that body goes about undertaking its tasks. The procedural requirements obviously do not compel the exercise of the State's sovereign powers, and do not purport to set standards to be followed in all areas of the state commission's endeavors.

[Reversed.]

Justice POWELL, concurring and dissenting.

[The Act] imposes unprecedented burdens on the States. As Justice O'Connor ably demonstrates, it intrusively requires them to make a place on their administrative agenda for consideration and potential adoption of federally proposed "standards." The statute does not simply ask States to consider quasi-legislative matters that Congress believes they would do well to adopt. It also prescribes administrative and judicial procedures that States must follow in deciding whether to adopt the proposed standards. At least to this extent, I think the PURPA violates the Tenth Amendment.

I.   Most, if not all, of the States have administrative bodies—usually commissions—that regulate electric and gas public utility companies. [Until] now, with limited exceptions, the federal government has not attempted to preempt this important state function, and certainly has not undertaken to prescribe the procedures by which state regulatory bodies make their decisions. The PURPA, for the first time, breaks with this longstanding deference to principles of federalism. Now, regardless of established procedures before state administrative regulatory agencies and of state law with respect to judicial review, the PURPA forces federal procedures on state regulatory institutions. [These requirements] intrude upon—in effect preempt—core areas of a State's administrative and judicial procedure.

In sustaining these provisions, [the] Court reasons that Congress can condition the utility regulatory activities of States on any terms it pleases since, under the Commerce Clause, Congress has the power to preempt completely all such activities. Under this "threat of preemption" reasoning, Congress—one supposes—could reduce the States to federal provinces. But as [National League of Cities] stated, and indeed as the structure of the Court's opinion today makes plain, the Commerce Clause and the Tenth Amendment embody distinct limitations on federal power. That Congress has satisfied the one demonstrates nothing as to whether Congress has satisfied the other.[1]

---

1. The Court cites Testa v. Katt, in support of the proposition that under some conditions the Federal Government may call upon state governmental institutions to decide matters of federal policy. But Testa recognized that, when doing so, Congress must respect the state institution's own decisionmaking structure and method. That opinion limited its holding to circumstances under which the state court has "jurisdiction adequate and appropriate *under established local* *law* to adjudicate this [federal] action." See Note, Utilization of State Courts to Enforce Federal Penal and Criminal Statutes: Developments in Judicial Federalism, 60 Harv.L.Rev. 966, 971 (1947) (nothing in Testa upsets "the traditional doctrine that Congress may not interfere with a state's sovereign right to determine and control the jurisdictional requirements of its own courts"). [Footnote by Justice Powell.]

"The general rule, bottomed deeply in belief in the importance of state control of state judicial procedure, is that federal law takes state courts as it finds them." Hart, The Relations Between State and Federal Law, 54 Colum.L.Rev. 489, 508 (1954). I believe the same principle must apply to other organs of state government. It may be true that the procedural provisions of the PURPA that prompt this dissent may not effect dramatic changes in the laws and procedures of some States. But I know of no other attempt by the Federal Government to supplant state prescribed procedures that in part define the nature of their administrative agencies. If Congress may do this, presumably it has the power to preempt state court rules of civil procedure and judicial review in classes of cases found to affect commerce. This would be the type of gradual encroachment hypothesized by Professor Tribe: "Of course, no one expects Congress to obliterate the states, at least in one fell swoop. If there is any danger, it lies in the tyranny of small decisions—in the prospect that Congress will nibble away at state sovereignty, bit by bit, until someday essentially nothing is left but a gutted shell."

I limit this dissent to the provisions of the PURPA identified above. Despite the appeal—and indeed wisdom—of Justice O'Connor's evocation of the principles of federalism, I believe precedents of this Court support the constitutionality of the substantive provisions of this Act on this facial attack. See [Virginia Surface Mining; Testa]. Accordingly, to the extent the procedural provisions may be separable, I would affirm in part and reverse in part.

Justice O'CONNOR, with whom the Chief Justice [BURGER] and Justice REHNQUIST join, concurring in part in the judgment and dissenting in part.

I agree with the Court that the Commerce Clause supported Congress' enactment of [PURPA]. I disagree, however, with much of the Court's Tenth Amendment analysis. Titles I and III of PURPA conscript state utility commissions into the national bureaucratic army. This result is contrary to the principles of National League of Cities, antithetical to the values of federalism, and inconsistent with our constitutional history. Accordingly, I dissent from subsections IVB and C of the Court's opinion.[1]

---

1. I concur in the Court's decision to uphold Title II, § 210 of PURPA against appellees' facial attack. As the Court explains, part of that section permits the [FERC] to exempt cogeneration and small power production facilities from otherwise applicable state and federal laws. This exemption authority does not violate the Tenth Amendment, for it merely preempts state control of private conduct, rather than regulating the "States as States."

Section 210's requirement that the States "implement" rules promulgated by the Secretary of Energy is more disturbing. [It] appears that state regulatory authorities may satisfy § 210's implementation requirement simply by adjudicating private disputes arising under that section. As the Court points out, the Mississippi Public Service Commission has jurisdiction over similar state disputes, and it is settled that a State may not exercise its judicial power in a manner that discriminates between analogous federal and state causes of action. See Testa v. Katt. Under these circumstances, but without foreclosing the possibility that particular applications of § 210's implementation provision might uncover hidden constitutional defects, I would not sustain appellees' facial attack on the provision.

Section 210 also authorizes FERC, electric utilities, cogenerators, and small power producers to "enforce" the above implementation provision against state utility commissions. As

I.   Titles I and III of PURPA require state regulatory agencies to decide whether to adopt a dozen federal standards governing gas and electric utilities. The statute describes, in some detail, the procedures state authorities must follow when evaluating these standards, but does not compel the States to adopt the suggested federal standards. The latter, deceptively generous feature of PURPA persuades the Court that the statute does not intrude impermissibly into state sovereign functions. The Court's conclusion, however, rests upon a fundamental misunderstanding of the role that state governments play in our federalist system.

State legislative and administrative bodies are not field offices of the national bureaucracy. Nor are they think tanks to which Congress may assign problems for extended study. Instead, each State is sovereign within its own domain, governing its citizens and providing for their general welfare. While the Constitution and federal statutes define the boundaries of that domain, they do not harness state power for national purposes. [Adhering] to these principles, the Court has recognized that the Tenth Amendment restrains congressional action that would impair "a State's ability to function as a State." [E.g., National League of Cities.] [Just] last Term this Court identified three separate inquiries underlying the result in National League of Cities. A congressional enactment violates the Tenth Amendment, we observed, if it regulates the " 'States as States,' " addresses "matters that are indisputably 'attribute[s] of state sovereignty,' " and "directly impair[s] [the States'] ability to 'structure integral operations in areas of traditional governmental functions.' " [2] [Virginia Surface Mining.] See also United Transportation Union.

Application of these principles to the present case reveals the Tenth Amendment defects in Titles I and III. Plainly those titles regulate the "States as States." While the statute's ultimate aim may be the regulation of private utility companies, PURPA addresses its commands solely to the States. Instead of requesting private utility companies to adopt lifeline rates, declining block rates, or the other PURPA standards, Congress directed state agencies to appraise the appropriateness of those standards. It is difficult to argue that a statute structuring the regulatory agenda of a state agency is not a regulation of the "State."

I find it equally clear that Titles I and III address "attribute[s] of state sovereignty." Even the Court recognizes that "the power to make decisions and to set policy is what gives the State its sovereign nature." The power to make decisions and set policy, however, embraces more than the ultimate au-

applied, it is conceivable that this enforcement provision would raise troubling federalism issues. Once again, however, I decline to accept appellees' facial challenge to the provision, preferring to consider the constitutionality of this provision in the setting of a concrete controversy. [Footnote by Justice O'Connor.]

2. In both [Virginia Surface Mining] and United Transportation Union we further noted that, even when these three requirements are met, "the nature of the federal interest advanced may be such that it justifies state submission." Neither of those cases involved such an exception to National League of Cities, and the Court has not yet explored the circumstances that might justify such an exception. [Footnote by Justice O'Connor.]

thority to enact laws; it also includes the power to decide which proposals are most worthy of consideration, the order in which they should be taken up, and the precise form in which they should be debated. PURPA intrudes upon all of these functions. It chooses twelve proposals, forcing their consideration even if the state agency deems other ideas more worthy of immediate attention. In addition, PURPA hinders the agency's ability to schedule consideration of the federal standards. Finally, PURPA specifies, with exacting detail, the content of the standards that will absorb the agency's time. If Congress routinely required the state legislatures to debate bills drafted by congressional committees, it could hardly be questioned that the practice would affect an attribute of state sovereignty. PURPA, which sets the agendas of agencies exercising delegated legislative power in a specific field, has a similarly intrusive effect.

Finally, PURPA directly impairs the States' ability to "structure integral operations in areas of traditional governmental functions." Utility regulation is a traditional function of state government, and the regulatory commission is the most integral part of that function. By taxing the limited resources of these commissions, and decreasing their ability to address local regulatory ills, PURPA directly impairs the power of state utility commissions to discharge their traditional functions efficiently and effectively.[3]

The Court sidesteps this analysis, suggesting tha the States may escape PURPA simply by ceasing regulation of public utilities. Even the Court recognizes that this choice "may be a difficult one," and that "it may be unlikely that the States will or easily can abandon regulation of public utilities to avoid PURPA's requirements."

In fact, the Court's "choice" is an absurdity, for if its analysis is sound, the Constitution no longer limits federal regulation of state governments. Under the Court's analysis, for example, [National League of Cities] would have been wrongly decided, because the States could have avoided the Fair Labor Standards Act by "choosing" to fire all employees subject to that Act and to close those branches of state government.[4] Similarly, Congress could

---

3. PURPA thus offends each of the criteria named in [Virginia Surface Mining]. I do not believe, moreover, that this is a case in which "the nature of the federal interest advanced may be such that it justifies state submission." See n. [2], supra. Whatever the ultimate content of that standard, it must refer, not only to the weight of the asserted federal interest, but also to the necessity of vindicating that interest in a manner that intrudes upon state sovereignty. In this case, the Government argues that PURPA furthers vital national interests in energy conservation. Although the congressional goal is a noble one, appellants have not shown that Congress needed to commandeer state utility commissions to achieve its aim. Consistent with the Tenth Amendment, Congress could have assigned

PURPA's tasks to national officials. Alternatively, it could have requested state commissions to comply with Titles I and III and directed the Secretary to shoulder the burden of any State choosing not to comply. [Footnote by Justice O'Connor.]

4. The Court attempts to distinguish National League of Cities. [In] that case, Congress had required the States to pay their employees specified amounts if they wished to continue regulating a variety of pre-emptible fields. Here, it has required the States to burden their officials with evaluation of a dozen legislative proposals if they wish to continue regulating private utilities. To me, the parallel is obvious, not "overstated." [I] am nevertheless confident that, as the Court itself stresses, today's deci-

dictate the agendas and meeting places of state legislatures, because unwilling States would remain free to abolish their legislative bodies. I do not agree that this dismemberment of state government is the correct solution to a Tenth Amendment challenge.

The choice put to the States by [the] statute upheld in [Virginia Surface Mining is] quite different from the decision PURPA mandates. [The] Surace Mining Act does not force States to choose between performing tasks set by Congress and abandoning all mining or land use regulation. That statute is "a program of cooperative federalism" because it allows the States to choose either to work with Congress in pursuit of federal surface mining goals or to devote their legislative resources to other mining and land use problems. By contrast, there is nothing "cooperative" about a federal program that compels state agencies either to function as bureaucratic puppets of the Federal Government or to abandon regulation of an entire field traditionally reserved to state authority. Yet this is the "choice" the Court today forces upon the States.

The Court defends its novel decision to permit federal conscription of state legislative power by citing [a few] cases upholding statutes that "in effect directed state decision-makers to take or to refrain from taking certain actions." Testa v. Katt is the most suggestive of these decisions. In Testa, the Court held that state trial courts may not refuse to hear a federal claim if "th[e] same type of claim arising under [state] law would be enforced by that State's courts." A facile reading of Testa might suggest that state legislatures must also entertain congressionally sponsored business, as long as the federal duties are similar to existing state obligations. Application of Testa to legislative power, however, vastly expands the scope of that decision. Because trial courts of general jurisdiction do not choose the cases that they hear, the requirement that they evenhandedly adjudicate state and federal claims falling within their jurisdiction does not infringe any sovereign authority to set an agenda.[5] As explained above, however, the power to choose subjects for legislation is a fundamental attribute of legislative power, and interference with this power unavoidably undermines state sovereignty. Accordingly, the existence of a congressional authority to "enlist [the state] judiciary [to] further federal ends" does not imply an equivalent power to impress state legislative bodies into federal service.

The Court, finally, reasons that because Congress could have preempted the entire field of intrastate utility regulation, the Constitution should not

sion is not intended to overrule National League of Cities. Instead, the novelty of PURPA's scheme merely seems to have obscured the relevance of National League of Cities to this case. [Footnote by Justice O'Connor.]

5. The Court suggests that the requirement that state courts adjudicate federal claims may, as a practical matter, undermine the capacity of those courts to decide state controversies. Whatever the force of that observation, it does not demonstrate Testa's relevance to this case. State legislative bodies possess at least one attribute of sovereignty, the power to set an agenda, that trial courts lack. This difference alone persuades me not to embrace the Court's expansion of Testa. [Footnote by Justice O'Connor.]

forbid PURPA's "less intrusive scheme." [6] The Court's evaluation of intrusiveness, however, is simply irrelevant to the constitutional inquiry. The Constitution permits Congress to govern only through certain channels. If the Tenth Amendment principles articulated in [National League of Cities and Virginia Surface Mining] foreclose PURPA's approach, it is no answer to argue that Congress could have reached the same destination by a different route. This Court's task is to enforce constitutional limits on congressional power, not to decide whether alternative courses would better serve state and federal interests.

I do not believe, moreover, that Titles I and III of PURPA are less intrusive than preemption. [7] When Congress preempts a field, it precludes only state legislation that conflicts with the national approach. The States usually retain the power to complement congressional legislation, either by regulating details unsupervised by Congress or by imposing requirements that go beyond the national threshold. Most importantly, after Congress preempts a field, the States may simply devote their resources elsewhere. This country does not lack for problems demanding legislative attention. PURPA, however, drains the inventive energy of state governmental bodies by requiring them to weigh its detailed standards, enter written findings, and defend their determinations in state court. While engaged in these congressionally mandated tasks, state utility commissions are less able to pursue local proposals for conserving gas and electric power. The States might well prefer that Congress simply impose the standards described in PURPA; this, at least, would leave them free to exercise their power in other areas.

Federal preemption is less intrusive than PURPA's approach for a second reason. Local citizens hold their utility commissions accountable for the choices they make. Citizens, moreover, understand that legislative authority usually includes the power to decide which ideas to debate, as well as which policies to adopt. Congressional compulsion of state agencies, unlike preemption, blurs the lines of political accountability and leaves citizens feeling that their representatives are no longer responsive to local needs.

The foregoing remarks suggest that, far from approving a minimally intrusive form of federal regulation, the Court's decision undermines the most valuable aspects as our federalism. Courts and commentators frequently have recognized that the fifty States serve as laboratories for the development of new social, economic, and political ideas. This state innovation is no judicial myth. When Wyoming became a State in 1890, it was the only State permit-

---

6. The Court's suggestion is somewhat disingenuous because Congress concluded that federal preemption of the matters governed by Titles I and III would be inappropriate. [Today's] decision, therefore, permits Congress to set state legislative agendas in a field that Congress might have occupied but expressly found unsuited to preemption. [Footnote by Justice O'Connor.]

7. In 1975, then Attorney General Edward H. Levi responded to a similar argument that the "greater" power of preemption includes the "lesser" power of demanding affirmative action from state governments. Attorney General Levi remarked that "it is an insidious point to say that there is more federalism by compelling a State instrumentality to work for the Federal Government." In a similar vein, he warned against "lov[ing] the States to their demise." [Footnote by Justice O'Connor.]

ting women to vote. That novel idea did not bear national fruit for another thirty years. Wisconsin pioneered unemployment insurance, while Massachusetts initiated minimum wage laws for women and minors. After decades of academic debate, state experimentation finally provided an opportunity to observe no-fault automobile insurance in operation. Even in the field of environmental protection, an area subject to heavy federal regulation, the States have supplemented national standards with innovative and far-reaching statutes. Utility regulation itself is a field marked by valuable state invention. PURPA, which commands state agencies to spend their time evaluating federally proposed standards and defending their decisions to adopt or reject those standards, will retard this creative experimentation.

In addition to promoting experimentation, federalism enhances the opportunity of all citizens to participate in representative government. [Citizens], however, cannot learn the lessons of self-government if their local efforts are devoted to reviewing proposals formulated by a far-away national legislature. If we want to preserve the ability of citizens to learn democratic processes through participation in local government, citizens must retain the power to govern, not merely administer, their local problems.

Finally, our federal system provides a salutary check on governmental power. As Justice Harlan once explained, our ancestors "were suspicious of every form of all-powerful central authority." To curb this evil, they both allocated governmental power between state and national authorities, and divided the national power among three branches of government. Unless we zealously protect these distinctions, we risk upsetting the balance of power that buttresses our basic liberties. In analyzing this brake on governmental power, Justice Harlan noted that "[t]he diffusion of power between federal and state authority [takes] on added significance as the size of the federal bureaucracy continues to grow." Today, the Court disregards this warning and permits Congress to kidnap state utility commissions into the national regulatory family. Whatever the merits of our national energy legislation, I am not ready to surrender this state legislative power to the [FERC].

II. [The] Court's result, moreover, is at odds with our constitutional history, which demonstrates that the Framers consciously rejected a system in which the national legislature would employ state legislative power to achieve national ends.

The principal defect of the Articles of Confederation [was] that the new National Government lacked the power to compel individual action. Instead, the central government had to rely upon the cooperation of state legislatures to achieve national goals. [The] Constitution cured this defect by permitting direct contact between the National Government and the individual citizen, a change repeatedly acknowleged by the delegates assembled in Philadelphia. [The] speeches and writings of the Framers suggest why they adopted this means of strengthening the National Government. Mason, for example, told the Convention that because "punishment could not [in the nature of things be executed on] the States collectively," he advocated a National Government that would "directly operate on individuals." [Thus], the Framers concluded that government by one sovereign through the agency of a second cannot be satisfactory. At one extreme, as under the Articles of Confederation, such a system is simply ineffective. At the other, it requires a degree of military force incompatible with stable government and civil liberty.[8] For this reason, the Framers concluded that "the execution of the laws of the [national government] should not require the intervention of the State Legislatures," The Federalist No. 16, and abandoned the Articles of Confederation in favor of direct national legislation.

At the same time that the members of the Constitutional Convention fashioned this principle, they rejected two proposals that would have given the national legislature power to supervise state governments directly. The first proposal would have authorized Congress "to call forth the force of the Union against any member of the Union failing to fulfill its duty under the articles thereof." The delegates never even voted on this suggestion. [The] second proposal received more favorable consideration. Virginia's Governor Randolph suggested that Congress should have the power "to negative all laws passed by the several States, contravening in the opinion of the National Legislature the articles of Union." On May 31, 1787, the Committee of the Whole approved this proposal without debate. A week later, Pinckney moved to extend the congressional negative to all state laws "which [Congress] should judge to be improper." Numerous delegates criticized this attempt to give Congress unbounded control over state lawmaking. [After] much debate, the Convention rejected Pinckney's suggestion. Late in July, the delegates reversed their approval of even Randolph's more moderate congressional veto. Several delegates now concluded that the negative would be "terrible to the States," "unnecessary," and "improper." Omission of the negative, however, left the new system without an effective means of adjusting conflicting state and national laws. To remedy this defect, the delegates adopted the Supremacy Clause. [Thus], the Framers substituted judicial review of state laws for congressional control of state legislatures.

While this history demonstrates the Framers' commitment to a strong central government, the means that they adopted to achieve that end are as instructive as the end itself.[9] Under the Articles of Confederation, the national legislature operated through the States. The Framers could have fortified the central government, while still maintaining the same system, if they had increased Congress' power to demand obedience from state legislatures. In time, this scheme might have relegated the States to mere departments of the National Government, a status the Court appears to endorse today. The

---

8. Henry M. Hart, Jr., agreed that the Framers were well aware "of the delicacy, and the difficulties of enforcement, of affirmative mandates from a federal government to the governments of the member states." Until the second half of this century, Congress apparently heeded this wisdom. "Federal law," Hart observed in 1954, "often says to the states, 'Don't do any of these things,' leaving outside the scope of its prohibition a wide range of alternative courses of action. But it is illuminating to observe how rarely it says, 'Do *this* thing,' leaving no choice but to go ahead and do it." [Hart, "The Relations Between State and Federal Law," 54 Colum.L.Rev. 489 (1954).] [Footnote by Justice O'Connor.]

9. [My] analysis of the Framers' intent does not detract from the proper role of federal power in a federalist system, but merely requires the exercise of that power in a manner that does not destroy state independence. [Footnote by Justice O'Connor.]

Framers, however, eschewed this course, choosing instead to allow Congress to pass laws directly affecting individuals, and rejecting proposals that would have given Congress military or legislative power over state governments. In this way, the Framers established independent state and national sovereigns. The National Government received the power to enact its own laws and to enforce those laws over conflicting state legislation. The States retained the power to govern as sovereigns in fields that Congress cannot or will not preempt. This product of the Constitutional Convention, I believe, is fundamentally inconsistent with a system in which either Congress or a state legislature harnesses the legislative powers of the other sovereign.

III.   During his last Term of service on this Court, Justice Black eloquently explained that our notions of federalism subordinate neither national nor state interests. [Younger v. Harris, 10th Ed., p. 1681; Ind.Rts., p. 1301.] [In] this case, I firmly believe that a proper "sensitivity to the legitimate interests of both State and National Governments" requires invalidation of Titles I and III of PURPA insofar as they apply to state regulatory authorities. . . .

EEOC v. WYOMING

460 U.S. ——, 103 S.Ct. 1054, 75 L.Ed.2d 18 (1983).

Justice BRENNAN delivered the opinion of the Court.

Under the Age Discrimination in Employment Act of 1967 (ADEA or Act), it is unlawful for an employer to discriminate against any employee or potential employee on the basis of age, except "where age is a bona fide occupational qualification reasonably necessary to the normal operation of the particular business, or where the differentiation is based on reasonable factors other than age." The question presented in this case is whether Congress acted constitutionally when, in 1974, it extended the definition of "employer" under [the] Act to include state and local governments. The [District Court], in an enforcement action brought by the Equal Employment Opportunity Commission (EEOC or Commission), held that, at least as applied to certain classes of state workers, the extension was unconstitutional. [We] now reverse.

I.   [Justice Brennan outlined the legislative history of the Act, including the 1974 extension to employees of state and local governments.]

II.   This case arose out of the involuntary retirement at age 55 of Bill Crump, a District Game Division supervisor for the Wyoming Game and Fish Department. Crump's dismissal was based on a Wyoming statute that conditions further employment for Game and Fish Wardens who reach the age 55 on "the approval of [their] employer." Crump filed a complaint with the EEOC, alleging that the Game and Fish Department had violated the Age Discrimination in Employment Act. After conciliation efforts [failed], the Commission filed suit [against] the State [seeking relief on] behalf of Mr. Crump and others similarly situated.

The District Court [dismissed] the suit. It held that the Age Discrimination in Employment Act violated the doctrine of Tenth Amendment immunity articulated in [National League of Cities], at least insofar as it regulated Wyoming's employment relationship with its game wardens and other law enforcement officials. . . .

III. The appellees have not claimed [that] Congress exceeded the scope of its affirmative grant of power under the Commerce Clause in enacting the ADEA. Rather, the District Court held and appellees argue that, at least with respect to state game wardens, application of the ADEA to the States is precluded by virtue of external constraints imposed on Congress's commerce powers by the Tenth Amendment.

A. [National League of Cities] struck down Congress's attempt to extend the wage and hour provisions of the Fair Labor Standards Act to state and local governments. National League of Cities was grounded on a concern that the imposition of certain federal regulations on state governments might, if left unchecked, "allow 'the National Government [to] devour the essentials of state sovereignty.' " It therefore drew from the Tenth Amendment an "affirmative limitation on the exercise of [congressional power under the Commerce Clause] akin to other commerce power affirmative limitations contained in the Constitution." The principle of immunity articulated in National League of Cities is a functional doctrine, however, whose ultimate purpose is not to create a sacred province of state autonomy, but to ensure that the unique benefits of a federal system in which the States enjoy a "separate and independent existence," not be lost through undue federal interference in certain core state functions. [Virginia Surface Mining] summarized the hurdles that confront any claim that a state or local governmental unit should be immune from an otherwise legitimate exercise of the federal power to regulate commerce: "[I]n order to succeed, a claim that congressional commerce power legislation is invalid under [National League of Cities] must satisfy *each* of three requirements. First, there must be a showing that the challenged statute regulates the 'States as States.' Second, the federal regulation must address matters that are indisputably 'attribute[s]' of state sovereignty.' And third, it must be apparent that the States' compliance with the federal law would directly impair their ability 'to structure integral operations in areas of traditional governmental functions." Moreover, "Demonstrating that these three requirements are met does not . . . guarantee that a Tenth Amendment challenge to congressional commerce power action will succeed. There are situations in which the nature of the federal interest advanced may be such that it justifies state submission."

The first requirement—that the challenged federal statute regulate the "States as States"—is plainly met in this case.[1] The second requirement—

1. It is worth emphasizing, however, that it is precisely this prong of the National League of Cities test that marks it as a specialized immunity doctrine rather than a broad limitation on federal authority. "[A] wealth of precedent attests to congressional authority to displace or pre-empt state laws regulating *private* activity affecting interstate commerce when these laws conflict with federal law. . . . Although such congressional enactments obviously curtail or prohibit the States' prerogatives to make legislative choices

that the federal statute address on "undoubted attribute of state sovereignty" —poses significantly more difficulties.[2]   We need not definitively resolve this issue, however, nor do we have any occasion to reach the final balancing step of the inquiry, [for] we are convinced that, even if Wyoming's decision to impose forced retirement on its game wardens does involve the exercise of an attribute of state sovereignty, the [Act] does not "directly impair" the State's ability to "structure integral operations in areas of traditional governmental functions."

    B.   The management of state parks is clearly a traditional state function.   As we have already emphasized, however, the purpose of the doctrine of immunity articulated in National League of Cities was to protect States from federal intrusions that might threaten their "separate and independent existence."   Our decision as to whether the federal law at issue here directly impairs the States' ability to structure their integral operations must therefore depend, as it did in National League of Cities itself, on considerations of degree.   [FERC v. Mississippi].   We conclude that the degree of federal intrusion in this case is sufficiently less serious than it was in National League of Cities so as to make it unnecessary for us to override Congress's express choice to extend its regulatory authority to the States.

    In this case, appellees claim no substantial stake in their retirement policy other than "assur[ing] the physical preparedness of Wyoming game wardens to perform their duties."   Under the ADEA, however, the State may still, at the very least, assess the fitness of its game wardens and dismiss those wardens whom it reasonably finds to be unfit.   Put another way, the Act requires the State to achieve its goals in a more individualized and careful manner than would otherwise be the case, but it does not require

---

respecting subjects the States may consider important, the Supremacy Clause permits no other result." [Virginia Surface Mining] [Footnote by Justice Brennan.]

2.   National League of Cities held that "there are attributes of sovereignty attaching to every state government which may not be impaired by Congress" and that "[o]ne undoubted attribute of state sovereignty is the States' power to determine the wages which shall be paid to those whom they employ in order to carry out their governmental functions, what hours those persons will work, and what compensation will be provided where those employees may be called upon to work overtime."   Precisely what it meant by an "undoubted attribute of state sovereignty" is somewhat unclear, however, and our subsequent cases [have] had little occasion to amplify on our understanding of the concept.

A State's employment relationship with its workers can, under certain circumstances, be one vehicle for the exercise of its core sovereign functions.   In National League of Cities, for example, the power to determine the wages of government workers was tied, among other things, to the exercise of the States' public welfare interest in providing jobs to persons who would otherwise be unemployed.   Moreover, some employment decisions are so clearly connected to the execution of underlying sovereign choices that they must be assimilated into them for purposes of the Tenth Amendment. [Such as the relationship between determining the hours of government workers and the unimpeded exercise of the State's role as provider of emergency services.]   But we are not to be understood to suggest that every state employment decision aimed simply at advancing a generalized interest in efficient management—even the efficient management of traditional state functions—should be considered to be an exercise of an "undoubted attribute of state sovereignty." [Footnote by Justice Brennan.]

the State to abandon those goals, or to abandon the public policy decisions underlying them.

Perhaps more important, appellees remain free under the ADEA to continue to do *precisely what they are doing now*, if they can demonstrate that age is a "bona fide occupational qualification" for the job of game warden. Thus, in distinct contrast to the situation in National League of Cities, even the State's discretion to achieve its goals *in the way it thinks best* is not being overridden entirely, but is merely being tested against a reasonable federal standard.

Finally, the Court's concern in National League of Cities was not only with the effect of the federal regulatory scheme on the particular decisions it was purporting to regulate, but also with the potential impact of that scheme on the States' ability to structure operations and set priorities over a wide range of decisions.[3] Indeed, National League of Cities spelled out in some detail how application of the federal wage and hour statute to the States threatened a virtual chain reaction of substantial and almost certainly unintended consequential effects on state decisionmaking. Nothing in this case, however, portends anything like the same wide-ranging and profound threat to the structure of State governance.

The most tangible consequential effect identified in National League of Cities was financial: forcing the States to pay their workers a minimum wage and an overtime rate would leave them with less money for other vital state programs. The test of such financial effect [does] not depend, however, on "particularized assessments of actual impact," which may vary from State to State and time to time, but on a more generalized inquiry, essentially legal rather than factual, into the direct and obvious effect of the federal legislation on the ability of the States to allocate their resources. In this case, we cannot conclude from the nature of the ADEA that it will have either a direct or an obvious negative effect on state finances. Older workers with seniority may tend to get paid more than younger workers without seniority, and may by their continued employment accrue increased benefits when they do retire. But these increased costs, even if they were not largely speculative in their own right, might very well be outweighed by a number of other factors: Those same older workers, as long as they remain employed, will not have to be paid any pension benefits at all, and will continue to contribute to the pension fund. And, when they do retire, they will likely, as an actuarial matter, receive benefits for fewer years than workers who retire early. Admittedly [the] costs of certain state health and other benefit plans would increase if they were automatically extended to older workers now forced to retire at an early age. But Congress, in passing the ADEA, included a provision specifically disclaiming a construction of the Act which would require that the health and similar benefits received by older workers be in all respects identical to those received by younger workers.

The second consequential effect identified in National League of Cities was on the States' ability to use their employment relationship with their

3. We do not mean to suggest that such consequential effects could be enough, by themselves, to invalidate a federal statute. [Footnote by Justice Brennan.]

citizens as a tool for pursuing social and economic policies beyond their immediate managerial goals.   Appellees, however, have claimed no such purposes for Wyoming's involuntary retirement statute.   Moreover, whatever broader social or economic purposes could be imagined for this [statute] would not, we are convinced, bring with them either the breadth or the importance of the state policies identified in National League of Cities.[4]

IV.   The extension of the ADEA to cover state and local governments, both on its face and as applied in this case, was a valid exercise of Congress's powers under the Commerce Clause.[5]

[Reversed and remanded.]

Justice STEVENS, concurring.

I.   [In] final analysis, we are construing the scope of the power granted to Congress by the Commerce Clause.   It is important to remember that this clause was the Framers' response to the central problem that gave rise to the Constitution itself.   [Justice] Rutledge described the origins and purpose of the Commerce Clause in these words:

> "If any liberties may be held more basic than others, they are the great and indispensable democratic freedoms secured by the First Amendment.   But it was not to assure them that the Constitution was framed and adopted.   Only later were they added, by popular demand.   It was rather to secure freedom of trade, to break down the barriers to its free flow, that the Annapolis Convention was called, only to adjourn with a view to Philadelphia.   Thus the generating source of the Constitution lay in the rising volume of restraints upon commerce which the Confederation could not check.   These were the proximate cause of our national existence down to today.

> "As evils are wont to do, they dictated the character and scope of their own remedy.   This lay specifically in the commerce clause.   No prohibition of trade barriers as among the states could have been effective of its own force or by trade agreements.   It had become apparent that such treaties were too difficult to negotiate and the process of

4.   Even if the minimal character of the federal intrusion in this case did not lead us to hold that the ADEA survives the third prong of the inquiry, it might still, when measured against the well-defined federal interest in the legislation, require us to find that the nature of that interest "justifies state submission."   We note, incidentally, that the strength of the federal interest underlying the Act is not negated by the fact that the federal government happens to impose mandatory retirement on a small class of its own workers.   Once Congress has asserted a federal interest, and once it has asserted the strength of that interest, we have no warrant for reading into the ebbs and flows of political decisionmaking a conclusion that Congress was insincere in that declaration, and must from

that point on evaluate the sufficiency of the federal interest as a matter of law rather than of psychological analysis.   [Footnote by Justice Brennan.]

5.   The Court's holding that the Act was valid under the Commerce Clause made it unnecessary for the Court to decide whether the Act was also valid under Congress's separate power under § 5 of the Fourteenth Amendment.   But the Court did specifically reaffirm (see Rome v. United States, 446 U.S. 156 (1980), printed at 10th Ed., p. 1066; Ind.Rts., p. 686) that proper exercises of the § 5 power are "not limited by the same Tenth Amendment constraints that circumscribe the exercise of [Commerce] Clause powers."   (Other § 5 aspects of the case are noted below, addition to 10th Ed., p. 1104; Ind.Rts., p. 724.)

securing them was too complex for this method to give the needed relief. Power adequate to make and enforce the prohibition was required. Hence, the necessity for creating an entirely new scheme of government. . . .

"So by a stroke as bold as it proved successful, they founded a nation, although they had set out only to find a way to reduce trade restrictions. So also they solved the particular problem causative of their historic action, by introducing the commerce clause in the new structure of power." *

There have been occasions when the Court has given a miserly construction to the Commerce Clause. But as the needs of a dynamic and constantly expanding national economy have changed, this Court has construed the Commerce Clause to reflect the intent of the Framers [to] confer a power on the national government adequate to discharge its central mission. In this process the Court has repeatedly repudiated cases that had narrowly construed the clause. The development of judicial doctrine has accommodated the transition from a purely local, to a regional, and ultimately to a national economy.

[In] the statutes challenged in this case and in [National League of Cities], Congress exercised its power to regulate the American labor market. There was a time when this Court would have denied that Congress had any such power, but that chapter in our judicial history has long been closed. Today, there should be universal agreement on the proposition that Congress has ample power to regulate the terms and conditions of employment throughout the economy. Because of the interdependence of the segments of the economy and the importance and magnitude of government employment, a comprehensive Congressional policy to regulate the labor market may require coverage of both public and private sectors to be effective.

Congress may not, of course, transcend specific limitations on its exercise of the commerce power that are imposed by other provisions of the Constitution. But there is no limitation in the text of the Constitution that is even arguably applicable to this case. The only basis for questioning the federal statute at issue here is the pure judicial fiat found in this Court's opinion in [National League of Cities]. Neither the Tenth Amendment, nor any other provision of the Constitution, affords any support for that judicially constructed limitation on the scope of the federal power granted to Congress by the Commerce Clause. [I] think it so plain that National League of Cities not only was incorrectly decided, but also is inconsistent with the central purpose of the Constitution itself, that it is not entitled to the deference that the doctrine of *stare decisis* ordinarily commands for this Court's precedents. Notwithstanding my respect for that doctrine, I believe that the law would be well served by a prompt rejection of National League of Cities' modern embodiment of the spirit of the Articles of Confederation. . . .

Chief Justice BURGER, with whom Justice POWELL, Justice REHNQUIST, and Justice O'CONNOR join, dissenting.

---

* The quotation is from a lecture delivered by Justice Rutledge in 1946. Justice Stevens served as law clerk to Justice Rutledge in 1947–48.

The Court decides today that Congress may dictate to the states, and their political subdivisions, detailed standards governing the selection of state employees, including those charged with protecting people and homes from crimes and fires. Although the opinion reads the Constitution to allow Congress to usurp this fundamental state function, I have re-examined that document and I fail to see where it grants to the national government the power to impose such strictures on the states either expressly or by implication. Those strictures are not required by any holding of this Court, and it is not wholly without significance that Congress has not placed similar limits on itself in the exercise of its own sovereign powers. Accordingly, I would hold the [Act] unconstitutional as applied to the states.

I.   [We] need not pause on the first prong of [the Virginia Surface Mining] test, for the legislation is indisputably aimed at regulating the states in their capacity as states. The Commission argues, however, that the legislation does not run counter to the other two prongs of the test. Turning then to prong two, whether the [Act] addresses matters that are 'attributes of state sovereignty,' we may assume that in enacting the Wyoming State Highway Patrol and Game and Fish Warden Retirement Act, Wyoming sought to assure the physical preparedness of its game wardens and others who enforce its laws. This goal is surely an attribute of sovereignty, for parks and recreation services were identified in National League of Cities as traditional state activities protected by the Tenth Amendment. Even more important, it is the essence of state power to choose—subject only to *constitutional* limits—who is to be part of the state government. If poachers destroy the fish and game reserves of Wyoming, it is not to the Congress that people are going to complain, but to state and local authorities who will have to justify their actions in selecting wardens. Since it is the state that bears the responsibility for delivering the services, it is clearly an attribute of state sovereignty to choose who will perform these duties.

To decide whether a challenged activity is an attribute of sovereignty, it is instructive to inquire whether other government entities have attempted to enact similar legislation. A finding that other governmental units have passed mandatory retirement laws, although not conclusive, is persuasive evidence that such laws are traditional methods for insuring an efficient workforce for certain governmental functions. [More] than one-half the states have retirement laws that, like the Wyoming [law], violate the Act. More important, Congress, while mandating compliance in the states, carefully preserved its own freedom to select employees on any basis it chooses. Although the Act was expressly made to apply to the national government, exceptions were built into the enactment. Certain categories of employment —such as law enforcement officers—were *explicitly* excluded, and in addition, the statute provides thta "[r]easonable exemptions to the provisions of this section may be established by the [Civil Service] Commission." I conclude that defining the qualifications of employees is an essential of sovereignty.

The third prong of the National League of Cities test is that the federal intrusion must impair the ability of the state to structure integral operations. [It] is beyond dispute that the statute can give rise to increased employment costs caused by forced employment of older individuals. Since these employees tend to be at the upper end of the pay scale, the cost of their wages while they are still in the work force is greater. And since most pension plans calculate retirement benefits on the basis of maximum salary or number of years of service, pension costs are greater when an older employee retires. The employer is also forced to pay more for insuring the health of older employees because, as a group, they inevitably carry a higher-than-average risk of illness. Since they are—especially in law enforcement—also more prone to on-the-job injuries, it is reasonable to conclude that the employer's disability costs are increased.

Non-economic hardships are equally severe. Employers are prevented from hiring those physically best able to do the job. Since older workers occupy a disproportionate share of the upper-level and supervisory positions, a bar on mandatory retirement also impedes promotion opportunities. Lack of such opportunities tends to undermine younger employees' incentive to strive for excellence, and impedes the state from fulfilling affirmative action objectives.

The Federal Government can hardly claim that the objectives of decreasing costs and increasing promotional opportunities are impermissible: many of the same goals are cited repeatedly to justify the "enclaves" of federal exceptions to the Act. For example, mandatory retirement is still the rule in the Armed Services and the Foreign Service. [Moreover, I] find it impossible to say that [the exceptions] provid[e] an adequate method for avoiding significant impairment to the state's ability to structure its integral governmental operations.

Since I am satisfied that the Act runs afoul of the three prongs of the National League of Cities test, I turn to the balancing test alluded to in Justice Blackmun's concurring opinion in National League of Cities, and in [Virginia Surface Mining.] The Commission argues that the federal interest in preventing unnecessary demands on the social security system and other maintenance programs, in protecting employees from arbitrary discrimination, and in eliminating unnecessary burdens on the free flow of commerce "is more than sufficient in the face of a Wyoming's bald assertion of a prerogative to be arbitrary."

It is simply not accurate to state that Wyoming is resting its challenge to the Act on a "sovereign" right to discriminate; [Wyoming] is asserting a right to set standards to meet local needs. Nor do [these] largely theoretical benefits to the Federal Government outweigh the very real danger that a fire may burn out of control because the firefighters are not physically able to cope; or that a criminal may escape because a law-enforcement officer's reflexes are too slow to react swiftly enough to apprehend an offender; or that an officer may be injured or killed for want of capacity to defend himself. These factors may not be real to Congress but it is not Congress' responsibility to prevent them; they are nonetheless real to the states. I would hold that Commerce Clause powers are wholly insufficient to bar the states from dealing with or preventing these dangers in a rational manner. Wyoming's solution is plainly a rational means. . . .

III.   [The] Framers did not give Congress the power to decide local employment standards because they wisely realized that as a body, Congress lacked the means to analyze the factors that bear on this decision, such as the diversity of occupational risks, climate, geography, and demography. Since local conditions generally determine how a job should be performed, and who should perform it, the authority and responsibility for making employment decisions must be in the hands of local governments, subject only to those restrictions unmistakably contemplated by the Fourteenth Amendment.

[And] even if Congress had infinite fact-finding means at its disposal, conditions in various parts of the country are too diverse to be susceptible to a uniformly applicable solution. Wyoming is a state with large sparsely populated areas, where law enforcement often requires substantial physical stamina; the same conditions are not always encountered by law enforcement officers in Rhode Island, which has far less land area, no mountains, and no wilderness. [Barring] states from making employment decisions tailored to meet specific local needs undermines the flexibility that has long allowed industrial states to live under the same flag as rural states, and small, densely populated states to coexist with large, sparsely populated ones.

The reserved powers of the states and Justice Brandeis' classic conception of the states as laboratories, New State Ice Co. v. Liebmann, 285 U.S. 262 (1932) (Brandeis, J., dissenting), are turned on their heads when national rather than state governments assert the authority to make decisions on the age standard of state law enforcement officers. Flexibility for experimentation not only permits each state to find the best solutions to its own problems, it is the means by which each state may profit from the experiences and activities of all the rest. Nothing in the Constitution permits Congress to force the states into a Procrustean [†] national mold that takes no account of local needs and conditions. That is the antithesis of what the authors of the Constitution contemplated for our federal system.

Justice POWELL, with whom Justice O'CONNOR joins, dissenting.

I join the Chief Justice's dissenting opinion, but write separately to record a personal dissent from Justice Stevens' novel view of our Nation's history.

I.   Justice Stevens begins his concurring opinion with the startling observation that the Commerce Clause "was the Framers' response to the *central problem* that gave rise to the Constitution itself." At a subsequent point in his opinion, he observes that "this Court has construed the Commerce Clause to reflect the *intent of the Framers* . . . to confer a power on the national government adequate to discharge its *central mission.*" Justice Stevens further states that "National League of Cities not only was incorrectly decided, but also is inconsistent with the *central purpose* of the Constitution itself . . . ."

---

† According to Greek legend, Procrustes forced all passing travellers to lie down on a bed. If the bed was too long, Procrustes stretched their bodies; if the bed was too short, he cut off their legs.

No one would deny that removing trade barriers between the States was *one* of the Constitution's purposes. I suggest, however, that there were other purposes of equal or greater importance motivating the statesmen who assembled in Philadelphia and the delegates who debated the ratification issue in the state conventions. No doubt there were differences of opinion as to the principal shortcomings of the Articles of Confederation. But one can be reasonably sure that few of the Founding Fathers thought that trade barriers among the States were "the central problem," or that their elimination was the "central mission" of the Constitutional Convention. Creating a national government within a federal system was far more central than any 18th century concern for interstate commerce.

It is true, of course, that this Court properly has construed the Commerce Clause, and extended its reach, to accommodate the unanticipated and unimaginable changes, particularly in transportation and communication, that have occurred [since] the Constitution was ratified. If Justice Stevens had written that the Founders' intent in adopting the Commerce Clause nearly two centuries ago is of little relevance to the world in which we live today, I would not have disagreed. But his concurring opinion purports to rely on their intent. I therefore write [to] place the Commerce Clause in proper historical perspective, and further to suggest that even today federalism is not, as Justice Stevens appears to believe, utterly subservient to that Clause.

II. The Constitution's central purpose was, as the name implies, to constitute a government. The most important provisions, therefore, are those in the first three Articles relating to the establishment of that government. The system of checks and balances, for example, is far more central to the larger perspective than any single power conferred on any branch. Indeed, the Virginia Plan, the initial proposal from which the entire Convention began its work, focuses on the framework of the national government without even mentioning the power to regulate commerce.

[Although] the "general Welfare" recognized [in the Preamble] could embrace the free flow of trade among States (despite the fact that the same language in the Articles of Confederation did not), it is clear that security "against foreign invasion [and] against dissentions between members of the Union" was of at least equal importance.

The power to achieve the purposes identified in the Preamble was not delegated solely to Congress. If, however, one looks at the powers that were so delegated, the position of the Commerce Clause hardly suggests that it was the "central" concern of the patriots who formed our Union. The enumeration of powers in Article I, § 8 begins with the "Power To lay and collect Taxes." This is followed by the power "to pay the Debts" of the United States. Then, consistent with the Preamble, comes the power to "provide for the common Defence and general Welfare." The power to regulate interstate commerce is only one among nearly a score of other powers that followed. [The] Commerce Clause was given no place of particular prominence. So much for what the Constitution's language and structure teach about the Framers' intent.

III. One would never know from the concurring opinion that the Constitution formed a federal system, comprising a national government with delegated powers and state governments that retained a significant measure of sovereign authority. [It] is impossible to believe that the Constitution would have been recommended by the Convention, must less ratified, if it had been understood that the Commerce Clause embodied the national government's "central mission," a mission to be accomplished even at the expense of regulating the personnel practices of state and local governments.

A.   The Bill of Rights imposes express limitations on national powers. The Tenth Amendment, in particular, explicitly recognizes the retained power of the States. [This] limitation was, of course, implicit in the Constitution as originally ratified. Even those who opposed the adoption of a Bill of Rights did not dispute the propriety of such a limitation. Rather, they argued that it was unnecessary, for the Constitution delegated certain powers to the central government, and those not delegated were necessarily retained by the States or the people. Furthermore, the inherent federal nature of the system is clear from the structure of the national government itself. Members of Congress and presidential electors are chosen by States. Representation in the Senate is apportioned by States, regardless of population. [The] initial ratification of the Constitution was accomplished on a state-by-state basis, and subsequent amendments require approval by three fourths of the States.

It was also clear from the contemporary debates that the Founding Fathers intended the Constitution to establish a federal system. [Justice Powell described various historical sources.]   .   .   .

IV.   Justice Stevens' concurring opinion recognizes no limitation on the ability of Congress to override state sovereignty in exercising its powers under the Commerce Clause. His opinion does not mention explicitly either federalism or state sovereignty. [Under] this view it is not easy to think of any state function—however sovereign—that could not be preempted.

Chapter 4

OTHER NATIONAL POWERS IN THE
1787 CONSTITUTION

10th ED., p. 213
Add to footnote **:

On the uniformity requirement, see United States v. Ptasynski, 462 U.S. —— (1983), discussed below, addition to 10th Ed., p. 356.

10th ED., p. 224
Add as footnote at end of Note 2:

On the necessity of ascertaining congressional purpose to determine if a tax violates the Uniformity Clause, see United States v. Ptasynski, 462 U.S. —— (1983), discussed below, addition to 10th Ed., p. 356.

10th ED., p. 237
Add to first paragraph of Note 2:

PENNHURST STATE SCHOOL v. HALDERMAN, 451 U.S. 1 (1981), suggests that the modern Court may be growing more reluctant to interpret federal-state grant programs as including conditions imposing affirmative obligations on the states. The case involved a grant program established by the Developmentally Disabled Assistance and Bill of Rights Act of 1974. Under the program, Congress provides funds to participating states to aid them in programs for the care and treatment of the mentally retarded. The Act's "bill of rights" provision states that mentally retarded persons "have a right to appropriate treatment, services, and habilitation" in "the setting that is least restrictive [of] personal liberty." The plaintiffs claimed that this provision creates rights that are judicially enforceable by private parties. Justice Rehnquist's majority opinion, however, held that the provision "simply does not create substantive rights." In the course of reaching this conclusion, he made some potentially significant comments on the relevant sources of power—§ 5 of the Fourteenth Amendment and the Spending Power. (The Fourteenth Amendment aspect of the case is further noted below, addition to 10th Ed., p. 1104; Ind. Rts., p. 724.)

Justice Rehnquist assessed the Spending Power as follows: "[O]ur cases have long recognized that Congress may fix the terms on which it shall disburse federal money to the States. Unlike legislation enacted under § 5, however, legislation enacted pursuant to the Spending Power is much in the nature of a contract: in return for federal funds, the States agree to comply with federally imposed conditions. The legitimacy of Congress' power to legislate under the Spending Power thus rests on whether the State voluntarily and knowingly accepts the terms of the 'contract.' [See, e.g., Steward Machine Co. v. Davis.] There can, of course, be no knowing acceptance if a State is unaware of the conditions or is unable to ascertain what is expected of it. Accordingly, if Congress intends to impose a condition on the grant of federal moneys, it must do so unambiguously.* By insisting that Congress speak with a clear voice, we enable the States to exercise their choice knowingly, cognizant of the consequences of their participation. [We] must carefully inquire, then, whether Congress in [the 'bill of rights' provision] imposed an obligation on the States to spend state money to fund certain rights as a condition of receiving federal moneys under the Act or whether it spoke merely in precatory terms." He concluded that the provision did "no more than express a congressional preference for certain kinds of treatment" and did not impose affirmative obligations on the states: "In sum, the court below failed to recognize the well-settled distinction between Congressional 'encouragement' of state programs and the imposition of binding obligations on the States. [Congress] was aware of the need of developmentally disabled persons and plainly understood the difference, financial and otherwise, between encouraging a specified type of treatment and mandating it."

Justice WHITE's partial dissent, joined by Justices Brennan and Marshall, insisted that the "bill of rights" provision *did* impose substantive conditions on the federal spending program: it "was intended by Congress to establish requirements which participating States had to meet in providing care to the developmentally disabled. The fact that Congress spoke in generalized terms rather than the language of regulatory minutia cannot make nugatory actions so carefully undertaken. [The provision] cannot be treated as only wishful thinking on the part of Congress. [It] clearly states rights which the developmentally disabled are to be provided as against a participating State," rights which the developmentally disabled can enforce in federal courts as private beneficiaries of the law. In implementing these rights, federal courts should determine what is "necessary to comply with the Act and then [permit] an appropriate period for the State to decide whether it preferred to give up federal funds and go its own route." And in a footnote replying to the majority's "contract" approach to grants-in-aid, Justice White commented: "None of the cases cited by the Court suggest, much less hold, that Congress is required to condition its grant of funds with contract-like exactitude."

---

* In a potentially important footnote at this point, Justice Rehnquist added: "There are limits on the power of Congress to impose conditions on the States pursuant to its Spending Power [e.g., Steward Machine Co.; Fullilove; see National League of Cities v. Usery]. Even the [plaintiffs], like the court below, recognize the 'constitutional difficulties' with imposing affirmative obligations on the States pursuant to the Spending Power. That issue, however, is not now before us."

Chapter 5

STATE REGULATION OF THE NATIONAL ECONOMY

10th ED., p. 295
Add to the Note, "Modern Balancing in Highway Cases":

The 1978 decision in Raymond (the principal case in text) was unanimous. Three years later (in Kassel, which follows), the Court invalidated a seemingly similar state regulation of highways. But, in contrast to Raymond, the Court in Kassel was sharply divided. There was no majority opinion to support the 6 to 3 decision. Justice Powell wrote a plurality opinion; Justice Brennan's concurring opinion supplied the necessary votes for the majority judgment. All of the opinions purported to accept and draw upon Raymond, but differed sharply about its implications.

In examining Kassel, consider the extent to which its level of scrutiny departs from that in Raymond. In view of Kassel, it is appropriate to repeat here, in modified form, the question with which the note in text begins: "In light of Bibb, Raymond [and, now, Kassel] what *is* the modern standard of review of state highway regulations challenged under the commerce clause?"

————

KASSEL v. CONSOLIDATED FREIGHTWAYS CORP.

450 U.S. 662, 101 S.Ct. 1309, 67 L.Ed.2d 580 (1981).

Justice POWELL announced the judgment of the Court and delivered an opinion in which Justice WHITE, Justice BLACKMUN, and Justice STEVENS joined.

The question is whether an Iowa statute that prohibits the use of certain large trucks within the State unconstitutionally burdens interstate commerce.

I. [Consolidated Freightways] is one of the largest common carriers in the country. [Among] other routes, Consolidated carries commodities through Iowa on Interstate 80, the principal east-west route linking New York, Chicago, and the West Coast, and on Interstate 35, a major north-south route.

Consolidated mainly uses two kinds of trucks. One consists of a three-axle tractor pulling a 40-foot two-axle trailer. This unit, commonly called a single, or "semi," is 55 feet in length overall. Such trucks have long been used on the Nation's highways. Consolidated also uses a two-axle tractor pulling a single-axle trailer which, in turn, pulls a single-axle dolly and a second single-axle trailer. This combination, known as a double, or twin, is 65 feet long overall. Many trucking companies, including Consolidated, increasingly prefer to use doubles to ship certain kinds of commodities. Doubles have larger capacities, and the trailers can be detached and routed separately if necessary. Consolidated would like to use 65-foot doubles on many of its trips through Iowa.

[Iowa], however, by statute restricts the length of vehicles that may use its highways. Unlike all other States in the West and Midwest, Iowa generally prohibits the use of 65-foot doubles within its borders. Instead, most truck combinations are restricted to 55 feet in length. Doubles,[1] mobile homes, trucks carrying vehicles such as tractors and other farm equipment, and singles hauling livestock, are permitted to be as long as 60 feet. Notwithstanding these restrictions, Iowa's statute permits cities abutting the state line by local ordinance to adopt the length limitations of the adjoining State. . . .

Because of Iowa's statutory scheme, Consolidated cannot use its 65-foot doubles to move commodities through the State. Instead, the company must do one of four things: (i) use 55-foot singles, (ii) use 60-foot doubles; (iii) detach the trailers of a 65-foot double and shuttle each through the State separately; or (iv) divert 65-foot doubles around Iowa. Dissatisfied with these options, Consolidated filed this suit in the District Court averring that Iowa's statutory scheme unconstitutionally burdens interstate commerce. Iowa defended the law as a reasonable safety measure enacted pursuant to its police power. The State asserted that 65-foot doubles are more dangerous than 55-foot singles and, in any event, that the law promotes safety and reduces road wear within the State by diverting much truck traffic to other States.[2]

In a 14-day trial, both sides adduced evidence on safety, and on the burden on interstate commerce imposed by Iowa's law. On the question of safety, the District Court found that the "evidence clearly establishes that the twin is as safe as the semi." [It] applied the standard we enunciated in [Raymond] and concluded that the state law impermissibly burdened interstate commerce. [T]he Court of Appeals agreed with the District Court. [W]e now affirm.

II. [A] state's power to regulate commerce is never greater than in matters traditionally of local concern. For example, regulations that touch upon safety—especially highway safety—are those that "the Court has been most reluctant to invalidate." Raymond. Indeed, "if safety justifications are not illusory, the court will not second guess legislative judgment about their importance in comparison with related burdens on interstate commerce." Raymond (Blackmun, J., concurring). Those who would challenge such bona fide safety regulations must overcome a "strong presumption of validity." [Bibb.]

But the incantation of a purpose to promote the public health or safety does not insulate a state law from Commerce Clause attack. Regulations designed for that salutary purpose nevertheless may further the purpose so mar-

---

1. The 60-foot double is not commonly used anywhere except in Iowa. It consists of a tractor pulling a large trailer, which in turn pulls a dolly attached to a small trailer. The odd-sized trailer used in the 60-foot double is not compatible for interchangeable use in other trailer combinations. [Footnote by Justice Powell.]

2. In this Court, Iowa places little or no emphasis on the constitutional validity of this second argument. [Footnote by Justice Powell.]

ginally, and interfere with commerce so substantially, as to be invalid under the Commerce Clause. In the Court's recent unanimous decision in Raymond, we declined to "accept the State's contention that the inquiry under the Commerce Clause is ended without a weighing of the asserted safety purpose against the degree of interference with interstate commerce." This "weighing" by a court requires—and indeed the constitutionality of the state regulation depends on—"a sensitive consideration of the weight and nature of the state regulatory concern in light of the extent of the burden imposed on the course of interstate commerce." Id.; accord, Pike v. Bruce Church, Inc.; Bibb; Southern Pacific.

III. Applying these general principles, we conclude that the Iowa truck-length limitations unconstitutionally burden interstate commerce. [This] case is Raymond revisited. Here, as in Raymond, the State failed to present any persuasive evidence that 65-foot doubles are less safe than 55-foot singles. Moreover, Iowa's law is now out of step with the laws of all other midwestern and western States. Iowa thus substantially burdens the interstate flow of goods by truck. In the absence of congressional action to set uniform standards,[3] some burdens associated with state safety regulations must be tolerated. But where, as here, the State's safety interest has been found to be illusory, and its regulations impair significantly the federal interest in efficient and safe interstate transportation, the state law cannot be harmonized with the Commerce Clause.[4]

A. Iowa made a more serious effort to support the safety rationale of its law than did Wisconsin in Raymond, but its effort was no more persuasive. As noted above, the District Court found that the "evidence clearly establishes that the twin is as safe as the semi." The record supports this finding.

The trial focused on a comparison of the performance of the two kinds of trucks in various safety categories. The evidence showed, and the District Court found, that the 65-foot double was at least the equal of the 55-foot single in the ability to brake, turn, and maneuver. The double, because of its axle placement, produces less splash and spray in wet weather. And, because of its articulation in the middle, the double is less susceptible to dangerous "off-tracking,"[5] and to wind.

None of these findings is seriously disputed by Iowa. Indeed, the State points to only three ways in which the 55-foot single is even arguably superior: singles take less time to be passed and to clear intersections; they may back up for longer distances; and they are somewhat less likely to jackknife.

The first two of these characteristics are of limited relevance on modern interstate highways. As the District Court found, the negligible difference in

---

3. The Senate last year [1980] passed a bill that would have pre-empted the field of truck lengths by setting a national limit of 65 feet. The House took no action before adjournment. [Footnote by Justice Powell.]

4. It is highly relevant that here, as in Raymond, the state statute contains exemptions that weaken the deference traditionally accorded to a state safety regulation. See § IV, infra. [Footnote by Justice Powell.]

5. "Off-tracking" refers to the extent to which the rear wheels of a truck deviate from the path of the front wheels while turning. [Footnote by Justice Powell.]

the time required to pass, and to cross intersections, is insignificant on 4-lane divided highways because passing does not require crossing into oncoming traffic lanes, Raymond, and interstates have few, if any, intersections. The concern over backing capability also is insignificant because it seldom is necessary to back up on an interstate. In any event, no evidence suggested any difference in backing capability between the 60-foot doubles that Iowa permits and the 65-foot doubles that it bans. Similarly, although doubles tend to jackknife somewhat more than singles, 65-foot doubles actually are less likely to jackknife than 60-foot doubles.

Statistical studies supported the view that 65-foot doubles are at least as safe overall as 55-foot singles and 60-foot doubles. One such study, which the District Court credited, reviewed Consolidated's comparative accident experience in 1978 with its own singles and doubles. [Iowa's] expert statistician admitted that this study provided "moderately strong evidence" that singles have a higher injury rate than doubles. Another study, prepared by the Iowa Department of Transportation at the request of the State legislature, concluded that "[s]ixty-five foot twin trailer combinations have not been shown by experiences in other states to be less safe than 60 foot twin trailer combinations or conventional tractor-semitrailers." Numerous insurance company executives, and transportation officials from the Federal Government and various States, testified that 65-foot doubles were at least as safe as 55-foot singles. Iowa concedes that it can produce no study that establishes a statistically significant difference in safety between the 65-foot double and the kinds of vehicles the State permits. [Nor] did Iowa present a single witness who testified that 65-foot doubles were more dangerous overall than the vehicles permitted under Iowa law. In sum, although Iowa introduced more evidence on the question of safety than did Wisconsin in Raymond, the record as a whole was not more favorable to the State.[6]

B. Consolidated, meanwhile, demonstrated that Iowa's law substantially burdens interstate commerce. Trucking companies that wish to continue to use 65-foot doubles must route them around Iowa or detach the trailers of the doubles and ship them through separately. Alternatively, trucking companies must use the smaller 55-foot singles or 60-foot doubles permitted under Iowa law. Each of these options engenders inefficiency and added expense. The record shows that Iowa's law added about $12.6 million each year to the costs of trucking companies. Consolidated alone incurred about $2 million per year in increased costs.

In addition to increasing the costs of the trucking companies (and, indirectly, of the service to consumers), Iowa's law may aggravate, rather than

6. In suggesting that Iowa's law actually promotes safety, the dissenting opinion ignores the findings of the courts below and relies on largely discredited statistical evidence. The dissent implies that a statistical study identified doubles as more dangerous than singles. At trial, however, the author of that study—Iowa's own statistician—conceded that his calculations were statistically biased, and therefore "not very meaningful."

The dissenting opinion also suggests that its conclusions are bolstered by the fact that the American Association of State Highway and Transportation Officials (AASHTO) recommends that States limit truck lengths. The dissent fails to point out, however, that AASHTO specifically recommends that States permit 65-foot doubles. [Footnote by Justice Powell.]

ameliorate, the problem of highway accidents. Fifty-five foot singles carry less freight than 65-foot doubles. Either more small trucks must be used to carry the same quantity of goods through Iowa, or the same number of larger trucks must drive longer distances to bypass Iowa. In either case, [the] restriction requires more highway miles to be driven to transport the same quantity of goods. Other things being equal, accidents are proportional to distance traveled. Thus, if 65-foot doubles are as safe as 55-foot singles, Iowa's law tends to *increase* the number of accidents, and to shift the incidence of them from Iowa to other States.

IV. Perhaps recognizing the weakness of the evidence supporting its safety argument, and the substantial burden on commerce that its regulations create, Iowa urges the Court simply to "defer" to the safety judgment of the State. It argues that the length of trucks is generally, although perhaps imprecisely, related to safety. The task of drawing a line is one that Iowa contends should be left to its legislature.

The Court normally does accord "special deference" to state highway safety regulations. Raymond. [Less] deference to the legislative judgment is due, however, where the local regulation bears disproportionately on out-of-state residents and businesses. Such a disproportionate burden is apparent here. Iowa's scheme, although generally banning large doubles from the State, nevertheless has several exemptions that secure to Iowans many of the benefits of large trucks while shunting to neighboring States many of the costs associated with their use.[7]

At the time of trial there were two particularly significant exemptions. First, singles hauling livestock or farm vehicles were permitted to be as long as 60 feet. [T]his provision undoubtedly was helpful to local interests. Cf. Raymond (exemption in Wisconsin for milk shippers). Second, cities abutting other States were permitted to enact local ordinances adopting the larger length limitation of the neighboring State. This exemption offered the benefits of longer trucks to individuals and businesses in important border cities without burdening Iowa's highways with interstate through traffic. Cf. Raymond (exemption in Wisconsin for shipments from local plants).

The origin of the "border cities exemption" also suggests that Iowa's statute may not have been designed to ban dangerous trucks, but rather to discourage interstate truck traffic. In 1974, the legislature passed a bill that would have permitted 65-foot doubles in the State. Governor Ray vetoed the bill. He said: "I find sympathy with those who are doing business in our state and whose enterprises could gain from increased cargo carrying ability by trucks. However, with this bill, the Legislature has pursued a course that would benefit only a few Iowa-based companies while providing a great advantage for out-of-state trucking firms and competitors at the expense of our Iowa citizens."[8] After the veto, the "border cities exemption" was immediately enacted and signed by the Governor.

---

7. As the District Court noted, diversion of traffic benefits Iowa by holding down (i) accidents in the State, (ii) auto insurance premiums, (iii) police staffing needs, and (iv) road wear. [Footnote by Justice Powell.]

8. [E]xceptions also are available to benefit Iowa truck makers and Iowa mobile home manufacturers or purchasers. Although these exemptions are not directly relevant to the controversy over the safety of 65-foot

It is thus far from clear that Iowa was motivated primarily by a judgment that 65-foot doubles are less safe than 55-foot singles. Rather, Iowa seems to have hoped to limit the use of its highways by deflecting some through traffic.[9] In the [lower courts], the State explicitly attempted to justify the law by its claimed interest in keeping trucks out of Iowa. The Court of Appeals correctly concluded that a State cannot constitutionally promote its own parochial interests by requiring safe vehicles to detour around it.

V. In sum, the statutory exemptions, their history, and the arguments Iowa has advanced in support of its law in this litigation, all suggest that the deference traditionally accorded a State's safety judgment is not warranted.[10] The controlling factors thus are the findings of the District Court, accepted by the Court of Appeals, with respect to the relative safety of the types of trucks at issue, and the substantiality of the burden on interstate commerce.

Because Iowa has imposed this burden without any significant countervailing safety interest [11] its statute violates the Commerce Clause.[12] . . .

Affirmed.

Justice BRENNAN, with whom Justice MARSHALL joins, concurring in the judgment.

Iowa's truck length regulation challenged in this case is nearly identical to the Wisconsin regulation struck down in [Raymond]. In my view the same Commerce Clause restrictions that dictated that holding also require invalidation of Iowa's regulation insofar as it prohibits 65-foot doubles.

doubles, they do contribute to the pattern of parochialism apparent in Iowa's statute. [Footnote by Justice Powell.]

9. The dissenting opinion insists that we defer to Iowa's truck-length limitations because they represent the collective judgment of the Iowa legislature. This position is curious because, as noted above, the Iowa legislature approved a bill legalizing 65-foot doubles. The bill was vetoed by the Governor, primarily for parochial rather than legitimate safety reasons. The dissenting opinion is at a loss to explain the Governor's interest in deflecting interstate truck traffic around Iowa. [Footnote by Justice Powell.]

10. Brotherhood of Locomotive Firemen v. Chicago, R. I. & P. R. Co., [10th Ed., p. 286], in its result, although perhaps not in all of its language, is consistent with the conclusion we reach today. There, the Arkansas "full-crew" laws were upheld against constitutional challenge because the Court easily perceived that they made nonillusory contributions to safety. Here, as in Raymond, there was no such evidence. This case and Raymond recognize, as the Court did

in Brotherhood, that States constitutionally may enact laws that demonstrably promote safety, even when those laws also burden the flow of commerce. [Footnote by Justice Powell.]

11. [The District Court] found that the statute did not discriminate against such commerce. Because the record fully supports the decision below with respect to the burden on interstate commerce, we need not consider whether the statute also operated to discriminate against that commerce. The latter theory was neither briefed nor argued in this Court. [Footnote by Justice Powell.]

12. Justice Rehnquist in dissent states that, as he reads the various opinions in this case, "only four Justices invalidate Iowa's law on the basis of the analysis in Raymond." It should be emphasized that Raymond, the analysis of which was derived from the Court's opinion in Pike v. Bruce Church, was joined by each of the eight Justices who participated. Today, Justice Brennan finds it unnecessary to reach the Raymond analysis because he finds the Iowa statute to be flawed for a threshold reason. [Footnote by Justice Powell.]

The reasoning bringing me to that conclusion does not require, however, that I engage in the debate between my Brothers Powell and Rehnquist over what the District Court record shows on the question whether 65-foot doubles are more dangerous than shorter trucks. With all respect, my Brothers ask and answer the wrong question.

For me, analysis of Commerce Clause challenges to state regulations must take into account three principles: (1) The courts are not empowered to second-guess the empirical judgments of lawmakers concerning the utility of legislation. (2) The burdens imposed on commerce must be balanced against the local benefits actually sought to be achieved by the State's lawmakers, and not against those suggested after the fact by counsel. (3) Protectionist legislation is unconstitutional under the Commerce Clause, even if the burdens and benefits are related to safety rather than economics.

I. Both the opinion of my Brother Powell and the opinion of my Brother Rehnquist are predicated upon the supposition that the constitutionality of a state regulation is determined by the factual record created by the State's lawyers in trial court. But that supposition cannot be correct, for it would make the constitutionality of state laws and regulations depend on the vagaries of litigation rather than on the judgments made by the State's lawmakers.

In considering a Commerce Clause challenge to a state regulation, the judicial task is to balance the burden imposed on commerce against the local benefits sought to be achieved by the State's *lawmakers*. In determining those benefits, a court should focus ultimately on the regulatory purposes identified by the lawmakers and on the evidence before or available to them that might have supported their judgment. See generally Minnesota v. Clover Leaf Creamery Co., [1981; noted below in this Supplement]. Since the court must confine its analysis to the purposes the lawmakers had for maintaining the regulation, the only relevant evidence concerns whether the lawmakers could rationally have believed that the challenged regulation would foster those purposes. See Brotherhood. It is not the function of the court to decide whether *in fact* the regulation promotes its intended purpose, so long as an examination of the evidence before or available to the lawmaker indicates that the regulation is not wholly irrational in light of its purposes.[1]

II. My Brothers Powell and Rehnquist make the mistake of disregarding the intention of Iowa's lawmakers and assuming that resolution of the

---

1. Moreover, I would emphasize that in the field of safety—and perhaps in other fields where the decisions of State lawmakers are deserving of a heightened degree of deference—the role of the courts is not to balance asserted burdens against intended benefits as it is in other fields. Compare Raymond (Blackmun, J., concurring) (safety regulation) with Pike v. Bruce Church, Inc. (regulation intended "to protect and enhance the reputation of growers within the State"). In the field of safety, once the court has established that the intended safety benefit is not illusory, insubstantial, or nonexistent, it must defer to the State's lawmakers on the appropriate balance to be struck against other interests. I therefore disagree with my Brother Powell when he asserts that the degree of interference with interstate commerce may in the first instance be "weighed" against the State's safety interests: "Regulations designed [to promote the public health or safety] nevertheless may further the purpose so marginally, *and interfere with commerce so substantially*, as to be invalid under the Commerce Clause" (emphasis added). [Footnote by Justice Brennan.]

case must hinge upon the argument offered by Iowa's attorneys: that 65-foot doubles are more dangerous than shorter trucks. They then canvass the factual record and findings of the courts below and reach opposite conclusions as to whether the evidence adequately supports that empirical judgment. I repeat: my Brothers Powell and Rehnquist have asked and answered the wrong question. For although Iowa's lawyers in this litigation have defended the truck length regulation on the basis of the safety advantages of 55-foot singles and 60-foot doubles over 65-foot doubles, Iowa's actual rationale for maintaining the regulation had nothing to do with these purported differences. Rather, Iowa sought to discourage interstate truck traffic on Iowa's highways. Thus, the safety advantages and disadvantages of the types and lengths of trucks involved in this case are irrelevant to the decision.[2]

2. My Brother Rehnquist claims that the "argument" that a Court should defer to the actual purposes of the lawmakers rather than to the post hoc justifications of counsel "has been consistently rejected by the Court in other contexts." Apparently, he has overlooked such cases as Allied Stores of Ohio, Inc. v. Bowers, 358 U.S. 522 (1959), where we described the rationale for our earlier decision in Wheeling Steel Corp. v. Glander, 337 U.S. 562 (1949):
"The statutes, on their face admittedly discriminatory against nonresidents, themselves declared their purpose. [Having] themselves specifically declared their purpose, the Ohio statute left no room to conceive of any other purpose for their existence. And the declared purpose having been found arbitrarily discriminatory against nonresidents, the Court could hardly escape the conclusion." And in Weinberger v. Wiesenfeld, we said: "This Court need not . . . accept at face value assertions of legislative purposes, when an examination of the legislative scheme and its history demonstrates that the asserted purpose could not have been a goal of the legislation." And in Murgia, we stated that a classification challenged as being discriminatory will be upheld only if it "rationally furthers the purpose identified by the State." See also [e.g.] Minnesota v. Clover Leaf Creamery Co.; Califano v. Goldfarb (plurality opinion).

The extent to which we may rely upon post hoc justifications of counsel depends on the circumstances surrounding passage of the legislation. Where there is no evidence bearing on the actual purpose for a legislative classification, our analysis necessarily focuses on the suggestions of counsel. Even then, "marginally more demand-ing scrutiny" is appropriate to "test the plausibility of the tendered purpose." Schweiker v. Wilson [1981] (Powell, J., dissenting). But where the lawmakers' purposes in enacting a statute are explicitly set forth, or are clearly discernible from the legislative history, this Court should not take—and, with the possible exception of United States Railroad Retirement Board v. Fritz [1980; printed below] (Brennan, J., dissenting), has not taken—the extraordinary step of disregarding the *actual* purpose in favor of some "imaginary basis or purpose." McGinnis v. Royster. The principle of separation of powers requires, after all, that we defer to the elected lawmakers' judgment as to the appropriate means to accomplish an end, not that we defer to the arguments of lawyers.

If, as here, the only purpose ever articulated by the State's lawmakers for maintaining a regulation is illegitimate, I consider it contrary to precedent as well as to sound principles of constitutional adjudication for the courts to base their analysis on purposes never conceived by the lawmakers. This is especially true where, as the dissent's strained analysis of the relative safety of 65-foot doubles to shorter trucks amply demonstrates, the post hoc justifications are implausible as well as imaginary. I would emphasize that, although my Brother Powell's plurality opinion does not give as much weight to the illegitimacy of Iowa's actual purpose as I do, both that opinion and this concurrence have found the actual motivation of the Iowa lawmakers in maintaining the truck length regulation highly relevant to, if not dispositive of, the case. [Footnote by Justice Brennan. Many of the cases relied on by Justice Brennan in this

My Brother Powell concedes that [Iowa] seems to have hoped to limit the use of its highways by deflecting some through traffic. This conclusion is more than amply supported by the record and the legislative history of the Iowa regulation.

Although the Court has stated that "[i]n no field [has] deference to state regulation been greater than that of highway safety," it has declined to go so far as to presume that size restrictions are inherently tied to public safety. [Raymond.] The Court has emphasized that the "strong presumption of validity" of size restrictions "cannot justify a court in closing its eyes to uncontroverted evidence of record," ibid—here the obvious fact that the safety characteristics of 65-foot doubles did not provide the motivation for either legislators or Governor in maintaining the regulation.

III.   Though my Brother Powell recognizes that the State's actual purpose in maintaining the truck length regulation was "to limit the use of its highways by deflecting some through traffic," he fails to recognize that this purpose, being *protectionist* in nature, is *impermissible* under the Commerce Clause.[3] .   .   .

Iowa may not shunt off its fair share of the burden of maintaining interstate truck routes, nor may it create increased hazards on the highways of neighboring States in order to decrease the hazards on Iowa highways. Such an attempt has all the hallmarks of the "[simple] protectionism" this Court has condemned in the economic area. Philadelphia v. New Jersey. Just as a State's attempt to avoid interstate competition in economic goods may damage the prosperity of the Nation as a whole, so Iowa's attempt to deflect interstate truck traffic has been found to make the Nation's highways as a whole more hazardous. That attempt should therefore be subject to "a virtually per se rule of invalidity." Ibid.

This Court's heightened deference to the judgments of state lawmakers in the field of safety is largely attributable to a judicial disinclination to weigh the interests of safety against other societal interests, such as the economic interest in the free flow of commerce. Thus, "if safety justifications are not illusory, the Court will not second-guess legislative judgment about their importance *in comparison with related burdens on interstate commerce.*" [Raymond] (Blackmun, J., concurring) (emphasis added). Here, the decision of Iowa's lawmakers to promote *Iowa's* safety and other interests at the direct expense of the safety and other interests of neighboring States merits no such deference. No special judicial acuity is demanded to perceive that this sort of parochial legislation violates the Commerce Clause. .   .   .

Justice REHNQUIST, with whom The Chief Justice [BURGER] and Justice STEWART join, dissenting.

The result in this case suggests, to paraphrase Justice Jackson, that the only state truck length limit "that is valid is one which this court has not been

---

footnote (and later in his opinion) are equal protection, not commerce clause, cases. The debate between him and Justice Rehnquist about the relevance of "actual purpose" also surfaces in several of the equal protection cases in this Supplement, below.]

3.   It is not enough to conclude, as my Brother Powell does, that "the deference traditionally accorded a State's safety judgment is not warranted." [Footnote by Justice Brennan.]

able to get its hands on." Jungersen v. Ostby & Barton Co., 335 U.S. 560, 572 (1949) (dissenting opinion). Although the plurality and concurring opinions strike down Iowa's law by different routes, I believe the analysis in both opinions oversteps our "limited authority to review state legislation under the commerce clause" [Brotherhood] and seriously intrudes upon the fundamental right of the States to pass laws to secure the safety of their citizens. .   .   .

I.   It is necessary to elaborate somewhat on the facts as presented in the plurality opinion to appreciate fully what the Court does today. Iowa's action in limiting the length of trucks which may travel on its highways is in no sense unusual. Every State in the Union regulates the length of vehicles permitted to use the public roads. Nor is Iowa a renegade in having length limits which operate to exclude the 65-foot doubles favored by Consolidated. These trucks are prohibited in other areas of the country as well, some 17 States and the District of Columbia, including all of New England and most of the Southeast. While pointing out that Consolidated carries commodities through Iowa on Interstate 80, "the principal east-west route linking New York, Chicago, and the West Coast," the plurality neglects to note that both Pennsylvania and New Jersey, through which Interstate 80 runs before reaching New York, also ban 65-foot doubles. In short, the persistent effort in the plurality opinion to paint Iowa as an oddity standing alone to block commerce carried in 65-foot doubles is simply not supported [by the facts].

II.   [Justice Rehnquist next turned to "the appropriate analysis to be applied."]   [The] Court very recently reaffirmed the long-standing view that "in no field [has] deference to state regulation been greater than that of highway safety." [Raymond.]   [Those] challenging a highway safety regulation must overcome a "strong presumption of validity." [Bibb.]

A determination that a state law is a rational safety measure does not end the Commerce Clause inquiry. A "sensitive consideration" of the safety purpose in relation to the burden on commerce is required. [Raymond.] When engaging in such a consideration the Court does not directly compare safety benefits to commerce costs and strike down the legislation if the latter can be said in some vague sense to "outweigh" the former. Such an approach would make an empty gesture of the strong presumption of validity accorded state safety measures, particularly those governing highways. It would also arrogate to this Court functions of forming public policy, functions which, in the absence of congressional action, were left by the Framers of the Constitution to state legislatures. [See Barnwell; Brotherhood; Bibb.] These admonitions are peculiarly apt when, as here, the question involves the difficult comparison of financial losses and "the loss of lives and limbs of workers and people using the highways." Brotherhood.[1]

---

1.   It should not escape notice that a majority of the Court goes on record today as agreeing that courts in Commerce Clause cases do not sit to weigh safety benefits against burdens on commerce when the safety benefits are not illusory. Even the plurality gives lip service to this principle. I do not agree with my Brother Brennan, however, that only those safety benefits somehow articulated by the legislature as *the* motivation for the challenged statute can be considered in supporting the state law. See infra. [Footnote by Justice Rehnquist.]

The purpose of the "sensitive consideration" referred to above is rather to determine if the asserted safety justification, although rational, is merely a pretext for discrimination against interstate commerce. We will conclude that it is if the safety benefits from the regulation are demonstrably trivial while the burden on commerce is great. [The] nature of the inquiry is perhaps best illustrated by examining those cases in which state safety laws have been struck down on Commerce Clause grounds. In Southern Pacific a law regulating train lengths was viewed by the Court as having "at most slight and dubious advantage, if any, over unregulated train lengths;" the lower courts concluded the law actually tended to *increase* the number of accidents by increasing the number of trains. In Bibb the contoured mudguards required by Illinois, alone among the States, had *no* safety advantages over conventional mudguards and, as in Southern Pacific, actually *increased* hazards. [The] cases thus demonstrate that the safety benefits of a state law must be slight indeed before it will be struck down under the dormant Commerce Clause.

III. There can be no doubt that the challenged statute is a valid highway safety regulation and thus entitled to the strongest presumption of validity against Commerce Clause challenges. [A]ll 50 States regulate the length of trucks which may use their highways. The American Association of State Highway and Transportation Officials (AASHTO) has consistently recommended length as well as other limits on vehicles.[2] There can also be no question that the particular limit chosen by Iowa—60 feet—is rationally related to Iowa's safety objective. Most truck limits are between 55 and 65 feet, and Iowa's choice is thus well within the widely accepted range.

Iowa adduced evidence supporting the relation between vehicle length and highway safety. The evidence indicated that longer vehicles take greater time to pass, thereby increasing the risks of accidents, particularly during the inclement weather not uncommon in Iowa.[3] Longer trucks are more likely to clog intersections, and although there are no intersections on the Interstate Highways, the order below went beyond the highways themselves and the concerns about greater length at intersections would arise "at every trip origin, every trip destination, every intermediate stop for picking up trail-

2. The plurality points out that "AASHTO specifically recommends that states permit 65-foot doubles." But in the absence of its adoption by the Iowa legislative process, an AASHTO recommendation as to a particular length limit remains exactly that: a recommendation which no State is bound to follow. [Footnote by Justice Rehnquist.]

3. Although greater passing time was offered as a safety justification in Raymond, the Court noted that the trucking companies there "produced *uncontradicted* evidence that the difference in passing time does not pose an appreciable threat to motorists traveling on limited access, four-lane divided highways" (emphasis supplied). That is not the case here. Iowa indicated before the trial court the connection between greater passing time and greater hazard, primarily the longer exposure to splash and spray. For a vehicle traveling at 55 miles per hour passing a truck traveling at 52 miles per hour, the additional exposure from a 65-foot truck as opposed to a 60-foot truck would be 92 feet and more than a full second. The greater passing distance and time would become even more significant off the Interstates when oncoming traffic is involved, and the District Court order permits the longer trucks to operate off the Interstates. [Footnote by Justice Rehnquist.]

ers, reconfiguring loads, change of drivers, eating, refueling—every intermediate stop would generate this type of situation." [Iowa also] introduced evidence that doubles are more likely than singles to jackknife or upset. In addition Iowa elicited evidence undermining the probative value of Consolidated's evidence. [E.g.,] Consolidated's evidence of the relative safety record of doubles may have been based in large part not on the relative safety of the vehicles themselves but on the experience of the drivers. [Additional summaries of evidence omitted.] In sum, there was sufficient evidence presented at trial to support the legislative determination that length is related to safety, and nothing in Consolidated's evidence undermines this conclusion.

The District Court approached the case as if the question were whether Consolidated's 65-foot trucks were as safe as others permitted on Iowa highways. [The] question, however, is whether the Iowa Legislature has acted rationally in regulating vehicle lengths and whether the safety benefits from this regulation are more than slight or problematical. [See, e.g., Barnwell.] [4]

The answering of the relevant question is not appreciably advanced by comparing trucks slightly over the length limit with those at the length limit. It is emphatically not our task to balance any incremental safety benefits from prohibiting 65-foot doubles as opposed to 60-foot doubles against the burden on interstate commerce. Lines drawn for safety purposes will rarely pass muster if the question is whether a slight increment can be permitted without sacrificing safety. The question is rather whether it can be said that the benefits flowing to Iowa from a rational truck length limitation are "slight or problematical." See Bibb. The particular line chosen by Iowa—60 feet—is relevant only to the question whether the limit is a rational one. Once a court determines that it is, it considers the overall safety benefits *from the regulation* against burdens on interstate commerce, and not any marginal benefits from the scheme the State established as opposed to that the plaintiffs desire. See Southern Pacific (train length law struck down because it "affords at most slight and dubious advantage, if any, *over unregulated train lengths*") (emphasis supplied); Barnwell.

4. The concurring opinion of my Brother Brennan mischaracterizes this dissent when it states that I assume "resolution of the case must hinge upon the argument offered by Iowa's attorneys: that 65-foot doubles are more dangerous than shorter trucks." I assume nothing of the sort. As noted in the immediately preceding paragraph, the point of this dissent is that the [lower courts] erred when they undertook to determine if the prohibited trucks were as safe as the permitted ones on the basis of evidence presented at trial. As I read this Court's opinions, the state must simply prove, aided by a "strong presumption of validity," that the safety benefits of its law are not illusory. I review the evidence presented at trial simply to demonstrate that Iowa made such a showing in this case, not because the validity of Iowa's law depends on its proving by a preponderance of the evidence that the excluded trucks are unsafe. As I thought was made clear, it is my view that Iowa must simply show a relation between vehicle length limits and safety, and that the benefits from its length limit are not illusory. Iowa's arguments on passing time, intersection obstruction, and problems at the scene of accidents have validity beyond a comparison of the 65- and 60-foot trucks. In sum, I fully agree with Justice Brennan that the validity of Iowa's length limit does not turn on whether 65-foot trucks are less safe than 60-foot trucks. [Footnote by Justice Rehnquist.]

The difficulties with the contrary approach are patent. While it may be clear that there are substantial safety benefits from a 55-foot truck as compared to a 105-foot truck, these benefits may not be discernible in 5-foot jumps. Appellee's approach would permit what could not be accomplished in one lawsuit to be done in ten separate suits, each challenging an additional five feet.

Any direct balancing of marginal safety benefits against burdens on commerce would make the burdens on commerce the sole significant factor, and make likely the odd result that similar state laws enacted for identical safety reasons might violate the Commerce Clause in one part of the country but not another. For example, Mississippi and Georgia prohibit trucks over 55 feet. Since doubles are not operated in the Southeast, the demonstrable burden on commerce may not be sufficient to strike down these laws, while Consolidated maintains that it is in this case, even though the doubles here are given an additional five feet. On the other hand, if Consolidated were to win this case it could shift its 65-foot doubles to routes leading into Mississippi or Georgia (both States border States in which 65-foot trucks are permitted) and claim the same constitutional violation it claims in this case. Consolidated Freightways, and not this Court, would become the final arbiter of the Commerce Clause.

It must be emphasized that there is nothing in the laws of nature which makes 65-foot doubles an obvious norm. Consolidated operates 65-foot doubles on many of its routes simply because that is the largest size permitted in many States through which Consolidated travels. Doubles can and do come in smaller sizes; indeed, when Iowa adopted the present 60-foot limit in 1963, it was in accord with AASHTO recommendations. Striking down Iowa's law because Consolidated has made a voluntary business decision to employ 65-foot doubles, a decision based on the actions of other state legislatures, would essentially be compelling Iowa to yield to the policy choices of neighboring States. Under our Constitutional scheme, however, there is only one legislative body which can pre-empt the rational policy determination of the Iowa Legislature and that is Congress. Forcing Iowa to yield to the policy choices of neighboring States perverts the primary purpose of the Commerce Clause, that of vesting power to regulate interstate commerce in Congress, where all the States are represented.   .   .   .[5]

The Court of Appeals felt compelled to reach the result it did in light of our decision in Raymond and the plurality agrees that "[t]his case is Raymond revisited."[6] Raymond, however, does not control this case. The Court in

5. The extent to which the assertion of a violation of the Commerce Clause is simply an effort to compel Iowa to yield to the decisions of its neighbors is clearest if one asks whether Iowa's law would violate the Commerce Clause if the 17 States which currently prohibit Consolidated's 65-foot doubles were not in the East and Southeast but rather surrounded Iowa. [Footnote by Justice Rehnquist.]

6. The concurring opinion begins by stating that the regulation involved here is "nearly identical" to the one struck down in Raymond, but then approaches the case in a completely different manner than the Court in Raymond. My Brother Brennan votes to strike down Iowa's law not because the safety benefits of Iowa's law are illusory—indeed, he specifically declines to consider the safety benefits—but because he views it as protectionist in nature. As I read the vari-

Raymond emphasized that "[o]ur holding is a narrow one, for we do not decide whether laws of other States restricting the operation of trucks over 55 feet long, or of double-trailer trucks, would be upheld if the evidence produced on the safety issue were not so overwhelmingly one-sided as in this case." The Raymond court repeatedly stressed that the State "made no effort to contradict [evidence] of comparative safety with evidence of its own," that the trucking companies' evidence was "uncontroverted," and that the State "virtually defaulted in its defense of the regulations as a safety measure." By contrast, both the District Court and the Court of Appeals recognized that Iowa "made an all out effort" and "zealously presented arguments" on its safety case. As noted, Iowa has adduced evidence sufficient to support its safety claim and has rebutted much of the evidence submitted by Consolidated.

Furthermore, the exception to the Wisconsin prohibition which the Court specifically noted in Raymond finds no parallel in this case. The exception in Raymond permitted oversized vehicles to travel from plant to plant in Wisconsin or between a Wisconsin plant and the border. [T]his discriminated on its face between Wisconsin industries and the industries of other States. The border cities exception to the Iowa length limit does not. Iowa shippers in cities with border city ordinances may use longer vehicles in interstate commerce, but interstate shippers coming into such cities may do so as well. Cities without border city ordinances may neither export nor import on oversized vehicles. Nor can the border cities exception be "[v]iewed realistically," as was the Wisconsin exception, to "be the product of compromise between forces within the State that seek to retain the State's general truck length limit, and industries within the State that complain that the general limit is unduly burdensome." Raymond. The Wisconsin exception was available to all Wisconsin industries wanting to ship out of State from Wisconsin plants. The border cities exception is of much narrower applicability: only five of Iowa's sixteen largest cities and only eight cities in all permit oversized trucks under the border cities exception. The population of the eight cities with border city ordinances is only 13 percent of the population of the State.

My Brother Brennan argues that the Court should consider only *the* purpose the Iowa legislators *actually* sought to achieve by the length limit, and not the purposes advanced by Iowa's lawyers in defense of the statute. This argument calls to mind what was said of the Roman Legions: that they may have lost battles, but they never lost a war, since they never let a war end until they had won it. The argument has been consistently rejected by the Court in other contexts, compare, e.g., United States Railroad Retirement Board v. Fritz [1980] with id. (Brennan, J., dissenting) and Michael M. v. Superior Court [1981] (plurality opinion) with id. (Brennan, J., dissenting) [both printed below], and Justice Brennan can cite no authority for the proposition that possible legislative purposes suggested by a state's lawyers should not be considered in Commerce Clause cases. The problems with a view such as that advanced in the concurring opinion are apparent. To name just a

ous opinions in this case, therefore, only four Justices invalidate Iowa's law on the basis of the analysis in Raymond. [Footnote by Justice Rehnquist.]

few, it assumes that individual legislators are motivated by one discernible "actual" purpose, and ignores the fact that different legislators may vote for a single piece of legislation for widely different reasons. How, for example, would a court adhering to the views expressed in the concurring opinion approach a statute, the legislative history of which indicated that 10 votes were based on safety considerations, 10 votes were based on protectionism, and the statute passed by a vote of 40–20? What would the *actual* purpose of the *legislature* have been in that case? . . . [7]

7. It is not a particularly pleasant task for the author of a dissent joined by two other Members of the Court to take issue with a statement made by the author of a concurrence in that same case which is joined by only one Member of the Court. Such fragmentation, particularly between two opinions neither of which command the adherence of a majority of the Court, cannot help but further unsettle what certainty there may be in the legal principles which govern our decision of commerce clause cases such as this and lay a foundation for similar uncertainty in other sorts of constitutional adjudication. Nonetheless, I feel obliged to take up the cudgels, however unwillingly, because Justice Brennan's concurrence, joined by Justice Marshall, is not only mistaken in its analysis but also in its efforts to interpret the meaning of today's decision.

Although both my Brother Brennan and I have cited cases from the equal protection area, it is not clear that the analysis of legislative purpose in that area is the same as in the present context. It may be more reasonable to suppose that proffered purposes of a statute, whether advanced by a legislature or post hoc by lawyers, cloak impermissible aims in Commerce Clause cases than in equal protection cases. Statutes generally favor one group at the expense of another, and the equal protection clause was not designed to proscribe this in the way that the Commerce Clause was designed to prevent local barriers to interstate commerce. Thus even if my Brother Brennan's arguments were supportable in Commerce Clause cases, that analysis would not carry over of its own force into the realm of equal protection generally.

But even in the Commerce Clause area, his arguments are unpersuasive. Allied Stores v. Bowers seems to me to cut against his position. . . .

Nor do the more recent decisions [—all equal protection cases—] cited by my Brother Brennan support his argument. For example, the fact that we *"need not* [accept] at face value assertions of legislative purposes, when an examination of the legislative scheme and its history demonstrates that the asserted purpose *could not* have been a goal of the legislation," [Weinberger v. Wiesenfeld] (emphasis supplied), hardly supports the proposition that we *cannot* consider assertions of legislative purpose which *could* have been a goal of the legislation, even though such purposes may not have been identified as goals by the legislature. To take another example, the upholding of the law in Murgia because it "rationally furthers the purpose identified by the State" certainly does not suggest that by "State" this Court meant only "legislature," and not the State's attorneys, or that *only* those purposes identified by the State could be considered in reviewing legislation.

Although Justice Brennan "would emphasize" the significance the plurality opinion attaches to the Governor's articulation of what is viewed as an impermissible purpose, this hardly supports the proposition that permissible purposes cannot be considered by a court unless they were somehow identified by the legislature as goals of the statute. The plurality opinion in fact examines the asserted safety purpose of the Iowa statute at some length. Indeed, Justice Brennan criticizes the plurality for examining the safety purpose and "disregarding the intention of Iowa's lawmakers."

Finally, Justice Brennan's statement that we have strayed from what he regards as the true faith in our recent decision in [Fritz], albeit over his vigorous dissent, does not aid his argument. His dissent, while undoubtedly vigorous, was not sufficiently persuasive to deter six Members of the Court from joining that opinion. [Footnote by Justice Rehnquist.]

Both the plurality and concurring opinions attach great significance to the Governor's veto of a bill passed by the Iowa Legislature permitting 65-foot doubles. Whatever views one may have about the significance of legislative motives, it must be emphasized that the law which the Court strikes down today was not passed to achieve the protectionist goals the plurality and the concurrence ascribe to the Governor. Iowa's 60-foot length limit was established in 1963, at a time when very few States permitted 65-foot doubles. Striking down legislation on the basis of asserted legislative motives is dubious enough, but the plurality and concurrence strike down the legislation involved in this case because of asserted impermissible motives for *not* enacting *other* legislation, motives which could not possibly have been present when the legislation under challenge here was considered and passed. Such action is, so far as I am aware, unprecedented in this Court's history.

Furthermore, the effort in both the plurality and concurring opinions to portray the legislation involved here as protectionist is in error. Whenever a State enacts more stringent safety measures than its neighbors, in an area which affects commerce, the safety law will have the incidental effect of deflecting interstate commerce to the neighboring States. Indeed, the safety and protectionist motives cannot be separated: The whole purpose of safety regulation of vehicles is to *protect* the State from unsafe vehicles. If a neighboring State chooses *not* to protect its citizens from the danger discerned by the enacting State, that is its business, but the enacting State should not be penalized when the vehicles it considers unsafe travel through the neighboring State.

The other States with truck length limits that exclude Consolidated's 65-foot doubles would not at all be paranoid in assuming that they might be next on Consolidated's "hit list." [8] The true problem with today's decision is that it gives no guidance whatsoever to these States as to whether their laws are valid or how to defend them. For that matter, the decision gives no guidance to Consolidated or other trucking firms either. Perhaps, after all is said and done, the Court today neither says nor does very much at all. We know only that Iowa's law is invalid and that the jurisprudence of the "negative side" of the Commerce Clause remains hopelessly confused.

8. Consolidated was a plaintiff in Raymond as well as this case. [Footnote by Justice Rehnquist.]

CONGRESS AND HIGHWAY SAFETY REGULATION

Although Kassel remains important for what it suggests regarding the standard of review for state highway regulations challenged under the commerce clause,* the precise issue before the Court in Kassel has been largely mooted by subsequent Congressional action. Both the Surface Transportation Assistance Act of 1982 (Pub.L. 97–424, 96 Stat. 2097) and the Department of Transportation Appropriations Act, 1983 (Pub.L. 97–369, 96 Stat. 1765) significantly displace state law in the field of truck weight, length, and width. The acts prescribe uniform weight and width requirements, and minimum length requirements, for trucks using the Interstate Highway System and other "qualifying" Federal-aid highways. Trailer lengths are for the first time regulated at the federal level. Under the acts, states must modify their laws to comport with the federal standards, and both injunctive relief and withholding of federal funds are available as remedies against non-complying states.

In the legislative history accompanying the uniform weight requirements, Congress indicated that the existence of differing weight laws in neighboring states imposed an "undue burden on interstate commerce." Does this congressional determination suggest that *all* state highway regulations should receive especially close scrutiny? Or does this evidence of congressional willingness to deal with the problem of state burdens on interstate commerce in the highway area indicate that Congress is fully able to protect its own prerogatives without the active assistance of the courts?

10th ED., p. 327
Add as footnote to Note 1:

a. For another strong statement by the modern Court condemning state restrictions on the export of natural resources, see the unanimous decision in New England Power Co. v. New Hampshire, 455 U.S. 331 (1982). The Company had for many years exported to out-of-state customers most of the hydroelectric energy generated at its power stations on the Connecticut River in New Hampshire. In 1980, a New Hampshire state agency withdrew the Company's authority to export the locally generated power. The agency acted pursuant to a state law banning the exportation of energy whenever the agency determined that the energy "is reasonably required for use within the state and that the public good requires that it be delivered for such use."

Chief Justice Burger's opinion concluded that the state ban violated the commerce clause and had not received congressional consent: "Our cases consistently have held that [the commerce clause] precludes a State from mandating that its

* Not surprisingly, lower courts have had difficulty in interpreting Kassel. The Third Circuit, in rejecting a Kassel-inspired challenge to a Pennsylvania law requiring periodic inspection of motor carrier vehicles, explicitly adopted the deferential standard articulated in Justice Rehnquist's dissent. American Trucking Associations, Inc. v. Larson, 683 F.2d 787 (3d Cir.), cert. denied 458 U.S. — (1982). But other courts have employed the balancing approach of the Kassel plurality. Swift Transportation, Inc. v. John, 546 F.Supp. 1185 (D.Ariz.1982); Gutridge v. Commonwealth, 532 F.Supp. 533 (E.D.Va. 1982.)

residents be given a preferred right of access, over out-of-state consumers, to natural resources located within its borders or to the products derived therefrom. E.g., [Hughes v. Oklahoma; Pennsylvania v. West Virginia; Philadelphia v. New Jersey]." He rejected New Hampshire's effort to distinguish the prior cases on the ground that the State "owned" the Connecticut River: "Whatever the extent of the State's proprietary interest in the river, the preeminent authority to regulate the flow of navigable waters resides with the federal government, which has licensed [the Company] to operate its Connecticut River hydroelectric plants. [The State's] purported 'ownership' of the Connecticut River therefore provides no justification for restricting or conditioning the use of these federally-licensed units. Moreover, New Hampshire has done more than regulate use of the resource it assertedly owns; it has restricted the sale of electric energy, a product entirely distinct from the river waters used to produce it. This product is manufactured by a private corporation using privately-owned facilities. Thus, New Hampshire's reliance on Reeves, Inc. v. Stake [addition to p. 328, below]—holding that a State may confine to its residents the sale of products it *produces*—is misplaced." (New Hampshire's strongest defense for its ban was that Congress, in the Federal Power Act, had expressly consented to the export restriction. The Court's rejection of that claim is noted below, addition to p. 356.)

b. See also the reiteration of the Court's skepticism about state export controls on natural resources in Sporhase v. Nebraska, 458 U.S. — (1982). The case is of special interest because it involved a state restriction on the export of ground water. Water is a scarce commodity in many states; Congress has long recognized the predominance of state law in the delineation of water rights; and advocates of state restraints in the interest of "conservation" have long maintained that the regulation of water resources enjoys a special, broad immunity from the typical commerce clause restrictions on state regulation of natural resources. But the Court's 7 to 2 decision in the Nebraska case, while acknowledging some state authority to restrict export of water, refused to accept the State's broadest immunity claims. The Court held unconstitutional a portion of a statutory restriction on the withdrawal of ground water from any well within Nebraska intended for use in an adjoining state.

Nebraska brought this action to enjoin appellants, owners of contiguous tracts of land in Nebraska and Colorado, from transferring water across the border without a permit. Appellants had pumped water from their well on their Nebraska tract in order to irrigate both their Nebraska and Colorado tracts. They had ignored a Nebraska permit requirement under which a state agency could issue a permit on finding not only that the withdrawal of the ground water was "reasonable," "not contrary to the conservation and use of ground water," and "not otherwise detrimental to the public welfare" but also that "the state in which the water is to be used grants reciprocal rights to withdraw and transport ground water from that state for use [in] Nebraska." Colorado did not grant such reciprocal rights; appellants accordingly could not have obtained the Nebraska permit because of the statute's reciprocity requirement. The Court concluded that the "reciprocity requirement does not survive the 'strictest scrutiny' reserved for facially discriminatory legislation. Hughes v. Oklahoma." [1]

Justice Stevens' majority opinion found that (1) ground water is an article of commerce and therefore subject to congressional regulation; [2] (2) the Nebraska restriction on the interstate transfer of ground water imposed an impermissible burden on commerce; and (3) Congress had not granted the states permission to engage in ground water regulation that otherwise would be impermissible. In reject-

1. The Court noted: "The reciprocity requirement cannot, of course, be justified as a response to another State's unreasonable burden on commerce. A. & P. Tea Co. v. Cottrell [1976; 10th Ed., p. 310]."

2. Justice Rehnquist's dissent charged the majority with "gratuitously undertak[ing]" to decide this first issue. Congress could clearly regulate ground water whether or not it consti-

tuted an "article of commerce"; all it needed to show was that a ground water overdraft had a substantial economic effect on interstate commerce. "It [is] wholly unnecessary to decide whether Congress could regulate groundwater overdraft in order to decide this case; since Congress has not undertaken such a regulation, I would leave the determination of its validity until such time as it is necessary to decide that question."

ing the Nebraska Supreme Court's contention that water is not an article of commerce, Justice Stevens rejected the state court's reliance on such cases as Geer and Hudson County Water (10th Ed., p. 327) which had rested on the "fiction" of state ownership of its water. Nebraska nevertheless argued that water was distinguishable from other natural resources because, under state law, the surface owner enjoys "a lesser ownership interest in the water than the captor of game birds or minnows" in Geer and Hughes v. Oklahoma (10th Ed., p. 328). Justice Stevens stated: "Although [Nebraska's] greater ownership interest may not be irrelevant to Commerce Clause analysis, it does not absolutely remove Nebraska ground water from such scrutiny. For [Nebraska's] argument is still based on the legal fiction of state ownership." Moreover, water was not distinguishable from other natural resources because it was "essential for human survival." Although the arguments for "state and local management of ground water" were strong, "the States' interests clearly have an interstate dimension." Most water supplies are used for agricultural purposes, and agricultural markets supplied by irrigated farms were "worldwide" and "provide the archetypical example of commerce among the several States." Nebraska's claims were relevant in Commerce Clause balancing, but they did not immunize the state regulation from such balancing.

Turning to that balancing, Justice Stevens recited the formula of Pike v. Bruce Church (see 10th Ed., pp. 296 and 327). He found Nebraska's purpose "to conserve and preserve diminishing sources of ground water" "unquestionably legitimate and highly important" as well as "genuine." He noted that "we are reluctant to condemn as unreasonable measures taken by a State to conserve and preserve for its own citizens this vital resource in times of severe shortage. [A] State's power to regulate the use of water in times and places of shortage for the purpose of protecting the health of its citizens—and not simply the health of its economy—is at the core of its police power. For Commerce Clause purposes, we have long recognized a difference between economic protectionism [and] health and safety regulation. [See Hood v. DuMond.]" The first three conditions in the permit scheme accordingly did not on their face "impermissibly burden interstate commerce." But the reciprocity provision did operate as "an explicit barrier to commerce. [The] State therefore bears the initial burden of demonstrating a close fit between the reciprocity requirement and its asserted local purpose. [Hughes v. Oklahoma; Dean Milk.]"

Justice Stevens concluded that the "reciprocity requirement fails to clear this initial hurdle. For there is no evidence that this restriction is narrowly tailored to the conservation and preservation rationale. Even though the supply of water in a particular well may be abundant [and] even though the most beneficial use of that water might be in another State, such water may not be shipped into a neighboring State that does not permit its water to be used in Nebraska." If it could be shown that Nebraska "as a whole suffers a water shortage, [then] the conservation and preservation purpose might be credibly advanced for the reciprocity provision. A demonstrably arid state conceivably might be able to marshall evidence to establish a close means-end relationship between even a total ban on the exportation of water and a purpose to conserve and preserve water. [Nebraska], however, does not claim that such evidence exists. We therefore are not persuaded that the reciprocity requirement—when superimposed on the first three restrictions in the statute— significantly advances the state's legitimate conservation and preservation interests; it surely is not narrowly tailored to serve that purpose. [It] does not survive the 'strictest scrutiny' reserved for facially discriminatory legislation. Hughes v. Oklahoma." 3

Justice Rehnquist, joined by Justice O'Connor, dissented. He emphasized "the traditional authority of a State over resources within its boundaries which are es-

---

3. Justice Stevens also rejected the claim that Congress had authorized the states "to impose otherwise impermissible burdens on interstate commerce in ground water." True, Congress had approved a number of interstate compacts dealing with water and had enacted 37 statutes deferring to state water law. But that did not demonstrate (with the degree of explicitness required for congressional "consent," see sec. 2 of this chapter) that "Congress wished to remove federal constitutional constraints on such state laws. The negative implications of the Commerce Clause, like the mandates of the Fourteenth Amendment, are ingredients of the *valid* state law to which Congress has deferred."

sential not only to the well-being, but often to the very lives of its citizens. In the exercise of this authority, a State may so regulate a natural resource so as to preclude that resource from attaining the status of an 'article of commerce' for the purposes of the negative impact of the Commerce Clause. It is difficult, if not impossible, to conclude that 'commerce' exists in an item that cannot be reduced to possession under state law and in which the State recognizes only a usufructuary right. 'Commerce' cannot exist in a natural resource that cannot be sold, rented, traded, or transferred, but only *used*. Of course, a State may not discriminate against interstate commerce when it regulates even such a resource. If the State allows indiscriminate intrastate commercial dealings in a particular resource, it may have a difficult task proving that an outright prohibition on interstate commercial dealings is not such a discrimination. I had thought that this was the basis for this Court's decisions in [e.g., Hughes v. Oklahoma.] [By] contrast, Nebraska so regulates groundwater that it cannot be said that the State permits any 'commerce,' intrastate or interstate, to exist in this natural resource. As [in] almost all of the Western States, [Nebraska] grants landowners only a right to *use groundwater on the land from which it has been extracted*."

Justice Rehnquist concluded: "[Since] Nebraska recognizes only a limited right to use groundwater on land owned by the appropriator, it cannot be said that 'commerce' in groundwater exists as far as Nebraska is concerned. Therefore, it cannot be said that [the statute] either discriminates against, or 'burdens,' interstate commerce. [The statute] is simply a regulation of the landowner's *right to use* groundwater extracted from lands he owns within Nebraska. Unlike the Court, I cannot agree that Nebraska's limitation upon a landowner's right to extract water from his land situated in Nebraska *for his own use* on land he owns in an adjoining State runs afoul of Congress' unexercised authority to regulate interstate commerce."

10th ED., p. 327
Add as footnote to Note 2:

Although the modern Court carefully scrutinizes state *regulations* burdening access to natural resources, it is very reluctant to intervene when the burdens on access arise from state *tax* laws. That reluctance is illustrated by Commonwealth Edison Co. v. Montana, 453 U.S. 609 (1981). There, the burden arose from a "severance tax" that Montana imposes on coal mined in the State.

Montana has approximately 25% of all known United States coal reserves, and more than 50% of the nation's low-sulfur coal reserves. Federal environmental legislation has sharply increased the demand for low-sulfur coal. Moreover, the Montana coal fields occupy a "pivotal" geographic position in the midwestern and northwestern energy markets. Consequently, Montana has supplied a growing percentage of the nation's coal.

In the late 1970's, during a period of energy scarcity, Montana drastically increased its severance tax on coal to a maximum of 30% of the "contract sales price." Montana's tax revision is typical of the behavior of the relatively few energy-rich states whose resources have become ever more important to the much larger number of energy-hungry, consuming states. To be sure, the tax is imposed at the same rate regardless of whether the coal is used in-state or out-of-state. But, since most of Montana's coal is exported, the tax burden is borne primarily by out-of-state consumers. As a result of the heightened tax, an ever-increasing percentage of Montana's revenue comes from its coal industry.

The challengers tried to persuade the Court that the Commerce Clause gives residents of one state a right of access at "reasonable" prices to resources located in a resource-abundant state. But the Court, by a 6 to 3 margin, was "not convinced that the Commerce Clause, of its own force, gives the residents of one State the right to control in this fashion the terms of resource development and depletion in a sister State."

The challengers also argued that Montana, by imposing the tax, "is [unconstitutionally] 'exploiting' its 'monopoly' position with respect to [coal]." Justice Marshall's majority opinion responded: "We [do not] share [the challengers'] apparent view that the Commerce Clause injects principles of antitrust law into the relations between the States. [Under the challengers' approach], the threshold questions [—i.e., whether a State enjoys a 'monopoly' position and whether the tax burden is shifted out-of-state—] would require complex factual inquiries about such issues as elasticity of demand for the product and alternate sources of supply." Thus, Justice Marshall was untroubled by the fact that the Montana trial court had not listened to any evidence before it ruled in favor of the tax. The majority's view was in essence that only in cases of explicit discrimination would the Court interfere. In effect, the majority left it to Congress to curb any "exploitation" by energy-rich states.

Justice Blackmun, joined by Justices Powell and Stevens, submitted a sharp dissent. He claimed that state severance taxes upon minerals are particularly susceptible to "tailoring"—i.e., shaping of the tax so that the major burden falls on out-of-state consumers—and that the challengers should have received a full trial of their claims. He commented: " 'Like a tollgate lying athwart a trade route, a severance or processing tax conditions access to natural resoucs.' Thus, to the extent that the taxing jurisdiction approaches a monopoly position in the mineral, and consumption is largely outside the State, such taxes are '[e]conomically and politically analogous to transportation taxes exploiting geographical position.' " He noted, moreover: "Several commentators have agreed that Montana and other similarly situated western States have pursued a policy of 'OPEC-like revenue maximization,' and that the Montana tax bears no reasonable relationship to the services and protection afforded by the State."

Justice Blackmun conceded that "the mere fact that the burden of a severance tax is largely shifted forward to out-of-state consumers does not, standing alone, make out a Commerce Clause violation." "But," he added, "the Clause *is* violated when, as [the challengers] allege is the case here, the State effectively selects 'a class of out-of-state taxpayers to shoulder a tax burden grossly in excess of any costs imposed directly or indirectly by such taxpayers on the State.' " While a trial would require "complex factual inquiries," "this threshold inquiry is [not] beyond judicial competence." It plainly is not beyond judicial competence, for example, to determine whether "the tax singles out [a] particular interstate activity and charges it with a grossly disproportionate share of the general costs of government." He concluded: "To be sure, the task is likely to prove to be a formidable one; but its difficulty does not excuse our failure to undertake it. This case poses extremely grave issues that threaten both to 'polarize the Nation,' and to reawaken 'the tendencies toward economic Balkanization' that the Commerce Clause was designed to remedy. See Hughes v. Oklahoma. It is no answer to say that the matter is better left to Congress."

10th ED., p. 328
Add to footnote * :

a. As noted in the Tenth Edition, the Court held near the end of the 1979–80 Term that South Dakota could confine to its residents the sale of cement produced in state-owned plants. Reeves, Inc. v. Stake, 447 U.S. 429 (1980). The majority in the 5 to 4 decision followed the Alexandria Scrap case, distinguished Hughes v. Oklahoma, and found that the State, as a "market participant" rather than a "regulator," was not subject to the strictures of the Commerce Clause when it adopted marketing policies barring out-of-state purchasers. A fuller explanation of the Justices' reasoning follows.

Justice Blackmun's majority opinion stated: "The basic distinction drawn in Alexandria Scrap between States as market participants and States as market regulators makes good sense and sound law. As that case explains, the Commerce Clause responds principally to state taxes and regulatory measures impeding free private trade in the national marketplace. There is no indication of a constitutional plan to limit the ability of the States themselves to operate freely in the free market.

"[Judicial restraint] in this area is also counseled by considerations of state sovereignty, the role of each State ' "as guardian and trustee for its people" ' and 'the long recognized right of trader or manufacturer, engaged in an entirely private business, freely to exercise his own independent discretion as to parties with whom he will deal.' Moreover, state proprietary activities may be, and often are, burdened with the same restrictions imposed on private market participants. Evenhandedness suggests that, when acting as proprietors, States should similarly share existing freedoms from federal constraints, including the inherent limits of the Commerce Clause. Finally, as this case illustrates, the competing considerations in cases involving state proprietary action often will be subtle, complex, politically charged, and difficult to assess under traditional Commerce Clause analysis. Given these factors, Alexandria Scrap wisely recognizes that, as a rule, the adjustment of interests in this context is a task better suited for Congress than this Court."

In rejecting the challenger's arguments, Justice Blackmun stated, inter alia: "First, petitioner protests that South Dakota's preference for its residents responds solely to the 'non-governmental objectiv[e]' of protectionism. Therefore, petitioner argues, the policy is per se invalid. See Philadelphia v. New Jersey. We find the label 'protectionism' of little help in this context. The State's refusal to sell to buyers other than South Dakotans is 'protectionist' only in the sense that it limits benefits generated by a state program to those who fund the state treasury and whom the State was created to serve. Petitioner's argument apparently also would characterize as 'protectionist' rules restricting to state residents the enjoyment of state educational institutions, energy generated by a state-run plant, police and fire protection, and agricultural improvement and business development programs. Such policies, while perhaps 'protectionist' in a loose sense, reflect the essential and patently unobjectionable purpose of state government—to serve the citizens of the State.

"Second, petitioner echoes the District Court's warning: 'If a state in this Union were allowed to hoard its commodities or resources for the use of their own residents only, a drastic situation might evolve. For example, Pennsylvania or Wyoming might keep their coal, the northwest its timber, and the mining states their minerals. The result being that embargo may be retaliated by embargo and commerce would be halted at state lines.' See, e.g., Baldwin v. Montana Fish & Game Comm'n. This argument, although rooted in the core purpose of the Commerce Clause, does not fit the present facts. Cement is not a natural resource, like coal, timber, wild game, or minerals. Cf. [Hughes v. Oklahoma]. It is the end product of a complex process whereby a costly physical plant and human labor act on raw materials. South Dakota has not sought to limit access to the State's limestone or other materials used to make cement. Nor has it restricted the ability of private firms or sister States to set up plants within its borders. Moreover, petitioner has not suggested that South Dakota possesses unique access to the materials needed to produce cement. Whatever limits might exist on a State's ability to invoke the Alexandria Scrap exemption to hoard resources which by happenstance are found there, those limits do not apply here.

"Third, it is suggested that the South Dakota program is infirm because it places South Dakota suppliers of ready-mix concrete at a competitive advantage in the out-of-state market; Wyoming suppliers, such as petitioner, have little chance against South Dakota suppliers who can purchase cement from the State's plant and freely sell beyond South Dakota's borders. The force of this argument is seriously diminished, if not eliminated, by several considerations. [E.g., the] argument necessarily implies that the South Dakota scheme would be unobjectionable if sales in other States were totally barred. It therefore proves too much, for it would tolerate even a greater measure of protectionism and stifling of interstate commerce than the challenged system allows.

"[In] its last argument, petitioner urges that, had South Dakota not acted, free market forces would have generated an appropriate level of supply at free market prices for all buyers in the region. Having replaced free market forces, South Dakota should be forced to replicate how the free market would have operated under prevailing conditions. This argument appears to us to be simplistic and speculative. The very reason South Dakota built its plant was because the free market had failed adequately to supply the region with cement. There is no indication, and no way to know, that private industry would have moved into petitioner's market area, and would have ensured a supply of cement to petitioner either prior to or during the 1978 construction season.

"[We] conclude, then, that the arguments for invalidating South Dakota's resident-preference program are weak at best. Whatever residual force inheres in them is more than offset by countervailing considerations of policy and fairness. Reversal would discourage similar state projects, even though this project demonstrably has served the needs of state residents and has helped the entire region for more than a half century. Reversal also would rob South Dakota of the intended benefit of its foresight, risk, and industry. Under these circumstances, there is no reason to depart from the general rule of Alexandria Scrap."

Justice Powell's dissent, joined by Justices Brennan, White and Stevens, insisted that South Dakota's sales policy "represents precisely the kind of economic protectionism that the Commerce Clause was intended to prevent.[1] The Court, however, finds no violation of the Commerce Clause solely because the State produces the cement. I agree with the Court that [South Dakota] may provide cement for its public needs without violating the Commerce Clause. But I cannot agree that South Dakota may withhold its cement from interstate commerce in order to benefit private citizens and businesses within the State."

Justice Powell explained his position as follows: "The Commerce Clause has proved an effective weapon against protectionism. [This] case presents a novel constitutional question. The Commerce Clause would bar legislation imposing on private parties the type of restraint on commerce adopted by South Dakota.[2] Conversely, a private business constitutionally could adopt a marketing policy that excluded customers who come from another State. This case falls between those polar situations. The State [engages] in a commercial enterprise and restricts its own interstate distribution. The question is whether the [state's] policy should be treated like state regulation of private parties or like the marketing policy of a private business.

"The application of the Commerce Clause to this case should turn on the nature of the governmental activity involved. If a public enterprise undertakes an 'integral operatio[n]' in areas of traditional governmental functions,' National League of Cities v. Usery, the Commerce Clause is not directly relevant. If, however, the State enters the private market and operates a commercial enterprise for the advantage of its private citizens, it may not evade the constitutional policy against economic Balkanization.

"This distinction derives from the power of governments to supply their own needs and from the purpose of the Commerce Clause itself, which is designed to protect 'the natural functioning of the interstate market.' In procuring goods and services for the operation of government, a State may act without regard to the private marketplace and remove itself from the reach of the Commerce Clause. But when a State itself becomes a participant in the private market for other purposes, the Constitution forbids actions that would impede the flow of interstate commerce. These categories recognize no more than the 'constitutional line between the State as government and the State as trader.' [E.g., New York v. United States.]

1. "By 'protectionism,' I refer to state policies designed to protect private economic interests within the State from the forces of the interstate market. I would exclude from this term policies relating to traditional governmental functions, such as education, and subsidy programs like the one at issue in [Alexandria Scrap]." [Footnote by Justice Powell.]

2. "The Court attempts to distinguish prior decisions that address Commerce Clause limitations on a State's regulation of natural resource exploitation. E.g., Hughes v. Oklahoma; Pennsylvania v. West Virginia. The Court contends that cement production, unlike the activities involved in those cases, 'is the end product of a complex process whereby a costly physical plant and human labor act on raw materials.' The Court's distinction fails in two respects. First, the principles articulated in the natural resources cases also have been applied in decisions involving agricultural production, notably milk processing. E.g., Hood v. Du Mond; Pike v. Bruce Church, Inc. More fundamentally, the Court's definition of cement production describes all sophisticated economic activity, including the exploitation of natural resources. The extraction of natural gas, for example, could hardly occur except through a 'complex process whereby a costly physical plant and human labor act on raw materials.'

"The Court also suggests that the Commerce Clause has no application to this case because South Dakota does not 'possess unique access to the materials needed to produce cement.' But in its regional market, South Dakota has unique access to *cement*. A cutoff in cement sales has the same economic impact as a refusal to sell resources like natural gas. Customers can seek other sources of supply, or find a substitute product, or do without. Regardless of the nature of the product the State hoards, the consumer has been denied the guarantee of the Commerce Clause that he 'may look [to] free competition from every producing area in the Nation to protect him from exploitation by any.' Hood v. Du Mond." [Footnote by Justice Powell.]

"The Court holds that South Dakota, like a private business, should not be governed by the Commerce Clause when it enters the private market. But precisely because South Dakota is a State, it cannot be presumed to behave like an enterprise 'engaged in an entirely private business.' A State frequently will respond to market conditions on the basis of political rather than economic concerns. To use the Court's terms, a State may attempt to act as a 'market regulator' rather than a 'market participant.' In that situation, it is a pretense to equate the State with a private economic actor. State action burdening interstate trade is no less state action because it is accomplished by a public agency authorized to participate in the private market.

"[Unlike] the market subsidies at issue in Alexandria Scrap, the marketing policy of the South Dakota Cement Commission has cut off interstate trade.[3] The State can raise such a bar when it enters the market to supply its own needs. In order to ensure an adequate supply of cement for public uses, the State can withhold from interstate commerce the cement needed for public projects. The State, however, has no parallel justification for favoring private, in-state customers over out-of-state customers. In response to political concerns that likely would be inconsequential to a private cement producer, South Dakota has shut off its cement sales to customers beyond its borders. That discrimination constitutes a direct barrier to trade 'of the type forbidden by the Commerce Clause, and involved in previous cases.' Alexandria Scrap. The effect on interstate trade is the same as if the state legislature had imposed the policy on private cement producers. The Commerce Clause prohibits this severe restraint on commerce."

b. Alexandria Scrap and Reeves provided the basis for the Court's decision in White v. Massachusetts Council of Construction Employers, Inc., 460 U.S. — (1983). At issue in White was an executive order of the mayor of Boston that "required that all construction projects funded in whole or in part by city funds, or funds which the city had the authority to administer, should be performed by a work force consisting of at least half *bona fide* residents of Boston." In upholding the requirement against a dormant commerce clause challenge, the Court specifically reaffirmed "the proposition that when a state or local government enters the market as a participant it is not subject to the restraints of the Commerce Clause."

The Massachusetts Supreme Court, in striking down the executive order, had relied on the significant impact on interstate commerce, as well as on the failure of the order to incorporate less restrictive alternatives. In reversing this decision, the Supreme Court, with Justice Rehnquist writing the opinion, made clear that these and other aspects of a balancing analysis are inappropriate when a city or state is a market participant. "If the city is a market participant, then the Commerce Clause establishes no barrier to conditions such as these which the city demands for its participation. Impact on out-of-state residents figures in the equation only after it is decided that the city is regulating the market rather than participating in it, for only in the former case need it be determined whether any burden on interstate commerce is permitted by the Commerce Clause."

Some of the projects at issue had been funded by federal grants, and the Court was unanimous in its conclusion that Congress had the power to "permit the type of parochial favoritism expressed in the order." As Justice Blackmun noted, concurring on this point, "Congress unquestionably has the power to authorize state or local discrimination against interstate commerce that otherwise would violate the dormant aspect of the Commerce Clause."

Justice Blackmun, however, joined by Justice White, dissented from the majority with respect to those projects funded by the city's own revenues. Unlike Alexandria Scrap and Reeves, he argued, the city's action here imposed restrictions on private firms, and therefore went beyond the limitations of market participation by the city. Responding to this objection, Justice Rehnquist's majority opinion concluded that the employees of private city contractors were in effect "working for the city," regardless of technical notions of privity of contract. But Justice Rehnquist did ac-

3. "One distinction between a private and a governmental function is whether the activity is supported with general tax funds, as was the case for the reprocessing program in Alexandria Scrap, or whether it is financed by the revenues it generates. In this case, South Dakota's cement plant has supported itself for many years. There is thus no need to consider the question whether a state-subsidized business could confine its sales to local residents." [Footnote by Justice Powell.]

knowledge "that there are some limits on a state or local government's ability to impose restrictions that reach beyond the immediate parties with which the government transacts business."

Because the issue was neither briefed nor argued in the Supreme Court, the Court mentioned but specifically refrained from deciding whether Boston's order would violate the Privileges and Immunities Clause of Art. IV, § 2, cl. 1: "The Citizens of each State shall be entitled to all Privileges and Immunities of Citizens in the several States." (On the Privileges and Immunities Clause of Art. IV, see Justice O'Connor's concurring opinion in Zobel v. Williams, printed below, addition to 10th Ed., p. 960; Ind.Rts., p. 580.)

c. Compare the invocation by a sharply divided Court of the Pike v. Bruce Church balancing standard—the standard printed at 10th Ed., p. 296—to invalidate a state regulation of commerce in Edgar v. MITE Corp., 457 U.S. 624 (1982). The case held unconstitutional the Illinois Business Take-Over Act, a law designed to regulate tender offers made to target companies that had certain specified contacts with Illinois. The only portions of Justice White's opinion that gained majority support were those holding (1) that the controversy was not moot and (2) that the state regulation violated the commerce clause under the Pike test. Citing Pike, Justice White stated that, "even when a state statute regulates interstate commerce indirectly, the burden imposed on that commerce must not be excessive in relation to the local interests served by the statute." He concluded that "the Illinois Act imposes a substantial burden on interstate commerce which outweighs its putative local benefits."

Justice White's opinion relied on another commerce clause ground as well: that the Illinois Act regulated interstate commerce "directly" by reaching "commerce wholly outside the state." That commerce clause basis did not gain majority support. Nor did a majority support Justice White's elaborate argument that the federal regulation of takeovers in the Williams Act of 1968 preempted the Illinois Act. The difficulty of gaining a majority to invalidate the Act under even the Pike v. Bruce Church basis is illustrated by Justice Powell's separate concurrence (one of five separate opinions in the case). Justice Powell voted to support the Pike aspect of Justice White's opinion even though he thought the case moot. He joined that part of Justice White's opinion only because of "the decision of a majority of the Court to reach the merits" and "because [the Pike rationale] leaves some room for state regulation of tender offers."

10th ED., p. 338
Add to footnote *:

In his opinion for the Court in Arkansas Elec. Cooperative Corp. v. Arkansas Public Serv. Comm'n, 461 U.S. —— (1983), Justice Brennan noted, in reference to the Pike v. Bruce Church balancing approach, that "this modern jurisprudence has usually, although not always, given more latitude to state regulation than the more categorical approach of which Attleboro was an example." The statement was made in the context of the Court's overruling the approach to state regulation of natural gas embodied in Public Utilities Comm'n v. Attleboro Steam & Elec. Co., 273 U.S. 83 (1927). Under the Attleboro test, the retail sale of natural gas was considered to have only an indirect effect on interstate commerce, and was therefore subject to state regulation. The wholesale sale of gas, however, was deemed to be directly related to interstate commerce, and thus beyond the reach of state regulation.

10th ED., p. 339
Add after Note 3:

3A. *A nonreturnable container law in the Supreme Court: The Clover Leaf Creamery case.* In MINNESOTA v. CLOVER LEAF CREAMERY CO., 449 U.S. 456 (1981), the Court rejected an attack on a state law which banned the retail sale of milk in plastic nonreturnable, nonrefillable containers, but permitted such sale in other nonreturnable containers, such as paperboard milk cartons. The state trial court invalidated the law on both equal protection and commerce clause grounds; the Minnesota Supreme Court affirmed the judgment, but did not reach the commerce clause issue. In reversing the state courts' invalidation, Justice BRENNAN's majority opinion rejected the commerce clause as well as the equal protection challenge.* (Justice Brennan explained that the majority reached the commerce clause issue "because of the obvious factual connection between the rationality analysis under the Equal Protection Clause and the balancing of interests under the Commerce Clause.")

The law's stated purpose was environmental: to promote resource conservation, ease solid waste disposal problems, and conserve energy. Nevertheless, the state trial court found that the "actual basis" of the law "was to promote the economic interests of certain segments of the local dairy and pulpwood industries." In contrast, the Minnesota Supreme Court scrutinized the law in terms of its articulated environmental purpose. The challengers' commerce clause arguments bore some resemblance to those advanced in the Oregon Bottle Case, the principal case in the casebook.

In rejecting the attack, Justice Brennan stated that environmental purposes do not shield state laws from commerce clause scrutiny. For example, if a purportedly environmental law "is in reality 'simple economic protectionism,' we have applied a 'virtually per se rule of invalidity.' Philadelphia v. New Jersey." † Moreover, even if a state environmental measure "regulates 'even-handedly,' and imposes only 'incidental' burdens on interstate commerce, the courts must nevertheless strike it down if 'the burden imposed on such commerce is clearly excessive in relation to the putative local benefits.' Pike v. Bruce Church, Inc."

Justice Brennan insisted that the milk container law "does not effect 'simple protectionism,' but 'regulates even-handedly' by prohibiting all milk retailers from selling their products in the [prohibited] containers, without regard to whether the milk, the containers, or the sellers are from outside the State." He continued: "Since the statute does not discriminate between interstate and intrastate commerce, the controlling question is whether the incidental burden imposed on interstate commerce by the [law] is 'clearly excessive in relation to the putative local benefits.' [Pike.] We conclude that it is not." He explained that conclusion as follows:

"The burden imposed on interstate commerce by the statute is relatively minor. Milk products may continue to move freely across the Minnesota border, and since most dairies package their products in more than one type of containers, the inconvenience of having to conform to different packaging requirements in Minnesota and the surrounding States should be slight. Within Minnesota, business will presumably shift from manufacturers of plastic nonreturnable containers to producers of paperboard cartons, refillable bot-

---

* The Court's disposition of the equal protection claim is discussed below, in addition to 10th Ed., p. 704; Ind. Rts., p. 324.

† Justice Brennan noted that "economic protectionism" could be found "on proof either of discriminatory effect, see Philadelphia v. New Jersey, or of discriminatory purpose, see Hunt v.

Washington State Apple Advertising Comm'n." He rejected a "discriminatory purpose" argument here (even though such an argument had been accepted by the state trial court) for the same reasons that he had rejected the argument in the equal protection context (as discussed below, addition to 10th Ed., p. 704; Ind. Rts., p. 324).

tles, and plastic pouches, but there is no reason to suspect that the gainers will be Minnesota firms, or the losers out-of-state firms.

"[Pulpwood] producers are the only Minnesota industry likely to benefit significantly from the Act at the expense of out-of-state firms. Respondents point out that plastic resin, the raw material used for making plastic nonreturnable milk jugs, is produced entirely by non-Minnesota firms, while pulpwood, used for making paperboard, is a major Minnesota product. Nevertheless, it is clear that respondents exaggerate the degree of burden on out-of-state interests, both because plastics will continue to be used in the production of plastic pouches, plastic returnable bottles, and paperboard itself, and because out-of-state pulpwood producers will presumably absorb some of the business generated by the Act.

"Even granting that the out-of-state plastics industry is burdened relatively more heavily than the Minnesota pulpwood industry, we find that this burden is not 'clearly excessive' in light of the substantial state interest in promoting conservation of energy and other natural resources and easing solid waste disposal problems. [We] find these local benefits ample to support Minnesota's decision under the Commerce Clause. Moreover, we find that no approach with 'a lesser impact on interstate activities' [Pike] is available. Respondents have suggested several alternative statutory schemes, but these alternatives are either more burdensome on commerce than the Act (as, for example, banning all nonreturnables) or less likely to be effective (as, for example, providing incentives for recycling).

"In [Exxon, 10th Ed., p. 313], we upheld a Maryland statute barring producers and refiners of petroleum products—all of which were out-of-state businesses—from retailing gasoline in the State. We stressed that the Commerce Clause 'protects the interstate market, not particular interstate firms, from prohibitive or burdensome regulations.' A nondiscriminatory regulation serving substantial state purposes is not invalid simply because it causes some business to shift from a predominantly out-of-state industry to a predominantly in-state industry. Only if the burden on interstate commerce clearly outweighs the State's legitimate purposes does such a regulation violate the Commerce Clause."

Justice POWELL dissented with regard to the commerce clause claim. He insisted that the Court should not have reached the commerce clause issue because only the state trial court, not the highest state court, had reached it. He accordingly urged that the case be remanded to the Minnesota Supreme Court "with instructions to consider specifically whether the statute discriminated impermissibly against interstate commerce." In his view, the highest state court had not scrutinized the trial court's finding regarding the "actual," seemingly discriminatory purpose of the state law; it had merely accepted the articulated legislative purpose and found the law invalid on equal protection grounds.**

** Justice Powell pointed out that commerce clause analysis "differs" from "rational basis" equal protection scrutiny: "Under the Commerce Clause, a court is empowered to disregard a legislature's statement of purpose if it considers it a pretext. See Dean Milk." He accordingly concluded that the majority had "no basis for *inferring* a rejection [by the highest state court] of the quite specific fact-findings by the trial court." The majority's conclusion thus seemed "flatly contrary to the only relevant specific findings of fact, i.e., those of the trial court. Accordingly, it was "unnecessary" and "inappropriate" to reach the commerce issue.

Justice STEVENS' dissent was primarily devoted to another, novel issue (noted above, as addition to 10th Ed. and Ind. Rts., p. 66), but he agreed with Justice Powell that the majority

should not have reached the commerce clause issue. Moreover, for reasons related to the major basis of his dissent, he urged that the Court should have respected the highest state court's fact findings. He argued that the Minnesota Supreme Court's equal protection conclusion, that the law was not rationally related to substantial state interests, undercut the majority's commerce clause premise that the law promoted ample "local benefits."

10th ED., p. 350
Add to footnote *:

The existence of unexercised authority may also suggest a congressional determination that such authority should not be exercised by anyone. "[A] federal decision to forgo regulation in a given area may imply an authoritative federal determination that the area is best left *un*regulated, and in that event would have as much pre-emptive force as a decision *to* regulate." Arkansas Elec. Cooperative Corp. v. Arkansas Public Serv. Comm'n, 461 U.S. —— (1983).

10th ED., p. 351
Add as footnote to Note 3b:

In recent decisions, the Court has repeatedly quoted a passage from the Florida Lime and Avocado case as a general summary of the modern preemption approach. See, e.g., Chicago & N.W. Tr. Co. v. Kalo Brick & Tile, 450 U.S. 311 (1981): "Preemption of state law by federal statute [is] not favored 'in the absence of persuasive reasons—either that the nature of the regulated subject matter permits no other conclusion, or that the Congress has unmistakably so ordained.' [Florida Lime & Avocado.]"

10th ED., p. 352
Add after Note 4 (before Sec. 2B):

APPLYING THE PREEMPTION FORMULAS

PACIFIC GAS & ELECTRIC CO. v. STATE ENERGY RESOURCES CONSERVATION & DEVELOPMENT COMM'N

461 U.S. ——, 103 S.Ct. 1713, 75 L.Ed.2d 752 (1983).

Justice WHITE delivered the opinion of the Court.

The turning of swords into plowshares has symbolized the transformation of atomic power into a source of energy in American society. To facilitate this development the federal government relaxed its monopoly over fissionable materials and nuclear technology, and in its place, erected a complex scheme to promote the civilian development of nuclear energy, while seeking to safeguard the public and the environment from the unpredictable risks of a new technology. Early on, it was decided that the states would continue their traditional role in the regulation of electricity production.

[This] case emerges from the intersection of the federal government's efforts to ensure that nuclear power is safe with the exercise of the historic state authority over the generation and sale of electricity. At issue is whether provisions in the 1976 amendments to California's Warren-Alquist Act, which condition the construction of nuclear plants on findings by the State Energy Resources Conservation and Development Commission that adequate storage facilities and means of disposal are available for nuclear waste, are preempted by the Atomic Energy Act of 1954, 42 U.S.C. § 2011, et seq.

I. A nuclear reactor must be periodically refueled and the "spent fuel" removed. This spent fuel is intensely radioactive and must be carefully stored. The general practice is to store the fuel in a water-filled pool at the reactor site. For many years, it was assumed that this fuel would be reprocessed; accordingly, the storage pools were designed as short-term holding facilities with limited storage capacities. As expectations for reprocessing remained unfulfilled, the spent fuel accumulated in the storage pools, creating the risk that nuclear reactors would have to be shutdown. This could occur if there were insufficient room in the pool to store spent fuel and also if there were not enough space to hold the entire fuel core when certain inspections or emergencies required unloading of the reactor. In recent years, the problem has taken on special urgency. [Government] studies indicate that a number of reactors could be forced to shut down in the near future due to the inability to store spent fuel.

There is a second dimension to the problem. Even with water-pools adequate to store safely all the spent fuel produced during the working lifetime of the reactor, permanent disposal is needed because the wastes will remain radioactive for thousands of years. There are both safety and economic aspects to the nuclear waste issue: first, if not properly stored, nuclear wastes might leak and endanger both the environment and human health; second, the lack of a long-term disposal option increases the risk that the insufficiency of interim storage space for spent fuel will lead to reactor-shutdowns, rendering nuclear energy an unpredictable and uneconomical adventure.

The California laws at issue here are responses to these concerns. In 1974, California adopted the Warren-Alquist State Energy Resources Conservation and Development Act. The Act requires that a utility seeking to build in California any electric power generating plant, including a nuclear power plant, must apply for certification to the State Energy Resources and Conservation Commission (Energy Commission). The Warren-Alquist Act was amended in 1976 to provide additional state regulation of new nuclear power plant construction.

Two sections of these amendments are before us. Section 25524.1(b) provides that before additional nuclear plants may be built, the Energy Commission must determine on a case-by-case basis that there will be "adequate capacity" for storage of a plant's spent fuel rods "at the time such nuclear facility requires such . . . storage." The law also requires that each utility provide continuous, on-site, "full core reserve storage capacity" in order to permit storage of the entire reactor core if it must be removed to permit repairs of the reactor. In short, § 25524.1(b) addresses the interim storage of spent fuel.

Section 25524.2 deals with the long-term solution to nuclear wastes. This section imposes a moratorium on the certification of new nuclear plants until the Energy Commission "finds that there has been developed and that the United States through its authorized agency has approved and there exists a demonstrated technology or means for the disposal of high-level nuclear waste." "Disposal" is defined as a "method for the permanent and terminal disposition of high-level nuclear waste . . . .".

In 1978, petitioners Pacific Gas and Electric Company and Southern California Edison Company filed this action in the [District] Court, requesting a declaration that numerous provisions of the Warren-Alquist Act, including the two sections challenged here, are invalid under the Supremacy Clause because they are preempted by the Atomic Energy Act. The Court of Appeals [affirmed] the District Court's ruling that the petitioners have standing to challenge the California statutes, and also agreed that the challenge to § 25524.2 is ripe for review. It concluded, however, that the challenge to § 25524.1(b) was not ripe "because we cannot know whether the Energy Commission will ever find a nuclear plant's storage capacity to be inadequate . . . .". On the merits, the court held that the nuclear moratorium provisions of § 25524.2 were not preempted because §§ 271 and 274(k) of the Atomic Energy Act constitute a Congressional authorization for states to regulate nuclear power plants "for purposes other than protection against radiation hazards." . . .

II. We agree that the challenge to § 25524.2 *is* ripe for judicial review, but that the questions concerning § 25524.1(b) are not. . . .

III. It is well-established that within Constitutional limits Congress may preempt state authority by so stating in express terms. Absent explicit preemptive language, Congress' intent to supercede state law altogether may be found from a "scheme of federal regulation so pervasive as to make reasonable the inference that Congress left no room to supplement it," "because the Act of Congress may touch a field in which the federal interest is so dominant that the federal system will be assumed to preclude enforcement of state laws on the same subject," or because "the object sought to be obtained by the federal law and the character of obligations imposed by it may reveal the same purpose." Fidelity Federal Savings & Loan Ass'n v. de la Cuesta, 458 U.S. —— (1982); Rice v. Santa Fe Elevator Corp. Even where Congress has not entirely displaced state regulation in a specific area, state law is preempted to the extent that it actually conflicts with federal law. Such a conflict arises when "compliance with both federal and state regulations is a physical impossibility," Florida Lime & Avocado Growers, Inc. v. Paul, or where state law "stands as an obstacle to the accomplishment and execution of the full purposes and objectives of Congress." Hines v. Davidowitz.

Petitioners [present] three major lines of argument as to why § 25524.2 is preempted. First, they submit that the statute—because it regulates construction of nuclear plants and because it is allegedly predicated on safety concerns—ignores the division between federal and state authority created by the Atomic Energy Act, and falls within the field that the federal government has preserved for its own exclusive control. Second, the statute, and the judgments that underlie it, conflict with decisions concerning the nuclear waste disposal issue made by Congress and the Nuclear Regulatory Commission. Third, the California statute frustrates the federal goal of developing nuclear technology as a source of energy. We consider each of these contentions in turn.

A. Even a brief perusal of the Atomic Energy Act reveals that, despite its comprehensiveness, it does not at any point expressly require the States to construct or authorize nuclear power plants or prohibit the States from deciding, as an absolute or conditional matter, not to permit the construction of any further reactors. Instead, petitioners argue that the Act is intended to preserve the federal government as the sole regulator of all matters nuclear, and that § 25524.2 falls within the scope of this impliedly preempted field. But as we view the issue, Congress, in passing the 1954 Act and in subsequently amending it, intended that the federal government should regulate the radiological safety aspects involved in the construction and operation of a nuclear plant, but that the States retain their traditional responsibility in the field of regulating electrical utilities for determining questions of need, reliability, cost and other related state concerns.

Need for new power facilities, their economic feasibility, and rates and services, are areas that have been characteristically governed by the States. [Thus,] "Congress legislated here in a field which the States have traditionally occupied . . . so we start with the assumption that the historic police powers of the States were not to be superseded by the Federal Act unless that was the clear and manifest purpose of Congress." [Rice.]

The Atomic Energy Act must be read, however, against another background. [Until] 1954 [the] use, control and ownership of nuclear technology remained a federal monopoly. The Atomic Energy Act of 1954 grew out of Congress' determination that the national interest would be best served if the Government encouraged the private sector to become involved in the development of atomic energy for peaceful purposes under a program of federal regulation and licensing. The Act implemented this policy decision by providing for licensing of private construction, ownership, and operation of commercial nuclear power reactors. The AEC, however, was given exclusive jurisdiction to license the transfer, delivery, receipt, acquisition, possession and use of nuclear materials. Upon these subjects, no role was left for the states.

The Commission, however, was not given authority over the generation of electricity itself, or over the economic question whether a particular plant should be built. [The] Nuclear Regulatory Commission (NRC), which now exercises the AEC's regulatory authority, does not purport to exercise its authority based on economic considerations, [and] [utility] financial qualifications are only of concern to the NRC if related to the public health and safety. It is almost inconceivable that Congress would have left a regulatory vacuum; the only reasonable inference is that Congress intended the states to continue to make these judgments. Any doubt that ratemaking and plant-need questions were to remain in state hands was removed by §

271, which provided: "Nothing in this chapter shall be construed to affect the authority or regulations of any Federal, State or local agency with respect to the generation, sale, or transmission of electric power produced through the use of nuclear facilities licensed by the Commission . . ."

[This] regulatory structure has remained unchanged, for our purposes, until 1965, when the following proviso was added to § 271: "*Provided*, that this section shall not be deemed to confer upon any Federal, State or local agency any authority to regulate, control, or restrict any activities of the Commission."

[This] account indicates that from the passage of the Atomic Energy Act in 1954 [to] the present day, Congress has preserved the dual regulation of nuclear-powered electricity generation: the federal government maintains complete control of the safety and "nuclear" aspects of energy generation; the states exercise their traditional authority over the need for additional generating capacity, the type of generating facilities to be licensed, land use, ratemaking, and the like.

The above is not particularly controversial. But deciding how § 25524.2 is to be construed and classified is a more difficult proposition. At the outset, we emphasize that the statute does not seek to regulate the construction or operation of a nuclear powerplant. It would clearly be impermissible for California to attempt to do so, for such regulation, even if enacted out of non-safety concerns, would nevertheless directly conflict with the NRC's exclusive authority over plant construction and operation. Respondents appear to concede as much. Respondents do broadly argue, however, that although safety regulation of nuclear plants by states is forbidden, a state may completely prohibit new construction until its safety concerns are satisfied by the federal government. We reject this line of reasoning. State safety regulation is not preempted only when it conflicts with federal law. Rather, the federal government has occupied the entire field of nuclear safety concerns, except the limited powers expressly ceded to the states. When the federal government completely occupies a given field or an identifiable portion of it, as it has done here, the test of preemption is whether "the matter on which the state asserts the right to act is in any way regulated by the federal government." [Rice.] A state moratorium on nuclear construction grounded in safety concerns falls squarely within the prohibited field. Moreover, a state judgment that nuclear power is not safe enough to be further developed would conflict directly with the countervailing judgment of the NRC that nuclear construction may proceed notwithstanding extant uncertainties as to waste disposal. A state prohibition on nuclear construction for safety reasons would also be in the teeth of the Atomic Energy Act's objective to insure that nuclear technology be safe enough for widespread development and use—and would be preempted for that reason.

That being the case, it is necessary to determine whether there is a non-safety rationale for § 25524.2. California has maintained [that] § 25524.2 was aimed at economic problems, not radiation hazards. The [California Assembly] explained that the lack of a federally approved method of waste disposal created a "clog" in the nuclear fuel cycle. Storage space was limited while more nuclear wastes were continuously produced. Without a permanent means of disposal, the nuclear waste problem could become critical leading to unpredictably high costs to contain the problem or, worse, shut-downs in reactors. [Although specific] indicia of California's intent in en-acting § 25524.2 are subject to varying interpretation, [we] should not become embroiled in attempting to ascertain California's true motive. First, inquiry into legislative motive is often an unsatisfactory venture. United States v. O'Brien [10th Ed., p. 244]. What motivates one legislator to vote for a statute is not necessarily what motivates scores of others to enact it. Second, it would be particularly pointless for us to engage in such in-quiry here when it is clear that the states have been allowed to retain au-thority over the need for electrical generating facilities easily sufficient to permit a state so inclined to halt the construction of new nuclear plants by refusing on economic grounds to issue certificates of public convenience in individual proceedings. In these circumstances, it should be up to Congress to determine whether a state has misused the authority left in its hands.

Therefore, we accept California's avowed economic purpose as the rationale for enacting § 25524.2. Accordingly, the statute lies outside the occupied field of nuclear safety regulation.

B. Petitioners' second major argument concerns federal regulation aimed at the nuclear waste disposal problem itself. It is contended that § 25524.2 conflicts with federal regulation of nuclear waste disposal, with the NRC's decision that it is permissible to continue to license reactors, not-withstanding uncertainty surrounding the waste disposal problem, and with Congress' recent passage of legislation directed at that problem.

Pursuant to its authority under the Act, the AEC, and later the NRC, promulgated extensive and detailed regulations concerning the operation of nuclear facilities and the handling of nuclear materials. [To] receive an NRC operating license, one must submit a safety analysis report, which in-cludes a "radioactive waste handling system." The regulations specify gen-eral design criteria and control requirements for fuel storage and handling and radioactive waste to be stored at the reactor site. In addition, the NRC has promulgated detailed regulations governing storage and disposal away from the reactor. NRC has also promulgated procedural requirements cov-ering license applications for disposal of high-level radioactive waste in geologic repositories.

Congress gave the Department of Energy the responsibility for "the es-tablishment of temporary and permanent facilities for the storage, manage-ment, and ultimate disposal of nuclear wastes." No such permanent disposal facilities have yet to be licensed, and the NRC and the Department of Energy continue to authorize the storage of spent fuel at reactor sites in pools of water. In 1977, the NRC was asked [to] halt reactor licensing until it had determined that there was a method of permanent disposal for high-level waste. The NRC concluded that, given the progress toward the development of disposal facilities and the availability of interim storage, it could continue to license new reactors.

The NRC's imprimatur, however, indicates only that it is safe to pro-ceed with such plants, not that it is economically wise to do so. Because the NRC order does not and could not compel a utility to develop a nuclear plant, compliance with both it and § 25524.2 are possible. Moreover, because the NRC's regulations are aimed at insuring that plants are safe, not necessarily that they are economical, § 25524.2 does not interfere with the objective of the federal regulation.

Nor has California sought through § 25524.2 to impose its own standards on nuclear waste disposal. The statute accepts that it is the federal responsibility to develop and license such technology. As there is no attempt on California's part to enter this field, one which is occupied by the federal government, we do not find § 25524.2 preempted any more by the NRC's obligations in the waste disposal field than by its licensing power over the plants themselves. . . .

C.   Finally, it is strongly contended that § 25524.2 frustrates the Atomic Energy Act's purpose to develop the commercial use of nuclear power. It is well established that state law is preempted if it "stands as an obstacle to the accomplishment of the full purposes and objectives of Congress." [Hines;   Florida Lime;   Fidelity Federal.]

There is little doubt that a primary purpose of the Atomic Energy Act was, and continues to be, the promotion of nuclear power. The Act itself states that it is a program "to encourage widespread participation in the development and utilization of atomic energy for peaceful purposes to the maximum extent consistent with the common defense and security and with the health and safety of the public." The House and Senate Reports confirmed that it was "a major policy goal of the United States" that the involvement of private industry would "speed the further development of the peaceful uses of atomic energy." The same purpose is manifest in the passage of the Price-Anderson Act, 42 U.S.C. § 2210, which limits private liability from a nuclear accident. The Act was passed "in order to protect the public and to encourage the development of the atomic energy industry .   . .". [It] is true, of course, that Congress has sought to simultaneously promote the development of alternative energy sources, but we do not view these steps as an indication that Congress has retreated from its oft-expressed commitment to further development of nuclear power for electricity generation.

The Court of Appeals is right [that] the promotion of nuclear power is not to be accomplished "at all costs." The elaborate licensing and safety provisions and the continued preservation of state regulation in traditional areas belie that. Moreover, Congress has allowed the States to determine— as a matter of economics—whether a nuclear plant vis-a-vis a fossil fuel plant should be built. The decision of California to exercise that authority does not, in itself, constitute a basis for preemption. Therefore, while the argument of petitioners and the United States has considerable force, the legal reality remains that Congress has left sufficient authority in the states to allow the development of nuclear power to be slowed or even stopped for economic reasons. Given this statutory scheme, it is for Congress to rethink the division of regulatory authority in light of its possible exercise by the states to undercut a federal objective. The courts should not assume the role which our system assigns to Congress.

[Affirmed.]

Justice BLACKMUN, with whom Justice STEVENS joins, concurring in part and concurring in the judgment.

I join the Court's opinion, except to the extent it suggests that a State may not prohibit the construction of nuclear power plants if the State is motivated by concerns about the safety of such plants. Since the Court finds that California was not so motivated, this suggestion is unnecessary to the Court's holding. More important, I believe the Court's dictum is wrong in several respects.

The Court takes the position that a State's safety-motivated decision to prohibit construction of nuclear power plants would be pre-empted for three distinct reasons. First, the Court states that "the Federal Government has occupied the entire field of nuclear safety concerns, except the limited powers expressly ceded to the States." Second, the Court indicates that "a state judgment that nuclear power is not safe enough to be further developed would conflict squarely with the countervailing judgment of the NRC . . . that nuclear construction may proceed notwithstanding extant uncertainties as to waste disposal." Third, the Court believes that a prohibition on construction of new nuclear plants would "be in the teeth of the Atomic Energy Act's objective to insure that nuclear technology be safe enough for widespread development and use." [I] cannot agree that a State's nuclear moratorium, even if motivated by safety concerns, would be pre-empted on any of these grounds.

I. First, Congress has occupied not the broad field of "nuclear safety concerns," but only the narrower area of how a nuclear plant should be constructed and operated to protect against radiation hazards. States traditionally have possessed the authority to choose which technologies to rely on in meeting their energy needs. Nothing in the Atomic Energy Act limits this authority, or intimates that a State, in exercising this authority, may not consider the features that distinguish nuclear plants from other power sources. On the contrary, § 271 of the Act indicates that States may continue, with respect to nuclear power, to exercise their traditional police power over the manner in which they meet their energy needs. There is, in short, no evidence that Congress had a "clear and manifest purpose," [Rice], to force States to be blind to whatever special dangers are posed by nuclear plants.
. . .

II. The Court's second basis for suggesting that States may not prohibit the construction of nuclear plants on safety grounds is that such a prohibition would conflict with the NRC's judgment that construction of nuclear plants may safely proceed. A flat ban for safety reasons, however, would not make "compliance with both federal and state regulations . . . a physical impossibility." [Florida Lime.] The NRC has expressed its judgment that it is safe to proceed with construction and operation of nuclear plants, but neither the NRC nor Congress has mandated that States do so.

III. A state regulation also conflicts with federal law if it "stands as an obstacle to the accomplishment and execution of the full purposes and objectives of Congress." [Hines.] The Court suggests that a safety-motivated state ban on nuclear plants would be pre-empted under this standard as well. But Congress has merely encouraged the development of nuclear technology so as to make another source of energy available to the States; Congress has not forced the States to accept this particular source. A ban on nuclear plant construction for safety reasons thus does not conflict with Congress' objectives or purposes.

The Atomic Energy Act was intended to promote the technological development of nuclear power, at a time when there was no private nuclear power industry. [The] Court makes much of the general statements of purpose in the Act and the legislative history, but those statements simply reflect Congress' desire to create a private nuclear power industry. Congress did not compel States to give preference to the eventual product of that industry or to ignore the peculiar problems associated with that product.

[In] sum, Congress has not required States to "go nuclear," in whole or in part. The Atomic Energy Act's twin goals were to promote the development of a technology and to ensure the safety of that technology. Although that Act reserves to the NRC decisions about how to build and operate nuclear plants, the Court reads too much into the Act in suggesting that it also limits the States' traditional power to decide what types of electric power to utilize. Congress simply has made the nuclear option available, and a State may decline that option for any reason. Rather than rest on the elusive test of legislative motive, therefore, I would conclude that the decision whether to build nuclear plants remains with the States. In my view, a ban on construction of nuclear power plants would be valid even if its authors were motivated by fear of a core meltdown or other nuclear catastrophe.

10th ED., p. 356

Add as footnote to Note 3b:

a.   For a recent reliance on the McCarran Act of 1945 [the McCarran-Ferguson Act sustained in the Prudential Insurance case], see Western & S.L.I. Co. v. Bd. of Equalization, 451 U.S. 648 (1981), rejecting a commerce clause challenge to a "retaliatory" state tax on out-of-state insurers. The challengers contended that the Act stops short of authorizing "anti-competitive state taxation that discriminates against out-of-state insurers." But Justice Brennan dismissed that argument, explaining that the Act "removes entirely any Commerce Clause restriction upon California's power to tax the insurance business." [However, the Court did entertain (and reject) an equal protection attack on the tax. Justice Brennan emphasized that the Act "altered [no] constitutional standards other than those derived from the Commerce Clause."]

b.   For a recent statement that congressional consent under Prudential Insurance Co. v. Benjamin must be explicit to be effective, see New England Power Co. v. New Hampshire, 455 U.S. 331 (1982). As noted above (addition to 10th Ed., p. 327), the New England Power decision voided, as impermissible under the commerce clause, a state ban on the export of locally generated hydroelectric power. The State argued that its restriction was nevertheless valid because § 201(b) of the Federal Power Act "expressly permits the State to prohibit the exportation of hydroelectric power produced within its borders." Chief Justice Burger's opinion for the unanimous Court found no such explicit consent.

Sec. 201(b) stated that the federal law was not to be read as depriving a state "of its lawful authority now exercised over the exportation of hydroelectric energy." In the Court's view, this was merely an anti-preemption provision; it was "in no sense an affirmative grant of power to the States to burden interstate commerce 'in a manner which would not otherwise be permissible.' [Nothing] in the legislative history or language of the statute evinces a congressional intent 'to alter the limits of state power otherwise imposed by the Commerce Clause,' or to modify the earlier holdings of this Court concerning the limits of state authority to restrain interstate trade. Rather, Congress' concern was simply 'to define the extent of the federal legislation's preemptive effect on state law.' " The Court emphasized that "when Congress has not 'expressly stated its intent and policy' to sustain state legislation from attack under the Commerce Clause, Prudential Ins. Co. v. Benjamin, we have no authority to rewrite its legislation based on mere speculation as to what Congress 'probably had in mind.' "

c. An especially strong statement of Congress' power to authorize "favoritism" or "discrimination" was made in White v. Massachusetts Council of Construction Employers, Inc., 460 U.S. —— (1983), quoted on this point above, addition to 10th Ed., p. 328.

d. Congressional power under the commerce clause to *validate* state legislation otherwise unconstitutional because it discriminates against interstate commerce should not be confused with congressional power to *enact* legislation that by its terms discriminates among states. For at least in terms of taxation, discriminatory congressional legislation is constrained by the Unformity Clause, which restricts Congress' power to tax under Art. I, § 8, cl. 1, by providing that all indirect taxes "shall be uniform throughout the United States." The Uniformity Clause was one of several measures adopted to forestall the possibility that the new national government would use its power to tax to single out certain states for especially harsh treatment. See Knowlton v. Moore, 178 U.S. 41 (1900).

Uniformity requires only that the tax operate "with the same force and effect in every place where the subject of it is found." Head Money Cases, 112 U.S. 580, 594 (1884). Thus there is no requirement that the thing taxed be distributed equally among the states, and taxes that disproportionately burden a particular state are not barred, as long as that state has not been singled out for special treatment. Moreover, it was also settled in the Head Money Cases that Congress possesses broad powers to define the subject of a tax by drawing distinctions between seemingly similar classes.

Not until United States v. Ptasynski, 462 U.S. —— (1983), did the Court have occasion to decide whether the Uniformity Clause prohibited Congress from defining the class of objects to be taxed in geographic terms. At issue in Ptasynski was that part of the Crude Oil Windfall Profit Tax Act of 1980, 26 U.S.C. §§ 4986 et seq., which excluded certain "exempt Alaskan oil" from the Act's coverage. Reversing a lower court ruling that an exemption framed in geographic terms violated the Uniformity Clause, the Court held that "[w]here Congress defines the subject of a tax in nongeographic terms, the Uniformity Clause is satisfied. We cannot say that when Congress uses geographic terms to identify the same subject, the classification is invalidated. The Uniformity Clause gives Congress wide latitude in deciding what to tax and does not prohibit it from considering geographically isolated problems. [But] where Congress does choose to frame a tax in geographic terms, we will examine the classification closely to see if there is actual geographic discrimination."

Applying this standard, Justice Powell's opinion for a unanimous Court found no prohibited geographic discrimination. Noting that the exemption covered less than 20% of Alaskan production, the Court concluded that the exemption was "not drawn on state political lines." Where Congress had made the exemption determination based on "neutral factors" of climate, ecology, location, and difficulty of extraction, there was no "indication that Congress sought to benefit Alaska for reasons that would offend the purpose of the clause."

Chapter 6

INTERGOVERNMENTAL IMMUNITIES AND
INTERSTATE RELATIONSHIPS

10th ED., p. 369
Add to the Notes on modern problems of tax immunities (after Note 3c):

4. *The modern Court's articulation of "a narrow approach to governmental tax immunity."* In UNITED STATES v. NEW MEXICO, 455 U.S. 720 (1982), the Justices unanimously rejected federal government contractors' claims of constitutional immunity from a range of state taxes. The Court took the occasion to confront at length "a recurring problem: to what extent may a State impose taxes on contractors that conduct business with the Federal Government?" In the course of Justice BLACKMUN's effort to delineate narrowly the scope of constitutional immunity from state taxation and to leave any broader immunities to congressional discretion, he reviewed the wavering line of precedents and offered a number of significant general statements designed to clarify this area of law:

"We have concluded that the confusing nature of our precedents counsels a return to the underlying constitutional principle. The one constant here, of course, is simple enough to express: a State may not, consistent with the Supremacy Clause, lay a tax 'directly upon the United States.' [But] the limits on the immunity doctrine are [as] significant as the rule itself. Thus, immunity may not be conferred simply because the tax has an effect on the United States, or even because the Federal Government shoulders the entire economic burden of the levy. That is the import of Alabama v. King & Boozer. [Similarly], immunity cannot be conferred simply because the state tax falls on the earnings of a contractor providing services to the Government. James v. Dravo Contracting Co. And where a use tax is involved, immunity cannot be conferred simply because the State is levying the tax on the use of federal property in private hands, even if the private entity is using the Government property to provide the United States with goods or services. In such a situation the contractor's use of the property 'in connection with commercial activities carried on for profit' is 'a separate and distinct taxable activity.' Indeed, immunity cannot be conferred simply because the tax is paid with Government funds.

"[What] the Court's cases leave room for, then, is the conclusion that tax immunity is appropriate in only one circumstance: when the levy falls on the United States itself, or an agency or instrumentality so closely connected to the Government that the two cannot realistically be viewed as separate entities, at least insofar as the activity being taxed is concerned. This view, we believe, comports with the principal purpose of the immunity doctrine, that of forestalling 'clashing sovereignty' [McCulloch], by preventing the States from laying demands directly on the Federal Government. As the federal

88

structure—along with the workings of the tax immunity doctrine*—has evolved, this command has taken on essentially symbolic importance, as the visible 'consequence of that [federal] supremacy which the constitution has declared.' McCulloch. At the same time, a narrow approach to governmental tax immunity accords with competing constitutional imperatives, by giving full range to each sovereign's taxing authority.

"Thus, a finding of constitutional tax immunity requires something more than the invocation of traditional agency notions: to resist the State's taxing power, a private taxpayer must actually 'stand in the Government's shoes.' [Granting] tax immunity only to entities that have been 'incorporated into the government structure' can forestall, at least to a degree, some of the manipulation and wooden formalism that occasionally have marked tax litigation—and that have no proper place in determining the allocation of power between co-existing sovereignties. [If] the immunity of federal contractors is to be expanded beyond its narrow constitutional limits, it is Congress that must take responsibility for the decision, by so expressly providing as respects contracts in a particular form, or contracts under particular programs. And this allocation of responsibility is wholly appropriate, for the political process is 'uniquely adapted to accommodating the competing demands' in this area. But absent congressional action, we have emphasized that the States' power to tax can be denied only under 'the clearest constitutional mandate.' " Applying these principles, Justice Blackmun concluded that none of the taxes challenged here was barred by any constitutional immunity.

This "narrow approach," however, does not appear to indicate that the Court will avoid scrutinizing closely those taxes alleged to discriminate against the federal government. In MEMPHIS BANK & TRUST CO. v. GARNER, 459 U.S. —— (1983), the Court restated its general approach: "Where [the] economic but not the legal incidence of the tax falls on the Federal Government, such a tax generally does not violate the constitutional immunity if it does not discriminate against holders of Federal property or those with whom the Federal Government deals. [A] state tax that imposes a greater burden on holders of federal property impermissibly discriminates against federal obligations."

For a unanimous Court, Justice MARSHALL applied this standard to a Tennessee tax on the net earnings of all banks doing business in the state. In calculating net earnings, interest on obligations of the United States and of states other than Tennessee was included, but interest on obligations of Tennessee and its political subdivisions was excluded. The disparity in treatment between Tennessee obligations and those of the United States led the Court to conclude that Tennessee had discriminated against federal obligations in favor of "otherwise comparable" state and local obligations, thus

---

* "With the abandonment of the notion that the economic—as opposed to the legal—incidence of the tax is relevant, it becomes difficult to maintain that federal tax immunity is designed to insulate federal operations from the effects of state taxation. It remains true, of course, that state taxes on contractors are constitutionally invalid if they discriminate against the Federal Government, or substantially interfere with its activities. . . ." [Footnote by Justice Blackmun.]

constituting "[impermissible discrimination] against the Federal Government and those with whom it deals."

The question of discrimination, however, is in this context an inquiry that is likely to be more practical than technical or formal. In WASHINGTON v. UNITED STATES, 460 U.S. —— (1983), the State of Washington was permitted to impose a tax that in some respects treated federal contractors as a separate category. Washington's general sales and use tax is imposed, in the case of construction projects, on the owner of the land, so that the tax as imposed includes not only construction materials, but the contractors' labor costs and markups as well. Because Washington could not tax directly the federal government where it was the landowner, Washington imposed, in the case of federal construction projects, a tax on the contractor for the materials used. The tax was thus less than the tax that was imposed on non-federal projects, because in the case of federal projects taxing the contractor meant that there was no tax on the contractor's labor costs and markups.

The United States argued that the imposition of a tax on contractors only in those cases where contractors worked for the federal government constituted a discriminatory tax on those who deal with the federal government. But the Court, in an opinion written by Justice REHNQUIST, upheld the tax, relying largely on the fact that the economic burden on federal construction projects remained less than the economic burden on non-federal projects. "The State does not discriminate against the Federal Government and those with whom it deals unless it treats someone else better than it treats them."

Thus the fact that federal contractors were treated specially was not dispositive. "[Washington] has merely accommodated for the fact that it may not impose a tax directly on the United States as the project owner. This the State may do without running afoul of the Supremacy Clause." Nor did the Court feel that the somewhat distinct treatment contained the possibility of abuse.† "As long as the tax imposed on those who deal with the federal government is an integral part of a tax system that applies to the entire state, there is little chance that the State will take advantage of the Federal Government by increasing the tax."

† Justice BLACKMUN, joined by Justices White, Marshall, and Stevens, dissented, primarily on the ground that, regardless of economic effect, the Supremacy Clause prohibits singling out the Federal Government and those with whom it deals for special tax treatment. "Now the Court, in order to prevent abuse, will have to dissect and carefully measure every state system that imposes its tax burden upon the United States."

The Court's holding that separate treatment is not per se invalid, with the Court available to correct abuses from taxation that is discriminatory in fact, is usefully compared with the Court's decision in Minneapolis Star and Tribune Co. v. Minnesota Comm'r of Revenue, printed below, addition to 10th Ed., p. 1325; Ind.Rts., p. 945. There the Court, for First Amendment reasons, prohibited a separate tax for newspapers, although it, like the tax in Washington v. United States, was compensatory for a tax exemption and was in fact less than the tax for which it was substituted. Justice Rehnquist's dissent in Minneapolis Star and Tribune echoes the same themes as his opinion for the Court in Washington v. United States.

10th ED., p. 369
Add to footnote *:

Note the elaborations of the principles of National League of Cities in a series of cases in the 1980s: Hodel v. Virginia Surface Min. & Recl. Ass'n, Inc., 452 U.S. 264 (1981); Hodel v. Indiana, 452 U.S. 314 (1981); United Transportation Union v. Long Island R. Co., 455 U.S. 678 (1982); FERC v. Mississippi, 456 U.S. 742 (1982); EEOC v. Wyoming, 460 U.S. —— (1983). All of these cases are printed above (addition to 10th Ed., p. 195).

10th ED., p. 370
Insert after Note 1:

1A. *State hostility to federal law.* As is implicit in the foregoing note, most questions of federal immunity from state regulation arise in the context of a generally applicable state requirement that may, as applied, interfere with federal law or policy. Occasionally, however, state action, like that in McCulloch itself, is specifically and intentionally directed against federal policy. For example, in NORTH DAKOTA v. UNITED STATES, 460 U. S. —— (1983), various North Dakota statutes were plainly enacted to slow down or control federal acquisition of easements in North Dakota pursuant to the Migratory Bird Conservation Act. Applying a standard of whether the state law was "hostile to federal interests," Justice Blackmun's opinion for the Court found that standard met here and thus denied effect to the North Dakota legislation.

10th ED., p. 373
Add as footnote to Note 3:

Note the sharp division on the Court about the relevance of Testa v. Katt in evaluating a Tenth Amendment challenge to the Public Utility Regulatory Policies Act of 1978, in FERC v. Mississippi, 456 U.S. 742 (1982) (printed above, addition to 10th Ed., p. 195).

10th ED., p. 379
Add to footnote *:

Note the extensive discussion of, and reliance on, the Privileges and Immunities Clause of Art. IV, § 2, in Justice O'Connor's concurring opinion in Zobel v. Williams, 457 U.S. 55 (1982), printed below, addition to 10th Ed., p. 960; Ind.Rts., p. 580.

Chapter 7

SEPARATION OF POWERS

10th ED., p. 397
Insert after Note 2b:

THE IRANIAN ASSETS CASE: DAMES & MOORE v. REGAN

The Steel Seizure Case received considerable attention in Justice REHNQUIST's prevailing opinion in DAMES & MOORE v. REGAN, 453 U.S. 654 (1981). The decision sustained the validity of President Carter's January 1981 Executive Agreement with Iran. The Agreement was negotiated in order to obtain the release of American hostages in Iran. Executive Orders issued pursuant to the Agreement provided, inter alia, for "nullification" of prejudgment attachments of Iranian assets. (The attachments had been obtained by creditors who had brought American court proceedings against Iran.) Moreover, the Orders required banks holding "blocked" Iranian assets—i.e., assets which were frozen in response to the hostage crisis—to transfer the assets to the Federal Reserve Bank, primarily for transfer to Iran.* The Orders also "suspended" all claims pending in American courts that could be presented to an Iran-United States Claims Tribunal for binding arbitration.

The Government defended its actions by relying in part on inherent executive powers under Art. II. But the Court's validation of the Executive Orders rested heavily on congressional approval of the presidential actions. With respect to the nullification of attachments and the transfer of blocked assets, the Court found "specific congressional authorization" in the International Emergency Economic Powers Act. With respect to the suspension of claims, the Court found no such "specific congressional authorization," but relied primarily on the "history of congressional acquiescence in conduct of the sort engaged in by the President." In the Court's view, Congress had "implicitly approved the practice of claim settlement by executive agreement."

---

* Of an estimated $12 billion in frozen Iranian assets, roughly $5 billion was used to pay off Iranian loan debts, and about $2.9 billion was returned to Iran as soon as the hostages were freed. Domestic branches of U. S. banks held over $2 billion in Iranian assets; $1 billion of this was transferred to an escrow account in England, and the remainder was returned to Iran. The escrow account was established, pursuant to the Agreement, for the purpose of securing payment of, and paying, any arbitral awards rendered against Iran by the Iran-United States Claims Tribunal, also established pursuant to the Agreement. The Tribunal has commenced adjudication of several hundred of those claims that exceed $250,000. The United States filed on behalf of some 2795 claimants who asked for less than $250,000. Legislation is pending (S. 1072) that would provide for individual adjudication of these latter claims by the United States Foreign Claims Settlement Commission in the event that the United States and Iran agree to settle all or part of them en bloc.

In the course of reaching these "narrow" conclusions, Justice Rehnquist referred repeatedly to the opinions in Youngstown, the Steel Seizure Case. Several times, he spoke approvingly of Justice Jackson's tripartite analysis. (Justice Rehnquist was once a law clerk to Justice Jackson.) But in a critical passage of the opinion, he quoted instead from Justice Frankfurter's concurrence in the Steel Seizure Case.

At one point, for example, Justice Rehnquist described the Jackson opinion in Youngstown as one "which both parties agree brings together as much combination of analysis and common sense as there is in this area." But Justice Rehnquist warned: "Although we have in the past and do today find Justice Jackson's classification of executive actions into three general categories analytically useful, we should be mindful of Justice Holmes' admonition, quoted by Justice Frankfurter in Youngstown, that 'The great ordinances of the Constitution do not establish and divide fields of black and white.' Justice Jackson himself recognized that his three categories represented 'a somewhat over-simplified grouping,' and it is doubtless the case that executive action in any particular instance falls, not neatly in one of three pigeon-holes, but rather at some point along a spectrum running from explicit congressional authorization to explicit congressional prohibition. This is particularly true as respects cases such as the one before us, involving responses to international crisis the nature of which Congress can hardly have been expected to anticipate in any detail."

Yet in confronting the most difficult issue in the case—the President's authority to suspend claims—Justice Rehnquist relied not on Justice Jackson's analysis, but rather on Justice Frankfurter's opinion in Youngstown. After finding no specific congressional authorization to suspend claims, Justice Rehnquist stated: "In light [of] the inferences to be drawn from the character of the legislation Congress has enacted in the area and from the history of acquiescence in executive claims settlement, [we] conclude that the President was authorized to suspend pending claims. [As] Justice Frankfurter pointed out in Youngstown, 'A systematic, unbroken executive practice, long pursued to the knowledge of Congress and never before questioned,[may] be treated as a gloss on "Executive Power" vested in the President by § 1 of Art. II.' Past practice does not, by itself, create power, but 'long-continued practice, known to and acquiesced in by Congress, would raise a presumption that the [action] has been [taken] in pursuance of its consent.' [Such a] practice is present here and such a presumption is also appropriate. In light of the fact that Congress may be considered to have consented to the President's action in suspending claims, we cannot say that action exceeded the President's powers. Our conclusion is buttressed by the fact that the means chosen by the President to settle the claims of American nationals provided an alternate forum, the Claims Tribunal, which is capable of providing meaningful relief."

Justice Rehnquist emphasized "the narrowness of our decision"† and

---

† The Court's effort to render a narrow decision was not confined to the ruling on suspension of claims. Justice Rehnquist described the Court's general approach to the case as follows: "We attempt to lay down no general 'guidelines' covering other situations not involved here, and attempt to confine the opinion only to the very questions necessary to decision of the case. [We] freely confess that we are obviously deciding only one more epi-

noted that this was not a situation "in which Congress has in some way resisted the exercise of presidential authority." He cautioned: "We do not decide that the President possesses plenary power to settle claims, even as against foreign governmental entities. [But] where, as here, the settlement of claims has been determined to be a necessary incident to the resolution of a major foreign policy dispute between our country and another, and where, as here, we can conclude that Congress acquiesced in the President's action, we are not prepared to say that the President lacks the power to settle such claims." ** [An additional note on this case appears below, addition to 10th Ed., p. 409.]

10th ED., p. 401
Add to the text on the Legislative Veto:

IMMIGRATION AND NATURALIZATION SERVICE v. CHADHA

462 U.S. ——, 103 S.Ct. ——, 76 L.Ed.2d —— (1983).

Chief Justice BURGER delivered the opinion of the Court.

[Each of these three consolidated cases] presents a challenge to the constitutionality of the provision in § 244(c)(2) of the Immigration and Nationality Act, 8 U.S.C. § 1254(c)(2), authorizing one House of Congress,

sode in the never-ending tension between the President exercising the executive authority in a world that presents each day some new challenge with which he must deal and the Constitution under which we all live and which no one disputes embodies some sort of system of checks and balances."

** The only issue in the case which evoked any dissent on the Court was whether the President's actions amounted to an unconstitutional "taking" under the Fifth Amendment's Just Compensation Clause. Justice Rehnquist found that the nullification of attachments and the transfer of the assets presented no Fifth Amendment difficulty. Central to this conclusion was his contention that "petitioner [the asserted creditor] did not acquire any 'property' interest in its attachments of the sort that would support a constitutional claim for compensation." With respect to the suspension of claims, he found the "taking" argument "not ripe for review." But he conceded "the possibility that the President's actions may effect a taking of petitioner's property." He accordingly proceeded to hold that in such an event petitioner would have

"a remedy at law in the Court of Claims under the Tucker Act, 28 U.S. C. § 1491."

Justice STEVENS' very brief concurrence argued that the jurisdictional question regarding the Court of Claims should not have been addressed. He considered the ruling inappropriate because "the possibility that requiring petitioner to prosecute its claim in another forum will constitute an unconstitutional 'taking' is so remote."

Justice POWELL's separate opinion, concurring and dissenting in part, was careful to rephrase the Court's holding in his own words: "The opinion makes clear that some claims may not be adjudicated by the Claims Tribunal, and that others may not be paid in full. [Should this occur, the Court permits the aggrieved party to] bring a 'taking' claim in the Court of Claims." Justice Powell also gave his view about how the Court of Claims should rule: "The Government must pay just compensation when it furthers the Nation's foreign policy goals by using as 'bargaining chips' claims lawfully held by a relatively few persons and subject to the jurisdiction of our courts. The extraordinary powers of the President and Congress upon

by resolution, to invalidate the decision of the Executive Branch, pursuant to authority delegated by Congress to the Attorney General of the United States, to allow a particular deportable alien to remain in the United States.

I.   Chadha is an East Indian who was born in Kenya and holds a British passport.   He was lawfully admitted to the United States in 1966 on a non-immigrant student visa.   His visa expired on June 30, 1972.   On October 11, 1973, the District Director of the Immigration and Naturalization Service ordered Chadha to show cause why he should not be deported for having "remained in the United States for a longer time than permitted."   Pursuant to § 242(b) of the Immigration and Nationality Act (Act), 8 U.S.C. § 1254(b), a deportation hearing was held before an immigration judge on January 11, 1974.   Chadha conceded that he was deportable for overstaying his visa and the hearing was adjourned to enable him to file an application for suspension of deportation under § 244(a)(1) of the Act.

[After] Chadha submitted his application for suspension of deportation, the deportation hearing was resumed on February 7, 1974.   On the basis of evidence adduced at the hearing, affidavits submitted with the application, and the results of a character investigation conducted by the INS, the immigration judge, on June 25, 1974, ordered that Chadha's deportation be suspended.   The immigration judge found that Chadha met the requirements of § 244(a)(1):   he had resided continuously in the United States for over seven years, was of good moral character, and would suffer "extreme hardship" if deported.

Pursuant to § 244(c)(1) of the Act, the immigration judge suspended Chadha's deportation and a report of the suspension was transmitted to Congress.   Section 244(c)(1) provides:

> "Upon application by any alien who is found by the Attorney General to meet the requirements of subsection (a) of this section the Attorney General may in his discretion suspend deportation of such alien. If the deportation of any alien is suspended under the provisions of this subsection, a complete and detailed statement of the facts and pertinent provisions of law in the case shall be reported to the Congress with the reasons for such suspension.   Such reports shall be submitted on the first day of each calendar month in which Congress is in session."

Once the Attorney General's recommendation for suspension of Chadha's deportation was conveyed to Congress, Congress had the power under § 244 (c)(2) of the Act to veto the Attorney General's determination that Chadha should not be deported.   Section 244(c)(2) provides:

> "(2) In the case of an alien specified in paragraph (1) of subsection (a) of this subsection—

which our decision rests cannot, in the circumstances of this case, displace the Just Compensation Clause of the Constitution."

The Court's Fifth Amendment holding on the nullification of attachments troubled Justice Powell. He refused to join the ruling that the nullification affected no protected property interests. Instead, he protested that the Court's ruling "may well be erroneous, and it certainly is premature with respect to many claims." In his view, all "taking" claims—in the attachment as well as in the claim suspension context—should have been left open for "resolution on a case-by-case basis [before] the Court of Claims."

if during the session of the Congress at which a case is reported, or prior to the close of the session of the Congress next following the session at which a case is reported, either the Senate or the House of Representatives passes a resolution stating in substance that it does not favor the suspension of such deportation, the Attorney General shall thereupon deport such alien or authorize the alien's voluntary departure at his own expense under the order of deportation in the manner provided by law. If, within the time above specified, neither the Senate nor the House of Representatives shall pass such a resolution, the Attorney General shall cancel deportation proceedings."

The June 25, 1974 order of the immigration judge suspending Chadha's deportation remained outstanding as a valid order for a year and a half. For reasons not disclosed by the record, Congress did not exercise the veto authority reserved to it under § 244(c)(2) until the first session of the 94th Congress. This was the final session in which Congress, pursuant to § 244(c) (2), could act to veto the Attorney General's determination that Chadha should not be deported. The session ended on December 19, 1975. Absent Congressional action, Chadha's deportation proceedings would have been cancelled after this date and his status adjusted to that of a permanent resident alien.

On December 12, 1975, Representative Eilberg, Chairman of the Judiciary Subcommittee on Immigration, Citizenship and International Law, introduced a resolution opposing "the granting of permanent residence in the United States to [six] aliens", including Chadha. The resolution was referred to the House Committee on the Judiciary. On December 16, 1975, the resolution was discharged from further consideration by the House Committee on the Judiciary and submitted to the House of Representatives for a vote. The resolution had not been printed and was not made available to other Members of the House prior to or at the time it was voted on. So far as the record before us shows, the House consideration of the resolution was based on Representative Eilberg's statement from the floor that

"[i]t was the feeling of the committee, after reviewing 340 cases, that the aliens contained in the resolution [Chadha and five others] did not meet these statutory requirements, particularly as it relates to hardship; and it is the opinion of the committee that their deportation should not be suspended."

The resolution was passed without debate or recorded vote. Since the House action was pursuant to § 244(c)(2), the resolution was not treated as an Article I legislative act; it was not submitted to the Senate or presented to the President for his action.

After the House veto of the Attorney General's decision to allow Chadha to remain in the United States, the immigration judge reopened the deportation proceedings to implement the House order deporting Chadha. [On] November 8, 1976, Chadha was ordered deported pursuant to the House action.

[Pursuant] to § 106(a) of the Act Chadha filed a petition for review of the deportation order in the United States Court of Appeals for the Ninth Circuit. The Immigration and Naturalization Service agreed with Chadha's position before the Court of Appeals and joined him in arguing that § 244 (c)(2) is unconstitutional. In light of the importance of the question, the Court of Appeals invited both the Senate and the House of Representatives to file briefs *amici curiae.*

After full briefing and oral argument, the Court of Appeals held that the House was without constitutional authority to order Chadha's deportation; accordingly it directed the Attorney General "to cease and desist from taking any steps to deport this alien based upon the resolution enacted by the House of Representatives." The essence of its holding was that § 244(c) (2) violates the constitutional doctrine of separation of powers.

We granted certiorari, [and] we now affirm.

II. Before we address the important question of the constitutionality of the one-House veto provision of § 244(c)(2), we first consider several challenges to the authority of this Court to resolve the issue raised. [The Court determined that it had appellate jurisdiction, that the one-house veto provision was severable from the remainder of § 244, that Chadha had standing to challenge the constitutionality of the one-house veto, that nothing other than a decision on the constitutionality of the one-house veto was likely to give Chadha his desired relief, that the Court of Appeals had proper jurisdiction of the case before it, and that a justiciable case or controversy existed.]

G

Political Question

It is also argued that this case presents a nonjusticiable political question because Chadha is merely challenging Congress' authority under the Naturalization Clause, U.S.Const. art. I, § 8, cl. 4, and the Necessary and Proper Clause. It is argued that Congress' Article I power "To establish a uniform Rule of Naturalization", combined with the Necessary and Proper Clause, grants it unreviewable authority over the regulation of aliens. The plenary authority of Congress over aliens under Art. I, § 8, cl. 4 is not open to question, but what is challenged here is whether Congress has chosen a constitutionally permissible means of implementing that power.

[A] brief review of those factors which may indicate the presence of a nonjusticiable political question satisfies us that our assertion of jurisdiction over this case does no violence to the political question doctrine. [Congress] apparently directs its assertion of nonjusticiability to [the existence of a textually demonstrable constitutional commitment of the issue to a coordinate political department. Baker v. Carr.] But if this turns the question into a political question virtually every challenge to the constitutionality of a statute would be a political question. Chadha indeed argues that one House of Congress cannot constitutionally veto the Attorney General's decision to allow him to remain in this country. No policy underlying the political question doctrine suggests that Congress or the Executive, or both acting in concert and in compliance with Art. I, can decide the constitutionality of a statute; that is a decision for the courts. [It] is correct that this controversy may, in a sense, be termed "political." But the presence of constitutional issues with significant political overtones does not automatically invoke the political question doctrine. Resolution of litigation challenging the constitutional authority of one of the three branches cannot be evaded by courts because the issues have political implications in the sense urged by Congress. Marbury v. Madison was also a "political" case, involving as it did claims under a judicial commission alleged to have been duly signed by the President but not delivered. But "courts cannot reject as 'no law suit' a bona fide controversy as to whether some action denominated 'political' exceeds constitutional authority." Baker v. Carr. . . .

III. A. We turn now to the question whether action of one House of Congress under § 244(c)(2) violates strictures of the Constitution. We begin, of course, with the presumption that the challenged statute is valid. Its wisdom is not the concern of the courts; if a challenged action does not violate the Constitution, it must be sustained.

[By] the same token, the fact that a given law or procedure is efficient, convenient, and useful in facilitating functions of government, standing alone, will not save it if it is contrary to the Constitution. Convenience and efficiency are not the primary objectives—or the hallmarks—of democratic government and our inquiry is sharpened rather than blunted by the fact that Congressional veto provisions are appearing with increasing frequency in statutes which delegate authority to executive and independent agencies:

> "Since 1932, when the first veto provision was enacted into law, 295 congressional veto-type procedures have been inserted in 196 different statutes as follows: from 1932 to 1939, five statutes were affected; from 1940–49, nineteen statutes; between 1950–59, thirty-four statutes; and from 1960–69, forty-nine. From the year 1970 through 1975, at least one hundred sixty-three such provisions were included in eighty-nine laws." Abourezk, The Congressional Veto: A Contemporary Response to Executive Encroachment on Legislative Prerogatives, 52 Ind.L.Rev. 323, 324 (1977).

[Justice] White undertakes to make a case for the proposition that the one-House veto is a useful "political invention," and we need not challenge that assertion. We can even concede this utilitarian argument although the long range political wisdom of this "invention" is arguable. [But] policy arguments supporting even useful "political inventions" are subject to the demands of the Constitution which defines powers and, with respect to this subject, sets out just how those powers are to be exercised.

Explicit and unambiguous provisions of the Constitution prescribe and define the respective functions of the Congress and of the Executive in the legislative process. Since the precise terms of those familiar provisions are critical to the resolution of this case, we set them out verbatim. Art. I provides:

> "All legislative Powers herein granted shall be vested in a Congress of the United States, which shall consist of a Senate *and* a House of Representatives." Art. I, § 1. (Emphasis added).

> "Every Bill which shall have passed the House of Representatives *and* the Senate, *shall*, before it become a Law, be presented to the President of the United States; . . ." Art. I, § 7, cl. 2. (Emphasis added).

"*Every* Order, Resolution, or Vote to which the Concurrence of the Senate and House of Representatives may be necessary (except on a question of Adjournment) *shall be* presented to the President of the United States; and before the Same shall take Effect, *shall be* approved by him, or being disapproved by him, *shall be* repassed by two thirds of the Senate and House of Representatives, according to the Rules and Limitations prescribed in the Case of a Bill." Art. I, § 7, cl. 3. (Emphasis added).

These provisions of Art. I are integral parts of the constitutional design for the separation of powers. [The] very structure of the articles delegating and separating powers under Arts. I, II, and III exemplify the concept of separation of powers and we now turn to Art. I.

B

The Presentment Clauses

The records of the Constitutional Convention reveal that the requirement that all legislation be presented to the President before becoming law was uniformly accepted by the Framers. Presentment to the President and the Presidential veto were considered so imperative that the draftsmen took special pains to assure that these requirements could not be circumvented. During the final debate on Art. I, § 7, cl. 2, James Madison expressed concern that it might easily be evaded by the simple expedient of calling a proposed law a "resolution" or "vote" rather than a "bill." 2 M. Farrand, The Records of the Federal Convention of 1787 301–302. As a consequence, Art. I, § 7, cl. 3 was added.

The decision to provide the President with a limited and qualified power to nullify proposed legislation by veto was based on the profound conviction of the Framers that the powers conferred on Congress were the powers to be most carefully circumscribed. It is beyond doubt that lawmaking was a power to be shared by both Houses and the President. In The Federalist No. 73, Hamilton focused on the President's role in making laws: "If even no propensity had ever discovered itself in the legislative body to invade the rights of the Executive, the rules of just reasoning and theoretic propriety would of themselves teach us that the one ought not to be left to the mercy of the other, but ought to possess a constitutional and effectual power of self-defense." See also The Federalist No. 51. In his Commentaries on the Constitution, Joseph Story makes the same point. 1 J. Story, Commentaries on the Constitution of the United States 614–615 (1858).

The President's role in the lawmaking process also reflects the Framers' careful efforts to check whatever propensity a particular Congress might have to enact oppressive, improvident, or ill-considered measures. The President's veto role in the legislative process was described later during public debate on ratification: "It establishes a salutary check upon the legislative body, calculated to guard the community against the effects of faction, precipitancy, or any impulse unfriendly to the public good which may happen to influence a majority of that body. . . . The primary inducement to conferring the power in question upon the Executive is to enable him to defend himself;

the secondary one is to increase the chances in favor of the community against the passing of bad laws through haste, inadvertence, or design." The Federalist No. 73 (A. Hamilton). . . .

C

Bicameralism

The bicameral requirement of Art. I, §§ 1, 7 was of scarcely less concern to the Framers than was the Presidential veto and indeed the two concepts are interdependent. By providing that no law could take effect without the concurrence of the prescribed majority of the Members of both Houses, the Framers reemphasized their belief, already remarked upon in connection with the Presentment Clauses, that legislation should not be enacted unless it has been carefully and fully considered by the Nation's elected officials. In the Constitutional Convention debates on the need for a bicameral legislature, James Wilson, later to become a Justice of this Court, commented: "Despotism comes on mankind in different shapes. Sometimes in an Executive, sometimes in a military one. Is there danger of a Legislative despotism? Theory & practice both proclaim it. If the Legislative authority be not restrained, there can be neither liberty nor stability; and it can only be restrained by dividing it within itself, into distinct and independent branches. In a single house there is no check, but the inadequate one, of the virtue & good sense of those who compose it."

Hamilton argued that a Congress comprised of a single House was antithetical to the very purposes of the Constitution. Were the Nation to adopt a Constitution providing for only one legislative organ, he warned: "we shall finally accumulate, in a single body, all the most important prerogatives of sovereignty, and thus entail upon our posterity one of the most execrable forms of government that human infatuation ever contrived. Thus we should create in reality that very tyranny which the adversaries of the new Constitution either are, or affect to be, solicitous to avert." The Federalist No. 22.

This view was rooted in a general skepticism regarding the fallibility of human nature later commented on by Joseph Story: "Public bodies, like private persons, are occasionally under the dominion of strong passions and excitements; impatient, irritable, and impetuous. . . . If [a legislature] feels no check but its own will, it rarely has the firmness to insist upon holding a question long enough under its own view, to see and mark it in all its bearings and relations to society."

These observations are consistent with what many of the Framers expressed, none more cogently than Hamilton in pointing up the need to divide and disperse power in order to protect liberty: "In republican government, the legislative authority necessarily predominates. The remedy for this inconveniency is to divide the legislature into different branches; and to render them, by different modes of election and different principles of action, as little connected with each other as the nature of their common functions and their common dependence on the society will admit." The Federalist No. 51.

However familiar, it is useful to recall that apart from their fear that special interests could be favored at the expense of public needs, the Framers were also concerned, although not of one mind, over the apprehensions of the smaller states. Those states feared a commonality of interest among the larger states would work to their disadvantage; representatives of the larger states, on the other hand, were skeptical of a legislature that could pass laws favoring a minority of the people. It need hardly be repeated here that the Great Compromise, under which one House was viewed as representing the people and the other the states, allayed the fears of both the large and small states.

We see therefore that the Framers were acutely conscious that the bicameral requirement and the Presentment Clauses would serve essential constitutional functions. The President's participation in the legislative process was to protect the Executive Branch from Congress and to protect the whole people from improvident laws. The division of the Congress into two distinctive bodies assures that the legislative power would be exercised only after opportunity for full study and debate in separate settings. The President's unilateral veto power, in turn, was limited by the power of two thirds of both Houses of Congress to overrule a veto thereby precluding final arbitrary action of one person. It emerges clearly that the prescription for legislative action in Art. I, §§ 1, 7 represents the Framers' decision that the legislative power of the Federal government be exercised in accord with a single, finely wrought and exhaustively considered, procedure.

IV. The Constitution sought to divide the delegated powers of the new federal government into three defined categories, legislative, executive and judicial, to assure, as nearly as possible, that each Branch of government would confine itself to its assigned responsibility. The hydraulic pressure inherent within each of the separate Branches to exceed the outer limits of its power, even to accomplish desirable objectives, must be resisted.

Although not "hermetically" sealed from one another, the powers delegated to the three Branches are functionally identifiable. When any Branch acts, it is presumptively exercising the power the Constitution has delegated to it. When the Executive acts, it presumptively acts in an executive or administrative capacity as defined in Art. II. And when, as here, one House of Congress purports to act, it is presumptively acting within its assigned sphere.

Beginning with this presumption, we must nevertheless establish that the challenged action under § 244(c)(2) is of the kind to which the procedural requirements of Art. I, § 7 apply. Not every action taken by either House is subject to the bicameralism and presentment requirements of Art. I. Whether actions taken by either House are, in law and fact, an exercise of legislative power depends not on their form but upon "whether they contain matter which is properly to be regarded as legislative in its character and effect." S.Rep.No.1335, 54th Cong., 2d Sess., 8 (1897).

Examination of the action taken here by one House pursuant to § 244 (c)(2) reveals that it was essentially legislative in purpose and effect. In purporting to exercise power defined in Art. I, § 8, cl. 4 to "establish an uniform Rule of Naturalization," the House took action that had the purpose and effect of altering the legal rights, duties and relations of persons, including the Attorney General, Executive Branch officials and Chadha, all outside the legislative branch. Section 244(c)(2) purports to authorize one House of Congress to require the Attorney General to deport an individual alien whose deportation otherwise would be cancelled under § 244. The one-House veto operated in this case to overrule the Attorney General and mandate Chadha's deportation; absent the House action, Chadha would remain in the United States. Congress has *acted* and its action has altered Chadha's status.

The legislative character of the one-House veto in this case is confirmed by the character of the Congressional action it supplants. Neither the House of Representatives nor the Senate contends that, absent the veto provision in § 244(c)(2), either of them, or both of them acting together, could effectively require the Attorney General to deport an alien once the Attorney General, in the exercise of legislatively delegated authority, had determined the alien should remain in the United States. Without the challenged provision in § 244(c)(2), this could have been achieved, if at all, only by legislation requiring deportation. Similarly, a veto by one House of Congress under § 244(c)(2) cannot be justified as an attempt at amending the standards set out in § 244(a)(1), or as a repeal of § 244 as applied to Chadha. Amendment and repeal of statutes, no less than enactment, must conform with Art. I.

The nature of the decision implemented by the one-House veto in this case further manifests its legislative character. After long experience with the clumsy, time consuming private bill procedure, Congress made a deliberate choice to delegate to the Executive Branch, and specifically to the Attorney General, the authority to allow deportable aliens to remain in this country in certain specified circumstances. It is not disputed that this choice to delegate authority is precisely the kind of decision that can be implemented only in accordance with the procedures set out in Art. I. Disagreement with the Attorney General's decision on Chadha's deportation—that is, Congress' decision to deport Chadha—no less than Congress' original choice to delegate to the Attorney General the authority to make that decision, involves determinations of policy that Congress can implement in only one way; bicameral passage followed by presentment to the President. Congress must abide by its delegation of authority until that delegation is legislatively altered or revoked.

Finally, we see that when the Framers intended to authorize either House of Congress to act alone and outside of its prescribed bicameral legislative role, they narrowly and precisely defined the procedure for such action. There are but four provisions in the Constitution, explicit and unambiguous, by which one House may act alone with the unreviewable force of law, not subject to the President's veto:

(a) The House of Representatives alone was given the power to initiate impeachments. Art. I, § 2, cl. 6;

(b) The Senate alone was given the power to conduct trials following impeachment on charges initiated by the House and to convict following trial. Art. I, § 3, cl. 5;

(c) The Senate alone was given final unreviewable power to approve or to disapprove presidential appointments. Art. II, § 2, cl. 2;

(d) The Senate alone was given unreviewable power to ratify treaties negotiated by the President. Art. II, § 2, cl. 2.

Clearly, when the Draftsmen sought to confer special powers on one House, independent of the other House, or of the President, they did so in explicit, unambiguous terms. These carefully defined exceptions from presentment and bicameralism underscore the difference between the legislative functions of Congress and other unilateral but important and binding one-House acts provided for in the Constitution. These exceptions are narrow, explicit, and separately justified; none of them authorize the action challenged here. On the contrary, they provide further support for the conclusion that Congressional authority is not to be implied and for the conclusion that the veto provided for in § 244(c)(2) is not authorized by the constitutional design of the powers of the Legislative Branch.

Since it is clear that the action by the House under § 244(c)(2) was not within any of the express constitutional exceptions authorizing one House to act alone, and equally clear that it was an exercise of legislative power, that action was subject to the standards prescribed in Article I. The bicameral requirement, the Presentment Clauses, the President's veto, and Congress' power to override a veto were intended to erect enduring checks on each Branch and to protect the people from the improvident exercise of power by mandating certain prescribed steps. To preserve those checks, and maintain the separation of powers, the carefully defined limits on the power of each Branch must not be eroded. To accomplish what has been attempted by one House of Congress in this case requires action in conformity with the express procedures of the Constitution's prescription for legislative action; passage by a majority of both Houses and presentment to the President.

The veto authorized by § 244(c)(2) doubtless has been in many respects a convenient shortcut; the "sharing" with the Executive by Congress of its authority over aliens in this manner is, on its face, an appealing compromise. In purely practical terms, it is obviously easier for action to be taken by one House without submission to the President; but it is crystal clear from the records of the Convention, contemporaneous writings and debates, that the Framers ranked other values higher than efficiency. The records of the Convention and debates in the States preceding ratification underscore the common desire to define and limit the exercise of the newly created federal powers affecting the states and the people. There is unmistakable expression of a determination that legislation by the national Congress be a step-by-step, deliberate and deliberative process.

The choices we discern as having been made in the Constitutional Convention impose burdens on governmental processes that often seem clumsy, inefficient, even unworkable, but those hard choices were consciously made by men who had lived under a form of government that permitted arbitrary governmental acts to go unchecked. There is no support in the Constitution or decisions of this Court for the proposition that the cumbersomeness and delays often encountered in complying with explicit Constitutional standards may be avoided, either by the Congress or by the President.

[Youngstown Sheet & Tube.] With all the obvious flaws of delay, untidiness, and potential for abuse, we have not yet found a better way to preserve freedom than by making the exercise of power subject to the carefully crafted restraints spelled out in the Constitution. . . .

[Affirmed.]

Justice POWELL, concurring in the judgment.

The Court's decision, based on the Presentment Clauses, Art. I, § 7, cl. 2 and 3, apparently will invalidate every use of the legislative veto. The breadth of this holding gives one pause. Congress has included the veto in literally hundreds of statutes, dating back to the 1930s. Congress clearly views this procedure as essential to controlling the delegation of power to administrative agencies. One reasonably may disagree with Congress' assessment of the veto's utility, but the respect due its judgment as a coordinate branch of Government cautions that our holding should be no more extensive than necessary to decide this case. In my view, the case may be decided on a narrower ground. When Congress finds that a particular person does not satisfy the statutory criteria for permanent residence in this country it has assumed a judicial function in violation of the principle of separation of powers. Accordingly, I concur in the judgment.

I. A. The Framers perceived that "[t]he accumulation of all powers legislative, executive and judiciary in the same hands, whether of one, a few or many, and whether hereditary, self appointed, or elective, may justly be pronounced the very definition of tyranny." The Federalist No. 47 (J. Madison). Theirs was not a baseless fear. Under British rule, the colonies suffered the abuses of unchecked executive power that were attributed, at least popularly, to an hereditary monarchy. During the Confederation, the States reacted by removing power from the executive and placing it in the hands of elected legislators. But many legislators proved to be little better than the Crown. [One] abuse that was prevalent during the Confederation was the exercise of judicial power by the state legislatures. The Framers were well acquainted with the danger of subjecting the determination of the rights of one person to the "tyranny of shifting majorities." [It] was to prevent the recurrence of such abuses that the Framers vested the executive, legislative, and judicial powers in separate branches. Their concern that a legislature should not be able unilaterally to impose a substantial deprivation on one person was expressed not only in this general allocation of power, but also in more specific provisions, such as the Bill of Attainder Clause, Art. I, § 9, cl. 3. [This] Clause, and the separation of powers doctrine generally, reflect the Framer's concern that trial by a legislature lacks the safeguards necessary to prevent the abuse of power.

B. The Constitution does not establish three branches with precisely defined boundaries. Rather, as Justice Jackson wrote, "[w]hile the Constitution diffuses power the better to secure liberty, it also contemplates that practice will integrate the dispersed powers into a workable government. It enjoins upon its branches separateness but interdependence, autonomy but reciprocity." [Youngstown Sheet & Tube.] [But] where one branch has impaired or sought to assume a power central to another branch, the Court has not hesitated to enforce the doctrine.

Functionally, the doctrine may be violated in two ways. One branch may interfere impermissibly with the other's performance of its constitutionally assigned function. See Nixon v. Administrator of General Services; United States v. Nixon. Alternatively, the doctrine may be violated when one branch assumes a function that more properly is entrusted to another. See [Youngstown Sheet & Tube.] This case presents the latter situation.

II. [On] its face, the House's action appears clearly adjudicatory. The House did not enact a general rule; rather it made its own determination that six specific persons did not comply with certain statutory criteria. It thus undertook the type of decision that traditionally has been left to other branches. Even if the House did not make a *de novo* determination, but simply reviewed the Immigration and Naturalization Service's findings, it still assumed a function ordinarily entrusted to the federal courts.

[The] impropriety of the House's assumption of this function is confirmed by the fact that its action raises the very danger the Framers sought to avoid—the exercise of unchecked power. In deciding whether Chadha deserves to be deported, Congress is not subject to any internal constraints that prevent it from arbitrarily depriving him of the right to remain in this country. Unlike the judiciary or an administrative agency, Congress is not bound by established substantive rules. Nor is it subject to the procedural safeguards, such as the right to counsel and a hearing before an impartial tribunal, that are present when a court or an agency adjudicates individual rights. The only effective constraint on Congress' power is political, but Congress is most accountable politically when it prescribes rules of general applicability. When it decides rights of specific persons, those rights are subject to "the tyranny of a shifting majority." . . .

Justice WHITE, dissenting.

Today the Court not only invalidates § 244(c)(2) of the Immigration and Nationality Act, but also sounds the death knell for nearly 200 other statutory provisions in which Congress has reserved a "legislative veto." For this reason, the Court's decision is of surpassing importance. And it is for this reason that the Court would have been well-advised to decide the case, if possible, on the narrower grounds of separation of powers, leaving for full consideration the constitutionality of other congressional review statutes operating on such varied matters as war powers and agency rulemaking, some of which concern the independent regulatory agencies.

The prominence of the legislative veto mechanism in our contemporary political system and its importance to Congress can hardly be overstated. It has become a central means by which Congress secures the accountability of executive and independent agencies. Without the legislative veto, Congress is faced with a Hobson's choice: either to refrain from delegating the necessary authority, leaving itself with a hopeless task of writing laws with the requisite specificity to cover endless special circumstances across the entire policy landscape, or in the alternative, to abdicate its lawmaking function to the executive branch and independent agencies. To choose the former leaves major national problems unresolved; to opt for the latter risks unaccountable policymaking by those not elected to fill that role. Accordingly, over the past five decades, the legislative veto has been placed in nearly 200 statutes.* The device is known in every field of governmental concern: reorganization, budgets, foreign affairs, war powers, and regulation of trade, safety, energy, the environment and the economy.

I. The legislative veto developed initially in response to the problems of reorganizing the sprawling government structure created in response to the Depression. The Reorganization Acts established the chief model for the legislative veto. When President Hoover requested authority to reorganize the government in 1929, he coupled his request that the "Congress be willing to delegate its authority over the problem (subject to defined principles) to the Executive" with a proposal for legislative review. He proposed that the Executive "should act upon approval of a joint committee of Congress or with the reservation of power of revision by Congress within some limited period adequate for its consideration." Congress followed President Hoover's suggestion and authorized reorganization subject to legislative review. Although the reorganization authority reenacted in 1933 did not contain a legislative veto provision, the provision returned during the Roosevelt Administration and has since been renewed numerous times. Over the years, the provision was used extensively. Presidents submitted 115 reorganization plans to Congress of which 23 were disapproved by Congress pursuant to legislative veto provisions.

Shortly after adoption of the Reorganization Act of 1939, Congress and the President applied the legislative veto procedure to resolve the delegation problem for national security and foreign affairs. World War II occasioned the need to transfer greater authority to the President in these areas. The legislative veto offered the means by which Congress could confer additional authority while preserving its own constitutional role. [Over] the quarter century following World War II, Presidents continued to accept legislative vetoes by one or both Houses as constitutional, while regularly denouncing provisions by which Congressional committees reviewed Executive activity. The legislative veto balanced delegations of statutory authority in new areas of governmental involvement: the space program, international agreements on nuclear energy, tariff arrangements, and adjustment of federal pay rates.

During the 1970's the legislative veto was important in resolving a series of major constitutional disputes between the President and Congress over claims of the President to broad impoundment, war, and national emergency powers. The key provision of the War Powers Resolution authorizes the termination by concurrent resolution of the use of armed forces in hostilities. A similar measure resolved the problem posed by Presidential claims of inherent power to impound appropriations. [Although] the War Powers Resolution was enacted over President Nixon's veto, the Impoundment Control Act was enacted with the President's approval. These statutes were followed by others resolving similar problems.

[The] legislative veto is more than "efficient, convenient, and useful." It is an important if not indispensable political invention that allows the President and Congress to resolve major constitutional and policy differences,

---

* An appendix to Justice White's dissent described a large number of the most important legislative veto provisions.

assures the accountability of independent regulatory agencies, and preserves Congress' control over lawmaking. Perhaps there are other means of accomodation and accountability, but the increasing reliance of Congress upon the legislative veto suggests that the alternatives to which Congress must now turn are not entirely satisfactory.

[The] history of the legislative veto also makes clear that it has not been a sword with which Congress has struck out to aggrandize itself at the expense of the other branches—the concerns of Madison and Hamilton. Rather, the veto has been a means of defense, a reservation of ultimate authority necessary if Congress is to fulfill its designated role under Article I as the nation's lawmaker. While the President has often objected to particular legislative vetoes, generally those left in the hands of congressional committees, the Executive has more often agreed to legislative review as the price for a broad delegation of authority. To be sure, the President may have preferred unrestricted power, but that could be precisely why Congress thought it essential to retain a check on the exercise of delegated authority.

II. For all these reasons, the apparent sweep of the Court's decision today is regretable. The Court's Article I analysis appears to invalidate all legislative vetoes irrespective of form or subject. Because the legislative veto is commonly found as a check upon rulemaking by administrative agencies and upon broad-based policy decisions of the Executive Branch, it is particularly unfortunate that the Court reaches its decision in a case involving the exercise of a veto over deportation decisions regarding particular individuals. Courts should always be wary of striking statutes as unconstitutional; to strike an entire class of statutes based on consideration of a somewhat atypical and more-readily indictable exemplar of the class is irresponsible.

[If] the legislative veto were as plainly unconstitutional as the Court strives to suggest, its broad ruling today would be more comprehensible. But, the constitutionality of the legislative veto is anything but clearcut. The issue divides scholars, courts, attorneys general, and the two other branches of the National Government. If the veto devices so flagrantly disregarded the requirements of Article I as the Court today suggests, I find it incomprehensible that Congress, whose members are bound by oath to uphold the Constitution, would have placed these mechanisms in nearly 200 separate laws over a period of 50 years.

The reality of the situation is that the constitutional question posed today is one of immense difficulty over which the executive and legislative branches—as well as scholars and judges—have understandably disagreed. That disagreement stems from the silence of the Constitution on the precise question: The Constitution does not directly authorize or prohibit the legislative veto. Thus, our task should be to determine whether the legislative veto is consistent with the purposes of Art. I and the principles of Separation of Powers which are reflected in that Article and throughout the Constitution. We should not find the lack of a specific constitutional authorization for the legislative veto surprising, and I would not infer disapproval of the mechanism from its absence. From the summer of 1787 to the present the government of the United States has become an endeavor far beyond the contemplation of the Framers. Only within the last half century has the complexity and size of the Federal Government's responsibilities grown so greatly that the Congress must rely on the legislative veto as the most effective if not the only means to insure their role as the nation's lawmakers. But the wisdom of the Framers was to anticipate that the nation would grow and new problems of governance would require different solutions. Accordingly, our Federal Government was intentionally chartered with the flexibility to respond to contemporary needs without losing sight of fundamental democratic principles. [In] my view, neither Article I of the Constitution nor the doctrine of separation of powers is violated by this mechanism by which our elected representatives preserve their voice in the governance of the nation.

III.   [There] is no question that a bill does not become a law until it is approved by both the House and the Senate, and presented to the President. Similarly, I would not hesitate to strike an action of Congress in the form of a concurrent resolution which constituted an exercise of original lawmaking authority. I agree with the Court that the President's qualified veto power is a critical element in the distribution of powers under the Constitution, widely endorsed among the Framers, and intended to serve the President as a defense against legislative encroachment and to check the "passing of bad laws through haste, inadvertence, or design." The Federalist No. 73 (A. Hamilton).

[This] does not, however, answer the constitutional question before us. The power to exercise a legislative veto is not the power to write new law without bicameral approval or presidential consideration. The veto must be authorized by statute and may only negative what an Executive department or independent agency has proposed. On its face, the legislative veto no more allows one House of Congress to make law than does the presidential veto confer such power upon the President. Accordingly, the Court properly recognizes that it "must establish that the challenged action under § 244(c)(2) is of the kind to which the procedural requirements of Art. I, § 7 apply" and admits that "not every action taken by either House is subject to the bicameralism and presentation requirements of Art. I."

A.   The terms of the Presentment Clauses suggest only that bills and their equivalent are subject to the requirements of bicameral passage and presentment to the President. [The] historical background of the Presentation Clause itself [reveals] only that the Framers were concerned with limiting the methods for enacting new legislation. The Framers were aware of the experience in Pennsylvania where the legislature had evaded the requirements attached to the passing of legislation by the use of "resolves," and the criticisms directed at this practice by the Council of Censors. There is no record that the Convention contemplated, let alone intended, that these Article I requirements would someday be invoked to restrain the scope of Congressional authority pursuant to duly-enacted law.

When the Convention did turn its attention to the scope of Congress' lawmaking power, the Framers were expansive. [McCulloch.]   .   .   .

B. The Court heeded this counsel in approving the modern administrative state. The Court's holding today that all legislative-type action must be enacted through the lawmaking process ignores that legislative authority is routinely delegated to the Executive branch, to the independent regulatory agencies, and to private individuals and groups. [The] wisdom and the constitutionality of these broad delegations are matters that still have not been put to rest. But for present purposes, [the] cases establish that by virtue of congressional delegation, legislative power can be exercised by independent agencies and Executive departments without the passage of new legislation. For some time, the sheer amount of law—the substantive rules, that regulate private conduct and direct the operation of government—made by the agencies has far outnumbered the lawmaking engaged in by Congress through the traditional process. There is no question but that agency rulemaking is lawmaking in any functional or realistic sense of the term. [These] regulations bind courts and officers of the federal government, may preempt state law, and grant rights to and impose obligations on the public. In sum, they have the force of law.

If Congress may delegate lawmaking power to independent and executive agencies, it is most difficult to understand Article I as forbidding Congress from also reserving a check on legislative power for itself. Absent the veto, the agencies receiving delegations of legislative or quasi-legislative power may issue regulations having the force of law without bicameral approval and without the President's signature. It is thus not apparent why the reservation of a veto over the exercise of that legislative power must be subject to a more exacting test. In both cases, it is enough that the initial statutory authorizations comply with the Article I requirements. . . .

C. The Court also takes no account of perhaps the most relevant consideration: However resolutions of disapproval under § 244(c)(2) are formally characterized, in reality, a departure from the status quo occurs only upon the concurrence of opinion among the House, Senate, and President. Reservations of legislative authority to be exercised by Congress should be upheld if the exercise of such reserved authority is consistent with the distribution of and limits upon legislative power that Article I provides.

1. [The] history of the Immigration Act makes clear that § 244(c)(2) did not alter the division of actual authority between Congress and the Executive. At all times, whether through private bills, or through affirmative concurrent resolutions, or through the present one-House veto, a permanent change in a deportable alien's status could be accomplished only with the agreement of the Attorney General, the House, and the Senate.

2. The central concern of the presentation and bicareralism requirements of Article I is that when a departure from the legal status quo is undertaken, it is done with the approval of the President and both Houses of Congress—or, in the event of a presidential veto, a two-thirds majority in both Houses. This interest is fully satisfied by the operation of § 244 (c)(2). The President's approval is found in the Attorney General's action in recommending to Congress that the deportation order for a given alien be suspended. The House and the Senate indicate their approval of the Executive's action by not passing a resolution of disapproval within the stat-

utory period.   Thus, a change in the legal status quo—the deportability of the alien—is consummated only with the approval of each of the three relevant actors.   The disagreement of any one of the three maintains the alien's pre-existing status: the Executive may choose not to recommend suspension; the House and Senate may each veto the recommendation.   The effect on the rights and obligations of the affected individuals and upon the legislative system is precisely the same as if a private bill were introduced but failed to receive the necessary approval.   .   .   .

IV.   [The] history of the separation of powers doctrine is [a] history of accomodation and practicality.   Apprehensions of an overly powerful branch have not led to undue prophylactic measures that handicap the effective working of the national government as a whole.   The Constitution does not contemplate total separation of the three branches of Government.   [Our] decisions reflect this judgment.   As already noted, the Court, recognizing that modern government must address a formidable agenda of complex policy issues, countenanced the delegation of extensive legislative authority to executive and independent agencies.   [I] do not suggest that all legislative vetoes are necessarily consistent with separation of powers principles.   A legislative check on an inherently executive function, for example that of initiating prosecutions, poses an entirely different question.   But the legislative veto device here—and in many other settings—is far from an instance of legislative tyranny over the Executive.   It is a necessary check on the unavoidably expanding power of the agencies, both executive and independent, as they engage in exercising authority delegated by Congress.

V.   I regret that I am in disagreement with my colleagues on the fundamental questions that this case presents.   But even more I regret the destructive scope of the Court's holding.   It reflects a profoundly different conception of the Constitution than that held by the Courts which sanctioned the modern administrative state.   Today's decision strikes down in one fell swoop provisions in more laws enacted by Congress than the Court has cumulatively invalidated in its history.   I fear it will now be more difficult "to insure that the fundamental policy decisions in our society will be made not by an appointed official but by the body immediately responsible to the people," Arizona v. California, 373 U.S. 546, 626 (1963) (Harlan, J., dissenting).   I must dissent.

Justice REHNQUIST, with whom Justice WHITE joins, dissenting.

A severability clause creates a presumption that Congress intended the valid portion of the statute to remain in force when one part is found to be invalid.   Because I believe that Congress did not intend the one-House veto provision of § 244(c)(2) to be severable, I dissent.

Section 244(c)(2) is an exception to the general rule that an alien's deportation shall be suspended when the Attorney General finds that statutory criteria are met.   It is severable only if Congress would have intended to permit the Attorney General to suspend deportations without it.   [By] severing § 244(c)(2), the Court permits suspension of deportation in a class of cases where Congress never stated that suspension was appropriate.   I do not believe we should expand the statute in this way without some clear indication that Congress intended such an expansion.

[The] Court finds that the legislative history of § 244 shows that Congress intended § 244(c)(2) to be severable because Congress wanted to relieve itself of the burden of private bills. But the history elucidated by the Court shows that Congress was unwilling to give the Executive Branch permission to suspend deportation on its own. Over the years, Congress consistently rejected requests from the Executive for complete discretion in this area. Congress always insisted on retaining ultimate control, whether by concurrent resolution, as in the 1948 Act, or by one-House veto, as in the present Act. Congress has never indicated that it would be willing to permit suspensions of deportation unless it could retain some sort of veto.

It is doubtless true that Congress has the power to provide for suspensions of deportation without a one-House veto. But the Court has failed to identify any evidence that Congress intended to exercise that power. On the contrary, Congress' continued insistence on retaining control of the suspension process indicates that it has never been disposed to give the Executive Branch a free hand.

[Because] I do not believe that § 244(c)(2) is severable, I would reverse the judgment of the Court of Appeals.

10th ED., p. 408
Add to Note 3a:

There have been further attempts to revitalize the delegation analysis of the Panama Refining and Schechter cases of the 1930s. Justice Rehnquist has recently urged that the delegation doctrine is a basis for invalidation of some modern congressional grants of authority to administrative agencies. See especially American Textile Mfrs. Inst. v. Donovan, 452 U.S. 490 (1981), which involved interpretation of the Occupational Safety and Health Act of 1970. The Act authorizes the Administrator (OSHA) to promulgate mandatory federal standards governing health and safety in the workplace. The most controversial provision, § 6(b)(5), states that OSHA "shall set the standard which most adequately assures, *to the extent feasible*, [that] no employee will suffer material impairment of health or functional capacity even if such employee has regular exposure to the hazard dealt with by such standard for the period of his working life." (Emphasis added.) The central issue in the case was OSHA's right or duty to engage in cost-benefit analysis before promulgating standards.

Justice Rehnquist's dissent, joined by Chief Justice Burger, argued that § 6(b)(5) "unconstitutionally delegated to the Executive Branch the authority to make the 'hard policy choices' properly the task of the legislature." * He insisted that the Act exceeded Congress' power "to delegate legislative authority to nonelected officials." In his view, inclusion of the phrase "to the extent feasible" "rendered what had been a clear, if somewhat unrealistic, statute into one so vague and precatory as to be an unconstitutional delega-

---

* Justice Rehnquist relied heavily on his concurring opinion in Industrial Union Dept. v. American Petrol. Inst., 448 U.S. 607 (1980). [The Industrial Union case involved the "benzene standard," a safeguard against cancer. The American Textile case dealt with the "cotton dust standard," a safeguard against "brown lung" disease.]

tion." He elaborated: "The words 'to the extent feasible' were used to mask a fundamental policy disagreement in Congress. I have no doubt that if Congress had been required to choose whether to mandate, permit, or prohibit the [Administrator] from engaging in a cost-benefit analysis, there would have been no bill for the President to sign." He added: "I do not mean to suggest that Congress, in enacting a statute, must resolve all ambiguities or must 'fill in all of the blanks.' Even the neophyte student of government realizes that legislation is the art of compromise. [But the typical compromise] is a far cry from this case, where Congress simply abdicated its responsibility for the making of a fundamental and most difficult policy choice— whether and to what extent 'the statistical possibility of future deaths should [be] disregarded in light of economic costs of preventing those deaths.' That is a 'quintessential legislative' choice and must be made by the elected representatives of the people, not by nonelected officials in the Executive Branch."

10th ED., p. 409
Add to Note 2:

Note also the Court's endorsement of the validity of the presidential actions taken pursuant to the January 1981 Executive Agreement entered into to obtain the release of American hostages in Iran. The Iranian Assets Case, Dames & Moore v. Regan, 453 U.S. 654 (1981), is more fully discussed above, addition to 10th Ed., p. 397. Justice Rehnquist's opinion found some of the challenged executive actions implementing the Agreement supported by specific congressional authorization and others by implied congressional consent and acquiescence.

With respect to the latter, Justice Rehnquist emphasized that "Congress has acquiesced in [the] longstanding practice of claims settlement by executive agreement." He defended that assertion in several ways. At one point, he invoked prior cases such as United States v. Pink, and argued that those cases "recognized that the President does have some measure of power to enter into executive agreements without obtaining the advice and consent of the Senate." He conceded that Pink had rested on the President's recognition power. But he also quoted from a broader ruling by Judge Learned Hand, Ozanic v. United States, 188 F.2d 228 (CA2 1951): "The constitutional power of the President extends to the settlement of mutual claims between a foreign government and the United States, at least when it is an incident to the recognition of that government; and it would be unreasonable to circumscribe it to such controversies. The continued mutual amity between this nation and other powers again and again depends upon a satisfactory compromise of mutual claims: the necessary power to make such compromises has existed from the earliest times and been exercised by the foreign offices of all civilized nations." *

10th ED., p. 434
Add to the second paragraph of footnote 2:
Gravel v. United States was discussed and distinguished in Harlow & Butterfield v. Fitzgerald, 457 U.S. 731 (1982) (noted below, addition to 10th Ed., p. 448),

---

* Note that the Executive Agreement in the Iranian Assets Case was *not* negotiated in connection with the recognition of a foreign government; but note also that the Iranian Assets ruling, rather than resting on inherent executive power under Art. II, relied primarily on congressional authorization or acquiescence.

where the Court refused to grant to White House aides the same "derivative" absolute immunity to which legislators' aides are entitled under Gravel.

10th ED., p. 448
Insert before Sec. 2C:

ABSOLUTE PRESIDENTIAL IMMUNITY
FROM CIVIL LIABILITY

The 5 to 4 decision in NIXON v. FITZGERALD, 457 U.S. ——— (1982), held that—at least "in the absence of explicit affirmative action by Congress"—"the President is absolutely immune from civil damages liability for his official acts." [1]   The case arose out of the following circumstances: Fitzgerald, a widely publicized "whistle blower" of the late 1960s, lost his position as a management analyst with the Department of the Air Force in 1970.   He had attained national prominence because of his testimony before a congressional subcommittee during which he exposed substantial cost overruns in the development of a military transport plane.   His testimony embarrassed and angered Defense Department officials and he lost his job.   In subsequent proceedings before the Civil Service Commission (CSC) and in the federal courts, Fitzgerald claimed that the loss of his job "represented unlawful retaliation for his truthful testimony."   The CSC found that Fitzgerald had been improperly removed from government service, but did not support his "retaliation" claim.   As finally amended, Fitzgerald's federal court complaint charging violation of his First Amendment and statutory rights named as defendants former President Nixon as well as other Nixon Administration officials.[2]

Justice POWELL, the author of the majority opinion, concluded that Nixon, "as a former President of the United States, is entitled to absolute immunity from damages liability predicated on his official acts.   We consider

---

1.   Could Congress change the absolute immunity established by this case through "express" legislation?   Justice Powell, in his majority opinion, left that question open.   He noted that Fitzgerald's statutory claim rested only on "implied" causes of action, so that "we need not address directly the immunity question as it would arise if Congress expressly had created a damages action against the President."   Contrast Chief Justice Burger's position: although he joined Justice Powell's opinion, he argued in his concurrence that the presidential immunity was mandated by the constitutional separation of powers and insisted: "[T]he Court's holding, in my view, effectively resolves [the congressional power] issue; once it is established that the Constitution confers absolute immunity, as the Court holds today, legislative action cannot alter that result.   Nothing in the Court's opinion is to be read as suggesting that a Constitutional holding of this Court can be legislatively overruled or

modified.   Marbury   v.   Madison." [Note the debate below (10th Ed., p. 1096; Ind.Rts., p. 716) on the congressional power to modify or overturn judicial determinations of constitutional rights under § 5 of the Fourteenth Amendment.]   Justice White, while dissenting from the majority's holding, in effect agreed with the Chief Justice on the issue of congressional power to alter the immunity: "We are never told [how] or why Congressional action could make a difference.   It is not apparent that any of the propositions relied upon by the majority to immunize the President would not apply equally to such a statutory cause of action;   nor does the majority indicate what new principles would operate to undercut those propositions."

2.   See Harlow & Butterfield v. Fitzgerald, a companion case to Nixon v. Fitzgerald, noted immediately following this case.

this immunity a functionally mandated incident of the President's unique office, rooted in the constitutional tradition of the separation of powers and supported by our history." In determining the scope of presidential immunity, he explained, the focus of the inquiry must be on historical analysis drawn from "our constitutional heritage and structure" as well as on "concerns of public policy."

In elaborating the reasons for absolute presidential immunity, Justice Powell emphasized the President's "unique position in the constitutional scheme." He distinguished earlier decisions granting only qualified immunity to persons holding such executive positions as governor and cabinet officer: "The President's unique status under the Constitution distinguishes him from other executive officials." He elaborated: "Because of the singular importance of the President's duties, diversion of his energies by concern with private lawsuits would raise unique risks to the effective functioning of government. As is the case with prosecutors and judges—for whom absolute immunity now is established—a President must concern himself with matters likely to 'arouse the most intense feelings.' [I]t is in precisely such cases that there exists the greatest public interest in providing an official 'the maximum ability to deal fearlessly and impartially with' the duties of his office. [Nor] can the sheer prominence of the President's office be ignored. In view of the visibility of his office and the effect of his actions on countless people, the President would be an easily identifiable target for suits for civil damages. Cognizance of this personal vulnerability frequently could distract a President from his public duties, to the detriment not only of the President and his office but also the Nation that the Presidency was designed to serve."

Justice Powell noted that courts "traditionally have recognized the President's constitutional responsibilities and status as factors counselling judicial deference and restraint." He conceded that "separation of powers doctrine does not bar every exercise of jurisdiction over the President. [See, e.g., United States v. Nixon.] But our cases also have established that a court, before exercising jurisdiction, must balance the constitutional weight of the interest to be served against the dangers of intrusion on the authority and functions of the Executive Branch. When judicial action is needed to serve broad public interests—as when the Court acts, not in derogation of the separation of powers, but to maintain their proper balance, cf. [The Steel Seizure Case], or to vindicate the public interest in an ongoing criminal prosecution, see United States v. Nixon—the exercise of jurisdiction has been warranted. In the case of this merely private suit for damages based on a President's official acts, we hold it is not." [3]

3. "The Court has recognized before that there is a lesser public interest in actions for civil damages than, for example, in criminal prosecutions. It never has been denied that absolute immunity may impose a regrettable cost on individuals whose rights have been violated. But, contrary to the suggestion of Justice White's dissent, it is not true that our jurisprudence ordinarily supplies a remedy in civil damages for every legal wrong. The dissent's objections on this ground would weigh equally against absolute immunity for any official. Yet the dissent makes no attack on the absolute immunity recognized for judges and prosecutors. . . ." [Footnote by Justice Powell.]

In a passage of his opinion that roused the special wrath of the dissenters, Justice Powell refused to follow the analysis typically applied in delineating the scope of the absolute immunity of other officials. The usual, "functional" approach limits absolute immunity to specified duties of the office, as Justice Powell conceded: "In defining the scope of an official's absolute privilege, this Court has recognized that the sphere of protected action must be related closely to the immunity's justifying purposes. Frequently our decisions have held that an official's absolute immunity should extend only to acts in performance of particular functions of his office." But he went on to insist that that approach was inappropriate with regard to the President: "In view of the special nature of the President's constitutional office and functions, we think it appropriate to recognize absolute Presidential immunity from damages liability for acts within the 'outer perimeter' of his official responsibility." He explained: "[T]he President has discretionary responsibilities in a broad variety of areas, many of them highly sensitive. In many cases it would be difficult to determine which of the President's innumerable 'functions' encompassed a particular action. In this case, for example, [Fitzgerald] argues that he was dismissed in retaliation for his testimony to Congress—a violation of [federal statutes]. The Air Force, however, has claimed that the underlying reorganization [which cost Fitzgerald his job] was undertaken to promote efficiency. Assuming that [Nixon] ordered the reorganization in which [Fitzgerald] lost his job, an inquiry into the President's motives could not be avoided under the kind of 'functional' theory asserted both by [Fitzgerald] and the dissent. Inquiries of this kind could be highly intrusive." Nor would Justice Powell accept the argument that Nixon would have acted "outside the outer perimeter of his duties" if he ordered Fitzgerald's discharge: "This construction would subject the President to trial on virtually every allegation that an action was unlawful, or was taken for a forbidden purpose. Adoption of this construction thus would deprive absolute immunity of its intended effect. It clearly is within the President's constitutional and statutory authority to prescribe the manner in which the Secretary will conduct the business of the Air Force. Because this mandate of office must include the authority to prescribe reorganizations and reductions in force, we conclude that [Nixon's] alleged wrongful acts lay well within the outer perimeter of his authority."

In conclusion, Justice Powell insisted: "A rule of absolute immunity for the President will not leave the nation without sufficient protection against misconduct on the part of the chief executive. There remains the constitutional remedy of impeachment. In addition, there are formal and informal checks on Presidential action that do not apply with equal force to other executive officials. The President is subjected to constant scrutiny by the press. Vigilant oversight by Congress also may serve to deter Presidential abuses of office, as well as to make credible the threat of impeachment. Other incentives to avoid misconduct may include a desire to earn re-election, the need to maintain prestige as an element of Presidential influence, and a President's traditional concern for his historical stature. The existence of alternative remedies and deterrents establishes that absolute immunity will not place the

President 'above the law.' [4]   For the President, as for judges and prosecutors, absolute immunity merely precludes a particular private remedy for alleged misconduct in order to advance compelling public ends." [5]

Justice WHITE, joined by Justices Brennan, Marshall and Blackmun, submitted a long and vehement dissent. He especially objected to the majority's failure to follow the usual approach in other absolute immunity cases. Citing Butz v. Economou, 438 U.S. 478 (1978), he stated that the Court had held that, "although public officials perform certain functions that entitle them to absolute immunity, the immunity attaches to particular functions— not to particular offices."   Here, by contrast, the majority had made "no effort to distinguish categories of presidential conduct that should be absolutely immune from other categories of conduct that should not qualify for that level of immunity.   The Court instead concludes that whatever the President does and however contrary to law he knows his conduct to be, he may, without fear of liability, injure federal employees or any other person within or without the government.   Attaching absolute immunity to the office of the President, rather than to particular activities that the President might perform, places the President above the law.   It is a reversion to the old notion that the King can do no wrong." [6]

Justice White charged that the majority's abandonment of "basic principles" tracing back to Marbury v. Madison rested on a judgment that had "few, if any, indicia of a judicial decision; it is almost wholly a policy choice, a choice that is without substantial support and that in all events is ambiguous in its reach and import.   [The] Court casually, but candidly, abandons the functional approach to immunity that has run through all of our decisions. Indeed, the majority turns this rule on its head by declaring that because the functions of the President's office are so varied and diverse and some of them

4. Justice Powell repudiated the dissent's "above the law" charge: "This contention is rhetorically chilling but wholly unjustified.   The remedy of impeachment demonstrates that the President remains accountable under law for his misdeeds in office. This case involves only a damages remedy. Although the President is not liable in civil damages for official misbehavior, that does not lift him 'above' the law. [It] is simple error to characterize an official as 'above the law' because a particular remedy is not available against him."

5. As noted earlier, Chief Justice BURGER, while joining Justice Powell's opinion, wrote separately "to underscore that the presidential immunity derives from and is mandated by the constitutional doctrine of separation of powers." He emphasized, too, that only civil liability was involved here: "It is one thing to say that a President must produce evidence rele-

vant to a criminal case, as in [e.g., United States v. Nixon], and quite another to say a President can be [held liable] for civil damages for dismissing a federal employee."

6. "It is ironic that this decision [placing the office of the President "beyond the law"] should come out at the time of the tenth anniversary of the Watergate affair. [The] majority vigorously protests this characterization of its position, arguing that the President remains subject to law in the form of impeachment proceedings. But the abandonment of the rule of law here is not in the results reached, but in the manner of reaching it. The majority fails to apply to the President those principles which we have consistently used to determine the scope and credibility of an absolute immunity defense. It does this because of some preconceived notion of the inapplicability of general rules of law to the President." [Footnote by Justice White.]

so profoundly important, the office is unique and must be clothed with of-
fice-wide, absolute immunity. This is policy, not law, and in my view, very
poor policy."

Justice White insisted, moreover, that the majority's "generalized absolute immunity" could not be sustained "when examined in the traditional
manner and in light of the traditional judicial sources." In an extensive examination of the conventional sources, he found no support for the arguments that "absolute immunity is an 'incidental power' of the Presidency, historically recognized as implicit in the Constitution," and that "absolute immunity is required by the separation of powers doctrine." [7] Justice White summarized the appropriate "functional" immunity approach he would apply as
follows: "The scope of immunity is determined by function, not office.
[Whatever] may be true of the necessity of [a] broad immunity in certain
areas of executive responsibility,[8] the only question that must be answered
here is whether the dismissal of employees falls within a constitutionally assigned executive function, the performance of which would be substantially
impaired by the possibility of a private action for damages. I believe it does
not." [9]

The immunity of presidential assistants. In a companion ruling to Fitzgerald v. Nixon, above, the Court refused to extend the broad presidential
immunity to the President's senior aides and advisers. Harlow & Butterfield
v. Fitzgerald, 457 U.S. 731 (1982). Fitzgerald's suit against Harlow and
Butterfield, aides in the Nixon White House, charged that they conspired to
violate Fitzgerald's constitutional and statutory rights as part of the same alleged conspiracy involved in Nixon v. Fitzgerald. Justice Powell's majority
opinion rejected the aides' claim that they were "entitled to a blanket protection of absolute immunity as an incident of their offices as Presidential aides."
He noted: "For executive officials in general, [our] cases make plain that
qualified immunity represents the norm." That rule, Justice Powell concluded, should be applied to Harlow and Butterfield as well: "It is no disparage-

---

7. Justice Powell's majority opinion responded: "In light of the fragmentary
character of the most important materials reflecting the Framers' intent,
we do think that the most compelling
arguments arise from the Constitution's separation of powers and the
judiciary's historic understanding of
that doctrine. But our primary reliance on constitutional structure and
judicial precedent should not be misunderstood. The best historical evidence clearly supports the Presidential immunity we have upheld. Justice White's dissent cites some other
materials, including ambiguous comments made at state ratifying conventions and the remarks of a single pub-
licist. But historical evidence must
be weighed as well as cited."

8. "I will not speculate on the presidential functions which may require

absolute immunity, but a clear example would be instances in which the
President participates in prosecutorial
decisions." [Footnote by Justice
White.]

9. Justice BLACKMUN, who joined
Justice White's dissent, also submitted
a separate dissent joined by Justices
Brennan and Marshall. He reiterated
the "unanswerable argument that no
man, not even the President, [is] absolutely and fully above the law."
And he argued that the case should
have been dismissed on the ground
that certiorari had been improvidently
granted because of a prior agreement
between Nixon and Fitzgerald, an
agreement which came close "to being
a wager on the outcome of the case."
[This aspect of the case is briefly noted below, addition to 10th Ed., p.
1655; Ind.Rts., p. 1275.]

ment of the offices held by [them] to hold that Presidential aides, like members of the Cabinet, generally are entitled only to a qualified immunity."

Justice Powell also rejected the claim that chief aides of the President were entitled to a "derivative" immunity by analogy to the rationale of Gravel v. United States (10th Ed., p. 434), where the Court had found aides to Members of Congress were entitled to some derivative immunity by extension of the legislators' immunity under the Speech and Debate Clause. Justice Powell stated: "The undifferentiated extension of absolute 'derivative' immunity to the President's aides [could] not be reconciled with the 'functional' approach that has characterized the immunity decisions of this Court, indeed including Gravel itself." Justice Powell also largely rejected a claim to an immunity "based on the 'special functions' of White House aides." He explained: "For aides entrusted with discretionary authority in such sensitive areas as national security or foreign policy, absolute immunity might well be justified to protect the unhesitating performance of functions vital to the national interest. But a 'special functions' rationale does not warrant a blanket recognition of absolute immunity for all Presidential aides in the performance of all their duties." [10]

---

10.   Harlow and Butterfield did prevail, however, in their argument that, if they were only entitled to qualified immunity, the standards for that immunity should be made more protective of officials, in order to "permit the defeat of insubstantial claims without resort to trial." In the past, the qualified "good faith" immunity had involved both "objective" and "subjective" aspects. Thus, under past decisions, a qualified immunity defense would fail if an official "*knew or reasonably should have known*" that the action he took within his sphere of official responsibility would violate the constitutional rights of the [plaintiff], *or* if he took the action *with malicious intention* to cause a deprivation of constitutional rights or other injury." But Justice Powell found that the latter, subjective element of the good faith defense had not succeeded in barring trials of insubstantial claims: "it now is clear that substantial costs attend the litigation of the subjective good faith of government officials." The Court accordingly concluded that "bare allegations of malice should not suffice to subject government officials either to the costs of trial or to the burdens of broad-reaching discovery. [We hold] that government officials performing discretionary functions generally are shielded from liability for civil damages insofar as their conduct does not violate clearly established statutory or constitutional rights of which a reasonable person would have known. Reliance on the objective reasonableness of an official's conduct, as measured by reference to clearly established law, should avoid excessive disruption of government and permit resolution of many insubstantial claims on summary judgment." (Several Justices submitted separate statements in the Harlow & Butterfield case, but only Chief Justice Burger refused to join Justice Powell's opinion of the Court. The Chief Justice's dissent thought the Gravel approach to legislators' aides was applicable to presidential aides as well: "I find it inexplicable why the Court makes no effort to demonstrate why the Chief Executive of the Nation should not be assured that senior staff aides will not have the same protection as the aides of Members of the House and Senate.")

Chapter 8

THE BILL OF RIGHTS AND THE STATES

10th ED., p. 498; IND. RTS., p. 118
Add as footnote to the sentence ending on line 3:

The Mapp holding should be taken with caution. In United States v. Calandra, 414 U.S. 338 (1974), the Court concluded that the exclusionary rule is "a judicially created remedy designed to safeguard Fourth Amendment rights generally through its deterrent effect, rather than a personal constitutional right of the party aggrieved." The vitality and scope of the exclusionary rule remain under attack. See United States v. Peltier, 422 U.S. 531 (1975); Illinois v. Gates, 462 U.S. —— (1983) (exclusionary rule is "an issue separate from the question whether Fourth Amendment rights of the party seeking to invoke the rule were violated by police conduct"). Is it self-evident that the Court has the authority to fashion remedial rules admittedly not *required* by the Constitution? Does the answer to this question vary with whether state or federal power is at issue? On these issues, see generally Monaghan, "Foreword: Constitutional Common Law," 89 Harv.L.Rev. 1 (1975).

Chapter 9

SUBSTANTIVE DUE PROCESS

10th ED., p. 552; IND. RTS., p. 172
Add to footnote 2:

The controversial issue left open by Agins v. Tiburon—whether a State may refuse to grant damages for inverse condemnation and limit the remedy to mere invalidation of the unconstitutional regulation—came before the Court in the following Term, but the majority failed to reach the merits, holding that the state court decision was not a "final judgment" in the jurisdictional sense. San Diego Gas & Electric Co. v. San Diego, 450 U.S. 621 (1981). Four Justices, however, did reach the merits and held that compensable "takings" could result from police power regulations, not only from formal condemnation proceedings.

Justice Brennan, joined by Justices Stewart, Marshall and Powell, criticized the California courts for failing "to recognize the essential similarity of 'regulatory takings' and other 'takings.'" He proposed that, "once a court finds that a ~~police~~ power regulation has effected a 'taking,' the government entity must pay just compensation for the period commencing on the date the regulation first effected the 'taking,' and ending on the date the government entity chooses to rescind or otherwise amend the regulation." (However, he rejected the argument that, once a regulatory "taking" has occurred, the government entity "must formally condemn [the] property and pay full fair market value.")

10th ED., p. 553; Ind. Rts., p. 173
Add to the Notes:

3. *A per se rule (rather than balancing) for "permanent physical occupations."* The 6 to 3 decision in LORETTO v. TELEPROMPTER MANHATTAN CATV CORP., 458 U.S. —— (1982), held that, when the government authorizes a "permanent physical occupation" (albeit a "minor" one) of an owner's property, there "is a taking without regard to the public interests that [the government action] may serve." The majority rejected as inappropriate here the balancing analysis typical in modern taking cases. The Court's newly articulated per se rule led it to invalidate a New York law

119

which provided that a landlord must permit a cable television company to install its cable facilities upon a landlord's rental property.[1] (The highest New York court, applying the balancing analysis typically used in modern cases to determine whether a regulation is a taking, had found no taking here. The Supreme Court disagreed both with the approach and the result.)

In defending the majority's per se rule applicable to all "permanent physical occupations," Justice MARSHALL stated: "Our constitutional history confirms the rule, recent cases do not question it, and the purposes of the Takings Clause compels its retention." He insisted that the decisions confirmed a distinction "between a permanent physical occupation, a physical invasion short of an occupation, and a regulation that merely restricts the use of property." Even Penn Central and its balancing approach did not in his view "repudiate the rule that a permanent physical occupation is a governmental action of such a unique character that it is a taking without regard to other factors that a court might ordinarily examine." Accordingly, "when the 'character of the governmental action' [Penn Central] is a permanent physical occupation of property, our cases uniformly have found a taking to the extent of the occupation, without regard to whether the action achieves an important public benefit or has only minimal economic impact on the owner." This rule was supported not only by tradition but by the policies of the Takings Clause. Justice Marshall asserted that "constitutional protection for the rights of private property cannot be made to depend on the size of the area permanently occupied," although "a court should consider the *extent* of the occupation as one relevant factor in determining the compensation due." He rejected the effort to defend the law as "simply a permissible regulation of the use of real property" and he insisted that the per se rule was not an undue interference with "the government's power to adjust landlord-tenant relationships."[2] In reaffirming "the traditional rule that a permanent physi-

---

1. Under the state law, which became effective in 1973, the landlord was not entitled to demand payment from the cable television beyond a "reasonable amount" set by a state commission. The state commission ruled that a one-time $1 payment was the normal fee to which a landlord was entitled. Before the law became effective, the Teleprompter Company typically obtained authorization from property owners along the cable's route, compensating the landlords at the standard rate of 5% of the gross revenues that the Company realized from the particular property.

The dissent claimed that the taking was only of about one-eighth of a cubic foot of space. The majority conceded that the invasion here was a "minor" intrusion on the property, but thought the "displaced volume" of the cables and related equipment was "in excess of 1½ cubic feet" and added: "In any event, these facts are not critical: whether the installation is a taking does not depend on whether the vol-

ume of space that it occupies is bigger than a bread box."

2. Justice Marshall argued that none of the cases sustaining the broad governmental power to regulate housing conditions in general, and landlord-tenant relationships in particular, without paying compensation involved situations where the government had authorized "the permanent occupation of the landlord's property by a third party." He added: "Consequently, our holding today in no way alters the analysis governing the State's power to require landlords to comply with building codes and provide utility connections, mailboxes, smoke detectors, fire extinguishers, and the like in the common area of a building. So long as these regulations do not require the landlord to suffer the physical occupation of a portion of his building by a third party, they will be analyzed under the multi-factor inquiry generally applicable to non-possessory governmental activity. See Penn Central."

cal occupation of property is a taking," he commented that, in such a situation, "the property owner entertains an historically-rooted expectation of compensation, and the character of the invasion is qualitatively more intrusive than perhaps any other category of property regulation."

In dissenting, Justice BLACKMUN, joined by Justices Brennan and White, condemned the decision as "curiously anachronistic" and formalistic and claimed that it could "undercut a carefully-considered legislative judgment concerning landlord-tenant relationships." In his view, "history teaches that takings claims are properly evaluated under a multifactor balancing test. By directing that all 'permanent physical occupations' automatically are compensable, [the] Court does not further equity so much as it encourages litigants to manipulate their factual allegations to gain the benefit of its per se rule. I do not relish the prospect of distinguishing the inevitable flow of certiorari petitions attempting to shoehorn insubstantial takings claims into today's 'set formula.' " He asserted, moreover, that the Court had not demonstrated how the New York law "impairs [private] rights in a manner *qualitatively* different from other garden-variety landlord-tenant legislation." He added: "[T]his Court long ago recognized that new social circumstances can justify legislative modification of a property owner's common-law rights, without compensation, if the legislative action serves sufficiently important public interests. [But] today's decision [represents] an archaic judicial response to a modern social problem." New York had responded to the technical advance of cable television with a law that "sought carefully to balance the interests of all private parties." But the majority had "reache[d] back in time for a per se rule that disrupts that legislative judgment." [3]

10th ED., p. 554; IND. RTS., p. 174
Add to footnote 4:

A unanimous Court found an unconstitutional taking in Webb's Fabulous Pharmacies, Inc. v. Beckwith, 449 U.S. 155 (1980). The case involved an aspect of the Florida interpleader scheme. In interpleader actions, funds may be deposited with the court pending resolution of the claims of contending creditors. Under state law, the clerk of the court was entitled not only to a fee based upon the size of the fund "for services rendered," but also to all interest accruing to the fund while on deposit with the court. In this case, the creditors challenged the clerk's claim to the interest, amounting to more than $100,000. In sustaining the clerk's retention of the interest, the state court found that there was "no unconstitutional taking because interest earned on the clerk of the circuit court's registry account is not private property."

In reversing, Justice Blackmun's opinion concluded that Florida could not "accomplish the result the county seeks simply by recharacterizing the principal as 'public money' because it is held temporarily by the court. The earnings of a fund are incidents of ownership of the fund itself and are property just as the fund itself is property. The state statute has the practical effect of appropriating for the county the value of the use of the fund for the period in which it is held in the registry. To put it another way: a State, by ipse dixit, may not transform private property into public property without compensation, even for the limited duration of the deposit in court. This is the very kind of thing that the Taking Clause of the Fifth Amendment was meant to prevent." He added: "We express no view as

3. In sustaining the law, the highest New York court, relying on the balancing analysis, had found that the legislation served legitimate police power purposes: "eliminating landlord fees and conditions that inhibit the development of [cable television], which has important educational and community benefits."

to the constitutionality of a statute that prescribes a county's retention of interest earned, where the interest would be the only return to the county for services it renders."

In United States v. Security Industrial Bank, 459 U.S. —— (1982), the Court was asked to determine whether a provision of the Bankruptcy Reform Act of 1978 could be applied to extinguish perfected non-possessory liens on personal property that had been perfected prior to the enactment of the statute. The Court, in an opinion by Justice Rehnquist, determined that such an interpretation of the Act would create substantial problems under the "takings" clause, and therefore avoided the constitutional problem by interpreting the Act as not applying to liens perfected prior to enactment.

10th ED., p. 569; IND. RTS., p. 189
Add after Note 2:

3. *Clarifying the standard of review.* Although both United States Trust and Allied Structural Steel appeared to presage rather strict scrutiny of state actions challenged under the Contract Clause, the standard of review seemed much more deferential in ENERGY RESERVES GROUP, INC. v. KANSAS POWER AND LIGHT CO., 459 U.S. —— (1983). Kansas Power and Light (KPL) was a party to a 1975 contract with Energy Reserves Group (ERG), pursuant to which ERG supplied natural gas to KPL at a price that was set in the contract, but which, according to the contract, could be raised to match any governmentally fixed price that exceeded the contract price. When Congress passed the Natural Gas Policy Act of 1978, Kansas responded by enacting the Kansas Natural Gas Price Protection Act, which in effect precluded ERG from using the price escalator clause in the contract to the full extent of the 1978 federal increase.

ERG claimed that the 1975 contract allowed it to take advantage of subsequent changes in governmental price ceilings, and the Kansas limitation therefore violated the Contract Clause by limiting a price increase that otherwise would have been permissible under the contract. The Court, however, unanimously rejected ERG's Contract Clause claim.

Justice BLACKMUN's opinion for the Court constructed a three-step inquiry from the Court's previous decisions, especially United States Trust and Allied Structural Steel. Justice Blackmun noted that the "threshold inquiry" is "whether the state law has, in fact, operated as a substantial impairment of a contractual relationship." Allied Structural Steel. The second step comes only "if the state regulation constitutes a substantial impairment." If that is the case, then "the State, in justification, must have a significant and legitimate public purpose behind the regulation." The final step, "once a legitimate public purpose has been identified," is to determine "whether the adjustment of 'the rights and responsibilities of contracting parties [is based] upon reasonable conditions and [is] of a character appropriate to the public purpose justifying [the legislation's] adoption.' United States Trust."

Turning to the first step of the inquiry, Justice Blackmun focused on the extent of state and federal regulation of the natural gas industry, and concluded that both ERG and the contract itself recognized the context of a heavily regulated industry. Because ERG knew at the time of contracting that it was subject to both state and federal regulation of prices, a change in those very regulations would not constitute the "substantial impairment" required to trigger the Contract Clause. "In short, ERG's reasonable expectations have not been impaired by the Kansas Act."

Justice POWELL's concurrence, joined by Chief Justice Burger and Justice Rehnquist, agreed that the threshold requirement of substantial impairment had not been satisfied, and would therefore go no further with the inquiry. The majority, however, also dealt with the remaining aspects of the standard, concluding that, even if there was an impairment, it was justified by Kansas's legitimate interests in regulating natural gas prices for the benefit of consumers. The Court also found, looking to the third part of the test, that Kansas had chosen appropriate means to serve its purpose. In applying the third part of the test, the Court specifically made mention of "the deference to which the Kansas Legislature's judgment is entitled."

Deference was even more evident in EXXON CORP. v. EAGERTON, 462 U.S. —— (1983), which made clear the limited applicability of the test extracted from United States Trust, Allied Structural Steel, and Energy Reserves Group. For a unanimous Court, Justice MARSHALL rejected the applicability of that test where the impairment of contractual obligations was merely the incidental by-product of "a generally applicable rule of conduct."

At issue in Exxon was an increase in the Alabama severance tax for oil and gas extracted from Alabama wells, coupled with a prohibition on passing through the increase from producers to purchasers. The producers challenged the pass-through prohibition as violative of the Contract Clause, because the prohibition would prevent the producers from taking advantage of provisions in existing contracts specifically allowing them to pass severance tax increases through to the purchasers. In rejecting the challenge, Justice Marshall drew a sharp distinction between laws specifically directed at contractual obligations, and those, like the Alabama law at issue, that merely had the *effect* of impairing contractual rights. "This Court has long recognized that a statute does not violate the Contract Clause simply because it has the effect of restricting, or even barring altogether, the performance of duties created by contracts entered into prior to its enactment. [Like] the laws upheld in [previous] cases, the pass-through prohibition did not prescribe a rule limited in effect to contractual obligations or remedies, but instead imposed a generally applicable rule of conduct. [The] prohibition applied to all oil and gas producers, regardless of whether they happened to be parties to sales contracts that contained [a pass-through provision.]" Thus, because the effect on existing contracts was "incidental to its main effect of shielding consumers from the burden of the tax increase," Justice Marshall found "sharply distinguishable" cases such as United States Trust and Allied Structural Steel, both of which involved laws "whose sole effect was to alter contractual duties." Because that was not the case here, Justice Marshall did not even resort to the previously-described three-part test in upholding the Alabama statute against the Contract Clause challenge.

10th ED., p. 570; IND. RTS., p. 190
Add to footnote 3:

Note also the discussion of the very limited bases for challenging retroactive federal tax legislation on due process grounds, in the per curiam opinion in United

v. Darusmont, 449 U.S. 292 (1981). Before discussing the criteria "for deter-
whether a particular tax is so harsh and oppressive as to be a denial of due
," the opinion stated as the general rule: "The Court consistently has held
tnat the application of an income tax statute to the entire calendar year in which
enactment took place does not per se violate the Due Process Clause of the Fifth
Amendment."

10th ED., p. 610; IND. RTS., p. 230
Add after Note 7:

8. *Proposed constitutional amendments on abortion, 1981–83.* In
1981, some members of Congress unveiled a novel response to Roe v. Wade:
a proposed Human Life Statute. That proposal is printed and discussed
below, addition to 10th Ed., p. 1099; Ind.Rts., p. 719. But, as noted there,
some "right-to-life" proponents doubted the constitutionality of legislative
action to curb the impact of Roe v. Wade and preferred attacking the decision via the constitutional amendment route.

The proposals have fallen into two categories: first, those embodying a
"States Rights" approach; second, those creating a new constitutional right
to personhood in the unborn. Those amendments embodying a "States
Rights" approach generally provide that no right to an abortion is secured
by the Constitution; the states are thus left free to adopt restrictions on
abortions as they see fit. Those amendments embodying the second, "right
to life," approach expand the definition of person as used in the Fifth and
Fourteenth Amendments. The right to personhood is declared variously to
attach "from the moment of fertilization" or "conception" or "at any stage
of biological development." Some of the proposed "right to life" amendments would permit abortions to prevent the death of the mother; others
would not. And some of them would extend the right beyond the coverage
of the Fifth and Fourteenth Amendments to provide against a deprivation
of life by "any person."

Although the Senate Judiciary Committee took favorable action on a
proposed amendment of the "States Rights" type during the 97th Congress
(S.J.Res. 110), the proposal was withdrawn by its sponsor (Senator Hatch)
before it could be voted in the late summer of 1982. As modified and approved by the Senate Judiciary Constitution Subcommittee in the 98th Congress, the same proposed amendment (S.J.Res. 3) now simply states: "A
right to abortion is not secured by the Constitution." The full Senate Judiciary Committee deadlocked 9–9 on the amendment when it voted on the
measure on April 19, 1983, and sent it to the Senate floor without a recommendation. The Senate rejected the amendment in a 50–49 vote on June
28, as abortion foes fell 18 votes short of the two-thirds needed for passage.
Other proposed amendments of the "right to life" variety have been introduced and referred to the House and Senate Judiciary Committees in the 98th
Congress.

9. *Reaffirmation of Roe.* In AKRON v. AKRON CENTER FOR
REPRODUCTIVE HEALTH, INC., 463 U.S. —— (1983), the Court went
beyond the particular issues of that case * to specifically reaffirm the hold-

---

* Other aspects of the case are discussed   Ind.Rts., p. 232, and addition to 10th
below, addition to 10th Ed., p. 612;   Ed., p. 614; Ind.Rts., p. 234.

ing in Roe v. Wade. Writing for the majority, Justice POWELL characterized Roe as holding "that the right of privacy, grounded in the concept of
personal liberty guaranteed by the Constitution, encompasses a woman's right
to decide whether to terminate her pregnancy." Before turning to the narrower issues presented by the case, Justice Powell noted that "arguments continue to be made [that] we erred in interpreting the Constitution." But the
majority refused to retreat from Roe. "Nonetheless, the doctrine of *stare
decisis*, while perhaps never entirely persuasive on a constitutional question,
is a doctrine that demands respect in a society governed by the rule of law.
We respect it today, and reaffirm Roe v. Wade." Justice Powell observed
that "[t]here are especially compelling reasons for adhering to *stare decisis*
in applying the principles of Roe v. Wade. That case was considered with
special care. It was first argued during the 1971 Term, and reargued—with
extensive briefing—the following Term. The decision was joined by the
Chief Justice and six other Justices. Since Roe was decided in February 1973,
the Court repeatedly and consistently has accepted and applied the basic
principle that a woman has a fundamental right to make the highly personal
choice whether or not to terminate her pregnancy."

In addition to reaffirming that "[t]he decision in Roe was based firmly on
[a] long-recognized and essential element of personal liberty," the Court
continued to employ the basic trimester division set forth in Roe. Although
acknowledging that medical developments within the past decade have made
second trimester abortions much safer, thus possibly changing the "compelling point" at which a state's interest may justify regulating abortion procedures, the Court declined to move the point away from the end of the first
trimester. "We think it prudent, however, to retain Roe's identification of
the beginning of the second trimester as the approximate time at which the
State's interest in maternal health becomes sufficiently compelling to justify
significant regulation of abortion." Referring to several medical studies,
Justice Powell concluded that "[t]he Roe trimester standard thus continues
to provide a reasonable legal framework for limiting a State's authority to
regulate abortions. Where the State adopts a health regulation governing
the performance of abortions during the second trimester, the determinative
question should be whether there is a reasonable medical basis for the regulation."

The Court's reaffirmation of Roe was prompted largely by the dissenting opinion of Justice O'CONNOR, joined by Justices White and Rehnquist.
Justice O'Connor stopped short of urging that the entire premise of Roe be
rejected, but she did argue that the basic trimester approach be overruled.
"Although respect for *stare decisis* cannot be challenged, 'this Court's considered practice [is] not to apply *stare decisis* as rigidly in constitutional as
in nonconstitutional cases.' Glidden Company v. Zdanok, 370 U.S. 530,
543 (1962). Although we must be mindful of the 'desirability of continuity of decision in constitutional questions . . . when convinced of
former error, this Court has never felt constrained to follow precedent. In
constitutional questions, when correction depends on amendment and not
upon legislative action this Court throughout its history has freely exercised
its powers to reexamine the basis of its constitutional decisions.' Smith v.
Allwright, 321 U.S. 649, 665 (1944)."

Thus freed from the compulsion of precedent, Justice O'Connor found the most fundamental flaw in Roe's three-stage structure to be its variability with scientific advances. "[I]t is apparent from the Court's opinion that neither sound constitutional theory nor our need to decide cases based on the application of neutral principles can accommodate an analytical framework that varies according to the 'stages' of pregnancy, where those stages, and their concomitant standards of review, differ according to the level of medical technology available when a particular challenge to state regulation occurs." "The Roe framework [is] clearly on a collision course with itself. As the medical risks of various abortion procedures decrease, the point at which the State may regulate for reasons of maternal health is moved further forward to actual childbirth. As medical science becomes better able to provide for the separate existence of the fetus, the point of viability is moved further back toward conception."

In place of an approach that varied with trimesters, Justice O'Connor urged that the standard be changed so that only regulations that were "unduly burdensome" to the right to have an abortion would be unconstitutional, "without reference to the particular 'stage' of pregnancy involved." (The "unduly burdensome" language comes from Bellotti v. Baird, discussed below, 10th Ed., p. 610; Ind.Rts., p. 230, and Maher v. Roe, discussed below, 10th Ed., p. 617; Ind.Rts., p. 237.) With respect to application of this standard, it is apparent that Justice O'Connor viewed a deferential judicial posture as most appropriate. "It is [difficult] to believe that this Court, without the resources available to those bodies entrusted with making legislative choices, believes itself competent to make these inquiries and to revise these standards every time the American College of Obstetricians and Gynecologists [or] similar group revises its views about what is and what is not appropriate medical procedure in this area." Thus, whether a state restriction was "unduly burdensome" would be a threshold inquiry, for "not every regulation that the State imposes must be measured against the State's compelling interests and examined with strict scrutiny." To Justice O'Connor, subjecting state regulations that were not "unduly burdensome" to only minimal scrutiny reflected the fact that "[t]he state interest in potential human life is [extant] throughout pregnancy. In Roe, the Court held that although the State had an important and legitimate interest in protecting potential life, that interest could not become compelling until the point at which the fetus was viable. The difficulty with this analysis is clear: *potential* life is no less potential in the first weeks of pregnancy than it is at viability or afterward. [The] choice of viability as the point at which the state interest in *potential* life becomes compelling is no less arbitrary than choosing any point before viability or any point afterward. Accordingly, I believe that the State's interest in protecting potential human life exists throughout the pregnancy."

10th ED., p. 612; IND. RTS., p. 232
Insert before Note 2:

    1A. *State regulation of abortions, 1983.* In a series of cases decided near the end of the 1982–1983 Term, the Court dealt with a wide variety of abortion regulations. One of these cases, AKRON v. AKRON CENTER

FOR REPRODUCTIVE HEALTH, INC., 462 U.S. —— (1983), provided the occasion for the Court's specific reaffirmation of Roe v. Wade. (This aspect of Akron is discussed at length above, addition to 10th Ed., p. 610; Ind.Rts., p. 230.) But in Akron the Court also confronted a number of specific restrictions on the abortion process. Perhaps the most important was Akron's requirement that any abortion performed after the first trimester be performed in a hospital. The effect of the Akron ordinance was to "prevent[] the performance of abortions in outpatient facilities that are not part of an acute-care, full-service hospital." Writing for the Court, Justice POWELL found the requirement excessively restrictive, even though it applied only after the first trimester. "We reaffirm today that a State's interest in health regulation becomes compelling at approximately the end of the first trimester. The existence of a compelling state interest in health, however, is only the beginning of the inquiry. The State's regulation may be upheld only if it is reasonably designed to further that state interest. [Roe] did not hold that it always is reasonable for a State to adopt an abortion regulation that applies to the entire second trimester. A State necessarily must have latitude in adopting regulations of general applicability in this sensitive area. But if it appears that during a substantial portion of the second trimester the State's regulation 'depart[s] from accepted medical practice,' [Roe], the regulation may not be upheld simply because it may be reasonable for the remaining portion of the trimester. Rather, the State is obligated to make a reasonable effort to limit the effect of its regulations to the period in the trimester during which its health interest will be furthered." Applying this standard, Justice Powell relied heavily on the current standards and research of the American College of Obstetricians and Gynecologists. Because various techniques now permitted safe outpatient abortions through most and perhaps all of the second trimester, and because hospitalization's cost "places a significant obstacle in the path of women seeking an abortion," Justice Powell concluded that the hospitalization requirement "imposed a heavy, and unnecessary, burden on women's access to a relatively inexpensive, otherwise accessible, and safe abortion procedure [Dilation and Evacuation], [and] therefore unreasonably infringes upon a women's constitutional right to obtain an abortion."

The Court in Akron invalidated a number of other abortion regulations. Among these were an "informed consent" requirement that mandated rather detailed warnings that a physician must give to the woman who is to have an abortion, as well as a 24 hour waiting period between signing the consent form and performance of the abortion. Justice Powell's majority opinion found the detailed catalogue of information required to be included in the physician's statement to the patient constitutionally defective. "First, it is fair to say that much of the information required is designed not to inform the woman's consent but rather to persuade her to withhold it altogether. [Among the requirements were a statement that life begins at conception, a description of the physiological characteristics of the unborn child, and a description of the severity and possible complications of abortion as a surgical procedure.] [An] additional, and equally decisive, objection [is] its intrusion upon the discretion of the pregnant woman's physician. This provision specifies a litany of information that the physician must recite to each woman regardless of whether in his judgment the information is relevant to her personal judgment." Although acknowledging that the state has a legitimate interest in obtaining informed consent, and that this could justify a requirement "that a physician make certain that his patient understands the physical and emotional implications of having an abortion," Justice Powell found that this provision was so detailed as to interfere unreasonably with the physician's advice upon which the woman is entitled to rely. Moreover, the Court also found the details of the consent scheme constitutionally infirm. It rejected the requirement that only the woman's physician could provide the information relating to consent because "[t]he State's interest is in ensuring that the woman's consent is informed and unpressured; the critical factor is whether she obtains the necessary information and counseling from a qualified person, not the identity of the person from whom she obtains it. [We] cannot say that the woman's consent to the abortion will not be informed if a physician delegates the counseling task to another qualified individual." The Court's view with respect to the waiting period was similar. "[I]f a woman, after appropriate counseling, is prepared to give her written informed consent and proceed with the abortion, a State may not demand that she delay the effectuation of that decision." [1]

Abortion regulations fared somewhat better in PLANNED PARENTHOOD ASS'N OF KANSAS CITY v. ASHCROFT, 462 U.S. ── (1983). Following Akron, the Court, with Justice POWELL again writing the opinion, invalidated Missouri's requirement that abortions after 12 weeks of pregnancy be performed in a hospital. But Justice Powell was joined by Chief Justice Burger and Justices O'Connor, White, and Rehnquist in upholding a requirement that a second physician be present for abortions performed after viability. "Preserving the life of a viable fetus that is aborted may not often be possible, but the State legitimately may choose to provide safeguards for the comparatively few instances of live birth that occur. We believe that the second-physician requirement reasonably furthers the State's compelling interest in protecting the lives of viable fetuses, ..." The same majority also upheld a requirement that any tissue removed be examined by a pathologist, and that the pathologist's report be filed with the state. "We think the cost of a tissue examination does not significantly burden a pregnant woman's abortion decision." [2]

SIMOPOULOS v. VIRGINIA, 462 U.S. ── (1983), clarified both Akron and Planned Parenthood with respect to the hospitalization require-

---

1. The Court also struck down on vagueness grounds a requirement that fetal remains be disposed of "in a humane and sanitary manner."

   Justice O'CONNOR filed a dissenting opinion, in which she was joined by Justices White and Rehnquist. Applying her "unduly burdensome" standard (see above, addition to 10th Ed., p. 610; Ind.Rts., p. 230), Justice O'Connor would have upheld all of the regulations invalidated by the majority.

2. Justice BLACKMUN, joined by Justices Brennan, Marshall, and Stevens, dissented with respect to the second-physician and pathology report holdings, arguing that in neither case had the state met its burden of showing that the requirements were "tailored to protect the State's legitimate interests."

Va Law defined "hospital" to include outpatient hospitals & clinics, so upheld

ment. Because Virginia's hospitalization requirement for second trimester abortions incorporated a definition of "hospital" that included outpatient hospitals and clinics, the Court, with Justice POWELL again writing for the majority, upheld the requirement. "Unlike the provisions at issue in City of Akron and Ashcroft, Virginia's statute and regulations do not require that the patient be hospitalized as an inpatient or that the abortion be performed in a full-service, acute-care hospital. Rather, the State's requirement that second-trimester abortions be performed in licensed clinics appears to comport with accepted medical practice, and leaves the method and timing of the abortion precisely where they belong—with the physician and the patient." [3]

10th ED., p. 614; IND. RTS., p. 234

Insert before Note 3:

2A. *Minors' abortions and parental notice requirements.* A Utah law requires physicians to "[n]otify, if possible," the parents or guardian of any minor upon whom an abortion is to be performed. In H. L. v. MATHE-SON, 450 U.S. 398 (1981), appellant attacked the law on its face in a class action which claimed to represent *all* unmarried minor women, including mature and emancipated ones. Chief Justice BURGER's majority opinion, however, insisted that appellant lacked standing to bring such a broad overbreadth challenge since she had not shown that she was "mature or emancipated." He accordingly limited the suit to the question of whether the statute was valid "(a) when the girl is living with and dependent upon her parents, (b) when she is not emancipated by marriage or otherwise, and (c) when she has made no claim or showing as to her maturity or as to her relations with her parents." [†] With review so narrowed, the Chief Justice had little difficulty finding the law constitutional: "As applied to the class properly before us, the statute plainly serves important state interests, is narrowly drawn to protect only those interests, and does not violate any guarantees of the Constitution."

In what the dissent described as a "cursory" examination of the merits, the Chief Justice noted that the law granted no "veto power over the minor's abortion decision" and found: "As applied to immature and dependent mi-

---

3. Simopoulos arose in the somewhat unusual context of an appeal of a criminal conviction for performing a second trimester abortion outside of a hospital. Justice O'Connor, joined by Justices White and Rehnquist, concurred in the judgment, agreeing that the conviction should be affirmed, but disagreeing "that the constitutional validity of the Virginia mandatory hospitalization requirement is contingent in any way on the trimester in which it is imposed." Justice Stevens dissented on the grounds that the Supreme Court of Virginia should be required to reconsider its ruling below in light of Akron.

† Justice Marshall's dissent, joined by Justices Brennan and Blackmun, argued that, under the Court's "prudential" standing considerations (see sec. 2 of the last chapter of the casebook) appellant should not be barred from raising her broad overbreadth challenge simply because she did not allege "that she herself falls within the statute's overbroad reach." Instead, she should be permitted to bring a facial attack by analogy to First Amendment overbreadth cases (see 10th Ed., p. 1185; Ind. Rts., p. 805), under which overbreadth challenges are permitted "without a showing that the moving party's conduct falls within the protected core."

nors, the statute plainly serves the important considerations of family integrity and protecting adolescents. [In addition], the statute serves a significant state interest by providing an opportunity for parents to supply essential medical and other information to a physician. [The law] is reasonably calculated to protect minors in appellant's class by enhancing the potential for parental consultation concerning a decision that has potentially traumatic and permanent consequences. [The possibility that] the requirement of notice to parents may inhibit some minors from seeking abortions is not a valid basis to void the statute. [The] Constitution does not compel a State to fine-tune its statutes so as to encourage or facilitate abortions." †

Justice MARSHALL's dissent, joined by Justices Brennan and Blackmun, thought the majority ruling "narrow" and found in it "a clear signal that more carefully drafted pleadings could secure both a plaintiff's standing to challenge the overbreadth of [the law] and success on the merits." ** He thought it clear that the parental notice requirement "burdens the minor's privacy right" and added: "None of the reasons offered by the State justifies this intrusion, for the statute is not tailored to serve them. Rather than serving to enhance the physician's judgment in cases such as appellant's, the statute prevents implementation of the physician's medical recommendation. Rather than promoting the transfer of information held by parents to the minor's physician, the statute neglects to require anything more than a communication from the physician moments before the abortion. Rather than respecting the private realm of family life, the statute invokes the criminal machinery of the State in an attempt to influence the interactions within the family."

Justice Marshall's discussion of the State's asserted interest in "protecting parental authority and family integrity" is also of interest. (See the next group of notes in this chapter, on "Substantive Due Process and Family Relations.") He noted that the "critical thrust" of most earlier decisions had been "to protect the privacy of individual families from unwarranted state in-

---

† In joining Chief Justice Burger's opinion, Justice POWELL, supported by Justice Stewart, adhered to his views in the 1979 Bellotti case and emphasized that the decision in this case left open the question of the constitutionality of the law as applied to such groups as mature minors. He commented: "Numerous and significant interests compete when a minor decides whether or not to abort her pregnancy. [The] circumstances relevant to the abortion decision by a minor can and do vary so substantially that absolute rules—requiring parental notice in all cases or in none—would create an inflexibility that often would allow for no consideration of the rights and interests [involved]." He viewed the dissenters' position as elevating "the decision of the minor and her physician to an absolute sta-

tus ignoring state and parental interests."

Justice STEVENS, concurring only in the judgment, thought the law constitutional on its face as applied to *all* minors. Relying on Danforth, he insisted that "the State's interest in protecting a young pregnant woman from the consequences of an incorrect abortion decision is sufficient to justify the parental-notice requirement" even as applied to mature minors.

** Chief Justice Burger disagreed with that "clear signal" perception, insisting that "there is no occasion to intimate or predict a view as to the proper resolution of some future case" raising issues the majority had excluded from consideration here.

trusion. Ironically, Utah invokes these decisions in seeking to justify state interference in the normal functioning of the family. Through its notice requirement, the State in fact enters the private realm of the family rather than leaving unaltered the pattern of interactions chosen by the family. Whatever its motive, state intervention is hardly likely to resurrect parental authority that the parents themselves are unable to preserve." He was equally unimpressed by the related claim that the statute safeguarded the parents' "reserved right [to] know of the important activities of their children." In his view, "when the threat to parental authority originates not from the State but from the minor child, invocation of 'reserved' rights of parents cannot sustain blanket state intrusion into family life such as that mandated [here]. Such a result not only runs counter to the private domain of the family; [it] also conflicts with the limits traditionally placed on parental authority. [Whatever] its importance elsewhere, parental authority deserves de minimis legal reinforcement where the minor's exercise of a fundamental right is burdened."

The Court dealt with minors' abortions and parental consent in two cases decided in the 1982–1983 Term. In AKRON v. AKRON CENTER FOR REPRODUCTIVE HEALTH, INC., 462 U.S. —— (1983), Justice POWELL's majority opinion relied on Planned Parenthood v. Danforth and Bellotti v. Baird to strike down Akron's requirement that abortions could be performed on women under the age of 15 only if there was written consent of her parents or an order of the court. Because there was no procedure for an individualized determination of whether a minor might be sufficiently mature or emancipated to make the decision for herself, Akron's requirement was determined to be constitutionally insufficient. But in PLANNED PARENTHOOD ASS'N OF KANSAS CITY v. ASHCROFT, 462 U.S. —— (1983), Justice POWELL wrote for a different majority in upholding a Missouri requirement of parental consent or a judicial alternative, because here the judicial procedure comported with the requirement that "the State must provide an alternative procedure whereby a pregnant minor may demonstrate that she is sufficiently mature to make the abortion decision herself or that, despite her immaturity, an abortion would be in her best interests." [Akron].*

10th ED., p. 633; IND. RTS., p. 253
Add to footnote 5:

Note also the consideration of hearing requirements in family law contexts in two 1981 decisions, Little v. Streater, 452 U.S. 1, and Lassiter v. Dept. of Social Services, 452 U.S. 18. Both cases are noted below (addition to 10th Ed., p. 948; Ind.Rts., p. 568). In Little, holding that an indigent defendant in a state-instigated paternity action was entitled to state-paid blood grouping tests, the unanimous decision noted the substantiality of the private interests implicated. Chief Justice Burger stated that the issue was "the creation of a parent-child relationship" and added: "This Court frequently has stressed the importance of familial bonds, whether or not legitimized by marriage, and accorded them constitutional protection." In Lassiter, the majority rejected an indigent mother's claim that she was entitled to counsel in a parental status termination proceeding. Instead, the Court left appointment-of-counsel claims to be determined on a case-by-case basis. Justice Stewart's majority opinion, while recognizing that the parent's interest was "an ex-

---

* Other aspects of Akron and Planned Parenthood are discussed more fully above, addition to 10th Ed., p. 610; Ind.Rts., p. 230, addition to 10th Ed., p. 612; Ind.Rts., p. 232.

tremely important one," nevertheless insisted that "the presumption that an indigent litigant has a right to appointed counsel" exists "only when, if he loses, he may be deprived of his physical liberty." Justice Blackmun's dissent, joined by Justices Brennan and Marshall, argued for an across-the-board right to counsel in termination proceedings and emphasized that "the Court has accorded a high degree of constitutional respect to a natural parent's interest [in] retaining the custody and companionship of the child."

10th ED., p. 635; IND. RTS., p. 255
Insert at beginning of footnote 7:

Note the discussion of the state interest in protecting parental authority and family autonomy in Justice Marshall's dissent in H. L. v. Matheson, 450 U.S. 398 (1981) (at the close of the addition to 10th Ed., p. 614; Ind.Rts., p. 234). The case involved a challenge to a state law requiring physicians to notify parents prior to performing abortions on minors.

10th ED., p. 635; IND. RTS., p. 255
Add to footnote 7:

Termination of parental rights. a.   In Doe v. Delaware, 450 U.S. 382 (1981). the Court avoided decision on a number of controversial questions pertaining to the termination of parental rights. The majority, in a summary per curiam disposition after oral argument, dismissed the appeal "for want of a properly presented federal question." Justice Brennan (joined by Justice White) and Justice Stevens submitted dissenting opinions.

The case was a challenge by natural parents to the constitutionality of Delaware's procedure for terminating parental rights upon findings that the parents were "not fitted to continue to exercise parental rights" and that termination of parental rights would be "in the best interests of the child." The challengers claimed that the "not fitted" standard was unconstitutionally vague and indefinite, that a higher standard of proof than mere "preponderance of the evidence" was required to terminate parental rights, and that substantive due process barred termination of parental rights in the absence of a demonstration of a compelling state interest, in the form of specific findings of existing or threatened injury to the child. Justice Brennan insisted that the dismissal of the appeal was "unprecedented and inexplicable," and Justice Stevens noted that the standard of proof question was "certain to reappear before us in the same form at a later date." [See the additional note on the jurisdictional aspects of this case (addition to 10th Ed. p. 1675; Ind. Rts., p. 1295).]

b.   Justice Stevens' prophecy in Doe v. Delaware proved accurate: the standard of proof issue soon resurfaced. In Santosky v. Kramer, 455 U.S. 745 (1982), a sharply divided Court held unconstitutional a New York provision permitting the termination of parental rights in their natural child upon a finding by a "fair preponderance of the evidence" that the child was "permanently neglected." Justice Blackmun's majority opinion insisted that due process "demands more than this. Before a State may sever completely and irrevocably the rights of parents in their natural child, due process requires that the State support its allegations by at least clear and convincing evidence."

In assessing the constitutional interests warranting due process protection, Justice Blackmun noted that "freedom of personal choice in matters of family life is a fundamental liberty interest protected by the Fourteenth Amendment." He added: "The fundamental liberty interest of natural parents in the care, custody, and management of their child does not evaporate simply because they have not been model parents or have lost temporary custody of their child to the State. [If] anything, persons faced with forced dissolution of their parental rights have a more critical need for procedural protections than do those resisting state intervention into ongoing family affairs. When the State moves to destroy weakened familial bonds, it must provide the parents with fundamentally fair procedures."

In delineating the kind of process "due" in these circumstances, Justice Blackmun relied on the three balancing factors of Mathews v. Eldridge (10th Ed., p. 668; Ind.Rts., p. 288). He concluded: "In parental rights termination proceedings, the private interest affected is commanding; the risk of error from using a preponderance standard is substantial; and the countervailing governmental interest favoring that standard is comparatively slight. Evaluation of the three Eldridge factors compels the conclusion that use of a 'fair preponderance of the evidence' standard in such proceedings is inconsistent with due process."

A sharp dissent by Justice Rehnquist, joined by Chief Justice Burger and Justices White and O'Connor, was particularly concerned that the majority had invited "further federal court intrusion into every facet of state family law." Justice Rehnquist elaborated: "The majority may believe that it is adopting a relatively unobtrusive means of ensuring that termination proceedings provide 'due process of law.' In fact, however, fixing the standard of proof as a matter of federal constitutional law will only lead to further federal court intervention in state schemes. [After] fixing the standard of proof, [the] majority will be forced to evaluate other aspects of termination proceedings with reference to that point. Having in this case abandoned evaluation of the overall effect of a scheme, and with it the possibility of finding that strict substantive standards or special procedures compensate for a lower burden of proof, the majority's approach will inevitably lead to the federalization of family law. Such a trend will only thwart state searches for better solutions in an area where this Court should encourage state experimentation." He insisted, moreover, that the majority had disregarded "New York's earnest effort to *aid* parents in regaining the custody of their children and a host of procedural protections placed around parental rights and interests. [Even] more worrisome, today's decision cavalierly rejects the considered judgment of the New York legislature in an area traditionally entrusted to state care."

10th ED., p. 643; IND. RTS., p. 263
Add as footnote at end of Note 1:

Noteworthy comments on state authority to prohibit minors' consensual sexual behavior appear in Michael M. v. Superior Court, 450 U.S. 464 (1981) (printed below, addition to 10th Ed., p. 885; Ind.Rts., p. 505). Justice Rehnquist's plurality opinion rejected an equal protection attack on California's statutory rape law, a law that makes men alone criminally liable. He noted: "We do not understand petitioner to question a state's authority to make sexual intercourse among teenagers a criminal act, at least on a gender-neutral basis." Justice Brennan's dissent countered that "our cases would not foreclose [a] privacy challenge" to the states' power to criminalize consensual sexual activity. He quoted from Eisenstadt v. Baird and added: "Minors, too, enjoy a right of privacy in connection with decisions affecting procreation. Thus, despite the suggestion of the plurality to the contrary, it is not settled that a State may rely on a pregnancy-prevention justification to make consensual sexual intercourse among minors a criminal act."

10th ED., p. 646; IND. RTS., p. 266
Insert before Sec. 4:

4. *Substantive due process, the mentally retarded, and the mentally ill.* In YOUNGBERG v. ROMEO, 457 U.S. 307 (1982), the Court considered "for the first time the substantive [due process] rights of involuntarily-committed mentally retarded persons." Romeo, a "profoundly retarded" man with the mental capacity of an 18-month old child, had been committed to a state institution at the behest of his mother. After Romeo's commitment, his mother became concerned about injuries he had suffered in the institution. She filed a § 1983 action as his "best friend" claiming that officials of the institution had violated his constitutional rights by failing to take appropriate measures to protect him against injuries. That suit presented the Court with the question whether Romeo had "substantive rights under the Due Process Clause [to] (i) safe conditions of confinement; (ii) freedom from bodily restraints; and (iii) training or 'habilitation.' "[1]

---

1. "Habilitation," a term of art in programs for the mentally retarded, focuses upon "training and development of needed skills."

Justice POWELL, in his opinion for the Court, had no difficulty finding constitutional support for the first two substantive rights claimed by Romeo.   Justice Powell found constitutionally protected liberty interests in
"safety" and "freedom of movement."   He noted that, since convicted criminals are entitled to safe conditions, "it must be unconstitutional to confine the
involuntarily committed—who may not be punished at all—in unsafe conditions."   And with respect to the "freedom from bodily restraint," he stated:
"This interest survives criminal conviction and incarceration.   Similarly, it
must also survive involuntary commitment."

Justice Powell found Romeo's third claim, to a "constitutional right to
minimally adequate habilitation," more troubling.   But that claim, too, was
supportable to a limited extent.   He explained: "In addressing the asserted
right to training, we start from established principles.   As a general matter, a
State is under no constitutional duty to provide substantive services for those
within its border.   See Harris v. McRae (publicly funded abortions); Maher
v. Roe (medical treatment).   [The] record reveals that [Romeo's] primary
needs are bodily safety and a minimum of physical restraint, and [Romeo]
claims training related to these needs.   As we have recognized that there is a
constitutionally protected liberty interest in safety and freedom from restraint,
training may be necessary to avoid unconstitutional infringement of those
rights.   [If], as seems the case, [Romeo] seeks only training related to safety
and freedom from restraints, this case does not present the difficult question
whether a mentally retarded person, involuntarily committed to a state institution, has some general constitutional right to training per se, even when no
type or amount of training would lead to freedom.   [In] the circumstances
presented by this case, [we] conclude that [Romeo's] liberty interests require
the State to provide minimally adequate or reasonable training to ensure safety and freedom from undue restraint."

But the fact that a liberty interest was implicated, Justice Powell noted,
did not necessarily demonstrate a due process violation: "In determining
whether a substantive right protected by the Due Process Clause has been violated, it is necessary to balance 'the liberty of the individual' and 'the demands of an organized society.'   Poe v. Ullman (Harlan, J., dissenting)."
Thus, "whether [Romeo's] constitutional rights have been violated must be
determined by balancing his liberty interests against the relevant state interests.   If there is to be any uniformity in protecting these interests, this balancing cannot be left to the unguided discretion of a judge or jury.   We therefore turn to consider the proper standard for determining whether a State adequately has protected the rights of the involuntarily-committed mentally retarded."

In articulating this standard, Justice Powell placed special emphasis on
the need to defer to professional judgments.   He relied heavily on an opinion
in the Court of Appeals stating that the "constitution only requires that the
courts make certain that professional judgment in fact was exercised.   It is
not appropriate for the courts to specify which of several professionally acceptable choices should have been made."   Although the involuntarily committed
were entitled to "more considerate treatment" than criminals, the State did

not have to meet a "compelling" or "substantial" necessity test. In Justice Powell's view, all that Romeo was entitled to was "minimally adequate training": "In this case, the minimally adequate training required by the Constitution is such training as may be reasonable in light of [Romeo's] liberty interests in safety and freedom from unreasonable restraints. In determining what is 'reasonable'—in this and in any case presenting a claim for training by a state—we emphasize that courts must show deference to the judgment exercised by a qualified professional. By so limiting judicial review, [interference] by the federal judiciary with the internal operations of [state] institutions should be minimized. Moreover, there certainly is no reason to think that judges or juries are better qualified than appropriate professionals in making such decisions. For these reasons, the decision, if made by a professional, is presumptively valid; liability may be imposed only when the decision by the professional is such a substantial departure from accepted professional judgment, practice or standards as to demonstrate that the person responsible actually did not base the decision on such a judgment. In an action for damages against a professional in his individual capacity, however, the professional will not be liable if he was unable to satisfy his normal professional standards because of budgetary constraints; in such a situation, good-faith immunity would bar liability." He summarized his conclusion as follows: "[T]he state is under a duty to provide [Romeo] with such training as an appropriate professional would consider reasonable to ensure his safety and to facilitate his ability to function free from bodily restraints. It may well be unreasonable not to provide training when training could significantly reduce the need for restraints or the likelihood of violence. [Romeo] thus enjoys constitutionally protected interest in conditions of reasonable care and safety, reasonably non-restrictive confinement conditions, and such training as may be required by these interests."

A concurrence by Justice BLACKMUN, joined by Justices Brennan and O'Connor, noted "two difficult and important issues" which he thought properly left unresolved by the Court's opinion. The first was whether the State could accept Romeo for "care and treatment" and then "constitutionally refuse to provide him any 'treatment,' as that term is defined by state law." [2] The "second difficult question left open today," Justice Blackmun noted, "is whether [Romeo] has an independent constitutional claim, grounded in the Due Process Clause of the Fourteenth Amendment, to that 'habilitation' or training necessary to *preserve* those basic self-care skills he possessed when he first entered [the state institution]—for example, the ability to dress himself

2. Chief Justice Burger's opinion concurring only in the judgment thought it "frivolous" for Romeo to contend "that, because state law purportedly creates a right to 'care and treatment,' he has a *federal substantive* right under the Due Process Clause to enforcement of this state right": "[W]ere every substantive right created by state law enforceable under the Due Process Clause, the distinction between state and federal law would quickly be obliterated." Justice

Blackmun insisted that the claim was not frivolous and argued: "If a state court orders a mentally retarded person committed for 'care *and* treatment,' [I] believe that due process might well bind the State to ensure that the conditions of his commitment bear some reasonable relation to each of these goals. In such a case, commitment without any 'treatment' whatsoever would not bear a reasonable relation to the purposes of the person's confinement."

and care for his personal hygiene. In my view, it would be consistent with the Court's reasoning today to include within the 'minimally adequate training required by the Constitution' such training as is reasonably necessary to prevent a person's pre-existing self-care skills from *deteriorating* because of his commitment".[3] Chief Justice BURGER, concurring only in the judgment, emphasized that he "would hold flatly that respondent has no constitutional right to training, or 'habilitation,' per se." He agreed with Justice Powell "that some amount of self-care instruction may be necessary to avoid unreasonable infringement of a mentally-retarded person's interest in safety and freedom from restraint." But he added that "it seems clear to me that the Constitution does not otherwise place an affirmative duty on the State to provide any particular kind of training or habilitation—even such as might be encompassed under the essentially standardless rubric 'minimally adequate training' to which the Court refers." [4]

10th ED., p. 665; IND. RTS., p. 285
Add as footnote to the sentence ending on line 1:

For a recent reliance on the cases discussed in this paragraph, see the Court's 7 to 2 decision in Connecticut Board of Pardons v. Dumschat, 452 U.S. 458 (1981). Chief Justice Burger's majority opinion held that the Board's practice of granting approximately 75% of the applications for commutation of life sentences did *not* create a constitutionally protected "liberty interest" or "entitlement." Accordingly, he rejected a prisoner's claim that the Board was required to state its reasons when denying such applications. Following the post-Paul v. Davis approach of reading "liberty" narrowly, he stated: "The ground for a constitutional claim, if any, must be found in statutes or other rules defining the obligations of the authority charged with exercising clemency."

Justice Stevens' dissent, joined by Justice Marshall, retorted that constitutionally protected liberty "is not merely 'a statutory creation of the State.' [I]ndividual liberty has far deeper roots." Similarly, Justice White's concurrence insisted that the precedents do *not* compel the conclusion that "all liberty interests entitled to constitutional protection must be found in state law."

3. Justice Blackmun agreed with Justice Powell that, on the record here, it was quite uncertain whether Romeo in fact sought any training "unrelated to safety and freedom from bodily restraints." But Justice Blackmun added: "If [Romeo] actually seeks habilitation in self-care skills not merely to reduce his aggressive tendencies, but also to maintain those basic self-care skills necessary to his personal autonomy within [the institution], I believe he is free on remand to assert that claim."

4. In another case decided on the same day as Youngberg v. Romeo, the Court had granted review "to determine whether involuntarily committed mental patients have a constitutional right to refuse treatment with antipsychotic drugs." Mills v. Rogers, 457 U.S. 291 (1982). But the Court did not reach the merits of that issue. Instead, it remanded the case to the Court of Appeals to determine whether an intervening state court decision (resting on both Massachusetts common law and the Federal Constitution) affected the proper disposition of this case. The Massachusetts decision had dealt with the rights of *noninstitutionalized* incompetent mental patients regarding involuntary treatment with antipsychotic drugs. Explaining the justifications for the remand, in the interest of avoiding unnecessary constitutional decisions, Justice Powell commented: "The parties agree that the Constitution recognizes a liberty interest in avoiding the unwanted administration of antipsychotic drugs. Assuming that they are correct in this respect, the substantive issue involves a definition of that protected constitutional interest, as well as identification of the conditions under which competing state interests might outweigh it. See [e.g., Youngberg v Romeo]."

10th ED., p. 666; IND. RTS., p. 286
Add after Note 2:

3. *State law as a source of "liberty" interests.* Although the Court has continued to narrow the range of liberty interests independently recognized by the Constitution, it has at the same time shown an increased willingness to look to state law as a source of liberty interests.

In HEWITT v. HELMS, 459 U.S. —— (1983), the issue arose in the context of the transfer of a prisoner from the general prison population to administrative segregation, a substantially more restrictive environment. The Court, in an opinion by Justice REHNQUIST, reaffirmed that "lawfully incarcerated persons retain only a narrow range of protected liberty interests." Relying on the need for special deference to administrative decisions in the prison context, Justice Rehnquist determined that "the transfer of an inmate to less amenable and more restrictive quarters for nonpunitive reasons is well within the terms of confinement ordinarily contemplated by a prison sentence." The Court thus refused to find any deprivation of a liberty "interest independently protected by the Due Process Clause," a determination that prompted a vigorous dissent by Justice STEVENS, joined by Justice Marshall and Justice Brennan.

The focus in Hewitt on conditions that might normally be expected to be the consequences of incarceration was echoed in OLIM v. WAKINEKONA, 461 U.S. —— (1983), involving transfer of a prisoner to an out-of-state prison. The Court, with Justice BLACKMUN writing the majority opinion, again refused to find in the transfer any deprivation of a liberty independently recognized by the Constitution. "Just as an inmate has no justifiable expectation that he will be incarcerated in any particular prison within a State, he has no justifiable expectation that he will be incarcerated in any particular State. [An] interstate prison transfer, including one from Hawaii to California, does not deprive an inmate of any liberty interest protected by the Due Process Clause in and of itself."

Finding the lack of an independently recognized liberty interest, however, is only the first step in the inquiry. For in both Hewitt and Olim the Court went on to examine carefully for the possibility that state law had created a liberty interest that would thus occasion procedural protection. In Olim the Court defined the focus of the inquiry as follows: "[A] State creates a protected liberty interest by placing substantive limitations on official discretion. An inmate must show 'that particularized standards or criteria guide the State's decisionmakers.' Connecticut Board of Pardons v. Dumschat (Brennan, J., concurring). If the decisionmaker is not 'required to base its decisions on objective and defined criteria,' but instead 'can deny the requested relief for any constitutionally permissible reason or for no reason at all,' the State has not created a constitutionally protected liberty interest."

Application of this standard caused the Court to find no deprivation of any liberty in Olim, because "the prison administrator's discretion to transfer an inmate is completely unfettered." But the Court did find a state-created liberty interest in Hewitt, relying largely on the fact that the relevant Pennsylvania statutes and regulations had not only mandated certain procedures prior to administrative segregation, but also had established "specific substantive predicates" before administrative segregation could be imposed. Having thus found the deprivation of a liberty in Hewitt, however, the Court went on to find the procedural protection afforded to be constitutionally sufficient. The Court determined that, in this context, an opportunity to present written evidence in a non-adversary setting was all that the Due Process Clause would require.

The Court thus reaffirmed in Hewitt that "liberty interests protected by the Fourteenth Amendment may arise from two sources—the Due Process Clause itself and the laws of the States. Meachum v. Fano." Although recent cases have suggested that the former source of liberty interests is narrowing, a trend confirmed by both Hewitt and Olim, Hewitt also suggests that the latter source may be expanding.

10th ED., p. 668; IND. RTS., p. 288
Insert after first paragraph of footnote 3:

Note also Logan v. Zimmerman Brush Co., 455 U.S. 422 (1982), where a unanimous Court found that the challenger had been deprived of a state-created property right without procedural due process. The Court held that a state may not "terminate a complainant's cause of action because a state official, for reasons beyond the complainant's control, failed to comply with the statutorily mandated procedure." The complainant, Logan, had filed a charge with a state commission claiming discrimination against the physically handicapped in violation of the Illinois Fair Employment Practices Act. After he filed his timely complaint, the commission failed to schedule a factfinding conference (designed to obtain evidence and explore the possibility of a negotiated settlement) within the 120-day period designated by the statute. The commission's delay was apparently due to inadvertence. The highest state court held that the time limit was mandatory and that the commission's failure to observe it deprived it of jurisdiction.

Justice Blackmun's opinion for the Court found that Logan's right to use the Act's adjudicatory procedures was a constitutionally protected state-created property interest. He conceded that a state was "free to create substantive defenses or immunities for use in adjudication—or to eliminate its statutorily created causes of action altogether." But the 120-day limitation "involves no such thing": "It is a procedural limitation on the claimant's ability to assert his rights, not a substantive element of [the] claim. Because the state scheme has deprived Logan of a property right, [we] turn to the determination of what process is due him." Justice Blackmun found that Logan was "entitled to have the Commission consider the merits of his charge, based upon the substantiality of the available evidence, before deciding whether to terminate his claim. [A] system or procedure that deprives persons of their claims in a random manner, as is apparently true [here], necessarily presents an unjustifiably high risk that meritorious claims will be terminated. And the State's interest in refusing [to consider Logan's claim] is, on this record, insubstantial." Logan was not to blame for the passing of the time limit; rather it was the commission's failure to convene a timely conference that resulted in the dismissal of Logan's case. Accordingly, Logan had been deprived of a "hearing appropriate to the nature of the case," in violation of procedural due process. (Justice Blackmun proceeded to write a separate opinion finding an equal protection violation as well. Five other Justices agreed that equal protection had been violated. The equal protection aspects of the case are fully explored below, addition to 10th Ed., p. 704; Ind. Rts., p. 324.)

10th ED., p. 669; IND. RTS., p. 289
Add to footnote 2:

For examples of applications of the Mathews v. Eldridge balancing analysis in family law contexts in the 1980s, see Little v. Streater, 452 U.S. 1 (1981) (holding that the state must pay for blood grouping tests in a state-involved paternity action against an indigent defendant); Lassiter v. Dept. of Social Services, 452 U.S. 18 (1981) (holding that due process does not require the appointment of counsel for indigent parents in every proceeding to terminate parental status); and Santosky v. Kramer, 455 U.S. 745 (1982) (holding that in state proceedings to terminate parental rights over their natural children because of "permanent neglect," a "fair preponderance of the evidence" standard is inadequate and that a state must support its allegations by "at least clear and convincing evidence"). These cases are noted further above (additions to 10th Ed., pp. 633 and 635; Ind.Rts., pp. 253 and 255).

In Landon v. Plasencia, 459 U.S. —— (1982), the Court held that the Matthews v. Eldridge balancing analysis applies to deportation proceedings, but did not find the record sufficient for it to decide whether the procedures at issue were constitutionally adequate. By contrast to deportation proceedings, however, the initial decision to admit or exclude an alien from the country is not governed by due process constraints. As the Court summarized in Landon: "[An] alien seeking initial admission to the United States requests a privilege and has no constitutional rights regarding his application, for the power to admit or exclude aliens is a sovereign prerogative. [However,] once an alien gains admission to our country and begins to develop the ties that go with permanent residence his constitutional status changes accordingly. [A] continuously present resident alien is entitled to a fair hearing [and due process] when threatened with deportation."

Chapter 10

EQUAL PROTECTION

10th ED., p. 692; IND. RTS., p. 312
Add to footnote 4:

During the 1980–1981 Term, extensive debates erupted in a remarkably large number of cases on the question of whether a legislature's "actual purpose" is relevant to the constitutionality of a challenged law. Most of the cases dealt with the content of deferential, rationality review in the equal protection context; one carried the debate over into the area of state regulation of interstate commerce. See, e.g., U. S. Railroad Retirement Bd. v. Fritz, 449 U.S. 166 (1980), and Schweiker v. Wilson, 450 U.S. 221 (1981) (both equal protection cases, noted as additions to the 10th Ed., p. 704; Ind.Rts., p. 324), and Kassel v. Consolidated Freightways Corp., 450 U.S. 662 (1981) (state regulation of commerce, noted as addition to 10th Ed., p. 295). Typically, Justice Brennan has contended that actual legislative purpose, not counsel's argument or judicial hypothesizing, should be determinative; Justice Rehnquist has insisted that a much more deferential stance is appropriate.

10th ED., p. 704; IND. RTS., p. 324
Add at end of sec. 1:

U. S. RAILROAD RETIREMENT BD. v. FRITZ

449 U.S. 166, 101 S.Ct. 453, 66 L.Ed.2d 368 (1980).

Justice REHNQUIST delivered the opinion of the Court.

[A lower federal court held unconstitutional a section of the Railroad Retirement Act of 1974.] The Act fundamentally restructured the railroad retirement system. The Act's predecessor statute, adopted in 1937, provided a system of retirement and disability benefits for persons who pursued careers in the railroad industry. Under that statute, a person who worked for both railroad and nonrailroad employers and who qualified for railroad retirement benefits and social security benefits received retirement benefits under both systems and an accompanying "windfall" benefit. The legislative history of the 1974 Act shows that the payment of windfall benefits threatened the railroad retirement system with bankruptcy by the year 1981. Congress therefore determined to place the system on a "sound financial basis" by eliminating future accruals of those benefits. Congress also enacted various transitional provisions, including a grandfather provision, § 231b(h), which expressly preserved windfall benefits for some classes of employees.

In restructuring the Railroad Retirement Act in 1974, Congress divided employees into various groups. *First*, those employees who lacked the requisite 10 years of railroad employment to qualify for railroad retirement benefits as of January 1, 1975, the changeover date, would have their retirement benefits computed under the new system and would not receive any windfall benefit. *Second*, those individuals already retired and already receiving dual benefits as of the changeover date would have their benefits computed under the old system and would continue to receive a windfall benefit. *Third*, those employees who had qualified for both railroad and social security benefits as of the changeover date, but who had not yet retired as of that date (and thus were not yet receiving dual benefits) were entitled to windfall benefits if they had (1) performed some railroad service in 1974, or (2) had a "current connection" with the railroad industry as of December 31, 1974, or (3) completed 25 years of railroad service as of December 31, 1974. § 231b(h)(1). *Fourth*, those employees who had qualified for railroad benefits as of the changeover date, but lacked a current connection with the railroad industry in 1974 and lacked 25 years of railroad employment, could obtain a lesser amount of windfall benefit if they had qualified for social security benefits as of the year (prior to 1975) they left railroad employment. § 231b(h)(2).

Thus, an individual who, as of the changeover date, was unretired and had 11 years of railroad employment and sufficient nonrailroad employment to qualify for social security benefits is eligible for the full windfall amount if he worked for the railroad in 1974 or had a current connection with the railroad as of December 31, 1974, or his later retirement date. But an unretired individual with 24 years of railroad service and sufficient nonrailroad service to qualify for social security benefits is not eligible for a full windfall amount unless he worked for the railroad in 1974, or had a current connection with the railroad as of December 31, 1974, or his later retirement date. And an employee with 10 years of railroad employment who qualified for social security benefits only after leaving the railroad industry will not receive a reduced windfall benefit while an employee who qualified for social security benefits prior to leaving the railroad industry would receive a reduced benefit. It was with these complicated comparisons that Congress wrestled in 1974.

Appellees filed this class action [seeking] a declaratory judgment that 45 U.S.C. § 231b(h) is unconstitutional under the Due Process Clause of the Fifth Amendment because it irrationally distinguishes between classes of annuitants. The District Court eventually certified a class of all persons eligible to retire between January 1, 1975 and January 31, 1977, who were permanently insured under the Social Security Act as of December 31, 1974, but who were not eligible to receive any "windfall component" because they had left the railroad industry before 1974, had no "current connection" with it at the end of 1974, and had less than 25 years of railroad service. Appellees contended below that it was irrational for Congress to have drawn a distinction between employees who had more than 10 years but less than 25 years of railroad employment simply on the basis of whether they had a "current connection" with the railroad industry as of the changeover date or as of the date of retirement. The District Court agreed with appellees that a differentiation based solely on whether an employee was "active" in a railroad business as of 1974 was not "rationally related" to the congressional purposes of insuring the solvency of the railroad retirement system and protecting vested benefits. We disagree and reverse.

The initial issue [is] the appropriate standard of judicial review to be applied when social and economic legislation enacted by Congress is challenged as being violative of the Fifth Amendment. [There] is no claim here that Congress has taken property in violation of the Fifth

Amendment, since railroad benefits, like social security benefits, are not contractual and may be altered or even eliminated at any time. [E.g.,] Flemming v. Nestor.* [And] the distinctions drawn in § 231b(h) do not burden fundamental constitutional rights or create "suspect" classifications, such as race or national origin .   .   ..

Despite the narrowness of the issue, this Court in earlier cases has not been altogether consistent in its pronouncements in this area. In Lindsley v. National Carbonic Gas Co. [1911], the Court said that "when the classification in such a law is called in question, if any state of facts reasonably can be conceived that would sustain it, the existence of that state of facts at the time that the law was enacted must be assumed." On the other hand, only nine years later in Royster Guano Co. v. Virginia [1920], the Court said that for a classification to be valid under the Equal Protection Clause it "must rest upon some ground of difference having a fair and substantial relation to the object of the legislation."

In more recent years, however, the Court in cases involving social and economic benefits has consistently refused to invalidate on equal protection grounds legislation which it simply deemed unwise or unartfully drawn. [See Dandridge v. Williams, Vance v. Bradley, and New Orleans v. Dukes. See also the earlier decision in Flemming v. Nestor (10th Ed., p. 239). And note a case "not dissimilar from the present one, in that the State was forced to make a choice which would undoubtedly seem inequitable to some members of the class"—Jefferson v. Hackney.]

Applying those principles to this case, the plain language of § 231b(h) marks the beginning and end of our inquiry.[1] There Congress determined that some of those who in the past received full windfall benefits would not continue to do so. Because Congress could have eliminated windfall benefits for all classes of employees, it is not constitutionally impermissible for Congress to have drawn lines between groups of employees for the purpose of phasing out those benefits. New Orleans v. Dukes.

---

* All of the cases cited in this opinion appear elsewhere in the casebook—mainly in this chapter.

1. This opinion and Justice Brennan's dissent cite a number of equal protection cases including Lindsley v. Natural Carbonic Gas Co., Royster Guano Co. v. Virginia, Flemming v. Nestor, Massachusetts Board of Retirement v. Murgia, New Orleans v. Dukes, Johnson v. Robison, U. S. Dept. of Agriculture v. Moreno, United States Dept. of Agriculture v. Murry, Weinberger v. Wiesenfeld, and James v. Strange. The most arrogant legal scholar would not claim that all of these cases applied a uniform or consistent test under the Equal Protection Clause. And realistically speaking, we can be no more certain that this opinion will remain undisturbed than were those who joined the opinion in Lindsley, Royster Guano Co., or any of the other cases referred to in this opinion and in the dissenting opinion. But like our predecessors and our successors, we are obliged to apply the equal protection component of the Fifth Amendment as we believe the Constitution requires and in so doing we have no hesitation in asserting, contrary to the dissent, that where social or economic regulations are involved, Dandridge v. Williams and Jefferson v. Hackney, together with this case, state the proper application of the test. The comments in the dissenting opinion about the proper cases for which to look for the correct statement of the equal protection rational basis standard, and about which cases limit earlier cases, are just that: comments in a dissenting opinion. [Footnote by Justice Rehnquist.]

The only remaining question is whether Congress achieved its purpose in a patently arbitrary or irrational way. The classification here is not arbitrary, says appellant, because it is an attempt to protect the relative equities of employees and to provide benefits to career railroad employees. Congress fully protected, for example, the expectations of those employees who had already retired and those unretired employees who had 25 years of railroad employment. Conversely, Congress denied all windfall benefits to those employees who lacked 10 years of railroad employment. Congress additionally provided windfall benefits, in lesser amount, to those employees with 10 years railroad employment who had qualified for social security benefits at the time they had left railroad employment, regardless of a current connection with the industry in 1974 or on their retirement date.

Thus, the only eligible former railroad employees denied full windfall benefits are those, like appellees, who had no statutory entitlement to dual benefits at the time they left the railroad industry, but thereafter became eligible for dual benefits when they subsequently qualified for social security benefits. Congress could properly conclude that persons who had actually acquired statutory entitlement to windfall benefits while still employed in the railroad industry had a greater equitable claim to those benefits than the members of appellees' class who were no longer in railroad employment when they became eligible for dual benefits. Furthermore, the "current connection" test is not a patently arbitrary means for determining which employees are "career railroaders," particularly since the test has been used by Congress elsewhere as an eligibility requirement for retirement benefits. Congress could assume that those who had a current connection with the railroad industry when the Act was passed in 1974, or who returned to the industry before their retirement, were more likely than those who had left the industry prior to 1974 and who never returned, to be among the class of persons who pursue careers in the railroad industry, the class for whom the Railroad Retirement Act was designed.

Where, as here, there are plausible reasons for Congress' action, our inquiry is at an end. It is, of course, "constitutionally irrelevant whether this reasoning in fact underlay the legislative decision," Flemming v. Nestor, because this Court has never insisted that a legislative body articulate its reasons for enacting a statute. This is particularly true where the legislature must necessarily engage in a process of line drawing. The "task of classifying persons for [benefits] inevitably requires that some persons who have an almost equally strong claim to favorite treatment be placed on different sides of the line," Mathews v. Diaz, and the fact that the line might have been drawn differently at some points is a matter for legislative, rather than judicial, consideration.

Finally, we disagree with the District Court's conclusion that Congress was unaware of what it accomplished or that it was misled by the groups that appeared before it. If this test were applied literally to every member of any legislature that ever voted on a law, there would be very few laws which would survive it. The language of the statute is clear, and we have historically assumed that Congress intended what it enacted. To be sure, appellees lost a political battle in which they had a strong interest, but this is neither the first nor the last time that such a result will occur in the legislative forum. What we have said is enough to dispose of the claims that Congress not only failed to accept appellees' argument as to restructuring in toto, but that such failure denied them [equal protection].

Reversed.

Justice STEVENS, concurring in the judgment.

In my opinion, Justice Brennan's criticism of the Court's approach to this case merits a more thoughtful response than that contained in footnote [1]. Justice Brennan correctly points out that if the analysis of legislative purpose requires only a reading of the statutory language in a disputed provision, and if any "conceivable basis" for a discriminatory classification will repel a constitutional attack on the statute, judicial review will constitute a mere tautological recognition of the fact that Congress did what it intended to do. Justice Brennan is also correct in reminding us that even though the statute is an example of "social and economic legislation," the challenge here is mounted by individuals whose legitimate expectations of receiving a fixed retirement income are being frustrated by, in effect, a breach of a solemn commitment by their government. When Congress deprives a small class of persons of vested rights that are protected—and, indeed, even enhanced [1]—for others who are in a similar though not identical position, I believe the Constitution requires something more than merely a "conceivable" or a "plausible" explanation for the unequal treatment.

I do not, however, share Justice Brennan's conclusion that every statutory classification must further an objective that can be confidently identified as the "actual purpose" of the legislature. Actual purpose is sometimes unknown. Moreover, undue emphasis on actual motivation may result in identically worded statutes being held valid in one State and invalid in a neighboring State.[2] I therefore believe that we must discover a correlation between the classification and either the actual purpose of the statute or a legitimate purpose that we may reasonably presume to have motivated an impartial legislature. If the adverse impact on the disfavored class is an apparent aim of the legislature, its impartiality would be suspect. If, however, the adverse impact may reasonably be viewed as an acceptable cost of achieving a larger goal, an impartial lawmaker could rationally decide that that cost should be incurred.

In this case, however, we need not look beyond the actual purpose of the legislature. As is often true, this legislation is the product of multiple and somewhat inconsistent purposes that led to certain compromises. One purpose was to eliminate in the future the benefit that is described by the Court as a "windfall benefit" and by Justice Brennan as an "earned dual benefit."

1. The 1974 Act provided increased benefits for spouses, widows, survivors and early retirees. [Footnote by Justice Stevens.]

2. Compare Rundlett v. Oliver, 607 F. 2d 495 (CA1 1979) (upholding Maine's statutory rape law) with Meloon v. Helgemoe, 564 F.2d 602 (CA1 1977),

cert. denied, 436 U.S. 950 (1978) (striking down New Hampshire's statutory rape law). [Footnote by Justice Stevens. For the Court's equal protection scrutiny of a statutory rape law, see Michael M. v. Superior Court, 450 U.S. 464 (1981) (addition to 10th Ed., p. 885; Ind. Rts., p. 505, below).]

That aim was incident to the broader objective of protecting the solvency of the entire railroad retirement program. Two purposes that conflicted somewhat with this broad objective were the purposes of preserving those benefits that had already vested and of increasing the level of payments to beneficiaries whose rights were not otherwise to be changed. As Justice Brennan emphasizes, Congress originally intended to protect *all* vested benefits, but it ultimately sacrificed some benefits in the interest of achieving other objectives.

Given these conflicting purposes, I believe the decisive questions are (1) whether Congress can rationally reduce the vested benefits of some employees to improve the solvency of the entire program while simultaneously increasing the benefits of others; and (2) whether, in deciding which vested benefits to reduce, Congress may favor annuitants whose railroad service was more recent than that of disfavored annuitants who had an equal or greater quantum of employment.

My answer to both questions is in the affirmative. The congressional purpose to eliminate dual benefits is unquestionably legitimate; that legitimacy is not undermined by the adjustment in the level of remaining benefits in response to inflation in the economy. As for the second question, some hardship—in the form of frustrated long-term expectations—must inevitably result from any reduction in vested benefits. Arguably, therefore, Congress had a duty—and surely it had the right to decide—to eliminate no more vested benefits than necessary to achieve its fiscal purpose. Having made that decision, any distinction it chose within the class of vested beneficiaries would involve a difference of degree rather than a difference in entitlement. I am satisfied that a distinction based upon currency of railroad employment represents an impartial method of identifying that sort of difference. Because retirement plans frequently provide greater benefits for recent retirees than for those who retired years ago—and thus give a greater reward for recent service than for past service of equal duration—the basis for the statutory discrimination is supported by relevant precedent. It follows, in my judgment, that the timing of the employees' railroad service is a "reasonable basis" for the classification as that term is used in Lindsley and Dandridge, as well as a "ground of difference having a fair and substantial relation to the object of the legislation" as those words are used in Royster Guano.   .   .   .

Justice BRENNAN, with whom Justice MARSHALL joins, dissenting.

[The] parties agree that the legal standard applicable to this case is the "rational basis" test. [The] Court today purports to apply this standard, but in actuality fails to scrutinize the challenged classification in the manner established by our governing precedents. I suggest that the mode of analysis employed by the Court in this case virtually immunizes social and economic legislative classifications from judicial review.

I. A legislative classification may be upheld only if it bears a rational relationship to a legitimate state purpose. [Vance v. Bradley; Murgia; New Orleans v. Dukes.] Perhaps the clearest statement of this Court's present approach to "rational basis" scrutiny may be found in Johnson v. Robison, 415 U.S. 361 (1974). In considering the constitutionality of limitations on the availability of educational benefits under the Veterans' Readjustment Benefits Act of 1966, eight Members of this Court agreed [on the Royster Guano Co. standard]. The enactments of Congress are entitled to a presumption of constitutionality, and the burden rests on those challenging a legislative classification to demonstrate that it does not bear the "fair and substantial relation to the object of the legislation" [Royster Guano Co.] required under the Constitution. Mathews v. Lucas.

Nonetheless, the rational basis standard "is not a toothless one," ibid, and will not be satisfied by flimsy or implausible justifications for the legislative classification, proffered after the fact by Government attorneys. See, e. g., Jimenez v. Weinberger; U. S. Dept. of Agriculture v. Moreno; U. S. Dept. of Agriculture v. Murry; James v. Strange. When faced with a challenge to a legislative classification under the rational basis test, the court should ask, first, what the purposes of the statute are, and second, whether the classification is rationally related to achievement of those purposes.

II.   The purposes of the Railroad Retirement Act of 1974 are clear, because Congress has commendably stated them in the House and Senate reports accompanying the Act. A section of the reports is entitled "Principal Purpose of the Bill." It notes generally that "[t]he bill provides for a complete restructuring of the Railroad Retirement Act of 1937, and will place it on a sound financial basis," [1] and then states: "Persons who already have vested rights under both the Railroad Retirement and the Social Security systems will in the future be permitted to receive benefits computed under both systems just as is true under existing law." Moreover, Congress explained that this purpose was based on considerations of fairness and the legitimate expectations of the retirees. [Thus], a "principal purpose" of the [Act], as explicitly stated by Congress, was to preserve the vested earned benefits of retirees who had already qualified for them. The classification at issue here, which deprives some retirees of vested dual benefits that they had earned prior to 1974, directly conflicts with Congress' stated purpose. As such, the classification is not only rationally unrelated to the congressional purpose; it is inimical to it.

III.   The Court today avoids the conclusion that § 231b(h) must be invalidated by deviating in three ways from traditional rational basis analysis. First, the Court adopts a tautological approach to statutory purpose, thereby avoiding the necessity for evaluating the relationship between the challenged classification and the legislative purpose. Second, it disregards the actual stated purpose of Congress in favor of a justification which was never suggested by any Representative or Senator, and which in fact conflicts with the stated congressional purpose. Third, it upholds the classification without any analysis of its rational relationship to the identified purpose.

A.   The Court states that "the plain language of § 231b(h) marks the beginning and end of our inquiry." This statement is strange indeed, for the

---

1. Of course, the legitimate governmental interest in restoring the Railroad Retirement system to fiscal soundness does not, in itself, serve to support the challenged classification in this case. At issue is why Congress discriminated among two classes of railroad retirees. The overall interest in saving money is irrelevant to this discrimination. [Footnote by Justice Brennan.]

"plain language" of the statute can tell us only what the classification is; it can tell us nothing about the purpose of the classification let alone the relationship between the classification and that purpose. Since § 231b(h) of the Act deprives appellees of their vested earned dual benefits, the Court apparently assumes that Congress must have *intended* that result. But by presuming purpose from result, the Court reduces analysis to tautology. It may always be said that Congress intended to do what it in fact did. If that were the extent of our analysis, we would find every statute, no matter how arbitrary or irrational, perfectly tailored to achieve its purpose. But equal protection scrutiny under the rational basis test requires the courts first to deduce the independent objectives of the statute, usually from statements of purpose and other evidence in the statute and legislative history, and second to analyze whether the challenged classification rationally furthers achievement of those objectives. The Court's tautological approach will not suffice.

B.   The Court analyzes the rationality of § 231b(h) in terms of a justification suggested by Government attorneys, but never adopted by Congress. The Court states that it is "constitutionally irrelevant whether this reasoning in fact underlay the legislative decision" [quoting Flemming v. Nestor (1960)]. In fact, however, equal protection analysis has evolved substantially on this question since Flemming was decided. Over the past 10 years, this Court has frequently recognized that the actual purposes of Congress, rather than the post hoc justifications offered by Government attorneys, must be the primary basis for analysis under the rational basis test. E.g., [Weinberger v. Wiesenfeld]. Thus, in San Antonio Ind. School Dist. v. Rodriguez, this Court stated that a challenged classification will pass muster under "rational basis" scrutiny only if it "rationally furthers some legitimate *articulated* state purpose" (emphasis added), and in Murgia, we stated that such a classification will be sustained only if it "rationally furthers the purpose *identified by the State.*" (Emphasis added.) [See also Johnson v. Robison; Califano v. Goldfarb.]

From these cases and others it is clear that this Court will no longer sustain a challenged classification under the rational basis test merely because Government attorneys can suggest a "conceivable basis" upon which it might be thought rational. The standard we have applied is properly deferential to the Legislative Branch: where Congress has articulated a legitimate governmental objective, and the challenged classification rationally furthers that objective, we must sustain the provision. In other cases, however, the courts must probe more deeply. Where Congress has expressly stated the purpose of a piece of legislation, but where the challenged classification is either irrelevant to or counter to that purpose, we must view any post hoc justifications proffered by Government attorneys with skepticism. A challenged classification may be sustained only if it is rationally related to achievement of an *actual* legitimate governmental purpose.

The Court argues that Congress chose to discriminate against appellees for reasons of equity, stating that "Congress could properly conclude that persons who had actually acquired statutory entitlement to windfall benefits while still employed in the railroad industry had a greater equitable claim to those benefits than the members of appellees' class who were no longer in railroad employment when they became eligible for dual benefits." [2]   This statement turns Congress' assessment of the equities on its head.   As I have shown, Congress expressed the view that it would be inequitable to deprive any retirees of any portion of the benefits they had been promised and that they had earned under prior law.   The Court is unable to cite even one statement in the legislative history by a Representative or Senator that makes the equitable judgment it imputes to Congress.   In the entire legislative history of the Act, the only persons to state that the equities justified eliminating appellees' earned dual benefits were representatives of railroad management and labor, whose self-serving interest in bringing about this result destroys any basis for attaching weight to their statements.

The factual findings of the District Court concerning the development of § 231b(h), amply supported by the legislative history, are revealing on this point.   In 1970, Congress established a commission to investigate the actuarial soundness of the Railroad Retirement system and to make recommendations for its reform.   The Commission was composed of one railroad management representative, one railroad labor representative, and three public representatives.   The Commission submitted a report in 1972, recommending, inter alia, that railroad retirees in the future no longer be permitted to earn full Railroad Retirement and Social Security benefits without offset. The Commission insisted, however, that "Individuals who have vested rights to social security benefits by virtue of permanently or fully insured status, but cannot exercise them because they are not at retirement age under railroad retirement, should be guaranteed an equivalent right in dollar terms to the staff tier portion of their benefits, including vested dual benefits.   .   .   ."

After receiving the Commission report, Congress asked railroad management and labor representatives to negotiate and submit a bill to restructure the Railroad Retirement system, which should "take into account the specific recommendations of the Commission on Railroad Retirement."   The members of this Joint Labor-Management Negotiating Committee were not appointed by public officials, nor did they represent the interests of the appellee class, who were no longer active railroaders or union members.

In an initial proposed restructuring of the system, the Joint Committee devised a means whereby the system's deficit could be completely eliminated without depriving retirees of vested earned benefits.   However, labor representatives demanded that benefits be increased for their current members, the cost to be offset by divesting the appellee class of a portion of the benefits they had earned under prior law.   As the District Court found: "Essentially, the railroad labor negotiators traded off the plaintiff class of beneficiaries to achieve added benefits for their current employees, even though doing so violated the basic Congressional purposes of the negotiations.   .   .   ."

2.   The Court's quoted justification fails on its face to support the challenged classification.   Despite the Court's apparent belief to the contrary, some members of the appellee class did "actually acquire statutory entitlement" to dual benefits while still employed in the railroad industry, but nevertheless were deprived of a portion of those benefits.   See § 231b(h)(2).   Under the Court's own reasoning, therefore, these persons were arbitrarily and impermissibly treated.   [Footnote by Justice Brennan.]

Congress conducted hearings to consider the Joint Committee's recommendations, but never directed its attention to their effect on persons in appellees' situation. In fact, the Joint Committee negotiators and Railroad Retirement Board members who testified at congressional hearings perpetuated the inaccurate impression that all retirees with earned vested dual benefits under prior law would retain their benefits unchanged. For example, Mr. William H. Dempsey, chairman of the management negotiators on the Joint Committee and principal witness at the hearings, told the Committee: "[P]rotection [will] be accorded to people who are on the rolls now receiving dual benefits and those who are vested under both systems as of January 1, 1975, the idea of the Commission being, and we agree with this, that these individuals had a right to rely upon the law as it existed when they were working. They had made their contributions. They have relied upon the law. They . . . should be protected."

Most striking is the following colloquy between Representative Dingell and Mr. Dempsey:

"Mr. DINGELL: Who is going to be adversely affected? Somebody has to get it in the neck on this. Who is going to be that lucky fellow?

"Mr. DEMPSEY: Well, I don't think so really. I think this is the situation in which every one wins. Let me explain. . . .

"Mr. DINGELL: Mr. Dempsey, I see some sleight of hand here but I don't see how it is happening. I applaud it but I would like to understand it. My problem is that you are going to go to a realistic system that is going to cost less but pay more in benefits. Now if you have accomplished this, I suggest we should put you in charge of the social security system." The Act was passed in the form drafted by the Joint Committee without any amendment relevant to this case.[3]

Of course, a misstatement or several misstatements by witnesses before Congress would not ordinarily lead us to conclude that Congress misapprehended what it was doing. In this instance, however, where complex legislation was drafted by outside parties and Congress relied on them to explain it, where the misstatements are frequent and unrebutted, and where no Member of Congress can be found to have stated the effect of the classification correctly, we are entitled to suspect that Congress may have been misled. As the District Court found: "At no time during the hearings did Congress even give a hint that it understood that the bill by its language eliminated an earned benefit of plaintiff's class."

Therefore, I do not think that this classification was rationally related to an *actual* governmental purpose.

C. The third way in which the Court has deviated from the principles of rational basis scrutiny is its failure to analyze whether the challenged classification is genuinely related to the purpose identified by the Court. Having suggested that "equitable considerations" underlay the challenged classifica-

---

3. Congress' unfortunate tendency to pass Railroad Retirement legislation drafted by labor and management representatives without adequate scruti- ny was criticized by the Commission on Railroad Retirement in its 1972 report. . . . [Footnote by Justice Brennan.]

tion—in direct contradiction to Congress' evaluation of those considerations, and in the face of evidence that the classification was the product of private negotiation by interested parties, inadequately examined and understood by Congress—the Court proceeds to accept that suggestion without further analysis.

An unadorned claim of "equitable" considerations is, of course, difficult to assess. It seems to me that before a court may accept a litigant's assertion of "equity," it must inquire what principles of equity or fairness might genuinely support such a judgment. But apparently the Court does not demand such inquiry, for it has failed to address any equitable considerations that might be relevant to the challenged classification. In my view, the following considerations are of greatest relevance to the equities of this case: (1) contribution to the system; (2) reasonable expectation and reliance; (3) need; and (4) character of service to the railroad industry. With respect to each of these considerations, I would conclude that appellees have as great an equitable claim to their earned dual benefits as do their more favored coworkers, who remain entitled to their earned dual benefits under § 231b(h).

Contribution to the system. The members of the appellee class worked in the railroad industry for more than 10 but fewer than 25 years, and also worked in nonrailroad jobs for the required number of years for vesting under Social Security—usually 40 quarters. During that time, they contributed to both the Railroad Retirement and Social Security systems, and met all requirements of the law for the vesting of benefits under those systems. In this respect, they are identical to their more favored coworkers, who contributed no more of their earnings to the systems than did appellees. On the basis of contributions to the systems, therefore, there is no reason for this discrimination.

Reasonable expectation and reliance. Throughout their working lives, appellees were assured that they would receive retirement benefits in accordance with the terms of the law as it then stood. No less than their more favored coworkers, they chose career paths and made calculations for their retirement based on these assurances. For Congress to change its rules and strip them of these benefits at the time of their retirement seems decidedly inequitable. [In] fact, this reliance was one of the principal reasons Congress resolved not to disturb the vested earned dual benefits of retirees.

Need. The appellee class is composed of fixed-income elderly people, no longer capable of re-entering the work force to reacquire benefits once earned but now lost. The average loss to the class members is about $88 per month, no small element in the monthly budget. The record provides no reason to suppose that members of the appellee class are any less likely to be in need than are their coworkers.

Character of service to the railroad industry. Members of the appellee class worked at least 10 years for the railroad industry by 1974, and many of them worked as long as 24 years. Their duration of railroad employment—surely the best measure of their service to the industry—was equal to that of their coworkers. In fact, some appellees worked *over twice as long* in the railroad industry as did some of those who retained their rights to a dual benefit. Admittedly, the members of the appellee class retired from railroad work prior to 1974, but the record shows that many left railroad work involuntarily, not because of a lack of commitment to the industry. Moreover, since one purpose of the Railroad Retirement system was to encourage railroad workers to retire early, so as to create positions for younger workers, it is hardly fair to fault the appellees now for having done so.

Even if I were able to accept the notion that Congress considered it equitable to deprive a class of railroad retirees of a portion of their vested earned benefits because they no longer worked for the railroad, I would still consider the means adopted in § 231b(h) irrational.[4] Under this provision, a retiree is favored by retention of his full vested earned benefits if he had worked so much as one day for a railroad in 1974. This is a plainly capricious basis for distinguishing among retirees, every one of whom had worked in the industry for at least *10 years*: the fortuity of one day of employment in a particular year should not govern entitlement to benefits earned over a lifetime.

I therefore conclude that the Government's proffered justification of "equitable considerations," accepted without question by the Court, cannot be defended. Rather, as the legislative history repeatedly states, equity and fairness demand that appellees, like their coworkers, retain the vested dual benefits they earned prior to 1974. A conscientious application of rational basis scrutiny demands, therefore, that § 231b(h) be invalidated.

IV. Equal protection rationality analysis does not empower the courts to second-guess the wisdom of legislative classifications. On this we are agreed, and have been for over 40 years. On the other hand, we are not powerless to probe beneath claims by Government attorneys concerning the means and ends of Congress. Otherwise, we would defer not to the considered judgment of Congress, but to the arguments of litigators. The instant case serves as an example of the unfortunate consequence of such misplaced deference. Because the Court is willing to accept a tautological analysis of congressional purpose, an assertion of "equitable" considerations contrary to the expressed judgment of Congress, and a classification patently unrelated to achievement of the identified purpose, it succeeds in effectuating neither equity nor congressional intent. . .. . *

THE CONTINUING EFFORTS TO DELINEATE THE CONTOURS OF DEFERENTIAL RATIONALITY REVIEW, 1980–83

Despite the majority's seeming commitment to an extremely deferential stance in Fritz, the Court continues to struggle with the problem of clarifying

---

4. Contrary to the Court's suggestion, this is not a "line-drawing" case, where the Congress must make a division at some point along an admittedly rationally conceived continuum. Here, Congress has isolated a particular class of retirees on the basis of a distinction that is utterly irrelevant to any actual or legitimate governmental purpose. [Footnote by Justice Brennan.]

* The debate between Justices Rehnquist and Brennan about the relevance of *actual* legislative purpose was renewed in several other cases later in the 1980–81 Term—not only in some of the equal protection decisions which follow but also in the context of state regulation of commerce, in Kassel v. Consolidated Freightways Corp., 450 U.S. 662 (1981) (printed as a principal case above, addition to 10th Ed., p. 295).

the precise degree of scrutiny appropriate for "rational basis" equal protection cases. As the decisions that follow indicate, debate persists about a number of recurring issues in rationality review. For example: How should the burdens of presenting data bearing on the validity of a challenged classification be allocated? To what extent should a challenged law be tested by the legislature's actual or articulated purposes rather than by purposes suggested by counsel or by conceivable purposes hypothesized by the courts? Should rationality review have any "bite"? To what extent does it? [1]

1. *The Clover Leaf Creamery case.* The Court's lineup was unusual when it rejected an equal protection attack in MINNESOTA v. CLOVER LEAF CREAMERY CO., 449 U.S. 456 (1981): No Justice dissented on the merits of the equal protection claim; and Justice Brennan, who has often dissented in modern rationality cases (e.g., Fritz), authored the majority opinion.

The challenged law banned the retail sale of milk in plastic nonreturnable, nonrefillable containers, but permitted such sale in other nonreturnable containers, such as paperboard cartons. The statute proclaimed that the ban was designed to promote resource conservation, ease solid waste disposal problems, and conserve energy.

The state trial court conducted extensive evidentiary hearings on the law's probable consequences. It found the evidence "in sharp conflict," but nevertheless thought itself "obliged to weigh and evaluate [the] evidence." It concluded that the law "would not succeed in effecting the Legislature's published policy goals." Moreover, it determined that, contrary to the stated statutory objective, the "actual basis" of the law was to promote "the economic interests of certain segments of the local dairy and pulpwood industries at the expense of the economic interests of other segments of the dairy industry and the plastics industry." For those reasons, the trial court invalidated the law on equal protection and commerce clause grounds.[2] Unlike the trial court, the Minnesota Supreme Court accepted the legislature's stated purpose. However, it engaged in an independent review of the evidence, and decided that "the evidence conclusively demonstrates that the discrimination against plastic nonrefillables is not rationally related to the Act's objectives."

---

1. Note especially the reflection of the continuing uncertainties in Justice Powell's dissent in the 5 to 4 ruling in Schweiker v. Wilson, 450 U.S. 221 (1981) (Note 2 below). A few months after joining Justice Rehnquist's majority opinion in Fritz, Justice Powell commented:

"The Court has employed numerous formulations for the 'rational basis' test. Members of the Court continue to hold divergent views on the clarity with which a legislative purpose must appear [Fritz], and about the degree of deference afforded the legislature in suiting means to ends, compare [Lindsley] with [Royster Guano Co.]." (Justice Powell's dissent in Schweiker

v. Wilson was of a considerably different tenor than that of the Rehnquist majority opinion which he had joined in Fritz.)

Compare the "rational basis" dialogue with the contemporaneous Court struggle to delineate the proper degree of "intermediate level" scrutiny applicable to the recent sex discrimination cases noted below. See, e.g., Michael M. v. Superior Court, 450 U.S. 464 (1981) (addition to 10th Ed., p. 885; Ind. Rts., p. 505).

2. The ultimate resolution of the commerce clause challenge is noted above, addition to 10th Ed., p. 339.

Justice BRENNAN rejected the equal protection challenge, insisting that the state courts' scrutiny of the evidence had been unduly intrusive. Under the "rational basis" test, he explained, the "narrow issue" was "whether the legislative classification between plastic and nonplastic nonreturnable milk containers is rationally related to achievement of the statutory purposes." He noted that the challengers had not questioned "the *theoretical* connection between a ban on plastic nonreturnables and the purposes articulated by the legislature; instead, they have argued that there is no *empirical* connection between the two." He responded: "But States are not required to convince the courts of the correctness of their legislative judgments." Rather, challengers have the burden of convincing courts "that the legislative facts on which [a] classification is apparently based could not reasonably be conceived to be true by the governmental decisionmaker. Vance v. Bradley." He elaborated: "Although parties challenging legislation under the Equal Protection Clause may introduce evidence supporting their claim that it is irrational, [they] cannot prevail so long as 'it is evident from all the considerations presented to [the legislature], and those of which we may take judicial notice, that the question is at least debatable.' [Carolene Products.] Where there was evidence before the legislature reasonably supporting the classification, litigants may not procure invalidation [merely] by tendering evidence in court that the legislature was mistaken."

Here, the State argued that the state judiciary had "impermissibly substituted its judgment for that of the legislature." The State advanced four arguments to show that the classification was "rationally related to the articulated statutory purposes." Justice Brennan examined each of the arguments [3] and agreed that the state courts had acted improperly.

3. In emphasizing the law's articulated purpose, Justice Brennan rejected the challengers' argument that the statute should be tested by its "actual," anticompetitive purpose as identified by the trial court. Justice Brennan replied: "We accept the contrary holding of the Minnesota Supreme Court that the articulated purpose of the Act is its actual purpose. In equal protection analysis, this Court will assume that the objectives articulated by the legislature are actual purposes of the statute, unless an examination of the circumstances forces us to conclude that they 'could not have been a goal of the legislation.' See Weinberger v. Wiesenfeld. Here, a review of the legislative history supports the Minnesota Supreme Court's conclusion that the principal purposes of the Act were to promote conservation and ease solid waste disposal problems. The contrary evidence cited by [the challengers] is easily understood, in context, as economic defense of an Act genuinely proposed for environmental reasons. We will not invalidate a state statute under the Equal Protection Clause merely because some legislators sought to obtain votes for the measure on the basis of its beneficial side effects on state industries." [Compare the Court's discussion of the relevance of "actual" legislative purposes a few months earlier (in Fritz, the principal case) and a few months later (in Schweiker v. Wilson, which follows).]

Note also Justice Brennan's formulation of "rational basis" equal protection standards in his majority opinion in Western & S.L.I. Co. v. Bd. of Equalization, 451 U.S. 648 (1981). Rejecting an equal protection challenge to a discriminatory state tax on out-of-state insurers, he stated: "In determining whether a challenged classification is rationally related to achievement of a legitimate state purpose, we must answer two questions: (1) Does the challenged legislation have a legitimate purpose?, and (2) Was it reasonable for the lawmakers to believe that use of the challenged classification would promote that purpose? [W]hether *in fact* the provision will accomplish its objectives is not the question: the Equal Protection Clause

The State argued, first, that the elimination of plastic milk jugs would encourage the use of environmentally superior containers and that the ban on plastic containers would "buy time during which environmentally preferable alternatives [might] be further developed." Justice Brennan found this approach "fully supported under our precedents." He noted that the "legislature [could] 'implement [its] program step by step.' [New Orleans v. Dukes]." He added: "The Equal Protection Clause does not deny the State [the] authority to ban one type of milk container conceded to cause environmental problems, merely because another type, already established in the market [and also environmentally undesirable], is permitted to continue in use. Whether *in fact* the Act will promote more environmentally desirable milk packaging is not the question: the Equal Protection Clause is satisfied by our conclusion that the Minnesota Legislature *could* rationally have decided that its ban on plastic nonreturnable milk jugs might force greater use of environmentally desirable alternatives."

Justice Brennan next turned to the State's argument that the law would "reduce the economic dislocation foreseen from the movement toward greater use of environmentally superior containers." The State contended that, although paperboard as well as plastic containers have environmental drawbacks, simultaneously banning both plastic and paperboard containers "would cause an enormous disruption in the milk industry." In contrast, banning plastic containers while continuing to permit the paperboard ones would "prevent the [dairy] industry from becoming reliant on the new container, while avoiding severe economic dislocation." Justice Brennan once again found this justification "supported by our precedents." He argued that the Dukes case was "not significantly different," and he elaborated the similarity by saying: "The state legislature concluded that nonreturnable, nonrefillable milk containers pose environmental hazards, and decided to ban the most recent entry into the field." As in Dukes, "[t]he fact that the legislature in effect 'grandfathered' paperboard containers, at least temporarily, does not make the Act's ban on plastic nonreturnables arbitrary or irrational."

The State's third argument was that the law would "help to conserve energy." The Minnesota Supreme Court had rejected this justification on the ground that the legislature had misunderstood the facts. That court insisted that, contrary to the legislative assumptions, the "production of plastic nonrefillables requires less energy than production of paper containers." Justice Brennan commented that the state court "may be correct that the Act is not a

is satisfied if we conclude that the [state legislature] *rationally could have believed* that the [law] would promote its objective. [Clover Leaf Creamery; Vance v. Bradley; Carolene Products.]"

See also Justice Marshall's recent, very deferential formulation of equal protection standards, in his opinion for the Court in Hodel v. Indiana, 452 U. S. 314 (1981) (addition to 10th Ed., p. 195). The case rejected a number of constitutional challenges to the Sur-

face Mining Act of 1977. Justice Marshall stated: "Social and economic legislation [that] does not employ suspect classifications or impinge on fundamental rights must be upheld against equal protection attack when the legislative means are rationally related to a legitimate governmental purpose. [Schweiker v. Wilson; Fritz.] Moreover, such legislation carries with it a presumption of rationality that can only be overcome by a clear showing of arbitrariness and irrationality."

sensible means of conserving energy," but added that the question was "at least debatable" in view of the evidence before the legislature, and that the state court accordingly had "erred in substituting its judgment for that of the legislature."

Finally the State argued that the law would ease solid waste disposal problems. Evidence before the legislature indicated that plastic containers occupy a greater volume in landfills than other nonreturnables, but the highest state court found that "plastic milk jugs in fact take up less space in landfills and present fewer solid waste disposal problems than do paperboard containers." Once again, Justice Brennan rejected the state court's approach: "[I]t is not the function of the courts to substitute their evaluation of legislative facts for that of the legislature." Accordingly, the state law passed "rational relation" scrutiny.[4]

2. *Schweiker v. Wilson.* During the 1980–81 Term, the clearest indication that Fritz, the principal case, does not mark the end of intense division on the Court about the importance of actual legislative purpose in "rational basis" equal protection review was a decision handed down only a few months after Fritz, SCHWEIKER v. WILSON, 450 U.S. 221 (1981). In Fritz, Justice Rehnquist's very deferential majority opinion searched for any "plausible reasons" for the legislative action, whether or not "this reasoning in fact underlay the legislative decision." Moreover, he asserted that "this Court has never insisted that a legislative body articulate its reasons for enacting a statute." Only two Justices dissented in Fritz.

Schweiker v. Wilson, by contrast, produced a much narrower, 5 to 4 decision. Justice Powell, who had silently joined Justice Rehnquist's majority opinion in Fritz, submitted a forceful dissent. He criticized the very deferential decisions [e.g., Flemming v. Nestor and McGowan v. Maryland] upon which the Fritz ruling had relied: "[T]hey do not describe the importance of actual legislative purpose in our analysis." He argued, moreover, that "post hoc hypotheses about legislative purpose, unsupported by the legislative history," should be received skeptically. His scrutiny accordingly paid considerable attention to "discernable" or "identifiable" legislative purposes.

Schweiker v. Wilson was an unsuccessful challenge to the exclusion of most patients in public mental institutions from eligibility for certain federal

---

4. The state courts also held that the law violated substantive due process. The Court rejected this claim as well: "From our conclusion under equal protection, [it] follows a fortiori that the Act does not violate the Fourteenth Amendment's Due Process Clause." [The Court also rejected a commerce clause challenge, discussed above, addition to 10th Ed., p. 339.]

Justice STEVENS dissented on an unusual ground (further discussed above, addition to 10th Ed., and Ind. Rts., p. 66). He insisted that the state courts were free under the Constitution to substitute their evaluation of the legislative facts for that of the state legislature, and he argued that the Court was improperly interfering with "the relationship between state legislatures and state courts" when it rebuked the state courts for doing so. He claimed that the state courts had applied "the correct federal equal protection standard" and that the Court had no business reversing simply "because it disagrees with the Minnesota courts' perception of their role in the State's lawmaking process." Justice Brennan rejected that "novel" argument as "without merit." [Justice Rehnquist did not participate in the decision.]

welfare benefits.   The case arose in the following statutory context: The federal Supplemental Security Income program (SSI) provides subsistence payments for needy persons who are aged, blind, or disabled.   Patients in public mental institutions are generally excluded from eligibility for full SSI payments.   However, most patients in public institutions are eligible for smaller SSI payments—"comfort allowances" of $25.00 per month, to enable the institutionalized needy "to purchase small comfort items not supplied by the institution."   But these "comfort payments" are offered only if a patient resides in a public institution that receives Medicaid funds on his or her behalf. This scheme was challenged in a class action representing all residents of public mental institutions between the ages of 21 and 65.   This group is ineligible for Medicaid support; accordingly, under the SSI system, it is not entitled to the monthly comfort payments available to inmates of other medical institutions, including mental patients in public medical hospitals and private institutions.

The challengers attacked the classification under "the equal protection component of the Fifth Amendment's Due Process Clause."   They argued that the scheme bore "no rational relationship to any legitimate objective of the SSI program."   Justice BLACKMUN's majority opinion rejected this challenge.[1]   He explained: "[T]he pertinent inquiry is whether the [classification] advances legitimate legislative goals in a rational fashion.   [Although] this rational basis standard is 'not a toothless one,' Mathews v. Lucas, it does not allow us to substitute our personal notions of good policy for those of Congress.   [As] long as the classificatory scheme chosen by Congress rationally advances a reasonable and identifiable governmental objective, we must disregard the existence of other methods of allocation that we, as individuals, perhaps would have preferred."

Justice Blackmun found sufficient indication in the "sparse" legislative record that "the decision to incorporate the Medicaid eligibility standards into the SSI scheme must be considered Congress' deliberate, considered choice." Accordingly, "we decline to regard such deliberate action as the result of inadvertence or ignorance."   He proceeded: "Having found the adoption of the Medicaid standards intentional, we deem it logical to infer from Congress' deliberate action an intent to further the same subsidiary purpose [in framing the SSI exclusion] that lies behind the Medicaid exclusion, which [was] adopted because Congress believed the States to have a 'traditional' responsibility to care for those institutionalized in public mental institutions.

1. The challengers also claimed that the classification warranted scrutiny at a level *higher* than that appropriate under rationality review, insisting that "because the statute classifies on the basis of mental illness, a factor that greatly resembles other characteristics that this Court has found inherently 'suspect,' [special] justification should be required for the congressional decision" to exclude most of the mentally ill.   The lower federal court accepted much of this argument, applied an "intermediate level of judicial scrutiny," and invalidated the provision.   Justice Blackmun, however, found it unnecessary to reach this issue, because he concluded "that this statute does not classify directly on the basis of mental health."   He emphasized: "[We] intimate no view as to what standard of review applies to legislation expressly classifying the mentally ill as a discrete group." This aspect of the case is further discussed below, addition to 10th Ed., p. 908; Ind. Rts., p. 528.

[We] cannot say that the belief that the States should continue to have the primary responsibility for making this small 'comfort money' allowance available to those residing in state-run institutions is an irrational basis for withholding from them federal general welfare funds." He added: "This Court has granted a 'strong presumption of constitutionality' to legislation conferring monetary benefits, because it believes that Congress should have discretion in deciding how to expend necessarily limited resources. Awarding this type of benefit inevitably involves the kind of line-drawing that will leave some comparably needy person outside the favored circle. We cannot say that it was irrational of Congress, in view of budgetary constraints, to decide that it is the Medicaid recipients in public institutions that are the most needy and the most deserving of the small monthly supplement."

Justice POWELL's strong dissent, joined by Justices Brennan, Marshall and Stevens, countered: "Congress thoughtlessly has applied a statutory classification developed to further legitimate goals of one welfare program [Medicaid] to another welfare program [SSI] serving entirely different needs. The result is an exclusion of wholly dependent people from minimal benefits, serving no government interest. This irrational classification violates the equal protection component of the Due Process Clause of the Fifth Amendment."

Justice Powell articulated his approach to rationality review as follows: "[The rationality] test holds two firmly established principles in tension. The Court must not substitute its view of wise or fair legislative policy for that of the duly elected representatives of the people [Vance v. Bradley; Dandridge v. Williams], but the equal protection requirement does place a substantive limit on legislative power. At a minimum, the legislature cannot arbitrarily discriminate among citizens. Enforcing this prohibition while avoiding unwarranted incursions on the legislative power presents a difficult task. No bright line divides the merely foolish from the arbitrary law. Given this difficulty, legislation properly enjoys a presumption of rationality, which is particularly strong for welfare legislation where the apportionment of scarce benefits in accordance with complex criteria requires painful, but unavoidable, line drawing.

"The deference to which legislative accommodation of conflicting interests is entitled rests in part upon the principle that the political process of our majoritarian democracy responds to the wishes of the people. Accordingly, an important touchstone for equal protection review of statutes is how readily a policy can be discerned which the legislature intended to serve. See, e.g., [Moreno; McGinnis v. Royster]. When a legitimate purpose for a statute appears in the legislative history or is implicit in the statutory scheme itself, a court has some assurance that the legislature has made a conscious policy choice. Our democratic system requires that legislation intended to serve a discernable purpose receive the most respectful deference. Yet, the question of whether a statutory classification discriminates arbitrarily cannot be divorced from whether it was enacted to serve an identifiable purpose. When a legislative purpose can be suggested only by the ingenuity of a government lawyer litigating the constitutionality of a statute, a reviewing court may be presented not so much with a legislative policy choice as its absence.

"In my view, the Court should receive with some skepticism post hoc hypotheses about legislative purpose, unsupported by the legislative history.[2] When no indication of legislative purpose appears other than the current position of the Secretary, the Court should require that the classification bear a 'fair and substantial relation' to the asserted purpose. See Royster Guano v. Virginia. This marginally more demanding scrutiny indirectly would test the plausibility of the tendered purpose, and preserve equal protection review as something more than 'a mere tautological recognition of the fact that Congress did what it intended to do.' Fritz (Stevens, J., concurring)."

Applying this approach to the challenged provision, Justice Powell commented: "Neither the structure of [the provision] nor its legislative history identifies or even suggests any policy plausibly intended to be served by denying appellees the small SSI allowance. [The] structure of the statute offers no guidance as to purpose because [the provision] is drawn in reference to the policies of Medicaid rather than to the policies of SSI. By mechanically applying the criteria developed for Medicaid, Congress appears to have avoided considering what criteria would be appropriate for deciding in which public institutions a person can reside and still be eligible for some SSI payment. The importation of eligibility criteria from one statute to another creates significant risks that irrational distinctions will be made between equally needy people."

The Government had argued: "Congress rationally could make the judgment that the States should bear the responsibility for any comfort allowance, because they already have the responsibility for providing treatment and minimal care." Justice Powell rejected this argument, stating: "There is no logical link [between] these two responsibilities." He elaborated: "[R]esidence in a *public mental* institution, as opposed to residence in a state *medical* hospital or a *private* mental hospital, bears no relation to any policy of the SSI program. [If] SSI pays a cash benefit relating to personal needs other than maintenance and medical care, it is irrelevant whether the State or the Federal Government is paying for the maintenance and medical care; the patients' need remains the same, the likelihood that the policies of SSI will be fulfilled remains the same." He accordingly concluded "that Congress had no rational reason for refusing to pay a comfort allowance to [the challengers], while paying it to numerous otherwise identically situated disabled indigents. This unexplained difference in treatment must have been a legislative oversight. I therefore dissent."

2. "Some of our cases suggest that the actual purpose of a statute is irrelevant, Flemming v. Nestor, and that the statute must be upheld 'if any state of facts reasonably may be conceived to justify' its discrimination. McGowan v. Maryland. Although these cases preserve an important caution, they do not describe the importance of actual legislative purpose in our analysis. We recognize that a legislative body rarely acts with a single mind and that compromises blur purpose. Therefore, it is appropriate to accord some deference to the executive's view of legislative intent, as similarly we accord deference to the consistent construction of a statute by the administrative agency charged with its enforcement. *Ascertainment of actual purpose to the extent feasible, however, remains an essential step in equal protection.*" [Footnote by Justice Powell. Emphasis added.]

3. *Logan v. Zimmerman Brush Co.* An unusual case in 1982, LO-GAN v. ZIMMERMAN BRUSH CO., 455 U.S. 422 (1982), demonstrated that the "mere rationality" strand of equal protection review retains "bite" despite Fritz's deferential tenor. Justice Blackmun's "opinion of the Court" in Logan was devoted entirely to sustaining the challenger's procedural due process attack on a state statutory scheme. That opinion for the unanimous Court did not mention the challenger's equal protection claim. But, in an unusual move, Justice Blackmun also submitted a separate opinion. That second Blackmun opinion, joined by Justices Brennan, Marshall and O'Connor, stated: "Although the Court [in the opinion written by Justice Blackmun himself] considered that it was unnecessary to discuss and dispose of the equal protection claim when the due process issue was being decided in Logan's favor, I regard the equal protection issue as sufficiently important to require comment on my part, particularly inasmuch as a majority of the Members of the Court are favorably inclined toward the claim." Justice Blackmun's separate opinion then explained why the challenged provision did not satisfy the minimum rationality standards of equal protection. And, in another separate opinion, Justice Powell, joined by Justice Rehnquist (who is typically the strongest defender of extemely deferential rationality review) stated that, even though he could not join Justice Blackmun's concurring opinion, he, too, agreed that the challenged law could not survive even the "minimal standard" of equal protection review. In short, six Justices voted to invalidate the law on "minimum rationality" equal protection grounds. Logan thus is a rare modern example of a case in which a majority agreed that a state law was irrational.[1]

The Logan case arose out of a proceeding under the Illinois Fair Employment Practices Act. The Act barred employment discrimination on the basis of physical handicap unrelated to ability. Logan filed a timely complaint with the State's Fair Employment Practices Commission claiming that he was discharged from employment because of his employer's belief that Logan's "short left leg made it impossible for him to perform his duties as a shipping clerk." Under ¶ 858(b) of the Act, the Commission was supposed to convene a "factfinding conference" within 120 days of the filing of the complaint. "Apparently through inadvertence," the Commission scheduled the conference for a date that was five days after the expiration of the statutory period. The Illinois Supreme Court found that the 120-day period was mandatory and that the failure to comply with it deprived the Commission of jurisdiction to consider Logan's complaint. Justice Blackmun's "opinion for the Court" held that this bar to considering the merits of Logan's claim was a violation of procedural due process (as more fully discussed above, addition to 10th Ed., p. 668; Ind. Rts., p. 288). As noted above,

---

1. Schweiker v. Wilson (the 1981 ruling in Note 2 above) had suggested—in view of the dissenting views of four of the Justices—that the very deferential scrutiny of Fritz might not be the last word on rationality review. Logan seems to confirm that, for six of the Justices, modern rationality review under the Equal Protection Clause is not always "toothless." It may also be of interest to note that Justice Blackmun, who had spoken for the deferential majority in Schweiker v. Wilson less than a year earlier, took the lead in articulating the equal protection flaw of the law challenged in Logan.

Justice Blackmun then proceeded to submit a separate opinion finding a violation of equal protection as well.

Justice BLACKMUN, joined by Justices Brennan, Marshall and O'Connor, explained his equal protection analysis as follows: "On its face, Logan's equal protection claim is an unconventional one. The Act's ¶ 858(b) establishes no explicit classifications and does not expressly distinguish between claimants, and the company therefore argues that Logan has no more been deprived of equal protection than anyone would be who is injured by a random act of governmental misconduct. As the Illinois Supreme Court interpreted the statute, however, ¶ 858(b) unambiguously divides claims—and thus, necessarily, claimants—into two discrete groups that are accorded radically disparate treatment. Claims processed within 120 days are given full consideration on the merits. [In] contrast, otherwise identical claims that do not receive a hearing within the statutory period are unceremoniously, and finally, terminated. Because the Illinois court recognized, in so many words, that the [Act] establishes two categories of claims, one may proceed to determine whether the classification drawn by the statute is consistent with the Fourteenth Amendment.

"For over a century, the Court has engaged in a continuing and occasionally almost metaphysical effort to identify the precise nature of the Equal Protection Clause's guarantees. [Here, Justice Blackmun cited the dissent in Schweiker v. Wilson.] At the minimum level, however, the Court 'consistently has required that legislation classify the persons it affects in a manner rationally related to legitimate governmental objectives.' Schweiker v. Wilson. This is not a difficult standard for a State to meet, when it is attempting to act sensibly and in good faith. But the 'rational-basis standard is "not a toothless one," ' id., quoting Mathews v. Lucas; the classificatory scheme must 'rationally advanc[e] a reasonable and identifiable governmental objective.' Schweiker v. Wilson. I see no need to explore the outer bounds of this test, for I find that the Illinois statute runs afoul of the lowest level of permissible equal protection scrutiny." Justice Blackmun proceeded to scrutinize the relationship between the statutory scheme and the State's purposes. He noted that the Act had "two express purposes: eliminating employment discrimination, and protecting [potential defendants] 'from unfounded charges of discrimination.' " He thought it "evident" that neither of these objectives was advanced by the Act's deadline provision. "Terminating potentially meritorious claims in a random manner obviously cannot serve to redress instances of discrimination. And it cannot protect employers from unfounded charges, for the frivolousness of a claim is entirely unrelated to the length of time the Commission takes to process that claim. [While] it may well be true that '[n]o bright line divides the merely foolish from the arbitrary law,' Schweiker v. Wilson (dissenting opinion), I have no doubt that ¶ 858(b) is patently irrational in the light of its stated purposes."

Justice Blackmun then turned to a "third rationale" recognized by Illinois' highest court: that the provision was "designed to further the 'just and expeditious resolutio[n]' of employment disputes." Justice Blackmun responded: "I cannot agree that terminating a claim that the State itself has

misscheduled is a rational way of expediting the resolution of disputes." [2]
He added: "Most important, the procedure at issue does not serve generally
to hasten the processing or ultimate termination of employment controversies.
Once the Commission has scheduled a factfinding conference and issued a
complaint, there are no statutory time limits at all on the length of time it can
take to resolve the claim. [It] is true, of course, that ¶ 858(b) serves to ex-
pedite the resolution of certain claims—those not processed within 120 days
—in a most obvious way, and in that sense it furthers the purpose of terminating disputes expeditiously. But it is not enough, under the Equal Protection Clause, to say that the legislature sought to terminate certain claims and
succeeded in doing so, for that is 'a mere tautological recognition of the fact
that [the legislature] did what it intended to do.' [Fritz (Stevens, J., concurring in the judgment).] This Court still has an obligation to view the
classificatory *system*, in an effort to determine whether the disparate treatment accorded the affected classes is arbitrary."

Justice Blackmun continued: "Here, that inquiry yields an affirmative
result. So far as the State's purpose is concerned, every [claimant's] charge,
when filed with the Commission, stands on the same footing. Yet certain ran-
domly selected claims, because processed too slowly by the State are irrevocably terminated without review. In other words, the State, converts similarly
situated claims into dissimilarly situated ones, and then uses this distinction as
the basis for its classification. This, I believe, is the very essence of arbitrary
state action. '[T]he Equal Protection Clause "imposes a requirement of
some rationality in the nature of the class singled out," ' and that rationality
is absent here. The Court faced an analogous situation in a case involving
sex-based classifications, and its conclusion there is applicable to the case before us now: giving preference to a discrete class 'merely to accomplish the
elimination of hearings on the merits, is to make the very kind of arbitrary
legislative choice forbidden by the Equal Protection Clause.' Reed v. Reed."

"Finally," Justice Blackmun noted, "it is possible that the Illinois Supreme Court meant to suggest that the deadline [can] be justified as a means
of thinning out the Commission's caseload, with the aim of encouraging the
Commission to convene timely hearings. This rationale, however, suffers
from the defect outlined above: it draws an arbitrary line between otherwise
identical claims. In any event, the State's method of furthering this purpose
—if this was in fact the legislative end—has so speculative and attenuated a
connection to its goal as to amount to arbitrary action. The State's rationale
must be something more than the exercise of a strained imagination; while
the connection between means and ends need not be precise, it, at the least,
must have some objective basis. That is not so here."

Justice POWELL's concurrence in the judgment, joined by Justice
Rehnquist, saw the case as "an isolated example of bureaucratic oversight,"

---

2. In a footnote at this point, Justice
Blackmun expressed some doubt that
the Illinois Supreme Court had really
defended the deadline provision on
this ground. He added: "In light of
my conclusions about the rationality
of such a justification, however, it is
irrelevant whether the Illinois Supreme Court intended to state that
this was the actual or articulated rationale for ¶ 858(b)'s deadline proviso.
I note that the rationales discussed in
the text have not been expressed by
the State's representatives; the Illinois Human Rights Commission, [the
successor to the earlier Commission],
by the State's Attorney General, has
filed a brief in this Court supporting
Logan."

"of little importance except to the litigants." To him, the issues presented were "too simple and straightforward to justify broad pronouncements on the law of procedural due process or of equal protection." He stated that he was "particularly concerned by the potential implications of the Court's expansive due process analysis." He accordingly urged that the case "should be decided narrowly on its unusual facts." [3]

Justice Powell nevertheless spent three paragraphs placing himself on record as finding the challenged law unconstitutional under the Equal Protection Clause. He thought "this unusual classification" was not "rationally related to a state interest that would justify it." He concluded: "This Court has held repeatedly that state created classifications must bear a rational relationship to legitimate governmental objectives. See, e.g., [Schweiker v. Wilson]. Although I do not join Justice Blackmun's separate opinion, I agree that the challenged statute, as construed and applied in this case, failed to comport with this minimal standard. I am concerned by the broad sweep of the Court's opinion, but I do join its judgment." [4]

3. "It is necessary for this Court to decide cases during almost every Term on due process and equal protection grounds. Our opinions in these areas often are criticized, with justice, as lacking consistency and clarity. Because these issues arise in varied settings, and opinions are written by each of nine Justices, consistency of language is an ideal unlikely to be achieved. Yet I suppose we would all agree—at least in theory—that unnecessarily broad statements of doctrine frequently do more to confuse than to clarify our jurisprudence. I have not always adhered to this counsel of restraint in my own opinion writing, and therefore imply no criticism of others. But it does seem to me that this is a case that requires a minimum of exposition." [Footnote by Justice Powell.]

4. In several cases during the 1981–82 Term, the Court rejected challenges under the rationality strand of equal protection. Thus, in G. D. Searle & Co. v. Cohn, 455 U.S. 404 (1982), a company challenged a New Jersey scheme under which unregistered foreign corporations, unlike registered foreign corporations and domestic ones, were not permitted to plead the statute of limitations (even though they could assert laches defenses). Justice Blackmun's majority opinion found the difference in treatment justified because unregistered foreign corporations are more difficult to locate and to serve with process. His only reference to a general standard of equal protection rationality review was that "a state statute is to be upheld against equal protection attack if it is rationally related to the achievement of legitimate governmental ends.

Schweiker v. Wilson." New Jersey's tolling provision readily satisfied "this constitutional minimum." Only Justice Stevens dissented on this aspect of the case. Addressing the "novel" equal protection issue here, he agreed that there was "a rational basis" for treating the corporations differently, but found "no legitimate state purpose to justify the special burden imposed on unregistered foreign corporations." He was troubled by the denial to the affected corporations of "the benefit of any statute of limitations": "Because there is a rational basis for *some* differential treatment, does it automatically follow that *any* differential treatment is constitutionally permissible? I think not; in my view the Constitution requires a rational basis for the special burden imposed on the disfavored class as well as a reason for treating that class differently." The availability of the laches defense did not satisfy him: "the defense merely lessens [the] adverse consequences [of the New Jersey laws]."

In Schweiker v. Hogan, 457 U.S. 569 (1982), the Court unanimously rejected an equal protection challenge to a federal-state welfare scheme which, as applied in Massachusetts, resulted "in a distribution of Medicaid benefits to recipients of Supplemental Security Income (SSI)—a class of aged, blind, or disabled persons who lack sufficient income to meet their basic needs [i.e., the categorically needy]—that is more generous than the distribution of such benefits to persons who are self-supporting [i.e., the medically needy]." Justice Stevens, without stating general standards of review, rejected the lower court's conclusion that the system "irrationally discriminate[d] between the categorically and the medically needy." He noted: "A belief that an act of Congress may be inequitable or unwise is of course an insufficient basis on which to conclude that it is unconstitutional." He accordingly rejected the argument "that if medical benefits are made available to a class of persons who are not categorically needy, it is constitutionally impermissible to deny them benefits if their income, after the deduction of incurred medical expenses, is lower than that of an individual who receives public assistance." He noted that the state had been free to deny *all medical benefits* to those not within the categorically needy class and concluded: "If a state may deny all benefits to the medically needy—while providing benefits to the categorically needy and rendering some persons who are on public assistance better off than others who are not—a State surely may narrow the gap between the two classes by providing partial benefits to the medically needy, even though certain members of that class may remain in a position less fortunate than those on public assistance."

In Exxon Corp. v. Eagerton, 462 U.S. —— (1983), a unanimous Court was concerned primarily with preemption and Contract Clause issues in a challenge to an Alabama severance tax increase coupled with a prohibition on passing that increase along to consumers. The case is discussed above, addition to 10th Ed., p. 569; Ind.Rts., p. 189. But Justice Marshall's opinion also rejected an equal protection challenge, and in the process set forth a characterization of the Court's "lenient standard of rationality." "Under that standard a statute will be sustained if the legislature could have reasonably concluded that the challenged classification would promote a legitimate state purpose."

Note also the reflection of the division on the Court about the current vitality of the Royster Guano-Reed v. Reed standard in Mesquite v. Aladdin's Castle, Inc., 455 U.S. 283 (1982). In Mesquite, the Court of Appeals had invalidated portions of a local ordinance governing coin-operated amusement establishments. The lower federal court had struck down, as irrational under equal protection standards, a provision stating that children under 17 years of age could not operate the amusement devices unless accompa-

nied by a parent or guardian. The Supreme Court majority refused to reach that issue on the merits because of uncertainty about whether the Court of Appeals had relied on federal or Texas standards of equal protection rationality. Justice Stevens' majority opinion, after noting that the Texas Constitution's equal protection provision might be "significantly broader than" the federal one, commented: "[I]t is important to take note of the Court of Appeals' interpretation of the Texas 'requirement of legislative rationality.' That interpretation seems to adopt a standard requiring that a legislative classification rest 'upon some ground of difference having a fair and substantial relationship to the object of the legislation.' This formulation is derived from this Court's opinion in [Royster Guano]. *But it is unclear whether this Court would apply the Royster Guano standard to the present case.* See [Fritz; Craig v. Boren]." [Emphasis added.] Justice Powell strongly disagreed, claiming that there was not "the slightest indication that the Court of Appeals was distinguishing between federal and state law." Moreover, he objected to the majority's view that the Royster Guano standard "may no longer be good law" and insisted that "this Court has never rejected either Royster Guano or Reed v. Reed. As stated in Fritz, '[t]he most arrogant legal scholar would not claim that all [Supreme Court] cases appl[y] a uniform or consistent test under equal protection principles.' In view of the example we have set, there is no reason to perceive inferences of divergent federal and state court views because of the failure of the Court of Appeals or Texas courts to use entirely consistent terminology." [See also Justice Rehnquist's discussion of deferential rationality review in his plurality opinion in Clements v. Fashing, 457 U.S. —— (1982), a ballot access case discussed below, addition to 10th Ed., p. 938; Ind. Rts., p. 558. Compare the application of equal protection criteria in Zobel v. Williams, 457 U.S. 55 (1982) (10th Ed., p. 960; Ind. Rts., p. 580). And note the extensive discussion of equal protection standards in Plyler v. Doe, 457 U.S. 202 (1982) (printed below, addition to 10th Ed., p. 897; Ind. Rts., p. 517), where the Court applied an intermediate standard of scrutiny in holding that Texas could not deny free public education to children of illegal aliens.]

10th ED., p. 714; IND. RTS., p. 334
Add to footnote 2:

Is the purposeful discrimination requirement applicable to claims under the Thirteenth Amendment (as it is under the Fourteenth)? The Court granted certiorari on this issue in Memphis v. Greene, 451 U.S. 100 (1981), but the majority found it unnecessary to resolve the question. However, Justice White's opinion concurring in the judgment did address the problem and concluded that the purposeful discrimination requirement does apply to Thirteenth Amendment claims. The case is noted below, addition to 10th Ed., p. 1057; Ind. Rts., p. 677.

10th ED., p. 725; IND. RTS., p. 345
Add to footnote 3:

As the Court pointed out in a statutory Title VII case, however, it is not necessary "to submit direct evidence of discriminatory intent. [As] in any lawsuit, the plaintiff may prove his case by direct or circumstantial evidence." U. S. Postal Service Bd. of Governors v. Aikens, 460 U.S. — (1983).

10th ED., p. 734; IND. RTS., p. 354
Add as foonote to majority opinion in Mobile:

In the wake of the Mobile decision, the Court's insistence on an intentional discrimination standard in § 2 cases came under severe attack in Congress. The House voted to substitute a "results" test, but the Senate balked. Ultimately, in extending the Voting Rights Act, Congress approved a compromise provision. See the fuller discussion of the Voting Rights Act extension (signed by the President on June 29, 1982) below (addition to 10th Ed., p. 1066; Ind. Rts., p. 686).

10th ED., p. 745; IND. RTS., p. 365
Add to footnote 13:

A sharply divided Court probed the requirements and implications of Mobile v. Bolden in ROGERS v. LODGE, 458 U.S. — (1982). The majority opinion affirmed the lower federal courts' holding that the at-large system of elections in Burke County, Georgia, violated the Fourteenth Amendment rights of the County's black citizens. The at-large system for electing the County's five-member Board of Commissioners was established in 1911. The County, a very large and predominantly rural one, had a slight majority of whites in the voting age population; no black candidate had ever been elected to the Board. The District Court, deciding the case prior to the Mobile decision, concluded that, while the present method of electing the Board was "racially neutral when adopted, [it] is being *maintained* for invidious purposes." It accordingly directed that the County be divided into five districts for purposes of electing County Commissioners. The Court of Appeals affirmed that judgment.

Justice WHITE, who wrote for the majority (but who had dissented in Mobile), relied heavily on the lower courts' findings and conclusions in affirming the rulings. With respect to the requisite adherence to the "purposeful discrimination" requirement of Mobile, he concluded that, "[a]lthough a tenable argument can be made to the contrary, we are not inclined to disagree with the Court of Appeals' conclusion that the District Court applied the proper legal standard." In his view, the District Court had "demonstrated its understanding of the controlling standard by observing that a determination of discriminatory intent is 'a requisite to a finding of unconstitutional vote dilution' under the Fourteenth and Fifteenth Amendments."

Justice White also upheld the District Court's findings and conclusions of fact: "We agree with the Court of Appeals that on the record before us, none of the factual findings are clearly erroneous." He reviewed briefly the types of circumstantial evidence the District Court had justifiably relied upon. For example, "although there had been black candidates, no black had ever been elected." Although "such facts are insufficient in themselves to prove purposeful discrimination absent other evidence such as proof that blacks have less opportunity to participate in the political processes," there was "supporting proof in this case [sufficient] to support an inference of intentional discrimination." For example, past discrimination had had an impact on "the ability of blacks to participate effectively in the political process" and "had prevented blacks from effectively participating in Democratic Party affairs and in primary elections." In addition, "elected officials of Burke County [had] been unresponsive and insensitive to the needs of the black community, which increased the likelihood that the political process was not equally open to blacks." Moreover, the at-large scheme, enacted by the state legislature, was in practice dependent upon the County's state representatives, and those representatives, the District Court found, had "retained a system which has minimized the ability of Burke County Blacks to participate in the political system." The Court found none of the District Court findings to be "clearly erroneous."

A long dissent by Justice STEVENS in large part elaborated the views in his concurrence in the Mobile case. He stated: "Despite my sympathetic appraisal of the Court's laudable goals,[1] I am unable to agree with its approach to the constitutional issue. [In] my opinion, this case raises questions that encompass more than the immediate plight of disadvantaged black citizens. I believe the Court errs by holding the structure of the local governmental unit unconstitutional without identifying an acceptable, judicially-manageable standard for adjudicating cases of this kind." As in Mobile, he argued that an objective rather than a subjective standard ought to apply. He suggested that the at-large system here might not survive scrutiny under a purely objective analysis, but data to support that argument, given the District Court's motivation approach, had not been developed in the record. And he insisted that, even if "the intent of the political majority" were controlling, "I could not agree that the only political groups that are entitled to protection [are] those defined by racial characteristics."

Justice Stevens reiterated his concern, expressed in Washington v. Davis as well as in Mobile, about the Court's "emphasis on subjective intent as a criterion for constitutional adjudication": "[I]n the long run constitutional adjudication that is premised on a case-by-case appraisal of the subjective intent of local decisionmakers cannot possibly satisfy the requirement of impartial administration of the law that is embodied in the Equal Protection Clause. [The] costs and the doubts associated with litigating questions of motive, which are often significant in routine trials, will be especially so in cases involving the 'motives' of legislative bodies." And he objected to the majority's application of motivation analysis here: "It is incongruous that subjective intent is identified as the constitutional standard and yet the persons who allegedly harbored an improper intent are never identified or mentioned. Undoubtedly, the evidence relied on by the Court proves that racial prejudice has played an important role in the history of Burke County and has motivated many wrongful acts by various community leaders. But unless that evidence is sufficient to prove that *every* governmental action was motivated by a racial animus, [the] Court has failed under its own test to demonstrate that the governmental structure of Burke County was maintained for a discriminatory purpose." He argued, too, that, although racial discrimination between individuals "is, at the very least, presumptively irrational," a "constitutional standard that gave special protection to political groups identified by racial characteristics would be inconsistent with the basic tenet of the Equal Protection Clause. [It] would be unrealistic to distinguish racial groups from other political groups on the ground that race is an irrelevant factor in the political process." He added: "[I]f the standard the Court applies today extends to all types of minority groups, it is either so broad that virtually every political device is vulnerable or it is so undefined that federal judges can pick and choose almost at will among those that will be upheld and those that will be condemned. [Any] suggestion that political groups in which black leadership predominates are in need of a permanent constitutional shield against the tactics of their political opponents underestimates the resourcefulness, the wisdom, and the demonstrated capacity of such leaders. I cannot accept the Court's constitutional holding."

In a briefer dissent, Justice POWELL, joined only by Justice Rehnquist, insisted that the approach endorsed by the majority was inconsistent with Mobile: "The [lower courts] based their findings of unconstitutional discrimination on the same factors held insufficient in Mobile. [Whatever] the wisdom of Mobile, the Court's opinion cannot be reconciled persuasively with that case. There are some variances in the largely sociological evidence presented in the two cases. But Mobile held

1. Justice Stevens stated that he did not think that there could be "any doubt about the constitutionality of an amendment to the Voting Rights Act that would require Burke County and other covered jurisdictions to abandon specific kinds of at-large voting schemes that perpetuate the effects of past discrimination. [South Carolina v. Katzenbach.] It might indeed be wise policy to accelerate the transition of minority groups to a position of political power commensurate with their voting strength by amending the Act to prohibit the use of multimember districts in all cover-

that this *kind* of evidence was not enough." For example, here, as in Mobile, the trial court had failed "to identify the state officials whose intent it considered relevant."

In a more general portion of his dissent, Justice Powell doubted the Court's heavy reliance "on the capacity of the federal district courts—essentially free from any standards propounded by this Court—to determine whether at-large voting systems" are being maintained for an "invidious purpose." He elaborated: "Federal courts thus are invited to engage in deeply subjective inquiries into the motivations of local officials in structuring local governments. Inquiries of this kind not only can be 'unseemly,' see Karst, The Costs of Motive-Centered Inquiry, 15 San Diego Law Rev. 1163 (1978); they intrude the federal courts—with only the vaguest constitutional direction—into an area of intensely local and political concern." He noted Justice Stevens' argument against the Court's subjective focus, stated that he agreed "with much of what he says," but added that he could not "share his views entirely." [2]

Justice Powell could not accept Justice Stevens' solution—deeming subjective intent "irrelevant in this area." He did not join Justice Stevens' opinion because he was "unwilling to abandon" the "purposeful discrimination" principle central in such cases as Washington v. Davis. Justice Powell added: "Nonetheless, I do agree with him that what he calls 'objective' factors should be the focus of inquiry in vote-dilution cases." Unlike the factors used by the lower courts here and in Mobile, "objective" factors were "direct, reliable, and unambiguous indices of discriminatory *intent*." Requiring "primary reliance" by lower courts on such factors to establish discriminatory intent "would prevent federal court inquiries into the *subjective* thought processes of local officials—at least until enough objective evidence had been presented to warrant discovery into subjective motivations in this complex, politically charged area." He concluded: "In the absence of proof of discrimination by reliance on the kind of objective factors identified by Justice Stevens, I would hold that the factors cited by the Court of Appeals are too attenuated as a matter of law to support an inference of discriminatory intent." [*]

10th ED., p. 754; IND. RTS., p. 374
Add to footnote 5:

Note the extensive discussion of the Hunter v. Erickson principle in the majority and dissenting opinions of two 1982 decisions considering state measures to curb mandatory busing in de facto school desegregation contexts. See Washington v. Seattle School Dist. No. 1, 458 U.S. ——, and Crawford v. Los Angeles Board of Education, 458 U.S. —— (both noted below, addition to 10th Ed., p. 773; Ind. Rts., p. 393).

ed jurisdictions." But the majority ruling here was "not based on either its own conception of sound policy or any statutory command" and he could not agree with the majority's view of constitutional requirements.

2. Justice Powell stated that he was in "fundamental agreement" with what he saw as Justice Stevens' "three principles": (1) that there should be a distinction between "state action that inhibits an individual's right to vote and state action that affects the political strength of various groups"; (2) that "vote-dilution cases of this kind are difficult [to] distinguish [from] other actions to redress gerrymanders"; and (3) "that the standard used to identify unlawful racial discrimination in this area should be defined in terms that are judicially manageable and reviewable. [This] is

inherently a political area, where the identification of a seeming violation does not necessarily suggest an enforceable judicial remedy—or at least none short of a system of quotas or group representation. Any such system, of course, would be antithetical to the principles of our democracy."

* See also the discussion of the "purposeful discrimination" requirement in General Building Contractors Assn. v. Pa., 458 U.S. —— (1982), holding that 42 U.S.C. § 1981, a Thirteenth Amendment-based statute, covers only cases of intentional discrimination. Justice Marshall, joined by Justice Brennan, argued in dissent that no purposeful discrimination requirement should be read into the statute. The case is noted below, footnote * to addition to 10th Ed., p. 1057; Ind. Rts., p. 677.

10th ED., p. 773; IND. RTS., p. 393
Insert before the Note:

STATE EFFORTS TO CURB BUSING

In two 1982 cases, the Court considered state measures adopted to curb mandatory busing programs which had been designed to eliminate de facto school segregation. The 5 to 4 decision in WASHINGTON v. SEATTLE SCHOOL DIST. NO. 1, 458 U.S. —, held such a state effort unconstitutional, despite Justice Powell's vehement opinion for the dissenters. But in CRAWFORD v. LOS ANGELES BOARD OF EDUCATION, 458 U.S. —, it was Justice Powell who wrote for the majority. The 8 to 1 decision in Crawford sustained California's prohibition of court-ordered busing to alleviate de facto segregation. (Only Justice Marshall dissented in the Crawford case.) Was the Washington ruling justifiable? If so, was the California case distinguishable?

1. *Washington v. Seattle School Dist. No. 1.* The Washington case invalidated a state initiative law, (Initiative 350) adopted in response to the Seattle School District's integration plan. The Seattle Plan had been designed to eliminate "racial imbalance" in the District's schools, in part through mandatory busing.[1] Justice BLACKMUN in his opinion for the majority, relied heavily on the 1969 decision in Hunter v. Erickson (10th Ed., p. 753; Ind. Rts., p. 373), a case that involved attempts to overturn fair housing legislation in Akron, Ohio. The central principle of Hunter, in Justice Blackmun's view, was that, although "the political majority may generally restructure the political process to place obstacles in the path of everyone seeking to secure the benefits of governmental action, [a] different analysis is required when the State allocates governmental power non-neutrally, by explicitly using the *racial* nature of a decision to determine the decisionmaking process. State action of this [kind] 'places *special* burdens on racial minorities within the governmental process,' thereby 'making it *more* difficult for certain racial and religious minorities [than for other members of the community] to achieve legislation that is in their interest.' " He concluded: "Initiative 350 must fall because it does 'not attemp[t] to allocate governmental power on the basis of any general principle,' [Hunter (Harlan, J., concurring).] Instead, it uses the racial nature of an issue to define the governmental decisionmaking structure, and thus imposes substantial and unique burdens on racial minorities." [2]

---

1. Initiative 350 stated that "no school board [shall] directly or indirectly require any student to attend a school other than the school which is geographically nearest or next nearest the student's place of residence [and] which offers the course of study pursued by such student." The initiative also enumerated several broad exceptions to this prohibition. Thus, a student could be assigned beyond his neighborhood school for special educational programs, or if the nearby-schools were overcrowded or unsafe, or if they lacked necessary physical facilities. However, the initiative did not "prevent any court of competent jurisdiction from adjudicating constitutional issues relating to the public schools" and thus did *not* bar judicial orders requiring mandatory busing in order to eliminate constitutionally prohibited de jure segregation.

2. Justice Blackmun rejected the dissent's charge that, under the majori-

Justice Blackmun rejected the argument that the initiative had no racial overtones: "We find it difficult to believe that [this argument] is seriously advanced, [for] despite its facial neutrality there is little doubt that the initiative was effectively drawn for racial purposes. [It] is beyond reasonable dispute [that] the initiative was enacted ' "because of," not merely "in spite of," its adverse effects upon' busing for integration. [Feeney."] Nor did he accept the view that "busing for integration, unlike the fair housing ordinance involved in Hunter, is not a peculiarly 'racial' issue at all." [3] He conceded that "proponents of mandatory integration cannot be classified by race," but insisted that "desegregation of the public schools [at] bottom inures primarily to the benefit of the minority, and is designed for that purpose. [For] present purposes, it is enough that minorities may consider busing for integration to be 'legislation that is in their interest.' Given the racial focus of Initiative 350, this suffices to trigger application of the Hunter doctrine."

Justice Blackmun emphasized that the practical effect of Initiative 350 was to work a reallocation of power similar to the kind condemned in Hunter. He explained: "The initiative removes the authority to address a racial problem—and only a racial problem—from the existing decisionmaking body, in such a way as to burden minority interests. Those favoring the elimination of de facto school segregation now must seek relief from the state legislature or from the statewide electorate. Yet authority over all other student assignment decisions, as well as over most other areas of educational policy, remains vested in the local school board. [As] in Hunter, then, the community's political mechanisms are modified to place effective decisionmaking authority over a racial issue at a different level of government." He rejected the arguments that the initiative had "not worked *any* reallocation of power," that it amounted "to nothing more than an unexceptional example of a State's intervention in its own school system," and that, "if the State is the body that usually makes decisions in this area, Initiative 350 worked a simple change in policy rather than a forbidden reallocation of power. Cf. [Crawford]." Justice Blackmun conceded that this seemed, "at first glance," a "potent argument." But he insisted that the issue here was "not whether Washington has the authority to intervene in the affairs of local school boards; it is, rather, whether the state has exercised that authority in a manner consistent with the Equal Protection Clause." In this case, Washington, by analogy to the Hunter case, had "chosen to make use of a more complex governmental structure, and a close examination both of the Washington statutes and of the Court's decisions in related areas convinces us that Hunter is fully applicable here.' He noted, for example, that, although Washington might have made all educational decisions on a statewide basis, it had, until the passage of the chal-

ty's view, "the State's attempt to repeal a desegregation program creates a racial classification, while 'identical action' by the Seattle School Board does not": "It is the State's race-conscious restructuring of its decision-making process that is impermissible, not the simple repeal of the Seattle Plan."

3. That argument was advanced by the United States, which, as Justice Blackmun noted, had "changed its position during the course of this litigation, and now supports the State."

lenged initiative, in fact "established the local school board, rather than the State, as the entity charged with making decisions of the type at issue here." Given the State's traditional emphasis on local control of schools, "we have little difficulty concluding that Initiative 350 worked a major reordering of the State's educational decisionmaking process. [By] placing power over desegregative busing at the state level, [the initiative] plainly 'differentiates between the treatment of problems involving racial matters and that afforded other problems in the same area.' ''

Justice Blackmun conceded, quoting from Crawford, that "the simple repeal or modification of desegregation or anti-discrimination laws, without more, never has been viewed as embodying a presumptively invalid racial classification." But Initiative 350, he insisted, "works something more than the 'mere repeal' of a desegregation law by the political entity that created it. It burdens all future attempts to integrate Washington schools in districts throughout the State, by lodging decisionmaking authority over the question at a new and remote level of government. [One] group cannot be subjected to a debilitating and often insurmountable disadvantage."

Finally, Justice Blackmun rejected the argument that Hunter had been "effectively overruled by more recent decisions of this Court." The defenders of the initiative argued that "Hunter applied a simple 'disparate impact' analysis: it invalidated a facially neutral ordinance because of the law's adverse effects upon racial minorities." They therefore argued that "Hunter was swept away, along with the disparate impact approach to equal protection, in Washington v. Davis and [Arlington Heights]." Justice Blackmun insisted, however, that the notion that the "purposeful discrimination" analysis somehow conflicted with Hunter "misapprehends the basis of the Hunter doctrine": "We have not insisted on a particularized inquiry into motivation in all equal protection cases: 'A racial classification, regardless of purported motivation, is presumptively invalid and can be upheld upon an extraordinary justification.' [Feeney.] And legislation of the kind challenged in Hunter similarly falls into an inherently suspect category. There is one immediate and crucial difference between Hunter and the [purposeful discrimination cases]." Cases such as Arlington Heights involved facially neutral classifications; the Hunter provision "dealt in explicitly racial terms." Justice Blackmun added: "This does not mean, of course, that every attempt to address a racial issue gives rise to an impermissible racial classification. See [Crawford]. But when the political process or the decisionmaking mechanism used to *address* racially conscious legislation—and only such legislation —is singled out for peculiar and disadvantageous treatment, the governmental action plainly 'rests on "distinctions based on race." ' And when the State's allocation of power places unusual burdens on the ability of racial groups to enact legislation specifically designed to overcome the 'special condition' of prejudice, the governmental action seriously 'curtail[s] the operation of those political processes ordinarily to be relied upon to protect minorities.' [Carolene Products footnote.]" Hunter accordingly rested on a central principle of the Fourteenth Amendment: "the prevention of meaningful and unjustified official distinctions based on race." Thus, a state requirement that anti-discrimination laws, "and only such laws, be passed by unanimous vote of the legislature would be constitutionally suspect." So would a requirement that laws to protect racial minorities "be confirmed by popular vote of the electorate as a whole, while comparable legislation is exempted from a similar procedure. The amendment addressed in Hunter—and [the] legislation at issue here—was less obviously pernicious than are these examples, but was no different in principle." True, Washington had a large interest in its system of education, and it "could have reserved to state officials the right to make all decisions in the areas of education. [It] has chosen, however, to use a more elaborate system; having done so, the State is obligated to operate that system within the confines of the Fourteenth Amendment. That, we believe, it has failed to do."

In dissenting, Justice POWELL, joined by Chief Justice Burger and Justices Rehnquist and O'Connor, objected to "the Court's unprecedented intrusion into the structure of a state government. The School Districts in this case were under no Federal Constitutional obligation to adopt mandatory busing programs. The [State], the governmental body ultimately responsible for the provision of public education, has determined that certain mandatory busing programs are detrimental to the education of its children. In my view, [the Fourteenth Amendment leaves the States] free to decide matters of concern to the State at the State, rather than local, level of government."

Justice Powell emphasized that there is no federal constitutional duty "to adopt mandatory busing in the absence of [unconstitutional, de jure segregation]." Thus, "a neighborhood school policy and a decision not to assign students on the basis of their race does not offend the Fourteenth Amendment."[4] Moreover, the Constitution does not "dictate to the States a particular division of authority [between] state and local governing bodies." He noted that the school district itself constitutionally could have cancelled its integration program at any time, "yet this Court holds that neither the legislature nor the people of the State of Washington could alter what the District had decided. [It] is a strange notion [that] local governmental bodies can forever preempt the ability of a State—the sovereign power—to address a matter of compelling concern to the State. The Constitution [does] not require such a bizarre result."[5]

4. "[Indeed], in the absence of a finding of segregation by the School District, mandatory busing on the basis of race raises constitutional difficulties of its own. Extensive pupil transportation may threaten liberty or privacy interests. See [Bakke (Powell opinion); Keyes (Powell opinion)]. Moreover, when a State or school board assigns students on the basis of their race, it acts on the basis of a racial classification, and we have consistently held that '[a] racial classification, regardless of purported motivation, is presumptively invalid and can be upheld only upon an extraordinary justification.' [Feeney.]" [Footnote by Justice Powell.]

5. In a footnote, Justice Powell stated: "The policies in support of neighborhood schooling are various but all of them are racially neutral. The people of the State legitimately could decide that unlimited mandatory busing places too great a burden on the liberty and privacy interests of families and students of all races. It might decide that the reassignment of students to distant schools, on the basis of race, was too great a departure from the ideal of racial neutrality in State action. And, in light of the experience with mandatory busing in other cities, the State might conclude that such a program ultimately would lead to greater racial imbalance in the schools."

The Hunter decision, so heavily relied upon by the majority, was deemed "simply irrelevant" by Justice Powell. The Washington initiative "simply does not place unique political obstacles in the way of racial minorities. In this case, unlike in Hunter, the political system has *not* been redrawn or altered. The authority of the State over the public school system [is] plenary. Thus, the State's political system is not altered when it adopts for the first time a policy, concededly within the area of its authority, for the regulation of local school districts. And certainly racial minorities are not uniquely or comparatively burdened by the State's adoption of a policy that would be lawful if adopted by any School District in the State. [Under the Court's] unprecedented theory of a vested constitutional right to local decisionmaking, the State apparently is now forever barred from addressing the perplexing problems of how best to educate fairly *all* children in a multiracial society where, as in this case, the local school board has acted first." [6] He added: "[This decision] deprives the State of Washington of all opportunity to address the unresolved questions resulting from extensive mandatory busing." [7]

2. *Crawford v. Los Angeles Board of Education.* In Crawford, the majority rejected an attack on a California constitutional amendment (Proposition I) designed to conform the state courts' power to order busing to that exercised by the federal courts under the Fourteenth Amendment.[1] The amendment to the California Constitution provided that state courts could not order mandatory pupil assignment or transportation unless a federal court would do so to remedy a violation of the federal Equal Protection Clause.[2]

6. "Even accepting the dubious notion that a State must demonstrate some past control over public schooling or race relations before now intervening in these matters, the Court's attempt to demonstrate that Initiative 350 represents a unique thrust by the State into these areas is unpersuasive. The Court's own discussion indicates the comprehensive character of the State's activity. [In] light of the wide range of regulation of the public schools by the State, it is wholly unclear what degree of prior concern or control by the State would satisfy the Court's new doctrine. . . ." [Footnote by Justice Powell.]

7. "[The Court] does say that '[i]t is the State's race-conscious restructuring of its decisionmaking process that is impermissible, not the simple repeal of the Seattle Plan.' Apparently the Court is saying that, despite what else may be said in its opinion, the people of the State—or the State legislature —may repeal the *Seattle plan*, even though neither the people nor the legislature validly may prescribe statewide standards. I perceive no logic in —and certainly no constitutional basis for—a distinction between repealing the Seattle plan of mandatory busing

and establishing a statewide policy to the same effect. The people of a State have far greater interest in the general problems associated with compelled busing for the purpose of integration than in the plan of a single school board." [Footnote by Justice Powell.]

1. Proposition I was ratified by the California voters in 1979. Prior to the adoption of the constitutional amendment, the California courts (relying on their interpretation of the state constitution's equal protection provision) had ordered busing in cases of de facto, not only de jure, segregation.

2. The amendment, enacted as a proviso to the California Constitution's due process and equal protection provisions, states: "[N]o court of this state may impose upon the State of California or any public entity, board, or official any obligation or responsibility with respect to the use of pupil school assignment or pupil transportation, (1) except to remedy a specific violation by such party that would also constitute a violation of the Equal Protection Clause of the 14th Amendment to the United States Constitution and (2)

In L.A. Busing was ordered by state courts under Calif = just law which permitted busing in both de facto and de jure situation.

The California amendment was adopted in the midst of controversy over court-ordered mandatory busing in Los Angeles. That state trial court's busing order had been affirmed by the California Supreme Court on the basis of an interpretation of the equal protection provision of the California Constitution which barred de facto, not merely de jure, school segregation.[3]

In writing the majority opinion which rejected the Fourteenth Amendment attack on the state constitutional amendment, Justice POWELL disagreed with the challengers' contention that "once a State chooses to do 'more' than the Fourteenth Amendment requires, it may never recede. We reject an interpretation of the Fourteenth Amendment so destructive of a state's democratic processes and of its ability to experiment. This interpretation has no support in the decisions of this Court." He thought it would be "paradoxical" to conclude that California, by adopting federal equal protection standards that provided for mandatory busing, had thereby violated the Fourteenth Amendment.[4]

Justice Powell rejected the challengers' claim that Proposition I employed an "explicit racial classification" and imposed a "race-specific" burden on minorities seeking to vindicate state-created rights. The claim was that, by limiting the power of state courts to enforce the state-created right to desegregated schools in de facto segregation situations, Proposition I created a "dual court system" which discriminated on the basis of race. The challengers emphasized that "other state created rights may be vindicated by the state courts without limitation on remedies." But Justice Powell insisted that Proposition I did not "embody a racial classification":[5] "It neither says nor implies that persons are to be treated differently on account of their race. [The] benefit it seeks to confer—neighborhood schooling—is made available regardless of race in the discretion of school boards. Indeed, even if Proposition I had a racially discriminatory effect, in view of the demographic mix of the [Los Angeles] District it is not clear which race or races would be affect-

Calif Am. "did not embody a racial classification"

3. Before the enactment of Proposition I, the California Supreme Court's reading of the state equal protection provision was that "school boards [bear] a constitutional obligation to take reasonable steps to alleviate segregation in the public schools, whether the segregation be de facto or de jure in origin."

4. Justice Powell noted that, "even after Proposition I, the California Constitution still imposes a greater duty of desegregation than does the Federal Constitution. The state courts [continue] to have an obligation under state law to order segregated school districts to use voluntary desegrega-

unless a federal court would be permitted under federal decisional law to impose that obligation or responsibility upon such party to remedy the specific violation of the Equal Protection Clause. . . ."

tion techniques, whether or not there has been a finding of intentional segregation. The school districts themselves retain a state law obligation to take reasonably feasible steps to desegregate, and they remain free to adopt reassignment and busing plans to effectuate desegregation." He added: "In this respect this case differs from the situation presented in [Washington]."

5. Justice Powell noted that, in Hunter v. Erickson, the Court had found that, although the law was neutral on its face, "the reality [was] that the law's impact [fell] on the minority." Justice Powell added: "In light of this reality and the distortion of the political process worked by the charter amendment [in Hunter], the Court considered that the amendment employed a racial classification despite its facial neutrality."

ed the most or in what way." (White students are in a minority in the Los Angeles school district.) Moreover, "discriminatory purpose" was necessary to show a Fourteenth Amendment violation. He added that "the simple repeal or modification of desegregation or anti-discrimination laws, without more, never has been viewed as embodying a presumptively valid racial classification." [6]

The challengers' central argument, however, was that Proposition I was not a "mere repeal" but rather was invalid under Hunter. Justice Powell replied: "We do not view Hunter as controlling here, nor are we persuaded by [the] characterization of Proposition I as something more than a mere repeal." Proposition I was less than a "repeal" of the California equal protection provision, since the California Constitution still placed upon school boards "a greater duty to desegregate than does the Fourteenth Amendment." Nor did Proposition I "distor[t] the political process for racial reasons" or "allocat[e] governmental or judicial power on the basis of a discriminatory principle. [Remedies] appropriate in one area of legislation may not be desirable in another. [A] 'dual court system'—one for the racial majority and one for the racial minority—is not established simply because civil rights remedies are different from those available in other areas. [In short], having gone beyond the requirements of the Federal Constitution, the State was free to return in part to the standard prevailing generally throughout the United States."

Finally, Justice Powell, like the California appellate court, rejected the challengers' claim that "Proposition I, if facially valid, was nonetheless unconstitutional because enacted with a discriminatory purpose." The state court had found that the voters might have been motivated by the amendment's stated purposes, "chief among them the educational benefits of neighborhood schooling," and that they might also have considered "that the extent of mandatory busing, authorized by state law, actually was aggravating rather than ameliorating the desegregation problem." The state court characterized the challengers' "claim of discriminatory intent on the part of millions of voters as but 'pure speculation.'" Justice Powell saw "no reason to differ with the conclusions of the state appellate court," pointing by analogy to the Court's deference to a state court's identification of discriminatory purpose in Reitman v. Mulkey. "Even if we could assume that Proposition I had a disproportionate, adverse affect on racial minorities, we see no reason to challenge the [state appellate court's] conclusion that the voters of the State were not motivated by a discriminatory purpose." [7]

6. "Of course, if the purpose of repealing legislation is to disadvantage a racial minority, the repeal is unconstitutional for this reason. See Reitman v. Mulkey [1967; printed at 10th Ed., p. 1015; Ind. Rts., p. 635.]" [Footnote by Justice Powell.]

7. A concurring opinion by Justice BLACKMUN, joined by Justice Brennan, supported Justice Powell's opinion and emphasized the "critical distinctions" between this case and

Washington. In Crawford, by contrast to Washington, there had been no restructuring of the state's decisionmaking process: "State courts do not create the rights they enforce; those rights originate elsewhere—in the state legislature, in the State's political subdivisions, or in the state constitution itself. When one of those rights is repealed, and therefore is rendered unenforceable in the courts, that action hardly can be said to restructure the State's decisionmaking

Justice MARSHALL, the sole dissenter, insisted at length that this case was indistinguishable from the companion Washington one. Both cases challenged state provisions "admittedly designed to substantially curtail, if not eliminate, the use of mandatory student assignment or transportation as a remedy for de facto segregation. [Because] I fail to see how a fundamental redefinition of the governmental decisionmaking structure with respect to the same racial issue can be unconstitutional when the state seeks to remove the authority from local school boards, yet constitutional when the state attempts to achieve the same result by limiting the power of its courts, I must dissent." He insisted that Hunter governed here as in the Washington case. The principles of Hunter and Washington, he claimed, led to the conclusion that Proposition I "works an unconstitutional reallocation of state power by depriving California courts of the ability to grant meaningful relief to those seeking to vindicate the state's guarantee against de facto segregation in the public schools." He thought Proposition I was sufficiently "racial" to invoke the Hunter doctrine because "minorities may consider busing for integration to be 'legislation that is in their interest'" [quoting the Washington opinion]. He noted that, after the adoption of Proposition I, "the only method of enforcing against a recalcitrant school board the state constitutional duty to eliminate racial isolation is to petition either the state legislature or the electorate as a whole. Clearly, the rules of the game have been significantly changed for those attempting to vindicate this constitutional right."

Justice Marshall insisted, moreover, that Proposition I was not a "mere repeal" within the meaning of any of the prior decisions. He argued that the only time that the Court had held that a "mere repeal" was not unconstitutional was in the Dayton school case (10th Ed., p. 776; Ind. Rts., p. 396), "a situation where a governmental entity rescinded its own prior statement of policy without affecting any existing educational policy." By contrast, in the three cases in which the Court had rejected "mere repeal" defenses—the Washington, Reitman v. Mulkey and Hunter decisions—"the alleged rescission was accomplished by a governmental entity other than the entity that had taken the initial action, and resulted in a drastic alteration of the substantive effect of existing policy. This case falls squarely within this latter category. [Proposition I] has placed an enormous barrier between minority children and the effective enjoyment of their constitutional rights, a barrier that is not placed in the path of those who seek to vindicate other rights granted by state law. [Certainly], Hunter and [Washington] cannot be distinguished on the ground that they concerned the reallocation of legislative power, whereas Proposition I redistributes the inherent power of a court to tailor the remedy to the violation. [Indeed], Proposition I, by denying full access to the only branch of government that has been willing to address this issue meaningfully, is far worse for those seeking to vindicate the plainly unpopular cause of

mechanism. While the California electorate may have made it more difficult to achieve desegregation when it enacted Proposition I, to my mind it did so not by working a structural change in the political *process* so much as by simply repealing the right to invoke a judicial busing remedy. Indeed, ruling for the [challengers] on a Hunter theory seemingly would mean that statutory affirmative action or antidiscrimination programs never could be repealed." Justice Blackmun also noted that the "political mechanisms that create and repeal the rights ultimately enforced by the courts were left entirely unaffected by Proposition I."

racial integration in the public schools than a simple reallocation of an often unavailable and unresponsive legislative process." [8]

8. Justice Marshall also criticized the majority's deference to the state appellate court on the issue of discriminatory purpose. He argued that the state court had rejected the discriminatory intent argument "[d]espite the absence of *any* factual record on this issue." Yet "this Court, in its haste to uphold the banner of 'neighborhood schools,' affirms a factual determination that was never made. Such blind allegiance to the conclusory statements of a lower court is plainly forbidden by our prior decisions." He thought the majority's reliance on Reitman v. Mulkey was "misplaced" because no factual findings had been made by the state court in this case.

10th ED., p. 774; IND. RTS., p. 394
Add to the Note (before Keyes):

Anti-busing proposals in Congress, 1981–83. Anti-busing proposals reemerged in Congress early in 1981. Supporters of efforts to curb busing were encouraged by the more conservative composition of Congress and by the Reagan Administration's anti-busing position. The most widely discussed proposal followed the pattern of the 1970s: the addition of anti-busing riders to funding bills. The House and the Senate both adopted anti-busing amendments to Justice Department spending authorization bills in 1981. The riders would have prevented the Department from bringing any lawsuit that could "directly or indirectly" lead to busing. On June 9, 1981, the House adopted Congressman Collins' anti-busing amendment by a better than 2 to 1 margin. On June 19, the Senate turned down Senator Weicker's effort to soften a similar rider proposed by Senator Helms. (President Reagan said he would sign legislation containing such a rider if it was finally enacted by Congress. No legislation containing such a rider, however, was finally enacted by the 97th Congress. In 1980, President Carter had vetoed bills that contained such riders.)

In the course of Senate debate on the 1981 rider, Senator Johnston of Louisiana proposed an anti-busing amendment that rested on a different, broader approach. Instead of simply curbing executive action to achieve busing, he relied on congressional power under § 5 of the Fourteenth Amendment as interpreted in Katzenbach v. Morgan. (See Sec. 4 of the next chapter.) The Johnston Amendment, known as the Neighborhood School Act, would have barred the courts from ordering busing in school cases except in narrowly defined circumstances. In most cases, the amendment would have prevented any federal court from ordering a student to be assigned or bused to a public school other than the one closest to the student's home. Exempted was busing "incident to the voluntary attendance of a student at a public school, including a magnet, vocational, technical or other school of specialized or individualized instruction." In defending his proposal, Senator Johnston argued that "it is time to recognize that [court-ordered busing] has not worked." (In addition to these proposals, congressional committees also had under consideration bills to curb federal courts jurisdiction in a number of controversial areas, including busing. None of the jurisdiction-limiting proposals were enacted into law during the 97th Congress. See addition to 10th Ed. and Ind.Rts., p. 57, above.)

The Johnston Amendment was adopted by the Senate in a 57–37 vote in March, 1982, but the House failed to act on it before the 97th Congress adjourned. Was it justifiable under the Morgan power? (The Johnston proposal rested not only on § 5 of the Fourteenth Amendment but also on the congressional power, under Art. III, § 1, pertaining to the jurisdiction of the lower federal courts. That aspect of the bill is noted further above, addition to 10th Ed. and Ind.Rts. p. 57.) *

Attempts to prohibit busing by amending the Constitution have continued. One proposed amendment that would prohibit any United States court from requiring "that any person be assigned to, or excluded from, any school on the basis of race, religion, or national origin" never emerged from committee in the 97th Congress. It was reintroduced (and again referred to committee) at the beginning of the 98th Congress. The proposed amendment rejected on the House floor in July 1979 was also reintroduced at the beginning of the 98th Congress and referred to Committee. No action appears likely on either proposal as of June 1983.

The two other anti-busing proposals pending in the 98th Congress attempt to curb school busing by statutorily limiting the jurisdiction of the federal courts. H.R.158, introduced by Congressman Hansen of Idaho,

* Just before adopting the Johnston proposal, the Senate turned down an alternative anti-busing bill sponsored by Senator Gorton, Republican of Washington. Senator Gorton's proposal, unlike the Johnston one, rested exclusively on the remedial power of Congress under § 5 of the Fourteenth Amendment. Moreover, the Gorton proposal specifically recognized the right, acknowledged by the Court ever since Brown v. Board of Education, to be free from de jure segregated schools. Senator Gorton's approach was to deal more directly with the problem of providing remedies for that constitutionally recognized right, in the exercise of congressional remedial power, and to avoid tampering with lower federal court jurisdiction. Was the Gorton approach on more solid constitutional footing than the Johnston one? Can the Court decisions regarding busing be viewed as delineations of "remedies" rather than creation of "rights"? (See the extensive constitutional discussion about the contending approaches in the Congressional Record for February 23, 1982, pp. S 955 et seq.)

Consider Attorney General Smith's letter of May 6, 1982, to Congressman Rodino, endorsing the constitutionality of S. 951, both on grounds of Art. III, § 1, as noted above (addition to 10th Ed. and Ind. Rts., p. 60), and (somewhat ambivalently and ambiguously) under § 5 of the Fourteenth Amendment. With respect to the latter, the Attorney General stated: "The limitation on busing remedies contained in the Neighborhood School Act would be authorized under § 5 to the extent that it does not prevent the inferior federal courts from adequately vindicating constitutional rights." He argued that under the Morgan case, the courts "would probably pay considerable deference to the congressional factfinding upon which the bill is ultimately based," although he conceded that there apparently was "no particularized research [presented] to the Senate which might have supported or undermined the specific limitations on federal court decrees." In his view, the Act would not be "interpreted to 'dilute' Fourteenth Amendment rights merely because it denies a certain form of relief in the inferior federal courts." He added, however, that, "although Congress can express its view through factfinding [that] busing is an ineffective remedial tool and that extensive busing is not necessary to remedy a constitutional violation, it is ultimately the responsibility of the courts to determine, after giving due consideration to the congressional findings, [whether] in a given case an effective remedy requires the use of mandatory busing in excess of the limitations set forth in [the bill]." [The Attorney General's concession that Congress could not, under § 5 of the Fourteenth Amendment, bar inferior federal courts from ordering mandatory busing when, in the judgment of the courts, "such busing is necessary to remedy a constitutional violation" apparently led him to rely with greater confidence on Art. III, § 1, the congressional power over lower federal court jurisdiction, as the ultimate constitutional support for the Neighborhood School Act.]

provides simply that "no court of the United States shall have jurisdiction to require the attendance at a particular school of any student because of race, color, creed, or sex." S.139, a bill to "provide for civil rights in public schools," was introduced by Senators Hatch and Thurmond. It provides that no lower federal court shall have jurisdiction to order the assignment or transportation to any public school, or the exclusion from any public school, of any student on the basis of race, color, or national origin. Any individual or school authority currently subject to a busing order is entitled to relief from that order unless four conditions are met— intentionally discriminatory pupil assignments would continue absent the original order; the totality of circumstances has not changed since the original order was entered; no other remedy would preclude the segregation; and the benefits of the order have clearly outweighed the costs. No action for relief from a busing order brought in state court could be removed to a federal court. S.139 relies on Congress' power under Art. III, § 1 and § 5 of the Fourteenth Amendment. (For a discussion of congressional power to limit lower federal court jurisdiction under Art. III, § 1, see 10th Ed. and Ind.Rts., p. 57 and addition to 10th Ed. and Ind. Rts., p. 57. Congressional power under § 5 of the Fourteenth Amendment is discussed in Sec. 4 of the next chapter.) S.139 is identical to a bill that was never reported out of the Senate Judiciary Committee in the 97th Congress, and it is unlikely that S.139 will be reported out in the 98th. H.R.158 currently has the same bleak prospects in the House Committee on the Judiciary.

10th ED., p. 801; IND. RTS., p. 421
Add as a footnote at the end of Wengler:

Note also the Justices' discussion of Kahn v. Shevin, Wengler, and other cases involving "benign" justifications for gender classifications, in Michael M. v. Superior Court, 450 U.S. 464 (1981) (printed below, as addition to 10th Ed., p. 885; Ind.Rts., p. 505). In Michael M., the Court rejected an equal protection challenge to California's statutory rape law, a law which makes men alone criminally liable. Note also the Court's forceful rejection of a "benign, compensatory" justification in striking down a state university's exclusion of a male from its all-female School of Nursing, in Mississippi University for Women v. Hogan, 458 U.S. —— (1982) (fully noted below, addition to 10th Ed., p. 884; Ind. Rts., p. 504).

10th ED., p. 862; IND. RTS., p. 482
Add to footnote * :

The Court managed to avoid decision on the merits in both Johnson and Minnick, the cases that had been expected to clarify the meaning of Fullilove. Johnson v. Chicago Bd. of Ed., 449 U.S. 915 (1981), the case challenging a school desegregation plan placing a ceiling on the percentage of minority enrollments, was remanded to the Court of Appeals "for further consideration in light of the subsequent developments described in the suggestion of mootness filed by respondents." (The parties had tentatively agreed on a revised plan in a related case after the Court had set this case for review.) The Johnson case reached the Court once more a year later; and, once again, the Court failed to reach the merits. In a 5 to 3 per curiam ruling, 457 U.S. 52 (1982), the majority, while agreeing with the lower court that the controversy was not moot, once again remanded so that Johnson could be consolidated with the related case, in order that a "complete factual record" could be developed. Justice Brennan voted to grant review and hear oral argument. Justice Rehnquist, joined by Justice Marshall, objected to the majority's failure to give adequate reasons for remanding the case.

Minnick v. Dept. of Corrections, 452 U.S. 105 (1981), the case challenging California's affirmative action plan for prison employees, evoked a fuller explanation from the Court. Justice Stevens' majority opinion dismissed the writ of certiorari on the ground that the state appellate court decision under review was not "final" in the sense of the jurisdictional statute. This conclusion was heavily influenced by "significant ambiguities in the record" concerning both the extent to which race and sex had been used in promotions and the State's justifications for the program. The Court noted, moreover, that there had been "significant developments" in the law: the trial court proceedings in Minnick had taken place before the Court's decision in Bakke. The majority accordingly decided "that we should not address the constitutional issues until the proceedings of the trial court are finally concluded and the state's appellate courts have completed their review of the trial court record." Justice Brennan concurred in the judgment.

Justice Stewart was the only one to reach the merits. He dissented, insisting that the State had unconstitutionally considered "a person's race in making promotion decisions." He quoted from his dissent in Fullilove and added: "So far as the Constitution goes, a private person may engage in any racial discrimination he wants [cf. Weber], but under the Equal Protection Clause, [a] sovereign State may never do so. [At this point, he added in a footnote: "It is self-evident folly to suppose that a person's race may constitutionally be taken into account, but that it must not be controlling."] And it is wholly irrelevant whether the State gives a 'plus' or 'minus' value to a person's race, whether the discrimination occurs in the decision to hire or fire or promote, or whether the discrimination is called 'affirmative action' or by some less euphemistic term." (In a separate notation, Justice Rehnquist agreed with the majority but stated: "If I viewed [the state court judgment] as 'final,' [I] would join the dissenting opinion of Justice Stewart.")

10th ED., p. 882; IND.RTS., p. 502
Add to footnote 3:

In Lehr v. Robertson, 463 U.S. —— (1983), the Court reiterated that an unwed father must demonstrate "a full commitment to the responsibilities of parenthood before his interest in personal contact with his child acquires substantial protection under the due process [and equal protection clauses.]" The father had argued that his child's adoption was invalid because he had neither received notice of the proceedings nor been given an opportunity to be heard. He also argued that the governing New York statute invidiously discriminated between the sexes by giving an unwed mother an absolute right to veto an adoption, but requiring that a putative father affirmatively come forward to demonstrate his commitment. In rejecting these claims, the Court held that because the father had previously "not come forward to participate in the rearing of the child," the due process clause protected only his opportunity to form a father-child relationship. And in rejecting the equal protection claim the Court concluded that where one parent has established a relationship with the child and the "other parent has either abandoned or never established a relationship, [a state is not prevented from] according the two parents different legal rights."

10th ED., p. 884; IND. RTS., p. 504
Insert after Note 2:

RECENT DEVELOPMENTS ON SEX DISCRIMINATION

In the Kirchberg case in 1981, below, the Court struck down a now superseded provision of Louisiana's community property law that gave a husband the unilateral right to dispose of jointly owned community property without his spouse's consent. On the same day, in the Michael M. case (the principal case that follows), the Court rejected an equal protection challenge to California's statutory rape law, a law which makes men alone criminally liable. In Kirchberg, the Court once again reiterated the "intermediate scrutiny" standard of Craig v. Boren. In the prevailing opinions in Michael M., by contrast, the references to Craig v. Boren seem considerably less emphatic and crisp. (Note also the decision two months later in Rostker v. Goldberg, upholding male-only draft registration. Rostker v. Goldberg is printed below, following Michael M. But see the 1982 decision in Mississippi University for Women v. Hogan, the last in the series

of cases in this section.) In examining these sex discrimination developments, consider whether the majority is retreating from the level of scrutiny
developed in the late 1970s.

KIRCHBERG v. FEENSTRA, 450 U.S. 455 (1981): Appellee Feenstra's husband executed a mortgage on the Feenstras' home as security on a
promissory note. He did not inform his wife of the mortgage, and her consent was not required because the law in effect at the time (1974) gave the
husband, as "head and master" of property jointly owned with his wife, exclusive control over its disposition. Justice MARSHALL delivered the
opinion of the Court. He approvingly recounted the Court of Appeals'
invalidation of Louisiana's old provision: "Because this provision explicitly discriminated on the basis of gender, the Court of Appeals properly inquired whether the provision was substantially related to the achievement of an important governmental objective. See, e.g., [Wengler;
Craig v. Boren]. The court noted that the State had advanced only one
justification for the provision—that '[one] of the two spouses has to
be designated as the manager of the community.' The court agreed that
the State had an interest in defining the manner in which community
property was to be managed, but found that the State had failed to show
why the mandatory designation of the husband as manager of the property
was necessary to further that interest." (The Court of Appeals limited its
ruling to prospective application only, in order to avoid "substantial hardship
with respect to property rights and obligations within the State of Louisiana.")

In affirming the judgment, Justice Marshall commented that the challenged provision "clearly embodies the type of express gender-based discrimination that we have found unconstitutional absent a showing that the classification is tailored to further an important governmental interest." He continued: "In defending the constitutionality [of the provision, the appellant]
does not claim that the provision serves any such interest.[1] Instead, appellant
attempts to distinguish this Court's decisions in cases such as Craig v. Boren
and Orr v. Orr [by] arguing that appellee Feenstra, as opposed to the disadvantaged individuals in those cases, could have taken steps to avoid the discriminatory impact of [the provision]." Under Louisiana law in effect in
1974, Mrs. Feenstra could have made a "declaration by authentic act" prohibiting her husband from executing a mortgage on her home without her consent. Appellant accordingly argued that Mrs. Feenstra, by failing to take advantage of this procedure, had become the "architect of her own predica-
ment" and therefore could not complain about the provision. But Justice
Marshall curtly dismissed this argument, admonishing that "appellant over-

1. Justice Marshall added in a footnote:
"Nor will this Court speculate about the
existence of such a justification.
'The burden [is] on those defending
the discrimination to make out the
claimed justification.' [Wengler.]
We note, however, that the failure of
the State to appeal from the decision
of the Court of Appeals, and the decision of the Louisiana legislature to
replace [the provision] with a gender-
neutral statute, suggest that appellant
would be hard-pressed to show that
the challenged provision substantially
furthered an important governmental
interest." [Louisiana's revision of its
community property law provides that
real property could not be encumbered
without the concurrence of both
spouses. However, the revision did
not take effect until 1980 and thus did
not apply to Mr. Feenstra's 1974 mortgage.]

looks the critical question: whether [the provision] substantially furthers an important government interest. [T]he 'absence of an insurmountable barrier' will not redeem an otherwise unconstitutionally discriminatory law. Trimble v. Gordon [in the next section of this chapter]. Instead, the burden remains on the party seeking to uphold a statute that expressly discriminates on the basis of sex to advance an 'exceedingly persuasive justification' for the challenged classification. [Feeney.]" Here, such a justification was lacking, so that the law was unconstitutional.[2]

Statute upheld

Challenge to Calif. Statutory making males criminally liable for sexual intercourse w females <18; vise versa but not

MICHAEL M. v. SUPERIOR COURT

450 U.S. 464, 101 S.Ct. 1200, 67 L.Ed.2d 437 (1981).

Justice REHNQUIST announced the judgment of the Court and delivered an opinion in which the Chief Justice [BURGER], Justice STEWART, and Justice POWELL joined.

17½ year old male charged under law with 16½ year female

The question presented in this case is whether California's "statutory rape" law, § 261.5 of the California Penal Code, violates the Equal Protection Clause. [The section] defines unlawful sexual intercourse as "an act of sexual intercourse accomplished with a female not the wife of the perpetrator, where the female is under the age of 18 years." The statute thus makes men alone criminally liable for the act of sexual intercourse.

Calif. courts applied scrutiny "strict" held The but based on gender justification valid

In July 1978, a complaint was filed in the Municipal Court of Sonoma County, Cal., alleging that petitioner, then a 17½ year old male, had had unlawful sexual intercourse with a female under the age of 18, in violation of § 261.5. The evidence adduced at a preliminary hearing showed that at approximately midnight on June 3, 1978, petitioner and two friends approached Sharon, a 16½ year old female, and her sister as they waited at a bus stop. Petitioner and Sharon, who had already been drinking, moved away from the others and began to kiss. After being struck in the face for rebuffing petitioner's initial advances, Sharon submitted to sexual intercourse with petitioner. [The lower state courts rejected petitioner's gender-discrimination challenge to the charge. The California Supreme Court applied "strict scrutiny," but nevertheless held the gender classification justified.]

Court discusses tests:

not inherently suspect thus not subjected not "strict to "strict scrutiny"

As is evident from our opinions, the Court has had some difficulty in agreeing upon the proper approach and analysis in cases involving challenges to gender-based classifications. [Unlike] the California Supreme Court, we have not held that gender-based classifications are "inherently suspect" and thus we do not apply so-called "strict scrutiny" to those classifications. Our cases have held, however, that the traditional minimum rationality test takes on a somewhat "sharper focus" when gender-based classifications are challenged. See Craig v. Boren (1976) (Powell, J., concurring). In Reed v. Reed, for example, the Court stated that a gender-based classification will be

2. Justice STEWART, joined by Justice Rehnquist, concurred only in the result, stating: "Since men and women were similarly situated for all relevant purposes with respect to the management and dispositon of community property, I agree that [the provision] violated the Equal Protection Clause."

but "sharper focus" substantial to impt gov function
Relnship

Craig v Boren:

upheld if it bears a "fair and substantial relationship" to legitimate state ends, while in Craig v. Boren, the Court restated the test to require the classification to bear a "substantial relationship" to "important governmental objectives."

Underlying these decisions is the principle that a legislature may not "make overbroad generalizations based on sex which are entirely unrelated to any differences between men and women or which demean the ability or social status of the affected class." But because the Equal Protection Clause does not "demand that a statute necessarily apply equally to all persons" or require "things which are different in fact [to] be treated in law as though they were the same" [Rinaldi v. Yeager], this Court has consistently upheld statutes where the gender classification is not invidious, but rather realistically reflects the fact that the sexes are not similarly situated in certain circumstances. Parham v. Hughes; Califano v. Webster; Schlesinger v. Ballard; Kahn v. Shevin. As the Court has stated, a legislature may "provide for the special problems of women." Weinberger v. Wiesenfeld.

Applying those principles to this case, the fact that the California Legislature criminalized the act of illicit sexual intercourse with a minor female is a sure indication of its intent or purpose to discourage that conduct. Precisely why the legislature desired that result is of course somewhat less clear. This Court has long recognized that "inquiries into congressional motives or purposes are a hazardous matter" [e.g., Palmer v. Thompson], and the search for the "actual" or "primary" purpose of a statute is likely to be elusive. [E.g., Arlington Heights.] Here, for example, the individual legislators may have voted for the statute for a variety of reasons. Some legislators may have been concerned about teenage pregnancies, others about protecting young females from physical injury or from the loss of "chastity," and still others about promoting various religious and moral attitudes towards premarital sex.

Calif's justification for law? to prevent illegitimate teenage pregnancies

The justification for the statute offered by the State, and accepted by the Supreme Court of California, is that the legislature sought to prevent illegitimate teenage pregnancies. That finding, of course, is entitled to great deference. Reitman v. Mulkey. And although our cases establish that the State's asserted reason for the enactment of a statute may be rejected, "if it could not have been a goal of the legislation," Weinberger v. Wiesenfeld, this is not such a case.

We are satisfied not only that the prevention of illegitimate pregnancy is at least one of the "purposes" of the statute, but that the State has a strong interest in preventing such pregnancy. At the risk of stating the obvious, teenage pregnancies, which have increased dramatically over the last two decades,[1] have significant social, medical and economic consequences for both the mother and her child, and the State.[2] Of particular concern to the State

---

1. In 1976 approximately one million 15–19 year olds became pregnant, one-tenth of all women in that age group. Two-thirds of the pregnancies were illegitimate. Illegitimacy rates for teenagers (births per 1,000 unmarried females) increased 75% for 14–17 year olds between 1961 and 1974 and 33% for 18–19 year olds. [Footnote by Justice Rehnquist.]

2. The risk of maternal death is 60% higher for a teenager under the age of 15 than for a woman in her early twenties. The risk is 13% higher for 15–19 year olds. The statistics fur-

is that approximately half of all teenage pregnancies end in abortion.[3] And of those children who are born, their illegitimacy makes them likely candidates to become wards of the State.[4]

We need not be medical doctors to discern that young men and young women are not similarly situated with respect to the problems and the risks of sexual intercourse. Only women may become pregnant and they suffer disproportionately the profound physical, emotional, and psychological consequences of sexual activity. The statute at issue here protects women from sexual intercourse at an age when those consequences are particularly severe.[5]

The question thus boils down to whether a State may attack the problem of sexual intercourse and teenage pregnancy directly by prohibiting a male from having sexual intercourse with a minor female.[6] We hold that such a statute is sufficiently related to the State's objectives to pass constitutional muster.

Because virtually all of the significant harmful and inescapably identifiable consequences of teenage pregnancy fall on the young female, a legislature

ther show that most teenage mothers drop out of school and face a bleak economic future. [Footnote by Justice Rehnquist.]

3. This is because teenagers are disproportionately likely to seek abortions. . . . [Footnote by Justice Rehnquist.]

4. The policy and intent of the California Legislature evinced in other legislation buttresses our view that the prevention of teenage pregnancy is a purpose of the statute. The preamble to the "Maternity Care for Minors Act," for example, states "The legislature recognizes that pregnancy among unmarried persons under 21 years of age constitutes an increasing social problem in California."

Subsequent to the decision below, the California Legislature considered and rejected proposals to render § 261.5 gender neutral, thereby ratifying the judgment of the California Supreme Court. That is enough to answer petitioner's contention that the statute was the "accidental by-product of a traditional way of thinking about women." Certainly this decision of the California Legislature is as good a source as is this Court in deciding what is "current" and what is "outmoded" in the perception of women. [Footnote by Justice Rehnquist.]

5. Although petitioner concedes that the State has a "compelling" interest in preventing teenage pregnancy, he contends that the "true" purpose of § 261.5 is to protect the virtue and chastity of young women. As such, the statute is unjustifiable because it rests on archaic stereotypes. What we have said above is enough to dispose of that contention. The question for us—and the only question under the Federal Constitution—is whether the legislation violates the Equal Protection Clause of the Fourteenth Amendment, not whether its supporters may have endorsed it for reasons no longer generally accepted. Even if the preservation of female chastity were one of the motives of the statute, and even if that motive be impermissible, petitioner's argument must fail because "it is a familiar practice of constitutional law that this Court will not strike down an otherwise constitutional statute on the basis of an allegedly illicit legislative motive." . . . [Footnote by Justice Rehnquist.]

6. We do not understand petitioner to question a state's authority to make sexual intercourse among teenagers a criminal act, at least on a gender-neutral basis. In Carey v. Population Services International (Brennan, J., plurality), four Members of the Court assumed for the purposes of that case that a State may regulate the sexual behavior of minors, while four other Members of the Court more emphatically stated that such regulation would be permissible. The Court has long recognized that a State has even broader authority to protect the physical, mental, and moral well-being of its youth than of its adults. [Footnote by Justice Rehnquist.]

legislature acting w[ithin] its authority when it acts to punish ... the [role], who suffers few of the consequences of his conduct.

1983 SUPPLEMENT

183

Not unreasonable to exclude females from punishment

acts well within its authority when it elects to punish only the participant who, by nature, suffers few of the consequences of his conduct. It is hardly unreasonable for a legislature acting to protect minor females to exclude them from punishment. Moreover, the risk of pregnancy itself constitutes a substantial deterrence to young females. No similar natural sanctions deter males. A criminal sanction imposed solely on males thus serves to roughly "equalize" the deterrents on the sexes.

We are unable to accept petitioner's contention that the statute is impermissibly underinclusive and must, in order to pass judicial scrutiny, be *broadened* so as to hold the female as criminally liable as the male. It is argued that this statute is not *necessary* to deter teenage pregnancy because a gender-neutral statute, where both male and female would be subject to prosecution, would serve that goal equally well. The relevant inquiry, however, is not whether the statute is drawn as precisely as it might have been, but whether the line chosen by the California Legislature is within constitutional limitations. Kahn v. Shevin.

In any event, we cannot say that a gender-neutral statute would be as effective as the statute California has chosen to enact. The State persuasively contends that a gender-neutral statute would frustrate its interest in effective enforcement. Its view is that a female is surely less likely to report violations of the statute if she herself would be subject to criminal prosecution.[7] In an area already fraught with prosecutorial difficulties, we decline to hold that the Equal Protection Clause requires a legislature to enact a statute so broad that it may well be incapable of enforcement.[8]

7. Petitioner contends that a gender-neutral statute would not hinder prosecutions because the prosecutor could take into account the relative burdens on females and males and generally only prosecute males. But to concede this is to concede all. If the prosecutor, in exercising discretion, will virtually always prosecute just the man and not the woman, we do not see why it is impermissible for the legislature to enact a statute to the same effect. [Footnote by Justice Rehnquist.]

8. The question whether a statute is *substantially* related to its asserted goals is at best an opaque one. It can be plausibly argued that a gender-neutral statute would produce fewer prosecutions than the statute at issue here. The dissent argues, on the other hand, that "even assuming that a gender neutral statute would be more difficult to enforce, [common] sense [suggests] that a gender-neutral statutory rape law is potentially a greater deterrent of sexual activity than a gender-based law, for the simple reason that a gender-neutral law subjects both men and women to crim-

inal sanctions and thus arguably has a deterrent effect on twice as many potential violators." Where such differing speculations as to the effect of a statute are plausible, we think it appropriate to defer to the decision of the California Supreme Court, "armed as it was with the knowledge of the facts and the circumstances concerning the passage and potential impact of [the statute], and familiar with the milieu in which that provision would operate." Reitman v. Mulkey.

It should be noted that two of the three cases relied upon by the dissent are readily distinguishable from the instant one. In both Navedo v. Preisser, 630 F.2d 636 (CA8 1980), and Meloon v. Helgemore, 564 F.2d 602 (CA1 1977), cert. denied, 436 U.S. 650 (1978), the respective governments asserted that the purpose of the statute was to protect young women from physical injury. Both courts rejected the justification on the grounds that there had been no showing that young females are more likely than males to suffer physical injury from sexual intercourse. They further held, contrary to our decision, that pregnancy prevention was not a "plausible" purpose

We similarly reject petitioner's argument that § 261.5 is impermissibly overbroad because it makes unlawful sexual intercourse with prepubescent females, who are, by definition, incapable of becoming pregnant. Quite apart from the fact that the statute could well be justified on the grounds that very young females are particularly susceptible to physical injury from sexual intercourse, it is ludicrous to suggest that the Constitution requires the California Legislature to limit the scope of its rape statute to older teenagers and exclude young girls.

There remains only petitioner's contention that the statute is unconstitutional as it is applied to him because he, like Sharon, was under 18 at the time of sexual intercourse. Petitioner argues that the statute is flawed because it presumes that as between two persons under 18, the male is the culpable aggressor. We find petitioner's contentions unpersuasive. Contrary to his assertions, the statute does not rest on the assumption that males are generally the aggressors. It is instead an attempt by a legislature to prevent illegitimate teenage pregnancy by providing an additional deterrent for men. The age of the man is irrelevant since young men are as capable as older men of inflicting the harm sought to be prevented.

In upholding the California statute we also recognize that this is not a case where a statute is being challenged on the grounds that it "invidiously discriminates" against females. To the contrary, the statute places a burden on males which is not shared by females. But we find nothing to suggest that men, because of past discrimination or peculiar disadvantages, are in need of the special solicitude of the courts. Nor is this a case where the gender classification is made "solely [for] administrative convenience," as in Frontiero v. Richardson, or rests on "the baggage of sexual stereotypes," as in Orr v. Orr. As we have held, the statute instead reasonably reflects the fact that the consequences of sexual intercourse and pregnancy fall more heavily on the female than on the male.

Affirmed.*

of the legislation. Thus neither court reached the issue presented here, whether the statute is substantially related to the prevention of teenage pregnancy. Significantly, Meloon has been severely limited by Rundlett v. Oliver, 607 F.2d 495 (CA1 1979), where the court upheld a statutory rape law on the ground that the State had shown that sexual intercourse physically injures young women more than males. Here, of course, even the dissent does not dispute that young women suffer disproportionately the deleterious consequences of illegitimate pregnancy. [Footnote by Justice Rehnquist.]

* Justice STEWART, who joined Justice Rehnquist's opinion, also submitted a separate opinion [omitted here]. His comparison of race and gender cases is of special interest: "The Constitution is violated when govenment, state or federal, invidiously classifies similarly situated people on the basis of the immutable characteristics with which they were born. Thus, detrimental racial classifications by government always violate the Constitution, for the simple reason that, so far as the Constitution is concerned, people of different races are always similarly situated. [See, e. g., Fullilove (dissenting opinion).] By contrast, while detrimental gender classifications by government often violate the Constitution, they do not always do so, for the reason that there are differences between males and females that the Constitution necessarily recognizes. In this case we deal with the most basic of these differences: females can become pregnant as the result of sexual intercourse; males cannot."

Blackmun Concurs (handwritten margin note)

Justice BLACKMUN, concurring in the judgment.

It is gratifying that the plurality recognizes that "[a]t the risk of stating the obvious, teenage pregnancies [have] increased dramatically over the last two decades" and "have significant social, medical and economic consequences for both the mother and her child, and the State." There have been times when I have wondered whether the Court was capable of this perception, particularly when it has struggled with the different but not unrelated problems that attend abortion issues. See, [e.g.], Beal v. Doe; Harris v. McRae; and today's opinion in H. L. v. Matheson [addition to 10th Ed., p. 614; Ind. Rts., p. 234, above].

Some might conclude that the two uses of the criminal sanction—here flatly to forbid intercourse in order to forestall teenage pregnancies, and in Matheson to prohibit a physician's abortion procedure except upon notice to the parents of the pregnant minor—are vastly different proscriptions. But the basic social and privacy problems are much the same. Both Utah's statute in Matheson and California's statute in this case are legislatively-created tools intended to achieve similar ends and addressed to the same societal concerns: the control and direction of young people's sexual activities. The plurality opinion impliedly concedes as much . . . .

I, however, cannot vote to strike down the California statutory rape law, for I think it is a sufficiently reasoned and constitutional effort to control the problem at its inception. For me, there is an important difference between this state action and a State's adamant and rigid refusal to face, or even to recognize, the "significant . . . consequences"—to the woman—of a forced or unwanted conception. [I] am persuaded that, although a minor has substantial privacy rights in intimate affairs connected with procreation, California's efforts to prevent teenage pregnancy are to be viewed differently from Utah's efforts to inhibit a woman from dealing with pregnancy once it has become an inevitability.

[The] plurality opinion in the present case points out the Court's respective phrasings of the applicable test in Reed v. Reed and in Craig v. Boren. I vote to affirm the judgment of the Supreme Court of California and to uphold the State's gender-based classification on that test and as exemplified by those two cases and by Schlesinger v. Ballard, Weinberger v. Wiesenfeld, and Kahn v. Shevin.

Passes (handwritten margin note)
Craig v Boren Test etc (handwritten margin note)
Mid Level Scrutiny? (handwritten margin note)

[I] think, too, that it is only fair, with respect to this particular petitioner, to point out that his partner, Sharon, appears not to have been an unwilling participant in at least the initial stages of the intimacies that took place the night of June 3, 1978. * Petitioner's and Sharon's nonacquaintance with each other before the incident; their drinking; their withdrawal from the others of the group; their foreplay, in which she willingly participated and seems to have encouraged; and the closeness of their ages (a difference of only one year and 18 days) are factors that should make this case an unattractive one to prosecute at all, and especially to prosecute as a felony,

---

* Justice Blackmun's very extensive quotations from the testimony at the preliminary hearing are omitted.

rather than as a misdemeanor chargeable under § 261.5. But the State has chosen to prosecute in that manner, and the facts, I reluctantly conclude, may fit the crime.

Justice BRENNAN, with whom Justices WHITE and MARSHALL join, dissenting.

I. It is disturbing to find the Court so splintered on a case that presents such a straightforward issue: whether the admittedly gender-based classification in Cal. Penal Code § 261.5 bears a sufficient relationship to the State's asserted goal of preventing teenage pregnancies to survive the "mid-level" constitutional scrutiny mandated by Craig v. Boren. Applying the analytical framework provided by our precedents, I am convinced that there is only one proper resolution of this issue: the classification must be declared unconstitutional. I fear that the plurality and Justices Stewart and Blackmun reach the opposite result by placing too much emphasis on the desirability of achieving the State's asserted statutory goal—prevention of teenage pregnancy—and not enough emphasis on the fundamental question of whether the sex-based discrimination in the California statute is *substantially* related to the achievement of that goal.[1]

II. After some uncertainty as to the proper framework for analyzing equal protection challenges to statutes containing gender-based classifications, this Court settled upon the proposition that a statute containing a gender-based classification cannot withstand constitutional challenge unless the classification is substantially related to the achievement of an important governmental objective. [Justice Brennan cited Craig v. Boren and seven subsequent cases applying it, including Kirchberg v. Feenstra (1981) (noted above, immediately preceding this case).] This analysis applies whether the classification discriminates against males or females. The burden is on the government to prove both the importance of its asserted objective and the substantial relationship between the classification and that objective. And the State cannot meet that burden without showing that a gender-neutral statute would be a less effective means of achieving that goal.[2]

The State of California vigorously asserts that the "important governmental objective" to be served by § 261.5 is the prevention of teenage pregnancy. It claims that its statute furthers this goal by deterring sexual activity by males—the class of persons it considers more responsible for causing those

---

1. None of the three opinions upholding the California statute fairly applies the equal protection analysis this Court has so carefully developed since Craig v. Boren. [All three] have a common failing. They overlook the fact that the State has not met its burden of proving that the gender discrimination in § 261.5 is *substantially* related to the achievement of the State's asserted statutory goal. My Brethren seem not to recognize that California has the burden of proving that a gender-neutral statutory rape law would be less effective than § 261.5 in deterring sexual activity lead-

ing to teenage pregnancy. Because they fail to analyze the issue in these terms, I believe they reach an unsupportable result. [Footnote by Justice Brennan.]

2. Gender-based statutory rape laws were struck down in Navedo v. Preisser, 630 F.2d 636 (CA8 1980), United States v. Hicks, 625 F.2d 216 (CA9 1980), and Meloon v. Helgemoe, 564 F.2d 602 (CA1 1977), cert. denied, 436 U.S. 950 (1978), precisely because the government failed to meet this burden of proof. [Footnote by Justice Brennan.]

pregnancies. But even assuming that prevention of teenage pregnancy is an important governmental objective and that it is in fact an objective of § 261.-5, California still has the burden of proving that there are fewer teenage pregnancies under its gender-based statutory rape law than there would be if the law were gender-neutral. To meet this burden, the State must show that because its statutory rape law punishes only males, and not females, it more effectively deters minor females from having sexual intercourse.[3]

The plurality assumes that a gender-neutral statute would be less effective than § 261.5 in deterring sexual activity because a gender-neutral statute would create significant enforcement problems. [But] the State must produce evidence that will persuade the Court that its assertion is true. The State has not produced such evidence in this case. Moreover, there are at least two serious flaws in the State's assertion that law enforcement problems created by a gender-neutral statutory rape law would make such a statute less effective than a gender-based statute in deterring sexual activity.

First, the experience of other jurisdictions, and California itself, belies the plurality's conclusion that a gender-neutral statutory rape law "may well be incapable of enforcement." [The] second flaw in the State's assertion is that even assuming that a gender-neutral statute would be more difficult to enforce, the State has still not shown that those enforcement problems would make such a statute less effective than a gender-based statute in deterring minor females from engaging in sexual intercourse. Common sense, however, suggests that a gender-neutral statutory rape law is potentially a *greater* deterrent of sexual activity than a gender-based law, for the simple reason that a gender-neutral law subjects both men and women to criminal sanctions and thus arguably has a deterrent effect on twice as many potential violators. Even if fewer persons were prosecuted under the gender-neutral law, as the State suggests, it would still be true that twice as many persons would be *subject* to arrest. The State's failure to prove that a gender-neutral law would be a less effective deterrent than a gender-based law, like the State's failure to prove that a gender-neutral law would be difficult to enforce, should have led this Court to invalidate § 261.5.

III. Until very recently, no California court or commentator had suggested that the purpose of California's statutory rape law was to protect young women from the risk of pregnancy. Indeed, the historical development of § 261.5 demonstrates that the law was initially enacted on the prem-

---

3. Petitioner has not questioned the State's constitutional power to achieve its asserted objective by criminalizing consensual sexual activity. However, I note that our cases would not foreclose such a privacy challenge.

The State is attempting to reduce the incidence of teenage pregnancy by imposing criminal sanctions on those who engage in consensual sexual activity with minor females. We have stressed, however, that "[i]f the right of privacy means anything, it is the right of the *individual*, married or single, to be free from unwarranted governmental intrusion into matters so fundamentally affecting a person as the decision whether to bear or beget a child." Eisenstadt v. Baird, 405 U.S. 438, 453 (1972). Minors, too, enjoy a right of privacy in connection with decisions affecting procreation. Carey v. Population Services Int'l. Thus, despite the suggestion of the plurality to the contrary, it is not settled that a State may rely on a pregnancy-prevention justification to make consensual sexual intercourse among minors a criminal act. [Footnote by Justice Brennan.]

ise that young women, in contrast to young men, were to be deemed legally incapable of consenting to an act of sexual intercourse. Because their chastity was considered particularly precious, those young women were felt to be uniquely in need of the State's protection. In contrast, young men were assumed to be capable of making such decisions for themselves; the law therefore did not offer them any special protection.

It is perhaps because the gender classification in California's statutory rape law was initially designed to further these outmoded sexual stereotypes, rather than to reduce the incidence of teenage pregnancies, that the State has been unable to demonstrate a substantial relationship between the classification and its newly asserted goal. But whatever the reason, the State has not shown that [its law] is any more effective than a gender-neutral law would be in deterring minor females from engaging in sexual intercourse. It has therefore not met its burden of proving that the statutory classification is substantially related to the achievement of its asserted goal.   .   .   .

Justice STEVENS, dissenting.

Local custom and belief—rather than statutory laws of venerable but doubtful ancestry—will determine the volume of sexual activity among unmarried teenagers. The empirical evidence cited by the plurality demonstrates the futility of the notion that a statutory prohibition will significantly affect the volume of that activity or provide a meaningful solution to the problems created by it. Nevertheless, as a matter of constitutional power, unlike my Brother Brennan, I would have no doubt about the validity of a state law prohibiting all unmarried teenagers from engaging in sexual intercourse. The societal interests in reducing the incidence of venereal disease and teenage pregnancy are sufficient, in my judgment, to justify a prohibition of conduct that increases the risk of those harms.

My conclusion that a nondiscriminatory prohibition would be constitutional does not help me answer the question whether a prohibition applicable to only half of the joint participants in the risk-creating conduct is also valid. It cannot be true that the validity of a total ban is an adequate justification for a selective prohibition; otherwise, the constitutional objection to discriminatory rules would be meaningless. The question in this case is whether the difference between males and females justifies this statutory discrimination based entirely on sex.[1]

---

1. Equal protection analysis is often said to involve different "levels of scrutiny." It may be more accurate to say that the burden of sustaining an equal protection challenge is much heavier in some cases than in others. Racial classifications, which are subjected to "strict scrutiny," are presumptively invalid because there is seldom, if ever, any legitimate reason for treating citizens differently because of their race. On the other hand, most economic classifications are presumptively valid because they are a necessary component of most regulatory programs. In cases involving discrim- ination between men and women, the natural differences between the sexes are sometimes relevant and sometimes wholly irrelevant. If those differences are obviously irrelevant, the discrimination should be treated as presumptively unlawful in the same way that racial classifications are presumptively unlawful. Cf. Califano v. Goldfarb (Stevens, J., concurring in the judgment). But if, as in this case, there is an apparent connection between the discrimination and the fact that only women can become pregnant, it may be appropriate to presume that the classification is law-

The fact that the Court did not immediately acknowledge that the capacity to become pregnant is what primarily differentiates the female from the male [2] does not impeach the validity of the plurality's newly-found wisdom. I think the plurality is quite correct in making the assumption that the joint act that this law seeks to prohibit creates a greater risk of harm for the female than for the male. But the plurality surely cannot believe that the risk of pregnancy confronted by the female—any more than the risk of venereal disease confronted by males as well as females—has provided an effective deterrent to voluntary female participation in the risk-creating conduct. Yet the plurality's decision seems to rest on the assumption that the California Legislature acted on the basis of that rather fanciful notion. In my judgment, the fact that a class of persons is especially vulnerable to a risk that a statute is designed to avoid is a reason for making the statute applicable to that class. The argument that a special need for protection provides a rational explanation for an exemption is one I simply do not comprehend.[3]

In this case, the fact that a female confronts a greater risk of harm than a male is a reason for applying the prohibition to her—not a reason for granting her a license to use her own judgment on whether or not to assume the risk. Surely, if we examine the problem from the point of view of society's interest in preventing the risk-creating conduct from occurring at all, it is irrational to exempt 50% of the potential violators. And, if we view the government's interest as that of a parens patriae seeking to protect its subjects from harming themselves, the discrimination is actually perverse. Would a rational parent making rules for the conduct of twin children of opposite sex simultaneously forbid the son and authorize the daughter to engage in conduct that is especially harmful to the daughter? That is the effect of this statutory classification. If pregnancy or some other special harm is suffered by one of the two participants in the prohibited act, that special harm no doubt would constitute a legitimate mitigating factor in deciding what, if any, punishment might be appropriate in a given case. But from the stand-

---

ful. This presumption, however, may be overcome by a demonstration that the apparent justification for the discrimination is illusory or wholly inadequate. Thus, instead of applying a "mid-level" form of scrutiny in all sex discrimination cases, perhaps the burden is heavier in some than in others. Nevertheless, as I have previously suggested, the ultimate standard in these, as in all other equal protection cases, is essentially the same. See Craig v. Boren (Stevens, J., concurring). Professor Cox recently noted that however the level of scrutiny is described, in the final analysis, "the Court is always deciding whether in its judgment the harm done to the disadvantaged class by the legislative classification is disproportionate to the public purposes the measure is likely to achieve." Cox, Book Review, 94 Harv.L.Rev. 700, 706 (1981). [Footnote by Justice Stevens.]

2. See General Electric Co. v. Gilbert (Stevens, J., dissenting). [Footnote by Justice Stevens.]

3. A hypothetical racial classification will illustrate my point. Assume that skin pigmentation provides some measure of protection against cancer caused by exposure to certain chemicals in the atmosphere and, therefore, that white employees confront a greater risk than black employees in certain industrial settings. Would it be rational to require black employees to wear protective clothing but to exempt whites from that requirement? It seems to me that the greater risk of harm to white workers would be a reason for including them in the requirement—not for granting them an exemption. [Footnote by Justice Stevens.]

point of fashioning a general preventive rule—or, indeed, in determining appropriate punishment when neither party in fact has suffered any special harm—I regard a total exemption for the members of the more endangered class as utterly irrational.

In my opinion, the only acceptable justification for a general rule requiring disparate treatment of the two participants in a joint act must be a legislative judgment that one is more guilty than the other. The risk-creating conduct that this statute is designed to prevent requires the participation of two persons—one male and one female. In many situations it is probably true that one is the aggressor and the other is either an unwilling, or at least a less willing, participant in the joint act. If a statute authorized punishment of only one participant and required the prosecutor to prove that that participant had been the aggressor, I assume that the discrimination would be valid. Although the question is less clear, I also assume, for the purpose of deciding this case, that it would be permissible to punish only the male participant, if one element of the offense were proof that he had been the aggressor, or at least in some respects the more responsible participant in the joint act. The statute at issue in this case, however, requires no such proof. The question raised by this statute is whether the State, consistently with the Federal Constitution, may always punish the male and never the female when they are equally responsible or when the female is the more responsible of the two.

It would seem to me that an impartial lawmaker could give only one answer to that question. The fact that the California Legislature has decided to apply its prohibition only to the male may reflect a legislative judgment that in the typical case the male is actually the more guilty party. Any such judgment must, in turn, assume that the decision to engage in the risk-creating conduct is always—or at least typically—a male decision. If that assumption is valid, the statutory classification should also be valid. But what is the support for the assumption? It is not contained in the record of this case or in any legislative history or scholarly study that has been called to our attention. I think it is supported to some extent by traditional attitudes toward male-female relationships. But the possibility that such an habitual attitude may reflect nothing more than an irrational prejudice makes it an insufficient justification for discriminatory treatment that is otherwise blatantly unfair. For, as I read this statute, it requires that one, and only one, of two equally guilty wrongdoers be stigmatized by a criminal conviction.

I cannot accept the State's argument that the constitutionality of the discriminatory rule can be saved by an assumption that prosecutors will commonly invoke this statute only in cases that actually involve a forcible rape but one that cannot be established by proof beyond a reasonable doubt. That assumption implies that a State has a legitimate interest in convicting a defendant on evidence that is constitutionally insufficient. Of course, the State may create a lesser-included offense that would authorize punishment of the more guilty party, but surely the interest in obtaining convictions on inadequate proof cannot justify a statute that punishes one who is equally or less guilty than his partner.[4]

4. Both Justice Rehnquist and Justice Blackmun apparently attach significance to the testimony at the preliminary hearing indicating that the peti-

Nor do I find at all persuasive the suggestion that this discrimination is adequately justified by the desire to encourage females to inform against their male partners. Even if the concept of a wholesale informant's exemption were an acceptable enforcement device, what is the justification for defining the exempt class entirely by reference to sex rather than by reference to a more neutral criterion such as relative innocence? Indeed, if the exempt class is to be composed entirely of members of one sex, what is there to support the view that the statutory purpose will be better served by granting the informing license to females rather than to males? If a discarded male partner informs on a promiscuous female, a timely threat of prosecution might well prevent the precise harm the statute is intended to minimize.

Finally, even if my logic is faulty and there actually is some speculative basis for treating equally guilty males and females differently, I still believe that any such speculative justification would be outweighed by the paramount interest in even-handed enforcement of the law. A rule that authorizes punishment of only one of two equally guilty wrongdoers violates the essence of the constitutional requirement that the sovereign must govern [impartially].

ROSTKER v. GOLDBERG

453 U.S. 57, 101 S.Ct. 2646, 69 L.Ed.2d 478 (1981)

Justice REHNQUIST delivered the opinion of the Court.

The question presented is whether the Military Selective Service Act violates the Fifth Amendment [in] authorizing the President to require the registration of males and not females.

I. [Section] 3 of the Act empowers the President, by proclamation, to require the registration of "every male citizen" and male resident aliens between the ages of 18 and 26. The purpose of this registration is to facilitate any eventual conscription. [The] MSSA registration provision serves no other purpose beyond providing a pool for subsequent induction.

Registration for the draft [was] discontinued in 1975. In early 1980, President Carter determined that it was necessary to reactivate the draft registration process.[1] The immediate impetus for this decision was the Soviet armed invasion of Afghanistan. [The] resulting crisis in Southwestern Asia convinced the President that the "time has come" "to use his present authority to require registration [as] a necessary step to preserving or enhancing our national security interests." The Selective Service System had been inactive,

---

tioner struck his partner. In light of the fact that the petitioner would be equally guilty of the crime charged in the complaint whether or not that testimony is true, it obviously has no bearing on the legal question presented by this case. The question is not whether "the facts [fit] the crime," Opinion of Blackmun, J.,— that is a question to be answered at trial—but rather, whether the statute defining the crime fits the constitutional requirement that justice be administered in an evenhanded fashion. [Footnote by Justice Stevens.]

1. The President did not seek conscription. Since the Act was amended to preclude conscription as of July 1, 1973, any actual conscription would require further congressional action. [Footnote by Justice Rehnquist.]

however, and funds were needed before reactivating registration. The President therefore recommended that funds be transferred from the Department of Defense to the separate Selective Service System. He also recommended that Congress take action to amend the MSSA to permit the [registration] and conscription of women as well as men.

Congress agreed that it was necessary to reactivate the registration process, and allocated funds for that purpose in a joint resolution which passed the House on April 22 and the Senate on June 12. The resolution did not allocate all the funds originally requested by the President, but only those necessary to register males. Although Congress considered the question at great length, it declined to amend the MSSA to permit the registration of women. On July 2, 1980, the President, by proclamation, ordered the registration of specified groups of young men. [Registration] was to commence on July 21, 1980. These events of last year breathed new life into a lawsuit which had been essentially dormant in the lower courts for nearly a decade.*

---

* Justice Rehnquist summarized the history of this lawsuit as follows: "[The suit] began in 1971 when several men subject to registration for the draft and subsequent induction into the Armed Services filed a complaint in the United States District Court for the Eastern District of Pennsylvania challenging the MSSA on several grounds. [Plaintiffs] contended that the Act amounted to a taking of property without due process, imposed involuntary servitude, violated rights of free expression and assembly, was unlawfully implemented to advance an unconstitutional war, and impermissibly discriminated between males and females. A three-judge district court was convened in 1974 to consider the claim of unlawful gender-based discrimination which is now before us. On July 1, 1974, the court declined to dismiss the case as moot, reasoning that although authority to induct registrants had lapsed, plaintiffs were still under certain affirmative obligations in connection with registration. Nothing more happened in the case for five years. Then, on June 6, 1979, the court clerk, acting pursuant to a local rule governing inactive cases, proposed that the case be dismissed. Additional discovery thereupon ensued, and defendants moved to dismiss on various justiciability grounds. The court denied the motion to dismiss, ruling that it did not have before it an adequate record on the operation of the Selective Service System and what action would be necessary to reactivate it. On July 1, 1980, the court certified a plaintiff class of 'all male persons who are registered or

subject to registration [or] are liable for training and service in the armed forces of the United States.'

"On Friday, July 18, 1980, three days before registration was to commence, the District Court issued an opinion finding that the Act violated the Due Process Clause [and] permanently enjoined the Government from requiring registration under the Act. The court initially determined that the plaintiffs had standing and that the case was ripe, determinations which are not challenged here by the Government. Turning to the merits, the court rejected plaintiffs' suggestions that the equal protection claim should be tested under 'strict scrutiny,' and also rejected defendants' argument that the deference due Congress in the area of military affairs required application of the traditional 'minimum scrutiny' test. Applying the 'important government interest' test articulated in Craig v. Boren, the court struck down the MSSA. The court stressed that it was not deciding whether or to what extent women should serve in combat, but only the issue of registration, and felt that this 'should dispel any concern that we are injecting ourselves in an inappropriate manner in military affairs.' The court then proceeded to examine the testimony and hearing evidence presented to Congress by representatives of the military and the Executive Branch, and concluded on the basis of this testimony that 'military opinion, backed by extensive study, is that the availability of women registrants would materially increase flexibility, not hamper it.' It rejected Congress' contrary de-

II. Whenever called upon to judge the constitutionality of an Act of Congress, [the] Court accords "great weight to the decisions of Congress." The Congress is a coequal branch of government whose members take the same oath we do to uphold the Constitution. [The] customary deference accorded the judgments of Congress is certainly appropriate when, as here, Congress specifically considered the question of the Act's constitutionality.

This is not, however, merely a case involving the customary deference accorded congressional decisions. The case arises in the context of Congress' authority over national defense and military affairs, and perhaps in no other area has the Court accorded Congress greater deference. In rejecting the registration of women, Congress explicitly relied upon its constitutional powers under Art. I, § 8, cls. 12–14. [This] Court has consistently recognized Congress' "broad constitutional power" to raise and regulate armies and navies, Schlesinger v. Ballard.

[Not] only is the scope of Congress' constitutional power in this area broad, but the lack of competence on the part of the courts is marked. [The] operation of a healthy deference to legislative and executive judgments in the area of military affairs is evident in several recent decisions of this Court. [E.g., Schlesinger v. Ballard.] None of this is to say that Congress is free to disregard the Constitution when it acts in the area of military affairs. In that area as any other Congress remains subject to the limitations of the Due Process Clause, but the tests and limitations to be applied may differ because of the military context. We of course do not abdicate our ultimate responsibility to decide the constitutional question, but simply recognize that the Constitution itself requires such deference to congressional choice. In deciding the question before us we must be particularly careful not to substitute our judgment of what is desirable for that of Congress, or our own evaluation of evidence for a reasonable evaluation by the Legislative Branch.

The District Court purported to recognize the appropriateness of deference to Congress when that body was exercising its constitutionally delegated authority over military affairs, but it stressed that "[w]e are not here concerned with military operations or day-to-day conduct of the military into which we have no desire to intrude." Appellees also stress that this case involves civilians, not the military, and that "the impact of registration on the military is only indirect and attenuated." We find these efforts to divorce registration from the military and national defense context, with all the deference called for in that context, singularly unpersuasive. [Congressional] judgments concerning registration and the draft are based on judgments concerning military operations and needs [and] the deference unquestionably due the latter judgments is necessarily required in assessing the

termination in part because of what it viewed as Congress' 'inconsistent positions' in declining to register women yet spending funds to recruit them and expand their opportunities in the military.

"The United States immediately filed a notice of appeal and the next day, Saturday, July 19, 1980, Justice Brennan, acting in his capacity as Circuit Justice for the Third Circuit, stayed the District Court's order enjoining commencement of registration. Registration began the next Monday. On December 1, 1980, we noted probable jurisdiction." [The case was decided on June 25, 1981.]

former as well. Although the District Court stressed that it was not intruding on military questions, its opinion was based on assessments of military need and flexibility in a time of mobilization. It would be blinking reality to say that our precedents requiring deference to Congress in military affairs are not implicated by the present case.

The Solicitor General argues, largely on the basis of [the] cases emphasizing the deference due Congress in the area of military affairs and national security, that this Court should scrutinize the MSSA only to determine if the distinction drawn between men and women bears a rational relation to some legitimate government purpose, see [Fritz], and should not examine the Act under the heightened scrutiny with which we have approached gender-based discrimination, see [Michael M.; Craig v. Boren; Reed v. Reed].[2] We do not think that the substantive guarantee of due process or certainty in the law will be advanced by any further "refinement" in the applicable tests as suggested by the Government. Announced degrees of "deference" to legislative judgments, just as levels of "scrutiny" which this Court announces that it applies to particular classifications made by a legislative body, may all too readily become facile abstractions used to justify a result. In this case the courts are called upon to decide whether Congress, acting under an explicit constitutional grant of authority, has by that action transgressed an explicit guarantee of individual rights which limits the authority so conferred. Simply labelling the legislative decision "military" on the one hand or "gender-based" on the other does not automatically guide a court to the correct constitutional result.

No one could deny that under the test of Craig v. Boren the Government's interest in raising and supporting armies is an "important governmental interest." Congress and its committees carefully considered and debated two alternative means of furthering that interest: the first was to register only males for potential conscription, and the other was to register both sexes. Congress chose the former alternative. When that decision is challenged on equal protection grounds, the question a court must decide is not which alternative it would have chosen had it been the primary decision-maker, but whether that chosen by Congress denies equal protection of the laws.

Nor can it be denied that the imposing number of cases from this Court previously cited suggest that judicial deference to such congressional exercise of authority is at its apogee when legislative action under the congressional authority to raise and support armies and make rules and regulations for their governance is challenged. [In] light of the floor debate and the report of the Senate Armed Services Committee, [it] is apparent that Congress was fully aware not merely of the many facts and figures presented to it by witnesses who testified before its committees, but of the current thinking as to the place of women in the Armed Services. In such a case, we cannot ignore Congress' broad authority conferred by the Constitution to raise and support armies when we are urged to declare unconstitutional its studied choice of one alternative in preference to another for furthering that goal.

---

2. It is clear that "[g]ender has never been rejected as an impermissible classification in all instances," Kahn v. Shevin. In making this observation the Court noted that "Congress has not so far drafted women into the Armed Services." Ibid. [Footnote by Justice Rehnquist.]

Congress acted deliberately, not "unthinkingly"

III. This case is quite different from several of the gender-based discrimination cases we have considered in that, despite appellees' assertions, Congress did not act "unthinkingly" or "reflexively and not for any considered reason." The question of registering women for the draft not only received considerable national attention and was the subject of wide-ranging public debate, but also was extensively considered by Congress in hearings, floor debate, and in committee. [The] House declined to provide for the registration of women when it passed the Joint Resolution allocating funds for the Selective Service System. When the Senate considered the Joint Resolution, it defeated, after extensive debate, an amendment which in effect would have authorized the registration of women.

[While] proposals to register women were being rejected in the course of transferring funds to register males, committees in both Houses which had conducted hearings on the issue were also rejecting the registration of women. [The] foregoing clearly establishes that the decision to exempt women from registration was not the "accidental by-product of a traditional way of thinking about women." Califano v. Webster. In Michael M., we rejected a similar argument because of action by the California Legislature considering and rejecting proposals to make a statute challenged on discrimination grounds gender-neutral. The cause for rejecting the argument is considerably stronger here. The issue was considered at great length, and Congress clearly expressed its purpose and intent. Contrast Califano v. Westcott.[3]

[Any] assessment of the congressional purpose and its chosen means must therefore consider the registration schemes as a prelude to a draft in a time of national emergency. Any other approach would not be testing the Act in light of the purposes Congress sought to achieve. Congress determined that any future draft, which would be facilitated by the registration scheme, would be characterized by a need for combat troops. [The] purpose of registration, therefore, was to prepare for a draft *of combat troops.*

purpose was to draft, if needed, combat troops

Women as a group, however, unlike men as a group, are not eligible for combat. The restrictions on the participation of women in combat in the Navy and Air Force are statutory. [The] Army and Marine Corps preclude the use of women in combat as a matter of established policy. Congress specifically recognized and endorsed the exclusion of women from combat in exempting women from registration. In the words of the Senate Report: "The principle that women should not intentionally and routinely engage in combat is fundamental, and enjoys wide support among our [people]." [The] President expressed his intent to continue the current military policy precluding women from combat, and appellees present their argument concerning registration against the background of such restrictions on the use of women in combat. Consistent with the approach of this Court in Schlesin-

3. Nor can we agree with the characterization of the MSSA in the Brief for Amicus Curiae National Organization of Women as a law which "coerce[s] or preclude[s] women as a class from performing tasks or jobs of which they are capable," or the suggestion that this case involves "[t]he exclusion of women from the military." Nothing in the MSSA restricts in any way the opportunities for women to volunteer for military service. [Footnote by Justice Rehnquist.]

ger v. Ballard, we must examine appellees' constitutional claim concerning registration with these combat restrictions firmly in mind.

The existence of the combat restrictions clearly indicates the basis for Congress' decision to exempt women from registration. The purpose of registration was to prepare for a draft of combat troops. Since women are excluded from combat, Congress concluded that they would not be needed in the event of a draft, and therefore decided [not to register them].[4] [The] District Court stressed that the military need for women was irrelevant to the issue of their registration. As that court put it: "Congress could not constitutionally require registration under MSSA of only black citizens or only white citizens, or single out any political or religious group simply because those groups contained sufficient persons to fill the needs of the Selective Service System." This reasoning is beside the point. The reason women are exempt from registration is not because military needs can be met by drafting men. This is not a case of Congress arbitrarily choosing to burden one of two similarly situated groups, such as would be the case with an all-black or all-white, or an all-Catholic or all-Lutheran, or an all-Republican or all-Democratic registration. Men and women, because of the combat restrictions on women, are simply not similarly situated for purposes of a draft or registration for a draft.

Congress' decision to authorize the registration of only men, therefore, does not violate the Due Process Clause. The exemption of women from registration is not only sufficiently but closely related to Congress' purpose in authorizing registration. See Michael M. (plurality); Craig v. Boren; Reed v. Reed. The fact that Congress and the Executive have decided that women should not serve in combat fully justifies Congress in not authorizing their registration, since the purpose of registration is to develop a pool of potential combat troops. As was the case in Schlesinger v. Ballard, "the gender classification is not invidious, but rather realistically reflects the fact that the sexes are not similarly situated" in this case. The Constitution requires that Congress treat similarly situated persons similarly, not that it engage in gestures of superficial equality.

In holding the MSSA constitutionally invalid the District Court relied heavily on the President's decision to seek authority to register women and the testimony of members of the Executive Branch and the military in support of that decision. As stated by the Administration's witnesses before Congress, however, the President's "decision to ask for authority to register women is based on equity." This was also the basis for the testimony by military officials. The Senate Report, evaluating the testimony before the Committee, recognized that "the argument for registration and induction of women [is] not based on military necessity, but on considerations of equity." Congress was certainly entitled, in the exercise of its constitutional powers to raise and

---

4. Justice Marshall's suggestion that since Congress focused on the need for combat troops in authorizing male-only registration, the Court could "be forced to declare the male-only registration program unconstitutional" in the event of a peacetime draft misreads our opinion. The perceived need for combat or combat-eligible troops in the event of a draft was not limited to a wartime draft. . . . [Footnote by Justice Rehnquist.]

regulate armies and navies, to focus on the question of military need rather than "equity." . . .[5]

Although the military experts who testified in favor of registering women uniformly opposed the actual drafting of women, there was testimony that in the event of a draft of 650,000 the military could absorb some 80,000 female inductees. The 80,000 would be used to fill noncombat positions, freeing men to go to the front. In relying on this testimony in striking down the MSSA, the District Court palpably exceeded its authority when it ignored Congress' considered response to this line of reasoning.

In the first place, assuming that a small number of women could be drafted for noncombat roles, Congress simply did not consider it worth the added burdens of including women in draft and registration plans. [Congress] also concluded that whatever the need for women for noncombat roles during mobilization, whether 80,000 or less, it could be met by volunteers. Most significantly, Congress determined that staffing non-combat positions with women during a mobilization would be positively detrimental to the important goal of military flexibility. [In] sum, Congress carefully evaluated the testimony that 80,000 women conscripts could be usefully employed in the event of a draft and rejected it in the permissible exercise of its constitutional responsibility. The District Court was quite wrong in undertaking an independent evaluation of this evidence, rather than adopting an appropriately deferential examination of *Congress'* evaluation of that evidence.

In light of the foregoing, we conclude that Congress acted well within its constitutional authority when it authorized the registration of men, and not women, under the Military Selective Service Act.

[Reversed.]

Justice WHITE, with whom Justice BRENNAN joins, dissenting.

I assume what has not been challenged in this case—that excluding women from combat positions does not offend the Constitution. Granting that, it is self-evident that if during mobilization for war, all noncombat military positions must be filled by combat-qualified personnel available to be moved into combat positions, there would be no occasion whatsoever to have any women in the Army, whether as volunteers or inductees. The Court appears to say that Congress concluded as much and that we should accept that judgment even though the serious view of the Executive Branch, including the responsible military services, is to the contrary. The Court's position in

5. The District Court also focused on what it termed Congress' "inconsistent positions" in encouraging women to volunteer for military service and expanding their opportunities in the service, on the one hand, and exempting them from registration and the draft on the other. This reasoning fails to appreciate the different purposes served by encouraging women volunteers and registration for the draft. Women volunteers do not occupy combat positions, so encouraging women to volunteer is not related to concerns about the availability of combat troops. In the event of a draft, however, the need would be for combat troops or troops which could be rotated into combat. Congress' positions are clearly not inconsistent and in treating them as such the District Court failed to understand Congress' purpose behind registration as distinguished from its purpose in encouraging women volunteers. [Footnote by Justice Rehnquist.]

this regard is most unpersuasive. I perceive little, if any, indication that Congress itself concluded that every position in the military, no matter how far removed from combat, must be filled with combat-ready men. Common sense and experience in recent wars, where women volunteers were employed in substantial numbers, belie this view of reality. It should not be ascribed to Congress, particularly in the face of the testimony of military authorities [that] there would be a substantial number of positions in the services that could be filled by women both in peacetime and during mobilization, even though they are ineligible for combat.

I would also have little difficulty agreeing to a reversal if all the women who could serve in wartime without adversely affecting combat readiness could predictably be obtained through volunteers. In that event, the equal protection component of the Fifth Amendment would not require the United States to go through, and a large segment of the population to be burdened with, the expensive and essentially useless procedure of registering women. But again I cannot agree with the Court that Congress concluded or that the legislative record indicates that each of the services could rely on women volunteers to fill all the positions for which they might be eligible in the event of mobilization. On the contrary, the record as I understand it supports the District Court's finding that the services would have to conscript ·at least 80,000 persons to fill positions for which combat-ready men would not be required.

[Of] course, the division among us indicates that the record in this respect means different things to different people, and I would be content to vacate the judgment below and remand for further hearings and findings on this crucial issue. Absent that, however, I cannot agree that the record supports the view that all positions for which women would be eligible in war time could and would be filled by female volunteers.

The Court also submits that because the primary purpose of registration and conscription is to supply combat troops and because the great majority of noncombat positions must be filled by combat-trained men ready to be rotated into combat, the absolute number of positions for which women would be eligible is so small as to be de minimis and of no moment for equal protection purposes, especially in light of the administrative burdens involved in registering all women of suitable age. There is some sense to this; but at least on the record before us, the number of women who could be used in the military without sacrificing combat-readiness is not at all small or insubstantial, and administrative convenience has not been sufficient justification for the kind of outright gender-based discrimination involved in registering and conscripting men but no women at all.

As I understand the record, then, in order to secure the personnel it needs during mobilization, the Government cannot rely on volunteers and must register and draft not only to fill combat positions and those noncombat positions that must be filled by combat-trained men, but also to secure the personnel needed for jobs that can be performed by persons ineligible for combat without diminishing military effectiveness. The claim is that in providing for the latter category of positions, Congress is free to register and draft only men. I discern no adequate justification for this kind of discrimination between men and women. Accordingly, with all due respect, I dissent.

Justice MARSHALL, with whom Justice BRENNAN joins, dissenting.

The Court today places its imprimatur on one of the most potent remaining public expressions of "ancient canards about the proper role of women." It upholds a statute that requires males but not females to register for the draft, and which thereby categorically excludes women from a fundamental civic obligation. Because I believe the Court's decision is inconsistent with the Constitution's guarantee of equal protection of the laws, I dissent.

I.   A.   [Although] the purpose of registration is to assist preparations for drafting civilians into the military, *we are not asked to rule on the constitutionality of a statute governing conscription.* [Consequently], we are not called upon to decide whether either men or women can be drafted at all, whether they must be drafted in equal numbers, in what order they should be drafted, or once inducted, how they are to be trained for their respective functions. In addition, this case does not involve a challenge to the statutes or policies that prohibit female members of the Armed Forces from serving in combat.[1] It is with this understanding that I turn to the task at hand.

B.   By now it should be clear that statutes like the MSSA, which discriminate on the basis of gender, must be examined under the "heightened" scrutiny mandated by Craig v. Boren. Under this test, a gender-based classification cannot withstand constitutional challenge unless the classification is substantially related to the achievement of an important governmental objective. [E.g., Kirchberg v. Feenstra.] This test applies whether the classification discriminates against males or females. The party defending the challenged classification carries the burden of demonstrating both the importance of the governmental objective it serves and the substantial relationship between the discriminatory means and the asserted end. Consequently, before we can sustain the MSSA, the Government must demonstrate that the gender-based classification it employs bears "a close and substantial relationship to [the achievement of] important governmental objectives." [Feeney.]

C.   [I] agree with the majority that "none could deny that [the] Government's interest in raising and supporting armies is an 'important governmental interest.'" Consequently, the first part of the Craig v. Boren test is satisfied. But the question remains whether the discriminatory means employed itself substantially serves the statutory end. In concluding that it does, the [majority notes that] the Court has accorded particular deference to decisions arising in the context of Congress' authority over military affairs. [But] even in the area of military affairs, deference to congressional judgments cannot be allowed to shade into an abdication of this Court's ultimate responsibility to decide constitutional questions. [When], as here, a federal law that classifies on the basis of gender is challenged as violating this constitutional guarantee, it is ultimately for this Court, not Congress, to decide

1.   [Appellees] do not concede the constitutional validity of these restrictions on women in combat, but they have taken the position that their validity is irrelevant, for purposes of this case. [Footnote by Justice Marshall.]

whether there exists the constitutionally required "close and substantial relationship" between the discriminatory means employed and the asserted governmental objective. In my judgment, there simply is no basis for concluding in this case that excluding women from registration is substantially related to the achievement of a concededly important governmental interest in maintaining an effective defense. The Court reaches a contrary conclusion only by using an "[a]nnounced degre[e] of 'deference' to legislative judgmen[t]" as a "facile abstractio[n] [to] justify a particular result." [Quoting majority opinion.]

II A. The Government does not defend the exclusion of women from registration on the ground that preventing women from serving in the military is substantially related to the effectiveness of the Armed Forces. Indeed, the successful experience of women serving in all branches of the Armed Services would belie any such claim. [The] justification for the MSSA's gender-based discrimination must therefore be found in considerations that are peculiar to the objectives of registration. The most authoritative discussion of Congress' reasons for declining to require registration of women is contained in the report prepared by the Senate Armed Services Committee on the Fiscal Year 1981 Defense Authorization Bill. [This] Court may appropriately look to the Report in evaluating the justification for the discrimination.

B. [The] Court's opinion offers [an] explanation of the relationship between the combat restrictions and Congress' decision not to require registration of women. The majority states that "[Congress] clearly linked the need for renewed registration with its views of the character of a subsequent draft." The Court also states that "Congress determined that any future draft, which would be facilitated by the registration scheme, would be characterized by a need for combat troops." The Court then reasons that since women are not eligible for assignment to combat, Congress' decision to exclude them from registration is not unconstitutional discrimination inasmuch as "[m]en and women, because of the combat restrictions on women, are simply not similarly situated for purposes of a draft or registration for a draft." There is a certain logic to this reasoning, but the Court's approach is fundamentally flawed.

In the first place, although the Court purports to apply the Craig v. Boren test, the "similarly situated" analysis the Court employs is in fact significantly different from the Craig v. Boren approach. Compare Kirchberg v. Feenstra (employing Craig v. Boren test) with id. (Stewart, J., concurring) (employing "similarly situated" analysis). The Court essentially reasons that the gender classification employed by the MSSA is constitutionally permissible because nondiscrimination is not necessary to achieve the purpose of registration to prepare for a draft of combat troops. In other words, the majority concludes that women may be excluded from registration because they will not be needed in the event of a draft.[2]

---

2. I would have thought the logical conclusion from this reasoning is that there is in fact no discrimination against women, in which case one must wonder why the Court feels compelled to pledge its purported fealty to the Craig v. Boren test. [Footnote by Justice Marshall.]

what question really is!

This analysis, however, focuses on the wrong question. The relevant inquiry under the Craig v. Boren test is not whether a *gender-neutral* classification would substantially advance important governmental interests. Rather, the question is whether the gender-based classification is itself substantially related to the achievement of the asserted governmental interest. Thus, the Government's task in this case is to demonstrate that excluding women from registration substantially furthers the goal of preparing for a draft of combat troops. Or, to put it another way, the Government must show that registering women would substantially impede its efforts to prepare for such a draft. Under our precedents, the Government cannot meet this burden without showing that a gender-neutral statute would be a less effective means of attaining this end. As the Court explained in Orr v. Orr, "Legislative classifications which distribute benefits and burdens on the basis of gender *carry the inherent risk of reinforcing sexual stereotypes about the 'proper place' of women and their need for special protection.* [Where], as here, the [Government's] purposes are as well served by a gender-neutral classification as one that gender classifies and therefore carries with it the baggage of sexual stereotypes, the [Government] cannot be permitted to classify on the basis of sexual stereotypes." In this case, the Government makes no claim that preparing for a draft of combat troops cannot be accomplished just as effectively by *registering* both men and women but *drafting* only men if only men turn out to be needed.[3] Nor can the Government argue that this alternative entails the additional cost and administrative inconvenience of registering women. This Court has repeatedly stated that the administrative convenience of employing a gender classification is not an adequate constitutional justification under the Craig v. Boren test.

administrative convenience not an adequate const just under Craig v Boren test

The fact that registering women in no way obstructs the governmental interest in preparing for a draft of combat troops points up a second flaw in the Court's analysis. The Court essentially reduces the question of the constitutionality of male-only *registration* to the validity of a hypothetical program for *conscripting* only men. The Court posits a draft in which *all* conscripts are either assigned to those specific combat posts presently closed to women or must be available for rotation into such positions. By so doing, the Court is able to conclude that registering women would be no more than a "gestur[e] of superficial equality," since women are necessarily ineligible for every position to be filled in its hypothetical draft. If it could indeed be guaranteed in advance that conscription would be reimposed by Congress only in circumstances where, and in a form under which, all conscripts would have to be trained for and assigned to combat or combat rotation positions from which women are categorically excluded, then it could be argued that registration of women would be pointless.

But of course, no such guarantee is possible. Certainly, nothing about the MSSA limits Congress to reinstituting the draft only in such circum-

---

3. Alternatively, the Government could employ a classification that is related to the statutory objective but is not based on gender, for example, combat eligibility. Under the current scheme, large subgroups of the male population who are ineligible for combat because of physical handicaps or conscientious objector status are nonetheless required to register. [Footnote by Justice Marshall.]

stances. For example, Congress may decide that the All-Volunteer Armed Forces are inadequate to meet the Nation's defense needs even in times of peace and reinstitute peacetime conscription. In that event, the hypothetical draft the Court relied on to sustain the MSSA's gender-based classification would presumably be of little relevance, and the Court could then be forced to declare the male-only registration program unconstitutional. This difficulty comes about because both Congress and the Court have lost sight of the important distinction between *registration* and *conscription.* Registration provides "an inventory of what the available strength is within the military qualified pool in this country." Conscription supplies the military with the personnel needed to respond to a particular exigency. The fact that registration is a first step in the conscription process does not mean that a registration law expressly discriminating between men and women may be justified by a valid conscription program which would, in retrospect, make the current discrimination appear functionally related to the program that emerged.

But even addressing the Court's reasoning on its own terms, its analysis is flawed because the entire argument rests on a premise that is demonstrably false. As noted, the majority simply assumes that registration prepares for a draft in which *every* draftee must be available for assignment to combat. But the majority's draft scenario finds no support in either the testimony before Congress, or more importantly, in the findings of the Senate Report. Indeed, the scenario appears to exist only in the Court's imagination, for even the Government represents only that "in the event of mobilization, *approximately two-thirds* of the demand on the induction system would be for *combat skills.*" For my part, rather than join the Court in imagining hypothetical drafts, I prefer to examine the findings in the Senate Report and the testimony presented to Congress.

C. [My] review of the findings contained in the Senate Report and the testimony presented at the congressional hearings demonstrates that there is no basis for the Court's representation that women are ineligible for *all* the positions that would need to be filled in the event of a draft. Testimony about personnel requirements in the event of a draft established that women could fill at least 80,000 of the 650,000 positions for which conscripts would be inducted. Thus, with respect to these 80,000 or more positions, the statutes and policies barring women from combat do not provide a reason for distinguishing between male and female potential conscripts; the two groups are, in the majority's parlance, "similarly situated." As such, the combat restrictions cannot by themselves supply the constitutionally required justification for the MSSA's gender-based classification. Since the classification precludes women from being drafted to fill positions for which they would be qualified and useful, the Government must demonstrate that excluding women from those positions is substantially related to the achievement of an important governmental objective.

III. The Government argues, however, that the "consistent testimony before Congress was to the effect that there is no military need to draft women." And the Government points to a statement in the Senate Report that "[b]oth the civilian and military leadership agreed that there was no military need to draft women. [The] argument for registration and induction of

women [is] not based on military necessity, but on considerations of equity."
In accepting the Government's contention, the Court asserts that the President's decision to seek authority to register women was based on "equity," and concludes that "Congress was certainly entitled, in the exercise of its constitutional powers to raise and regulate armies and navies, to focus on the question of military need rather than 'equity.'" In my view, a more careful examination of the concepts of "equity" and "military need" is required.

[By] "considerations of equity," the military experts acknowledged that female conscripts can perform as well as male conscripts in certain positions, and that there is therefore no reason why one group should be totally excluded from registration and a draft. Thus, what the majority so blithely dismisses as "equity" is nothing less than the Fifth Amendment's guarantee of equal protection of the laws which "requires that Congress treat similarly situated persons similarly." Moreover, whether Congress could subsume this constitutional requirement to "military need" in part depends on precisely what the Senate Report meant by "military need." [However] the "military need" statement in the Senate Report is understood, it does not provide the constitutionally required justification for the total exclusion of women from registration and draft plans.

[IV] Recognizing the need to go beyond the "military need" argument, the Court asserts that "Congress determined that staffing noncombat positions with women during a mobilization would be positively detrimental to the important goal of military flexibility." None would deny that preserving "military flexibility" is an important governmental interest. But to justify the exclusion of women from registration and the draft on this ground, there must be a further showing that staffing even a limited number of noncombat positions with women would impede military flexibility. I find nothing in the Senate Report to provide any basis for the Court's representation that Congress believed this to be the case. [I] cannot agree with the Court's attempt to "interpret" the Senate Report's conclusion that drafting *very large numbers* of women would impair military flexibility, as proof that Congress reached the entirely different conclusion that drafting a limited number of women would adversely affect military flexibility.

[V.] [The] majority asserts that even "assuming that a small number of women could be drafted for noncombat roles, Congress simply did not consider it worth the added burdens of including women in draft and registration plans." In actual fact, the conclusion the Senate Report reached is significantly different from the one the Court seeks to attribute to it. The specific finding by the Senate Report was that "[i]f the law required women to be drafted *in equal numbers* with men, mobilization would be severely impaired because of strains on training facilities and administrative systems." There was, however, no suggestion at the congressional hearings that simultaneous induction of *equal* numbers of males and female conscripts was either necessary or desirable. The Defense Department recommended that women be included in registration and draft plans, with the number of female draftees and the timing of their induction to be determined by the military's personnel requirements. In endorsing this plan, the Department gave no indication that such a draft would place any strains on training and administrative facilities.

[The] Senate Report simply failed to consider the possibility that a limited number of women could be drafted because of its conclusion that [the] MSSA does not authorize drafting different numbers of men and women and its speculation on judicial reaction to a decision to register women. But since Congress was free to amend [the Act], and indeed would have to undertake new legislation to authorize any draft, the matter cannot end there. Furthermore, the Senate Report's speculation that a statute authorizing differential induction of male and female draftees would be vulnerable to constitutional challenge is unfounded. The unchallenged restrictions on the assignment of women to combat, the need to preserve military flexibility, and the other factors discussed in the Senate Report provide more than ample grounds for concluding that the discriminatory means employed by such a statute would be substantially related to the achievement of important governmental objectives. Since Congress could have amended [the Act] to authorize differential induction of men and women based on the military's personnel requirements, the Senate Report's discussion about "added burdens" that would result from drafting equal numbers of male and female draftees provides no basis for concluding that the total exclusion of women from registration and draft plans is substantially related to the achievement of important governmental objectives. In sum, neither the Senate Report itself nor the testimony presented at the congressional hearings provides any support for the conclusion the Court seeks to attribute to the Report—that drafting a limited number of women, with the number and the timing of their induction and training determined by the military's personnel requirements, would burden training and administrative facilities.

VI. After reviewing the discussion and findings contained in the Senate Report, the most I am able to say of the Report is that it demonstrates that drafting *very large numbers* of women would frustrate the achievement of a number of important governmental objectives that relate to the ultimate goal of maintaining "an adequate armed strength [to] insure the security of this Nation." Or to put it another way, the Senate Report establishes that induction of a large number of men but only a limited number of women, as determined by the military's personnel requirements, would be substantially related to important governmental interests. But the discussion and findings in the Senate Report do not enable the Government to carry its burden of demonstrating that *completely* excluding women from the draft by excluding them from registration substantially furthers important governmental objectives.

In concluding that the Government has carried its burden in this case, the Court adopts "an appropriately deferential examination of *Congress'* evaluation of [the] evidence." The majority then proceeds to supplement Congress' actual findings with those the Court apparently believes Congress could (and should) have made. Beyond that, the Court substitutes hollow shibboleths about "deference to legislative decisions" for constitutional analysis. It is as if the majority has lost sight of the fact that "it is the responsibility of this Court to act as the ultimate interpreter of the Constitution." (Powell v.

McCormack. Congressional enactments in the area of military affairs must, like all other laws, be *judged* by the standards of the Constitution. [In] an attempt to avoid its constitutional obligation, the Court today "pushes back the limits of the Constitution" to accommodate an Act of Congress. . . .

MISSISSIPPI UNIVERSITY FOR WOMEN v. HOGAN, 458 U.S. —— (1982): The 5 to 4 decision in this case sustained a man's equal protection challenge to the State's policy of excluding men from the Mississippi University for Women (MUW) School of Nursing. MUW, founded in 1884 (to provide for the "Education of White Girls"), is the oldest state-supported all-female university in the nation. Its School of Nursing was established in 1971. Hogan, a registered nurse in Columbus, Miss., where MUW is located, was denied admission to the School's baccalaureate program. He was told he could only audit courses and would have to go to one of the State's coeducational nursing schools elsewhere in Mississippi to obtain credits toward a degree.

In sustaining Hogan's attack on the School of Nursing's single-sex admissions policy,[1] Justice O'CONNOR, writing for the majority, applied the heightened level of scrutiny articulated in Craig v. Boren and rejected the State's effort to justify its system as "benign" and "compensatory." She sketched the framework for her analysis by stating "several firmly-established principles": "That this statute discriminates against males rather than against females does not exempt it from scrutiny or reduce the standard of review.[2] [Moreover], the party seeking to uphold a statute that classifies individuals on the basis of their gender must carry the burden of showing an 'exceedingly

---

1. Justice O'Connor repeatedly stated the ruling as a "narrow" one limited to MUW's professional nursing school: "[W]e decline to address the question of whether MUW's admissions policy, as applied to males seeking admission to schools other than the School of Nursing, violates the Fourteenth Amendment." But Justice Powell's dissent (noted more fully below) expressed doubt that the majority's analysis could be so limited. He thought the majority's limit on the scope of its ruling would be "welcome" if it left "MUW free to remain an all-women's university in each of its other schools and departments— which include four schools and more than a dozen departments." But in his view, the "logic of the Court's entire opinion [appears] to apply sweepingly to the entire university." As he saw it, "the issue properly before us is the single-sex policy of the University. [I] see no principled way—in light of the Court's rationale—to reach a different result with respect to other MUW schools and departments." But he added that, "given the Court's insistence that its decision applies only to the School of Nursing,

it is my view that the Board and officials of MUW may continue to operate the remainder of the University on a single-sex basis without fear of personal liability. The standard of such liability is whether the conduct of the official 'violate[s] clearly established statutory or constitutional rights of which a reasonable person would have known.' The Court today leaves in doubt the reach of its decision."

2. "Without question, MUW's admissions policy worked to Hogan's disadvantage. Although Hogan could have attended classes and received credit in one of Mississippi's state-supported coeducational nursing programs, none of which was located in Columbus, he could attend only by driving a considerable distance from his home. A similarly situated female would not have been required to choose between foregoing credit and bearing that inconvenience. [The] policy of denying males the right to obtain credit toward a baccalaureate degree [imposed] upon Hogan 'a burden he would not bear were he female.' " [Footnote by Justice O'Connor.]

persuasive justification' for the classification. [Kirchberg v. Feenstra; Feeney.] The burden is met only by showing that the classification serves 'important governmental objectives and that the discriminatory means employed' are 'substantially related to the achievement of those objectives.' [Wengler.]"

Justice O'Connor continued: "Although the test for determining the validity of a gender-based classification is straightforward, it must be applied free of fixed notions concerning the roles and abilities of males and females. Care must be taken in ascertaining whether the statutory objective itself reflects archaic and stereotypic notions. [If] the State's objective is legitimate and important, we must next determine whether the requisite direct, substantial relationship between objective and means is present. [The] need for the requirement is amply revealed by reference to the broad range of statutes already invalidated by this Court, statutes that relied upon the simplistic, outdated assumption that gender could be used as a 'proxy for other, more germane bases of classification,' Craig v. Boren, to establish a link between objective and classification."

Under this analysis, Justice O'Connor found, the MUW scheme could not survive scrutiny. She rejected the State's primary justification, that the single-sex admissions policy "compensates for discrimination against women and, therefore, constitutes educational affirmative action." [3] She conceded that, in "limited circumstances, a gender-based classification favoring one sex can be justified if it intentionally and directly assists members of the sex that is disproportionately burdened." But such a "benign" justification requires "searching analysis." [E.g., Weinberger v. Wiesenfeld.] A state can establish a "compensatory purpose" justification "only if members of the gender benefited by the classification actually suffer a disadvantage related to the classification. [E.g., Califano v. Webster; Schlesinger v. Ballard.]" Here, however, the State had made "no showing that women lacked opportunities to obtain training in the field of nursing or to attain positions of leadership in that field when the MUW School of Nursing opened its doors or that women currently are deprived of such opportunities." She noted, for example, that, in 1970, "women earned 94 percent of the nursing baccalaureate degrees conferred in Mississippi and 98.6 percent of the degrees earned nationwide. [And] the labor force reflects the same predominance of women in nursing. [Accordingly], [r]ather than compensate for discriminatory barriers faced by women, MUW's policy of excluding males [tends] to perpetuate the stereotyped view of nursing as an exclusively woman's job. [MUW's] admissions policy lends credibility to the old view that women, not men, should become nurses, and makes the assumption that nursing is a field for women a self-fulfilling prophecy. Thus, we conclude that, although the

3. "In its Reply Brief, the State understandably retreated from its contention that MUW was founded to provide opportunities for women which were not available to men. Apparently, the impetus for founding MUW came not from a desire to provide women with advantages superior to those offered men, but rather [from] a desire to provide white women in Mississippi access to state-supported higher learning. [In] Mississippi, as elsewhere in the country, women's colleges were founded to provide some form of higher education for the academically disenfranchised." [Footnote by Justice O'Connor.]

State recited a 'benign, compensatory purpose,' it failed to establish that the alleged objective is the actual purpose underlying the discriminatory classification."[4]

Moreover, MUW's policy failed "the second part of the equal protection test, for the State has made no showing that the gender-based classification is substantially and directly related to its proposed compensatory objective. To the contrary, MUW's policy of permitting men to attend classes as auditors fatally undermines its claim that women, at least those in the School of Nursing, are adversely affected by the presence of men. [The] record in this case is flatly inconsistent with the claim that excluding men from the School of Nursing is necessary to reach any of MUW's educational goals. Thus, considering both the asserted interest and the relationship between the interest and the methods used by the State, we conclude that the State has fallen far short of establishing the 'exceedingly persuasive justification' needed to sustain the gender-based classification." [5]

Finally, Justice O'Connor rejected the argument that Congress had specifically authorized single-sex schools. Title IX of the Education Amendments Act of 1972, prohibiting gender discrimination in education programs that receive federal financial assistance, exempted undergraduate institutions if they "traditionally and continually from [their] establishment [have] had a policy of admitting only students of one sex." The State argued that this was a valid limit on the Equal Protection Clause enacted under the congressional power granted by § 5 of the Fourteenth Amendment. Justice O'Connor expressed doubt that Congress had intended to exempt colleges "from any constitutional obligation"; she thought that the provision "at most" exempted colleges from the requirements of Title IX. But even if Congress "envisioned a constitutional exemption, the State's argument would fail." Congress' power under § 5, though "broad," was "limited to adopting measures to enforce the guarantees of the Amendment; § 5 grants Congress

---

4. "Even were we to assume that discrimination against women affects their opportunity to obtain an education or to obtain leadership roles in nursing, the challenged policy nonetheless would be invalid, for the State has failed to establish that the legislature intended the single-sex policy to compensate for any perceived discrimination. Cf. Califano v. Webster. The State has provided no evidence whatever that the Mississippi legislature has ever attempted to justify its differing treatment of men and women seeking nurses' training. . . ." [Footnote by Justice O'Connor.]

5. "Justice Powell's dissent suggests that a second objective is served by the gender-based classification in that Mississippi has elected to provide women a choice of educational environments. Since any gender-based classification provides one class a benefit or choice not available to the other class, however, that argument begs the question. The issue is not whether the benefited class profits from the classification, but whether the State's decision to confer a benefit only upon one class by means of a discriminatory classification is substantially related to achieving a legitimate and substantial goal." [Footnote by Justice O'Connor.]

Justice Powell responded to this comment as follows: "This is *not* the issue in this case. Hogan is not complaining about any benefit conferred upon women. Nor is he claiming discrimination because Mississippi offers no all-male college. As his brief states: 'Joe Hogan does not ask to attend an all-male college which offers a Bachelor of Science in nursing; he asks only to attend MUW' and he asks this only for his personal convenience."

no power to restrict, abrogate, or dilute these guarantees." [Quoting Justice Brennan's footnote [1] in Katzenbach v. Morgan.] Justice O'Connor added: "The fact that the language of [the exemption] applies to MUW provides the State no solace: '[A] statute apparently governing a dispute cannot be applied by judges consistently with their obligations, when such an application of the statute would conflict with the Constitution. Marbury v. Madison.' Younger v. Harris." [6]

Justice POWELL, joined by Justice Rehnquist, submitted the most extensive dissent. He argued that the majority had unduly curtailed valuable diversity in higher education, that the heightened standard of review was inappropriate here, that a "rational basis" standard should govern, and that "[t]his simply is not a sex discrimination case. The Equal Protection Clause was never intended to be applied to this kind of case." In elaborating those conclusions, he objected to the Court's condemnation of the State's effort "to provide women with a traditionally popular and respected choice of educational environment. It does so in a case instituted by one man, who represents no class, and whose primary concern is personal convenience." The Court's emphasis on "sexual stereotyp[ing]," he insisted, had "no application whatever to [Hogan] or to the 'wrong' of which he complains. At best this is anomalous. And ultimately the anomaly reveals legal error—that of applying a heightened equal protection standard, developed in cases of genuine sexual stereotyping, to a narrowly utilized state classification that provides an *additional* choice for women." Moreover, the Mississippi system should survive review even if a heightened standard of scrutiny were applied.

Reviewing the history of single-sex education, Justice Powell insisted that the "sexual segregation of students has been a reflection of, rather than an imposition upon, the preference of those subject to the policy." He noted that "generations of Americans, including scholars, have thought—wholly without regard to any discriminatory animus—that there were distinct advantages in this type of higher education." He conceded that coeducational institutions are now far more numerous, but argued that "their numerical predominance does not establish—in any sense properly cognizable by a court— that individual preferences for single-sex education are misguided or illegitimate, or that a State may not provide its citizens with a choice." He argued that the heightened standard of review generally applicable to sex discrimination was inappropriate here: "In no previous case have we applied it to invalidate state efforts to *expand* women's choices. Nor are there prior sex discrimination decisions by this Court in which a male plaintiff [had] the choice of an equal benefit." He insisted: "By applying heightened equal protection analysis to this case,[7] the Court frustrates the liberating spirit of the Equal

6. See also the additional note on the "Morgan power" aspect of this case below, addition to 10th Ed., p. 1104; Ind. Rts., p. 724.

7. "Even the Court does not argue that the appropriate standard here is 'strict scrutiny'—a standard that none . of our 'sex discrimination' cases ever has adopted. Sexual segregation in

education differs from the tradition typified by [Plessy v. Ferguson], of 'separate but equal' *racial* segregation. It was characteristic of racial segregation that segregated facilities were offered, not as alternatives to increase the choices available to blacks, but as the *sole* alternative. MUW stands in sharp contrast. Of Mississippi's eight public universities and 16 public jun-

Protection Clause. It forbids the States from providing women with an opportunity to choose the type of university they prefer."

Since Justice Powell did not view the case as "presenting a serious equal protection claim," he thought a "rational basis analysis" was appropriate. But even if heightened scrutiny were applied, the record demonstrated that the gender-based distinction served "an important governmental objective by means that are substantially related to its achievement." He found the State's purpose of affording a choice "legitimate and substantial." And he rejected the majority's argument that MUW perpetuated stereotypes about nursing as a woman's job, noting that the School of Nursing was founded 90 years after the single-sex campus itself: "This hardly supports a link between nursing as a woman's profession and MUW's single-sex admission policy." He concluded: "[Mississippi's] accommodation [of] student choices is legitimate because it is completely consensual and is important because it permits students to decide for themselves the type of college education they think will benefit them most. Finally, Mississippi's policy is substantially related to its long-respected objective." The Court's decision ran counter to the traditional American "respect for diversity." All that was involved here was one man's claim to "a right to attend the college in his home community." [8]

10th ED., p. 885; IND. RTS., p. 505
Add as footnote at end of Note 3:

The expiration (and aftermath) of ERA. At midnight on June 30, 1982, the extended period for the ratification of the proposed 27th Amendment, the Equal Rights Amendment, expired. Thirty-five states had endorsed the amendment, but with the approval of three more required for ratification, supporters and opponents alike agreed that the measure had been defeated. The defeat left ERA proponents uncertain as to how best to proceed. Although some ERA proponents contemplated statutory alternatives to a constitutional amendment, most have joined in an attempt to recommence the process of amending the Constitution with an Equal Rights Amendment. H.J. Res. 1 and S.J. Res. 10, both introduced in the 98th Congress in January 1983, propose constitutional amendments identical to the one submitted to the states on March 22, 1972. As of June 1983 there had been no formal action in either house on either proposal.

ior colleges, only MUW considers sex as a criterion for admission. Women consequently are free to select a coeducational education environment for themselves if they so desire; their attendance at MUW is not a matter of coercion." [Footnote by Justice Powell.]

8. In a separate dissenting notation, Chief Justice BURGER, while agreeing generally with Justice Powell's dissent, emphasized that the holding was "limited to the context of a professional nursing school." He, unlike Justice Powell, read the majority opinion to suggest that "a State might well be justified in maintaining, for example, the option of an all-women's business school or liberal arts program." In another dissent, Justice BLACKMUN noted that the State had not "closed the doors of its educational system to males like Hogan" and added: "I have come to suspect that

it is easy to go too far with rigid rules in this area of claimed sex discrimination, and to lose—indeed destroy—values that mean much to some people by forbidding the State from offering them a choice while not depriving others of an alternate choice. Justice Powell [advances] this theme well." Like Justice Powell, he was skeptical about the asserted narrowness of the majority opinion: "[T]here is inevitable spillover from the Court's ruling today. That ruling, it seems to me, places in constitutional jeopardy any state-supported educational institution that confines its student body in any area to members of one sex, even though the State elsewhere provides an equivalent program to the complaining applicant. [I] hope that we do not lose all values that some think are worthwhile (and are not based on differences of race or religion) and relegate ourselves to needless conformity."

10th ED., p. 894; IND. RTS., p. 514
Insert after Ambach v. Norwick (before the Notes):

ALIENAGE RESTRICTIONS IN PUBLIC EMPLOYMENT, 1982: PROBATION OFFICERS AND OTHER "PEACE OFFICERS"

The 5 to 4 decision in CABELL v. CHAVEZ–SALIDO, 454 U.S. 432 (1982), continued the Court's recent tendency to apply quite deferential scrutiny to citizenship requirements for state employment. The challengers were lawfully admitted resident aliens who sought to become "Deputy Probation Officers, Spanish-speaking." They were denied employment because California law imposed a citizenship requirement for the positions they sought. One statutory provision required all "peace officers" to be American citizens; another provision designated probation officers as "peace officers." A lower federal court (ruling after Foley and Ambach) had held the statutory scheme unconstitutional both facially and as applied. The Court reversed, insisting that this bar to aliens was permissible under the Sugarman-Foley-Ambach line of cases.

Justice WHITE, writing for the majority, began with a renewed attempt to make sense of the wavering line of precedents. He noted that "to say that the decisions do not fall into a neat pattern is not to say that they fall into no pattern. In fact, they illustrate a not unusual characteristic of legal development: broad principles are articulated, narrowed when applied to new contexts, and finally replaced when the distinctions they rely upon are no longer tenable." He elaborated: "The cases through Graham dealt for the most part with attempts by the states to retain certain economic benefits exclusively for citizens. Since Graham, the Court has confronted claims distinguishing between the economic and sovereign functions of government. This distinction has been supported by the argument that although citizenship is not a relevant ground for the distribution of economic benefits, it is a relevant ground for determining membership in the political community. [While] not retreating from the position that restrictions on lawfully resident aliens that primarily affect economic interests are subject to heightened judicial scrutiny, we have concluded that strict scrutiny is out of place when the restriction primarily serves a political function. [The] exclusion of aliens from basic governmental processes is not a deficiency in the democratic system but a necessary consequence of the community's process of political self-definition." He emphasized the centrality of the "distinction between the economic and political functions of government," a distinction that he conceded "may be difficult to apply in particular cases."

Justice White proceeded to delineate a "two-step process," allegedly inherent in Sugarman, to evaluate claims that "a particular restriction on legally resident aliens serves political and not economic goals": "First, the specificity of the classification will be examined: a classification that is substantially over or underinclusive tends to undercut the governmental claim that the classification serves legitimate political ends.[1] [Second], even if the classification is sufficiently tailored, it may be applied in the particular case only to [those who] 'perform functions that go to the heart of representative government.' "

Applying this approach, Justice White rejected the lower court's invalidation of the requirement that all "peace officers" be citizens and concluded that the restriction challenged here "passes both of the Sugarman tests." The lower court had found the restriction overinclusive by noting that more than seventy positions were classified as "peace officers" under California law and that at least some of these classifications could not be justified under the state power to define its "political community," "no matter how liberally that category is viewed." [2] Justice White criticized that argument as applying "a standard of review far stricter than that approved in Sugarman and later cases." Even if the citizenship requirement could not be applied to each of the seventy positions, to invalidate the entire law if it was "overinclusive at all" was to apply an erroneous standard. The proper inquiry, he asserted, was "whether the restriction reaches so far and is so broad and haphazard as to belie the state's claim that it is only attempting to ensure that an important function of government be in the hands of those having the 'fundamental legal bond of citizenship.' Under this standard, the classifications used need not be precise; there need only be a substantial fit. Our examination of the California scheme convinces us that it is sufficiently tailored to withstand a facial challenge."

In Justice White's view, "[e]ven a casual reading [of the law] makes clear that the unifying character of all categories of peace officers is their law enforcement function. [Although] some of these categories may have only a tenuous connection to traditional police functions of law enforcement, the questionable classifications are comparatively few in number. [Foley] made clear that a state may limit the exercise of the sovereign's coercive police powers over the members of the community to citizens. The California statutes at issue here are an attempt to do just that. They are sufficiently tailored in light of that aim to pass the lower level of scrutiny we articulated as the ap-

---

1. Justice White viewed the classification in Sugarman as deficient because of such overinclusiveness and underinclusiveness: "The classification in Sugarman itself—all members of the competitive civil service—could not support the claim that it was an element in 'the State's broad power to define its political community' because it indiscriminately swept in menial occupations, while leaving out some of the state's most important political functions." '

2. The lower court had commented: "There appears to be no justification whatever for excluding aliens [from] holding public employment as cemetery sextons, furniture and bedding inspectors, livestock identification inspectors and toll service employees."

propriate equal protection standard for such an exercise of sovereign power in Sugarman." [3]

Justice White also rejected the lower court's invalidation of the citizenship requirement "as applied" to deputy probation officers. He explained: "In reaching this conclusion, [the lower court] focused too narrowly on a comparison of the characteristics and functions of probation officers with those of the state troopers at issue in Foley and the teachers in Ambach. Foley and Ambach did not describe the outer limits of permissible citizenship requirements." For example, those cases had not barred citizenship requirements for judges or jurors. "Definition of the important sovereign functions of the political community is necessarily the primary responsibility of the representative branches of government, subject to limited judicial review."

Examining the functions of probation officers, Justice White found that "they, like the state troopers [in Foley], sufficiently partake of the sovereign's power to exercise coercive force over the individual that they may be limited to citizens. Although the range of individuals over whom [a probation officer exercises] supervisory authority is limited, the powers of the probation officer are broad with respect to those over whom [he exercises] that authority. [In] carrying out these responsibilities the probation officer necessarily has a great deal of discretion that, just like that of the police officer and the teacher, must be exercised, in the first instance, without direct supervision." He accordingly concluded: "One need not take an overly idealistic view of the educational functions of the probation officer [to] recognize that the probation officer acts as an extension of the judiciary's authority to set the conditions under which particular individuals will lead their lives and of the executive's authority to coerce obedience to those conditions. From the perspective of the probationer, his probation officer may personify the state's sovereign powers; from the perspective of the larger community, the probation officer may symbolize the political community's control over, and thus responsibility for, those who have been found to have violated the norms of the social order. From both of these perspectives, a citizenship requirement may seem an appropriate limitation on those who would exercise and, therefore, symbolize this power of the political community over those who fall within its jurisdiction."

3. In a footnote, Justice White pointed out that an underinclusiveness challenge was also inappropriate here, despite "some language in Sugarman indicating that such an argument is appropriate." He conceded that Sugarman had suggested that "a statutory exclusion of aliens from a particular form of public employment will be evaluated in light of the entire framework of public employment positions open and closed to aliens"; but he added that "clearly our subsequent cases have not adopted that position." He explained: "Thus, in both Foley and Ambach only the specific governmental functions directly at issue were considered." In Sugarman, underinclusiveness arguments were relevant because the "competitive civil service" classification had covered a "wide variety of governmental functions": "Such a sweeping and apparently indiscriminate categorization raises legitimate questions of arbitrariness that are not raised when the state limits a particular and important governmental function—e.g., coercive police power—to citizens. When we deal with such a specific category, underinclusiveness arguments are relevant only within the category: Are there, for example, individuals who exercise the state's coercive police power that are not required to be citizens? In this respect, the California statutory scheme is not substantially underinclusive."

Justice BLACKMUN's dissent, joined by Justices Brennan, Marshall and Stevens, charged the majority with "misstating the standard of review it has long applied to alienage classifications" and concluded that "today's decision rewrites the Court's precedents, ignores history, defies common sense, and reinstates the deadening mantle of state parochialism in public employment." In Justice Blackmun's view, "California's exclusion of these [challengers] from the position of deputy probation officer stems solely from state parochialism and hostility toward foreigners who have come to this country lawfully. I find it ironic that the Court invokes the principle of democratic self-government to exclude from the law enforcement process individuals who have not only resided here lawfully, but who now desire merely to help the State enforce its laws. [The law] violates [their] rights to equal treatment and an individualized determination of fitness."

In supporting these conclusions, Justice Blackmun took issue at length with the majority's position regarding the standard of review appropriate under the prior cases. He insisted that a "stringent standard" was appropriate under Sugarman and its progeny: barriers against permanent resident aliens had to be "carefully examined in order to determine whether [the claimed governmental] interest is legitimate and substantial [and] whether the means adopted to achieve the goal are necessary and precisely drawn." He insisted: "The Court's analysis fundamentally distorts Sugarman. That decision did not condone a looser standard for review of classifications barring aliens from 'political' jobs." Nor was more lenient review justified by the post-Sugarman cases. While Foley and Ambach did explore "the boundaries of a State's power to define its political community, those cases have not altered this stringent standard of review."

As Justice Blackmun interpreted the heightened standard of review propounded in Sugarman, "a state statute that bars aliens from political positions lying squarely within the political community nevertheless violates the Equal Protection Clause if it excludes aliens from other public jobs in an unthinking or haphazard manner. The statutes at issue here represent just such an unthinking and haphazard exercise of state power. [Exactly] like the statutes struck down in Sugarman, California's statutory exclusion of aliens is fatally overinclusive and underinclusive. It bars aliens from employment in numerous public positions where the State's proffered justification has little, if any, relevance. At the same time, it allows aliens to fill other positions that would seem naturally to fall within the state's asserted purpose."

Nor did Justice Blackmun find any justification for the majority position under the Sugarman exception. In his view, the Sugarman exception permitted states to impose citizenship requirements for certain public offices that "perform functions that go to the heart of representative government"; yet that exception was "exceedingly narrow" as originally understood. Foley and Ambach had broadened the exception somewhat, to be sure. But, Justice Blackmun insisted, "I cannot embrace the Court's unsupported assertion that 'Foley and Ambach did not describe the outer limits of permissible citizenship requirements.' From the Court's analysis in Foley and Ambach, one must conclude that a State may not invoke Sugarman's narrow exception without making a substantial showing."

In Justice Blackmun's view, the permissible scope of state citizenship requirements for public employment after Foley and Ambach should be read as follows: The State must "show that it has historically reserved a particular executive position for its citizens as a matter of its 'constitutional prerogativ[e].' Furthermore, the State must demonstrate that the public employee in that position exercises plenary coercive authority and control over a substantial portion of the citizen population. The public employee must exercise this authority over his clientele without intervening judicial or executive supervision. Even then, the State must prove that citizenship 'bears some rational relationship to the special demands of the particular position.'" He insisted: "Without such a rigorous test, Sugarman's exception swallows Sugarman's rule. Yet the Court does not apply such a rigorous test today." Instead, the majority had applied a "nebulous standard" and had not demonstrated that deputy probation officers perform "important sovereign functions of the political community."

Justice Blackmun found it impossible to equate the functions of probation officers "with the discretionary duties of policemen, judges, and jurors." Moreover, California's "inflexible exclusion of aliens from deputy probation officer positions is inconsistent with its tolerance of aliens in other roles integral to the criminal justice system." For example, "a criminal defendant in California may be represented at trial and on appeal by an alien attorney, have his case tried before an alien judge and appealed to an alien justice, and then have his probation supervised by a county probation department headed by an alien. I find constitutionally absurd the Court's suggestion that the same defendant cannot be entrusted to the supervised discretion of a resident alien deputy probation officer." In short, California had "identified no characteristic of permanent resident aliens *as a class* which disables them from performing the job of deputy probation officer. [Indeed], the State advances no rational reason why these [challengers], native Spanish-speakers with graduate academic degrees, are not superbly qualified to act as probation officers for Spanish-speaking probationers, some of whom themselves may not be citizens." *

10th ED., p. 897; IND. RTS., p. 517
Add to footnote 1:

The relevance of federal preemption principles in alienage cases was emphasized in TOLL v. MORENO, 458 U.S. —— (1982). There, the District Court had invalidated a state restriction on certain aliens by relying on equal protection principles as well as the Supremacy Clause. The Court's majority opinion, written by Justice Brennan, rested solely on the Supremacy Clause and therefore found it unnecessary to reach the equal protection issue. In the course of his opinion, Justice BRENNAN stated: "Commentators have noted [that] many of the Court's decisions concerning alienage classifications, such as Takahashi, are better explained in preemption than equal protection terms." And he commented: "Takahashi and Graham stand for the broad principle that 'state regulation not congressionally sanctioned that discriminates against aliens lawfully admitted to the country is impermissible if it imposes additional burdens not contemplated by Congress.'" (He added in a footnote: "Our cases do recognize, however, that a State, in the course of defining

---

* For a heated encore of the argument regarding the issue of whether recent alienage cases have undercut the "heightened scrutiny" developed in the early 1970s for alienage classifica-tions, see the confrontation between Justices Rehnquist and Blackmun in Toll v. Moreno, 458 U.S. —— (1982), discussed immediately below.

its political community, may, in appropriate circumstances, limit the participation of noncitizens in the State's political and governmental functions. See, e.g., Cabell v. Chavez-Salido; Ambach v. Norwick; Foley v. Connelie; Sugarman v. Dougall."

The case involved the University of Maryland's policy of granting preferential treatment for purposes of tuition and fees to students with "in-state" status. The University permitted citizens and "immigrant aliens" to obtain in-state status upon a showing of domicile within the State; but "nonimmigrant aliens," even if domiciled in Maryland, were not eligible for such status. The Court held the University's in-state policy invalid under the Supremacy Clause "insofar as the policy categorically denies in-state status to domiciled nonimmigrant aliens who hold G-4 visas." In reaching that result, Justice Brennan relied entirely on federal legislation. The basic immigration laws speak of two classes of aliens, "immigrant" and "nonimmigrant." With respect to nonimmigrants, the law establishes various categories, including the G-4 category. For many of the nonimmigrant categories, Congress has precluded the covered alien from establishing domicile in the United States. "But significantly," Justice Brennan noted, "Congress has allowed G-4 aliens—employees of various international organizations, and their immediate families—to enter the country on terms permitting the establishment of domicile in the United States. In light of Congress' explicit decision not to bar G-4 aliens from acquiring domicile, the State's decision to deny 'in-state' status to G-4 aliens *solely* on account of the G-4 alien's federal immigration status surely amounts to an ancillary 'burden not contemplated by Congress' in admitting these aliens to the United States." (He also relied in part on the federal government's "additional affirmative step of conferring special tax privileges [including exemption from state taxes] on G-4 aliens.")[1]

Justice REHNQUIST, joined by Chief Justice Burger, submitted a lengthy dissent. He not only took exception to the majority's preemption approach ("the fact that a state statute can be said to discriminate against aliens does not, standing alone, demonstrate that the statute is preempted, absent some form of congressional sanction"), but he also challenged at length the equal protection arguments relied upon by the lower courts and not reached by the majority. He asserted that several recent decisions made it clear that "not every alienage classification is subject to strict scrutiny. In my view, the classification [involved here] cannot fairly be called 'suspect,' and therefore I would ask only whether it rests upon a rational basis. [I] believe it does."

Justice Rehnquist reviewed the history of "heightened" scrutiny for alienage classifications since Graham v. Richardson. That case, he stated, rested simply on the notion that aliens as a class were "a prime example of a 'discrete and insular minority.' " From subsequent cases, "[o]ne could infer that rigorous judicial scrutiny normally was necessary because aliens were barred from asserting their interests in the governmental body responsible for imposing burdens upon them. More recent decisions have established, however, that the political powerlessness of aliens is itself a consequence of distinctions on the basis of alienage that are constitutionally permissible." In view of Foley v. Connelie, Cabell v. Chavez-Salido and Ambach v. Norwick, there was "reason to doubt whether political powerlessness is any longer a legitimate reason for treating aliens as a 'suspect class' deserving of 'heightened judicial solicitude.' " In his view, the recent decisions merely reflected "the judgment that alienage, or the other side of the coin, citizenship, is for certain important state purposes a constitutionally relevant characteristic and therefore cannot always be considered invidious in the same manner as race or national origin." He noted, too, that in all earlier alienage cases the question was the permissible distinction a state might draw "between citizens and permanent resident aliens." Here, however, "the question is whether the State can distinguish between two groups, [one] of which consists of citizens and [immigrant] aliens," and the other of

1. Justice O'CONNOR submitted a brief opinion agreeing with the majority's preemption finding, but on a narrower ground: "I conclude that the Supremacy Clause does not prohibit the University from charging out-of-state tuition to those G-4 aliens who are exempted by federal law from federal taxes only." In this case, however, the alien challengers were exempt from state as well as federal taxes. "Imposition of out-of-state tuition on such aliens conflicts with federal law exempting them from state taxes, since, after all, the University admits that it seeks to charge the higher tuition in order to recover costs that state income taxes normally would cover."

nonimmigrant aliens and others (including citizens) who do not pay state taxes. And under the proper rationality standard, that scheme readily passed constitutional muster.

Justice Rehnquist's comments on equal protection scrutiny drew a vehement response in a concurring opinion by Justice BLACKMUN, who noted that the Court's ruling provided "an eloquent and sufficient answer to Justice Rehnquist's dissent: despite the vehemence with which his opinion is written, Justice Rehnquist has persuaded only one Justice to [join] his position." He continued: "But because the dissent attempts to plumb the Court's psyche,[2] I feel compelled to add comments addressed to Justice Rehnquist's ruminations on equal protection. In particular, I cannot leave unchallenged his suggestion that the Court's decisions holding resident aliens to be a 'suspect class' no longer are good law." He elaborated: "[Justice Rehnquist's] exegesis of the Court's reasons for according aliens 'suspect class' status is simplistic to the point of caricature. By labeling aliens a 'discrete and insular minority,' Graham v. Richardson, the Court did something more than provide an historical description of their political standing." Instead, it was a combination of factors—"disparate treatment accorded a class of 'similarly circumstanced' persons who historically have been disabled by the prejudice of the majority"—that "led the Court to conclude that alienage classifications 'in themselves supply a reason to infer antipathy' [Feeney] and therefore demand close judicial scrutiny."

Nor had the more recent decisions, such as Foley v. Connelie, undercut that basic approach: "The idea that aliens may be denied political rights is not a recently-discovered concept or a newly-molded principle that can be said to have eroded the prior understanding. To the contrary, the Court always has recognized that aliens may be denied the use of the mechanisms of self-government, and *all* of the alienage cases have been decided against the backdrop of that principle." In short, the Court's alienage cases were "not irreconcilable or inconsistent with one another. For while the Court has recognized [that] alienage may be taken into account when it is relevant—that is, when classifications bearing on political interests are involved—'[t]he distinction between citizens and aliens [ordinarily is] *irrelevant* to private activity,' Ambach v. Norwick (emphasis added). And it hardly need be demonstrated that governmental distinctions based on irrelevant characteristics cannot stand. If this dual aspect of alienage doctrine is unique, it is because aliens constitute a unique class."

Justice Blackmun added that he found "preposterous" Justice Rehnquist's suggestion that, "because States do not violate the Constitution when they exclude aliens from participation in the government of the community, the aliens' powerlessness therefore is constitutionally irrelevant. [Since Carolene Products] it never has been suggested that the *reason* for a discrete class' political powerlessness is significant; instead, the *fact* of powerlessness is crucial, for in combination with prejudice it is the minority group's inability to assert its political interests that 'curtail[s] the operation of those political processes ordinarily to be relied upon to protect minorities.' [If] anything, the fact that aliens constitutionally may be—and generally are—formally and completely barred from participating in the process of self-government makes particularly profound the need for searching judicial review of classifications grounded on alienage." He noted that no opinion had ever endorsed Justice Rehnquist's "lone dissent in Sugarman," echoed today: "Of course, one cannot condemn another for sticking to his guns. Barring a radical change in the Court's reasoning in cases concerning alienage, however, one can expect that today's equal protection writing by Justice Rehnquist will join his opinion in Sugarman, to use his phrase, as 'lifeless words on the pages of these Reports.' " [Justice Rehnquist had used that phrase in referring to Vlandis v. Kline ("an irrebuttable presumption" case in the last Note in this chapter).][3]

2. "The Justice opines that '[i]f the Court has eschewed strict scrutiny in the "political process" [alienage-equal protection] cases, it may be because the Court is becoming uncomfortable with the categorization of aliens as a suspect class.' " [Footnote by Justice Blackmun.]

3. Justice Rehnquist in turn responded to this attack by Justice Blackmun by asserting that Justice Blackmun "misunderstands my point. I have observed that the political powerlessness of aliens is the result of state-created classifications which this Court has upheld as constitutional. One may nevertheless conclude, as Justice Blackmun does, that the political pow-

10th ED., p. 897; IND. RTS., p. 517
Insert before Sec. 3C:

[handwritten: Fails a substantial state interest test]

| ILLEGAL ALIENS: |
| ACCESS TO EDUCATION |

[handwritten: alien ed.]

[handwritten: May Texas deny free public education to undocumented alien children? No]

PLYLER v. DOE

457 U.S. 202, 102 S.Ct. 2382, 72 L.Ed.2d 786 (1982).*

Justice BRENNAN delivered the opinion of the Court.

[handwritten: Question]

The question presented by these cases is whether, consistent with [equal protection], Texas may deny to undocumented school-age children the free public education that it provides to children who are citizens of the United States or legally admitted aliens.

I. Since the late nineteenth century, the United States has restricted immigration into this country. Unsanctioned entry into the United States is a crime, and those who have entered unlawfully are subject to deportation. But despite the existence of these legal restrictions, a substantial number of persons have succeeded in unlawfully entering the United States, and now live within various States, including [Texas]. In May 1975, the Texas legislature revised its education laws to withhold from local school districts any state funds for the education of children who were not "legally admitted" into the United States. The 1975 revision also authorized local school districts to deny enrollment in their public schools to children not "legally ad-

[handwritten margin: Unsanctioned entry to US is a crime + subject to deportation]

[handwritten margin: Texas Ed. Laws withhold funds from local school districts for education of ch. not legally admitted to US]

erlessness of aliens is still a reason for applying strict scrutiny to alienage classifications. My point, to which Justice Blackmun's concurrence is unresponsive, is that a classification which is constitutionally relevant to many important state purposes should not be considered 'suspect.' It is beside the point [that] alienage may be irrelevant for some other purposes. Were this consideration conclusive, all state classifications would be considered 'suspect' [because] every classification is relevant to some purposes and irrelevant to others."

* Decided together with Texas v. Certain Named and Unnamed Undocumented Alien Children.

Plyler v. Doe was a class action on behalf of certain school-children of Mexican origin residing in Smith County, Texas, who could not establish that they had been legally admitted into the United States. The suit attacked the exclusion of the children from the public schools of the Tyler Independent School District. Since 1977, the District had required "undocumented"

children to pay a "full tuition fee" in order to enroll. The lower federal courts held that the exclusion of the children from free public education violated the Equal Protection Clause.

The companion case, the Alien Children Litigation, was a consolidated action against state and local officials. There, too, the District Court and the Court of Appeals found an equal protection violation. The Court of Appeals rejected claims that Texas law was preempted by federal law and policy. The Supreme Court did not rule on the preemption argument: "In light of our disposition of the Fourteenth Amendment issue, we have no occasion to reach this claim."

The lower court injunctions remained in effect while the Supreme Court considered the appeals. Although state officials had initially predicted that 100,000 children of illegal aliens would enroll in Texas schools as a result of the injunctions, in fact only 12,000 attended Texas public schools in the 1980–81 school year and 18,000 in the 1981–82 year. See The New York Times, June 16, 1982.

mitted" to the country. These cases involve constitutional challenges to those provisions. . . .

[II] The Fourteenth Amendment provides that "No State [shall] deprive any person of life, liberty, or property, without due process of law; nor deny to *any person within its jurisdiction* the equal protection of the laws." Appellants argue at the outset that undocumented aliens, because of their immigration status, are not "persons within the jurisdiction" of the State of Texas, and that they therefore have no right to the equal protection of Texas law. We reject this argument. Whatever his status under the immigration laws, an alien is surely a *person* in any ordinary sense of that term. Aliens, even aliens whose presence in this country is unlawful, have long been recognized as "persons" guaranteed due process of law by the Fifth and Fourteenth Amendments. Indeed, we have clearly held that the Fifth Amendment protects aliens whose presence in this country is unlawful from invidious discrimination by the Federal Government.[1] Mathews v. Diaz.

Appellants seek to distinguish our prior cases, emphasizing that the Equal Protection Clause directs a State to afford its protection to persons *within its jurisdiction* while the Due Process Clauses [contain] no such assertedly limiting phrase. In appellants' view, persons who have entered the United States illegally are not "within the jurisdiction" of a State even if they are present within a State's boundaries and subject to its laws. Neither our cases nor the logic of the Fourteenth Amendment supports that constricting construction of the phrase "within its jurisdiction." We have never suggested that the class of persons who might avail themselves of the equal protection guarantee is less than coextensive with that entitled to due process. To the contrary, we have recognized that both provisions were fashioned to protect an identical class of persons, and to reach every exercise of State authority. [Yick Wo v. Hopkins.]

[There] is simply no support for appellants' suggestion that "due process" is somehow of greater stature than "equal protection" and therefore available to a larger class of persons. To the contrary, each aspect of the Fourteenth Amendment reflects an elementary limitation on state power. To permit a State to employ the phrase "within its jurisdiction" in order to identify subclasses of persons whom it would define as beyond its jurisdiction, thereby relieving itself of the obligation to assure that its laws are designed and applied equally to those persons, would undermine the principal purpose for which the Equal Protection Clause was incorporated in the Fourteenth Amendment. The Equal Protection Clause was intended to work nothing less than the abolition of all caste- and invidious class-based legislation. That objective is fundamentally at odds with the power the State asserts here to classify persons subject to its laws as nonetheless excepted from its protection.

Although the congressional debate concerning § 1 of the Fourteenth Amendment was limited, that debate clearly confirms the understanding that

---

1. It would be incongruous to hold that the United States, to which the Constitution assigns a broad authority over both naturalization and foreign affairs, is barred from invidious discrimination with respect to unlawful aliens, while exempting the States from a similar limitation. [Footnote by Justice Brennan.]

the phrase "within its jurisdiction" was intended in a broad sense to offer the guarantee of equal protection to all within a State's boundaries, and to all upon whom the State would impose the obligations of its laws. Indeed, it appears from those debates that Congress, by using the phrase "person within its jurisdiction," sought expressly to ensure that the equal protection of the laws was provided to the alien population. [Use] of the phrase "within its jurisdiction" thus does not detract from, but rather confirms, the understanding that the protection of the Fourteenth Amendment extends to anyone, citizen or stranger, who *is* subject to the laws of a State, and reaches into every corner of a State's territory. That a person's initial entry into a State, or into the United States, was unlawful, and that he may for that reason be expelled, cannot negate the simple fact of his presence within the State's territorial perimeter. Given such presence, he is subject to the full range of obligations imposed by the State's civil and criminal laws. And until he leaves the jurisdiction—either voluntarily, or involuntarily in accordance with the Constitution and laws of the United States—he is entitled to the equal protection of the laws that a State may choose to establish.

Our conclusion that the illegal aliens who are plaintiffs in these cases may claim the benefit of the Fourteenth Amendment's guarantee of equal protection only begins the inquiry. The more difficult question is whether the Equal Protection Clause has been violated by the refusal of the State of Texas to reimburse local school boards for the education of children who cannot demonstrate that their presence within the United States is lawful, or by the imposition by those school boards of the burden of tuition on those children. It is to this question that we now turn.

(III.) [In] applying the Equal Protection Clause to most forms of state action, we thus seek only the assurance that the classification at issue bears some fair relationship to a legitimate public purpose. But we would not be faithful to our obligations [if] we applied so deferential a standard to every classification. The Equal Protection Clause was intended as a restriction on state legislative action inconsistent with elemental constitutional premises. Thus we have treated as presumptively invidious those classifications that disadvantage a "suspect class," [2] or that impinge upon the exercise of a "fundamental right." [3] With respect to such classifications, it is appropriate to en-

---

2. Several formulations might explain our treatment of certain classifications as "suspect." Some classifications are more likely than others to reflect deep-seated prejudice rather than legislative rationality in pursuit of some legitimate objective. Legislation predicated on such prejudice is easily recognized as incompatible with the constitutional understanding that each person is to be judged individually and is entitled to equal justice under the law. Classifications treated as suspect tend to be irrelevant to any proper legislative goal. Finally, certain groups, indeed largely the same groups, have historically been "relegated to such a position of political powerlessness as to command extraor-

dinary protection from the majoritarian political process." [Carolene Products.] The experience of our Nation has shown that prejudice may manifest itself in the treatment of some groups. Our response to that experience is reflected in the Equal Protection Clause of the Fourteenth Amendment. Legislation imposing special disabilities upon groups disfavored by virtue of circumstances beyond their control suggests the kind of "class or caste" treatment that the Fourteenth Amendment was designed to abolish. [Footnote by Justice Brennan.]

3. In determining whether a class-based denial of a particular right is deserving of strict scrutiny under the

force the mandate of equal protection by requiring the State to demonstrate that its classification has been precisely tailored to serve a compelling governmental interest. In addition, we have recognized that certain forms of legislative classification, while not facially invidious, nonetheless give rise to recurring constitutional difficulties; in these limited circumstances we have sought the assurance that the classification reflects a reasoned judgment consistent with the ideal of equal protection by inquiring whether it may fairly be viewed as furthering a substantial interest of the State.[4] We turn to a consideration of the standard appropriate for the evaluation of [the Texas law].

A. Sheer incapability or lax enforcement of the laws barring entry into this country, coupled with the failure to establish an effective bar to the employment of undocumented aliens, has resulted in the creation of a substantial "shadow population" of illegal migrants—numbering in the millions—within our borders.[5] This situation raises the specter of a permanent caste of undocumented resident aliens, encouraged by some to remain here as a source of cheap labor, but nevertheless denied the benefits that our society makes available to citizens and lawful residents. The existence of such an underclass presents most difficult problems for a Nation that prides itself on adherence to principles of equality under law.[6]

Equal Protection Clause, we look to the Constitution to see if the right infringed has its source, explicitly or implicitly, therein. But we have also recognized the fundamentality of participation in state "elections on an equal basis with other citizens in the jurisdiction" even though "the right to vote, *per se*, is not a constitutionally protected right." With respect to suffrage, we have explained the need for strict scrutiny as arising from the significance of the franchise as the guardian of all other rights. [Footnote by Justice Brennan.]

4. See Craig v. Boren; Lalli v. Lalli. This technique of "intermediate" scrutiny permits us to evaluate the rationality of the legislative judgment with reference to well-settled constitutional principles. [Only] when concerns sufficiently absolute and enduring can be clearly ascertained from the Constitution and our cases do we employ this standard to aid us in determining the rationality of the legislative choice. [Footnote by Justice Brennan.]

5. The Attorney General recently estimated the number of illegal aliens within the United States at between 3 and 6 million. In presenting to both the Senate and House of Representatives several presidential proposals for reform of the immigration laws [in July, 1981]—including one to "le-galize" many of the illegal entrants currently residing in the United States by creating for them a special status under the immigration laws—the Attorney General [William French Smith] noted that this subclass is largely composed of persons with a permanent attachment to the nation, and that they are unlikely to be displaced from our territory. . . . [Footnote by Justice Brennan.]

6. We reject the claim that "illegal aliens" are a "suspect class." No case in which we have attempted to define a suspect class has addressed the status of persons unlawfully in our country. Unlike most of the classifications that we have recognized as suspect, entry into this class, by virtue of entry into this country, is the product of voluntary action. Indeed, entry into the class is itself a crime. In addition, it could hardly be suggested that undocumented status is a "constitutional irrelevancy." With respect to the actions of the federal government, alienage classifications may be intimately related to the conduct of foreign policy, to the federal prerogative to control access to the United States, and to the plenary federal power to determine who has sufficiently manifested his allegiance to become a citizen of the Nation. No State may independently exercise a like power. But if the Federal Government has by

The children who are plaintiffs in these cases are special members of this underclass. Persuasive arguments support the view that a State may withhold its beneficence from those whose very presence within the United States is the product of their own unlawful conduct. These arguments do not apply with the same force to classifications imposing disabilities on the minor children of such illegal entrants. At the least, those who elect to enter our territory by stealth and in violation of our law should be prepared to bear the consequences, including, but not limited to, deportation. But the children of those illegal entrants are not comparably situated. Their "parents have the ability to conform their conduct to societal norms," and presumably the ability to remove themselves from the State's jurisdiction; but the children who are plaintiffs in these cases "can affect neither their parents' conduct nor their own status." Trimble v. Gordon. Even if the State found it expedient to control the conduct of adults by acting against their children, legislation directing the onus of a parent's misconduct against his children does not comport with fundamental conceptions of justice. [Weber.]

Of course, undocumented status is not irrelevant to any proper legislative goal. Nor is undocumented status an absolutely immutable characteristic since it is the product of conscious, indeed unlawful, action. But [the Texas law] is directed against children, and imposes it discriminatory burden on the basis of a legal characteristic over which children can have little control. It is thus difficult to conceive of a rational justification for penalizing these children for their presence within the United States. Yet that appears to be precisely the effect of [the law].

Public education is not a "right" granted to individuals by the Constitution. [Rodriguez.] But neither is it merely some governmental "benefit" indistinguisable from other forms of social welfare legislation. Both the importance of education in maintaining our basic institutions, and the lasting impact of its deprivation on the life of the child, mark the distinction. [Meyer v. Nebraska; Schempp; Ambach v. Norwick; Yoder.] [In] addition, education provides the basic tools by which individuals might lead economically productive lives to the benefit of us all. In sum, education has a fundamental role in maintaining the fabric of our society. We cannot ignore the significant social costs borne by our Nation when select groups are denied the means to absorb the values and skills upon which our social order rests.

In addition to the pivotal role of education in sustaining our political and cultural heritage, denial of education to some isolated group of children poses an affront to one of the goals of the Equal Protection Clause: the abolition of governmental barriers presenting unreasonable obstacles to advancement on the basis of individual merit. Paradoxically, by depriving the children of any disfavored group of an education, we foreclose the means by which that group might raise the level of esteem in which it is held by the majority. But more directly, "education prepares individuals to be self-reliant and self-sufficient participants in society." [Yoder.] Illiteracy is an enduring disability. The inability to read and write will handicap the individ-

uniform rule prescribed what it believes to be appropriate standards for the treatment of an alien subclass, the States may, of course, follow the federal direction. See De Canas v. Bica, 424 U.S. 351 (1976). [Footnote by Justice Brennan.]

ual deprived of a basic education each and every day of his life. The ines-
timable toll of that deprivation on the social, economic, intellectual and psychological well-being of the individual, and the obstacle it poses to individual
achievement, makes it most difficult to reconcile the cost or the principle of a
status-based denial of basic education with the framework of equality embodied in the Equal Protection Clause.[7] What we said 28 years ago in Brown v.
Board of Education still holds true: "Today, education is perhaps the most
important function of state and local governments. . . . "

B. These well-settled principles allow us to determine the proper level
of deference to be afforded [in this case]. Undocumented aliens cannot be
treated as a suspect class because their presence in this country in violation of
federal law is not a "constitutional irrelevancy." Nor is education a fundamental right; a State need not justify by compelling necessity every variation
in the manner in which education is provided to its population. But more is
involved in this case than the abstract question whether [this law] discriminates against a suspect class, or whether education is a fundamental right.
[This law] imposes a lifetime hardship on a discrete class of children not accountable for their disabling status. The stigma of illiteracy will mark them
for the rest of their lives. By denying these children a basic education, we
deny them the ability to live within the structure of our civic institutions, and
foreclose any realistic possibility that they will contribute in even the smallest
way to the progress of our Nation. In determining the rationality of [this
law], we may appropriately take into account its costs to the Nation and to
the innocent children who are its victims. In light of these countervailing
costs, the discrimination contained in [this law] can hardly be considered rational unless it furthers some substantial goal of the State.

IV. It is the State's principal argument, and apparently the view of the
dissenting Justices, that the undocumented status of these children *vel non* establishes a sufficient rational basis for denying them benefits that a State
might choose to afford other residents. The State notes that while other aliens are admitted "on an equality of legal privileges with all citizens under
non-discriminatory laws," [Takahashi], the asserted right of these children to
an education can claim no implicit congressional imprimatur.[8] Indeed, on

7. Because the State does not afford
noncitizens the right to vote, and may
bar noncitizens from participating in
activities at the heart of its political
community, appellants argue that denial of a basic education to these children is of less significance than the
denial to some other group. Whatever the current status of these children, the courts below concluded that
many will remain here permanently
and that some indeterminate number
will eventually become citizens. The
fact that many will not is not decisive, even with respect to the importance of education to participation in
core political institutions. [In] addition, although a noncitizen "may be
barred from full involvement in the

political arena, he may play a role—
perhaps even a leadership role—in
other areas of import to the community." Nyquist v. Mauclet. Moreover,
the significance of education to our
society is not limited to its political
and cultural fruits. The public
schools are an important socializing
institution, imparting those shared
values through which social order and
stability are maintained. [Footnote
by Justice Brennan.]

8. If the constitutional guarantee of
equal protection was available only to
those upon whom Congress affirmatively granted its benefit, the State's
argument would be virtually unanswerable. But the Equal Protection

the State's view, Congress' apparent disapproval of the presence of these children within the United States [provides] authority for its decision to impose upon them special disabilities. Faced with an equal protection challenge respecting the treatment of aliens, we agree that the courts must be attentive to congressional policy; the exercise of congressional power might well affect the State's prerogatives to afford differential treatment to a particular class of aliens. But we are unable to find in the congressional immigration scheme any statement of policy that might weigh significantly in arriving at an equal protection balance concerning the State's authority to deprive these children of an education.

[Congress] has developed a complex scheme governing admission to and status within our borders. The obvious need for delicate policy judgments has counselled the Judicial Branch to avoid intrusion into this field. [Mathews v. Diaz.] But this traditional caution does not persuade us that unusual deference must be shown the classification embodied [in the Texas law]. The States enjoy no power with respect to the classification of aliens. [As] we recognized in De Canas v. Bica, the States do have some authority to act with respect to illegal aliens, at least where such action mirrors federal objectives and furthers a legitimate state goal. In De Canas, the State's program reflected Congress' intention to bar from employment all aliens except those possessing a grant of permission to work in this country. In contrast, there is no indication that the disability imposed by [Texas] corresponds to any identifiable congressional policy. The State does not claim that the conservation of state educational resources was ever a congressional concern in restricting immigration. More importantly, the classification [used here] does not operate harmoniously within the federal program.

[To] be sure, [these] children are subject to deportation. But there is no assurance that a child subject to deportation will ever be deported. [In] light of the discretionary federal power to grant relief from deportation, a State cannot realistically determine that any particular undocumented child will in fact be deported until after deportation proceedings have been completed. It would of course be most difficult for the State to justify a denial of education to a child enjoying an inchoate federal permission to remain.

We are reluctant to impute to Congress the intention to withhold from these children, for so long as they are present in this country through no fault of their own, access to a basic education. In other contexts, undocumented status, coupled with some articulable federal policy, might enhance State authority with respect to the treatment of undocumented aliens. But in the area of special constitutional sensitivity presented by this case, and in the absence of any contrary indication fairly discernible in the present legislative record, we perceive no national policy that supports the State in denying these children an elementary education. The State may borrow the federal classification. But to justify its use as a criterion for its own discriminatory policy, the

Clause operates of its own force to protect anyone "within [the State's] jurisdiction" from the State's arbitrary action. See Part II, supra. The question we examine in text is whether the federal *disapproval* of the presence of these children assists the State in overcoming the presumption that denial of education to innocent children is not a rational response to legitimate state concerns. [Footnote by Justice Brennan.]

State must demonstrate that the classification is reasonably adapted to "*the purposes for which the state desires to use it.*" Oyama v. California (emphasis added). We therefore turn to the state objectives that are said to support [the Texas law].

V. Appellants argue that the classification at issue furthers an interest in the "preservation of the state's limited resources for the education of its lawful residents." Of course, a concern for the preservation of resources standing alone can hardly justify the classification used in allocating those resources. Graham v. Richardson. The State must do more than justify its classification with a concise expression of an intention to discriminate. Apart from the asserted state prerogative to act against undocumented children solely on the basis of their undocumented status—an asserted prerogative that carries only minimal force in the circumstances of this case—we discern three colorable state interests that might support [this law].

First, appellants appear to suggest that the State may seek to protect [itself] from an influx of illegal immigrants. While a State might have an interest in mitigating the potentially harsh economic effects of sudden shifts in population,[9] [this law] hardly offers an effective method of dealing with an urgent demographic or economic problem. There is no evidence in the record suggesting that illegal entrants impose any significant burden on the State's economy. To the contrary, the available evidence suggests that illegal aliens underutilize public services, while contributing their labor to the local economy and tax money to the State fisc. The dominant incentive for illegal entry into [Texas] is the availability of employment; few if any illegal immigrants come to this country, or presumably to [Texas], in order to avail themselves of a free education. Thus, even making the doubtful assumption that the net impact of illegal aliens on the economy of the State is negative, we think it clear that "[c]harging tuition to undocumented children constitutes a ludicrously ineffectual attempt to stem the tide of illegal immigration," at least when compared with the alternative of prohibiting the employment of illegal aliens.

Second, while it is apparent that a state may "not [reduce] expenditures for education by barring [some arbitrarily chosen class of] children from its schools," Shapiro v. Thompson, appellants suggest that undocumented children are appropriately singled out for exclusion because of the special burdens they impose on the State's ability to provide high quality public education. But the record in no way supports the claim that exclusion of undocumented children is likely to improve the overall quality of education in the State.[10] [Of] course, even if improvement in the quality of education were a

9. Although the State has no direct interest in controlling entry into this country, that interest being one reserved by the Constitution to the Federal Government, unchecked unlawful migration might impair the State's economy generally, or the State's ability to provide some important service. Despite the exclusive federal control of this Nation's borders, we cannot conclude that the States are without any power to deter the influx of persons entering the United States against Federal law, and whose numbers might have a discernible impact on traditional state concerns. [Footnote by Justice Brennan.]

10. Nor does the record support the claim that the educational resources of the State are so direly limited that some form of "educational *triage*"

likely result of barring some *number* of children from the schools of the State, the State must support its selection of *this* group as the appropriate target for exclusion. In terms of educational cost and need, however, undocumented children are "basically indistinguishable" from legally resident alien children.

Finally, appellants suggest that undocumented children are appropriately singled out because their unlawful presence within the United States renders them less likely than other children to remain within the boundaries of the State, and to put their education to productive social or political use within the State. Even assuming that such an interest is legitimate, it is an interest that is most difficult to quantify. The State has no assurance that any child, citizen or not, will employ the education provided by the State within the confines of the State's borders. In any event, the record is clear that many of the undocumented children disabled by this classification will remain in this country indefinitely, and that some will become lawful residents or citizens of the United States. It is difficult to understand precisely what the State hopes to achieve by promoting the creation and perpetuation of a subclass of illiterates within our boundaries, surely adding to the problems and costs of unemployment, welfare, and crime. It is thus clear that whatever savings might be achieved by denying these children an education, they are wholly insubstantial in light of the costs involved to these children, the State, and the Nation.

VI. If the State is to deny a discrete group of innocent children the free public education that is offers to other children residing within its borders, that denial must be justified by a showing that it furthers some substantial state interest. No such showing was made here.

[Affirmed.]

Justice MARSHALL, concurring.

While I join the Court opinion, I do so without in any way retreating from my opinion in [Rodriguez]. I continue to believe that an individual's interest in education is fundamental. Furthermore, I believe that the facts of these cases demonstrate the wisdom of rejecting a rigidified approach to equal protection analysis, and of employing an approach that allows for varying levels of scrutiny depending upon "the constitutional and societal importance of the interest adversely affected and the recognized invidiousness of the basis upon which the particular classification is drawn." [Ibid.] It continues to be my view that a class-based denial of public education is utterly incompatible with [equal protection].

Justice BLACKMUN, concurring.

I join the opinion and judgment of the Court. Like Justice Powell, I believe that the children involved in this litigation "should not be left on the streets uneducated." I write separately, however, because in my view the nature of the interest at stake is crucial to the proper resolution of this case.

The "fundamental rights" aspect of the Court's equal protection analysis —the now-familiar concept that governmental classifications bearing on certain interests must be closely scrutinized—has been the subject of some controversy. [E.g., Shapiro (Harlan, J., dissenting).] [Others] have noted that strict scrutiny under the Equal Protection Clause is unnecessary when classifications infringing enumerated constitutional rights are [involved]. [Rodriguez (Stewart, J., concurring).] [Still] others have suggested that fundamental rights are not properly a part of equal protection analysis at all, because they are unrelated to any defined principle of equality.[1]

These considerations, combined with doubts about the judiciary's ability to make fine distinctions in assessing the effects of complex social policies, led the Court in Rodriguez to articulate a firm rule: fundamental rights are those that "explicitly or implicitly [are] guaranteed by the Constitution." [I] joined Justice Powell's opinion for the Court in Rodriguez, and I continue to believe that it provides the appropriate model for resolving most equal protection disputes. Classifications infringing substantive constitutional rights necessarily will be invalid, if not by force of the Equal Protection Clause, then through operation of other provisions of the Constitution. Conversely, classifications bearing on nonconstitutional interests—even those involving "the most basic economic needs of impoverished human beings," Dandridge v. Williams—generally are not subject to special treatment under the Equal Protection Clause, because they are not distinguishable in any relevant way from other regulations in "the area of economics and social welfare."

With all this said, however, I believe the Court's experience has demonstrated that the Rodriguez formulation does not settle every issue of "fundamental rights" arising under the Equal Protection Clause. Only a pedant would insist that there are *no* meaningful distinctions among the multitude of social and political interests regulated by the States, and Rodriguez does not stand for quite so absolute a proposition. To the contrary, Rodriguez implicitly acknowledged that certain interests, though not constitutionally guaranteed, must be accorded a special place in equal protection analysis. Thus, the Court's decisions long have accorded strict scrutiny to classifications bearing on the right to vote in state elections. [The] right to vote is accorded extraordinary treatment because it is, in equal protection terms, an extraordinary right: a citizen cannot hope to achieve any meaningful degree of individual political equality if granted an inferior right of participation in the political process. Those denied the vote are relegated, by state fiat, in a most basic way to second-class status.

It is arguable, of course, that the Court never should have applied fundamental rights doctrine in the fashion outlined above. Justice Harlan, for one, maintained that strict equal protection scrutiny was appropriate only when racial or analogous classifications were at issue. [Shapiro] (dissenting opinion). But it is too late to debate that point, and I believe that accepting the principle of the voting cases—the idea that state classifications bearing on certain interests pose the risk of allocating rights in a fashion inherently contrary to any notion of "equality"—dictates the outcome here. As both Justice

---

1. See, e.g., Perry, Modern Equal Protection: A Conceptualization and Appraisal, 79 Colum.L.Rev. 1023, 1075– 1083 (1979). [Footnote by Justice Blackmun.]

Blackmun argues in analogy to voting "right", higher level of scrutiny needed.

Powell and The Chief Justice observe, the Texas scheme inevitably will create "a subclass of illiterate persons"; where I differ with The Chief Justice is in my conclusion that this makes the statutory scheme unconstitutional as well as unwise.

In my view, when the State provides an education to some and denies it to others, it immediately and inevitably creates class distinctions of a type fundamentally inconsistent with those purposes, mentioned above, of [equal protection]. Children denied an education are placed at a permanent and insurmountable competitive disadvantage, for an uneducated child is denied even the opportunity to achieve. And when those children are members of an identifiable group, that group—through the State's action—will have been converted into a discrete underclass. Other benefits provided by the State, such as housing and public assistance, are of course important; to an individual in immediate need, they may be more desirable than the right to be educated. But classifications involving the complete denial of education are in a sense unique, for they strike at the heart of equal protection values by involving the State in the creation of permanent class distinctions. Cf. Rodriguez, (Marshall, J., dissenting). In a sense, then, denial of an education is the analogue of denial of the right to vote; the former relegates the individual to second-class social status; the latter places him at a permanent political disadvantage.

"Denial of Education is analog of denial of right to vote"

This conclusion is fully consistent with Rodriguez. The Court there reserved judgment on the constitutionality of a state system that "occasioned an absolute denial of educational opportunities to any of its children." [Rodriguez] held, and the Court now reaffirms, that "a State need not justify by compelling necessity every variation in the manner in which education is provided to its population." Similarly, it is undeniable that education is not a "fundamental right" in the sense that it is constitutionally guaranteed. Here, however, the State has undertaken to provide an education to most of the children residing within its borders. And, in contrast to the situation in Rodriguez, it does not take an advanced degree to predict the effects of a complete denial of education upon those children targeted by the State's classification. In such circumstances, the voting decisions suggest that the State must offer something more than a rational basis for its classification.[2]

[thus] State must offer something more than a rational basis for its classification

[Whatever] the State's power to classify deportable aliens [—and] whatever the Federal Government's ability to draw more precise and more acceptable alienage classifications—the statute at issue here sweeps within it a substantial number of children who will in fact, and who may well be entitled to, remain in the United States. Given the extraordinary nature of the interest involved, this makes the classification here fatally imprecise. And, as the Court demonstrates, the Texas legislation is not otherwise supported by any substantial interests. . . .

Justice POWELL, concurring.

2. The Court concludes that [the law] must be invalidated "unless it furthers some substantial goal of the State." Since the statute fails to survive this level of scrutiny, as the Court demonstrates, there is no need to determine whether a more probing level of review would be appropriate. [Footnote by Justice Blackmun.]

Powell Concurs

I join the opinion of the Court, and write separately to emphasize the unique character of the case before us. The classification in question severely disadvantages children who are the victims of a combination of circumstances. Access from Mexico into this country [is] readily available and virtually uncontrollable. Illegal aliens are attracted by our employment opportunities, and perhaps by other benefits as well. This is a problem of serious national proportions, as the Attorney General recently has recognized. Perhaps because of the intractability of the problem, Congress—vested by the Constitution with the responsibility of protecting our borders and legislating with respect to aliens—has not provided effective leadership in dealing with this problem.[1] It therefore is certain that illegal aliens will continue to enter the United States [and] an unknown percentage of them will remain here. I agree with the Court that their children should not be left on the streets uneducated.

heightened review is proper

Although the analogy is not perfect, our holding today does find support in decisions of this Court with respect to the status of illegitimates. [See Weber.] [In] this case, [Texas] effectively denies to the school age children of illegal aliens the opportunity to attend the free public schools that the State makes available to all residents. They are excluded only because of a status resulting from the violation by parents or guardians of our immigration laws and the fact that they remain in our country unlawfully. The respondent children are innocent in this respect. They can "affect neither their parents' conduct nor their own status." Trimble v. Gordon.

Craig v Boren Test Proper

Our review in a case such as this is properly heightened. See id. Cf. Craig v. Boren. The classification at issue deprives a group of children of the opportunity for education afforded all other children simply because they have been assigned a legal status due to a violation of law by their parents. These children thus have been singled out for a lifelong penalty and stigma. A legislative classification that threatens the creation of an underclass of future citizens and residents cannot be reconciled with one of the fundamental purposes of the Fourteenth Amendment. In these unique circumstances, the Court properly may require that the State's interests be substantial and that the means bear a "fair and substantial relation" to these interests.[3] See Lalli

1. [The] federal government has "broad constitutional powers [over immigration]." [Takahashi.] [Indeed], even equal protection analysis in this area is based to a large extent on an underlying theme of preemption and exclusive federal power over immigration. See [Takahashi]. Given that the states' power to regulate in this area is so limited, and that this is an area of such peculiarly strong federal authority, the necessity of federal leadership seems evident. [Footnote by Justice Powell.]

2. I emphasize the Court's conclusion that strict scrutiny is not appropriately applied to this classification. This exacting standard of review has been

reserved for instances in which a "fundamental" constitutional right or a "suspect" classification is present. Neither is present in this case, as the Court holds. [Footnote by Justice Powell.]

3. The Chief Justice argues in his dissenting opinion that this heightened standard of review is inconsistent with the Court's decision in [Rodriguez]. But in Rodriguez no group of children was singled out by the State and then penalized because of their parent's status. Rather, funding for education varied across the State because of the tradition of local control. Nor, in that case, was any group of children totally deprived of all educa-

v. Lalli. [In] my view, the State's denial of education to these children bears no substantial relation to any substantial state interest. The [lower courts] that addressed this case concluded that the classification could not satisfy even the bare requirements of rationality. One need not go so far to conclude that the exclusion of appellee's class [4] of children from state-provided education is a type of punitive discrimination based on status that is impermissible under the Equal Protection Clause.

In reaching this conclusion, I am not unmindful of what must be the exasperation of responsible citizens and government authorities in Texas and other states similarly situated. Their responsibility, if any, for the influx of aliens is slight compared to that imposed by the Constitution on the federal government.[5] So long as the ease of entry remains inviting, and the power to deport is exercised infrequently by the federal government, the additional expense of admitting these children to public schools might fairly be shared by the federal and state governments. But it hardly can be argued rationally that anyone benefits from the creation within our borders of a subclass of illiterate persons many of whom will remain in the State, adding to the problems and costs of both State and National Governments attendant upon unemployment, welfare and crime.

Chief Justice BURGER, with whom Justice WHITE, Justice REHN-QUIST, and Justice O'CONNOR join, dissenting.

4 Dissenters

Were it our business to set the Nation's social policy, I would agree without hesitation that it is senseless for an enlightened society to deprive any children—including illegal aliens—of an elementary education. I fully agree that it would be folly—and wrong—to tolerate creation of a segment of society made up of illiterate persons, many having a limited or no command of our language.[1] However, the Constitution does not constitute us as "Platonic

tion as in this case. If the resident children of illegal aliens were denied welfare assistance, made available by government to all other children who qualify, this also—in my opinion—would be an impermissible penalizing of children because of their parents' status. [Footnote by Justice Powell.]

4. The classes certified in these cases included all undocumented school-age children of Mexican origin residing in the school district or the State. Even so, it is clear that neither class was thought to include mature Mexican minors who were solely responsible for violating the immigration laws. [A] different case would be presented in the unlikely event that a minor, old enough to be responsible for illegal entry and yet still of school age, entered this country illegally on his own volition. [Footnote by Justice Powell.]

5. In addition, the states' ability to respond on their own to the problems caused by this migration may be limited by the principles of preemption that apply in this area. . . . [Footnote by Justice Powell.]

1. It does not follow, however, that a State should bear the costs of educating children whose illegal presence in this country results from the default of the political branches of the federal government. A State has no power to prevent unlawful immigration, and no power to deport illegal aliens; those powers are reserved exclusively to Congress and the Executive. If the federal government, properly chargeable with deporting illegal aliens, fails to do so, it should bear the burdens of their presence here. Surely if illegal alien children can be identified for purposes of this litigation, their parents can be identified for purposes of prompt deportation. [Footnote by Chief Justice Burger.]

Guardians" nor does it vest in this Court the authority to strike down laws because they do not meet our standards of desirable social policy, "wisdom," or "common sense." We trespass on the assigned function of the political branches [when] we assume a policymaking role as the Court does today. The Court makes no attempt to disguise that it is acting to make up for Congress' lack of "effective leadership" in dealing with the serious national problems caused by the influx of uncountable millions of illegal aliens across our borders. [But] it is not the function of the judiciary to provide "effective leadership" simply because the political branches of government fail to do so. The Court's holding today manifests the justly criticized judicial tendency to attempt speedy and wholesale formulation of "remedies" for the failures—or simply the laggard pace—of the political processes of our system of government. The Court employs, and in my view abuses, the Fourteenth Amendment in an effort to become an omnipotent and omniscient problem solver. That the motives for doing so are noble and compassionate does not alter the fact that the Court distorts our constitutional function to make amends for the defaults of others.

I.   In a sense, the Court's opinion rests on such a unique confluence of theories and rationales that it will likely stand for little beyond the results in these particular cases. Yet the extent to which the Court departs from principled constitutional adjudication is nonetheless disturbing. I have no quarrel with the conclusion that the Equal Protection Clause of the Fourteenth Amendment *applies* to aliens who, after their illegal entry into this country, are indeed physically "within the jurisdiction" of a State. However, as the Court concedes, this "only begins the inquiry." The Equal Protection Clause does not mandate identical treatment of different categories of persons. The dispositive issue in these cases, simply put, is whether, for purposes of allocating its finite resources, a State has a legitimate reason to differentiate between persons who are lawfully within the State and those who are unlawfully there. The distinction [Texas] has drawn—based not only upon its own legitimate interests but on classifications established by the federal government in its immigration laws and policies—is not unconstitutional.

A.   The Court acknowledges that, except in those cases when state classifications disadvantage a "suspect class" or impinge upon a "fundamental right," the Equal Protection Clause permits a State "substantial latitude" in distinguishing between different groups of persons. Moreover, the Court expressly—and correctly—rejects any suggestion that illegal aliens are a suspect class or that education is a fundamental right. Yet by patching together bits and pieces of what might be termed quasi-suspect-class and quasi-fundamental-rights analysis, the Court spins out a theory custom-tailored to the facts of these cases. In the end, we are told little more than that the level of scrutiny employed to strike down the Texas law applies only when illegal alien children are deprived of a public education.[2] If ever a court was guilty of an unabashedly result-oriented approach, this case is a prime example.

2.   The Court implies, for example, that the Fourteenth Amendment would not require a State to provide welfare benefits to illegal aliens. [Footnote by Chief Justice Burger.]

(1) The Court first suggests that these illegal alien children [are] entitled to special solicitude under the Equal Protection Clause because they lack "control" over or "responsibility" for their unlawful entry into this country. Similarly, the Court appears to take the position that [the law] is presumptively "irrational" because it has the effect of imposing "penalties" on "innocent" children.[3] However, the Equal Protection Clause does not preclude legislators from classifying among persons on the basis of factors and characteristics over which individuals may be said to lack "control." Indeed, in some circumstances persons generally, and children in particular, may have little control over or responsibility for such things as their ill-health, need for public assistance, or place of residence. Yet a state legislature is not barred from considering, for example, relevant differences between the mentally-healthy and the mentally-ill, or between the residents of different counties,[4] simply because these may be factors unrelated to individual choice or to any "wrongdoing." The Equal Protection Clause [is] not an all-encompassing "equalizer" designed to eradicate every distinction for which persons are not "responsible."

The Court does not presume to suggest that appellees' purported lack of culpability for their illegal status prevents them from being deported or otherwise "penalized" under federal law. Yet would deportation be any less a "penalty" than denial of privileges provided to legal residents? Illegality of presence in the United States does not—and need not—depend on some amorphous concept of "guilt" or "innocence" concerning an alien's entry. Similarly, a State's use of federal immigration status as a basis for legislative classification is not necessarily rendered suspect for its failure to take such factors into account.

The Court's analogy to cases involving discrimination against illegitimate children [is] grossly misleading. The State has not thrust any disabilities upon appellees due to their "status of birth." Rather, appellees' status is predicated upon the circumstances of their concededly illegal presence in this country, and is a direct result of Congress' obviously valid exercise of its "broad constitutional powers" in the field of immigration and naturalization. This Court has recognized that in allocating governmental benefits to a given

---

3. Both the opinion of the Court and Justice Powell's concurrence imply that appellees are being "penalized" because their *parents* are illegal entrants. However, Texas has classified appellees on the basis of *their own* illegal status, not that of their parents. Children born in this country to illegal alien parents, including some of appellees' siblings, are not excluded from the Texas schools. Nor does Texas discriminate against appellees because of their Mexican origin or citizenship. Texas provides a free public education to countless thousands of Mexican immigrants who are lawfully in this country. [Footnote by Chief Justice Burger.]

4. Appellees "lack control" over their illegal residence in this country in the same sense as lawfully resident children lack control over the school district in which their parents reside. Yet in [Rodriguez], we declined to review under "heightened scrutiny" a claim that a State discriminated against residents of less wealthy school districts in its provision of educational benefits. There was no suggestion in that case that a child's "lack of responsibility" for his residence in a particular school district had any relevance to the proper standard of review of his claims. The result was that children lawfully here but residing in different counties received different treatment. [Footnote by Chief Justice Burger.]

class of aliens, one "may take into account the character of the relationship between the alien and this country." Mathews v. Diaz. When that "relationship" is a federally-prohibited one, there can, of course, be no presumption that a State has a constitutional duty to include illegal aliens among the recipients of its governmental benefits.

(2) The second strand of the Court's analysis rests on the premise that, although public education is not a constitutionally-guaranteed right, "neither is it merely some governmental 'benefit' indistinguishable from other forms of social welfare legislation." Whatever meaning or relevance this opaque observation might have in some other context,[5] it simply has no bearing on the issues at hand. Indeed, it is never made clear what the Court's opinion means on this score.

The importance of education is beyond dispute. Yet we have held repeatedly that the importance of a governmental service does not elevate it to the status of a "fundamental right" for purposes of equal protection analysis. [Rodriguez] expressly rejected the proposition that state laws dealing with public education are subject to special scrutiny under the Equal Protection Clause. Moreover, the Court points to no meaningful way to distinguish between education and other governmental benefits in this context. Is the Court suggesting that education is more "fundamental" than food, shelter, or medical care? The Equal Protection Clause guarantees similar treatment of similarly situated persons, but it does not mandate a constitutional hierarchy of governmental services. [The] central question in these cases, as in every equal protection case not involving truly fundamental rights "explicitly or implicitly guaranteed by the Constitution," is whether there is some legitimate basis for a legislative distinction between different classes of persons. The fact that the distinction is drawn in legislation affecting access to public education—as opposed to legislation allocating other important governmental benefits, such as public assistance, health care, or housing—cannot make a difference in the level of scrutiny applied.

(B.) Once it is conceded—as the Court does—that illegal aliens are not a suspect class, and that education is not a fundamental right, our inquiry should focus on and be limited to whether the legislative classification at issue bears a rational relationship to a legitimate state purpose. [E.g., Vance v. Bradley; Dandridge v. Williams]. The State contends primarily that [its law] serves to prevent undue depletion of its limited revenues available for education, and to preserve the fiscal integrity of the State's school financing system against an ever-increasing flood of illegal aliens. [Of] course such fiscal concerns alone could not justify discrimination against a suspect class or an arbitrary and irrational denial of benefits to a particular group of persons. Yet I assume no member of this Court would argue that prudent conservation

5. In support of this conclusion, the Court's opinion strings together quotations drawn from cases addressing such diverse matters as the right of individuals under the Due Process Clause to learn a foreign language, Meyer v. Nebraska; the First Amendment prohibition against state-mandated religious exercises in the public schools, [Schempp]; and state impingements upon the free exercise of religion, [Yoder]. However, not every isolated utterance of this Court retains force when wrested from the context in which it was made. [Footnote by Chief Justice Burger.]

of finite state revenues is *per se* an illegitimate goal. Indeed, the numerous classifications this Court has sustained in social welfare legislation were invariably related to the limited amount of revenues available to spend on any given program or set of programs. The significant question here is whether the requirement of tuition from illegal aliens who attend the public schools—as well as from residents of other States, for example—is a rational and reasonable means of furthering the State's legitimate fiscal ends.[6]

Without laboring what will undoubtedly seem obvious to many, it simply is not "irrational" for a State to conclude that it does not have the same responsibility to provide benefits for persons whose very presence in the State and this country is illegal as it does to provide for persons lawfully present. By definition, illegal aliens have no right whatever to be here, and the State may reasonably, and constitutionally, elect not to provide them with governmental services at the expense of those who are lawfully in the State. [The] Court has failed to offer even a plausible explanation why illegality of residence in this country is not a factor that may legitimately bear upon the bona fides of state residence and entitlement to the benefits of lawful residence.[7]

It is significant that the federal government has seen fit to exclude illegal aliens from numerous social welfare programs, such as the food stamp program, the old age assistance, aid to families with dependent children, aid to the blind, aid to the permanently and totally disabled, and supplemental security income programs, the medicare hospital insurance benefits program and the medicaid hospital insurance benefits for the aged and disabled program. Although these exclusions do not conclusively demonstrate the constitutionality of the State's use of the same classification for comparable purposes, at the very least they tend to support the rationality of excluding illegal alien residents of a State from such programs so as to preserve the State's finite revenues for the benefit of lawful residents.

---

6. The Texas law might also be justified as a means of deterring unlawful immigration. While regulation of immigration is an exclusively federal function, a State may take steps, consistent with federal immigration policy, to protect its economy and ability to provide governmental services from the "deleterious effects" of a massive influx of illegal immigrants. The Court maintains that denying illegal aliens a free public education is an "ineffectual" means of deterring unlawful immigration, at least when compared to a prohibition against the employment of illegal aliens. Perhaps that is correct, but it is not dispositive: the Equal Protection Clause does not mandate that a State choose either the most effective and all-encompassing means of addressing a problem or none at all. Texas might rationally conclude that more significant "demographic or economic problems" are engendered by the illegal entry into the State of entire families of aliens for indefinite periods than by the periodic sojourns of single adults who intend to leave the State after short-term or seasonal employment. It blinks reality to maintain that the availability of governmental services such as education plays no role in an alien family's decision to enter, or remain in, this country; certainly, the availability of a free bilingual public education might well influence an alien to bring his children rather than travel alone for better job opportunities. [Footnote by Chief Justice Burger.]

7. The Court's opinion is disingenuous when it suggests that the State has merely picked a "disfavored group" and arbitrarily defined its members as nonresidents. Appellees' "disfavored status" stems from the very fact that federal law explicitly prohibits them from being in this country. . . . [footnote by Chief Justice Burger.]

The Court maintains—as if this were the issue—that "barring undocumented children from local schools would not necessarily improve the quality of education provided in those schools." However, the legitimacy of barring illegal aliens from programs such as medicare or medicaid does not depend on a showing that the barrier would "improve the quality" of medical care given to persons lawfully entitled to participate in such programs. [T]here can be no doubt that very large added costs will fall on the State or its local school districts as a result of the inclusion of illegal aliens in the tuition-free public schools. The State may, in its discretion, use any savings resulting from its tuition requirement to "improve the quality of education" in the public school system, or to enhance the funds available for other social programs, or to reduce the tax burden placed on its residents; each of these ends is "legitimate." The State need not show, as the Court implies, that the incremental cost of educating illegal aliens will send it into bankruptcy, or have a "grave impact on the quality of education"; that is not dispositive under a "rational basis" scrutiny. In the absence of a constitutional imperative to provide for the education of illegal aliens, the State may "rationally" choose to take advantage of whatever savings will accrue from limiting access to the tuition-free public schools to its own lawful residents, excluding even citizens of neighboring States. Denying a free education to illegal alien children is not a choice I would make were I a legislator. Apart from compassionate considerations, the long-range costs of excluding any children from the public schools may well outweigh the costs of educating them. But that is not the issue; the fact that there are sound *policy* arguments against the Texas legislature's choice does not render that choice an unconstitutional one.

II. The Constitution does not provide a cure for every social ill, nor does it vest judges with a mandate to try to remedy every social problem. Lindsay v. Normet. Moreover, when this Court rushes in to remedy what it perceives to be the failings of the political processes, it deprives those processes of an opportunity to function. When the political institutions are not forced to exercise constitutionally allocated powers and responsibilities, those powers, like muscles not used, tend to atrophy. Today's cases, I regret to say, present yet another example of unwarranted judicial action which in the long run tends to contribute to the weakening of our political processes.

Congress [bears] primary responsibility for addressing the problems occasioned by the millions of illegal aliens flooding across our southern border. [While] the "specter of a permanent caste" of illegal Mexican residents of the United States is indeed a disturbing one, it is but one segment of a larger problem, which is for the political branches to solve. I find it difficult to believe that Congress would long tolerate such a self-destructive result—that it would fail to deport these illegal alien families or to provide for the education of their children. Yet instead of allowing the political processes to run their course—albeit with some delay—the Court seeks to do Congress' job for it, compensating for congressional inaction. It is not unreasonable to think that this encourages the political branches to pass their problems to the judiciary. The solution to this seemingly intractable problem is to defer to the political processes, unpalatable as that may be to some.

10th ED., p. 908; IND. RTS., p. 528
Add to footnote *:

Should classifications based on mental illness trigger heightened scrutiny? SCHWEIKER v. WILSON, 450 U.S. 221 (1981) (more fully noted above, addition to 10th Ed., p. 704; Ind.Rts., p. 324), was an attack on provisions of the federal Supplemental Security Income (SSI) program. The program provides small "comfort allowances" for most, but not all, disabled patients in public hospitals. However, inmates of public mental institutions between the ages of 21 and 64 are not entitled to these "comfort" payments, because eligibility for SSI comfort payments is tied to coverage under Medicaid, and this group is not covered by Medicaid. This exclusion was challenged as a violation of equal protection requirements.

The challengers argued, inter alia, that the statutory scheme should "be subjected to a heightened standard of review" because the mentally ill "historically have been subjected to purposeful unequal treatment; they have been relegated to a position of political powerlessness; and prejudice against them curtails their participation in the pluralist system and strips them of political protection against discriminatory legislation." The District Court accepted that argument and struck down the provision.

But Justice BLACKMUN's majority opinion reversed, stating: "[W]e intimate no view as to what standard of review applies to legislation expressly classifying the mentally ill as a discrete group" because "this statute does not classify directly on the basis of mental health." He explained: "The statute does not isolate the mentally ill or subject them, as a discrete group, to special or subordinate treatment. At the most, [it] incidentally denies a small monthly comfort benefit to a certain number of persons suffering from mental illness; but in so doing it imposes equivalent deprivation on other groups who are not mentally ill, while at the same time benefiting substantial numbers of the mentally ill." He argued that "Congress made a distinction not between the mentally ill and a group composed of nonmentally ill, but between residents in public institutions receiving Medicaid funds for their care and residents in such institutions not receiving Medicaid funds." He continued: "To the extent that the statute has an indirect impact upon the mentally ill as a subset of publicly institutionalized persons, this record certainly presents no statistical support for a contention that the mentally ill as a class are burdened disproportionately to any other class affected by the classification. [Moreover, the challengers] have failed to produce any evidence that the intent of Congress was to classify on the basis of mental health. [As] in Jefferson v. Hackney, the indirect deprivation worked by this legislation upon [the] class, whether or not the class is considered 'suspect,' does not without more move us to regard it with a heightened scrutiny. Cf. [Feeney]." Justice Blackmun found that the scheme readily passed muster under the "rational basis" standard.

Justice POWELL's dissent, joined by Justices Brennan, Marshall and Stevens, also applied the rationality test but concluded that the exclusion was invalid. His only comment on the "heightened scrutiny" claim came in a footnote: "The Court too quickly dispatches the argument that [the statute] classifies on the basis of mental illness. While it is true that not all mentally ill people are denied the benefit, and that some people denied the benefit are not mentally ill, it is inescapable that appellees are denied the benefit because they are patients in mental institutions. Only the mentally ill are treated in mental institutions. While I would agree that there is no indication that Congress intended to punish or slight the mentally ill, the history of Medicaid demonstrates Congress' disinclination to involve the federal government in state treatment of mental illness in public institutions. Because I find the classification irrational, I do not reach the question whether classifications drawn in part on the basis of mental health require heightened scrutiny as appellees suggest."

10th ED., p. 908; IND. RTS., p. 528
Insert after Lalli v. Lalli (before Sec. 4):

ILLEGITIMACY CLASSIFICATIONS IN THE 1980s

MILLS v. HABLUETZEL, 456 U.S. 91 (1982), and PICKETT v. BROWN, 462 U.S. —— (1983), indicate that, despite the meandering course of decisions in the 1970s, the Court continues to accord illegitimacy classifi-

cations more than deferential scrutiny.   In Mills, the Court struck down a
Texas aw requiring that a paternity suit to identify the natural father of an
illegitimate child for the purpose of obtaining child support must be brought
before the child is one year old.   (Texas imposes no time limit on the right
of a legitimate child to sue for support.)   The one-year limit at issue in
Mills was Texas' 'less than generous'' response to Gomez v. Perex, 409 U.S.
535 (1973), which had invalidated a Texas rule denying *any* support rights
to illegitimate children.   In Mills, the Justices once again found Texas'
scheme unsatisfactory: the Court held that the special burden imposed on
illegitimate children by the one-year limit was "not justified by the State's
interest in avoiding the prosecution of stale or fraudulent claims."

Justice REHNQUIST (who had vehemently opposed any special scrutiny of illegitimacy classifications in Trimble v. Gordon, 10th Ed., p. 900;
Ind.Rts., p. 520) wrote for the Court in Mills.   He stated: "If Gomez and
the equal protection principles which underlie it are to have any meaning, it
is clear that the support opportunity provided by the State to illegitimate children must be more than illusory.   The period for asserting the right to support must be sufficiently long to permit those who normally have an interest
in such children to bring an action on their behalf despite the difficult personal, family, and financial circumstances that often surround the birth of a
child outside of wedlock.   It would hardly satisfy the demands of equal protection and the holding of Gomez to remove an 'impenetrable barrier' to support, only to replace it with an opportunity so truncated that few could utilize
it effectively."   He added, however, that the State was not required to "adopt
procedures for illegitimate children that are coterminous with those accorded
legitimate children.   Paternal support suits on behalf of illegitimate children
contain an element that such suits for legitimate children do not contain:
proof of paternity.   [T]he problems of proving paternity have been recognized repeatedly by this Court.   Therefore, in support suits by illegitimate
children more than in support suits by legitimate children, the State has an interest in preventing the prosecution of stale or fraudulent claims, and may
impose greater restrictions on the former than it imposes on the latter.   Such
restrictions will survive equal protection scrutiny to the extent they are substantially related to a legitimate state interest.   See Lalli v. Lalli; Trimble v.
Gordon; Mathews v. Lucas.*   The State's interest in avoiding the litigation of
stale or fraudulent claims will justify those periods of limitation that are sufficiently long to present a real threat of loss or diminution of evidence, or an
increased vulnerability to fraudulent claims."

Applying these principles to the issue in Mills, Justice Rehnquist drew
"two related requirements" from the Equal Protection Clause: "First, the period for obtaining support granted by Texas to illegitimate children must be
sufficiently long in duration to present a reasonable opportunity for those with
an interest in such children to assert claims on their behalf.   Second, any time
limitation placed on that opportunity must be substantially related to the
State's interest in avoiding the litigation of stale or fraudulent claims."   Under these criteria, the one-year right granted by Texas constituted a denial of

---

* Reviewing these precedents, Justice
  Rehnquist commented: "There is no
  reason to think that the factual differences between those cases and the
present case call for a variation of
the general principle which those cases have laid down."

equal protection. The time limit did not provide illegitimate children "with an adequate opportunity to obtain support," in light of the obvious "obstacles to such suits that confront unwed mothers during the child's first year." Moreover, "this unrealistically short time limitation is not substantially related to the State's interest in avoiding the prosecution of stale or fraudulent claims. [We] can conceive of no evidence essential to paternity suits that invariably will be lost in only one year, nor is it evident that the passage of twelve months will appreciably increase the likelihood of fraudulent claims."

Five of the Justices expressed concern that Justice Rehnquist, despite his willingness to invalidate the one-year limit, might in the future be unduly deferential to longer time limits. Their concern was aroused by a concluding footnote to the Court's opinion in which Justice Rehnquist noted that, after the commencement of the Mills litigation, Texas had amended its time limit provision "to increase to four years the period for asserting paternity claims" on behalf of illegitimate children. Justice Rehnquist commented: "The restrictions imposed by States to control problems of proof [often] take the form of statutes of limitation. [Because] such statutes 'are by definition arbitrary,' they are best left to legislative determination and control. Normally, therefore, States are free to set periods of limitation without fear of violating some provision of the Constitution. In this case, however, the [one-year] limitation period enacted by the Texas legislature has the unusual effect of emasculating a right which the Equal Protection Clause requires the State to provide to illegitimate children."

In response to this comment, Justice O'CONNOR, joined by Chief Justice Burger and Justices Brennan and Blackmun, submitted a concurring opinion: "Although I agree with the Court's analysis and result, I write separately because I fear that the opinion may be misinterpreted as approving the four-year statute of limitation now used in Texas." She elaborated: "[I]t is not only birth-related circumstances that compel the conclusion that the statutory distinction in this case [is] unconstitutional. [E.g.], the strength of the asserted state interest is undercut by the countervailing state interest in ensuring that genuine claims for child support are satisfied. [It] is also significant to the result today that a paternity suit is one of the few Texas causes of action not tolled during the minority of the plaintiff. Of all the difficult proof problems that may arise in civil actions generally, paternity, an issue unique to illegitimate children, is singled out for special treatment." She thought there was reason "to question whether the burden placed on illegitimates is designed to advance permissible state interests." Moreover, "the practical obstacles to filing suit within one year of birth could as easily exist several years after the birth of the illegitimate child." She accordingly concluded: "A review of the factors used in deciding that the one-year statute of limitation cannot withstand an equal protection challenge indicates that longer periods of limitation for paternity suits also may be unconstitutional. [There] is nothing special about the first year following birth that compels the decision in this case. Because I do not read the Court's decision as prejudging the constitutionality of longer periods of limitation, I join it." †

---

† In a separate notation concurring only in the judgment, Justice POW-ELL stated that he, too, was "concerned, for the reasons persuasively

The Court consolidated its approach in Pickett v. Brown, decided a year after Mills. The Tennessee statute at issue in Pickett was for all practical purposes identical to the Texas law before the Court in Mills, except that Tennessee set a two-year limitation period rather than the one-year limit invalidated in Mills. Writing for a now unanimous Court, Justice BRENNAN reaffirmed the Mills standard of a substantial relationship to a legitimate state interest, and determined that "the principles discussed in Mills require us to invalidate this limitations period on equal protection grounds." Relying heavily on Justice O'Connor's concurring opinion in Mills, Justice Brennan found that the two-year limitation was still insufficient to provide illegitimate children with "an adequate opportunity to gain support," and in addition also failed to meet the second part of the Mills test. The Court held that the two-year period was not "substantially related to the State's interest in avoiding the litigation of stale or fraudulent claims" because it was too small a difference from a one-year period, because in some instances the same reasoning would apply to claims brought on behalf of legitimate children, who were nevertheless not restricted by the two-year period, and because "the State's interest in preventing the litigation of stale or fraudulent paternity claims has become more attenuated as scientific advances in blood testing have alleviated the problems of proof surrounding paternity actions."

10th ED., p. 924; IND. RTS., p. 544
Add to footnote 11:

Note the extensive discussion of the reach of the Rodriguez approach in the several opinions in Plyler v. Doe, 457 U.S. 202 (1982), where the majority struck down Texas' attempt to bar the children of illegal aliens from access to free public education. Plyler v. Doe is printed above, addition to 10th Ed., p. 897; Ind.Rts., p. 517.

10th ED., p. 932; IND. RTS., p. 552
Add after Note 1c:

d. *Ball v. James.* In BALL v. JAMES, 451 U.S. 355 (1981), a sharply divided Court applied the Salyer exception to the "one-person one-vote" rule and sustained the constitutionality of a "one-acre one-vote" scheme for electing the directors of a large water reclamation district in Arizona. The dissenters insisted that the majority had unjustifiably departed from the Kramer-Cipriano-Kolodziejski line of cases.

Arizona's Salt River District finances most of its water operations by selling electricity to several hundred thousand Arizona residents, including the inhabitants of a large part of metropolitan Phoenix. The water district in the Salyer case, by contrast, covered a sparsely populated agricultural area. Justice STEWART's majority opinion nevertheless concluded that the Salyer restriction of voting to landowners was also valid in the Arizona district. Moreover, he exercised the deferential "rationality" review of Salyer rather than the strict scrutiny of Kramer. He conceded that the services provided by the Arizona district "are more diverse and affect far more people than those of the [district in Salyer]," but insisted that

stated by Justice O'Connor, that the Court's opinion may be read as pre-

judging the constitutionality of longer periods of limitation."

the Arizona district "simply does not exercise the sort of governmental powers that invoke" the one-person one-vote principle. He noted that the Arizona district "cannot enact any laws governing the conduct of citizens, nor does it administer such normal functions of government as the maintenance of streets, the operation of schools, or sanitation, health, or welfare services." He commented that "the provision of electricity is not a traditional element of governmental sovereignty, Jackson v. Metropolitan Edison Co. [10th Ed., p. 992; Ind.Rts., p. 612], and so is not in itself the sort of general or important governmental function that would make the government provider subject to [the one-person one-vote rule]." And he rejected the argument that "the sheer size of the power operations and the great number of people they affect serve to transform the District here into an entity of general governmental power." Rather, he found the functions of the district to be "of the narrow, special sort which justifies a departure from the popular election requirement." He concluded "that the voting scheme for the District is constitutional because it bears a reasonable relationship to its statutory objectives." *

Justice WHITE's dissent, joined by Justices Brennan, Marshall and Blackmun, insisted that the majority had misapplied the limited exception recognized in Salyer and concluded: "An analysis of the two relevant factors required by Salyer [—limited purpose and insubstantial effect on nonvoters—] demonstrates that the Salt River District possesses significant governmental authority and has a sufficiently wide effect on nonvoters to require application of the strict scrutiny mandated by Kramer." He emphasized: "With respect to energy management and the provision of water and electricity, the District's power is immense. [To] conclude that the effect of the District's operations in this case is substantially akin to that in Salyer ignores reality. [T]he District is an integral governmental actor providing important governmental services to residents of the District. To conclude otherwise is to ignore the urban reality of the District's operations." He objected, moreover, to the majority's suggestion that the provision of electricity and water was not a "sufficiently governmental" function. That, he claimed, was "a distinctly odd view of the reach of municipal services in this day and age." Emphasizing the district's effect on "the daily lives of thousands of citizens," he objected to their exclusion from meaningful participation in the conduct of the district's operations.

10th ED., p. 938; IND. RTS., p. 558
Insert before Sec. 4C:

6. *Limiting strict scrutiny in ballot access cases: Public officials' candidacies.* In CLEMENTS v. FASHING, 457 U.S. —— (1982), Justice REHNQUIST's plurality opinion announced that "[n]ot all ballot access restrictions require 'heightened' equal protection scrutiny" and sustained two

---

* Justice POWELL joined the majority but noted in a concurring opinion that, although the Kramer holding was unaffected by either Salyer or Ball, "it must be evident that some of the reasoning in that case has been questioned." (The majority opinion had noted that, although strict scrutiny was applied in Kramer, merely deferential, rationality review was used in Salyer.)

Texas constitutional provisions limiting a public official's ability to become a candidate for another public office. One provision (§ 19) required certain officeholders to complete their current terms of office before they could be eligible to serve in the state legislature.[1] Another, "automatic resignation" provision (§ 65) mandated that, if holders of certain state and county offices whose unexpired term exceeded one year became candidates for any other state or federal office, "such announcement or such candidacy [would] constitute an automatic resignation of the office then held."[2] The "automatic resignation" provision was challenged by four officials whose candidacies for higher judicial office were allegedly inhibited by the state barrier. One of the challengers (a Justice of the Peace) also attacked the state restriction on candidacies for the legislature.[3]

In rejecting the equal protection attack, Justice Rehnquist's plurality opinion (joined by Chief Justice Burger and Justices Powell and O'Connor) began by explaining why the challenged provisions did not "deserve 'scrutiny' more vigorous than that which the traditional [equal protection rationality] principles would require."[4] He insisted that, in recent years, the Court had departed from "traditional equal protection analysis" only in "two essentially separate, although similar, lines of ballot access cases. One line [involves] classifications based on wealth. [Clearly], the challenged provisions in the instant case involve neither filing fees nor restrictions that invidiously burden those of lower economic status. [Bullock v. Carter; Lubin v. Panish.] The second line [involves] classification schemes that impose burdens on new or small political parties or independent candidates. See, e.g., Illinois Elections Bd. v. Socialist Workers Party; Storer v. Brown; American Party of Texas v.

---

1. Art. III, § 19, of the Texas Constitution provides: "No judge of any court, Secretary of State, Attorney General, clerk of any court of record, or any person holding a lucrative office under the United States, or this State, or any foreign government shall during the term for which he is elected or appointed, be eligible for the Legislature."

2. Art. XVI, Sec. 65, of the Texas Constitution provides: "[I]f any of the officers named herein shall announce their candidacy, or shall in fact become a candidate, in any General, Special or Primary Election, for any office of profit under the laws of this State or the United States other than the office then held, at any time when the unexpired term of the office then held shall exceed one (1) year, such announcement or such candidacy shall constitute an automatic resignation of the office then held." Sec. 65 covers the following state and county offices: "District Clerks, County Clerks, County Judges, County Treasurers, Criminal District Attorneys, County Surveyors, Inspectors of Hides and Animals, County Commissioners, Justices of the Peace, Sheriffs, Assessors and Collectors of Taxes, District Attorneys, County Attorneys, Public Weighers, and Constables."

3. These officeholder-challengers were joined by 20 voters who alleged that they would vote for the officeholder-challengers were they to become candidates.

4. Justice Rehnquist stated those principles as follows: "Under traditional equal protection principles, distinctions need only be drawn in such a manner as to bear some rational relationship to a legitimate state end. Classifications are set aside only if they are based solely on reasons totally unrelated to the pursuit of the State's goals and only if no grounds can be conceived to justify them. See, e.g., [McDonald; McGowan]. We have departed from traditional equal protection principles only when the challenged statute places burdens upon 'suspect classes' of persons or on a constitutional right that is deemed to be 'fundamental.' [Rodriguez.]"

White; Jenness v. Fortson; Williams v. Rhodes." He added: "The provisions [challenged here] do not contain any classification that imposes special burdens on minority political parties or independent candidates. The burdens placed on [these] candidates [in] no way depend upon political affiliation or political viewpoint."

In determining whether heightened scrutiny should nevertheless apply here, he examined "the nature of the interests that are affected and the extent of the burden these provisions place on candidacy." He limited his examination of § 19, the barrier to candidacies for the legislature, solely to the situation of the challenger who was a Justice of the Peace. The Justice of the Peace served for a four-year term. To Justice Rehnquist, the length of the term in effect established "a maximum 'waiting period' of two years for candidacy by a Justice of the Peace for the Legislature" and therefore placed only "a de minimis burden on the political aspirations of a *current* officeholder." He insisted: "A 'waiting period' is hardly a significant barrier to candidacy. [This] sort of insignificant interference with access to the ballot need only rest on a rational predicate in order to survive a challenge under the Equal Protection Clause." And the minimum rationality requirement was readily met here: "[The] provision furthers Texas' interests in maintaining the integrity of the State's Justices of the Peace.[5] By prohibiting candidacy for the Legislature until completion of one's term of office, § 19 seeks to ensure that a Justice of the Peace will neither abuse his position nor neglect his duties because of his aspirations for higher office." Nor did he find any flaw in the provision "because it burdens only those officeholders who desire to run for the Legislature." He relied on the "one step at a time" philosophy of Williamson v. Lee Optical Co.

Justice Rehnquist disposed of the equal protection challenge to the "automatic resignation" provision even more summarily: "The burdens that § 65 imposes on candidacy are even less substantial than those imposed by § 19. The two provisions [serve] essentially the same state interests." He was not impressed by the District Court's view that the classification was unconstitutional "because Texas has failed to explain sufficiently why some elected public officials are subject to [the barrier] and why others are not." The challengers had failed to show "that there is no rational predicate to the classification scheme." Again, he invoked the "one step at a time" rationale: the barrier had been enacted in connection with the extension of certain terms of office from two to four years; that the State did not go further in applying the automatic resignation provision to those officeholders whose terms were not extended, [absent] an invidious purpose, is not the sort of malfunctioning of the State's lawmaking process forbidden by the Equal Protection Clause. A regulation is not devoid of a rational predicate simply because it happens to be incomplete. See Williamson v. Lee Optical Co." [6]

5. "The State's particular interest in maintaining the integrity of the judicial system could support § 19 even if such a restriction could not survive constitutional scrutiny with regard to any other officeholder." [Footnote by Justice Rehnquist.]

6. In the only portion of Justice Rehnquist's discussion of the merits that gained majority rather than plurality support (because Justice Stevens joined that part of the opinion), Justice Rehnquist also rejected a First Amendment challenge. Relying on his discussion of the equal protec-

In a separate opinion, Justice STEVENS agreed with the rejection of the equal protection claim but gave different reasons for doing so. He objected to the general discussion of the "level of scrutiny" problem: "Unfortunately that analysis may do more to obfuscate than to clarify the inquiry. This case suggests that a better starting point may be a careful identification of the character of the federal interest in equality that is implicated by the State's discriminatory classification. In my opinion, the disparate treatment in this case is not inconsistent with any federal interest that is protected by the Equal Protection Clause." Here, "the disparate treatment of different officeholders [was] entirely a function of the different offices that they occupy"; there was "no suggestion that the attributes of the offices have been defined to conceal an intent to discriminate on the basis of personal characteristics." The central question, then, was "whether there is any federal interest in requiring a State to define the benefits and burdens of different elective state offices in any particular manner. In my opinion there is not." He explained that conclusion as follows: "I see no reason why a State may not provide that certain offices [will] be filled [by] persons who may not seek other office until they have fulfilled their duties in the first. There may be no explanation for these classifications that a federal judge would find to be 'rational.' But they do not violate the Equal Protection Clause because there is no federal requirement that a State fit the emoluments or the burdens of different elective state offices into any particular pattern. The reason, then, that appellees may be treated differently from other officeholders is that they occupy different offices."

Justice Stevens added: "As in so many areas of the law, it is important to consider each case individually. In the situation presented, however, I believe that there is no federal interest in equality that requires the [State] to treat the different classes as if they were the same. This reasoning brings me to the same conclusion that Justice Rehnquist has reached. It avoids, however, the danger of confusing two quite different questions.[7] Justice Rehnquist has demonstrated that there is a 'rational basis' for imposing the burdens at issue [here]. He has not, however, adequately explained the reasons, if any, for imposing those burdens on some offices but not others. With respect to the latter inquiry, the plurality is satisfied to note that the State may approach its goals 'one step at a time.' In my judgment, this response is simply another way of stating that there need be no justification at

tion arguments, he stated: "The State's interests in this regard are sufficient to warrant the de minimis interference with appellees' interests in candidacy." He cited "another reason" for rejecting the First Amendment challenge: "Appellees are *elected* state officeholders who contest restrictions on partisan political activity. [The barriers here] represent a far more limited restriction on political activity than this Court has upheld with regard to *civil servants.* See CSC v. Letter Carriers; Broadrick v. Oklahoma; United Public Workers v. Mitchell."

7. "See Westen, The Empty Idea of Equality, 95 Harv.L.Rev. 537 (1982). Professor Westen's article is valuable because it illustrates the distinction between concern with the substantive import of a state restriction and concern with any disparate impact that it may produce. In recognizing that distinction, however, it is important not to lose sight of the fact that the Equal Protection Clause has independent significance in protecting the federal interest in requiring States to govern impartially." [Footnote by Justice Stevens.]

all for treating two classes differently during the interval between the first step and the second step—an interval that, of course, may well last forever. Although such an approach is unobjectionable in a case involving the differences between different public offices, I surely could not subscribe to Justice Rehnquist's formulation of the standard to be used in evaluating state legislation that treats different classes of persons differently." [8]

Justice BRENNAN, joined by Justices Marshall, Blackmun and White, strongly disagreed with Justice Rehnquist's rejection of the equal protection claim. He concluded that the challenged provisions could not "survive even minimal equal protection scrutiny." [9] Even applying rationality review, he could find "no genuine justification" for the challenged classifications: "[N]either the State nor the plurality offers any justification for *differential* treatment of various classes of officeholders, and the search for such justification makes clear that the classifications embodied in these provisions lack any meaningful relationship to the State's asserted or supposed interests." For example, he could find no relationship "between the burden placed on the class of all state, federal, and foreign officeholders seeking legislative seats and the asserted state interests. [It] is beyond dispute that the class is substantially overbroad." He also objected at length to Justice Rehnquist's use of the "one step at a time" approach: "the plurality today gives new meaning to the term 'legal fiction.' " For example, the barrier to running for the legislature has been on the books since 1876: "There is no legislative history [to] suggest that it is part of a larger, more equitable regulatory scheme. And in the 106 years that have passed since [its] adoption, the Texas legislature has adopted no comparable bar to candidacy for other offices." The "one step at a time" justification was available only "where the record demonstrates that such 'one step at a time' regulation is in fact being undertaken. I cannot subscribe [to] the plurality's wholly fictional one-step-at-a-time justification. [The] haphazard reach and isolated existence [of this barrier] strikes me as the very sort of 'arbitrary scheme or plan' that we distinguished from an as-yet-uncompleted design in McDonald v. Board of Election, a case the plurality relies on to support the classification in this case." Similarly, the "automatic resignation" provision "restricts the candidacy only of an unexplained and seemingly inexplicable collection of administrative, execu-

---

8. Justice Brennan's dissent took issue with a portion of this passage in Justice Stevens' opinion: "Justice Stevens argues in his concurrence that there is no federal interest in requiring the State to treat different elective state offices in a fair and equitable manner. I agree [that] the State may define *many* of the 'benefits and burdens of different elective state offices' in a dissimilar manner without [persuading a federal judge that it is acting rationally], so long as such classifications do not mask any racial or otherwise impermissible discrimination. But where the differential treatment concerns a restriction on the right to seek public office—a right protected by the First Amendment—that Amendment supplies the federal interest in equality that may be lacking where the State is simply determining salary, hours, or working conditions of its own employees."

9. Justice Brennan addressed the "level of scrutiny" problem in ballot access cases generally only in a footnote: "It is worth noting [that] the plurality's analysis of the level of scrutiny to be applied to these restrictions gives too little consideration to the impact of our prior cases. Although we have never defined candidacy as a

tive, and judicial officials." There was no explanation "why the State has a greater interest in having the undivided attention of a 'public weigher' than of a state criminal court judge, or any reason why the State has greater interest in preventing the abuse of office by an 'Inspector of Hides and Animals' than by a Justice of the Texas Supreme Court. Yet in each instance [the provision] applies to the former office and not to the latter." Once again, the "one step at a time" rationale was unavailing: the provision could not "in any realistic sense be upheld as one step in an evolving scheme." [10]

7. *Hints of a new approach.* Justice STEVENS' majority opinion in ANDERSON v. CELEBREZZE, 460 U.S. —— (1983), suggests a rather different methodology for ballot access cases. At issue was an Ohio statute that required independent candidates to file their petitions and related materials by March 20 if they wished a place on the November ballot. John Anderson, independent candidate for President in 1980, challenged the statute on two grounds. First, he claimed that the early filing deadline was so early that it represented an excess restriction on access to the ballot, one that was not justified by any legitimate state interest. Second, by imposing a filing deadline for independents without requiring comparable action for the nominee of a political party, the statute impermissibly discriminated against independent candidates.

The Court upheld Anderson's claim, finding that Ohio's asserted interests in voter education, equal treatment for partisan and independent candidates, and political stability were either illegitimate or too remotely related

fundamental right, we have clearly recognized that restrictions on candidacy impinge on First Amendment rights of candidates and voters. See, e.g., Illinois Elections Bd. v. Socialist Workers Party; Lubin v. Panish; American Party of Texas v. White; Bullock v. Carter; Williams v. Rhodes. With this consideration in mind, we have applied strict scrutiny in reviewing most restrictions on ballot access. [The] plurality dismisses our prior cases as dealing with only two kinds of ballot access restrictions —classifications based on wealth and classifications imposing burdens on new or small political parties or independent candidates. But strict scrutiny was required in those cases because of their impact on the First Amendment *rights* of candidates and voters, see Storer v. Brown, not because the *class* of candidates or voters that was burdened was somehow suspect. The plurality offers no explanation as to why the restrictions at issue here, which completely bar some candidates from running and require other candidates to give up their present employment, are less 'substantial' in their impact on candidates and their supporters than, for example, the $700 filing fee at issue in Lubin.

In my view, some greater deference may be due the State because these restrictions affect only public employees, but this does not suggest that, in subjecting these classifications to equal protection scrutiny, we should completely disregard the vital interests of the candidates and the citizens whom they represent in a political campaign."

10. Justice Brennan also sustained the separate First Amendment challenge to § 19, but Justice White did not join that part of his opinion. Justice Brennan criticized the majority for failing to address "the crucial question: What justification does the State have for this restriction and how does this provision address the State's asserted interests?" He elaborated: "[T]o survive scrutiny under the First Amendment, a restriction on political campaigning by government employees must be narrowly tailored and substantially related to furthering the State's asserted interest." The restriction on candidacy for the legislature, he concluded, was "not narrowly tailored to conform to the State's asserted interest. Nor does it further those interests in a meaningful way."

to the early filing deadline to justify such a substantial barrier to independent candidates. More important than the particular result, however, were two significant departures in approach from previous ballot access cases.

Most noteworthy, especially in light of the skepticism evidenced in Rodriguez with respect to fundamental rights analysis in the equal protection area, was the Court's specific decision to rule on First Amendment and not equal protection grounds. "[We] base our conclusions directly on the First and Fourteenth Amendments and do not engage in a separate Equal Protection Clause analysis. We rely, however, on the analysis in a number of our prior election cases resting on the Equal Protection Clause. [These] cases, applying the 'fundamental rights' strand of equal protection analysis, have identified the First [Amendment] rights implicated by restrictions on the eligibility of voters and candidates, and have considered the degree to which the State's restrictions further legitimate state interests. [Williams; Bullock; Lubin; Ilinois Elections Bd.]"

The Court also made clear that ballot access cases would be decided by an individualized weighing of the various interests involved. "Constitutional challenges to specific provisions of a State's election laws [cannot] be resolved by any 'litmus-paper test' that will separate valid from invalid restrictions. Storer. Instead, a court [must] first consider the character and magnitude of the asserted injury to the [First Amendment rights] that the plaintiff seeks to vindicate. It then must identify and evaluate the precise interests put forward by the State as justifications for the burden imposed. [The] Court must not only determine the legitimacy and strength of each of those interests; it also must consider the extent to which those interests make it necessary to burden the plaintiff's rights. Only after weighing all these factors is the reviewing court in a position to decide whether the challenged provision is unconstitutional." *

10th ED., p. 946; IND. RTS., p. 566
Add to footnote 3:

In Bearden v. Georgia, 461 U.S. —— (1983), the Court relied on Williams and Tate to hold that probation may not be revoked for mere nonpayment of a fine. Probation may be revoked for nonpayment of a fine only if it is determined that there had been no bona fide efforts to pay, "or that adequate alternative forms of punishment did not exist." Of particular interest in Justice O'Connor's majority opinion is the discussion of the relationship between due process and equal protection principles. "There is no doubt that the State has treated the petitioner differently from a person who did not fail to pay the imposed fine and therefore did not violate probation. To determine whether this differential treatment violates the Equal Protection Clause, one must determine whether, and under what circumstances, a defendant's indigent status may be considered in the decision whether to revoke probation. This is substantially similar to asking directly the due process question of whether and when it is fundamentally unfair or arbitrary for the State to revoke probation when an indigent is unable to pay the fine." At this point Justice O'Connor

---

* Justice REHNQUIST's dissenting opinion, joined by Justices White, Powell, and O'Connor, focused primarily on the similarities between this case and Storer v. Brown. The dissenters were unpersuaded by the Court's attempts to distinguish Storer, and were also unconvinced that this restriction in fact impeded the efforts of Anderson or other independent candidates. Interestingly, however, the dissent expressed no disagreement with the Court's characterization of the case as a First Amendment case rather than an equal protection case, and did not take issue with generalized balancing approach set forth by Justice Stevens.

added a footnote that articulated a preference for a due process inquiry. "A due process approach has the advantage in this context of directly confronting the intertwined question of the role that a defendant's financial background can play in determining an appropriate sentence. When the court is initially considering what sentence to impose, a defendant's level of financial resources is a point on a spectrum rather than a classification. Since indigency in this context is a relative term rather than a classification, [the] more appropriate question is whether consideration of a defendant's financial background in setting or resetting a sentence is so arbitrary or unfair as to be a denial of due process."

10th ED., p. 948; IND. RTS., p. 568
Add to the Notes:

3. *Little.* The unanimous decision in LITTLE v. STREATER, 452 U.S. 1 (1981), followed Boddie and distinguished Kras and Ortwein in holding that an indigent defendant in a paternity action was entitled to state-subsidized blood grouping tests.* The case arose in the following circumstances: An unmarried mother receiving welfare assistance reported to a state agency that defendant was the father of her child. (Welfare regulations required her to make such a report.) The state agency then helped her to bring a paternity suit against the defendant. (Welfare regulations required her to bring suit.) Defendant, pursuant to a state statute, moved to order blood grouping tests on the mother and her child.†
Under the state law, the moving party—i.e., defendant—was required to pay for the tests. Defendant asserted that he was indigent and asked that the State be ordered to pay for the tests. That request was denied; consequently, no blood grouping tests were performed. Defendant lost the paternity suit and was ordered to pay child support.

In holding that the denial of state-paid tests violated due process in this case, Chief Justice BURGER applied the balancing criteria of Mathews v. Eldridge (noted at the end of the previous chapter in the text) and emphasized "the unique quality of blood grouping tests as a source of exculpatory evidence." Moreover, he stressed "the State's prominent role in the litigation." This was not simply "a common dispute between private parties"; rather, "the State's involvement [was] considerable and manifest, giving rise to a constitutional duty." Further, paternity proceedings in Connecticut, although characterized by the State as "civil," in fact "have 'quasi-criminal' overtones." Moreover, without blood grouping tests, a paternity defendant is under a "distinct disadvantage" under Connecticut's evidentiary rules, because "his testimony alone is insufficient to overcome the plaintiff's prima facie case." Thus, without the tests, "the risk is not inconsiderable that an indigent defendant [will] be erroneously adjudged the father."

The Chief Justice accordingly concluded that. without the tests, "an indigent defendant, who faces the State as an adversary [and] who must overcome the evidentiary burden Connecticut imposes, lacks 'a meaningful opportunity to be heard.' [Boddie.]" Therefore, in the case at hand, the "fundamental fairness" requirement of the Due Process Clause had not been satisfied. The Chief Justice distinguished Kras and Ortwein: "Kras and Ortwein emphasized the availability of other relief and the less 'fundamental' charac-

---

* Since the Court found a violation of due process, it deemed it unnecessary to consider defendant's equal protection challenge.

† Such tests might have established that defendant *was not* the child's father; they could not have proven that he *was* the father.

ter of the private interests at stake than those implicated in Boddie. Because [defendant] has no choice of an alternative forum and his interests, as well as those of the child, are constitutionally significant [because "the creation of a parent-child relationship" was at stake], this case is comparable to Boddie rather than to Kras and Ortwein." **

10th ED., p. 960; IND. RTS., p. 580
Add after the Notes:

For a rare modern case examining a right to travel claim in a context other than durational residence requirements, see JONES v. HELMS, 452 U.S. 412 (1981). Georgia law makes a parent's willful abandonment of a dependent child a crime. The crime is a misdemeanor if all of the events take place in Georgia; but it becomes a felony if the parent leaves the State after abandoning the child in Georgia. The challenger contested the constitutionality of this "enhanced punishment of those parents who [leave Georgia] after abandoning their children."

The Court of Appeals sustained the challenge: it considered the law an infringement of the "fundamental right to travel" and accordingly applied "strict scrutiny." But Justice STEVENS' opinion for the Court rejected the lower court's analysis, insisting that the enhancement provision "did not penalize the exercise of the constitutional right to travel." He explained: "Despite the fundamental nature of [the right to travel], there nonetheless are situations in which a State may prevent a citizen from leaving. Most obvious is the case in which a person has been convicted of a crime within a State. We are aware of nothing in our prior cases or in the language of the Federal Constitution that suggests that a person who has committed an offense punishable by imprisonment has an unqualified federal right to leave the jurisdiction prior to arrest or conviction." Here, the challenger had pleaded guilty to the charge. Justice Stevens concluded from this that the challenger's "own misconduct had qualified his right to travel interstate before he sought to exercise that right."

Justice Stevens was then able to find a "significant" difference between this case and prior right to travel decisions, from Crandall v. Nevada to the modern durational residence cases: "In all of those cases, the statute at issue imposed a burden on the exercise of the right to travel by citizens whose right to travel had not been qualified in any way. In contrast, in this case, [the challenger's] criminal conduct within [Georgia] necessarily qualified his right thereafter freely to travel interstate. [Moreover, the earlier cases are inapposite because] the question presented by this case is not whether Georgia can justify disparate treatment of residents and nonresidents, or of new and old residents. Rather the question is whether the State may enhance the misdemeanor of child abandonment to a felony if a resident offender leaves

---

** Compare with Little the divided decision, on the same day, in Lassiter v. Dept. of Social Services, 452 U.S. 18 (1981), rejecting the claim of the petitioner—an indigent mother involved in a state court parental status termination proceeding—that she was entitled to counsel. The majority left the appointment of counsel in termination proceedings to be determined on a case-by-case basis. Justice Stevens and Justice Blackmun (joined by Justices Brennan and Marshall) submitted dissents arguing that counsel must be provided in *all* termination cases.

the State after committing the offense. Presumably the commission of the misdemeanor of child abandonment would not justify a permanent restriction on the offender's freedom to leave the jurisdiction. But a restriction that is rationally related to the offense itself [must] be within the State's power. Thus, although a simple penalty for leaving a State is plainly impermissible, if departure aggravates the consequences of conduct that is otherwise punishable, the State may treat the entire sequence of events, from the initial offense to departure from the State, as more serious than its separate components." Here, the scheme rested on a legitimate purpose: "to cause parents to support their children." And there was no basis for questioning the legislative judgment that the statute would serve this purpose. Accordingly, there was no "impermissible infringement" of the right to travel.

Having rejected any basis for strict scrutiny, Justice Stevens had no difficulty turning aside the equal protection attack. The law applied equally to all parents residing in Georgia, and there had been no showing of discriminatory enforcement. Moreover, the challenger's claim that less restrictive means were available to the State was beside the point: "Because we have concluded that [the law] does not infringe [upon] fundamental rights," "the State need not employ the least restrictive, or even the most effective or wisest, means to achieve its legitimate ends."

Justice BLACKMUN concurred only in the judgment. Unlike Justice Stevens, he acknowledged that the Georgia scheme "clearly penalizes [the challenger's] exercise of his constitutional right to travel." But he thought the penalty justified "by the State's special interest in law enforcement in this context." He explained: "The challenged [law] is concerned primarily with restitution rather than punishment, and the core criminal conduct, willful abandonment and continuing nonsupport, is markedly more difficult to redress once the offending parent leaves the jurisdiction. A restriction that reasonably discourages departure may therefore be justified as tailored to further the precise remedial objective of the criminal law." He emphasized that "the objective advanced here is not identical to the more general goal of improving the administration of criminal justice." And he added: "I doubt that a State constitutionally may impose greater penalties for all crimes simply because the accused leaves the jurisdiction." *

* Justice WHITE joined the Court's opinion, but also submitted a separate statement. He contended that the Court had vindicated his position at the time of Shapiro v. Thompson: that such cases could be decided directly on right to travel grounds "without implicating the Equal Protection Clause at all." Such an approach, he thought, was being followed by the Court here: "[The Court] first finds that whatever restriction on interstate travel is imposed by the challenged Georgia provision, the State's interest in enforcing its child support laws is sufficient to justify the restriction. The opinion then finds that the equal protection claim is without substance because there is at least a rational basis for the State's classification."

10th ED., p. 960; IND. RTS., p. 580
Insert before Sec. 4E:

"bona fide" residency requirement upheld

MARTINEZ v. BYNUM

461 U.S. —, 103 S.Ct. 1838, 75 L.Ed.2d 879 (1983).

diff than durational residence requirement

Justice POWELL delivered the opinion of the Court.

This case involves a facial challenge to the constitutionality of the Texas residency requirement governing minors who wish to attend public free schools while living apart from their parents or guardians.

I. Roberto Morales was born in 1969 in McAllen, Texas, and is thus a United States citizen by birth. His parents are Mexican citizens who reside in Reynosa, Mexico. He left Reynosa in 1977 and returned to Mc-Allen to live with his sister, petitioner Oralia Martinez, for the primary purpose of attending school in the McAllen Independent School District. Although Martinez is now Morales's custodian, she is not—and does not desire to become—his guardian.[1] As a result, Morales is not entitled to tuition-free admission to the McAllen schools. Section 21.031(b) and (c) of the Texas Education Code would require the local school authorities to admit him if he or "his parent, guardian, or the person having lawful control of him" resided in the school district, but § 21.031(d) denies tuition-free admission for a minor who lives apart from a "parent, guardian, or other person having lawful control of him under an order of a court" if his presence in the school district is "for the primary purpose of attending the public free schools."[2] Respondent McAllen Independent School District therefore denied Morales's application for admission in the fall of 1977.

In December 1977 Martinez, as next friend of Morales, [instituted] the present action in the [District Court] against the Texas Commissioner of Education [and] various local school officials in those districts. After a hearing on the merits, the District Court granted judgment for the defendants. The court concluded that § 21.031(d) was justified by the State's "legitimate interest in protecting and preserving the quality of its educational system and the right of its own bona fide residents to attend state schools on a preferred tuition basis." [The Court of Appeals] affirmed.

II. This Court frequently has considered constitutional challenges to residence requirements. On several occasions the Court has invalidated requirements that condition receipt of a benefit on a minimum period of residence within a jurisdiction, but it always has been careful to distinguish such durational residence requirements from bona fide residence requirements. In Shapiro v. Thompson, for example, the Court invalidated one-year durational residence requirements that applicants for public assistance

Morales born in Texas of Mexican parents. At age 8, returned to Texas to live w sister Martinez for purpose of attending Texas schools.

Texas Law prohibited free tuition admission unless parents or guardian lived w/in school dist. (Sister not a "guardian")

preserve quality of ed.

Dist. Court upheld § Texas Law. Ct. Appeals affirmed.

Court has distinguished durational residence requirements from bona fide residence requirements

---

1. [The] Texas Family Code defines "custodian" as "the adult with whom the child resides." "Guardian" is defined as "the person who, under court order, is the guardian of the person of the child or the public or private agency with whom the child has been placed by a court." [Footnote by Justice Powell.]

2. [Although] the "special purpose" test was not codified in § 21.031(d) until 1977, it had been a feature of Texas common law since at least 1905. . . . [Footnote by Justice Powell.]

benefits were required to satisfy despite the fact that they otherwise had "met the test for residence in their jurisdictions." Justice Brennan, writing for the Court, stressed that "[t]he residence requirement and the one-year waiting-period requirement are distinct and independent prerequisites for assistance," and carefully "impl[ied] no view of the validity of waiting-period *or* residence requirements determining eligibility to vote, eligibility for tuition-free education, to obtain a license to practice a profession, to hunt or fish, and so forth." In Dunn v. Blumstein, the Court similarly invalidated Tennessee laws requiring a prospective voter to have been a state resident for one year and a county resident for three months, but it explicitly distinguished these durational residence requirements from bona fide residence requirements. This was not an empty distinction. Justice Marshall, writing for the Court, again emphasized that "States have the power to require that voters be bona fide residents of the relevant political subdivision."

[We] specifically have approved bona fide residence requirements in the field of public education. The Connecticut statute before us in Vlandis v. Kline, for example, was unconstitutional because it created an irrebuttable presumption of nonresidency for state university students whose legal addresses were outside of the State before they applied for admission. The statute violated the Due Process Clause because it in effect classified some bona fide state residents as nonresidents for tuition purposes. But we "fully recognize[d] that a State has a legitimate interest in protecting and preserving . . . the right of its own bona fide residents to attend [its colleges and universities] on a preferential tuition basis." This "legitimate interest" permits a "State [to] establish such reasonable criteria for in-state status as to make virtually certain that students who are not, in fact, bona fide residents of the State, but who have come there solely for educational purposes cannot take advantage of the in-state rates." Last Term, in Plyler v. Doe, we reviewed an aspect of [the] statute at issue in this case. Although we invalidated the portion of the statute that excluded undocumented alien children from the public free schools, we recognized the school districts' right "to apply . . . established criteria for determining residence."

[A] bona fide residence requirement, appropriately defined and uniformly applied, furthers the substantial state interest in assuring that services provided for its residents are enjoyed only by residents. Such a requirement with respect to attendance in public free schools does not violate the Equal Protection Clause.[3] It does not burden or penalize the constitutional right of interstate travel, for any person is free to move to a State and to establish residence there. A bona fide residence requirement simply

---

3. A bona fide residence requirement implicates no "suspect" classification, and therefore is not subject to strict scrutiny. Indeed, there is nothing invidiously discriminatory about a bona fide residence requirement if it is uniformly applied. Thus the question is simply whether there is a rational basis for it.

This view assumes, of course, that the "service" that the State would deny to nonresidents is not a fundamental right protected by the Constitution. A State, for example, may not refuse to provide counsel to an indigent nonresident defendant at a criminal trial where a deprivation of liberty occurs. As we previously have recognized, however, "[p]ublic education is not a 'right' granted to individuals by the Constitution." [Plyler] [Footnote by Justice Powell.]

requires that the person *does* establish residence before demanding the services that are restricted to residents.

There is a further, independent justification for local residence requirements in the public-school context. [The] provision of primary and secondary education [is] one of the most important functions of local government. Absent residence requirements, there can be little doubt that the proper planning and operation of the schools would suffer significantly. The State thus has a substantial interest in imposing bona fide residence requirements to maintain the quality of local public schools.

III. The central question we must decide here is whether § 21.031(d) is a bona fide residence requirement. Although the meaning may vary according to context, "residence" generally requires both physical presence and an intention to remain.[4] As the Supreme Court of Maine explained over a century ago, "When . . . a person voluntarily takes up his abode in a given place, with intention to remain permanently, or for an indefinite period of time; or, to speak more accurately, when a person takes up his abode in a given place, without any present intention to remove therefrom, such place of abode becomes his residence. . . ." Inhabitants of Warren v. Inhabitants of Thomaston, 43 Me. 406 (1857). This classic two-part definition of residence has been recognized as a minimum standard in a wide range of contexts time and time again.

In [Vlandis] we approved a more rigorous domicile test as a "reasonable standard for determining the residential status of a student." That standard was described as follows: " 'In reviewing a claim of in-state status, the issue becomes essentially one of domicile. In general, the domicile of an individual is his true, fixed and permanent home and place of habitation. It is the place to which, whenever he is absent, he has the intention of returning.' " This standard could not be applied to school-age children in the same way that it was applied to college students. But at the very least, a school district generally would be justified in requiring school-age children or their parents to satisfy the traditional, basic residence criteria—i.e., to live in the district with a bona fide intention of remaining there—before it treated them as residents.

Section 21.031 is far more generous than this traditional standard. It compels a school district to permit a child such as Morales to attend school without paying tuition if he has a bona fide intention to remain in the school district indefinitely, for he then would have a reason for being there other than his desire to attend school: his intention to make his home in the district. Thus § 21.031 grants the benefits of residency to all who satisfy the traditional requirements. The statute goes further and extends these benefits to many children even if they (or their families) do not intend to remain in the district indefinitely. As long as the child is not living in the district for the sole purpose of attending school, he satisfies the statutory

---

4. Contrary to the suggestion in the dissent, we have said nothing about domicile. The Texas statute, like many similar ones, speaks only in terms of residence. We hold simply that a State may impose bona fide residence requirements for tuition-free admission to its public schools. Our conclusion is supported by the fact that several States have recognized the "intention to remain" requirement in this context. [Footnote by Justice Powell.]

Statute Upheld

test. For example, if a person comes to Texas to work for a year, his children will be eligible for tuition-free admission to the public schools. Or if a child comes to Texas for six months for health reasons, he would qualify for tuition-free education. In short, § 21.031 grants the benefits of residency to everyone who satisfies the traditional residence definition and to some who legitimately could be classified as nonresidents. Since there is no indication that this extension of the traditional definition has any impermissible basis, we certainly cannot say that § 21.031(d) violates the Constitution.

Affirmed.

Brennan Concurs but emphasizes only a facial challenge

Justice BRENNAN, concurring.

I join the Court's opinion. I write separately, however, to stress that this case involves only a facial challenge to the constitutionality of the Texas statute. In upholding the statute, the Court does not pass on its validity as applied to children in a range of specific factual contexts. In particular, the Court does not decide whether the statute is constitutional as applied to Roberto Morales, a United States citizen whose parents are non-resident aliens. If this question were before the Court, I believe that a different set of considerations would be implicated which might affect significantly an analysis of the statute's constitutionality.

Marshall Dissents

Justice MARSHALL, dissenting.

Shortly after petitioner Roberto Morales reached his eighth birthday, he left his parents' home in Reynosa, Mexico and returned to his birthplace, McAllen, Texas. He planned to make his home there with his married sister in order to attend school and learn English. Morales has resided with his sister in McAllen for the past five years and intends to remain with her until he has completed his schooling. The Texas statute grants free public education to every school-age child who resides in Texas except for one who lives apart from his parents or guardian for educational purposes. Accordingly, Morales has been refused free admission to the schools in the McAllen district.

The majority upholds the classification embodied in the Texas statute on the ground that it applies only to the class of children who are considered *non*-residents. The majority's approach reflects a misinterpretation of the Texas statute, a misunderstanding of the concept of residence, and a misapplication of this Court's past decisions concerning the constitutionality of residence requirements. In my view, the statutory classification, which deprives some children of an education because of their motive for residing in Texas, is not adequately justified by the asserted state interests. . . . .

The Court does not address the constitutionality of the classification contained in the statute. Instead, it upholds as constitutional on its face a statute that denies free public education only to a portion of the children actually described in the Texas statute: children who reside in the State solely for the purpose of attending the local schools *and* who also intend to leave the district after the completion of their education. By inferring that children will not be excluded from the local free schools if they "intend to remain indefinitely" in the district, the Court is able to characterize the Texas statute as imposing a "traditional residence standard." Having characterized the statute in this fashion, the Court then reasons that because a bona fide residence requirement has been upheld in numerous contexts, the Texas statute is *a fortiori* permissible since it does not deny free education to "resident" children, but only to non-resident children whose presence is motivated by the availability of free education.

By its terms the Texas statute applies to any child whose presence in the district is motivated primarily by a desire to obtain free education. The statute draws no further distinction between those who intend to leave upon the completion of their education and those who do not. No Texas court has adopted the narrowing interpretation on which this Court relies. [The] Court nevertheless proceeds to address the constitutionality of the statute as newly interpreted. For the reasons elaborated below, I believe the majority errs in its approach to that question.

II. In the Court's view, because the Texas statute employs a "traditional" residence requirement in a uniform fashion, and indeed is even more generous since it permits some "non-residents" to obtain free education, the statute need be subjected only to the most minimal judicial scrutiny normally accorded bona fide residence requirements. For the reasons stated below, this conclusion rests on a number of false assumptions and misconceptions. The Court mistakenly equates the Texas statute with a residence requirement, when in fact the statute, as reinterpreted by the Court, imposes a standard even more difficult to meet than a domicile requirement for access to public education. Moreover, even if it were permissible to provide free education only to those residents who intend to remain in the State, the Texas statute does not impose that restriction uniformly.

A. The majority errs in reasoning that, because "intent to remain indefinitely" in a State is a "traditional" component of many State residence requirements, the imposition of that restriction on free public education is presumptively valid. The standard described by the Court is not the traditional standard for determining residence, but is, if anything, the standard for determining domicile. Although this Court's prior cases suggest that, as a general matter, a State may reserve its educational resources for its residents, there is no support for the view that a State may close its schools to all but *domiciliaries.*

A difference between the concepts of residence and domicile has long been recognized. A person is generally a resident of any state with which he has a well-settled connection. ["Intent] to remain indefinitely" in the State need not be shown in order to be considered a resident of a state. [On] the other hand, an individual has only one domicile, which is generally the state with which he is currently most closely connected, but which may be a state with which he was closely connected in the past. Traditionally, an individual has been said to acquire a new domicile when he resides in a State with "the absence of any intention to live elsewhere," or with " 'the absence of any present intention of not residing permanently or indefinitely in' the new abode." The concept of domicile has typically been reserved for purposes that clearly require general recognition of a single State with which the individual, actually or presumptively, is most closely connected.

The majority errs in assuming that, as a general matter, States are free to close their schools to all but domiciliaries of the State. To begin with, it is clear that *residence*, not domicile, is the traditional standard of eligibility for lower school education, just as residence often has been used to determine whether an individual is subject to State income tax, whether his property in the State is exempt from attachment, and whether he is subject to jury duty. Moreover, this Court's prior decisions which speak of the constitutionality of a bona fide *residence* standard provide no support for the majority's assumption. . . .

B. Even assuming that a State may constitutionally deny free public education to all persons, including residents, who fail to meet the traditional standard for acquiring a domicile, this is not what the Texas statute does. Section 23.021(d) operates to deny public education to some persons who meet the traditional standard. As interpreted by the Court, the Texas statute denies free public education to any child who intends to leave the district at some point in the future. Yet such an intention does not preclude an individual from being considered a domiciliary under the prevailing conception of domicile.

When a person lives in a single geographical area, which is the center of his domestic, social and civil life, that place has all the indicia of his domicile, and will generally be so regarded irrespective of his intent to make a home somewhere else in the distant future. . . . .

C. Even if it were permissible to deny free education to residents who expect to leave the State at some future date, the statute could not escape constitutional scrutiny because it does not apply this test uniformly. Under § 21.031, the public free schools of Texas are generally open to any child who is a resident of the State. Admission is not limited to residents who intend to remain indefinitely in Texas. [The] only exception is children who live apart from their parents or legal guardians for educational purposes. Those children, unlike all others, must intend to remain indefinitely in a particular school district in the State in order to attend its schools.

Because the intent requirement is applied to only one class of children, it cannot be characterized as a bona fide residence requirement. As the majority recognizes, a State may not pick and choose among classes of State inhabitants to decide which will be subject to particularly difficult or preclusive eligibility standards. . . .

III. I continue to believe that, in analyzing a classification under the Equal Protection Clause, the appropriate level of scrutiny depends on "the constitutional and societal importance of the interest adversely affected and the recognized invidiousness of the basis upon which the particular classification is drawn." [San Antonio v. Rodriguez (Marshall, J., dissenting).] It has become increasingly clear that the approach actually taken in our cases focuses "upon the character of the classification in question, the relative importance to individuals in the class discriminated against of the governmental benefits that they do not receive, and the asserted state interests in support of the classification." Dandridge v. Williams (Marshall, J., dissenting). See, e.g., Mississippi University For Women v. Hogan; Plyler v. Doe; Zobel v. Williams. In my view, § 23.031 cannot withstand the careful scrutiny that I believe is warranted under the Equal Protection Clause.

A. The interest adversely affected by § 21.031, a child's education, is one which I continue to regard as fundamental. [Rodriguez (Marshall, J., dissenting)]. The fundamental importance of education is reflected in "the unique status accorded public education by our society, and by the close relationship between education and some of our most basic constitutional values." Last Term's decision in Plyler v. Doe is the most recent decision of this Court to recognize the special importance of education. [Therefore,] simply on the ground that § 21.031 significantly impedes access to education, I would subject the statutory classification to careful scrutiny.

B. The Texas statute is not narrowly tailored to achieve a substantial state interest. The State of Texas does not attempt to justify the classification by reference to its interest in the safety and well-being of children within its boundaries. The State instead contends that the principle purpose of the classification is to preserve educational and financial resources for those most closely connected to the State. The classification of children according to their motive for residing in the State cannot be justified as a narrowly tailored means of limiting public education to children "closely connected" with the State. Under the Texas scheme, some children who are "residents" of the State in every sense of that word are nevertheless denied an education. Other children whose only connection with the State is their physical presence are entitled to free public education as long as their presence is not motivated by a desire to obtain a free education. A child residing in the State for any other reason, no matter how ephemeral, will receive a free education even if he plans to leave before the end of the school year. Whatever interest a State may have in preserving its educational resources for those who have a sufficiently close connection with the State, that interest does not justify a crude statutory classification which grants and withholds public education on a basis which is related only in a haphazard way to the extent of that child's connection with the State.

. . . .

Finally, whatever the magnitude of the problems associated with fluctuations in the student population because of migration from without the State, the motive-requirement of § 21.031 (d) is simply not narrowly tailored to further the state interest in minimizing fluctuations. Just as there is nothing to suggest that the number of children who enter Texas for educational purposes will vary significantly from year to year, there is certainly nothing to suggest that their number will vary to a greater extent than the number who enter for all other purposes. Moreover, once children enter the State for educational purposes, they are likely to be the among the most stable members of the school-age population. It is by definition a matter of primary importance to such children that they remain in the district until they complete their schooling. All other children, to whom attending the local schools is a matter of comparative unimportance, may have little tie to the State or to a particular district within the State during their school years. Indeed, under the Texas statute a child who resides in the State for any purpose other than to attend the local schools is entitled to free education even if he expressly intends to remain for less than a year. Yet a child who resides in the State in order to attend its schools is denied an education even if he intends to remain until he has completed twelve full years of primary and secondary education. This disparate treatment cannot be justified by any alleged state concern over fluctuating student populations. . . .

ZOBEL v. WILLIAMS

457 U.S. 55, 102 S.Ct. 2309, 72 L.Ed.2d 672 (1982).

Chief Justice BURGER delivered the opinion of the Court.

The question presented on this appeal is whether a statutory scheme by which a State distributes income derived from its natural resources to the adult citizens of the State in varying amounts, based on the length of each citizen's residence, violates the equal protection rights of newer state citizens. The Alaska Supreme Court sustained the constitutionality of the statute. [We] reverse.

The 1967 discovery of large oil reserves on state-owned land in the Prudhoe Bay Area of Alaska resulted in a windfall to the State. The State, which had a total budget of $124 million in 1969, before the oil revenues began to flow into the state coffers, received $3.7 billion in petroleum revenues during the 1981 fiscal year.[1] This income will continue, and most likely grow for some years in the future. Recognizing that its mineral reserves, although large, are finite and that the resulting income will not continue in perpetuity, the State took steps to assure that its current good fortune will bring long range benefits. To accomplish this Alaska in 1976 adopted a constitutional amendment establishing the Permanent Fund into which the State must deposit at least 25% of its mineral income each year. The amendment prohibits the legislature from appropriating any of the principal of the fund but permits use of the fund's earnings for general governmental purposes.

In 1980, the legislature enacted a dividend program to distribute annually a portion of the Fund's earnings directly to the State's adult residents. Under the plan, each citizen 18 years of age or older receives one dividend unit for each year of residency subsequent to 1959, the first year of statehood. The statute fixed the value of each dividend unit at $50 for the 1979 fiscal year; a one-year resident thus would receive one unit, or $50, while a resident of Alaska since it became a State in 1959 would receive 21 units, or $1,050. The value of a dividend unit will vary each year depending on the income of the Permanent Fund and the amount of that income the State allocates for other purposes. The State now estimates that the 1985 fiscal year dividend will be nearly four times as large as that for 1979.

1. [The] 1980 census reports that Alaska's adult population is 270,265; per capita 1981 oil revenues amount to $13,632 for each adult resident. Petroleum revenues now amount to 89% of the State's total government revenue. [Footnote by Chief Justice Burger.]

2. The infusion of Permanent Fund earnings into state general revenues also led the Alaska legislature to enact a statute giving residents a one-third exemption from state income taxes for each year of residence; this operated to exempt entirely anyone with three or more years of residency.

Appellants, residents of Alaska since 1978, brought this suit in 1980 challenging the dividend distribution plan as violative of their right to equal protection guarantees and their constitutional right to migrate to Alaska, to establish residency there and thereafter to enjoy the full rights of Alaska citizenship on the same terms as all other citizens of the State. . . .[2]

I. The Alaska dividend distribution law is quite unlike the durational residency requirements we examined in [Sosna; Maricopa; Dunn v. Blumstein; Shapiro.] Those cases involved laws which required new residents to reside in the State a fixed minimum period to be eligible for certain benefits available on an equal basis to all other residents. The asserted purpose of the durational residency requirements was to assure that only persons who had established *bona fide* residence received rights and benefits provided for residents. The Alaska statute does not impose any threshold waiting period on those seeking dividend benefits; persons with less than a full year of residency are entitled to share in the distribution. Nor does the statute purport to establish a test of the *bona fides* of state residence. Instead, the dividend statute creates fixed, permanent distinctions between an ever increasing number of perpetual classes of concededly *bona fide* residents, based on how long they have been in the State.

Appellants established residence in Alaska two years before the dividend law was passed. [They] challenge the distinctions made within the class of persons who were residents when the dividend scheme was enacted in 1980. The distinctions appellants attack include the preference given to persons who were residents when Alaska became a State in 1959 over all those who have arrived since then, as well as the distinctions made between all *bona fide* residents who settled in Alaska at different times during the 1959 to 1980 period.[3]

When a State distributes benefits unequally, the distinctions it makes are subject to scrutiny under the Equal Protection Clause of the Fourteenth Amendment.[4] Generally, a law will survive that scrutiny if the distinction it makes rationally furthers a legitimate state purpose. Some particularly invidious distinctions are subject to more rigorous scrutiny. Appellants claim that the distinctions made by the Alaska law should be subjected to the higher level of scrutiny applied to the durational residency requirements in [Sha-

The Alaska Supreme Court [held] that this statute violated the State Constitution's equal protection clause. . . . [Footnote by Chief Justice Burger.]

3. The Alaska statute does not simply make distinctions between native born Alaskans and those who migrate to Alaska from other states; it does not discriminate only against those who have recently exercised the right to travel, as did the statute involved in Shapiro v. Thompson. The Alaska statute also discriminates among long-time residents and even native born residents. For example, a person born in Alaska in 1962 would have received $100 less than someone who was born in the State in 1960. Of course the native Alaskan born in 1962 would also receive $100 less than the person who moved to the State in 1960.

The statute does not involve the kind of discrimination which the Privileges and Immunities Clause of Art. IV was designed to prevent. That Clause "was designed to insure to a citizen of State A who ventures into State B the same privileges which the citizens of State B enjoy." Toomer v. Witsell [10th Ed., p. 375]. The Clause is thus not applicable to this case. [Footnote by Chief Justice Burger. Compare Justice O'Connor's concurrence, below.]

[Margin handwritten notes: State asserts it need only meet minimum rationality test. It cannot pass that, need not decide if enhanced scrutiny needed. State gives Three Purposes. 1st Two not rationally related to the distinctions made.]

piro and Maricopa]. The State, on other hand, asserts that the law need only meet the minimum rationality test. In any event, if the statutory scheme cannot pass even the minimal test proposed by the State, we need not decide whether any enhanced scrutiny is called for.

A. The State advanced [three] purposes justifying the distinctions made by the dividend program: (a) creation of a financial incentive for individuals to establish and maintain residence in Alaska; (b) encouragement of prudent management of the Permanent Fund; and (c) apportionment of benefits in recognition of undefined "contributions of various kinds, both tangible and intangible, which residents have made during their years of residency."[5]

As the Alaska Supreme Court apparently realized, the first two state objectives [are] not rationally related to the distinctions Alaska seeks to make between newer residents and those who have been in the State since 1959. Assuming arguendo that granting increased dividend benefits for each year of continued Alaska residence might give some residents an incentive to stay in the state in order to reap increased dividend benefits in the future, the State's interest is not in any way served by granting greater dividends to persons for their residency during the 21 years prior to the enactment.[6] Nor does the State's purpose of furthering the prudent management of the Permanent Fund and the state's resources support retrospective application of its plan to the date of statehood. On this score the state's contention is straightforward: "[If] residents believed that twenty years from now they would be required to share permanent fund income on a per capita basis with the large population that Alaska will no doubt have by then, the temptation would be great to urge the legislature to provide immediately for the highest possible return on the investments of the permanent fund principal, which would require investments in riskier ventures." The State similarly argues that equal

[Margin handwritten notes: right to travel derives from = protection]

4. The Alaska courts considered whether the dividend distribution law violated appellants' constitutional right to travel. The right to travel and to move from one state to another has long been accepted, yet both the nature and the source of that right has remained obscure. In addition to protecting persons against the erection of actual barriers to interstate movement, the right to travel, when applied to residency requirements, protects new residents of a state from being disadvantaged because of their recent migration or from otherwise being treated differently from longer-term residents. In reality, right to travel analysis refers to little more than a particular application of equal protection analysis. Right to travel cases have examined, in equal protection terms, state distinctions between newcomers and longer-term residents. See [Maricopa; Dunn v. Blumstein; Shapiro]. This case also involves distinctions between residents based on when they arrived in the State and is therefore also subject to equal protec-

tion analysis. [Footnote by Chief Justice Burger.]

5. These purposes were enumerated in the first section of the act creating the dividend distribution plan. [Thus] we need not speculate as to the objectives of the legislature. [Footnote by Chief Justice Burger.]

6. In fact, newcomers seem more likely to become dissatisfied and to leave the State than well-established residents; it would thus seem that the State would give a larger, rather than a smaller, dividend to new residents if it wanted to discourage emigration. The separation of residents into classes hardly seems a likely way to persuade new Alaskans that the State welcomes them and wants them to stay. Of course, the State's objective of reducing population turnover cannot be interpreted as an attempt to inhibit migration into the State without encountering insurmountable constitutional difficulties. See [Shapiro]. [Footnote by Chief Justice Burger.]

per capita distribution would encourage rapacious development of natural resources. Even if we assume that the state interest is served by increasing the dividend for each year of residency beginning with the date of enactment, is it rationally served by granting greater dividends in varying amounts to those who resided in Alaska during the 21 years prior to enactment? We think not.

The last of the State's objectives—to reward citizens for past contributions—alone was relied upon by the Alaska Supreme Court to support the retrospective application of the law to 1959. However, that objective is not a legitimate state purpose. A similar "past contributions" argument was made and rejected in [Shapiro]. [This] reasoning would permit the State to apportion all benefits and services according to the past tax [or intangible] contributions of its citizens. *The Equal Protection Clause prohibits such an apportionment of state services."* (Emphasis added.) [See also Vlandis v. Kline.]

If the States can make the amount of a cash dividend depend on length of residence, what would preclude varying university tuition on a sliding scale based on years of residence—or even limiting access to finite public facilities, eligibility for student loans, for civil service jobs, or for government contracts by length of domicile? Could States impose different taxes based on length of residence? Alaska's reasoning could open the door to state apportionment of other rights, benefits and services according to length of residency.[7] It would permit the states to divide citizens into expanding numbers of permanent classes. Such a result would be clearly impermissible.[8]

II. We need not consider whether the State could enact the dividend program prospectively only. Invalidation of a portion of a statute does not necessarily render the whole invalid unless it is evident that the legislature would not have enacted the legislation without the invalid portion. [Here], the legislation expressly provides that invalidation of any portion of the statute renders the whole invalid. [It] is of course for the Alaska courts to pass on the severability clause of the statute.

III. The only apparent justification for the retrospective aspect of the program, "favoring established residents over new residents," is constitutionally unacceptable. Vlandis v. Kline. In our view Alaska has shown no valid state interests which are rationally served by the distinction it makes between citizens who established residence before 1959 and those who have become residents since then. We hold that the Alaska dividend distribution plan violates the guarantees of [equal protection].

[Reversed.] *

7. Apportionment would thus be prohibited only when it involves "fundamental rights" and services deemed to involve "basic necessities of life." See [Maricopa]. [Footnote by Chief Justice Burger.]

8. Starns v. Malkerson, cannot be read as a contrary decision of this Court. First, summary affirmance by this Court is not to be read as an adoption of the reasoning supporting the judgment under review. Moreover, [we] considered the Minnesota one-year residency requirement [for in-state tuition benefits] examined in Starns a test of bona fide residence, not a return on prior contributions to the commonwealth. [Footnote by Chief Justice Burger.]

* While this case was pending in the Supreme Court, the Alaska legislature passed a stand-by bill providing for the distribution of $1,000 to each resident of Alaska who has lived in the State for at least six months. (Under this system, unlike that invalidated in

Justice BRENNAN, with whom Justice MARSHALL, Justice BLACK-MUN, and Justice POWELL join, concurring.

I join the opinion of the Court, and agree with its conclusion. [I] write separately only to emphasize that the pervasive discrimination embodied in the Alaska distribution scheme gives rise to constitutional concerns of somewhat larger proportions than may be evident on a cursory reading of the Court's opinion. In my view, these concerns might well preclude even the prospective operation of Alaska's scheme.

I. I agree with Justice O'Connor that these more fundamental defects in the Alaska dividend-distribution law are, in part, reflected in what has come to be called the "right to travel." [1] That right—or, more precisely, the federal interest in free interstate migration—is clearly, though indirectly, affected by the Alaska dividend-distribution law, and this threat to free interstate migration provides an independent rationale for holding that law unconstitutional. At the outset, however, I note that the frequent attempts to assign the right to travel some textual source in the Constitution seem to me to have proven both inconclusive and unnecessary. In light of the unquestioned historic recognition of the principle of free interstate migration, and of its role in the development of the Nation, we need not feel impelled to "ascribe the source of this [fundamental] right to travel interstate to a particular constitutional provision." [Shapiro.] [As] is clear from our cases, the right to travel achieves its most forceful expression in the context of equal protection analysis. But if, finding no citable passage in the Constitution to assign as its source, some might be led to question the independent vitality of the principle of free interstate migration, I find its unmistakable essence in that document that transformed a loose confederation of States into one Nation. A scheme of the sort adopted by Alaska is inconsistent with the Federal structure even in its prospective operation.

The Court today reaffirms the important principle that, at least with respect to a durational-residency discrimination, a State's desire "to reward citizens for past contributions" is "clearly not a legitimate state purpose." I do not think it "odd," [see Justice O'Connor's concurrence] that the Court disclaims reliance on the "right to travel" as the source of this limitation on state

---

Zobel, the amount of each payment does *not* depend on the recipient's years of residence.) On June 16, 1982—two days after the Court's decision in Zobel—Gov. Jay Hammond signed the stand-by legislation. The first checks went out the next day. Although Gov. Hammond was reported to be unhappy with the Zobel ruling, he announced that the new scheme would achieve much of what he had wanted when he proposed the Permanent Fund and the dividend scheme: "I wanted to curb the runaway growth of government. [B]elieve you me, [the] politicians would have sopped up every penny of it if we hadn't stopped them." An opponent of the payout scheme countered: "We should be investing in legacies for the future such as hydro projects, roads and bridges." See The New York Times, June 18, 1982.

1. What is notably at stake in this case, and what clearly must be taken into account in determining the constitutionality of this legislative scheme, is the *national* interest in a fluid system of interstate movement. It may be that national interests are not always easily translated into individual rights, but where the "right to travel" is involved, our cases leave no doubt that it will trigger intensified equal protection scrutiny. . . . [Footnote by Justice Brennan.]

power. In my view, the acknowledged illegitimacy of that state purpose has a different heritage—it reflects not the structure of the Federal Union but the idea of constitutionally protected equality. See [e.g., Shapiro]. [T]he Alaska plan discriminates against the recently naturalized citizen, in favor of the Alaska citizen of longer duration; it discriminates against the eighteen year old native resident, in favor of all residents of longer duration. If the Alaska plan were limited to discriminations such as these, and did not purport to apply to migrants from sister States, interstate travel would not be noticeably burdened—yet those discriminations would surely be constitutionally suspect.

The Fourteenth Amendment guarantees the equal protection of the law to anyone who may be within the territorial jurisdiction of a State. That Amendment does not suggest by its terms that equal treatment might be denied a person depending upon how long that person *has been* within the jurisdiction of the State. The Fourteenth Amendment does, however, expressly recognize one elementary basis for distinguishing between persons who may be within a State's jurisdiction at any particular time—by setting forth the requirements for state citizenship. But it is significant that the Citizenship Clause of the Fourteenth Amendment expressly equates citizenship only with simple residence. That Clause does not provide for, and does not allow for, degrees of citizenship based on length of residence. And the Equal Protection Clause would not tolerate such distinctions. In short, as much as the right to travel, equality of citizenship is of the essence in our republic.

[It] is, of course, elementary that the Constitution does not bar the States from making reasoned distinctions between citizens: Insofar as those distinctions are rationally related to the legitimate ends of the State they present no constitutional difficulty, as our equal protection jurisprudence attests. But we have never suggested that duration of residence *vel non* provides a valid justification for discrimination. To the contrary, discrimination on the basis of residence must be supported by a valid state interest independent of the discrimination itself. To be sure, allegiance and attachment may be rationally measured by length of residence—length of residence may, for example, be used to test the *bona fides* of citizenship—and allegiance and attachment may bear some rational relationship to a very limited number of legitimate state purposes. [E.g., the seven year citizenship requirement to run for governor in New Hampshire.] But those instances in which length of residence could provide a legitimate basis for distinguishing one citizen from another are rare.

Permissible discriminations between persons must bear a rational relationship to their *relevant* characteristics. While some imprecision is unavoidable in the process of legislative classification, the ideal of equal protection requires attention to individual merit, to individual need. In almost all instances, the business of the State is not with the past, but with the present: to remedy continuing injustices, to fill current needs, to build on the present in order to better the future. The past actions of individuals may be relevant in assessing their present needs; past actions may also be relevant in predicting current ability and future performance. In addition, to a limited extent, recognition and reward of past public service has independent utility for the State, for such recognition may encourage other people to engage in comparably meritorious service. But even the idea of rewarding past public service offers scarce support for the "past contribution" justification for durational residence classifications since length of residence has only the most tenuous relation to the *actual* service of individuals to the State.

Thus, the past contribution rationale proves much too little to provide a rational predicate for discrimination on the basis of length of residence. But it also proves far too much, for "it would permit the State to apportion all benefits and services according to the [past] contributions of its citizens." [Shapiro.] In effect, then, the past-contribution rationale is so far-reaching in its potential application, and the relationship between residence and contribution to the State so vague and insupportable, that it amounts to little more than a restatement of the criterion for discrimination that it purports to justify. But while duration of residence has minimal utility as a measure of things that are, in fact, constitutionally relevant, resort to duration of residence as the basis for a distribution of state largesse does closely track the constitutionally untenable position that the longer one's residence, the worthier one is of the State's favor. In my view, it is difficult to escape from the recognition that underlying any scheme of classification on the basis of duration of residence, we shall almost invariably find the unstated premise that "some citizens are more equal than others." We rejected that premise and, I believe, implicitly rejected most forms of discrimination based upon length of residence, when we adopted the Equal Protection Clause.

Justice O'CONNOR, concurring in the judgment.

The Court strikes Alaska's distribution scheme, purporting to rely solely upon [equal protection]. The phrase "right to travel" appears only fleetingly in the Court's analysis. [The] Court's reluctance to rely explicitly on a right to travel is odd, because its holding depends on the assumption that Alaska's desire "to reward citizens for past contributions [is] not a legitimate state purpose." Nothing in the Equal Protection Clause itself, however, declares this objective illegitimate. Instead, as a full reading of [Shapiro] and Vlandis v. Kline reveals, the Court has rejected this objective only when its implementation would abridge an interest in interstate travel or migration.

I respectfully suggest, therefore, that the Court misdirects its criticism when it labels Alaska's objective illegitimate. A desire to compensate citizens for their prior contributions is neither inherently invidious nor irrational. Under some circumstances, the objective may be wholly reasonable.[1] Even a generalized desire to reward citizens for past endurance, particularly in a State where years of hardship only recently have produced prosperity, is not innate-

1. A State, for example, might choose to divide its largesse among all persons who previously have contributed their time to volunteer community organizations. If the State graded its dividends according to the number of years devoted to prior community service, it could be said that the State intended "to reward citizens for past contributions." Alternatively, a State might enact a tax credit for citizens who contribute to the State's ecology by building alternative fuel sources or establishing recycling plants. If the State made this credit retroactive, to benefit those citizens who launched these improvements before they became fashionable, the State once again would be rewarding past contributions. The Court's opinion would dismiss these objectives as wholly illegitimate. I would recognize them as valid goals and inquire only whether their implementation infringed any constitutionally protected interest. [Footnote by Justice O'Connor.]

ly improper. The difficulty is that plans enacted to further this objective necessarily treat new residents of a State less favorably than the longer-term residents who have past contributions to "reward." This inequality [conflicts] with the constitutional purpose of maintaining a Union rather than a mere "league of States." The Court's task, therefore, should be (1) to articulate this constitutional principle, explaining its textual sources, and (2) to test the strength of Alaska's objective against the constitutional imperative. By choosing instead to declare Alaska's purpose wholly illegitimate, the Court establishes an uncertain jurisprudence. What makes Alaska's purpose illegitimate? Is the purpose illegitimate under all circumstances? What other state interests are wholly illegitimate? Will an "illegitimate" purpose survive review if it becomes "important" or "compelling"? [2] These ambiguities in the Court's analysis prompt me to develop my own approach to Alaska's scheme.

Alaska's distribution plan distinguishes between long-term residents and recent arrivals. Stripped to its essentials, the plan denies non-Alaskans settling in the State the same privileges afforded longer-term residents. The Privileges and Immunities Clause of Article IV, which guarantees "[t]he Citizens of each [State] all Privileges and Immunities of Citizens in the several States," addresses just this type of discrimination. [See 10th Ed., pp. 374–79.] Accordingly, I would measure Alaska's scheme against the principles implementing the Privileges and Immunities Clause. In addition to resolving the particular problems raised by Alaska's scheme, this analysis supplies a needed foundation for many of the "right to travel" claims discussed in the Court's prior opinions.

I. Our opinions teach that Article IV's Privileges and Immunities Clause "was designed to insure to a citizen of State A who ventures into State B the same privileges which the citizens of State B enjoy." Toomer v. Witsell [10th Ed., p. 375.] The Clause protects a nonresident who enters a State to work, to hunt commercial game, or to procure medical services. A fortiori, the Privileges and Immunities Clause should protect the "citizen of State A who ventures into State B" to settle there and establish a home. In this case, Alaska forces nonresidents settling in the State to accept a status inferior to that of old-timers. In effect, [the] State told its citizens: "Your status depends upon the date on which you established residence here. Those of you who migrated to the State cannot share its bounty on the same basis as those who were here before you." Surely this scheme imposes one of the "disabilities of alienage" prohibited by Article IV's Privileges and Immunities Clause.

It could be argued that Alaska's scheme does not trigger the Privileges and Immunities Clause because it discriminates among classes of residents, rather than between residents and nonresidents. This argument, however,

---

2. The Court's conclusion that Alaska's scheme lacks a rational basis masks a puzzling aspect of its analysis. By refusing to extend any legitimacy to Alaska's objective, the Court implies that a program designed to reward prior contributions will never survive equal protection scrutiny. For example, the programs described in n. 1, supra, could not survive the Court's analysis even if the State demonstrat-ed a compelling interest in rewarding volunteer activity or promoting conservation measures. The Court's opinion, although purporting to apply a deferential standard of review, actually insures that any governmental program depending upon a "past contributions" rationale will violate the Equal Protection Clause. [Footnote by Justice O'Connor.]

(Marginal handwritten notes: "Would invoke Privileges and Immunities Clause")

misinterprets the force of Alaska's distribution system. Alaska's scheme classifies citizens on the basis of their former residential status, imposing a relative burden on those who migrated to the State after 1959. Residents who arrived in Alaska after that date have a less valuable citizenship right than do the old-timers who preceded them. Citizens who arrive in the State tomorrow will receive an even smaller claim on Alaska's resources. The fact that this discrimination unfolds after the nonresident establishes residency does not insulate Alaska's scheme from scrutiny under the Privileges and Immunities Clause. Each group of citizens who migrated to Alaska in the past, or chooses to move there in the future, lives in the State on less favorable terms than those who arrived earlier. The circumstance that some of the disfavored citizens already live in Alaska does not negate the fact that "the citizen of State A who ventures into [Alaska]" to establish a home labors under a continuous disability.

If the Privileges and Immunities Clause applies to Alaska's distribution system, then our prior opinions describe the proper standard of review. [See Baldwin v. Montana Fish & Game Comm'n, 10th Ed., p. 378.] [Once] the Court ascertains that discrimination burdens an "essential activity," it will test the constitutionality of the discrimination under a two-part test. First, there must be "something to indicate that non-citizens constitute a peculiar source of the evil at which the statute is aimed." Second, the Court must find a "substantial relationship" between the evil and the discrimination practiced against the noncitizens.

Certainly the right infringed in this case is "fundamental." [It] is difficult to imagine a right more essential to the Nation as a whole than the right to establish residence in a new State. [Alaska's] encumbrance on the right of nonresidents to settle in that State, therefore, must satisfy the dual standard identified [above]. Alaska has not shown that its new residents are the "peculiar source" of any evil addressed by its disbursement scheme. The State does not argue that recent arrivals constitute a particular source of its population turnover problem. [Nor] is there any evidence that new residents, rather than old, will foolishly deplete the State's mineral and financial resources. Finally, although Alaska argues that its scheme compensates residents for their prior tangible and intangible contributions to the State, nonresidents are hardly a peculiar source of the "evil" of partaking in current largesse without having made prior contributions. A multitude of native Alaskans—including children and paupers—may have failed to contribute to the State in the past. Yet the State does not dock paupers for their prior failures to contribute, and it awards every person over the age of 18 dividends equal to the number of years that person has lived in the State.

Even if new residents were the peculiar source of these evils, Alaska has not chosen a cure that bears a "substantial relationship" to the malady. As the dissenting judges below observed, Alaska's scheme gives the largest dividends to residents who have lived longest in the State. The dividends awarded to new residents may be too small to encourage them to stay in Alaska. The size of these dividends appears to give new residents only a weak interest in prudent management of the State's resources. As a reward for prior contributions, finally, Alaska's scheme is quite ill-suited. While the phrase "substantial relationship" does not require mathematical precision, it demands at least some recognition of the fact that persons who have migrated to Alaska may have contributed significantly more to the State, both before and after their arrival, than have some natives. For these reasons, I conclude that Alaska's disbursement scheme violates Article IV's Privileges and Immunities Clause. I thus reach the same destination as the Court, but along a course that more precisely identifies the evils of the challenged statute.

II.   The analysis outlined above might apply to many cases in which a litigant asserts a right to travel or migrate interstate.[3] To historians, this would come as no surprise. Article IV's Privileges and Immunities Clause has enjoyed a long association with the rights to travel and migrate interstate.

The Clause derives from Article IV of the Articles of Confederation. The latter expressly recognized a right of "free ingress and egress to and from any other State." [While] the Framers of our Constitution omitted the reference to "free ingress and egress," they retained the general guaranty of "privileges and immunities." [Commentators] have assumed that the Framers omitted the express guaranty merely because it was redundant, not because they wished to excise the right from the Constitution. [Early] opinions by the Justices of this Court also traced a right to travel or migrate interstate to Article IV's Privileges and Immunities Clause. [E.g., Corfield v. Coryell.] History, therefore, supports assessment of Alaska's scheme, as well as other infringements of the right to travel, under the Privileges and Immunities Clause. This Clause may not address every conceivable type of discrimination that the Court previously has denominated a burden on interstate travel. I believe, however, that application of [the Clause] to controversies involving the "right to travel" would at least begin the task of reuniting this elusive right with the constitutional principles it embodies. Because I believe that Alaska's distribution scheme violates [the Clause], I concur in the Court's [judgment].

Justice REHNQUIST, dissenting.

Alaska's dividend distribution scheme represents one State's effort to apportion unique economic benefits among its citizens. Although the wealth received from the oil deposits of Prudhoe Bay may be quite unlike the eco-

Rehnquist
Dissents

---

3. Any durational residency requirement, for example, treats nonresidents who have exercised their right to settle in a State differently from longer-term residents. This is not to say, however, that all such requirements would fail scrutiny under the Privileges and Immunities Clause. The durational residency requirement upheld in [Sosna] (one year to obtain divorce), for example, would have survived under the analysis outlined above. In Sosna the State showed that nonresidents were a peculiar source of the evil addressed by its durational residency requirement. Those persons could misrepresent their at-

tachment to Iowa and obtain divorces that would be susceptible to collateral attack in other States. Iowa adopted a reasonable response to this problem by requiring nonresidents to demonstrate their bona fide residency for one year before obtaining a divorce. I am confident that the analysis developed [above and in Hicklin v. Orbeck, 10th Ed., p. 378] will adequately identify other legitimate durational residency requirements. [Footnote by Justice O'Connor.]

Would Justice O'Connor's analysis apply to a state's preference for employing its own residents? See White v. Massachusetts Council of Construction Em-

An economic regulation, thus presumptively valid—

nomic resources enjoyed by most States, Alaska's distribution of that wealth is in substance no different from any other State's allocation of economic benefits. The distribution scheme being in the nature of economic regulation, I am at a loss to see the rationality behind the Court's invalidation of it as a denial of equal protection. This Court has long held that state economic regulations are presumptively valid, and violate the Fourteenth Amendment only in the rarest of circumstances [E.g., New Orleans v. Dukes; Fritz.]

Despite the highly deferential approach which we invariably have taken toward state economic regulations, the Court today finds the retroactive aspect of the Alaska distribution scheme violative of the Fourteenth Amendment. [But] the illegitimacy of a State's recognizing the past contributions of its citizens has been established by the Court only in certain cases considering an infringement of the right to travel, and the majority itself rightly declines to apply the strict scrutiny analysis of those right-to-travel cases. The distribution scheme at issue in this case impedes no person's right to travel to and settle in Alaska; if anything, the prospect of receiving annual cash dividends would encourage immigration to Alaska. The State's [reward-for-past-contributions] justification cannot, therefore, be dismissed simply by quoting language [from] right-to-travel cases which have no relevance to the question before us.

Lochnerism

So understood, this case clearly passes equal protection muster. There can be no doubt that the state legislature acted rationally when it concluded that dividends retroactive to the year of statehood would "recognize the 'contributions of various kinds, both tangible and intangible,' which residents have made during their years of state residency." Nor can there be any doubt that Alaska, perhaps more than any other State in the Union, has good reason for recognizing such contributions. Because the distribution scheme is thus rationally based, I dissent from its invalidation under the guise of equal protection analysis.[1] In striking down the Alaskan scheme, the Court seems momentarily to have forgotten "the principle that the Fourteenth Amendment gives the federal courts no power to impose upon the States their view of what constitutes wise economic or social policy." Dandridge v. Williams.

ployers, Inc., 460 U.S. —— (1983), discussed above, addition to 10th Ed., p. 328. See generally Simson, "Discrimination Against Nonresidents and the Privileges and Immunities Clause of Article IV," 128 U.Pa.L.Rev. 379 (1979).

1. I also disagree with the suggestion of Justice O'Connor that the Alaska distribution scheme contravenes the Privileges and Immunities Clause of Art. IV of the Constitution. That Clause assures that *nonresidents* of a State shall enjoy the same privileges and immunities as residents enjoy. Toomer v. Witsell. We long ago held that the Clause has no application to a citizen of the State whose laws are complained of. [Slaughter-House Cases.] [Footnote by Justice Rehnquist.]

Chapter 11

THE POST–CIVIL WAR AMENDMENTS AND CIVIL RIGHTS LEGISLATION

10th ED., p. 999; IND. RTS., p. 619
Add as footnote at end of Note on White Primary Cases (before Shelley):

Another offshoot of the public function doctrine is the principle that delegation of traditional public functions to religious entities may violate the Establishment Clause of the First Amendment. In Larkin v. Grendel's Den, Inc., printed below, addition to 10th Ed., p. 1581; Ind. Rts., p. 1201, the Court struck down on Establishment Clause grounds what it perceived as a delegation of the zoning function to churches. The Court in Larkin made no mention of any of the public function or other state action cases.

10th ED., p. 1018; IND. RTS., p. 638
Add to footnote 1:

See also the discussion of Hunter v. Erickson (and of Reitman v. Mulkey) in the two 1982 decisions considering state measures to curb mandatory busing in de facto school segregation contexts: Washington v. Seattle School Dist. No. 1, 458 U.S. —— (1982) and Crawford v. Los Angeles Board of Education, 458 U.S. —— (1982) (both noted below, addition to 10th Ed., p. 773; Ind.Rts., p. 393).

10th ED., p. 1028; IND. RTS., p. 648
Insert before Sec. 3:

STATE ACTION DOCTRINE IN 1982

In three cases decided in the summer of 1982, the Court returned to the complexities of state action doctrine. In two of the cases—Blum v. Yaretsky and Rendell-Baker v. Kohn—the majority followed in the footsteps of the Burger Court's efforts in in the 1970s to circumscribe the scope of the state action concept. Thus, Justice Rehnquist, the author of the major "narrowing" opinions of the preceding decade—Jackson v. Metropolitan Edison Co. (1974) and Flagg Bros., Inc. v. Brooks (1978)—was in the majority in Blum and Rendell-Baker, and Justices Marshall and Brennan dissented. But the third 1982 case—Lugar v. Edmondson Oil Company—produced a strikingly different alignment: Justices Brennan and Marshall were in the majority in that 5 to 4 decision: Justice Rehnquist, the author of the major 1970s cases, was now in dissent (as were Chief Justice Burger and Justice Powell, who had been with the majority in most Burger Court state action decisions). Justice Powell's dissent in Lugar accused the new majority of undermining "fundamental distinctions between the common-sense categories of state and private conduct." As an added illustration of the unusual voting pattern in Lugar, it is noteworthy that Justice White, who had dissented in Flagg Bros., wrote the majority opinion. (Justice White concurred in the judgments in Blum and Rendell-Baker.) In examining these opinions, consider whether the reformulations of the traditional Burger Court position in Blum and Rendell-Baker clarify the reach of the modern state action doctrine; and whether Lugar is truly inconsistent with the usual Burger Court approach.

1. *Blum v. Yaretsky.* Justice Rehnquist, the author of the majority opinion in BLUM v. YARETSKY, 457 U.S. —— (1982), stated the issue as follows: "Respondents represent a class of Medicaid patients challenging decisions by the nursing homes in which they reside to discharge or

transfer patients without notice or an opportunity for a hearing. The question is whether the State may be held responsible for those decisions so as to subject them to the strictures of the Fourteenth Amendment." He concluded that "respondents have failed to establish 'state action' in the nursing homes' decisions to discharge or transfer Medicaid patients to lower levels of care. Consequently, they have failed to prove that petitioners have violated rights secured by the Fourteenth Amendment." The case involved the administration of the Medicaid program under 1965 amendments to the Social Security Act, which provide federal financial assistance to states that choose to reimburse certain medical costs incurred by the poor. New York is a participating state. It provides Medicaid assistance to eligible persons who receive care in private nursing homes, which are designated as either "skilled nursing facilities" (SNFs) or "health related facilities" (HRFs). HRFs provide less extensive and generally less expensive medical care than SNFs. The state reimburses nursing homes chosen by Medicaid patients. The portion of this litigation considered on the merits by the Court was a class action challenging facility-initiated discharges and transfers to lower levels of care. Respondents, the challengers, claimed that they did not receive adequate notice and hearings before they were discharged from SNFs or transferred to HRFs. In order to establish a due process claim, they had to demonstrate that the transfer or discharge action constituted "state action" under the Fourteenth Amendment. They succeeded in that demonstration in the lower courts, but failed in the Supreme Court. The challengers sued state officials responsible for administering the Medicaid program in New York, claiming that the private nursing homes' medical reports that underlay discharge or transfer decisions were in fact part and parcel of the state scheme.

In rejecting that argument, Justice Rehnquist articulated his framework for state action analysis as follows: "[R]espondents [have] named as defendants state officials responsible for administering the Medicaid program in New York. These officials are also responsible for regulating nursing homes in the State. [But] respondents are not challenging particular state regulations or procedures, and their arguments concede that the decision to discharge or transfer a patient originates not with state officials, but with [private] nursing homes. [Their] lawsuit, therefore, seeks to hold state officials liable for the actions of private parties, and the injunctive relief they have obtained requires the State to adopt regulations that will prohibit the private conduct of which they complain.

"This case is obviously different from those cases in which the defendant is a private party and the question is whether his conduct has sufficiently received the imprimatur of the state so as to make it 'state' action. [See, e.g., Flagg Bros.; Jackson; Moose Lodge.] It also differs from other 'state action' cases in which the challenged conduct consists of enforcement of state laws or regulations by state officials who are themselves parties in the lawsuit; in such cases the question typically is whether the private motives which trigger the enforcement of those laws can fairly be attributed to the State. But both these types of cases shed light upon the analysis necessary to resolve the present case.

"First, although it is apparent that nursing homes in New York are extensively regulated, '[t]he mere fact that a business is subject to state regulation does not by itself convert its action into that of the State.' [The] complaining party must also show that 'there is a sufficiently close nexus between the State and the challenged action of the regulated entity so that the action of the latter may be fairly treated as that of the State itself. [Jackson.] The purpose of this requirement is to assure that constitutional standards are invoked only when it can be said that the State is *responsible* for the specific conduct of which the plaintiff complains. The importance of this assurance is evident when, as in this case, the complaining party seeks to hold the State liable for the actions of private parties.

"Second, [our] precedents indicate that a State normally can be held responsible for a private decision only when it has exercised coercive power or has provided such significant encouragement, either overt or covert, that the choice must in law be deemed to be that of the State. Mere approval of or acquiescence in the initiatives of a private party is not sufficient to justify holding the State responsible for those initiatives under the terms of the Fourteenth Amendment. [See Flagg Bros.; Jackson.] Third, the required nexus may be present if the private entity has exercised powers that are 'traditionally the exclusive prerogative of the State.' [Jackson.]"

Applying these principles to the Blum case, Justice Rehnquist considered and rejected in sequence all of the proferred arguments for finding state action. He began by repudiating the Court of Appeals' basis for finding state action. That court had reasoned that "state action was present in the discharge or transfer decisions implemented by the nursing homes because the State responded to those decisions by adjusting the patient's Medicaid benefits." Justice Rehnquist replied: "Respondents, however, do not challenge the adjustment of benefits, but the discharge or transfer of patients. [That] the State responds to such actions by adjusting benefits does not render it *responsible* for those actions. The decisions about which respondents complain are made by physicians and nursing home administrators, all of whom are concededly private parties. There is no suggestion that those decisions were influenced in any degree by the State's obligation to adjust benefits in conformity with changes in the cost of medically necessary care."

The challengers had also argued that state action should be found because "the State 'affirmatively commands' [the] discharge or transfer [of] patients who are thought to be inappropriately placed in their nursing facilities." Justice Rehnquist, however, concluded that "our review of the statutes and regulations [does not] support respondents' characterization of them" In his view, the regulations did not demonstrate that "the State is responsible for the decision to discharge or transfer particular patients. Those decisions ultimately turn on medical judgments made by private parties according to professional standards that are not established by the State."[1] Justice

---

1. Justice Rehnquist found some similarity between this case and a decision earlier in the Term, Polk County v. Dodson, 454 U.S. 312 (1981), holding that a public defender did not act "under color of" state law within the meaning of § 1983 when representing an indigent defendant in a state criminal proceeding: "Although the public defender was employed by the State and appointed by the State to represent the respondent, we concluded that '[t]his assignment entailed functions and obligations in no way dependent on state authority.' The decisions made by the public defender in the course of representing his client were framed in accordance with professional canons of ethics rather than dictated by any rule of conduct im-

Rehnquist also rejected the contention that "even if the State does not command the transfers at issue, it reviews and either approves or rejects them on the merits." Again, the "regulations [did] not bear this construction"; "nothing in the regulations authorizes the officials to approve or disapprove decisions [regarding] particular patients. [Adjustments] in benefit levels in response to a decision to discharge or transfer a patient [do] not constitute approval or enforcement of that decision. [T]his degree of involvement is too slim a basis on which to predicate a finding of state action in the [discharge or transfer] decision itself."

Justice Rehnquist was equally unimpressed by respondents' reliance on Burton for "the rather vague generalization that such a relationship exists between the State and the nursing homes it regulates that the State may be considered a joint participant in the homes' discharge and transfer of Medicaid patients." The respondents argued that "State subsidization of the operating and capital costs of the facilities, payment of the medical expenses of more than 90% of of the patients in the facilities, and the licensing of the facilities than 90% of the patients in the facilities, and the licensing of the facilities tion." Justice Rehnquist replied: "But accepting all these assertions as true, we are nonetheless unable to agree that the State is responsible for the decisions challenged [here]. [P]rivately owned enterprises providing services that the State would not necessarily provide, even though they are extensively regulated, do not fall within the ambit of Burton. [Jackson.] That programs undertaken by the State result in substantial funding of the activities of a private entity is no more persuasive than the fact of regulation of such an entity in demonstrating that the State is responsible for decisions made by the entity in the course of its business." Justice Rehnquist concluded by rejecting respondents' "public function" argument—the claim that under the Jackson standard, "nursing homes perform a function that has been 'traditionally the exclusive prerogative of the State.' " Neither the statutes nor the state constitution mandated the provision of medical care. "Even if respondents' characterization of the State's duties were correct, however, it would not follow that decisions made in the day-to-day administration of a nursing home are the kind of decisions traditionally and exclusively made by the sovereign for and on behalf of the public."

Justice WHITE invoked his decision in Lugar (Note 3 below) to justify his concurrence in the judgment. Under Lugar, he noted, "respondents must show that the transfer or discharge is made on the basis of some rule of decision for which the state is responsible. It is not enough to show that the state takes certain actions in response to this private decision. The rule of decision implicated in the actions at issue here appears to be nothing more than a medical judgment."

Justice BRENNAN, joined by Justice Marshall, submitted a lengthy dissent, insisting that the majority had departed "from the Burton precept," had ignored "the nature of the regulatory framework," and had accordingly failed "to perceive the decisive involvement of the State in the private conduct challenged by the respondents." He elaborated: "In an era of active government

posed by the State. The same is true of nursing home decisions to discharge or transfer particular patients be-cause the care they are receiving is medically inappropriate."

intervention to remedy social ills, the true character of the State's involvement in, and coercive influence over, the activities of private parties, often through complex and opaque regulatory frameworks, may not always be apparent. But if the task that the Fourteenth Amendment assigns to the courts is thus rendered more burdensome, the courts' obligation to perform that task faithfully [is] rendered more, not less important." The ultimate question as he saw it was whether the defendant "has brought the force of the State to bear against [the] plaintiff in a manner the Fourteenth Amendment was designed to inhibit. Where the defendant is a government employee, this inquiry is relatively straightforward. But in deciding whether 'state action' is present in actions performed directly by persons other than government employees, what is required is a realistic and delicate appraisal of the State's involvement in the total context of the action taken. [Burton; see Lugar.]" [2]

In his extensive review of the Medicaid scheme as applied to nursing homes, Justice Brennan concluded that "the level-of-care decisions at issue in this case, even when characterized as the 'independent' decision of the nursing home, have far less to do with the exercise of independent professional judgment than they have to do with the *State's* desire to save money. [An] accurate and realistic appraisal of the procedures actually employed in [New York] leaves no doubt that not only has the State established the system of treatment levels [in] order to further its own fiscal goals, but that the State prescribes with as much precision as is possible the standards by which individual determinations are to be made." He insisted: "[N]ot only does the program implement the State's fiscal goals, but, to paraphrase the Court, 'These requirements [make] the State responsible for actual decisions to discharge or transfer particular patients.' Where, as here, a private party acts on behalf of the State to implement state policy, his action is state action."

Justice Brennan added: "Quite apart from the State's specific involvement in the transfer decisions at issue in this case, the nature of the nursing home as an institution, sustained by State and Federal funds, and pervasively regulated by the State so as to ensure that it is properly implementing the governmental undertaking to provide assistance to the elderly and disabled that is embodied in the Medicaid program, undercuts the Court's sterile approach to the state action inquiry in this case. [The] degree of interdependence between the state and the nursing home is far more pronounced than it was between the State and the private entity in [Burton]. The State subsidizes practically all of the operating and capital costs of the facility. [Even] more striking is the fact that the residents of those homes are, by definition, utterly dependent on the State for their support and their placement For many, the totality of their social network is the nursing home community. Within that environment, the nursing home operator is the immediate authority, the provider of food, clothing, shelter, and health care, and in every significant respect, the functional equivalent of a State. Cf. Marsh v. Alabama. Surely, in this context we must be especially alert to those situations in which the State 'has elected to place its power, property and prestige behind' the actions of the nursing home owner. See [Burton]."

2. Justice Brennan insisted that the "imprint of state power on the private party's actions" in Blum was "even more significant" than that found to justify a finding of state action in Lugar.

"Yet, whatever might be the status of the nursing home operator where the State has simply left the resident in his charge, while paying for the resident's support and care, it is clear that the State has not simply left nursing home patients to the care of nursing home operators. [The central question at this stage is] whether the State has brought its force to bear against the plaintiffs through the office of these private parties. In answering that question we may safely assume that when the State chooses to perform its governmental undertakings through private institutions, [not] every action of those private parties is state action. But when the State directs, supports, and encourages those private parties to take specific action, that is state action. We may hypothesize many decisions of nursing home operators that affect patients, but are not attributable to the State. But [with] respect to the level-of-care determination, the State does everything but pay the nursing home operator a fixed salary. Because the State is clearly responsible for the specific conduct of petitioners about which respondents complain, and because this renders petitioners state actors for purposes of the Fourteenth Amendment, I dissent."

2. *Rendell-Baker v. Kohn.* Chief Justice BURGER's majority opinion in RENDELL–BAKER v. KOHN, 457 U.S. —— (1982), closely tracked Justice Rehnquist's approach in Blum. The Court held that "a private school, whose income is derived primarily from public sources and which is regulated by public authorities," could not be considered as engaging in state action when it discharged certain employees. The employees brought this federal civil rights action under § 1983 claiming that school officials had violated their constitutional rights by firing them from the staff of a small private school for "maladjusted" students. "The core issue [in] this case," the Chief Justice emphasized, "is not whether petitioners were discharged because of their speech or without adequate procedural protections, but whether the school's action in discharging them can fairly be seen as state action." After examining all of the alleged indicia of state action, he concluded that the school and its officials were not subject to federal constitutional guarantees.

Quoting from Blum, the Chief Justice emphasized that a state can be held responsible for a private decision "only when it has exercised coercive power or has provided such significant encouragement, either overt or covert, that the choice must in law be deemed to be that of the State." The fact that the school, like the nursing homes in Blum, depended on public funding, was not enough: "the school's receipt of public funds does not make the discharge decisions acts of the state." The Chief Justice added: "The school, like the nursing homes, is not fundamentally different from many private corporations whose business depends primarily on contracts to build roads, bridges, dams, ships, or submarines for the government. Acts of such private contractors do not become acts of the government by reason of their significant or even total engagement in performing public contracts." No more helpful to the employees was the extensive state regulation of the school: "Here the decisions to discharge the petitioners were not compelled or even influenced by any state regulation. Indeed, in contrast to the extensive regulation of the school generally, the various regulators showed relatively little interest in the school's personnel matters." [3]

Nor was the Chief Justice persuaded by a "public function" argument. The *"exclusive* prerogative of the State" criterion of the Jackson case was not satisfied here: "There can be no doubt that the education of maladjusted high school students is a public function, but that is only the beginning of the inquiry. [While state law] demonstrates that the State intends to provide services for such students at public expense, [t]hat legislative policy choice in no way makes these services the exclusive province of the State." Finally, the Chief Justice found no "symbiotic relationship" between the school and the State similar to the relationship found in Burton. Unlike the special relationship of the private restaurant to the state in Burton, here "the school's fiscal relationship with the State is not different from that of many contractors performing services for the government."

As in Blum, Justice WHITE concurred only in the judgment. He stated: "For me, the critical factor is the absence of any allegation that the employment decision was itself based upon some rule of conduct or policy put forth by the State. [The] employment decision remains, therefore, a private decision not fairly attributable to the state."

Justice MARSHALL, joined by Justice Brennan, insisted in dissent that the holding "simply cannot be justified" : "The state has delegated to the [school] its statutory duty to educate children with special needs. The school receives almost all of its funds from the state, and is heavily regulated. This nexus between the school and the state is so substantial that the school's action must be considered State action." He relied especially on the "symbiotic relationship" approach of Burton, insisting that "an examination of the facts and circumstances leads inexorably to the conclusion that the actions of the [school] should be attributed to the State; it is difficult to imagine a closer relationship between a government and a private enterprise." Moreover, the fact that "the school is providing a substitute for public education" seemed to him "also an important indicium of state action. [The] fact that a private entity is providing a vital public function, when coupled with other factors demonstrating a close connection with the State, may justify a finding of state action. Cf. Evans v. Newton."

Justice Marshall summarized his position as follows: "When an entity is not only heavily regulated and funded by the State, but also provides a service that the State is required to provide, there is a very close nexus with the State. Under [such] circumstances, it is entirely appropriate to treat the entity as an arm of the State. Cf. Smith v. Allwright. [Indeed], I would conclude that the actions challenged here were under color of state law, even if I believed that the sole basis for state action was the fact that the school was providing

---

3. One of the employees, a vocational counselor, held a position for which appointments were subject to the approval of a state agency that provided grant money. But the Chief Justice viewed that as a "limited role" by the state, "not comparable to the role played by the public officials in [Lugar, Note 3 below]." He noted that the state agency had no power to hire or discharge a counselor who had the qualifications specified in the school's grant application; and the discharged counselor here did have those qualifications.

[statutorily mandated] services.[4] [The] decision in this case marks a return to empty formalism in state action doctrine. Because I believe that the state action requirement must be given a more sensitive and flexible interpretation, [I] dissent."

    3. *Lugar v. Edmondson Oil Company.* Justice Rehnquist and Chief Justice Burger, the authors of the majority opinions in Blum and Rendell-Baker, were among the dissenters in the third case of the 1982 state action trilogy, LUGAR v. EDMONDSON OIL COMPANY, 457 U.S. ——. Lugar was the latest of a long series of cases (from Sniadach in 1969 through Flagg Bros. in 1978) considering creditors' summary remedies.[5] The case arose when Edmondson sued in a state court to collect a debt from Lugar, the operator of a truck stop. Ancillary to that action, Edmondson sought prejudgment attachment of some of Lugar's property. The prejudgment attachment procedure required only that Edmondson allege, in an ex parte petition, a belief that Lugar might dispose of his property in order to defeat his creditors. Acting upon that petition, a clerk of the state court issued a writ of attachment, which was then executed by the county sheriff. The writ effectively sequestered Lugar's property, although he retained possession. Pursuant to the law, a hearing on the propriety of the attachment and levy was later conducted. About a month after the levy, a state court ordered the attachment dismissed because Edmondson had failed to establish the statutory grounds for attachment alleged in its petition. Lugar then brought a § 1983 action against Edmondson and its president. Lugar alleged that in attaching his property the defendants had acted jointly with the state to deprive him of property without due process of law. The complaint was construed to allege a due process violation both from a misuse of the Virginia attachment procedure and from the statutory procedure itself. The Court, in a 5 to 4 decision, concluded that Lugar "did present a valid cause of action under § 1983 insofar as he challenged the constitutionality of the Virginia statute; he did not, insofar as [he] alleged only misuse or abuse of the statute."

    In delineating the governing state action principles, Justice WHITE, who wrote the majority opinion, stated: "Our cases [have] insisted that the conduct allegedly causing the deprivation of a federal right be fairly attributable to the state. These cases reflect a two-part approach to this question of 'fair attribution'. First, the deprivation must be caused by the exercise of some right or privilege created by the state or by a rule of conduct imposed by the state or by a person for whom the state is responsible. [Second], the party charged with the deprivation must be a person who may fairly be said to be a state actor. This may be because he is a state official, because he has acted together with or has obtained significant aid from state officials, or because his conduct is otherwise chargeable to the state. Without a limit such as this, private parties could face constitutional litigation whenever they seek to rely on some state rule governing their interactions with the community surrounding them.

4.   Justice Marshall objected to the majority's analogy between the school and most private contractors: "Although shipbuilders and dambuilders, like the school, may be dependent on government funds, they are not so closely supervised by the government. And unlike most private contractors, the school is performing a statutory duty of the State."

5.   See footnote 10, 10th Ed., p. 994; Ind.Rts., p. 614.

"Although related, these two principles are not the same. They collapse into each other when the claim of a constitutional deprivation is directed against a party whose official character is such as to lend the weight of the state to his decisions. The two principles diverge when the constitutional claim is directed against a party without such apparent authority, i.e., against a private party. The difference between the two inquiries is well illustrated by comparing [Moose Lodge] with Flagg Brothers. In [Moose Lodge], the decision to discriminate could not be ascribed to any governmental decision; those governmental decisions that did affect Moose Lodge were unconnected with its discriminatory policies. Flagg Brothers focused on the other component of the state action principle. [Undoubtedly] the state was responsible for the statute. The response of the Court, however, focused not on the terms of the statute but on the character of the defendant to the § 1983 suit: Action by a private party pursuant to this statute, without something more, was not sufficient to justify a characterization of that party as a 'state actor.' The Court suggested that that 'something more' which would convert the private party into a state actor might vary with the circumstances of the case. This was simply a recognition that the Court has articulated a number of different factors or tests in different contexts: e.g., the 'public function' test; the 'state compulsion' test; the 'nexus' test; and, in the case of prejudgment attachments, a 'joint action' test, Flagg Brothers.[6] Whether these different tests are actually different in operation or simply different ways of characterizing the necessarily fact-bound inquiry that confronts the Court in such a situation need not be resolved here. See Burton."

Applying that analysis to this case, Justice White stated: "[T]he first question is whether the claimed deprivation has resulted from the exercise of a right or privilege having its source in state authority. The second question is whether, under the facts of this case, respondents [Edmondson and its president], who are private parties, may be appropriately characterized as 'state actors.'" In answering the first question, Justice White focused on one count in Lugar's complaint that seemed to challenge the procedures used by Edmondson under state law and could be read to challenge "the state statute as procedurally defective under the Fourteenth Amendment." That count satisfied Justice White's first requirement in his state action analysis: "While private misuse of a state statute does not describe conduct that can be attributed to the state, the procedural scheme created by the statute obviously is the product of state action. This is subject to constitutional restraints and properly may be addressed in a § 1983 action, if the second element of the state action requirement is met as well." And that second requirement was also met: "[W]e have consistently held that a private party's joint participation with state officials in the seizure of disputed property is sufficient to characterize that party as a 'state actor' for purposes of the Fourteenth Amendment. [The lower court] erred in holding that in this context 'joint participation' required something more than invoking the aid of state officials to take advan-

---

6. "Contrary to the suggestion of the dissent, we do not hold today that 'a private party's mere invocation of state legal procedures constitutes "joint participation" or "conspiracy" with state officials satisfying the § 1983 requirement of action under color of law.' The holding today, as the above analysis makes clear, is limited to the particular context of prejudgment attachment." [Footnote by Justice White.]

tage of state created attachment procedures. That holding is contrary to the conclusions we have reached as to the applicability of due process standards to such procedures. Whatever may be true in other contexts, this is sufficient when the state has created a system whereby state officials will attach property on the ex parte application of one party to a private dispute." [7]

Chief Justice BURGER, dissenting, concluded that "it cannot be said that the actions of [Edmondson] are fairly attributable to the State." He elaborated: "[Edmondson] did no more than invoke a presumptively valid state prejudgment attachment procedure available to all. Relying on a dubious 'but for' analysis, the Court erroneously concludes that the subsequent procedural steps taken by the State in attaching a putative debtor's property in some way transforms [Edmondson's] acts into actions of the State. This case is no different from the situation in which a private party commences a lawsuit and secures injunctive relief which, even if temporary, may cause significant injury to the defendant. Invoking a judicial process, of course, implicates the State and its officers, but does not transform essentially private conduct into actions of the State. [The] Court's opinion expands the reach of [§ 1983] beyond anything intended by Congress."

In a longer dissent, Justice POWELL, joined by Justices Rehnquist and O'Connor, found the Court's decision to be "a disquieting example of how expansive judicial decisionmaking can ensnare a person who had every reason to believe he was acting in strict accordance with law. [This] decision is as unprecedented as it is implausible. [Nor] is the Court's analysis consistent with the mode of inquiry prescribed by our cases." Justice Powell insisted that "our cases do not establish that a private party's mere invocation of state legal procedures constitutes 'joint participation' or 'conspiracy' with state officials satisfying the Sec. 1983 requirement of action under color of law. [Instead], recent decisions make clear that independent, private decisions made in the context of litigation cannot be said to occur under color of law." [8]

10th ED., p. 1051; IND. RTS., p. 671
Insert at beginning of footnote 1:

In Parratt v. Taylor, 451 U.S. 527 (1981), Justice Rehnquist's majority opinion reexamined Monroe v. Pape and concluded that § 1983 is not limited to intentional deprivations of constitutional rights; rather, § 1983 also authorizes actions for "mere negligence."

7. In finding Flagg Bros. distinguishable, the majority relied in part on the fact that the creditor's remedy involved in Flagg Bros. (a warehouseman's sale pursuant to a statutory warehouseman's lien) could be exercised without the intervention of a state official, but simply pursuant to state procedures. Here, by contrast, the issuance and execution of the writ of attachment pursuant to Edmondson's suit was undertaken by state officials.

8. "The Court avers that its holding 'is limited to the particular context of prejudgment attachment.' However welcome, this limitation lacks a principled basis. It is unclear why a private party engages in state action when filing papers seeking an attachment of property, but not when seeking other relief (e.g., injunction), or when summoning police to investigate a suspected crime." [Footnote by Justice Powell.]

10th ED., p. 1052; IND. RTS., p. 672
Add as footnote after the third line of the text:

But the majority in Newport v. Fact Concerts, Inc., 453 U.S. 247 (1981), ruled that a municipality may *not* be held liable for punitive damages under § 1983. Apart from the issue of municipal immunity, however, punitive damages are generally available in § 1983 actions. Smith v. Wade, 461 U.S. —— (1983).

10th ED., p. 1057; IND. RTS., p. 677
Add to Note 2a:

42 U.S.C. § 1982, the provision successfully invoked in the Jones and Sullivan cases, was also involved in MEMPHIS v. GREENE, 451 U.S. 100 (1981), but the Court held that the plaintiffs could not recover under either § 1982 or the Thirteenth Amendment itself. Black residents sued Memphis because it had closed a street at the border between a white and a black neighborhood. The Court of Appeals held the street closing invalid because it adversely affected the plaintiffs' right to hold and enjoy their property, in violation of § 1982. The Supreme Court granted review to determine whether proof of discriminatory purpose is necessary in § 1982 and Thirteenth Amendment cases, as it is under the Fourteenth Amendment (see sec. 2 of the preceding chapter). But the majority found it unnecessary to reach these issues. Instead, Justice STEVENS' opinion for the Court reexamined the record at length and set aside the lower court's interpretation of the facts.

Justice Stevens thought that the street closing caused only minor inconvenience and emphasized that it rested on legitimate police power concerns rather than an improper purpose: "The city's decision [was] motivated by its interest in protecting the safety and tranquility of a residential neighborhood. [The] city has conferred a benefit on certain white property owners but there is no reason to believe that it would refuse to confer comparable benefit on black property owners. The closing has not affected the value of property owned by black citizens, but it has caused some slight inconvenience to black motorists." Under this view of the record, there was no violation of § 1982. Although earlier cases had "broadly defined the property rights protected by § 1982," those decisions had all involved "the right of black persons to hold and acquire property on an equal basis with white persons and the right of blacks not to have property interests impaired because of their race." Here, there was nothing in the record to show that the city's action "depreciated the value of property owned by black citizens" or "severely restricted access to black homes." Rather, the city had merely required black residents to use "one public street rather than another": "We need not assess the magnitude of that injury to conclude that it does not involve any impairment to the kind of property interests that we have identified as being within the reach of § 1982."

Turning to the self-executing effect of the Thirteenth Amendment, the Court left open, as it had in Jones, "the question whether § 1 of the Amendment by its own terms did anything more than abolish slavery." Justice Stevens concluded that "a review of the justification for the official action challenged in this case demonstrates that its disparate impact on black citizens could not, in any event, be fairly characterized as a badge or incident of slavery." He stated: "The [safety and tranquility interests] motivating the city's action [are] sufficient to justify an adverse impact on motorists who are somewhat inconvenienced by the street closing. That inconvenience cannot be equated to an actual restraint on the liberty of black citizens that is in any sense comparable to the odious practice the Thirteenth Amendment was designed to eradicate." Nor was he persuaded that a finding of a Thirteenth Amendment violation here could "rest, not on the actual consequences of the closing, but rather on the symbolic significance of the fact that most of the drivers who will be inconvenienced by the action are black." The inconvenience here was a function of residence, not race: "Because urban neighborhoods are so frequently characterized by a common ethnic or racial heritage, a regulation's adverse impact on a particular neighborhood will often have a disparate effect on an identifiable ethnic or racial group. To regard an inevitable consequence of that kind as a form of stigma so severe as to violate the Thirteenth Amendment would trivialize the great purpose of that charter of freedom." He accordingly found that the impact of the street closing was "a routine burden of citizenship; it does not reflect a violation of the Thirteenth Amendment." *

* Justice WHITE, who submitted an opinion concurring in the judgment, was the only member of the Court to examine fully the issue on which certiorari had been granted. He argued that "[p]urposeful racial discrimination" was the focus of § 1982, and contended that this interpretation was supported by the legislative history of the Civil Rights Act of 1866: "[N]othing in the legislative history [suggests] that Congress was concerned with facially neutral measures which happened to have an incidental impact on former slaves." He concluded that a violation of § 1982 requires some "showing of racial animus or an intent to discriminate on the basis of race."

Justice Marshall's dissent, while purporting not to reach the "discriminatory purpose" issue, nevertheless devoted a footnote to disagreeing with Justice White's position: "I do not believe that his arguments support his conclusion." Justice Marshall found no basis for concluding that Congress sought only to bar action based on "discriminatory intent." He added that, even if purposeful discrimination had to be shown, "it is enough for me if the evidence raises an inference of intent and the government fails to rebut it with a sufficiently strong explanation." Here, on his reading of the record (discussed in text), the inference of discriminatory intent had not been adequately rebutted.

In 1982, the Court settled the issue left open by most of the Justices in Memphis v. Greene. GENERAL BUILDING CONTRACTORS ASSN., INC. v. PA., 458 U.S. —— (1982), held that a suit under § 1981 (the companion law

to § 1982) requires "proof of discriminatory intent" and does not reach "practices that merely result in a disproportionate impact on a particular class."

The suit grew out of racial discrimination in the construction industry. The lower court found purposeful discrimination by the unions but not by the petitioners, who were contractors and their trade associations. Nevertheless, the lower court imposed liability on the contractors as well. The discriminatory practices occurred in the operation of an exclusive union "hiring hall" (utilized pursuant to bargaining contracts between the union and the petitioners) and in the administration of an apprenticeship program (administered by a committee which was funded by the trade associations and half of whose members were appointed by the trade associations). Justice REHNQUIST's majority opinion concluded that, absent proof of discriminatory intent, injunctive liability could not be imposed vicariously on the petitioners for the discriminatory conduct of the union. He rejected any liability on the basis of respondeat superior and refused to find that the law imposed a "nondelegable duty" on the employers to ensure that there was no discrimination in the union's selection of the workforce. (Justice Stevens filed a separate opinion concurring in part and concurring in the judgment. Justice O'Connor, joined by Justice Blackmun, also filed a separate opinion, even though she joined all of the majority's opinion.)

Justice MARSHALL's dissent, joined by Justice Brennan, insisted that there

Justice MARSHALL's dissent, joined by Justices Brennan and Black-mun, took a very different view of the record. He agreed that if the city had merely engaged in a "policy decision" to close a street "for valid municipal reasons," the Court's result would be correct. But he added that "the evidence in this case, combined with a dab of common sense, paints a far different picture from the one emerging from the majority's opinion. In this picture a group of white citizens has decided to act to keep Negro citizens from traveling through their urban 'utopia,' and the city has placed its seal of approval on the scheme. It is this action that I believe is forbidden." He especially criticized the majority for ignoring "the plain and powerful symbolic message of the 'inconvenience,'" and he added: "I cannot subscribe to the majority's apparent view that the city's erection of this 'monument to racial hostility' amounts to nothing more than a 'slight inconvenience.' [This case involves] precisely the kind of evidence of intent that we deemed probative in Arlington Heights (10th Ed., p. 720; Ind. Rts., p. 340]. [The plaintiffs] are being sent a clear, though sophisticated, message that because of their race, they are to stay out of the all-white enclave [and] should instead take the long way around in reaching their destinations. [Combined] with this message are the prospects of increased police harassment and of a decline in their property values."

On this view of the facts, he readily found a violation of § 1982 if the provision was "given the broad reading that our cases require." He argued that "a proper reading of the record demonstrates substantial harm to [plaintiffs'] property rights as a result of the establishment of [the] barrier." And, he insisted, the legislative history of § 1982 "also supports my conclusion that the carving out of racial enclaves within a city is precisely the kind of injury that the statute was enacted to prevent." He added: "[I do not] wish to imply that the Act prevents government from ever closing a street when the effect is to inflict harm on Negro property owners. But because of our Nation's sad legacy of discrimination and the broad remedial purpose of § 1982, I believe that official actions whose effects fall within its terms ought to be closely scrutinized. When, as here, the decisionmaker takes action with full knowledge of its enormously disproportionate racial impact, I believe that § 1982 requires that the government carry a heavy burden in order to

was no "purposeful intent" requirement in § 1981: "Nothing in the statutory language implies that a right denied because of sheer insensitivity, or a pattern of conduct that disproportionately burdens the protected class of persons, is entitled to any less protection than one denied because of racial animus." Moreover, the majority had "virtually ignore[d] Congress' broad remedial purposes." Congress had sought "a major revolution in the prevailing social order. It is inconceivable that the Congress which enacted [this law] intended to absolve employers from even injunctive liability imposed as a result of intentional discrimination practiced by the persons to whom they had delegated their authority to hire employees." He accused the majority of shutting its eyes "to reality, ignoring the manner in which racial discrimination most often infects our society. Today, although flagrant examples of intentional discrimination still exist, discrimination more often occurs 'on a more sophisticated and subtle level,' the effects of which are often as cruel and 'devastating as the most crude form of discrimination.'" He argued, too, that the petitioners should be held liable even if an intentional discrimination requirement were appropriate.

justify its action. [There] is no need to suggest here just how great the government's burden should be, because the reason set forth by the city for the closing [could] not, on the facts of this case, survive any but the most minimal scrutiny." †

10th ED., p. 1066; IND. RTS., p. 686
Add to footnote 9:

Extension of the Voting Rights Act. With § 5 of the Voting Rights Act of 1965 scheduled to expire in August 1982, efforts began in Congress early in 1981 to extend it once again, this time for ten years. The debate began with consideration of § 5, the "preclearance" provision. But the focus of controversy soon shifted to § 2 and the issue of the appropriate standard of proof for identifying laws that "deny or abridge" the right to vote. The Supreme Court's ruling in 1980, in Mobile v. Bolden (10th Ed., p. 728; Ind.Rts., p. 348), had determined that § 2 required proof of a discriminatory intent, not merely a discriminatory result. Civil rights groups, arguing for a "results" standard, maintained that the Court's intent test imposed an unduly burdensome litigation obstacle. Supporters of the Court's decision countered that discrimination, by its very nature, must be intentional and that the "results" standard would eventually lead to the establishment of racial quotas and proportional representation in elections.

In November 1981, the House, siding with civil rights advocates, adopted the results standard for § 2, indefinitely extended § 5's "preclearance" requirement, and modified § 4 to make it easier for affected jurisdictions to "bail out" from coverage under § 5. In the Senate, conservative lawmakers supported by the Reagan Administration mounted strong opposition to the House's "results" language until Kansas Republican Robert Dole proposed a compromise. The Dole Compromise endorsed judicial attention to "results" as one factor in the consideration of the "totality of circumstances" relevant to a § 2 discrimination claim. However, the Compromise carefully qualified the results standard in order to mollify conservatives' concerns about racial quotas and proportional representation by providing: "The extent to which members of a protected class have been elected to office is one 'circumstance' which may be considered [by the courts in § 2 cases]: Provided, that nothing in this [law] establishes a right to have members of a protected class elected in numbers equal to their proportion in the population." [On the "preclearance" issue, the indefinite extension of § 5 by the House was reduced to 25 years. After 1984, moreover, a jurisdiction now subject to § 5 may "bail out" (under § 4) upon demonstrating a history of affirmative voting rights policies.] After nearly unanimous approval in both houses, the compromise extension of the Voting Rights Act was signed into law by President Reagan on June 29, 1982.

† Justice Marshall reached the Thirteenth Amendment issue only in a footnote. Although he recognized that the majority claimed to have left open the question of whether the Thirteenth Amendment by its own terms did anything more than abolish slavery, Justice Marshall stated: "Assuming with the majority that the Amendment would, even without implementing legislation, ban more than the mere practice of slavery, I would conclude that official action causing harm of the magnitude suffered here plainly qualifies as a 'badge or incident' of slavery, at least as those terms were understood by the Reconstruction Congress." He pointed out that essentially the same persons had framed both the Thirteenth Amendment and the 1866 Civil Rights Act and concluded that "because the [street closing] is forbidden [by] § 1982, it is a fortiori a violation of the Thirteenth Amendment as well. Of course, this should not be taken as an argument that Congress *cannot* under § 2 of the Thirteenth Amendment enact legislation forbidding more than would § 1 of the Amendment standing alone. I simply suggest that Congress *did not* do so when it enacted § 1 of the Civil Rights Act of 1866. I also do not mean to imply that all municipal decisions that affect Negroes adversely and benefit whites are prohibited by the Thirteenth Amendment. I would, however, insist that the government carry a heavy burden of justification before I would sustain against Thirteenth Amendment challenge conduct as egregious as erection of a barrier to prevent predominently-Negro traffic from entering a historically all-white neighborhood."

10th ED., p. 1099; IND. RTS., p. 719
Insert before Note 4:

3A. *Invoking the Morgan power, 1981–83: The "Human Life Statute."*
Fifteen years after the Morgan decision, the scope of the legislative power
suggested by that ruling attracted an unprecedented degree of interest in Congress. Opponents of various Court decisions turned to the Morgan rationale in
framing legislative responses to the judicial rulings. The most controversial
proposal was the proposed "Human Life Statute," introduced by Senator
Helms and Congressman Hyde (S. 158, H.R. 900, 97th Cong., 1st Sess.).
The Helms-Hyde bill was designed to authorize broader state control of abortions or, at least, to express congressional displeasure with the Roe v. Wade
decision and to prompt the Court to reconsider it.[1] Sec. 1 of the bill
provides: [2]

"The Congress finds that present-day scientific evidence indicates a significant likelihood that actual human life exists from conception.[3]

"The Congress further finds that the fourteenth amendment to the Constitution of the United States was intended to protect all human beings.

"Upon the basis of these findings, and in the exercise of the powers of
the Congress, including its power under section 5 of the fourteenth amendment to the Constitution of the United States, the Congress hereby declares
that for the purpose of enforcing the obligation of the States under the fourteenth amendment not to deprive persons of life without due process of law,
human life shall be deemed to exist from conception, without regard to race,
sex, age, health, defect, or condition of dependency; and for this purpose
'person' shall include all human life as defined herein."

Senator East's Subcommittee on the Separation of Powers of the Senate
Judiciary Committee approved the bill by a 3 to 2 vote on July 9, 1981.
However, full Senate consideration of the proposal was postponed because
of the position of Senator Hatch, one of the Senators in the majority. Senator Hatch stated that he had "serious constitutional reservations" about the
bill and that he preferred a constitutional amendment to bar abortions.
(See addition to 10th Ed., p. 610; Ind.Rts. p. 234, above). Although the
97th Congress took no final action on the Helms-Hyde proposal before
adjournment, the proposal was re-introduced in substantially the same form
at the beginning of the 98th Congress and has been placed on the Senate
calendar.

Is the proposed "Human Life Statute" constitutional? Before approving
the proposal, Senator East's Subcommittee held extensive hearings on that
question. Among the proponents was Stephen H. Galebach, a young Washington lawyer who had advocated such legislation in Galebach, "A Human
Life Statute," The Human Life Review 5 (1981) [reprinted in 127 Cong.

---

1. Court-ordered busing in school desegregation cases was a second major
area for congressional invocation of
the Morgan rationale. See addition
to 10th Ed., p. 774; Ind.Rts., p. 394,
above.

2. Sec. 2 of the bill, which would eliminate lower federal court jurisdiction

in abortion cases, is printed above, addition to 10th Ed. and Ind.Rts., p. 60.

3. Before S. 158 was approved by a
Senate Subcommittee in July 1981, the
first paragraph of § 1 was revised to
read: "The Congress finds that the
life of each human being begins at
conception."

Rec. 5289 (daily ed., Jan. 19, 1981)]. Galebach argues that § 1 of the proposal is constitutional despite Roe v. Wade. He claims that the Court's refusal in Roe v. Wade to treat the fetus as a person was merely a decision resting on the incapacity of the judiciary to decide the question of when human life begins, and that, under § 5 of the Fourteenth Amendment, Congress is the appropriate body to resolve that question. He explores at length the line of cases beginning with Morgan. He states, for example: "A [congressional] determination that unborn children are human life [fully] justifies the correlative determination that they are persons. The latter determination, however, collides with the Supreme Court's holding in Roe v. Wade that the unborn are not persons. But that holding makes sense only in light of the Court's inability to decide whether the unborn are human life. Informed by a congressional determination that life begins at conception, the Court might well reach a different conclusion. Still, the potential conflict raises serious constitutional questions. Does the Roe v. Wade holding as to 'person' deprive Congress of power to pass contrary legislation? If Congress does pass legislation declaring unborn children to be human life and persons, should the Court defer to Congress' determination?"

Galebach answers these questions by defending congressional power: under the Morgan line of cases, he insists, Congress is the "co-enforcer of the Fourteenth Amendment." He claims that *both* rationales in Morgan permit Congress to include unborn children within the protections of the Fourteenth Amendment without regard to whether the judiciary would find them to be persons. And he even sees such legislation as consistent with the Morgan dissent: "[W]hether the Court follows the standard of the Morgan majority, or the stricter review standard of the minority, the result in this case is the same: the Supreme Court's interpretation of 'person' in Roe v. Wade does not bar Congress from taking a different view based on its determination that human life begins or is likely to begin at conception." He adds: "When Congress has greater competence than the courts, Congress should take the lead in defining the content of Fourteenth Amendment rights." Finally, in discussing the impact of the proposal, he comments that "the suggested statute would create a situation in which states have a compelling state interest in the protection of unborn life sufficient to justify anti-abortion statutes should states choose to enact them." [4]

Is Galebach's reasoning persuasive? Sharp criticisms of his proposed invocation of the Morgan power have been voiced by pro-choice groups and by some legal scholars. Professor Laurence H. Tribe, for example, has stated that if the proposal were read as overruling Roe v. Wade, it would be clearly

---

4. Galebach elaborates: "The task of adjusting the meaning of 'life' and 'person' to accord with changing evidence and views of life is properly a task for Congress. Not only is the line between life and non-life a difficult one, more appropriately drawn by the legislature than by the courts; it is a line that the Roe v. Wade opinion itself explicitly declared the courts unable to draw. If Congress draws the line at conception, the courts have no independent basis on which to draw a line different from that drawn by Congress. Under the approach of Katzenbach v. Morgan, followed as recently as last term by the Supreme Court, the Court's prior definition of 'person' in Roe v. Wade poses no greater barrier to congressional enforcement action than the Lassiter holding posed to Congress' nationwide prohibition of literacy tests."

unconstitutional.[5] Is such a position defensible without repudiating some of the statements in Katzenbach v. Morgan? Other scholars, such as former Solicitor General Robert H. Bork, have rested their assertions that the proposal is unconstitutional on their conclusion that some of the broad statements regarding congressional power in Katzenbach v. Morgan are themselves wrong. For a careful, balanced review of the arguments for and against the proposal, see Lewis and Rosenberg, "Legal Analysis of Congress' Authority to Enact a Human Life Statute" (Congressional Research Service, The Library of Congress, Feb. 20, 1981).[7]

10th ED., p. 1104; IND. RTS., p. 724
Add to the Notes:

6. *Subsequent developments.* a. A year after his dissent in Rome v. United States, Justice Rehnquist found another context in which to suggest a narrow view of the Morgan power. This time, however, he spoke for a majority. The case, PENNHURST STATE SCHOOL v. HALDERMAN, 451 U.S. 1 (1981), involved the interpretation of the Developmentally Disabled Assistance and Bill of Rights Act of 1975. This Act established a federal-state grant program providing financial assistance to programs for the care and treatment of the mentally retarded. The Act's "bill of rights" provision states that mentally retarded persons "have a right to appropriate treatment, services, and habilitation" in "the setting that is least restrictive [of] personal liberty." The Court of Appeals found that Congress had enacted the law "pursuant to both § 5 of the Fourteenth Amendment and the Spending Power," and that the "bill of rights" provision created substantive rights judicially enforceable by private litigants.

Justice REHNQUIST's majority opinion reversed, holding that the "bill of rights" provision "simply does not create substantive rights." He accordingly found it unnecessary to address the constitutional issue of whether Congress had the power to impose such affirmative obligations on states. But in the course of "discerning congressional intent," Justice Rehnquist discussed "the appropriate test for determining when Congress intends to enforce

5. See also Ely and Tribe, "Let There Be Life," The New York Times (March 17, 1981): "Senator Jesse A. Helms wasn't conceived yesterday, and his constitutional advisers undoubtedly have explained to him why an attempt to overrule Roe v. Wade by statute must fail."

7. See also Gordon, "The Nature and Uses of Congressional Power under Section Five of the Fourteenth Amendment to Overcome Decisions of the Supreme Court," 72 Northwestern L.Rev. 656 (1977). Professor Gordon states: "Congress has power to overturn the empirical findings of the Court; but it can do so only as long as it does not infringe on the norma-

tive component of the judicial decision. Were Congress to make an empirical 'finding' that an abortion procedure that was difficult or relatively unavailable was safer, thereby banning the generally available one, its legislation could not stand. In that case its empirical finding would undermine the normative principle of the woman's autonomy over her body." Compare Note, "Congressional Power to Enforce Due Process Rights," 80 Colum.L.Rev. 1265 (1980). For other efforts to rely on the Morgan power in legislative proposals under consideration in 1982, see the antibusing efforts (noted as addition to 10th Ed., p. 774; Ind.Rts., p. 394).

[Fourteenth Amendment] guarantees." He stated: "Because [enforcing] legislation imposes congressional policy on a State involuntarily, and because it often intrudes on traditional state authority, we should not quickly attribute to Congress an unstated intent to act under its authority to enforce the Fourteenth Amendment. Our previous cases are wholly consistent with that view, since Congress in those cases expressly articulated its intent to legislate pursuant to § 5. [See, e.g., Morgan.] Those cases, moreover, involved statutes which simply prohibited certain kinds of state conduct. The case for inferring intent is at its weakest where, as here, the rights asserted impose *affirmative* obligations on the States to fund certain services, since we may assume that Congress will not implicitly attempt to impose massive financial obligations on the States." *

b.　In EEOC v. WYOMING, 460 U.S. —— (1983), the Court clarified its position regarding the evidence necessary to show Congressional reliance on § 5. Although the Court's disposition of the commerce clause and Tenth Amendment issues (see above, addition to 10th Ed., p. 195) made it possible to avoid the § 5 issue, Justice BRENNAN's majority opinion nevertheless sought to correct a significant misconception. The lower court had taken Pennhurst to require of Congress an explicit reliance on § 5 in plain § 5 language. In response, Justice Brennan described Pennhurst as containing no such requirement. "It is in the nature of our review of congressional legislation defended on the basis of Congress's powers under § 5 of the Fourteenth Amendment that we be able to discern some legislative purpose or factual predicate that supports the exercise of that power. That does not mean, however, that Congress need anywhere recite the words 'section 5' or 'Fourteenth Amendment' or 'equal protection.' [The] rule of statutory construction invoked in Pennhurst was, like all rules of statutory construction, a tool with which to divine the meaning of otherwise ambiguous statutory intent."

The majority did not deal further with the § 5 question, but Chief Justice BURGER's dissent, joined by Justices Powell, Rehnquist, and O'Connor, contended that imposing restrictions on the mandatory retirement laws of the states was beyond Congress's § 5 power. "Since it was ratified after the Tenth Amendment, the Fourteenth Amendment is not subject to the constraints [of National League of Cities.] [But] this does not mean that Congress has been given a 'blank check' to intrude into details of

---

* In a footnote to this passage, Justice Rehnquist added: "There is of course a question whether Congress would have the power to create the rights and obligations found by the court below. Although the court below held that '[the provision] does not go beyond what has been judicially declared to be the limits of the Fourteenth Amendment,' this Court has never found that the involuntarily committed have a constitutional 'right to treatment,' much less the voluntarily committed. Thus, [several parties] argue that legislation which purports to create against the States not only a right to treatment, but one in the least restrictive setting, is not 'appropriate' legislation within the meaning of § 5. Because we conclude that [the provision] creates no rights whatsoever, we find it unnecessary to consider that question." (Justice White's partial dissent, joined by Justices Brennan and Marshall, agreed that the provision was not enacted pursuant to congressional power under the Fourteenth Amendment, but rather under the Spending Power. For the Court's comments on the Spending Power aspects of the case, see above, addition to 10th Ed., p. 237.)

states' governments at will. [Congress] may act [under § 5] only where a violation lurks. The flaw in the Commission's analysis is that in this instance, no one—not the Court, not the Congress—has determined that mandatory retirement plans violate any rights protected by [the civil war] amendments." The Chief Justice then outlined the Court's deferential rational-basis approach to age discrimination claims, as embodied in Murgia and Bradley (above, 10th Ed., p. 697; Ind.Rts., p. 319). Concluding that the Age Discrimination in Employment Act did not therefore enforce the Court's definition of equal protection guarantees, the Chief Justice also rejected the argument that this case came within the scope of Morgan. "Nor can appellant claim that Congress has used the powers we recognized in [City of Rome; Oregon v. Mitchell; Jones v. Mayer; South Carolina v. Katzenbach; Katzenbach v. Morgan] to enact legislation that prohibits conduct not in itself unconstitutional because it considered the prohibition necessary to guard against encroachment of guaranteed rights or to rectify past discrimination. There has been no finding [that] the abrogated state law infringed on rights identified by this Court. Nor did Congress use, as it did in [Morgan], its 'specially informed legislative competence' to decide that the state law it invalidated was too intrusive on federal rights to be an appropriate means to achieve the ends sought by the state. [Allowing] Congress to protect constitutional rights statutorily that it has independently defined fundamentally alters our scheme of government." The Chief Justice went on to refer to the Court's refusal in Oregon v. Mitchell to allow Congressional control over state elections. This provided ample precedent to refuse to allow the § 5 power to be used to encroach on areas traditionally and constitutionally left to the states. "[This] same reasoning leads inevitably to the conclusion that Congress lacked power to apply the Age Act to the states. There is no hint in the body of the Constitution ratified in 1789 or in the relevant amendments that every classification based on age is outlawed. Yet there is much in the Constitution and the relevant amendments to indicate that states retain sovereign powers not expressly surrendered, and these surely include the power to choose the employees they feel are best able to serve and protect their citizens."

c. Note also the potentially important, narrow view of the Morgan power (with heavy reliance on footnote [1] of Justice Brennan's opinion in Morgan) in MISSISSIPPI UNIVERSITY FOR WOMEN v. HOGAN, 458 U.S. —— (1982), (more fully noted above, addition to 10th Ed., p. 884; Ind.Rts., p. 504). In that case, Justice O'CONNOR's majority opinion found that a state university had unconstitutionally excluded a male applicant from its women-only School of Nursing. The State offered as an added justification the argument that Congress, in Title IX of the Education Amendments of 1972, had authorized the university's discrimination by exempting undergraduate institutions that traditionally have used single-sex admissions policies from the gender discrimination prohibition of Title IX. The exemption provision in Title IX, the State argued, was "a congressional limitation upon the broad prohibitions of the Equal Protection Clause of the Fourteenth Amendment." Justice O'Connor rejected that claim summarily: Even if the statute were read as attempting to provide a "constitutional exemption, the

State's argument would fail." Sec. 5 of the Fourteenth Amendment gave Congress broad power, to be sure; but Congress' power " 'is limited to adopting measures to enforce the guarantees of the Amendment; § 5 grants Congress no power to restrict, abrogate, or dilute these guarantees.' Katzenbach v. Morgan [quoting Justice Brennan's footnote]. Although we give deference to congressional decisions and classifications, neither Congress nor a State can validate a law that denies the rights guaranteed by the Fourteenth Amendment. The fact that the language of [the exemption provision] applies to the [University] provides the State no solace: '[A] statute apparently governing a dispute cannot be applied by judges, consistently with their obligations, when such an application of the statute would conflict with the Constitution. Marbury v. Madison.' Younger v. Harris."

Chapter 12

FREEDOM OF EXPRESSION: BASIC THEMES

10th ED., p. 1176; IND. RTS., p. 796
Add to text, at footnote 2:

Compare the majority's disposition of the constitutional challenges in a later passport case, Haig v. Agee, 453 U.S. 280 (1981) (further discussed below, addition to 10th Ed., p. 1676; Ind. Rts., p. 1296). The case involved a State Department regulation permitting the Secretary of State to revoke a passport if he "determines that the national's activities abroad are causing or are likely to cause serious damage to the national security or the foreign policy of the United States." The Secretary of State had relied on this regulation to revoke the passport of Philip Agee, a former CIA agent who was engaged in a campaign "to expose CIA officers and agents"; Agee challenged the revocation on both statutory and constitutional grounds. (The Court's rejection of the statutory challenge is discussed below, addition to 10th Ed., p. 1676; Ind. Rts., p. 1296.)

Chief Justice Burger gave only brief consideration to Agee's constitutional challenges, which included, inter alia, First Amendment and freedom to travel claims. (Justice Brennan's dissent criticized the Chief Justice's "whirlwind treatment of Agee's constitutional claims.") On the right to travel issue, the Chief Justice emphasized that "the *freedom* to travel outside the United States must be distinguished from the *right* to travel within the United States." Citing Aptheker, he remarked: "It is 'obvious and unarguable' that no governmental interest is more compelling than the security of the Nation. [Measures] to protect the secrecy of our Government's foreign intelligence operations plainly serve these interests."

Turning to the free speech claim, Chief Justice Burger stated: "Assuming arguendo that First Amendment protections reach beyond our national boundaries, Agee's First Amendment claim has no foundation." The Chief Justice conceded that the revocation of Agee's passport rested in part on the content of his speech—"specifically, his repeated disclosures of intelligence operations and names of intelligence personnel." "However," Chief Justice Burger added, citing Near v. Minnesota, "Agee's disclosures, among other things, have the declared purpose of obstructing intelligence operations and the recruiting of intelligence personnel. They are clearly not protected by the Constitution. The mere fact that Agee is also engaged in criticism of the Government does not render his conduct beyond the reach of the law. To the extent the revocation of his passport operates to inhibit Agee, 'it is an inhibition of *action*,' rather than of speech." [1] Moreover, the Chief Justice

---

1. In support of the last sentence, Chief Justice Burger cited (and quoted from) Chief Justice Warren's opinion in an earlier passport case, Zemel v. Rusk, 381 U.S. 1 (1965). For an additional comment on the use of the "speech"-"conduct" distinction in the Agee case, see below, addition to 10th Ed., p. 1270; Ind.Rts., p. 890.

stated (relying once again on Aptheker): "The protection accorded beliefs standing alone is very different from the protection accorded conduct. [E.g., Aptheker.]" He elaborated: "Beliefs and speech are only part of Agee's 'campaign to fight the United States CIA.' In that sense, this case contrasts markedly with the facts in [Aptheker]."

Justice Brennan's dissent, joined by Justice Marshall, rested largely on disagreement with the majority's statutory interpretation approach. The dissent addressed the Court's treatment of the constitutional issues only in a footnote. Justice Brennan asserted that the Court's handling of Agee's constitutional claims was unwarranted, "either because [the majority's statements] are extreme oversimplifications of constitutional doctrine or mistaken views of the law and facts of this case." One of his complaints was that "the Court seems to misunderstand the prior precedents of this Court, for Agee's speech is undoubtedly protected by the Constitution. However, it may be that [his] First Amendment right to speak is outweighed by the Government's interest in national security. The point [Agee] makes, and one that is worthy of plenary consideration, is that revocation of his passport obviously does implicate First Amendment rights by chilling his right to speak, and therefore the Court's responsibility must be to balance that infringement against the asserted governmental interests to determine whether the revocation contravenes the First Amendment." [2]

10th ED., p. 1183; IND. RTS., p. 803
Add to footnote 3:

Consider the recent discussion and application of the Brandenburg incitement standard in NAACP v. Claiborne Hardware Co., 458 U.S. —— (1982).

In that case, as more fully discussed below (addition to 10th Ed., p. 1425; Ind. Rts., p. 1045, the Court set aside, on First Amendment grounds, a very large damage judgment imposed on alleged participants in an economic boycott by black citizens of white merchants in a Mississippi county. The boycott sought to secure

2. In June 1982, as a response to the problem of "naming names" reflected in Agee, Congress enacted the Intelligence Identities Protection Act (50 U.S.C. § 421, Pub.L. 97–200). The Act imposes fines and jail terms for divulging information that is sufficient to identify intelligence operatives. Its most controversial provision extends the sanctions beyond former government employees like Agee to anyone who, "with reason to believe that such activities would impair or impede the foreign intelligence activities of the United States, discloses any information that identifies an individual as a covert agent," provided that the disclosure is part of a "pattern of activities intended to identify or expose covert action." [Some supporters of the law admitted that their major target was publications such as the "Covert Action Information Bulletin," whose revelations of agents' names had allegedly resulted in several injuries and at least one death. (The "Bulle-

tin" apparently stopped publishing names early in 1982.)]
The congressional consideration of the Act spurred an extensive First Amendment debate. Opponents argued that, in any appropriate First Amendment balancing, only an *intent* to endanger the national security would outbalance the protections of the First Amendment. They also objected to what they feared was a precedent for criminalizing the publication of nonclassified information. Proponents of the law insisted that simple negligence—"reason to know" of the risk created—was sufficient to tip the constitutional scales in favor of the validity of the law. Congress adopted the negligence standard; but the Conference Committee Report made special efforts to interpret the statutory language as exempting routine news reporting. See generally 40 Cong.Quar.Weekly Report 641 (March 20, 1982); 4 National Law Journal, No. 42, p. 3 (June 28, 1982).

compliance by both civic and business leaders with a lengthy list of demands for equality and racial justice. One of the defendants was Charles Evers, the Field Secretary of the NAACP, who helped organize the local chapter of the NAACP and took a leading role in the boycott. One of the arguments advanced to defend the imposition of liability on Evers was that "a finding that his public speeches were likely to incite lawless action could justify holding him liable for unlawful conduct that in fact followed within a reasonable period." (One of Evers' speeches had been recorded by the police and was reproduced at length as an Appendix to the Court's opinion.) In one speech, Evers stated that boycott violators would be "disciplined" by their own people. The portion of Justice Stevens' opinion rejecting the incitement rationale for imposing liability on Evers follows. Is that passage a persuasive application of Brandenburg and the concept of incitement, or does it significantly modify the Brandenburg incitement standard? Justice Stevens stated:

"While many of the comments in Evers' speeches might have contemplated 'discipline' in the permissible form of social ostracism, it cannot be denied that references [e.g.] to the possibility that necks would be [broken] implicitly conveyed a sterner message. In the passionate atmosphere in which the speeches were delivered, they might have been understood as inviting an unlawful form of discipline or, at least, as intending to create a fear of violence whether or not improper discipline was specifically intended.

"It is clear that 'fighting words'—those that provoke immediate violence—are not protected by the First Amendment. [Chaplinsky.] Similarly, words that create an immediate panic are not entitled to constitutional protection. [Schenck (the "falsely shouting fire" metaphor).] This Court has made clear, however, that mere *advocacy* of the use of force or violence does not remove speech from the protection of the First Amendment. [Justice Stevens quoted from Brandenburg, including its incitement test.]

"The emotionally charged rhetoric of Charles Evers' speeches did not transcend the bounds of protected speech set forth in Brandenburg. The lengthy addresses generally contained an impassioned plea for black citizens to unify, to support and respect each other, and to realize the political and economic power available to them. In the course of those pleas, strong language was used. *If that language had been followed by acts of violence, a substantial question would be presented whether Evers could be held liable for the consequences of that unlawful conduct.* In this case, however, [almost all] acts of violence identified in 1966 occurred weeks or months after the April 1, 1966 speech; the chancellor made no finding of any violence after the challenged 1969 speech. Strong and effective extemporaneous rhetoric cannot be nicely channeled in purely dulcet phrases. An advocate must be free to stimulate his audience with spontaneous and emotional appeals for unity and action in a common cause. When such appeals do not incite lawless action, they must be regarded as protected speech. To rule otherwise would ignore the 'profound national commitment' that 'debate on public issues should be uninhibited, robust, and wide-open.' [New York Times.]" [Emphasis added.]

10th ED., p. 1183; IND. RTS., p. 803
Insert after Note 2 on Brandenburg:

3. *The reach of Brandenburg.* Both "advocacy" and "incitement" describe speech that in some way *urges* people to action. But does Brandenburg apply as well to the communication of *information* that may lead to criminal acts, such as instructions for manufacturing illegal drugs, plans for the security system at Fort Knox, or information relating to the construction of illegal (in private hands) bombs or weapons? Do the dangers involved in the dissemination of this type of information fit into the Brandenburg model? Does the presence or absence of some "political" component make a difference? Consider in this context the Intelligence Identities Protection Act (addition to 10th Ed., p. 1176; Ind.Rts., p. 796) and United States v. Progressive, Inc. (10th Ed., p. 1515; Ind.Rts., p. 1135). See generally Greenawalt, "Speech and Crime," 1980 Am.B.Found.Res.J. 645.

Apart from the particular question of factual rather then normative statements, does the foregoing suggest that there may be dangers so great as to outweigh even the strongest First Amendment values, yet still not susceptible of characterization in Brandenburg terms?   In New York v. Ferber, 458 U.S. —— (1982) (addition to 10th Ed., p. 1373; Ind.Rts., p. 993), and in Globe Newspaper Co. v. Superior Court, 457 U.S. 596 (1982) (addition to 10th Ed., p. 1545; Ind.Rts., p. 1165), the Court alluded to a "compelling" interest in protecting children.   Is the range of compelling interests broader than the incitement to riot situation envisaged by Brandenburg?   Can compelling interests in general outweigh the First Amendment?   Is it possible that Brandenburg, and the test it sets forth, is representative rather than exclusive?

10th ED., p. 1189; IND. RTS., p. 809
Add to footnote 9:

In Kolender v. Lawson, 461 U.S. —— (1983), the Court struck down on vagueness grounds a California statute "that requires persons who loiter or wander on the streets to provide a 'credible and reliable' identification and to account for their presence when requested by a peace officer . . .". The majority opinion of Justice O'Connor relied heavily on the special justification for the vagueness doctrine found in Smith v. Goguen. "Although the [vagueness] doctrine focuses both on actual notice to citizens and arbitrary enforcement, we have recognized recently that the more important aspect of vagueness doctrine 'is not actual notice, but the other principal element of the doctrine—the requirement that a legislature establish minimal guidelines to govern law enforcement.' " Although Justice O'Connor did not ariculate specific dangers, she did note that "Our concern here is based upon the 'potential for arbitrarily suppressing First Amendment liberties . . . . .' Shuttlesworth v. Birmingham." (Shuttlesworth is discussed below, 10th Ed., p. 1273; Ind.Rts., p. 893.) Justice White's dissent, joined by Justice Rehnquist, took issue with the majority's "cryptic" and "vague reference to potential suppression of First Amendment liberties." In the absence of a specific identification of the way in which this statute might implicate the First Amendment, he argued, a criminal statute should not be struck down on vagueness grounds "unless it is 'impermissibly vague in all of its applications.' Hoffman Estates v. Flipside, 455 U.S. 489 (1982)."

10th ED., p. 1195; IND. RTS., p. 815
Add to footnote 18:

Note Justice White's important elaboration (and, arguably, extension) of his "substantial overbreadth" approach of Broadrick in rejecting an overbreadth attack on a New York law directed at child pornography. See New York v. Ferber, 458 U.S. —— (1982), considered fully below, addition to 10th Ed., p. 1373; Ind.Rts., p. 993.

10th ED., p. 1219; IND. RTS., p. 839
Add as footnote to Note 3 (on Schaumburg):

For another invalidation of a regulation of charitable solicitations, see Larson v. Valente, 456 U.S. 228 (1981) (more fully noted below, addition to 10th Ed., p. 1566; Ind.Rts., p. 1186). The state regulation attacked in that case exempted religious organizations from Minnesota's registration and disclosure requirements for charitable solicitations, but only if the religious organization received more than half of its total contributions from its members. This "fifty per cent" rule was challenged by members of the Unification Church (the "Moonies"). The Court sustained the challenge but did not rely on the free speech guarantee, as it had in Schaumburg. Instead, it relied on the Establishment Clause.

[handwritten: Note Test Applied]

[handwritten: Rule upheld restricting sitedown the place and manner of soliciting on Fairgrounds]

SOLICITING ON STATE FAIR GROUNDS

HEFFRON v. INT'L SOC. FOR KRISHNA CONSC.

452 U.S. 640, 101 S.Ct. 2559, 69 L.Ed.2d 298 (1981).*

Justice WHITE delivered the opinion of the Court.

The question presented [is] whether a State [may] require a religious organization desiring to distribute and sell religious literature and to solicit donations at a state fair to conduct those activities only at an assigned location within the fairgrounds even though application of the rule limits the religious practices of the organization. *[handwritten: ① whether State may restrict soliciting and distribution of literature by Religious Org to specified place on fairgrounds?]*

I. Each year, the Minnesota Agricultural Society, a public corporation organized under the laws of Minnesota, operates a state fair on a 125-acre state-owned tract located in St. Paul, Minn. [The] Society is authorized to make all "bylaws, ordinances, and rules, not inconsistent with law, which it may deem necessary or proper for the government of the fair grounds." Under this authority, the Society promulgated Minnesota State Fair Rule 6.05 which provides in relevant part that: *[handwritten: State Agricultural Society made Rule requiring licence and making violation a misdemeanor.]*

> "Sale or distribution of any merchandise, including printed or written material except under license issued [by] the Society and/or from a duly-licensed location, shall be a misdemeanor."

As Rule 6.05 is construed and applied by the Society, "all persons, groups or firms which desire to sell, exhibit or distribute materials during the annual State Fair must do so only from fixed locations on the fairgrounds." Although the Rule does not prevent organizational representatives from walking about the fairgrounds and communicating the organization's views with fair patrons in face-to-face discussions, it does require that any exhibitor conduct its sales, distribution, and fund solicitation operations from a booth rented from the Society. Space in the fairgrounds is rented to all comers in a nondiscriminatory fashion on a first-come, first-served basis with the rental charge based on the size and location of the booth.[1] The rule applies alike to nonprofit, charitable, and commercial enterprises. *[handwritten: Rule Applied as restricting to fixed locations. Requires rental of Booth in a non discriminating first-come; first served basis]*

[R]espondents International Society for Krishna Consciousness, Inc. (ISKCON), an international religious society espousing the views of the Krishna religion, and Joseph Beca, head of the Minneapolis ISKCON temple, filed suit [to invalidate] Rule 6.05, both on its face and as applied, [under] the First Amendment. [Specifically], ISKCON asserted that the Rule would suppress the practice of Sankirtan, one of its religious rituals, which enjoins its members to go into public places to distribute or sell religious literature and to *[handwritten: Krishna's Challenge Rule on face and as applied]*

---

* Examination of this case may be postponed to 10th Ed., p. 1296; Ind. Rts., p. 916, below, for consideration with other materials pertaining to access to "nontraditional" public places.

1. [The] propriety of the fee is not an issue in the present case. Cf. Cox v. New Hampshire. [Footnote by Justice White.]

solicit donations for the support of the Krishna religion.[2] [The trial court [up-held the] constitutionality of the Rule]. [T]he Minnesota Supreme Court re-versed, holding that Rule 6.05, as applied to respondents, unconstitutionally restricted the Krishnas' religious practice of Sankirtan. [We granted certio-rari] in light of the important constitutional issues presented and the conflict-ing results reached in similar cases in various lower courts.

II. The State does not dispute that the oral and written dissemination of the Krishnas' religious views and doctrines is protected by the First Amendment. [Schneider; Lovell.] Nor does it claim that this protection is lost because the written materials sought to be distributed are sold rather than given away or because contributions or gifts are solicited in the course of propagating the faith. Our cases indicate as much. [Murdock; Schaum-burg.]

It is also common ground, however, that the First Amendment does not guarantee the right to communicate one's views at all times and places or in any manner that may be desired. [E.g., Adderley; see Cox v. Louisiana.] [T]he activities of ISKCON, like those of others protected by the First Amendment, are subject to reasonable time, place, and manner restrictions. [Grayned; Adderley; Cox v. New Hampshire.] "We have often approved restrictions of that kind provided that they are justified without reference to the content of the regulated speech, that they serve a significant governmental interest, and that in doing so they leave open ample alternative channels for communication of the information." [Virginia Pharmacy.] The issue here [is] whether Rule 6.05 is a permissible restriction on the place and manner of communicating the views of the Krishna religion, more specifically, whether the Society may require the members of ISKCON who desire to practice Sankirtan at the State Fair to confine their distribution, sales, and so-licitation activities to a fixed location.

A major criterion for a valid time, place, and manner restriction is that the restriction "may not be based upon either the content or subject matter of the speech." Rule 6.05 qualifies in this respect, since [the] Rule applies evenhandedly to all who wish to distribute and sell written materials or to so-licit funds. No person or organization, whether commercial or charitable, is permitted to engage in such activities except from a booth rented for those purposes.[3]

---

2. In performing Sankirtan, ISKCON members "often greet members of the public by giving them flowers or small American flags." For the pur-pose of this lawsuit, respondents did not assert any right to seek contribu-tions in return for these "greetings gifts," nor did they seek to dance, chant, or engage in any other activi-ties besides the distribution and sale of literature and the solicitation of donations. [Footnote by Justice White.]

3. Respondents do argue that because the rule requires ISKCON to await expressions of interest from fair pa-trons before it may distribute, sell, or solicit funds, the regulation is not content-neutral in that it prefers lis-tener-initiated exchanges to those originating with the speaker. The ar-gument is interesting but has little force. This aspect of the rule is in-herent in the determination to confine exhibitors to fixed locations; it applies to all exhibitors alike and it does not invalidate the rule as a reasonable time, place, and manner regulation. [Footnote by Justice White.]

Nor does Rule 6.05 suffer from the more covert forms of discrimination that may result when arbitrary discretion is vested in some governmental authority. The method of allocating space is a straightforward first-come, first-served system. The Rule is not open to the kind of arbitrary application that this Court has condemned as inherently inconsistent with a valid time, place, and manner regulation because such discretion has the potential for becoming a means of suppressing a particular point of view. See [e.g., Shuttlesworth v. Birmingham; Cox v. Louisiana; Hague v. CIO].

A valid time, place, and manner regulation must also serve a significant governmental interest. Here, the principal justification asserted by the State in support of Rule 6.05 is the need to maintain the orderly movement of the crowd given the large number of exhibitors and persons attending the Fair.[4] The fairgrounds comprise a relatively small area of 125 acres, the bulk of which is covered by permanent buildings, temporary structures, parking lots, and connecting thoroughfares. There were some 1400 exhibitors and concessionaires renting space for the 1977 and 1978 Fairs, chiefly in permanent and temporary buildings. The Fair is designed to exhibit to the public an enormous variety of goods, services, entertainment and other matters of interest. This is accomplished by confining individual exhibitors to fixed locations, with the public moving to and among the booths or other attractions, using streets and open spaces provided for that purpose. Because the Fair attracts large crowds—an average of 115,000 patrons on weekdays and 160,000 on Saturdays and Sundays—it is apparent that the State's interest in the orderly movement and control of such an assembly of persons is a substantial consideration.

As a general matter, it is clear that a State's interest in protecting the "safety and convenience" of persons using a public forum is a valid governmental objective. Furthermore, consideration of a forum's special attributes is relevant to the constitutionality of a regulation since the significance of the governmental interest must be assessed in light of the characteristic nature and function of the particular forum involved. See, e.g., [Grayned; Lehman]. This observation bears particular import in the present case since respondents make a number of analogies between the fairgrounds and city streets, which have "immemorially been held in trust for the use of the public [and] have been used for purposes of assembly, communicating thoughts between citizens, and discussing public questions." [Hague v. CIO.] But it is clear that there are significant differences between a street and the fairgrounds. A street is continually open, often uncongested, and constitutes not only a necessary conduit in the daily affairs of a locality's citizens, but also a place where people may enjoy the open air or the company of friends and

---

4. Petitioners assert two other state interests in support of the Rule. First, petitioners claim that the Rule forwards the State's valid interest in protecting its citizens from fraudulent solicitations, deceptive or false speech, and undue annoyance. See [Schaumburg; Cantwell]. Petitioners also forward the State's interest in protecting the fairgoers from being harrassed or otherwise bothered, on the grounds that they are a captive audience. In light of our holding that the Rule is justified solely in terms of the State's interest in managing the flow of the crowd, we do not reach whether these other two purposes are constitutionally sufficient to support the imposition of the Rule. [Footnote by Justice White.]

neighbors in a relaxed environment. The Minnesota Fair [is] a temporary event attracting great numbers of visitors who come to the event for a short period to see and experience the host of exhibits and attractions at the Fair. The flow of the crowd and demands of safety are more pressing in the context of the Fair. As such, any comparisons to public streets are necessarily inexact.

The Minnesota Supreme Court recognized that the State's interest in the orderly movement of a large crowd and in avoiding congestion was substantial and that Rule 6.05 furthered that interest significantly. Nevertheless, the [court] declared that the case did not turn on the "importance of the state's undeniable interest in preventing the widespread disorder that would surely exist if no regulation such as Rule 6.05 were in effect" but upon the significance of the State's interest in avoiding whatever disorder would likely result from granting members of ISKCON an exemption from the Rule. Approaching the case in this way, the court concluded that although some disruption would occur from such an exemption, it was not of sufficient concern to warrant confining the Krishnas to a booth. The court also concluded that, in any event, the rule was not essential to the furtherance of the State's interest in crowd control, which could adequately be served by less intrusive means.

As we see it, the Minnesota Supreme Court took too narrow a view of the State's interest in avoiding congestion and maintaining the orderly movement of fair patrons on the fairgrounds. The justification for the Rule should not be measured by the disorder that would result from granting an exemption solely to ISKCON. That organization and its ritual of Sankirtan have no special claim to First Amendment protection as compared to that of other religions who also distribute literature and solicit funds.[5] None of our cases suggest that the inclusion of peripatetic solicitation as part of a church ritual entitles church members to solicitation rights in a public forum superior to those of members of other religious groups that raise money but do not purport to ritualize the process. Nor for present purposes do religious organizations enjoy rights to communicate, distribute, and solicit on the fairgrounds superior to those of other organizations having social, political, or other ideological messages to proselytize. These nonreligious organizations seeking support for their activities are entitled to rights equal to those of religious groups to enter a public forum and spread their views, whether by soliciting funds or by distributing literature.

If Rule 6.05 is an invalid restriction on the activities of ISKCON, it is no more valid with respect to the other social, political, or charitable organizations that have rented booths at the Fair and confined their distribution, sale, and fund solicitation to those locations. Nor would it be valid with respect to other organizations that did not rent booths, either because they were unavailable due to a lack of space or because they chose to avoid the expense involved, but that would in all probability appear in the fairgrounds to dis-

5. Respondents do not defend the limited approach of the Minnesota Supreme Court. They concede that whatever exemption they were entitled to under the First Amendment would apply to other organizations seeking similar rights to take part in certain protected activities in the public areas of the fairgrounds. [Footnote by Justice White.]

tribute, sell, and solicit if they could freely do so. The question would also inevitably arise as to what extent the First Amendment also gives commercial organizations a right to move among the crowd to distribute information about or to sell their wares as respondents claim they may do.

ISKCON desires to proselytize at the fair because it believes it can successfully communicate and raise funds. In its view, this can be done only by intercepting fair patrons as they move about, and if success is achieved, stopping them momentarily or for longer periods as money is given or exchanged for literature. This consequence would be multiplied many times over if Rule 6.05 could not be applied to confine such transactions by ISKCON and others to fixed locations. Indeed, the court below agreed that without Rule 6.05 there would be widespread disorder at the fairgrounds. The court also recognized that some disorder would inevitably result from exempting the Krishnas from the Rule. Obviously, there would be a much larger threat to the State's interest in crowd control if all other religious, nonreligious, and noncommercial organizations could likewise move freely about the fairgrounds distributing and selling literature and soliciting funds at will.

Given these considerations, we hold that the State's interest in confining distribution, selling, and fund solicitation activities to fixed locations is sufficient to satisfy the requirement that a place or manner restriction must serve a substantial state interest. By focusing on the incidental effect of providing an exemption from Rule 6.05 to ISKCON, the Minnesota Supreme Court did not take into [account] the fact that any such exemption cannot be meaningfully limited to ISKCON, and as applied to similarly situated groups would prevent the State from furthering its important concern with managing the flow of the crowd. In our view, the Society may apply its Rule and confine the type of transactions at issue to designated locations without violating the First Amendment.

For similar reasons, we cannot agree with the Minnesota Supreme Court that Rule 6.05 is an unnecessary regulation because the State could avoid the threat to its interest posed by ISKCON by less restrictive means, such as penalizing disorder or disruption, limiting the number of solicitors, or putting more narrowly drawn restrictions on the location and movement of ISKCON's representatives. As we have indicated, the inquiry must involve not only ISKCON, but also all other organizations that would be entitled to distribute, sell or solicit if the booth rule may not be enforced with respect to ISKCON. Looked at in this way, it is quite improbable that the alternative means suggested by the Minnesota Supreme Court would deal adequately with the problems posed by the much larger number of distributors and solicitors that would be present on the fairgrounds if the judgment below were affirmed.

For Rule 6.05 to be valid as a place and manner restriction, it must also be sufficiently clear that alternative forums for the expression of respondents' protected speech exist despite the effects of the Rule. Rule 6.05 is not vulnerable on this ground. First, the Rule does not prevent ISKCON from practicing Sankirtan anywhere outside the fairgrounds. More importantly, the Rule has not been shown to deny access within the forum in question. Here, the Rule does not exclude ISKCON from the fairgrounds, nor does it deny that organization the right to conduct any desired activity at some point within the forum. Its members may mingle with the crowd and orally propagate their views. The organization may also arrange for a booth and distribute and sell literature and solicit funds from that location on the fairgrounds itself. The Minnesota State Fair is a limited public forum in that it exists to provide a means for a great number of exhibitors temporarily to present their products or views, be they commercial, religious, or political, to a large number of people in an efficient fashion. Considering the limited functions of the Fair and the [confined] area within which it operates, we are unwilling to say that Rule 6.05 does not provide ISKCON and other organizations with an adequate means to sell and solicit on the fairgrounds. The First Amendment protects the right of every citizen to "reach the minds of willing listeners and to do so there must be opportunity to win their attention." Kovacs v. Cooper. Rule 6.05 does not unnecessarily limit that right within the fairgrounds.[6]

[Reversed and remanded.]

Justice BRENNAN, with whom Justice MARSHALL and Justice STEVENS join, concurring in part and dissenting in part.

As the Court recognizes, the issue in this case is whether [Rule 6.05] constitutes a reasonable time, place, and manner restriction. [T]he Court considers, inter alia, whether the regulation serves a significant governmental interest and whether that interest can be served by a less intrusive restriction. The Court errs, however, in failing to apply its analysis separately to each of the protected First Amendment activities restricted by Rule 6.05. Thus, the Court fails to recognize that some of the State's restrictions may be reasonable while others may not.

Rule 6.05 restricts three types of protected First Amendment activity: distribution of literature, sale of literature, and solicitation of funds. [The] State advances three justifications for its booth rule. The justification relied upon by the Court today is the State's interest in maintaining the orderly movement of the crowds at the fair. The second justification [is] the State's interest in protecting its fairgoers from fraudulent, deceptive, and misleading solicitation practices. The third justification, based on the "captive audience" doctrine, is the State's interest in protecting its fairgoers from annoyance and harrassment.

6. Given this understanding of the nature of the Fair, we reject respondents' claim that Rule 6.05 effects a total ban on protected First Amendment activities in the open areas of the fairgrounds. In effect, respondents seek to separate, for constitutional purposes, the open areas of the fairgrounds from that part of the fairgrounds where the booths are located. For the reasons stated in text, we believe respondents' characterization of the Rule is plainly incorrect. The booths are not secreted away in some nonaccessible location. but are located within the area of the fairgrounds where visitors are expected, and indeed encouraged, to pass. Since respondents are permitted to solicit funds and distribute and sell literature from within the fairgrounds, albeit from a fixed location, it is inaccurate to say that Rule 6.05 constitutes a ban on such protected activity in the relevant public forum. Accordingly, the only question is the Rule's validity as a time, place, and manner restriction. [Footnote by Justice White.]

I quite agree with the Court that the State has a significant interest in maintaining crowd control on its fairgrounds. I also have no doubt that the State has a significant interest in protecting its fairgoers from fraudulent or deceptive solicitation practices. Indeed, because I believe on this record that this latter interest is substantially furthered by a Rule that restricts sales and solicitation activities to fixed booth locations, where the State will have the greatest opportunity to police and prevent possible deceptive practices, I would hold that Rule 6.05's restriction on those particular forms of First Amendment expression is justified as an antifraud measure. Accordingly, I join the judgment of the Court insofar as it upholds Rule 6.05's restriction on sales and solicitations. However, because I believe that the booth rule is an overly intrusive means of achieving the State's interest in crowd control, and because I cannot accept the validity of the State's third asserted justification,[1] I dissent from the Court's approval of Rule 6.05's restriction on the distribution of literature.

As our cases have long noted, once a governmental regulation is shown to impinge upon basic First Amendment rights, the burden falls on the government to show the validity of its asserted interest and the absence of less intrusive alternatives. See, e.g., [Schneider]. The challenged "regulation must be narrowly tailored to further the State's legitimate interest." [Grayned]. Minnesota's Rule 6.05 does not meet this test.

[Significantly], each and every fairgoer, whether political candidate, concerned citizen, or member of a religious group, is free to give speeches, engage in face-to-face advocacy, campaign, or proselytize. No restrictions are placed on any fairgoer's right to speak at any time, at any place, or to any person.[2] Thus, if on a given day 5,000 members of ISKCON came to the fair and paid their admission fees, all 5,000 would be permitted to wander throughout the fairgrounds, delivering speeches to whomever they wanted, about whatever they wanted. Moreover, because this right does not rest on Sankirtan or any other religious principle,[3] it can be exercised by every politi-

---

1. Because fairgoers are fully capable of saying "no" to persons seeking their attention and then walking away, they are not members of a captive audience. They have no general right to be free from being approached. See [Schaumburg; Martin v. Struthers]. [Footnote by Justice Brennan.]

2. A state fair is truly a marketplace of ideas and a public forum for the communication of ideas and information. [Despite] the Court's suggestion to the contrary, a fair is surely a "natural and proper place[] for the dissemination of information and opinion." [Schneider.] In no way could I agree that respondents' desired "manner of expression is basically incompatible with the normal activity" of the fair. [Footnote by Justice Brennan.]

3. I am somewhat puzzled by the Court's treatment of the Sankirtan issue. Respondents' complaint [alleges] that Rule 6.05, on its face and as applied, violates both the Free Exercise and the Free Speech Clauses. In their brief and in oral argument, however, respondents emphasize that they do not claim any special treatment because of Sankirtan, but are willing to rest their challenge wholly upon their general right to free speech, which they concede is identical to the right enjoyed by every other religious, political, or charitable group. There is therefore no need for the Court to discuss Sankirtan.

Having chosen to discuss it, however, the Court does so in a manner that is seemingly inconsistent with prior case law. The parties have stipulated that members of ISKCON have a unique "duty to perform a religious ritual

cal candidate, partisan advocate, and common citizen who has paid the price of admission. All share the identical right to move peripatetically and speak freely throughout the fairgrounds.

Because of Rule 6.05, however, as soon as a proselytizing member of ISKCON hands out a free copy of the Bhagavad-Gita to an interested listener, or a political candidate distributes his campaign brochure to a potential voter, he becomes subject to arrest and removal from the fairgrounds. This constitutes a significant restriction on First Amendment rights. By prohibiting distribution of literature outside the booths, the fair officials sharply limit the number of fairgoers to whom the proselytizers and candidates can communicate their messages. Only if a fairgoer affirmatively seeks out such information by approaching a booth does Rule 6.05 fully permit potential communicators to exercise their First Amendment rights.

In support of its crowd control justification,[4] the State contends that if fairgoers are permitted to distribute literature, large crowds will gather, blocking traffic lanes and causing safety problems. [But] the State has failed to provide any support for these assertions. It has made no showing that relaxation of its booth rule would create additional disorder in a fair that is already characterized by the robust and unrestrained participation of hundreds of thousands of wandering fairgoers. If fairgoers can make speeches, engage in face-to-face proselytizing, and buttonhole prospective supporters, they can surely distribute literature to members of their audience without significantly adding to the State's asserted crowd control problem. The record is devoid of any evidence that the 125-acre fairgrounds could not accommodate peripatetic distributors of literature just as easily as it now accommodates peripatetic speechmakers and proselytizers.

Relying on a general, speculative fear of disorder, the [State] has placed a significant restriction on respondents' ability to exercise core First Amendment rights. This restriction is not narrowly drawn to advance the State's interests, and for that reason is unconstitutional. "[U]ndifferentiated fear or

(margin handwritten notes:) Not narrowly Drawn so unconst

Rule is not narrowly drawn to advance State interests so not constitutional

known as Sankirtan, which consists of going out into public places, to disseminate or sell religious literature and to solicit contributions to support the publishing, religious, and educational functions of Krishna Consciousness." The Court, however, disparages the significance of this ritual, stating without explanation or supporting authority: "[ISKCON] and its ritual of Sankirtan have no special claim to First Amendment protection as compared to that of other religions who also distribute literature and solicit funds. . . ."

Our cases are clear that governmental regulations which interfere with the exercise of specific religious beliefs or principles should be scrutinized with particular care. See, e.g., Sherbert v. Verner. [See also Wisconsin v. Yoder.] I read the Court as accepting these precedents, and merely holding that even if Sankirtan is "conduct protected by the Free Exercise Clause," it is entitled to no greater protection than other forms of expression protected by the First Amendment that are burdened to the same extent by Rule 6.05. [Footnote by Justice Brennan.]

4. Other than the "captive audience" justification, the only interest seriously asserted by the State in support of its restriction on distribution of literature is its interest in crowd control. At oral argument, counsel for the State expressly declined to advance an antilittering objective, and virtually conceded that the antifraud rationale would not apply unless the communicator sought to obtain money from the fairgoers. [Footnote by Justice Brennan.]

apprehension of disturbance is not enough to overcome the right to freedom of expression." [Tinker.] If the State had a reasonable concern that distribution in certain parts of the fairgrounds—for example, entrances and exits—would cause disorder, it could have drafted its rule to prohibit distribution of literature at those points. If the State felt it necessary to limit the number of persons distributing an organization's literature, it could, within reason, have done that as well. It had no right, however, to ban all distribution of literature outside the booths. [Because] I believe that the State could have drafted a more narrowly-drawn restriction on the right to distribute literature without undermining its interest in maintaining crowd control on the fairgrounds, I would affirm that part of the judgment below that strikes down Rule 6.05 as it applies to distribution of literature.

Blackman concurring + dissenting

Justice BLACKMUN, concurring in part and dissenting in part.

For the reasons stated by Justice Brennan, I believe that [Rule 6.05] is unconstitutional as applied to the distribution of literature. I also agree, however, that the Rule is *constitutional* as applied to the sale of literature and the solicitation of funds. I reach this latter conclusion by a different route than does Justice Brennan, for I am not persuaded that, under the Court's precedents, the State's interest in protecting fairgoers from fraudulent solicitation or sales practices justifies Rule 6.05's restrictions of those activities.[1]

Also says unconstit. as applied to distribution of literature

In [Schaumburg], the Court stressed that a community's interest in preventing fraudulent solicitations must be met by narrowly drawn regulations that do not unnecessarily interfere with First Amendment freedoms. It there held that possibility of fraud in "door-to-door" or "on-street" solicitations could be countered "by measures less intrusive than a direct prohibition on solicitation," such as disclosure provisions and penal laws prohibiting fraudulent misrepresentations. I see no reason why the same considerations are not applicable here. There is nothing in this record to suggest that it is more difficult to police fairgrounds for fraudulent solicitations than it is to police an entire community's streets; just as fraudulent solicitors may "melt into a crowd" at the fair, so also may door-to-door solicitors quickly move on after consummating several transactions in a particular neighborhood. Indeed, since respondents have offered to wear identifying tags, and since the fairgrounds are an enclosed area, it is at least arguable that it is easier to police the fairgrounds than a community's streets.

Nonetheless, I believe that the State's substantial interest in maintaining crowd control and safety on the fairgrounds does justify Rule 6.05's restriction on solicitation and sales activities not conducted from a booth. As the Court points out, "[t]he flow of the crowd and demands of safety are more pressing in the context of the Fair" than in the context of a typical street. While I agree with Justice Brennan that the State's interest in order does not justify restrictions upon distribution of literature, I think that common-sense

State interest of crowd control reason uphold

1. It should be stressed that Rule 6.05 does not prevent respondents from wandering throughout the fairgrounds and directing interested donors or purchasers to their booth. Thus, it is in fact only the exchange of money, rather than the solicitation per se of contributions or of purchases, that is limited to a booth. Accordingly, I use the terms "solicitation" and "sales" to connote only the actual exchange of money, rather than the act of requesting that the fairgoer purchase literature or make a contribution at the booth. [Footnote by Justice Blackmun.]

differences between literature distribution, on the one hand, and solicitation and sales, on the other, suggest that the latter activities present greater crowd control problems than the former. The distribution of literature does not require that the recipient stop in order to receive the message the speaker wishes to convey; instead, the recipient is free to read the message at a later time. For this reason, literature distribution may present even fewer crowd control problems than the oral proselytizing that the State already allows upon the fairgrounds. [In contrast], sales and the collection of solicited funds not only require the fairgoer to stop, but also "engender additional confusion [because] they involve acts of exchanging articles for money, fumbling for and dropping money, making change, etc." Rules restricting the exchange of money to booths have been upheld in analogous contexts, see, e.g., International Society for Krishna Consciousness v. Eaves, 601 F.2d 809, 828–829 (CA5 1979) (Atlanta airports), and for similar reasons I would uphold Rule 6.05 insofar as it applies to solicitation and sales.*

10th ED., p. 1220; IND. RTS., p. 840
Add as footnote to Note 1:

Note the recent important invocation of the Chaplinsky approach in the Court's decision to classify "child pornography as a category of material outside the protection of the First Amendment." See New York v. Ferber, 458 U.S. —— (1982), fully considered below, addition to 10th Ed., p. 1373; Ind.Rts., p. 993.

10th ED., p. 1229; IND. RTS., p. 849
Add to footnote *:

Note the heavy reliance on the Chaplinsky categorization approach in New York v. Ferber, 458 U.S. —— (1982), "classifying child pornography as a category of material outside the protection of the First Amendment." The case is considered fully below, addition to 10th Ed., p. 1373; Ind.Rts., p. 993.

10th ED., p. 1239; IND. RTS., p. 859
Add to footnote *:

On the relationship between the First Amendment and equal protection, see also Regan v. Taxation With Representation of Washington, 461 U.S. —— (1983), discussed fully below, addition to 10th Ed., p. 1481; Ind.Rts., p. 1101, and Perry Education Ass'n v. Perry Local Educators' Ass'n, 460 U.S. —— (1983), printed below, addition to 10th Ed., p. 1325; Ind.Rts., p. 945.

10th ED., p. 1248; IND. RTS., p. 868
After Young v. American Mini Theatres:

THE LIMITS OF AMERICAN MINI THEATRES

SCHAD v. MT. EPHRAIM

452 U.S. 61, 101 S.Ct. 2176, 68 L.Ed.2d 671 (1981).

Justice WHITE delivered the opinion of the Court.

In 1973, appellants began operating an adult bookstore in the commercial zone in the Borough of Mount Ephraim in Camden County, N. J. The store sold adult books, magazines and films. Amusement licenses shortly issued permitting the store to install coin-operated devices by virtue of which a customer could sit in a booth, insert a coin and watch an adult film. In 1976, the store introduced an additional coin-operated mechanism permitting

---

* Note the discussion of Heffron in Metromedia, Inc. v. San Diego, 453 U.S. 490 (1981), a recent decision involving a First Amendment attack on bill- board regulation. The case is printed below, addition to 10th Ed., p. 1262; Ind.Rts., p. 882.

the customer to watch a live dancer, usually nude, performing behind a glass panel. Complaints were soon filed against appellants charging that the bookstore's exhibition of live dancing violated § 99–15B of Mount Ephraim's zoning ordinance, which described the permitted uses in a commercial zone.[1]

[Appellants were found guilty in the state trial court and were fined.] [T]he court recognized that "live nude dancing is protected by the First Amendment" but was of the view that "First Amendment guarantees are not involved" since the case "involves solely a zoning ordinance" under which "[l]ive entertainment is simply not a permitted use in any establishment" whether the entertainment is a nude dance or some other form of live presentation. Reliance was placed on the statement in [American Mini Theatres] that "[t]he mere fact that the commercial exploitation of material protected by the First Amendment is subject to zoning and other licensing requirements is not a sufficient reason for invalidating these ordinances." [In this Court, appellants'] principal claim is that the imposition of criminal penalties under an ordinance prohibiting all live entertainment, including nonobscene, nude dancing, violated their rights of free expression guaranteed by the [First Amendment]. [We] now set aside appellants' convictions.

(I) As the Mount Ephraim code has been construed by the [state courts], "live entertainment," including nude dancing, is "not a permitted use in any establishment" in the Borough of Mount Ephraim. By excluding live entertainment throughout the Borough, the Mount Ephraim ordinance prohibits a wide range of expression that has long been held to be within the protections of the [First Amendment.] Entertainment, as well as political and ideological speech, is protected; motion pictures, programs broadcast by radio and television and live entertainment, such as musical and dramatic works, fall within the First Amendment guarantee. Nor may an entertainment program be prohibited solely because it displays the nude human figure. "Nudity alone" does not place otherwise protected material outside the mantle of the First Amendment. Jenkins v. Georgia; Southeastern Promotions; Erznoznik. [Furthermore], nude dancing is not without its First Amendment protections from official regulation.

Whatever First Amendment protection should be extended to nude dancing, live or on film, however, the Mount Ephraim ordinance prohibits all live entertainment in the Borough: no property in the Borough may be principally used for the commercial production of plays, concerts, musicals, dance or any other form of live entertainment. Because appellants' claims are rooted in the First Amendment, they are entitled to rely on the impact of the ordinance on the expressive activities of others as well as their own. "Because

---

1. Sec. 99–15B provided:

"B. Principal permitted uses on the land and in buildings.

"(1) Offices and banks; taverns; restaurants and luncheonettes for sit-down dinners only and with no drive-in facilities; automobile sales; retail stores, such as but not limited to food, wearing apparel, millinery, fabrics, hardware, lumber, jewelry, paint, wallpaper, appliances, flowers, gifts, books, stationery, pharmacy, liquors, cleaners, novelties, hobbies and toys; repair shops for shoes, jewels, clothes and appliances; barbershops and beauty salons; cleaners and laundries; pet stores; and nurseries. . . .

"(2) Motels."

Section 99–4 of the zoning ordinance provided that "[a]ll uses not expressly permitted in this chapter are prohibited."

[Handwritten margin notes: "Shad guilty in state court & fined." "live dancing violated zoning ordinance; not among 'permitted uses'" "State court felt 1st Am not involved, case solely a zoning ordinance" "D's claim criminal penalty under ordinance violates 1st Am." "Convictions set aside" "city excluded throughout the Borough" "Live entertainment is protected" "nudity alone does not place Outside 1st Am" "D's can rely on overbreadth challenge" "Ordinance prohibits also, plays, concerts, musicals etc"]

overbroad laws, like vague ones, deter privileged activities, our cases firmly establish appellant's standing to raise an overbreadth challenge." [Grayned.]

II. The First Amendment requires that there be sufficient justification for the exclusion of a broad category of protected expression as one of the permitted commercial uses in the Borough. The justification does not appear on the face of the ordinance since the ordinance itself is ambiguous with respect to whether live entertainment is permitted: § 99–15B purports to specify only the "principal" permitted uses in commercial establishments, and its listing of permitted retail establishments is expressly nonexclusive; yet, § 99–4 declares that all uses not expressly permitted are forbidden. The state courts at least partially resolved the ambiguity by declaring live entertainment to be an impermissible commercial use. [They responded to the First Amendment challenge by relying on the zoning power.]

The power of local governments to zone and control land use is undoubtedly broad and its proper exercise is an essential aspect of achieving a satisfactory quality of life in both urban and rural communities. But the zoning power is not infinite and unchallengeable; it "must be exercised within constitutional limits." Accordingly, it is subject to judicial review; and, as is most often the case, the standard of review is determined by the nature of the right assertedly threatened or violated rather than by the power being exercised or the specific limitation imposed. Where property interests are adversely affected by zoning, the courts generally have emphasized the breadth of municipal power to control land use and have sustained the regulation if it is rationally related to legitimate state concerns and does not deprive the owner of economically viable use of his property. [Beyond] that, as is true of other ordinances, when a zoning law infringes upon a protected liberty, it must be narrowly drawn and must further a sufficiently substantial government interest. [See Schneider; Schaumburg; Moore v. East Cleveland.] Because the ordinance challenged in this case significantly limits communicative activity within the Borough, we must scrutinize both the interests advanced by the Borough to justify this limitation on protected expression and the means chosen to further those interests.

As an initial matter, this case is not controlled by American Mini Theatres. Although the Court there stated that a zoning ordinance is not invalid merely because it regulates activity protected under the First Amendment, it emphasized that the challenged restriction on the location of adult movie theaters imposed a minimal burden on protected speech. The restriction did not affect the number of adult movie theaters that could operate in the city; it merely dispersed them. The Court did not imply that a municipality could ban all adult theaters—much less all live entertainment or all nude dancing—from its commercial districts citywide. Moreover, it was emphasized in that case that the evidence presented to the Detroit Common Council indicated that the concentration of adult movie theaters in limited areas led to deterioration of surrounding neighborhoods, and it was concluded that the city had justified the incidental burden on First Amendment interests resulting from merely dispersing, but not excluding, adult theaters.

In this case, however, Mount Ephraim has not adequately justified its substantial restriction of protected activity.[2] None of the justifications assert-ed in this Court was articulated by the state courts and none of them with-stands scrutiny. First, the Borough contends that permitting live entertain-ment would conflict with its plan to create a commercial area that caters only to the "immediate needs" of its residents and that would enable them to pur-chase at local stores the few items they occasionally forgot to buy outside the Borough. No evidence was introduced below to support this assertion, and it is difficult to reconcile this characterization of the Borough's commercial zones with the provisions of the ordinance. Section 99–15A expressly states that the purpose of creating commercial zones was to provide areas for "local and *regional* commercial operations." (Emphasis added.) The range of permitted uses goes far beyond providing for the "immediate needs" of the residents. Motels, hardware stores, lumber stores, banks, offices, and car showrooms are permitted in commercial zones. The list of permitted "retail stores" is nonexclusive, and it includes such services as beauty salons, barber shops, cleaners, and restaurants. Virtually the only item or service that may not be sold in a commercial zone is entertainment, or at least live entertainment.[3] The Borough's first justification is patently insufficient.

Court applies strict scrutiny of city's justifications

plan to create area serving local needs (not enough)

Second, Mount Ephraim contends that it may selectively exclude com-mercial live entertainment from the broad range of commercial uses permit-ted in the Borough for reasons normally associated with zoning in commercial districts, that is, to avoid the problems that may be associated with live enter-tainment, such as parking, trash, police protection, and medical facilities. The Borough has presented no evidence, and it is not immediately apparent as a matter of experience, that live entertainment poses problems of this na-ture more significant than those associated with various permitted uses; nor does it appear that the Borough's zoning authority has arrived at a defensible conclusion that unusual problems are presented by live entertainment. Cf. [American Mini Theatres].[4] We do not find it self-evident that a theater,

parking, police protection, trash, etc. (not enough)

2. If the New Jersey courts had ex-pressly interpreted this ordinance as banning all entertainment, we would reach the same result. [Footnote by Justice White.]

3. At present, this effect is somewhat lessened by the presence of at least three establishments that are permit-ted to offer live entertainment as a nonconforming use. These uses ap-parently may continue indefinitely, since the Mount Ephraim Code does not require nonconforming uses to be terminated within a specified period of time. The Borough's decision to permit live entertainment as a non-conforming use only undermines the Borough's contention that live enter-tainment poses inherent problems that justify its exclusion. [Footnote by Justice White.]

4. Mount Ephraim also speculates that the Borough may have concluded that live nude dancing is undesirable. It is noted that in California v. LaRue, 409 U. S. 109 (1972), this Court identi-fied a number of problems that Cali-fornia sought to eliminate by prohibit-ing certain explicitly sexual entertain-ment in bars and in nightclubs li-censed to serve liquor. This specual-tion lends no support to the chal-lenged ordinance. First, § 99–15B ex-cludes all live entertainment, not just live nude dancing. Even if Mount Ephraim might validly place restric-tions on certain forms of live nude dancing under a narrowly drawn ordi-nance, this would not justify the ex-clusion of all live entertainment or, insofar as this record reveals, even the nude dancing involved in this case. Second, the regulation challenged in California v. LaRue was adopted only after the Department of Alcoholic

for example, would create greater parking problems than would a restaurant. Even less apparent is what unique problems would be posed by exhibiting live nude dancing in connection with the sale of adult books and films, particularly since the bookstore is licensed to exhibit nude dancing on films. It may be that some forms of live entertainment would create problems that are not associated with the commercial uses presently permitted in Mount Ephraim. Yet this ordinance is not narrowly drawn to respond to what might be the distinctive problems arising from certain types of live entertainment, and it is not clear that a more selective approach would fail to address those unique problems if any there are. The Borough has not established that its interests could not be met by restrictions that are less intrusive on protected forms of expression.

The Borough also suggests that § 99–15B is a reasonable "time, place and manner" restriction; yet it does not identify the municipal interests making it reasonable to exclude all commercial live entertainment but to allow a variety of other commercial uses in the Borough.[5] [Under Grayned v. Rockford], the initial question in determining the validity of the exclusion as a time, place and manner restriction is whether live entertainment is "basically incompatible with the normal activity [in the commercial zones]." As discussed above, no evidence has been presented to establish that live entertainment is incompatible with the uses presently permitted by the Borough. Mount Ephraim asserts that it could have chosen to eliminate all commercial uses within its boundaries. Yet we must assess the exclusion of live entertainment in light of the commercial uses Mount Ephraim allows, not in light of what the Borough might have done.[6]

To be reasonable, time, place and manner restrictions not only must serve significant state interests but also must leave open adequate alternative channels of communication. Here, the Borough totally excludes all live entertainment, including nonobscene nude dancing that is otherwise protected by the First Amendment. As we have observed, American Mini Theatres did not purport to approve the total exclusion from the city of theaters showing adult, but not obscene, materials. It was carefully noted in that case that the number of regulated establishments was not limited and that "[t]he situation would be quite different if the ordinance had the effect of suppresing, or greatly restricting access to, lawful speech."

The Borough nevertheless contends that live entertainment in general and nude dancing in particular are amply available in close-by areas outside

Beverage Control had determined that significant problems were linked to the activity that was later regulated. Third, in California v. LaRue the Court relied heavily on the State's power under the Twenty-first Amendment. [Footnote by Justice White.]

5. Mount Ephraim argued in its brief that nonlive entertainment is an adequate substitute for live entertainment. This contention was apparently abandoned at oral argument, since the Borough's counsel stated that the ordinance bans all commercial enter-

tainment. At any rate, the argument is an inadequate response to the fact that live entertainment, which the ordinance bans, is protected by the First Amendment. [Footnote by Justice White.]

6. Thus, our decision today does not establish that every unit of local government entrusted with zoning responsibilities must provide a commercial zone in which live entertainment is permitted. [Footnote by Justice White.]

the limits of the Borough. Its position suggests the argument that if there were countywide zoning, it would be quite legal to allow live entertainment in only selected areas of the county and to exclude it from primarily residential communities, such as the Borough of Mount Ephraim. This may very well be true, but the Borough cannot avail itself of that argument in this case. There is no countywide zoning in Camden County, and Mount Ephraim is free under state law to impose its own zoning restrictions, within constitutional limits. Furthermore, there is no evidence in this record to support the proposition that the kind of entertainment appellants wish to provide is available in reasonably nearby areas. The courts below made no such findings; and at least in their absence, the ordinance excluding live entertainment from the commercial zone cannot constitutionally be applied to appellants so as to criminalize the activities for which they have been fined. "[O]ne is not to have the exercise of his liberty of expression in appropriate places abridged on the plea that it may be exercised in some other place." Schneider.

[Reversed.]

Justice BLACKMUN, concurring.

I join the Court's opinion, but write separately to address two points that I believe are sources of some ambiguity in this still emerging area of the law. First, I would emphasize that the presumption of validity that traditionally attends a local government's exercise of its zoning powers carries little, if any, weight where the zoning regulation trenches on rights of expression protected under the First Amendment. [After] today's decision, it should be clear that where protected First Amendment interests are at stake, zoning regulations have [no] "talismanic immunity from constitutional challenge." [American Mini Theatres (concurring opinion).]

My other observation concerns the suggestion that a local community should be free to eliminate a particular form of expression so long as that form is available in areas reasonably nearby. In Mini Theatres, the Court dealt with locational restrictions imposed by a political subdivision [that] preserved reasonable access to the regulated form of expression within the boundaries of that same subdivision. It would be a substantial step beyond Mini Theatres to conclude that a town or county may legislatively prevent its citizens from engaging in or having access to forms of protected expression that are incompatible with its majority's conception of the "decent life" solely because these activities are sufficiently available in other locales. I do not read the Court's opinion to reach, nor would I endorse, that conclusion.*

Were I a resident of Mount Ephraim, I would not expect my right to attend the theater or to purchase a novel to be contingent upon the availability of such opportunities in "nearby" Philadelphia, a community in whose decisions I would have no political voice. Cf. [Southeastern Promotions]. Similarly, I would not expect the citizens of Philadelphia to be under any obligation to provide me with access to theaters and bookstores simply because Mount Ephraim previously had acted to ban these forms of "entertainment."

* I need not address here the weight to be given other arguments invoked by local communities as a basis for restricting protected forms of expression. [Footnote by Justice Blackmun.]

This case does not require articulation of a rule for evaluating the meaning of "reasonable access" in different contexts. The scope of relevant zoning authority varies widely across our country, as do geographic configurations and types of commerce among neighboring communities, and this issue will doubtless be resolved on a case-by-case basis. For now, it is sufficient to observe that in attempting to accommodate a locality's concern to protect the character of its community life, the Court must remain attentive to the guarantees of the First Amendment, and in particular to the protection they afford to minorities against the "standardization of ideas [by] dominant political or community groups." Terminiello v. Chicago.

Justice POWELL, with whom Justice STEWART joins, concurring.

I join the Court's opinion as I agree that Mt. Ephraim has failed altogether to justify its broad restriction of protected expression. This is not to say, however, that some communities are not free—by a more carefully drawn ordinance—to regulate or ban all commercial public entertainment. In my opinion, such an ordinance could be appropriate and valid in a residential community where all commercial activity is excluded. Similarly, a residential community should be able to limit commercial establishments to essential "neighborhood" services permitted in a narrowly zoned area. But the Borough of Mt. Ephraim failed to follow these paths. The ordinance before us was not carefully drawn and, as the Court points out, it is sufficiently over- and under-inclusive that any argument about the need to maintain the residential nature of this community fails as a justification.

Justice STEVENS, concurring in the judgment.

The record in this case leaves so many relevant questions unanswered that the outcome, in my judgment, depends on the allocation of the burden of persuasion. If the case is viewed as a simple attempt by a small residential community to exclude the commercial exploitation of nude dancing from a "setting of tranquility," (Burger, C. J., dissenting), it would seem reasonable to require appellants to overcome the usual presumption that a municipality's zoning enactments are constitutionally valid. [On] the other hand, if one starts, as the Court does, from the premise that "appellants' claims are rooted in the First Amendment," it would seem reasonable to require the Borough to overcome a presumption of invalidity. [Neither] of these characterizations provides me with a satisfactory approach to this case. For appellants' business is located in a commercial zone, and the character of that zone is not unequivocally identified either by the text of the Borough's zoning ordinance or by the evidence in the record. And even though the foliage of the First Amendment may cast protective shadows over some forms of nude dancing, its roots were germinated by more serious concerns that are not necessarily implicated by a content-neutral zoning ordinance banning commercial exploitation of live entertainment. Cf. [American Mini Theatres].

One of the puzzling features of this case is that the character of the prohibition the Borough seeks to enforce is so hard to ascertain. Because the written zoning ordinance purports to ban all commercial uses except those that are specifically listed—and because no form of entertainment is listed— literally it prohibits the commercial exploitation not only of live entertainment, but of motion pictures and inanimate forms as well. But the record indicates that what actually happens in this commercial zone may bear little resemblance to what is described in the text of the zoning ordinance.

The commercial zone in which appellants' adult bookstore is located is situated along the Black Horse Pike, a north-south artery on the eastern fringe of the Borough.[1] The parties seem to agree that this commercial zone is relatively small; presumably, therefore, it contains only a handful of commercial establishments. Among these establishments are Al-Jo's, also known as the Club Al-Jo, My Dad's, and Capriotti's, all of which offer live entertainment.[2] In addition, the zone contains the Mount Ephraim Democratic Club, the Spread Eagle Inn, and Giuseppi's. The record also contains isolated references to establishments known as the Villa Picasso and Millie's. Although not mentioned in the record, Mount Ephraim apparently also supports a commercial motion picture theater.[3]

The record reveals very little about the character of most of these establishments. [The] one fact that does appear with clarity [is] that, in 1973, appellants were issued an amusement license that authorized them to exhibit adult motion pictures which their patrons viewed in private booths in their adult bookstore. Borough officials apparently regarded this business as lawful under the zoning ordinance and compatible with the immediate neighborhood until July of 1976 when appellants repainted their exterior sign and modified their interior exhibition.

Without more information about this commercial enclave on Black Horse Pike, one cannot know whether the change in appellants' business in 1976 introduced cacophony into a tranquil setting or merely a new refrain in a local replica of Place Pigalle. If I were convinced that the former is the correct appraisal of this commercial zone, I would have no hesitation in agreeing with The Chief Justice that even if the live nude dancing is a form

---

1. At oral argument in this Court, counsel for the appellants asserted that the commercial zone extends for 250 feet on either side of the Black Horse Pike, and that the remainder of the Borough is zoned for residential use. The Chief Justice, in dissent, apparently relies upon counsel's description of Mount Ephraim's zoning pattern in support of his contention that Mount Ephraim is a quiet, "'bedroom' community" into which appellants have thrust the disruptive influence of nude dancing. However, counsel's assertion is unsupported by the record in this case, and indeed is inconsistent with the Borough's zoning ordinance. The Zoning Map of the Borough of Mount Ephraim indicates that, rather than containing a single commercial zone, Mount Ephraim in fact contains four commercial zones. [The] record does not reveal to what extent, if any, the three additional commercial zones have been commercially developed, but it is apparent from the Borough's Code that Mount Ephraim either has accepted or is prepared to accept a greater degree of commercial development than that presently found in the vicinity of appellants' bookstore. [Footnote by Justice Stevens.]

2. My Dad's, which is located directly across the street from appellants' bookstore, features a musical combo that plays music from a stage; a vocalist also performs there on occasion. Capriotti's, a dinner club/discotheque, and Al-Jo's also feature live performances by musical groups. The Borough permits live entertainment in these establishments as a prior nonconforming use. [Footnote by Justice Stevens.]

3. Counsel for both parties informed the Court at oral argument that a motion picture theater is in operation in Mount Ephraim. The theater apparently is located near and to the east of appellants' bookstore. According to counsel for the Borough, the theater is permitted as a prior nonconforming use. [Footnote by Justice Stevens.]

of expressive activity protected by the First Amendment, the Borough may prohibit it.[4] But when the record is opaque, as this record is, I believe the Borough must shoulder the burden of demonstrating that appellants' introduction of live entertainment had an identifiable adverse impact on the neighborhood or on the Borough as a whole. It might be appropriate to presume that such an adverse impact would occur if the zoning plan itself were narrowly drawn to create categories of commercial uses that unambiguously differentiated this entertainment from permitted uses. However, this open-ended ordinance affords no basis for any such presumption.

The difficulty in this case is that we are left to speculate as to the Borough's reasons for proceeding against appellants' business, and as to the justification for the distinction the Borough has drawn between live and other forms of entertainment. While a municipality need not persuade a federal court that its zoning decisions are correct as a matter of policy, when First Amendment interests are implicated, it must at least be able to demonstrate that a uniform policy in fact exists and is applied in a content-neutral fashion. Presumably, municipalities may regulate expressive activity—even protected activity—pursuant to narrowly-drawn content-neutral standards; however, they may not regulate protected activity when the only standard provided is the unbridled discretion of a municipal official. Compare Saia v. New York with Kovacs v. Cooper.[5] Because neither the text of the zoning ordinance, nor the evidence in the record, indicates that Mount Ephraim applied narrowly-drawn content-neutral standards to the appellants' business, for me this case involves a criminal prosecution of appellants simply because one of their employees has engaged in expressive activity that has been assumed arguendo to be protected by the First Amendment.[6] Accordingly, and without endorsing the overbreadth analysis employed by the Court, I concur in its judgment.

Chief Justice BURGER, with whom Justice REHNQUIST joins, dissenting. . . .

4. The Chief Justice states: "It is clear that, in passing the statute challenged here, the citizens of the Borough of Mount Ephraim meant only to preserve the basic character of their community. It is just as clear that, by thrusting its live nude dancing shows on this community, the appellant alters and damages that community over its objections."

The problem with The Chief Justice's analysis, in my judgment, is that "the basic character of [the] community" is not at all clear on the basis of the present record. Although Mount Ephraim apparently is primarily a residential community, it is also a community that in 1973 deemed an adult bookstore that exhibited adult motion pictures, or "peep shows," not inconsistent with its basic character. I simply cannot say with confidence that the addition of a live nude dancer to this commercial zone in 1976 produced a dramatic change in the community's character. [Footnote by Justice Stevens.]

5. The open-ended character of the prohibition in the Mount Ephraim Code presents an opportunity for the exercise of just such unbridled discretion. The Borough has, at different stages of this litigation, advanced two different interpretations of that prohibition. According to one, all commercial entertainment is prohibited within the boundaries of Mount Ephraim; according to the other, only commercial live entertainment is prohibited. Appellants have suggested yet a third possible interpretation. They maintain that the prohibition is applied only against live nude dancing. [Footnote by Justice Stevens.]

6. Like Justice Powell, I have no doubt that some residential communities may, pursuant to a carefully drawn ordinance, regulate or ban commercial

Dissent

The residents of this small enclave chose to maintain their town as a placid, "bedroom" community of a few thousand people. To that end, they passed an admittedly broad regulation prohibiting certain forms of entertainment. Because I believe that a community of people are—within limits—masters of their own environment, I would hold that, as applied, the ordinance is valid.

At issue here is the right of a small community to ban an activity incompatible with a quiet, residential atmosphere. [Mount Ephraim] did nothing more than employ traditional police power to provide a setting of tranquility. [T]he issue *in the case that we have before us* is not whether Mount Ephraim may ban traditional live entertainment, but whether it may ban nude dancing, which is used as the "bait" to induce customers into the appellants' book store. When, and if, this ordinance is used to prevent a high school performance of "The Sound of Music," for example, the Court can deal with that problem.

An overconcern about draftsmanship and overbreadth should not be allowed to obscure the central question before us. It is clear that, in passing the statute challenged here, the citizens [of] Mount Ephraim meant only to preserve the basic character of their community. It is just as clear that, by thrusting its live nude dancing shows on this community, the appellant alters and damages that community over its objections. As applied in this case, therefore, the statute speaks directly and unequivocally. It may be that, as applied in some other case, this statute would violate the First Amendment, but, since such a case is not before us, we should not decide it.

Even assuming that the "expression" manifested in the nude dancing that is involved here is somehow protected speech under the First Amendment, [Mount Ephraim] is entitled to regulate it. Here, as in American Mini Theatres, the zoning ordinance imposes a minimal intrusion on genuine rights of expression; only by contortions of logic can it be made otherwise. Mount Ephraim is a small community on the periphery of two major urban centers [Philadelphia and Camden] where this kind of entertainment may be found acceptable. The fact that nude dancing has been totally banned in this community is irrelevant. "Chilling" this kind of show business in this tiny residential enclave can hardly be thought to show that the appellants' "message" will be prohibited in nearby—and more sophisticated —cities. The fact that a form of expression enjoys some constitutional protection does not mean that there are not times and places inappropriate for its exercise. The towns and villages of this nation are not, and should not be forced into, a mold cast by this Court. Citizens should be free to choose to shape their community so that it embodies their conception of the "decent life." This will sometimes mean deciding that certain forms of activity—factories, gas stations, sports stadia, bookstores, and surely live nude shows— will not be allowed. That a community is willing to tolerate such a commercial use as a convenience store, a gas station, a pharmacy, or a delicatessen

public entertainment within their boundaries. Surely, a municipality zoned entirely for residential use need not create a special commercial zone solely to accommodate purveyors of entertainment. Cf. Valley View Village v. Proffett, 221 F.2d 412, 417–418 (CA6 1955) (Stewart, J.) (zoning ordinance that provides only for residential use is not per se invalid). Mount Ephraim, however, is not such a municipality. [Footnote by Justice Stevens.]

does not compel it also to tolerate every other "commercial use," including pornography peddlers and live nude shows.

[To] say that there is a First Amendment right to impose every form of expression on every community, including the kind of "expression" involved here, is sheer nonsense. To enshrine such a notion in the Constitution ignores fundamental values that the Constitution ought to protect. To invoke the First Amendment to protect the activity involved in this case trivializes and demeans that great Amendment.*

10th ED., p. 1258; IND. RTS., p. 878
Add to footnote 4:

For a recent application of the themes of offensiveness and intrusiveness, see Bolger v. Youngs Drug Products Corp., 463 U.S. —— (1983), discussed below, addition to 10th Ed., p. 1406; Ind.Rts., p. 1026.

10th ED., p. 1262; IND. RTS., p. 882
Add after the Note (before Sec. 2F):

BILLBOARD REGULATIONS: TWO–TIER ANALYSIS IN 1981

METROMEDIA, INC. v. SAN DIEGO

453 U.S. 490, 101 S.Ct. 2882, 69 L.Ed.2d 800 (1981)

Justice WHITE announced the judgment of the Court and delivered an opinion in which Justice STEWART, Justice MARSHALL and Justice POWELL join.

This case involves the validity of an ordinance [of] San Diego, Cal., imposing substantial prohibitions on the erection of outdoor advertising displays within the city.

(I) Stating that its purpose was "to eliminate hazards to pedestrians and motorists brought about by distracting sign displays" and "to preserve and improve the appearance of the City," San Diego enacted an ordinance to prohibit "outdoor advertising display signs." † ["Advertising display signs"] include any sign that "directs attention to a product, service or activity, event, person, institution or business."

The ordinance provides two kinds of exceptions to the general prohibition: on-site signs and signs falling within 12 specified categories. On-site signs are defined as those "designating the name of the owner or occupant of the premises upon which such signs are placed, or identifying such premises; or signs advertising goods manufactured or produced or services rendered on the premises upon which such signs are placed." The specific categories exempted from the prohibition include government signs and "temporary politi-

---

* Note the frequent references to Schad in several of the opinions in Metromedia, Inc. v. San Diego, 453 U.S. 490 (1981), where the Court considered First Amendment challenges to a billboard regulation. The case is printed below, addition to 10th Ed., p. 1262; Ind.Rts., p. 882.

† The California Supreme Court subsequently defined the term "advertising display sign" as "a rigidly assembled sign, display, or device permanently affixed to the ground or permanently attached to a building or other inherently permanent structure constituting, or used for the display of, a commercial or other advertisement to the public."

cal campaign signs"† Under this scheme, on-site commercial advertising is permitted, but other commercial advertising and noncommercial communications using fixed-structure signs are everywhere forbidden unless permitted by one of the specified exceptions.

Appellants are companies that were engaged in the outdoor advertising business in San Diego at the time the ordinance was passed. Each owns a substantial number of outdoor advertising displays (approximately 500 to 800) within the city. These signs are all located in areas zoned for commercial and industrial purposes, most of them on property leased by the owners to appellants for the purpose of maintaining billboards. Each sign [has] a fair market value of between $2,500 and $25,000. Space on the signs was made available to "all comers" and the copy on each sign changed regularly, usually monthly. [Although] the purchasers of advertising space on appellants' signs usually seek to convey a commercial message, their billboards have also been used to convey a broad range of noncommercial political and social messages.

Appellants brought suit in state court to enjoin enforcement of the ordinance. [They prevailed in the lower courts, but the California Supreme Court upheld the ordinance against a First Amendment attack.]

II. [We] have not given plenary consideration to cases involving First Amendment challenges to statutes or ordinances limiting the use of billboards, preferring on several occasions summarily to affirm decisions sustaining state or local legislation directed at billboards. [Justice White noted several summary dispositions between 1969 and 1979.] . . .

III. This Court has often faced the problem of applying the broad principles of the First Amendment to unique forums of expression. See, e.g., [Consolidated Edison v. Public Service Comm'n]. Even a cursory reading of these opinions reveals that at times First Amendment values must yield to other societal interests. These cases support the cogency of Justice Jackson's remark in Kovacs v. Cooper: Each method of communicating ideas is "a law unto itself" and that law must reflect the "differing natures, values, abuses and dangers" of each method. We deal here with the law of billboards.

Billboards are a well-established medium of communication, used to convey a broad range of different kinds of messages. [The] record in this case indicates that besides the typical commercial uses, San Diego billboards have been used [for a variety of public interest and political messages]. But whatever its communicative function, the billboard remains a "large, immobile, and permanent structure which like other structures is subject [to] regulation." Moreover, because it is designed to stand out and apart from its surroundings, the billboard creates a unique set of problems for land-use planning and development. Billboards, then, like other media of

---

† Justice White summarized the exempted categories as follows: government signs; signs located at public bus stops; signs manufactured, transported or stored within the city, if not used for advertising purposes; commemorative historical plaques; religious symbols; signs within shopping malls; for-sale and for-lease signs; signs on public and commercial vehicles; signs depicting time, temperature, and news; approved temporary, off-premises, subdivision directional signs; and "temporary political campaign signs."

[Handwritten margin notes: Challenge is by companies in outdoor adv. business owning outdoor display. / 500-800 signs w/in city, each having value 2.5k → 25k / commercial, political and social messages displayed / Calif S.C. upheld ordinance / Each Medium is a "Law unto Itself" / we deal here with "Law of Billboards." / Exempted Signs]

communication, combine communicative and noncommunicative aspects. As with other media, the government has legitimate interests in controlling the noncommunicative aspects of the medium, but [the First Amendment fore-closes] a similar interest in controlling the communicative aspects. Because regulation of the noncommunicative aspects of a medium often impinges to some degree on the communicative aspects, it has been necessary for the courts to reconcile the government's regulatory interests with the individual's right to expression. [Performance] of this task requires a particularized inquiry into the nature of the conflicting interests at stake here, beginning with a precise appraisal of the character of the ordinance as it affects communication.

As construed by the California Supreme Court, the ordinance restricts the use of certain kinds of outdoor signs. That restriction is defined in two ways: first, by reference to the structural characteristics of the sign; second, by reference to the content, or message, of the sign. Thus, the regulation only applies to a "permanent structure constituting, or used for the display of, a commercial or other advertisement to the public." Within that class, the only permitted signs are those (1) identifying the premises on which the sign is located, or its owner or occupant, or advertising the goods produced or services rendered on such property and (2) those within one of the specified exemptions to the general prohibition, such as temporary political campaign signs. To determine if any billboard is prohibited by the ordinance, one must determine how it is constructed, where it is located, and what message it carries.

Thus, under the ordinance (1) a sign advertising goods or services available on the property where the sign is located is allowed; (2) a sign on a building or other property advertising goods or services produced or offered elsewhere is barred; (3) noncommercial advertising, unless within one of the specific exceptions, is everywhere prohibited. The occupant of property may advertise his own goods or services; he may not advertise the goods or services of others, nor may he display most noncommercial messages.

IV) Appellants' principal submission is that enforcement of the ordinance will eliminate the outdoor advertising business in San Diego and that the [First Amendment bars] the elimination of this medium of communication. Appellants contend that the city may bar neither all off-site commercial signs nor all noncommercial advertisements and that even if it may bar the former, it may not bar the latter. [Because] our cases have consistently distinguished between the constitutional protection afforded commercial as opposed to noncommercial speech, in evaluating appellants' contention we consider separately the effect of the ordinance on commercial and noncommercial speech.

The extension of First Amendment protections to purely commercial speech is a relatively recent development in First Amendment jurisprudence. [The "commercial speech" developments are more fully considered in Sec. 3 of the next chapter.] [In Virginia Pharmacy (1976)], we plainly held that speech proposing no more than a commercial transaction enjoys a substantial degree of First Amendment protection: A state may not completely suppress the dissemination of truthful information about an entirely lawful activity merely because it is fearful of that information's effect upon its disseminators and its recipients. That decision, however, did not equate commercial and noncommercial speech for First Amendment purposes; indeed, it expressly indicated the contrary.

[In Central Hudson (1980), we] adopted a four-part test for determining the validity of government restrictions on commercial speech as distinguished from more fully protected speech. (1) The First Amendment protects commercial speech only if that speech concerns lawful activity and is not misleading. A restriction on otherwise protected commercial speech is valid only if it (2) seeks to implement a substantial governmental interest, (3) directly advances that interest, and (4) reaches no farther than necessary to accomplish the given objective. Appellants agree that the proper approach to be taken in determining the validity of the restrictions on commercial speech is that which was articulated in Central Hudson, but assert that the San Diego ordinance fails that test. We do not agree.

There can be little controversy over the application of the first, second, and fourth criteria. There is no suggestion that the commercial advertising at issue here involves unlawful activity or is misleading. Nor can there be substantial doubt that the twin goals that the ordinance seeks to further—traffic safety and the appearance of the city—are substantial governmental goals. It is far too late to contend otherwise with respect to either traffic safety, Railway Express Agency, Inc. v. New York, or esthetics, see [e.g., Belle Terre v. Boraas]. Similarly, we reject appellants' claim that the ordinance is broader than necessary and, therefore, fails the fourth part of the Central Hudson test. If the city has a sufficient basis for believing that billboards are traffic hazards and are unattractive, then obviously the most direct and perhaps the only effective approach to solving the problems they create is to prohibit them. The city has gone no farther than necessary in seeking to meet its ends. Indeed, it has stopped short of fully accomplishing its ends: It has not prohibited all billboards, but allows on-site advertising and some other specifically exempted signs.

The more serious question, then, concerns the third of the Central Hudson criteria: Does the ordinance "directly advance" governmental interests in traffic safety and in the appearance of the city? It is asserted that the record is inadequate to show any connection between billboards and traffic safety. The California Supreme Court noted the meager record on this point but held "as a matter of law that an ordinance which eliminates billboards designed to be viewed from the streets and highways reasonably relates to traffic safety." Noting that "billboards are intended to, and undoubtedly do, divert a driver's attention from the roadway" and that whether the "distracting effect contributes to traffic accidents invokes an issue of continuing controversy," the California Supreme Court agreed with many other courts that a legislative judgment that billboards are traffic hazards is not manifestly unreasonable and should not be set aside. We likewise hesitate to disagree with the accumulated, common-sense judgments of local lawmakers and of the many reviewing courts that billboards are real and substantial hazards to traffic safety.[1]

---

1. Justice White's footnote at this point cited 11 state and lower federal court decisions accepting the traffic hazard rationale and 3 decisions rejecting the rationale.

There is nothing here to suggest that these judgments are unreasonable. [See the Railway Express case (10th Ed., p. 681; Ind. Rts., p. 301).]

We reach a similar result with respect to the second asserted justification for the ordinance—advancement of the city's esthetic interests. It is not speculative to recognize that billboards by their very nature, wherever located and however constructed, can be perceived an "esthetic harm." San Diego, like many other States and municipalities, has chosen to minimize the presence of such structures. Such esthetic judgments are necessarily subjective, defying objective evaluation, and for that reason must be carefully scrutinized to determine if they are only a public rationalization of an impermissible purpose. But there is no claim in this case that San Diego has as an ulterior motive the suppression of speech, and the judgment involved here is not so unusual as to raise suspicions in itself.

It is nevertheless argued that the city denigrates its interest in traffic safety and beauty and defeats its own case by permitting on-site advertising and other specified signs. Appellants question whether the distinction between on-site and off-site advertising on the same property is justifiable in terms of either esthetics or traffic safety. The ordinance permits the occupant of property to use billboards located on that property to advertise goods and services offered at that location; identical billboards, equally distracting and unattractive, that advertise goods or services available elsewhere are prohibited even if permitting the latter would not multiply the number of billboards. Despite the apparent incongruity, this argument has been rejected at least implicity, in all of the cases sustaining the distinction between off-site and on-site commercial advertising. We agree with those cases and with our own [summary dispositions in recent years].

In the first place, whether on-site advertising is permitted or not, the prohibition of off-site advertising is directly related to the stated objectives of traffic safety and esthetics. This is not altered by the fact that the ordinance is underinclusive because it permits on-site advertising. Second, the city may believe that off-site advertising, with its periodically changing content, presents a more acute problem than does on-site advertising. See [Railway Express]. Third, San Diego has obviously chosen to value one kind of commercial speech—on-site advertising—more than another kind of commercial speech—off-site advertising. The ordinance reflects a decision by the city that the former interest, but not the latter, is stronger than the city's interests in traffic safety and esthetics. The city has decided that in a limited instance —on-site commercial advertising—its interests should yield. We do not reject that judgment. As we see it, the city could reasonably conclude that a commercial enterprise—as well as the interested public—has a stronger interest in identifying its place of business and advertising the products or services available there than it has in using or leasing its available space for the purpose of advertising commercial enterprises located elsewhere. See [e.g., Railway Express (Jackson, J., concurring)]. It does not follow from the fact that the city has concluded that some commercial interests outweigh its municipal interests in this context that it must give similar weight to all other commercial advertising. Thus, off-site commercial billboards may be prohibited while on-site commercial billboards are permitted.

The constitutional problem in this area requires resolution of the conflict between the city's land-use interests and the commercial interests of those seeking to purvey goods and services within the city. In light of the above analysis, we cannot conclude that the city has drawn an ordinance broader than is necessary to meet its interests, or that it fails directly to advance substantial government interests. In sum, insofar as it regulates commercial speech the San Diego ordinance meets the constitutional requirements of Central Hudson.

V. It does not follow, however, that San Diego's general ban on signs carrying noncommercial advertising is also valid under the [First Amendment]. The fact that the city may value commercial messages relating to on-site goods and services more than it values commercial communications relating to off-site goods and services does not justify prohibiting an occupant from displaying its own ideas or those of others.

As indicated above, our recent commercial speech cases have consistently accorded noncommercial speech a greater degree of protection than commercial speech. San Diego effectively inverts this judgment, by affording a greater degree of protection to commercial than to noncommercial speech. There is a broad exception for on-site commercial advertisements, but there is no similar exception for noncommercial speech. The use of on-site billboards to carry commercial messages related to the commercial use of the premises is freely permitted, but the use of otherwise identical billboards to carry noncommercial messages is generally prohibited. The city does not explain how or why noncommercial billboards located in places where commercial billboards are permitted would be more threatening to safe driving or would detract more from the beauty of the city. Insofar as the city tolerates billboards at all, it cannot choose to limit their content to commercial messages; the city may not conclude that the communication of commercial information concerning goods and services connected with a particular site is of greater value than the communication of noncommercial messages.

Furthermore, the ordinance contains exceptions that permit various kinds of noncommercial signs, whether on property where goods and services are offered or not, that would otherwise be within the general ban. A fixed sign may be used to identify any piece of property and its owner. Any piece of property may carry or display religious symbols, commemorative plaques of recognized historical societies and organizations, signs carrying news items or telling the time or temperature, signs erected in discharge of any governmental function, or temporary political campaign signs.[2] No other noncommercial or ideological signs meeting the structural definition are permitted, regardless of their effect on traffic safety or esthetics.

Although the city may distinguish between the relative value of different categories of commercial speech, the city does not have the same range of

2. In this sense, this case presents the opposite situation from that in Lehman and Greer v. Spock, 424 U.S. 828 (1976). In both of those cases a government agency had chosen to prohibit from a certain forum speech relating to political campaigns, while other kinds of speech were permitted. In both cases this Court upheld the prohibition, but both cases turned on unique fact situations involving government-created forums and have no application here. [Footnote by Justice White.]

choice in the area of noncommercial speech to evaluate the strength of, or distinguish between, various communicative interests. See [e.g., Mosley]. With respect to noncommercial speech, the city may not choose the appropriate subjects for public discourse: "To allow a government the choice of permissible subjects for public debate would be to allow that government control over the search for political truth." Consolidated Edison. Because some noncommercial messages may be conveyed on billboards throughout the commercial and industrial zones, San Diego must similarly allow billboards conveying other noncommercial messages throughout those zones.[3]

Finally, we reject appellee's suggestion that the ordinance may be appropriately characterized as a reasonable "time, place and manner" restriction. The ordinance does not generally ban billboard advertising as an unacceptable "manner" of communicating information or ideas; rather, it permits various kinds of signs. Signs that are banned are banned everywhere and at all times. We have observed that time, place and manner restrictions are permissible if "they are justified without reference to the content of the regulated speech, [serve] a significant governmental interest, [and] leave open ample alternative channels for communication of the information." [Virginia Pharmacy.] Here, it cannot be assumed that "alternative channels" are available, for the parties stipulated to just the opposite: "Many businesses, politicians and other persons rely upon outdoor advertising because other forms of advertising are insufficient, inappropriate and prohibitively expensive." [It] is apparent as well that the ordinance distinguishes in several ways between permissible and impermissible signs at a particular location by reference to their content. Whether or not these distinctions are themselves constitutional, they take the regulation out of the domain of time, place, and manner restrictions. See [Consolidated Edison].

VI. Despite the rhetorical hyperbole of The Chief Justice's dissent, there is a considerable amount of common ground between the approach taken in this opinion and that suggested by his dissent. Both recognize that

3. Because a total prohibition of outdoor advertising is not before us, we do not indicate whether such a ban would be consistent with the First Amendment. But see [Schad, printed above, addition to 10th Ed., p. 1248; Ind.Rts., p. 868] on the constitutional problems created by a total prohibition of a particular expressive forum, live entertainment in that case. Despite Justice Stevens' insistence to the contrary, we do not imply that the ordinance is unconstitutional because it "does not abridge enough speech."

Similarly, we need not reach any decision in this case as to the constitutionality of the federal Highway Beautification Act of 1965. That Act, like the San Diego ordinance, permits on-site commercial billboards in areas in which it does not permit billboards with noncommercial messages. However, unlike the San Diego ordinance, which prohibits billboards conveying noncommercial messages throughout the city, the federal law does not contain a total prohibition of such billboards in areas adjacent to the Interstate and primary highway systems. As far as the Federal Government is concerned, such billboards are permitted adjacent to the highways in areas zoned industrial or commercial under state law or in unzoned commercial or industrial areas. Regulation of billboards in those areas is left primarily to the States. For this reason, the decision today does not determine the constitutionality of the federal statute. Whether, in fact, the distinction is constitutionally significant can only be determined on the basis of a record establishing the actual effect of the Act on billboards conveying noncommercial messages. [Footnote by Justice White.]

each medium of communication creates a unique set of First Amendment problems, both recognize that the city has a legitimate interest in regulating the noncommunicative aspects of a medium of expression, and both recognize that the proper judicial role is to conduct "a careful inquiry into the competing concerns of the State and the interests protected by the guarantee of free expression." Our principal difference with his dissent is that it gives so little weight to the latter half of this inquiry.[4]

Discussion of Burger's dissent

The Chief Justice [writes:] "Although we must ensure that any regulation of speech 'further[s] a sufficiently substantial government interest' [given] a reasonable approach to a perceived problem, this Court's duty [is] to determine whether the legislative approach is essentially neutral to the messages conveyed and leaves open other adequate means of conveying those messages."[5] Despite his belief that this is "the essence of democracy," this has never been the approach of this Court when a legislative judgment is challenged as an unconstitutional infringement of First Amendment rights.[6]

By "essentially neutral," The Chief Justice may mean either or both of two things. He may mean that government restrictions on protected speech are permissible so long as the government does not favor one side over another on a subject of public controversy. This concept of neutrality was specifically rejected by the Court last Term [in Consolidated Edison]. There, the Court dismissed the Commission's contention that a prohibition of all discussion, regardless of the viewpoint expressed, on controversial issues of public policy does not unconstitutionally suppress freedom of speech. "The First

4. Justice Stevens' suggested standard seems to go even further than The Chief Justice in ignoring the private interests protected by the First Amendment. He suggests that regulation of speech is permissible so long as it is not biased in favor of a particular position and leaves open "ample" means of communication. Nowhere does he suggest that the strength or weakness of the government's interests is a factor in the analysis. [Footnote by Justice White.]

5. The Chief Justice correctly notes that traditional labels should not be substituted for analysis and, therefore, he correctly rejects any simple classification of the San Diego ordinance as either a "prohibition" or a "time, place, and manner restriction." These "labels" or "categories," however, have played an important role in this Court's analysis of First Amendment problems in the past. The standard The Chief Justice himself adopts appears to be based almost exclusively on prior discussions of time, place and manner restrictions. See [e.g.] Heffron [printed earlier in this Supplement, addition to 10th Ed., p. 1219; Ind.Rts., p. 839]; Consolidated Edison.

But this Court has never held that the less strict standard of review applied to time, place, and manner restrictions is appropriately used in every First Amendment case, or that it is the most that the First Amendment requires of government legislation which infringes on protected speech. If this were the case, there would be no need for the detailed inquiry this Court consistently pursues in order to answer the question of whether a challenged restriction is in fact a time, place, and manner restriction—the same standard of review would apply regardless of the outcome of that inquiry. As we demonstrated above, the San Diego ordinance is not such a restriction and there is, therefore, no excuse for applying a lower standard of First Amendment review to that ordinance. [Footnote by Justice White.]

6. Nor has this Court ever accepted the view that it must defer to a legislative judgment that a particular medium of communication is "offensive" and "intrusive," merely because "other means [of communication] are available." [Footnote by Justice White.]

Amendment's hostility to content-based regulation extends not only to restrictions on particular viewpoints, but also to prohibition of public discussion of an entire topic." On the other hand, The Chief Justice may mean by neutrality that government restrictions on speech cannot favor certain communicative contents over others. As a general rule, this, of course, is correct, see, e.g., [Mosley]; Carey v. Brown. The general rule, in fact, is applicable to the facts of this case: San Diego has chosen to favor certain kinds of messages—such as on-site commercial advertising, and temporary political campaign advertisements—over others. Except to imply that the favored categories are for some reason de minimis in a constitutional sense, his dissent fails to explain why San Diego should not be held to have violated this concept of First Amendment neutrality.

Taken literally The Chief Justice's approach would require reversal of the many cases striking down antisolicitation statutes on First Amendment grounds: In each of them the city would argue that preventing distribution of leaflets rationally furthered the city's interest in limiting litter, applied to all kinds of leaflets, and hence did not violate the principle of government neutrality and left open alternative means of communication. See, e.g., Martin v. Struthers; [Schneider]. Despite the dissent's assertion to the contrary, however, it has been this Court's consistent position that democracy stands on a [stronger] footing when courts protect First Amendment interests against legislative intrusion, rather than deferring to merely rational legislative judgments in this area.

Because The Chief Justice misconceives the nature of the judicial function in this situation, he misunderstands the significance of the city's extensive exceptions to its billboard prohibition. He characterizes these exceptions as "essentially negligible," and then opines that it borders on the frivolous to suggest that in "allowing such signs but forbidding noncommercial billboards, the city has infringed freedom of speech." That, of course, is not the nature of this argument.

There can be no question that a prohibition on the erection of billboards infringes freedom of speech: The exceptions do not create the infringement, rather the general prohibition does. But the exceptions to the general prohibition are of great significance in assessing the strength of the city's interest in prohibiting billboards. We conclude that by allowing commercial establishments to use billboards to advertise the products and services they offer, the city necessarily has conceded that some communicative interests, e.g., on-site commercial advertising, are stronger than its competing interests in esthetics and traffic safety. It has nevertheless banned all noncommercial signs except those specifically excepted.

The Chief Justice agrees that in allowing the exceptions to the rule the city has balanced the competing interests, but he argues that we transgress the judicial role by independently reviewing the relative values the city has assigned to various communicative interests. He seems to argue that although the Constitution affords a greater degree of protection to noncommercial than to commercial speech, a legislature need not make the same choices. This position makes little sense even abstractly, and it surely is not consistent with our cases or with The Chief Justice's own argument that statutes challenged on First Amendment grounds must be evaluated in light of the unique facts and circumstances of the case. Governmental interests are only revealed and given concrete force by the steps taken to meet those interests. If the city has concluded that its official interests are not as strong as private interests in commercial communications, may it nevertheless claim that those same official interests outweigh private interests in noncommercial communications? Our answer, which is consistent with our cases, is in the negative.

VII. Because the San Diego ordinance reaches too far into the realm of protected speech, we conclude that it is unconstitutional on its face.[7]

[Reversed and remanded.] [8]

Justice BRENNAN, with whom Justice BLACKMUN joins, concurring in the judgment.

Believing that "a total prohibition of outdoor advertising is not before us," the plurality does not decide "whether such a ban would be consistent with the First Amendment." Instead, it concludes that San Diego may ban all billboards containing commercial speech messages without violating the First Amendment, thereby sending the signal to municipalities that bifurcated billboard regulations prohibiting commercial messages but allowing noncommercial messages would pass constitutional muster. I write separately because I believe this case in effect presents the total ban question, and because I believe the plurality's bifurcated approach itself raises serious First Amendment problems and relies on a distinction between commercial and noncommercial speech unanticipated by our prior cases.

I. [This] billboard regulation bans all commercial and noncommercial billboard advertising with a few limited exceptions. . . .

II. [Where] the plurality and I disagree is in the characterization of the San Diego ordinance and thus in the appropriate analytical framework to apply. The plurality believes that the question of a total ban is not presented in this case because the ordinance contains exceptions to its general prohibition. In contrast, my view is that the *practical* effect of the San Diego ordinance is to eliminate the billboard as an effective medium of communication for the speaker who wants to express the sorts of messages described in ¶ 23

7. Appellants contend that the ordinance will effectively eliminate their businesses and that this violates the Due Process Clause. We do not know, however, what kind of ordinance, if any, San Diego will seek to enforce in place of that which we invalidate today. In any case, any question of unconstitutional "takings" aside, the Due Process Clause does not afford a greater degree of protection to appellants' business than does the First Amendment. Since we hold that the First Amendment interests in commercial speech are not sufficient to prevent the city from prohibiting off-site commercial advertisements, no different result should be reached under the Due Process Clause. [Footnote by Justice White.]

8. Although the ordinance contains a severability clause, determining the meaning and application of that clause are properly responsibilities of the state courts. [Since] our judgment is based essentially on the inclusion of noncommercial speech within the prohibitions of the ordinance, the California courts may sustain the ordinance by limiting its reach to commercial speech, assuming the ordinance is susceptible to this treatment. [Footnote by Justice White.]

of the Joint Stipulation,* and that the exceptions do not alter the overall character of the ban. Unlike the on-premise sign, the off-premise billboard "is, generally speaking, made available to 'all-comers,' in a fashion similar to newspaper or broadcasting advertising. It is a forum for the communication of messages to the public." Joint Stipulation ¶ 22(c).[1] Speakers in San Diego no longer have the opportunity to communicate their messages of general applicability to the public through billboards. None of the exceptions provides a practical alternative for the general commercial or noncommercial billboard advertiser.

[The] characterization of the San Diego regulation as a total ban of a medium of communication has more than semantic implications, for it suggests a First Amendment analysis quite different from the plurality's. Instead of relying on the exceptions to the ban to invalidate the ordinance, I would apply the tests this Court has developed to analyze content-neutral prohibitions of particular media of communication.[2] Most recently, in [Schad], this Court assessed "the substantiality of the governmental interests asserted" and "whether those interests could be served by means that would be less intrusive on activity protected by the First Amendment," in striking down the Borough's total ban on live commercial entertainment. Schad merely articulated an analysis applied in previous cases concerning total bans of media of expression. E.g., [Schneider; Martin v. Struthers]. [In] the case of billboards, I would hold that a city may totally ban them if it can show that a sufficiently substantial governmental interest is directly furthered by the total ban, and that any more narrowly drawn restriction, i.e., anything less than a total ban, would promote less well the achievement of that goal.

Applying that test to the instant case, I would invalidate the San Diego ordinance. The city has failed to provide adequate justification for its substantial restriction on protected activity. See [Schad]. First, although I have no quarrel with the substantiality of the city's interest in traffic safety, the city has failed to come forward with evidence demonstrating that billboards, actually impair traffic safety in San Diego. Although the plurality hesitates "to

---

* Paragraph 23 of the Joint Stipulation of the parties stated that billboards in San Diego had been used "to advertise national and local products, goods and services, new products being introduced to the consuming public, to publicize the 'City in Motion' campaign of the City of San Diego, to communicate messages from candidates for municipal, state and national offices, including candidates for judicial office, to propose marriage, to seek employment, to encourage the use of seat belts, to denounce the United Nations, to seek support for Prisoners of War and Missing in Action, to promote the United Crusade and a variety of other charitable and socially-related endeavors and to provide directions to the traveling public."

1. Perusal of the photographs of billboards included in the Appendix to

the Jurisdictional Statement filed in this Court reveals the wide range of noncommercial messages communicated through billboards, including the following: "Welcome to San Diego[:] Home of 1,100 Underpaid Cops"; "Support San Diego's No-Growth Policy[:] Spend Your Money in Los Angeles!"; "Voluntary Integration, Better Education By Choice"; "Support America's First Environment Strike. Don't Buy Shell!"; and "Get US out! of the United Nations." [Footnote by Justice Brennan.]

2. Different factors come into play when the challenged legislation is simply a time, place, or manner regulation rather than a total ban of a particular medium of expression. [Footnote by Justice Brennan.]

disagree with the accumulated, common sense judgments of local lawmakers and of the many reviewing courts that billboards are real and substantial hazards to traffic safety," I would not be so quick to accept legal conclusions in other cases as an adequate substitute for evidence *in this case* that banning billboards directly furthers traffic safety.[3] Moreover, the ordinance is not narrowly drawn to accomplish the traffic safety goal. Although it contains an exception for signs "not visible from any point on the boundary of the premises," billboards not visible from the street but nevertheless visible from the "boundary of the premises" are not exempted from the regulation's prohibition.

Second, I think that the city has failed to show that its asserted interest in aesthetics is sufficiently substantial in the commercial and industrial areas of San Diego. [It] is no doubt true that the appearance of certain areas of the city would be enhanced by the elimination of billboards, but "it is not immediately apparent as a matter of experience" that their elimination in all other areas as well would have more than a negligible impact on aesthetics. The Joint Stipulation reveals that "[s]ome sections of the City of San Diego are scenic, some blighted, some containing strips of vehicle related commercial uses, some contain new and attractive office buildings, some functional industrial development and some areas contain older but useful commercial establishments." A billboard is not *necessarily* inconsistent with oil storage tanks, blighted areas, or strip development. Of course, it is not for a court to impose its own notion of beauty on San Diego. But before deferring to a city's judgment, a court must be convinced that the city is seriously and comprehensively addressing aesthetic concerns with respect to its environment. Here, San Diego has failed to demonstrate a comprehensive coordinated effort in its commercial and industrial areas to address other obvious contributors to an unattractive environment. In this sense the ordinance is underinclusive. See [Erznoznik]. Of course, this is not to say that the city must address all aesthetic problems at the same time, or none at all. [But] if billboards alone are banned and no further steps are contemplated or likely, the commitment of the city to improving its physical environment is placed in doubt. By showing a comprehensive commitment to making its physical environment in commercial and industrial areas more attractive, and by allowing only narrowly tailored exceptions, if any,[4] San Diego could demonstrate that its inter-

---

3. Not one of the 11 cases cited by the plurality in its footnote [1] stands for the proposition that reviewing courts have determined that "billboards are real and substantial hazards to traffic safety." These 11 cases merely apply the minimal scrutiny rational relationship test and the presumption of legislative validity to hold that it would not be *unreasonable* or *inconceivable* for a legislature or city government to conclude that billboards are traffic hazards. [Therefore], when the majority states that "there is nothing here to suggest that these judgments are unreasonable," it is really saying that there is nothing un-reasonable about other courts finding that there is nothing unreasonable about a legislative judgment. This is hardly a sufficient finding under the heightened scrutiny appropriate for this case. . . . [Footnote by Justice Brennan.]

4. Appellants argue that the exceptions to the total ban, such as for on-premise signs, undercut the very goals of traffic safety and aesthetics that the city claims as paramount, and therefore invalidate the whole ordinance. But obviously, a city can have special goals the accomplishment of which would conflict with the overall goals

est in creating an aesthetically pleasing environment is genuine and substantial. This is a requirement where, as here, there is an infringement of important constitutional consequence. I have little doubt that some jurisdictions will easily carry the burden of proving the substantiality of their interest in aesthetics. For example, the parties acknowledge that a historical community such as Williamsburg, Va. should be able to prove that its interests in aesthetics and historical authenticity are sufficiently important that the First Amendment value attached to billboards must yield. [I] express no view on whether San Diego or other large urban areas will be able to meet the burden. But San Diego failed to do so here, and for that reason I would strike down its ordinance.

III. The plurality's treatment of the commercial-noncommercial distinction in this case is mistaken in its factual analysis of the San Diego ordinance, and departs from this Court's precedents. In Part IV of its opinion, the plurality concludes that the San Diego ordinance is constitutional insofar as it regulates commercial speech. Under its view, a city with merely a reasonable justification could pick and choose between those commercial billboards it would allow and those it would not, or could totally ban all commercial billboards.[5] In Part V, the plurality concludes, however, that the San Diego ordinance as a whole is unconstitutional because, inter alia, it affords a greater degree of protection to commercial than to noncommercial speech.

[The] plurality apparently reads the on-site premises exception as limited solely to commercial speech. I find no such limitation in the ordinance

addressed by the total billboard ban. It would make little sense to say that a city has an all-or-nothing proposition—either ban all billboards or none at all. Because I conclude that the San Diego ordinance impermissibly infringes First Amendment rights in that the city has failed to justify the ordinance sufficiently in light of substantial governmental interests, I need not decide, as the plurality does in Part V of its opinion, whether the exceptions to the total ban constitute independent grounds for invalidating the regulation. However, if a city can justify a total ban, I would allow an exception only if it directly furthers an interest that is at least as important as the interest underlying the total ban, if the exception is no broader than necessary to advance the special goal, and if the exception is narrowly drawn so as to impinge as little as possible on the overall goal. To the extent that exceptions rely on content-based distinctions, they must be scrutinized with special care.

[My] views in this case make it unnecessary to decide the permissibility of the on-premise exception, but it is not inconceivable that San Diego could incorporate an exception to its overall ban to serve the identification interest without violating the Constitution. I also do not decide the validity of the other exceptions to the San Diego regulation. [Footnote by Justice Brennan.]

5. The plurality comments that "the city could reasonably conclude that a commercial enterprise—as well as the interested public—has a stronger interest in identifying its place of business and advertising the products or services available there than it has in using or leasing its available space for the purpose of advertising commercial enterprises located elsewhere." But [Central Hudson] demands more than a rational basis for preferring one kind of commercial speech over another. Moreover, this case does not present legislation implicating the "commonsense differences" between commercial and noncommercial speech that "'suggest that a different degree of protection is necessary to insure that the flow of truthful and legitimate commercial information is unimpaired.'" There is no suggestion that San Diego's billboard ordinance is designed to deal with "false or misleading signs." [Footnote by Justice Brennan.]

[T]he on-site exception allows "signs designating the name of the owner or occupant of the premises upon which such signs are placed, or identifying such premises; or signs advertising goods manufactured or produced or services rendered on the premises upon which such signs are placed." As I read the ordinance, the content of the sign depends strictly on the identity of the owner or occupant of the premises. If the occupant is a commercial enterprise, the substance of a permissible identifying sign would be commercial. If the occupant is an enterprise usually associated with noncommercial speech, the substance of the identifying sign would be noncommercial. Just as a supermarket or barbershop could identify itself by name, so too could a political campaign headquarters or a public interest group. I would also presume that, if a barbershop could advertise haircuts, a political campaign headquarters could advertise "Vote for Brown," or "Vote for Proposition 13."

More importantly, I cannot agree with the plurality's view that an ordinance totally banning commercial billboards but allowing noncommercial billboards would be constitutional.[6] For me, such an ordinance raises First Amendment problems at least as serious as those raised by a total ban, for it gives city officials the right—before approving a billboard—to determine whether the proposed message is "commercial" or "noncommercial." Of course the plurality is correct when it observes that "our cases have consistently distinguished between the constitutional protection afforded commercial as opposed to noncommercial speech," but it errs in assuming that a *governmental unit* may be put in the position in the first instance of deciding whether the proposed speech is commercial or noncommercial. In individual cases, this distinction is anything but clear. Because making such determinations would entail a substantial exercise of discretion by city officials, it presents a real danger of curtailing noncommercial speech in the guise of regulating commercial speech.

[It] is one thing for a court to classify in specific cases whether commercial or noncommercial speech is involved, but quite another—and for me dispositively so—for a city to do so regularly for the purpose of deciding what messages may be communicated by way of billboards. Cities are equipped to make traditional police power decisions, not decisions based on the content of speech. I would be unhappy to see city officials dealing with the following series of billboards and deciding which ones to permit: the first billboard contains the message "Visit Joe's Ice Cream Shoppe"; the second, "Joe's Ice Cream Shoppe uses only the highest quality dairy products"; the third, "Because Joe thinks that dairy products are good for you, please shop at Joe's

6. Of course, as a matter of marketplace economics, such an ordinance may prove the undoing of *all* billboard advertising, both commercial and noncommercial. It may well be that no company would be able to make a profit maintaining billboards used solely for noncommercial messages. Although the record does not indicate how much of appellant's income is produced by noncommercial communicators, it would not be unreasonable to assume that the bulk of its customers advertise commercial messages. Therefore, noncommercial users may represent such a small percentage of the billboard business that it would be impossible to stay in business based upon their patronage alone. Therefore, the plurality's prescription may represent a de facto ban on both commercial and noncommercial billboards. This is another reason to analyze this case as a "total ban" case. [Footnote by Justice Brennan.]

Shoppe"; and the fourth, "Joe says to support dairy price supports: they mean lower prices for you at his Shoppe." Or how about some San Diego Padres baseball fans—with no connection to the team—who together rent a billboard and communicate the message "Support the San Diego Padres, a great baseball team." May the city decide that a United Automobile Workers billboard with the message "Be a patriot—do not buy Japanese-manufactured cars" is "commercial" and therefore forbid it? What if the same sign is placed by Chrysler? [7]

I do not read our recent line of commercial cases as authorizing this sort of regular and immediate line-drawing by governmental entities. If anything, our cases recognize the difficulty in making a determination that speech is either "commercial" or "noncommercial." "The line between ideological and nonideological speech is impossible to draw with accuracy." [Lehman (Brennan, J., dissenting).] I have no doubt that those who seek to convey commercial messages will engage in the most imaginative of exercises to place themselves within the safe haven of noncommercial speech, while at the same time conveying their commercial message. Encouraging such behavior can only make the job of city officials—who already are inclined to ban billboards—that much more difficult and potentially intrusive upon legitimate noncommercial expression. . . .

Chief Justice BURGER, dissenting.

Today the Court takes an extraordinary—even a bizarre—step by severely limiting the power of a city to act on risks it perceives to traffic safety and the environment posed by large, permanent billboards. Those joining the plurality opinion invalidate a city's effort to minimize these traffic hazards and eyesores simply because, in exercising rational legislative judgment, it has chosen to permit a narrow class of signs that serve special needs.

Relying on simplistic platitudes about content, subject matter, and the dearth of other means to communicate, the billboard industry attempts to escape the real and growing problems every municipality faces in protecting safety and preserving the environment in an urban area. The Court's disposition of the serious issues involved exhibits insensitivity to the impact of these billboards on those who must live with them and the delicacy of the legislative judgments involved in regulating them. American cities desiring to mitigate the dangers mentioned must, as a matter of *federal constitutional law*, elect between two unsatisfactory options: (a) allowing all "noncommercial" signs, no matter how many, how dangerous, or how damaging to the environment; or (b) forbidding signs altogether. Indeed, lurking in the recesses of today's opinions is a not-so-veiled threat that the second option, too, may soon be withdrawn. This is the long arm and voracious appetite of federal power —this time judicial power—with a vengeance, reaching and absorbing traditional concepts [of] local authority.

7. These are not mere hypotheticals that can never occur. The Oil, Chemical and Atomic Workers Int'l Union, AFL–CIO, actually placed a billboard advertisement stating: "Support America's First Environment Strike. Don't Buy Shell!" What if Exxon had placed the advertisement? Could Shell respond in kind? [Footnote by Justice Brennan.]

(1). [1] fear that those joining in today's disposition have become mesmerized with broad, but not controlling, language appearing in our prior opinions but now torn from its original setting. [It] is not really relevant whether the San Diego ordinance is viewed as a regulation regarding time, place, and manner, or as a total prohibition on a medium with some exceptions defined, in part, by content. Regardless of the label we give it, we are discussing a very simple and basic question: the authority of local government to protect its citizens' legitimate interests in traffic safety and the environment by eliminating distracting and ugly structures from its buildings and roadways, to define which billboards actually pose that danger, and to decide whether, in certain instances, the public's need for information outweighs the dangers perceived. The billboard industry's superficial sloganeering is no substitute for analysis, and the plurality and the concurring opinions adopt much of that approach uncritically. Generally constitutional principles indeed apply, but "each case ultimately must depend on its own specific facts." [Erznoznik.]

(2)(a) [The] uniqueness of the medium, the availability of alternative means of communication, and the public interest the regulation serves are important factors to be weighed; and the balance very well may shift when attention is turned from one medium to another. Regulating newspapers, for example, is vastly different from regulating billboards. Some level of protection is generally afforded to the medium a speaker chooses, but as we have held just this past week in [Heffron], "the First Amendment does not guarantee the right to communicate one's views at all times and places or in any manner that may be desired." (Emphasis added). [See also Justice Black in Adderley.] In the 1979 Term, we once again reaffirmed that restrictions are valid if they "serve a significant governmental interest and leave ample alternative channels for communication." [Consolidated Edison.] The Court has continued to apply this same standard almost literally to this day in [Heffron]. Accord, [Schad].

(b). San Diego adopted its ordinance to eradicate what it perceives—and what it has a right to perceive—as ugly and dangerous eyesores thrust upon its citizens. [Having] acknowledged the legitimacy of local governmental authority, the plurality largely ignores it. As the plurality also recognizes, the means the city has selected to advance these goals are sensible and do not exceed what is necessary to eradicate the dangers seen. The means chosen to effectuate legitimate governmental interests are not for this Court to select. "These are matters for the legislative judgment controlled by public opinion." Kovacs v. Cooper (Frankfurter, J., concurring). The plurality ignores this Court's seminal opinions in Kovacs by substituting their judgment for that of city officials and disallowing a ban on one offensive and intrusive means of communication when other means are available. Although we must ensure that any regulation of speech "further[s] a sufficiently substantial government interest" [Schad], given a reasonable approach to a perceived problem, this Court's duty is not to make the primary policy decisions but instead is to determine whether the legislative approach is essentially neutral to the messages conveyed and leaves open other adequate means of conveying those messages. This is the essence of both democracy and federalism, and we gravely damage both when we undertake to throttle legislative discretion and judgment at the "grass roots" of our system.

(c). [Of course] the city has restricted one form of communication and this action implicates the First Amendment. But to say the ordinance presents a First Amendment *issue* is not necessarily to say that it constitutes a First Amendment *violation*. The plurality confuses the Amendment's coverage with the scope of its protection. In the process of eradicating the perceived harms, the ordinance here in no sense suppresses freedom of expression, either by discriminating among ideas or topics or by suppressing discussion generally. [Moreover], aside from a few narrow and essentially negligible exceptions, San Diego has not differentiated with regard to topic.

[The] messages conveyed on San Diego billboards—whether commercial, political, social, or religious—are not inseparable from the billboards that carry them. These same messages can reach an equally large audience through a variety of other media: newspapers, television, radio, magazines, direct mail, pamphlets, etc. True, these other methods may not be so "eye-catching"—or so cheap—as billboards, but there has been no suggestion that billboards heretofore have advanced any particular viewpoint or issue disproportionately to advertising generally. Thus, the ideas billboard advertisers have been presenting are not *relatively* disadvantaged vis-à-vis the messages of those who heretofore have chosen other methods of spreading their views. It borders on the frivolous to suggest that the San Diego ordinance infringes on freedom of expression, given the wide range of alternative means available.

(3) (a). The plurality concludes that a city may constitutionally exercise its police power by eliminating off-site *commercial* billboards; they reach this result by following our recent cases holding that commercial speech, while protected by the Constitution, receives less protection than "noncommercial" —i.e., political, religious, social—speech. But as the plurality giveth, they also taketh away—and, in the process take away virtually everything.

In a bizarre twist of logic, the plurality seems to hold that *because* San Diego has recognized the hardships of its ordinance on certain special needs of citizens and, therefore, exempted a few narrowly defined classes of signs from the ordinance's scope, [the] ordinance violates the First Amendment. From these dubious premises, the plurality has given every city, town, and village in this country desiring to respond to the hazards posed by billboards a choice between two equally unsatisfactory alternatives: (a) banning all signs of any kind whatsoever, or (b) permitting all "noncommercial" signs, no matter how numerous, how large, how damaging to the environment, or how dangerous to motorists and pedestrians. Otherwise, the municipality must give up and do nothing in the face of an ever-increasing menace to the urban environment. Indeed, the plurality hints—and not too subtly—that the first option might be withdrawn if any city attempts to invoke it. See [footnote [3] in the plurality opinion]. This result is insensitive to the needs of the modern urban dweller and devoid of valid constitutional foundations.

(b)   The exceptions San Diego has provided—the presence of which is the plurality's sole ground for invalidating the ordinance—are few in number, are narrowly tailored to peculiar public needs, and do not remotely endanger freedom of speech. [Where] the ordinance does differentiate among topics, it simply allows such noncontroversial things as conventional signs identifying a business enterprise, time-and-temperature signs, historical markers, and for-sale signs. It borders—if not trespasses—on the frivolous to suggest that, by allowing such signs but forbidding noncommercial billboards, the city has infringed freedom of speech. [A] city's simultaneous recognition of the need for certain exceptions permitting limited forms of communication, purely factual in nature and neutral as to the speaker, should not wholly deprive the city of its ability to address the balance of the [problem.]

(c). The fatal flaw in the plurality's logic comes when they conclude that San Diego, by exempting on-site commercial signs, thereby has "afford-[ed] a greater degree of protection to commercial than to noncommercial speech." The "greater degree of protection" our cases have given noncommercial speech establishes a narrower range of constitutionally permissible regulation. To say [noncommercial] speech receives a greater degree of *constitutional* protection, however, does not mean that a legislature is forbidden to afford differing degrees of *statutory* protection when the restrictions on each form of speech—commercial and noncommercial—otherwise pass constitutional muster under the standards respectively applicable.

No case in this Court creates, as the plurality suggests, a hierarchy of types of speech in which if one type is actually protected through legislative judgment, the Constitution compels that judgment be exercised in favor of all types ranking higher on the list. When a city chooses to impose looser restrictions in one area than it does in another analogous area—even one in which the Constitution more narrowly constrains legislative discretion—it neither undermines the constitutionality of its regulatory scheme nor renders its legislative choices ipso facto irrational. A city does not thereby "conced[e] that some communicative interests [are] stronger than its competing interests in esthetics and traffic safety," ante; it has only declined, in one area, to exercise its powers to the full extent the Constitution permits. The Constitution does not require any governmental entity to reach the limit of permissible regulation solely because it has chosen to do so in a related area. Cf. Williamson v. Lee Optical Co. The plurality today confuses the degree of constitutional protection—i.e., the strictness of the test applied—with the outcome of legislative judgment.

By allowing communication of certain commercial ideas via billboards, but forbidding noncommercial signs altogether, a city does not necessarily place a greater "value" on commercial speech. In these situations, the city is simply recognizing that it has greater latitude to distinguish among various forms of commercial communication when the same distinctions would be impermissible if undertaken with regard to noncommercial speech. Indeed, when adequate alternative channels of communication are readily available so that the message may be freely conveyed through other means, a city arguably is more faithful to the Constitution by treating all noncommercial speech the same than by attempting to impose the same classifications in noncommercial as it has in commercial areas. To undertake the same kind of balancing and content judgment with noncommercial speech that is permitted with commercial speech is far more likely to run afoul of the First Amendment.

Thus, we may, consistent with the First Amendment, hold that a city may—and perhaps must—take an all-or-nothing approach with noncommercial speech yet remain free to adopt selective exceptions for commercial speech, as long as the latter advance legitimate governmental interests. Indeed, it is precisely *because* "the city does not have the same range of choice in the area of noncommercial speech to evaluate the strength of, or distinguish between, various communicative interests" that a city should be commended, not condemned, for treating all noncommercial speech the same.

(4). The Court today unleashes a novel principle, unnecessary and, indeed, alien to First Amendment doctrine announced in our earlier cases. As Justice Stevens cogently observes, the plurality, "somewhat ironically, concludes that the ordinance is an unconstitutional abridgment of speech because it does not abridge enough speech." (Emphasis added.) The plurality gravely misconstrues the commercial-noncommercial distinction of earlier cases when they hold that the preferred position of noncommercial speech compels a city to impose the same or greater limits on commercial as on noncommercial speech. The Court today leaves the modern metropolis with a series of Hobson's choices and rejects basic concepts of federalism. [This] is indeed "an exercise of raw judicial power," Doe v. Bolton (White, J., dissenting), and is far removed from the high purposes of the First Amendment.

Justice REHNQUIST, dissenting.

I agree substantially with the views expressed in the dissenting opinions of The Chief Justice and Justice Stevens and make only these two additional observations: (1) In a case where city planning commissions and zoning boards must regularly confront constitutional claims of this sort, it is a genuine misfortune to have the Court's treatment of the subject be a virtual Tower of Babel, from which no definitive principles can be clearly drawn; and (2) I regret even more keenly my contribution to this judicial clangor, but find that none of the views expressed in the other opinions written in the case come close enough to mine to warrant the necessary compromise to obtain a Court opinion.

In my view, the aesthetic justification alone is sufficient to sustain a total prohibition of billboards within a community, regardless of whether the particular community is "a historic community such as Williamsburg" or one as unsightly as the older parts of many of our major metropolitan areas. Such areas should not be prevented from taking steps to correct, as best they may, mistakes of their predecessors. Nor do I believe that the limited exceptions contained in the San Diego ordinance are the type which render this statute unconstitutional. The closest one is the exception permitting billboards during political campaigns, but I would treat this as a virtually self-limiting exception which will have an effect on the aesthetics of the city only during the periods immediately prior to a campaign. As such, it seems to me a reasonable outlet, limited as to time, for the free expression which the First and Fourteenth Amendments were designed to protect.

Unlike Justice Brennan, I do not think a city should be put to the task of convincing a local judge that the elimination of billboards would have more than a negligible impact on aesthetics. Nothing in my experience on the bench has led me to believe that a judge is in any better position than a city or county commission to make decisions in an area such as aesthetics. Therefore, little can be gained in the area of constitutional law, and much lost in the process of democratic decisionmaking, by allowing individual judges in city after city to second-guess such legislative or administrative determinations.

Stevens Dissent

Justice STEVENS, dissenting.

If enforced as written, the ordinance at issue in this case will eliminate the outdoor advertising business [in] San Diego. The principal question presented is, therefore, whether a city may prohibit this medium of communication. Instead of answering that question, the plurality focuses its attention on the exceptions from the total ban and, somewhat ironically, concludes that the ordinance is an unconstitutional abridgment of speech because it does not abridge enough speech.[1]

plurality holds ordinance unconst. because it does not abridge enough speech!

The plurality first holds that a total prohibition of the use of "outdoor advertising display signs" for commercial messages, other than those identifying or promoting a business located on the same premises as the sign, is permissible. I agree with the conclusion that the constitutionality of this prohibition is not undercut by the distinction San Diego has drawn between on-site and off-site commercial signs, and I therefore join Parts I through IV of Justice White's opinion. I do not, however, agree with the reasoning which leads the plurality to invalidate the ordinance because San Diego failed to include a total ban on the use of billboards for both commercial and noncommercial messages.

[Although] it is possible that some future applications of the San Diego ordinance may violate the First Amendment, I am satisfied that the ordinance survives the challenges that these appellants have standing to raise. Unlike the plurality, I do not believe that this case requires us to decide any question concerning the kind of signs a property owner may display on his own premises. I do, however, believe that it is necessary to confront the important question, reserved by the plurality, whether a city may entirely ban one medium of communication. My affirmative answer to that question leads me to the conclusion that the San Diego ordinance should be upheld; that conclusion is not affected by the content-neutral exceptions that are the principal subject of the debate between the plurality and The Chief Justice.

Dissent should uphold

I. [I do not believe that appellants] have any standing to assert the purely hypothetical claims of property owners whose on-site advertising is entirely unaffected by the application of the ordinance at issue in this case. This case involves only the use of permanent signs in areas zoned for commercial and industrial purposes. It is conceivable that some public spirited or eccentric businessman might want to use a permanent sign on his commercial property to display a noncommercial message. The record, however, discloses no such use in the past, and it seems safe to assume that such uses in

---

1. That is the effect of both Justice White's reaction to the exceptions from a total ban and Justice Brennan's concern about the city's attempt to differentiate between commercial and noncommercial messages, although both of their conclusions purportedly rest on the character of the abridgment rather than simply its quantity. [Footnote by Justice Stevens.]

the future will be at best infrequent.   Rather than speculate about hypothetical cases that may be presented by property owners not now before the Court, I would judge this ordinance on the basis of its effect on the outdoor advertising market and save for another day any questions concerning its possible effect in an entirely separate market.   . . .[2]

II   [The] parties have stipulated, correctly in my view, that the net effect of the city's ban on billboards will be a reduction in the total quantity of communication in San Diego.   If the ban is enforced, some present users of billboards will not be able to communicate in the future as effectively as they do now.   This ordinance cannot, therefore, be sustained on the assumption that the remaining channels of communication will be just as effective for all persons as a communications marketplace which includes a thousand or more large billboards available for hire.   The unequivocal language of the First Amendment [could] surely be read to foreclose any law reducing the quantity of communication within a jurisdiction.   I am convinced, however, that such a reading would be incorrect.   My conviction is supported by a hypothetical example, by the Court's prior cases, and by an appraisal of the healthy character of the communications market.

Archaeologists use the term "graffiti" to describe informal inscriptions on tombs and ancient monuments.   The graffito was familiar in the culture of Egypt and Greece, in the Italian decorative art of the 15th-century, and it survives today in some subways and on the walls of public buildings.   It is an inexpensive means of communicating political, commercial, and frivolous messages to large numbers of people; some creators of graffiti have no effective alternate means of publicly expressing themselves.   Nevertheless, I believe a community has the right to decide that its interests in protecting property from damaging trespasses and in securing beautiful surroundings outweigh the countervailing interest in uninhibited expression by means of words and pictures in public places.   If the First Amendment categorically protected the marketplace of ideas from any quantitative restraint, a municipality could not outlaw graffiti.   Our prior decisions are not inconsistent with this proposition.   [Kovacs v. Cooper] at least stands for the proposition that a municipality may enforce a rule that curtails the effectiveness of a particular means of communication [—loudspeakers].   Kovacs, I believe, forecloses any claim that a prohibition of billboards must fall simply because it has some limiting effect on the communications market.[3]

2.   Ironically, today the plurality invalidates this ordinance—not because it is too broad—but rather because it is not broad enough.   It assumes for the purpose of decision that a repeal of all exceptions, including the exception for on-site advertising, would cure the defects it finds in the present ordinance.   However, because neither the appellants nor the on-site advertisers would derive any benefits from a repeal of the exception for on-site commercial signs, the plurality's reliance on the overbreadth doctrine to support vicarious standing in this case is curious indeed.   [Footnote by Justice Stevens.]

3.   Our decisions invalidating ordinances prohibiting or regulating door-to-door solicitation and leafletting are not to the contrary.   In those cases, the state interests the ordinances purported to serve—for instance, the prevention of littering or fraud—were only indirectly furthered by the regulation of communicative activity.   In many of the cases, the ordinances provided for a licensing scheme, rather than a blanket prohibition.   The dis-

[Because] the legitimacy of the interests supporting a city-wide zoning plan designed to improve the entire municipality are beyond dispute, in my judgment the constitutionality of the prohibition of outdoor advertising involves two separate questions. First, is there any reason to believe that the regulation is biased in favor of one point of view or another, or that it is a subtle method of regulating the controversial subjects that may be placed on the agenda for public debate? Second, is it fair to conclude that the market which remains open for the communication of both popular and unpopular ideas is ample and not threatened with gradually increasing restraints? In this case, there is not even a hint of bias or censorship in the city's actions. Nor is there any reason to believe that the overall communications market in San Diego is inadequate.

[If] one is persuaded, as I am, that a wholly impartial total ban on billboards would be permissible, it is difficult to understand why the exceptions in San Diego's ordinance present any additional threat to the interests protected by the First Amendment. The plurality suggests that, because the exceptions are based in part on the subject matter of noncommercial speech, the city somehow is choosing the permissible subjects for public debate. While this suggestion is consistent with some of the broad dictum in [Consolidated Edison], it does not withstand analysis in this case.

The essential concern embodied in the First Amendment is that government not impose its viewpoint on the public or select the topics on which public debate is permissible. The San Diego ordinance simply does not implicate this concern. Although Consolidated Edison broadly identified regulations based on the subject matter of speech as impermissible content-based regulations, essential First Amendment concerns were implicated in that case because the government was attempting to limit discussion of controversial topics, and thus was shaping the agenda for public debate. The neutral exceptions in the San Diego ordinance do not present this danger.

To the extent that the exceptions relate to subject matter at all, I can find no suggestion on the face of the ordinance that San Diego is attempting to influence public opinion or to limit public debate on particular issues. Except for the provision allowing signs to be used for political campaign purposes for limited periods, none of the exceptions even arguably relates to any controversial subject matter. As a whole they allow a greater dissemination of information than could occur under a total ban. [The] exception for political campaign signs presents a different question. For I must assume that these signs may be just as unsightly and hazardous as other off-site billboards. Nevertheless, the fact that the community places a spe-

cretion thus placed in the hands of municipal officials was found constitutionally offensive because of the risk of censorship. In addition, because many of these cases involved the solicitation efforts of the Jehovah's Witnesses, the Court was properly sensitive to the risk that the ordinances could be used to suppress unpopular viewpoints.

In this case, as the plurality acknowledges, the ban on billboards directly serves, and indeed is necessary to further, the city's legitimate interests in traffic safety and aesthetics. San Diego's ordinance places no discretion in any municipal officials, and there is no reason to suspect that the ordinance was designed or is being applied to suppress unpopular viewpoints. [Footnote by Justice Stevens.]

cial value on allowing additional communication to occur during political campaigns is surely consistent with the interests the First Amendment was designed to protect. Of course, if there were reason to believe that billboards were especially useful to one political party or candidate, this exception would be suspect. But nothing of that sort is suggested by this record. In the aggregate, therefore, it seems to me that the exceptions in this ordinance cause it to have a less serious effect on the communications market than would a total ban.

In sum, I agree with The Chief Justice that nothing more than a rather doctrinaire application of broad statements that were made in other contexts may support a conclusion that this ordinance is unconstitutional because it includes a limited group of exceptions that neither separately nor in the aggregate compromise "our zealous adherence to the principle that the government may not tell the citizen what he may or may not say." [American Mini Theatres] (opinion of Stevens, J.). None of the exceptions is even arguably "conditioned upon the sovereign's agreement with what a speaker may intend to say." Ibid. Accordingly, and for the reasons stated in greater detail by The Chief Justice, I respectfully dissent.

10th ED., p. 1270; IND. RTS., p. 890
Add as footnote to Note 3:

Note the recent reemergence of the "speech"-"conduct" distinction in Chief Justice Burger's majority opinion in Haig v. Agee, 453 U.S. 280 (1981) (more fully discussed in additions to 10th Ed., p. 1676; Ind. Rts., p. 1296 and 10th Ed., p. 1176; Ind. Rts., p. 796). The Secretary of State had revoked the passport of Philip Agee, a former CIA agent whose activities abroad had resulted in exposure of alleged undercover CIA agents and intelligence sources in foreign countries. The Secretary had acted pursuant to a regulation permitting passport revocation where "the Secretary determines that the national's activities abroad are causing or are likely to cause serious damage to the national security or the foreign policy of the United States." Chief Justice Burger devoted most of his opinion to the argument that Congress had implicitily authorized the regulation and the executive action. He gave only cursory attention to a range of constitutional challenges.

One of the constitutional claims rested on the First Amendment. The Chief Justice's rejection of that claim included the statement: "To the extent the revocation of [Agee's] passport operates to inhibit [him], 'it is an inhibition of *action*,' rather than of speech. Zemel v. Rusk, 381 U.S. 1 (1965). Agee is as free to criticize the United States Government as he was when he held the passport." [Ironically, Chief Justice Burger, in reviving the "speech"-"action" distinction in this context, relied on the language of his predecessor, Chief Justice Warren, the author of the Zemel decision. In Zemel, another passport case, Chief Justice Warren had stated: "There are few restrictions on action which could not be clothed by ingenious argument in the garb of decreased data flow." Contrast Justice Powell's comment on this approach in Saxbe v. Washington Post Co., 417 U.S. 843 (1974): "[T]he dichotomy between speech and action, while often helpful to analysis, is too uncertain to serve as the dispositive factor in charting the outer boundaries of First Amendment concerns."]

Justice Brennan's dissent, although primarily devoted to the statutory issue, objected in a footnote to the majority's "whirlwind treatment of Agee's constitutional claims" and its "extreme oversimplifications of constitutional doctrine." With respect to Chief Justice Burger's use of the "speech"-"action" distinction, Justice Brennan commented: "Under the Court's rationale, I would suppose that a 40-year prison sentence imposed upon a person who criticized the Government's food stamp policy would represent only an 'inhibition of action.' After all, the individual would remain free to criticize the United States Government, albeit from a jail cell."

10th ED., p. 1271; IND. RTS., p. 891
Add after second paragraph of footnote 1:

The Court again relied on the vagueness doctrine to strike down a loitering and identification statute in Kolender v. Lawson, 461 U.S. —— (1983), discussed above, addition to 10th Ed., p. 1189; Ind.Rts., p. 809.

10th ED., p. 1272; IND. RTS., p. 892
Insert after Note 3 (before section on permit requirements):

UNITED STATES v. GRACE

461 U.S. ——, 103 S.Ct. 1702, 75 L.Ed.2d 736 (1983).

[This case, which concerns picketing on the grounds and surrounding sidewalks of the Supreme Court, is printed below, addition to 10th Ed., p. 1296; Ind.Rts., p. 916.]

10th ED., p. 1278; IND. RTS., p. 898
Add as footnote to the first paragraph of Sec. 2G:

In addition to the cases discussed in Sec. 2G, see Heffron v. Int'l Soc. for Krishna Consc., 452 U.S. 640 (1981), a case involving access rights of Hare Krishna proselytizers to state fair grounds. Justice White's majority opinion commented that "[t]he Minnesota State Fair is a *limited* public forum . . . ." (Emphasis added.) The case is printed above, addition to 10th Ed., p. 1219; Ind. Rts., p. 839. Public forum doctrine is also discussed extensively in Perry Education Ass'n v. Perry Local Educators' Ass'n, 460 U.S. —— (1983), dealing with a claim of access to a school system's internal mail system and mailboxes. The case is printed below, addition to 10th Ed., p. 1325; Ind.Rts., p. 945.

10th ED., p. 1287; IND. RTS., p. 907
Insert after the Note on Grayned (before Lehman):

Content neutrality and access to public university facilities. In WIDMAR v. VINCENT, 454 U.S. 263 (1981), the Court exercised the strict scrutiny it typically applies to content-based exclusions from public forums to hold that a state university that makes its facilities generally available for the activities of registered student groups may not constitutionally bar a group desiring to use the facilities for religious worship and discussion. The case arose when the University of Missouri at Kansas City, relying on its policy of prohibiting the use of its facilities "for purposes of religious worship or religious teaching," barred a student religious group from meeting anywhere on University grounds. The Court rejected the University's argument that its interest in promoting the separation of church and state was adequate to survive First Amendment strict scrutiny.[1]

In explaining the application of free speech principles here, Justice POWELL's majority opinion stated: "Through its policy of accommodating their meetings, the University has created a forum generally open for use by student groups. Having done so, the University has assumed an obligation to justify its discriminations and exclusions under applicable constitutional norms.[2] The Constitution forbids a State to enforce certain exclusions from a

[1]. The Court's discussion of separation of church and state principles is noted with the Establishment Clause materials below, as addition to 10th Ed., p. 1565; Ind. Rts., p. 1185.

[2]. Justice Powell elaborated in a footnote: "This Court has recognized that the campus of a public university, at least for its students, possesses many of the characteristics of a public fo-

forum generally open to the public, even if it was not required to create the forum in the first place. The University's institutional mission, which it describes as providing a '*secular* education' to its students, does not exempt its actions from constitutional scrutiny. With respect to persons entitled to be there, our cases leave no doubt that the First Amendment rights of speech and association extend to the campuses of state universities.

"Here the University of Missouri has discriminated against student groups and speakers based on their desire to use a generally open forum to engage in religious worship and discussion. These are forms of speech and association protected by the First Amendment. See, e.g., [Heffron; Saia]. In order to justify discriminatory exclusion from a public forum based on the religious content of a group's intended speech, the University must therefore satisfy the standard of review appropriate to content-based exclusions. It must show that its regulation is necessary to serve a compelling state interest and that it is narrowly drawn to achieve that end."

After rejecting the University's separation of church and state defense (as discussed in the additional note below), Justice Powell concluded by returning to free speech principles. He emphasized: "Our holding in this case in no way undermines the capacity of the University to establish reasonable time, place, and manner regulations. [See, e.g., Grayned.] Nor do we question the right of the University to make academic judgments as to how best to allocate scarce resources or 'to determine for itself on academic grounds who may teach, what may be taught, how it shall be taught, and who may be admitted to study.' [Sweezy v. New Hampshire.] Finally, we affirm the continuing validity of cases that recognize a University's right to exclude even First Amendment activities that violate reasonable campus rules or substantially interfere with the opportunity of other students to obtain an education. The basis for our decision is narrow. Having created a forum generally open to student groups, the University seeks to enforce a content-based

rum. See generally [Police Dept. v. Mosley]. At the same time, however, our cases have recognized that First Amendment rights must be analyzed 'in light of the special characteristics of the school environment.' [Tinker.] We continue to adhere to that view. A university differs in significant respects from public forums such as streets or parks or even municipal theaters. A university's mission is education, and decisions of this Court have never denied its authority to impose reasonable regulations compatible with that mission upon the use of its campus and facilities. We have not held, for example, that a campus must make all of its facilities equally available to students and nonstudents alike, or that a university must grant free access to all of its grounds or buildings."

[A few months after Widmar, the Court confronted but did not decide a case involving a nonstudent's access claim to the grounds of a *private* university. Princeton University v. Schmid, 455 U.S. 100 (1982). Schmid, a nonstudent, had been convicted of criminal trespass for distributing political materials on the Princeton University campus without getting the permission of University officials. The New Jersey Supreme Court sustained Schmid's claim that his *state* constitutional rights of speech and assembly had been violated. The state courts had permitted Princeton University to intervene, and Princeton sought review in the U.S. Supreme Court, insisting that its speech and property rights had been infringed by the highest state court's ruling. The Court's per curiam ruling dismissed the appeal for lack of Art. III jurisdiction, emphasizing mootness and Princeton's lack of federal standing. Cf. Doremus v. Board of Educ., 10th Ed., p. 1651; Ind. Rts., p. 1271.]

exclusion of religious speech. Its exclusionary policy violates the fundamental principle that a state regulation of speech should be content-neutral, and the University is unable to justify this violation under applicable constitutional standards."

In an opinion concurring only in the judgment, Justice STEVENS took issue with the majority's approach: "In my opinion, the use of the terms 'compelling state interest' and 'public forum' to analyze the question presented in this case may needlessly undermine the academic freedom of public universities." [3] Justice Stevens elaborated: "Today most major colleges and universities are operated by public authority. Nevertheless, their facilities are not open to the public in the same way that streets and parks are. University facilities—private or public—are maintained primarily for the benefit of the student body and the faculty. In performing their learning and teaching missions, the managers of the university routinely make countless decisions based on the content of communicative materials. They select books for inclusion in the library, they hire professors on the basis of their academic philosophies, they select courses for inclusion in the curriculum, and they reward scholars for what they have written. In addition, in encouraging students to participate in extracurricular activities, they necessarily make decisions concerning the content of these activities.

"Because every university's resources are limited, an educational institution must routinely make decisions concerning the use of the time and space that is available for extracurricular activities. In my judgment, it is both necessary and appropriate for those decisions to evaluate the content of a proposed student activity. I should think it obvious, for example, that if two groups of 25 students requested the use of a room at a particular time—one to view Mickey Mouse cartoons and the other to rehearse an amateur performance of Hamlet—the First Amendment would not require that the room be reserved for the group that submitted its application first. Nor do I see why a university should have to establish a 'compelling state interest' to defend its decision to permit one group to use the facility and not the other. In my opinion, a university should be allowed to decide for itself whether a program that illuminates the genius of Walt Disney should be given precedence over one that may duplicate material adequately covered in the classroom. Judgments of this kind should be made by academicians, not by federal judges, and their standards for decision should not be encumbered with ambiguous phrases like 'compelling state interest.'

"Thus, I do not subscribe to the view that a public university has no greater interest in the content of student activities than the police chief has in the content of a soap box oration on Capitol Hill. A university legitimately may regard some subjects as more relevant to its educational mission than others. But the university, like the police officer, may not allow its agreement or disagreement with the viewpoint of a particular speaker to determine whether access to a forum will be granted. If a state university is to deny recognition to a student organization—or is to give it a lesser right to use

---

3. Justice Powell responded to this concern by calling it "unjustified": "Our holding is limited to the context of a public forum created by the University itself."

school facilities than other student groups—it must have a valid reason for doing so."

Despite his different standard of review, Justice Stevens found the University decision unjustified. He explained: "I believe that the University may exercise a measure of control over the agenda for student use of school facilities [without] needing to identify so-called 'compelling state interests.' Quite obviously, however, the University could not allow a group of Republicans or Presbyterians to meet while denying Democrats or Mormons the same privilege. It seems apparent that the policy under attack would allow groups of young philosophers to meet to discuss their skepticism that a Supreme Being exists, or a group of political scientists to meet to debate the accuracy of the view that religion is the 'opium of the people.' If school facilities may be used to discuss anti-clerical doctrine, it seems to me that comparable use by a group desiring to express a belief in God must also be permitted. The fact that their expression of faith includes ceremonial conduct is not, in my opinion, a sufficient reason for suppressing their discussion entirely."

Justice WHITE, the sole dissenter, disagreed not only with the majority's Establishment Clause approach (as discussed in the additional note below) but also with its free speech analysis. He objected to the argument that, "because religious worship uses speech, it is protected by the Free Speech Clause of the First Amendment.[4] Not only is it protected, [the challengers] argue, but religious worship qua speech is not different from any other variety of protected speech as a matter of constitutional principle. I believe that this proposition is plainly wrong. Were it right, the Religion Clauses would be emptied of any independent meaning in circumstances in which religious practice took the form of speech. Although the majority describes this argument as 'novel,'[5] I believe it to be clearly supported by our previous cases."

4. In a footnote at this point, Justice White commented that it was "surprising that the majority assumes this proposition to require no argument." The precedents did not support Justice Powell's reasoning, he insisted. For example, "Heffron and Saia involved the communication of religious views to a non-religious public audience. Talk about religion and about religious beliefs, however, is not the same as religious services of worship."

5. The majority opinion elaborated its "novel" accusation as follows: "The dissent does not deny that speech *about* religion is speech entitled to the general protections of the First Amendment. It does not argue that descriptions of religious experiences fail to qualify as 'speech.' Nor does it repudiate last Term's decision in [Heffron], which assumed that religious appeals to nonbelievers constituted protected 'speech.' Rather, the dissent seems to attempt a distinction between the kinds of religious speech explicitly protected by our cases and a new class of religious 'speech act[s],' comprising 'worship.' There are at least three difficulties with this distinction. First, the dissent fails to establish that the distinction has intelligible content. [Second], even if the distinction drew an arguably principled line, it is highly doubtful that it would lie within the judicial competence to administer. [Finally], the dissent fails to establish the *relevance* of the distinction on which it seeks to rely. [It] gives no reason why the Establishment Clause, or any other provision of the Constitution, would require different treatment for religious speech designed to win religious converts, see Heffron, than for religious worship by persons already converted. It is far from clear that the State gives greater support in the latter case than in the former."

Note also an additional response to Justice White's dissent, in another footnote to Justice Powell's majority opinion: "As the dissent emphasizes, the

Justice White elaborated: "If the majority were right that no distinction may be drawn between verbal acts of worship and other verbal acts, [a number of prior decisions] would have to be reconsidered. Although I agree that the line may be difficult to draw in many cases, surely the majority cannot seriously suggest that no line may ever be drawn. If that were the case, the majority would have to uphold the University's right to offer a class entitled 'Sunday Mass.' Under the majority's view, such a class would be—as a matter of constitutional principle—indistinguishable from a class entitled 'The History of the Catholic Church.' There may be instances in which a state's attempt to disentangle itself from religious worship would intrude upon secular speech about religion. In such a case the state's action would be subject to challenge under the Free Speech Clause of the First Amendment. This is not such a case. This case involves religious worship only; the fact that that worship is accomplished through speech does not add anything to [the challengers'] argument. That argument must rely upon the claim that the state's action impermissibly interferes with the free exercise of respondents' religious practices. Although this is a close question, I conclude that it does not." In explaining that conclusion, Justice White insisted that in this instance the burden on free exercise was "minimal" and that therefore "the state need do no more than demonstrate that the regulation furthers some permissible state end. The state's interest in avoiding claims that it is financing or otherwise supporting religious worship—in maintaining a definitive separation between church and state—is such an end. [Thus], I believe the interest of the state is sufficiently strong to justify the imposition of the minimal burden on [the challengers'] ability freely to exercise their religious beliefs." [6]

Establishment Clause requires the State to distinguish between 'religious' speech—speech undertaken or approved by the State, the primary effect of which is to support an Establishment of Religion—and 'nonreligious' speech—speech undertaken or approved by the State, the primary effect of which is not to support an Establishment of Religion. This distinction is required by the plain text of the Constitution. It is followed in our cases. The dissent attempts to equate this distinction with its view of an alleged constitutional difference between religious 'speech' and religious 'worship.' We think that the distinction advanced by the dissent lacks a foundation in either the Constitution or in our cases, and that it is judicially unmanageable."

6. Note also Justice White's comment in a footnote: "I know of no precedent holding that simply because a public forum is open to all kinds of speech—including speech about religion—it must be open to regular religious worship services as well. I doubt that the state need stand by and allow its public forum to become a church for any religious sect that chooses to stand on its right of access to that forum."

10th ED., p. 1296; IND. RTS., p. 916
Add after the Note (before Sec. 2H):

ACCESS TO THE JUDICIAL ENVIRONS

UNITED STATES v. GRACE

461 U.S. —, 103 S.Ct. 1702, 75 L.Ed.2d 736 (1983).

Justice WHITE delivered the opinion of the Court.

In this case we must determine whether 40 U.S.C. § 13k, which prohibits, among other things, the "display [of] . . . any flag, banner, or device designed or adapted to bring into public notice any party, organization, or movement" in the United States Supreme Court building and on its grounds, violates the First Amendment.

I. In May 1978 appellee Thaddeus Zywicki, standing on the sidewalk in front of the Supreme Court building, distributed leaflets to passersby. The leaflets were reprints of a letter to the editor of The Washington Post from a United States Senator concerning the removal of unfit judges from the bench. A Supreme Court police officer approached Zywicki and told him, accurately, that Title 40 of the United States Code prohibited the distribution of leaflets on the Supreme Court grounds, which includes the sidewalk. Zywicki left. [On two occasions in 1980 Zywicki again tried to pass out leaflets in front of the Court, but left after being told to do so by a Court police officer.]

[Around] noon on March 17, 1980, appellee Mary Grace entered upon the sidewalk in front of the Court and began to display a four foot by two and a half foot sign on which was inscribed the verbatim text of the First Amendment. A Court police officer approached Grace and informed her that she would have to go across the street if she wished to display the sign. Grace was informed that Title 40 of the United States Code prohibited her conduct and that if she did not cease she would be arrested. Grace left the grounds.

On May 13, 1980, Zywicki and Grace filed the present suit. [The] Court of Appeals determined that the District Court's dismissal for failure to exhaust administrative remedies was erroneous and went on to strike down § 13k on its face as an unconstitutional restriction on First Amendment rights in a public place.

II. Section 13k prohibits two distinct activities; it is unlawful either "to parade, stand, or move in processions or assemblages in the Supreme Court Building or grounds," or "to display therein any flag, banner, or device designed or adapted to bring into public notice any party, organization, or movement." Each appellee appeared individually on the public sidewalks to engage in expressive activity and it goes without saying that the threat of arrest to which each appellee was subjected was for violating the prohibition against the display of a "banner or device." Accordingly, our view is limited to the latter portion of the statute. Likewise, the controversy presented by appellees concerned their right to use the public side-walks surrounding the Court building for the communicative activities they sought to carry out, and we shall address only whether the proscriptions of § 13k are constitutional as applied to the public sidewalks. [We] agree with the United States that the statute covers the particular conduct of Zywicki or Grace and that it is therefore proper to reach the constitutional question involved in this case.

III. It is [true] that "public places" historically associated with the free exercise of expressive activities, such as streets, sidewalks, and parks, are considered, without more, to be "public forums." See [Perry Education Assn. v. Perry Local Educator's Assn. (printed below, addition to 10th Ed., p. 1325; Ind.Rts., p. 945); Cox v. New Hampshire; Hague v. CIO.] In such places, the government's ability to permissibly restrict expressive conduct is very limited: the government may enforce reasonable time, place, and manner regulations as long as the restrictions "are content-neutral, are narrowly tailored to serve a significant government interest, and leave open ample alternative channels of communication." [Perry]. Additional restrictions such as an absolute prohibition on a particular type of expression will be upheld only if narrowly drawn to accomplish a compelling governmental interest.

Publicly owned or operated property does not become a "public forum" simply because members of the public are permitted to come and go at will. See Greer v. Spock. Although whether the property has been "generally opened to the public" is a factor to consider in determining whether the government has opened its property to the use of the people for communicative purposes, it is not determinative of the question. We have regularly rejected the assertion that people who wish "to propagandize protests or views have a constitutional right to do so whenever and however and wherever they please." Adderly v. Florida. See, e.g., [Cox I; Cox II.] There is little doubt that in some circumstances the Government may ban the entry on to public property that is not a "public forum" of all persons except those who have legitimate business on the premises. The Government, "no less than a private owner of property, has the power to preserve the property under its control for the use to which it is lawfully dedicated." [Adderly.]

IV. It is argued that the Supreme Court building and grounds fit neatly within the description of non-public forum property. Although the property is publicly owned, it has not been traditionally held open for the use of the public for expressive activities. As Greer v. Spock teaches, the property is not transformed into "public forum" property merely because the public is permitted to freely enter and leave the grounds at practically all times and the public is admitted to the building during specified hours. Under this view it would be necessary only to determine that the restrictions imposed by § 13k are reasonable in light of the use to which the building and grounds are dedicated and that there is no discrimination on the basis of content. We need not make that judgment at this time, however, because § 13k covers the public sidewalks as well as the building and grounds inside the sidewalks. As will become evident, we hold that § 13k may not be applied to the public sidewalks.

The prohibitions imposed by § 13k technically cover the entire grounds of the Supreme Court as defined in § 13p. That section describes the Court grounds as extending to the curb of each of the four streets enclosing the block on which the building is located. Included within this small geographical area, therefore, are not only the building, the plaza and surrounding promenade, lawn area, and steps, but also the sidewalks. The sidewalks comprising the outer boundaries of the Court grounds are indistinguishable from any other sidewalks in Washington, D.C., and we can discern no reason why they should be treated any differently. Sidewalks, of course, are among those areas of public property that traditionally have been held open to the public for expressive activities and are clearly within those areas of public property that may be considered, generally without further inquiry, to be public forum property. In this respect, the present case differs from Greer v. Spock. In Greer, the streets and sidewalks at issue were located within an enclosed military reservation, Fort Dix, New Jersey, and were thus separated from the streets and sidewalks of the city itself. That is not true of the sidewalks surrounding the Court. There is no separation, no fence, and no indication whatever to persons stepping from the street to the curb and sidewalks that serve as the perimeter of the Court grounds that they have entered some special type of enclave. In U. S. Postal Service v. Greenburgh Civic Assns., we stated that "Congress . . . may not by its own *ipse dixit* destroy the "public forum" status of streets and parks which have historically been public forums. . . ." The inclusion of the public sidewalks within the scope of § 13k's prohibition, however, results in the destruction of public forum status that is at least presumptively impermissible. Traditional public forum property occupies a special position in terms of First Amendment protection and will not lose its historically recognized character for the reason that it abuts government property that has been dedicated to a use other than as a forum for public expression. . . .

V. The goverment submits that § 13k qualifies as a reasonable time, place, and manner restriction which may be imposed to restrict communicative activities on public-forum property such as sidewalks. The argument is that the inquiry should not be confined to the Supreme Court grounds but should focus on "the vicinity of the Supreme Court" or "the public places of Washington, D.C." Viewed in this light, the Government contends that there are sufficient alternative areas within the relevant forum, such as the streets around the Court or the sidewalks across those streets to permit § 13k to be considered a reasonable "place" restriction having only a minimal impact on expressive activity. We are convinced, however, that the section, which totally bans the specified communicative activity on the public sidewalks around the Court grounds, cannot be justified as a reasonable place restriction primarily because it has an insufficient nexus with any of the public interests that may be thought to undergird § 13k.

[Based] on its provisions and legislative history, it is fair to say that the purpose of the Act was to provide for the protection of the building

---

Handwritten margin notes:

Sec 13k may not be applied to the sidewalk

Sidewalks included in area covered by Sec 13k. but indistinguishable from any other Wash DC Sidewalks

In Spock, sidewalks were w/in a military base.

Gov. argues there are sufficient other places w/in the relevant forum eg across the street.

Cannot be justified because of insufficient nexus w/ public interest asserted

Thus not a reasonable time & place restriction

Purpose was to protect grounds + person to maintain proper order + decorum of Court

and grounds and of the persons and property therein, as well as the maintenance of proper order and decorum. Section 13k was one of the provisions apparently designed for these purposes.

[We] do not denigrate the necessity to protect persons and property or to maintain proper order and decorum within the Supreme Court grounds, but we do question whether a total ban on carrying a flag, banner or device on the public sidewalks substantially serves these purposes. There is no suggestion, for example, that appellees' activities in any way obstructed the sidewalks or access to the Building, threatened injury to any person or property, or in any way interfered with the orderly administration of the building or other parts of the grounds. As we have said, the building's perimeter sidewalks are indistinguishable from other public sidewalks in the city that are normally open to the conduct that is at issue here and that § 13k forbids. A total ban on that conduct is no more necessary for the maintenance of peace and tranquility on the public sidewalks surrounding the building than on any other sidewalks in the city.

[The] United States offers another justification for § 13k that deserves our attention. It is said that the federal courts represent an independent branch of the Government and that their decision-making processes are different from those of the other branches. Court decisions are made on the record before them and in accordance with the applicable law. The views of the parties and of others are to be presented by briefs and oral argument. Courts are not subject to lobbying, judges do not entertain visitors in their chambers for the purpose of urging that cases be resolved one way or another, and they do not and should not respond to parades, picketing or pressure groups. Neither, the Government urges, should it appear to the public that the Supreme Court is subject to outside influence or that picketing or marching, singly or in groups, is an acceptable or proper way of appealing to or influencing the Supreme Court. Hence, we are asked to hold that Congress was quite justified in preventing the conduct in dispute here from occurring on the sidewalks at the edge of the Court grounds.

Gov argues Courts should be protected from pressure groups + from appearance of influence

Purpose good, but not served by statute,

As was the case with the maintenance of law and order on the Court grounds, we do not discount the importance of this proffered purpose for § 13k. But, again, we are unconvinced that the prohibitions of § 13k that are at issue here sufficiently serve that purpose to sustain its validity insofar as the public sidewalks on the perimeter of the grounds are concerned. Those sidewalks are used by the public like other public sidewalks. There is nothing to indicate to the public that these sidewalks are part of the Supreme Court grounds or are in any way different from other public sidewalks in the city. We seriously doubt that the public would draw a different inference from a lone picketer carrying a sign on the sidewalks around the building than it would from a similar picket on the sidewalks across the street.

(H) 13k is unconst. as applied to the Sidewalks

[We] hold that under the First Amendment [§ 13k] is unconstitutional as applied to [the] sidewalks. Of course, this is not to say that those sidewalks, like other sidewalks, are not subject to reasonable time, place and manner restrictions, either by statute or by regulations.

[Affirmed in part and vacated in part.]

but not to say that sidewalks not subject to reasonable t, p, m rest's

Justice MARSHALL, concurring in part and dissenting in part.

I would hold [§ 13k] unconstitutional on its face. The statute in no way distinguishes the sidewalks from the rest of the premises, and excising the sidewalks from its purview does not bring it into conformity with the First Amendment. Visitors to this Court do not lose their First Amendment rights at the edge of the sidewalks.

[When] a citizen is "in a place where [he] has every right to be," Brown v. Louisiana, he cannot be denied the opportunity to express his views simply because the government has not chosen to designate the area as a forum for public discussion. While the right to conduct expressive activities in such areas as streets, parks, and sidewalks is reinforced by their traditional use for purposes of assembly, that right ultimately rests on the principle that "one who is rightfully on a street which the state has left open to the public carries with him there *as elsewhere* the constitutional right to express his views in an orderly fashion." Jamison v. Texas, 318 U.S. 413 (1943). Every citizen lawfully present in a public place has a right to engage in peaceable and orderly expression that is not incompatible with the primary activity of the place in question, whether that place is a school, a library, a private lunch counter, the grounds of a statehouse, the grounds of the United States Capitol, a bus terminal, an airport, or a welfare center. As we stated in [Grayned], "[t]he crucial question is whether the manner of expression is basically incompatible with the normal activity of a particular place at a particular time." "[O]ne is not to have the exercise of his liberty of expression in appropriate places abridged on the plea that it may be exercised in some other place." [Schneider,]

I see no reason why the premises of this Court should be exempt from this basic principle. It would be ironic indeed if an exception to the Constitution were to be recognized for the very institution that has the chief responsibility for protecting constitutional rights. I would apply to the premises of this Court the same principle that this Court has applied to other public places. . . .

So sweeping a prohibition is scarcely necessary to protect the operations of this Court, and in my view cannot constitutionally be applied either to the Court grounds or to the areas inside the Court building that are open to the public. . . .

Justice STEVENS, dissenting in part and concurring in part.

[I] see no reason to stretch the language of the statute to encompass the activities of either Zywicki or Grace. As a matter of statutory interpretation, we should not infer that Congress intended to abridge free expression in circumstances not plainly covered by the language of the statute. As a matter of judicial restraint, we should avoid the unnecessary adjudication of constitutional questions. . . .

ACCESS TO STATE FAIR GROUNDS

HEFFRON v. INT'L SOC. FOR KRISHNA CONSC.

452 U.S. 640, 101 S.Ct. 2559, 69 L.Ed.2d 298 (1981).

[This case is printed above, addition to 10th Ed., p. 1219; Ind. Rts. p. 839.]

ACCESS TO HOME LETTER BOXES

U. S. POSTAL SERVICE v. GREENBURGH CIVIC ASSNS.

453 U.S. 114, 101 S.Ct. 2676, 69 L.Ed.2d 517 (1981).

Justice REHNQUIST delivered the opinion of the Court.

We noted probable jurisdiction to decide whether the [District Court] correctly determined that 18 U.S.C. § 1725, which prohibits the deposit of unstamped "mailable matter" in a letter box approved by the United States Postal Service, unconstitutionally abridges the First Amendment rights of certain civic associations in Westchester County, N. Y. . . . .

I. Appellee Council of Greenburgh Civic Associations is an umbrella organization for a number of civic groups in Westchester County, N. Y. Appellee Saw Mill Valley Civic Association is one of the Council's member groups. In June 1976, the Postmaster in White Plains, N. Y., notified the Chairman of the Saw Mill Valley Civic Association that the association's practice of delivering messages to local residents by placing unstamped notices and pamphlets in the letter boxes of private homes was in violation of 18 U.S.C. § 1725.* [In] February 1977, appellees filed this suit in the District Court for declaratory and injunctive relief from the Postal Service's threatened enforcement of § 1725. Appellees contended that the enforcement of § 1725 would inhibit their communication with residents of the town of Greenburgh and would thereby deny them the freedom of speech and freedom of the press secured by the First Amendment.

The District Court initially dismissed the complaint for failure to state a claim on which relief could be granted. On appeal, however, the Court of

---

*Sec. 1725 (initially enacted in 1934) provides: "Whoever knowingly and willfully deposits any mailable matter such as statements of accounts, circulars, sale bills, or other like matter, on which no postage has been paid, in any letter box established, approved, or accepted by the Postal Service for the receipt or delivery of mail matter on any mail route with intent to avoid payment of lawful postage thereon, shall for each such offense be fined not more than $300.00."

Appeals for the Second Circuit reversed and remanded the case to the District Court to give the parties "an opportunity to submit proof as to the extent of the handicap to communication caused by enforcement of the statute in the area involved, on the one hand, and the need for the restriction for protection of the mails, on the other." In light of this language, it was not unreasonable for the District Court to conclude that it had been instructed to "try" the statute, much as more traditional issues of fact are tried by a court, and that is what the District Court proceeded to do.

In the proceedings on remand, the Postal Service offered three general justifications for § 1725: (1) that § 1725 protects mail revenues; (2) that it facilitates the efficient and secure delivery of the mails; and (3) that it promotes the privacy of mail patrons. More specifically, the Postal Service argued that elimination of § 1725 could cause the overcrowding of mailboxes due to the deposit of civic association notices. Such overcrowding would in turn constitute an impediment to the delivery of the mails. Testimony was offered that § 1725 aided the investigation of mail theft by restricting access to letter boxes, thereby enabling postal investigators to assume that anyone other than a postal carrier or a householder who opens a mailbox may be engaged in the violation of the law.

[The] Postal Service introduced testimony that it would incur additional expense if § 1725 were either eliminated or held to be inapplicable to civic association materials. If delivery in mailboxes were expanded to permit civic association circulars—but not other types of nonmailable matter such as commercial materials—mail carriers would be obliged to remove and examine individual unstamped items found in letter boxes to determine if their deposit there was lawful. Carriers would also be confronted with a larger amount of unstamped mailable matter which they would be obliged to separate from outgoing mail. [The] final justification offered by the Postal Service [was] that the statute provided significant protection for the privacy interests of postal customers. Section 1725 provides postal customers the means to send and receive mails without fear of their correspondence becoming known to members of the community.

The Postal Service also argued at trial that the enforcement of § 1725 left appellees with ample alternative means of delivering their message. The appellees can deliver their messages either by paying postage, by hanging their notices on doorknobs, by placing their notices under doors or under a doormat, by using newspaper or nonpostal boxes affixed to houses or mailbox posts, by telephoning their constituents, by engaging in person-to-person delivery in public areas, by tacking or taping their notices on a door post or letter box post, or by placing advertisements in local newspapers. . . .

The District Court found the above arguments of the Postal Service insufficient to sustain the constitutionality of § 1725, at least as applied to these appellees. [The court] based its decision on several findings. The court initially concluded that because civic associations generally have small cash reserves and cannot afford the applicable postage rates, mailing of the appellees' message would be financially burdensome. Similarly, because of the relatively slow pace of the mail, use of the mails at certain times would impede the appellees' ability to communicate quickly with their constituents. [The] court also found that none of the alternative means of delivery suggested by the Postal Service were "nearly as effective as placing civic association flyers in approved mailboxes; so that restriction on the [appellees'] delivery methods to such alternatives also constitutes a serious burden on [appellees'] ability to communicate with their constituents." . . . [1]

II. The present case is a good example of Justice Holmes' aphorism that "a page of history is worth a volume of logic." For only by review of the history of the postal system and its present statutory and regulatory scheme can the constitutional challenge to § 1725 be placed in its proper context. [Justice Rehnquist's "review of the history of the postal system" is omitted.]

[Congress] has established a detailed statutory and regulatory scheme to govern this country's vast postal system. [Acting under statutory authority], the Postal Service has provided by regulation that both urban and rural postal customers must provide appropriate mail receptacles meeting detailed specifications concerning size, shape and dimensions. A letter box provided by a postal customer which meets the Postal Service's specifications [becomes] part of the Postal Service's nationwide system for the receipt and delivery of mail.

[It] is not without irony that this elaborate system of regulation, coupled with the historic dependence of the Nation on the Postal Service, has been the causal factor which led to this litigation. For it is because of the very fact that virtually every householder wishes to have a mailing address and a receptacle in which mail sent to that address will be deposited by the Postal Service that the letter box or other mail receptacle is attractive to those who wish to convey messages within a locality but do not wish to purchase the stamp or pay such other fee as would permit them to be transmitted by the Postal Service. To the extent that the "alternative means" eschewed by the appellees and found to be inadequate alternatives by the District Court are in fact so, it is in no small part attributable to the fact that the typical mail patron first

---

1. The District Court reasoned that the alternative methods suggested by the Postal Service were inadequate because they can result in the civic notices either being lost or damaged as a result of wind, rain or snow. Weatherstripping on doors may prevent the flyers from being placed under the door. Use of plastic bags for protection of the civic notices is both time consuming and "relatively expensive for a small volunteer organization." Deposit of materials outside may cause litter problems as well as arouse resentment among residents because it informs burglars that no one is home. Alternative methods which depend on reaching the occupant personally are less effective because their success depends on the mere chance that the person called or visited will be home at any given time. The court also found that enforcement of § 1725 against civic associations "does not appear so necessary or contribute to enforcement of the anti-theft, anti-fraud, or Private Express statutes that this interest outweighs the [appellees'] substantial interest in expedient and economical communication with their constituents." Based on the above, the District Court concluded that "the cost to free expression of imposing this burden on [appellees] outweighed the showing made by the Postal Service of its need to enforce the statute to promote effective delivery and protection of the mails." [Footnote by Justice Rehnquist.]

looks for written communications from the "outside world" not under his doormat, or inside the screen of his front door, but in his letter box.

[Postal Service regulations], however, provide that letter boxes and other receptacles designated for the delivery of mail "shall be used exclusively for matter which bears postage." Section 1725 merely reinforces this regulation. [Nothing] in any of the legislation or regulations [requires] any person to become a postal customer. Anyone is free to live in any part of the country without having letters or packages delivered or received by the Postal Service by simply failing to provide the receptacle for those letters and packages which the statutes and regulations require. [What] the legislation and regulations do require is that those persons who *do* wish to receive and deposit their mail at their home or business do so under the direction and control of the Postal Service.

III. [This Court has] recognized the broad power of Congress to act in matters concerning the posts. [However] broad the postal power conferred by Art. I may be, it may not of course be exercised by Congress in a manner that abridges the freedom of speech or of the press. [In] addressing appellees' claim, we note that we are not here confronted with a regulation which in any way prohibits individuals from going door-to-door to distribute their message or which vests unbridled discretion in a governmental official to decide whether or not to permit the distribution to occur. We are likewise not confronted with a regulation which in any way restricts the appellees' right to use the mails. [Admittedly], if appellees do choose to mail their notices, they will be required to pay postage in a manner identical to other Postal Service patrons, but appellees do not challenge the imposition of a fee for the services provided by the Postal Service.

What is at issue in this case is solely the constitutionality of an Act of Congress which makes it unlawful for persons to use, without payment of a fee, a letter box which has been designated an "authorized depository" of the mail by the Postal Service. [W]hen a letter box is so designated, it becomes an essential part of the Postal Service's nationwide system for the delivery and receipt of mail. In effect, the postal customer, although he pays for the physical components of the "authorized depository," agrees to abide by the Postal Service's regulations in exchange for the Postal Service agreeing to deliver and pick up his mail.

Appellees' claim is undermined by the fact that a letter box, once designated an "authorized depository," does not at the same time undergo a transformation into a "public forum" of some limited nature to which the First Amendment guarantees access to all comers. There is neither historical nor constitutional support for the characterization of a letter box as a public forum. [It] is difficult to accept appellees' assertion that because it may be somewhat more efficient to place their messages in letter boxes there is a First Amendment right to do so. The underlying rationale of appellees' argument would seem to foreclose Congress or the Postal Service from requiring in the future that all letter boxes contain locks with keys being available only to the homeowner and the mail carrier. Such letter boxes are presently found in many apartment buildings, and we do not think their presence offends the First Amendment. [Letter boxes] which lock, however, have the same effect on civic associations who wish access to them as does the enforcement of § 1725. Such letter boxes also accomplish the same purpose—that is, they protect mail revenues while at the same time facilitating the secure and efficient delivery of the mails. We do not think the First Amendment prohibits Congress from choosing to accomplish these purposes through legislation as opposed to lock and key.

Indeed, it is difficult to conceive of any reason why this Court should treat a letter box differently for First Amendment access purposes than it has in the past treated the military base in Greer v. Spock, the jail or prison in [e.g.] Adderley v. Florida, or the advertising space made available in city rapid transit cars in [Lehman]. In all these cases, this Court recognized that the First Amendment does not guarantee access to property simply because it is owned or controlled by the government. In Greer v. Spock, the Court cited approvingly from its earlier opinion in Adderley v. Florida, wherein it explained that "The State, no less than a private owner of property, has power to preserve the property under its control for the use to which it is lawfully dedicated." [2]

This Court has not hesitated in the past to hold invalid laws which it concluded granted too much discretion to public officials as to who might and who might not solicit individual homeowners, or which too broadly inhibited the access of persons to traditional First Amendment forums such as the public streets and parks. See, [e.g., Schaumburg; Lovell; Mosley]. But it is a giant leap from the traditional "soap box" to the letter box designated as an authorized depository of the United States mails, and we do not believe the First Amendment requires us to make that leap.[4]

2. Justice Brennan argues that a letter box is a public forum because: "[the] mere deposit of mailable matter without postage is not 'basically incompatible' with the 'normal activity' for which a letter box is used, i.e., deposit of mailable matter with proper postage or mail delivery by the postal service. On the contrary, the mails and the letter boxes are specifically used for the communication of information and ideas and thus surely constitute a public forum appropriate for the exercise of First Amendment rights subject to reasonable time, place, and manner restrictions such as those embodied in § 1725." Justice Brennan's analysis assumes that simply because an instrumentality "is used for the communication of ideas or information," it thereby becomes a public forum. Our cases provide no support for such a sweeping proposition. Certainly, a bulletin board in a cafeteria at Fort Dix is "specifically used for the communication of information and ideas," but such a bulletin board is no more a "public forum" than are the street corners and parking lots found not to be so at the same military base. Greer v. Spock.

Likewise, the advertising space made available in public transportation in the City of Shaker Heights is "specifically used for the communication of information and ideas," but that fact alone was not sufficient to transform that space into a "public forum" for First Amendment purposes. [Lehman.]

[For] the reasons we have stated at length in our opinion, we think the appellees' First Amendment activities are wholly incompatible with the maintenance of a nationwide system for the safe and efficient delivery of mail. The history of the postal system and the role the letter box serves within that system supports this conclusion, and even Justice Brennan acknowledges that a "significant governmental interest" is advanced by the restriction imposed by § 1725. [Footnote by Justice Rehnquist.]

4. Justice Marshall in his dissent states that he disagrees "with the Court's assumption that if no public forum is involved, the only First Amendment challenges to be considered are whether the regulation is

(not necessary to apply first place + manner test)

not a public forum

(also)

no regulation on basis of content

thus law upheld on that basis

IV. It is thus unnecessary for us to examine § 1725 in the context of a "time, place, and manner" restriction on the use of the traditional "public forums" referred to above. This Court has long recognized the validity of reasonable time, place, and manner regulations on such a forum so long as the regulation is content neutral, serves a significant governmental interest, and leaves open adequate alternative channels for communication. But since a letter box is not traditionally such a public forum, the elaborate analysis engaged in by the District Court was, we think, unnecessary. To be sure, if a governmental regulation is based on the content of the speech or the message, that action must be scrutinized more carefully to ensure that communication has not been prohibited " 'merely because public officials disapprove the speakers' view.' " [Consolidated Edison Co. v. PSC.] But in this case there simply is no question that § 1725 does not regulate speech on the basis of content. While the analytical line between a regulation of the "time, place, and manner" in which First Amendment rights may be exercised in a traditional public forum, and the question of whether a particular piece of personal or real property owned or controlled by the government is in fact a "public forum" may blur at the edges, we think the line is nonetheless a workable one. We likewise think that Congress may, in exercising its authority to develop and operate a national postal system, properly legislate with the generality of cases in mind, and should not be put to the test of defending in one township after another the constitutionality of a statute under the traditional "time, place, and manner" analysis. This Court has previously acknowledged that the "guarantees of the First Amendment" have never meant "that people who want to propagandize their protests or views have a constitutional right to do so whenever and however they please." Greer v. Spock, quoting Adderley v. Florida. If Congress and the Postal Service are to operate as efficiently as possible a system for the delivery of mail, [they] must obviously adopt regulations of general character having uniform applicability throughout the more than 3 million square miles which the United States embraces. In so doing, the Postal Service's authority to impose regulations cannot be made to depend on all of the variations of climate, population, density, and other factors that may vary significantly within a distance of less than 100 miles.

content-based [and] reasonable." The First Amendment prohibits Congress from "abridging freedom of speech, or of the press," and its ramifications are not confined to the "public forum" first noted in Hague v. CIO. What we hold is the principle reiterated by cases such as Adderley v. Florida and Greer v. Spock, that property owned or controlled by the government which is *not* a public forum may be subject to a prohibition of speech, leafleting, picketing, or other forms of communication without running afoul of the First Amendment. Admittedly, the government must act reasonably in imposing such restrictions, and the prohibition must be content-neutral. But, for the reasons stated in our opinion, we think it cannot be questioned that § 1725 is both a reasonable and content-neutral regulation.

Even Justice Marshall's dissent recognizes that the government may defend the regulation here on a ground other than simply a "time, place, and manner" basis. For example, he says in dissent that "The question, then, is whether this statute burdens any First Amendment rights enjoyed by appellees. If so, it must be determined whether this burden is justified by a significant governmental interest substantially advanced by the statute." We think § 1725 satisfies even the test articulated by Justice Marshall. [Footnote by Justice Rehnquist.]

(V.) [While] Congress no more than a suburban township may not by its own ipse dixit destroy the "public forum" status of streets and parks which have historically been public forums, we think that for the reasons stated a letter box may not properly be analogized to streets and parks. It is enough for our purposes that neither the enactment nor the enforcement of § 1725 was geared in any way to the content of the message sought to be placed in the letter box.

Reversed.

Justice BRENNAN, concurring in the judgment.

Brennan Concurs in Result

I concur in the judgment, but not in the Court's opinion. I believe the Court errs in not determining whether § 1725 is a reasonable time, place, and manner restriction on appellees' exercise of their First Amendment rights, as urged by the Government, and in resting its judgment instead on the conclusion that a letter box is not a public forum. In my view, this conclusion rests on an improper application of the Court's precedents and ignores the historic role of the mails as a national medium of communication.

Should determine whether a reasonable time, place, manner restriction

I. [Despite] the burden on appellees' rights, I conclude that the statute is constitutional because it is a reasonable time, place, and manner regulation. First, § 1725 is content-neutral. [Second,] the burden on expression advances a significant governmental interest—preventing loss of mail revenues. The District Court's finding that the "failure to enforce the statute as to [appellees] would [not] result in a *substantial* loss of revenue" may be true, but that conclusion overlooks the obvious cumulative effect that the District Court's ruling would have if applied across the country. Surely, the Government is correct when it argues that the Postal Service "is not required to make a case-by-case showing of a compelling need for the incremental revenue to be realized from charging postage to each organization or individual who desires to use the postal system to engage in expression protected by the First Amendment." Third, there are "ample alternative channels for communication." Appellees may, for example, place their circulars under doors or attach them to doorknobs. Simply because recipients may find 82% of materials left in the letter box, but only 70–75% of materials otherwise left at the residence, is not a sufficient reason to conclude that alternative means of delivery are not "ample."

Applies Test
• Content neutral
• Sig gov Int
• Ample Alternative channels

(II.) The Court declines to analyze § 1725 as a time, place, and manner restriction. Instead, it concludes that a letter box is not a public forum. [I] believe that the Court's conclusion ignores the proper method of analysis in determining whether property owned or directly controlled by the Government is a public forum. Moreover, even if the Court were correct that a letter box is not a public forum, the First Amendment would still require the Court to determine whether the burden on appellees' exercise of their First Amendment rights is supportable as a reasonable time, place, and manner restriction.

A. For public forum analysis, "[t]he crucial question is whether the manner of expression is basically incompatible with the normal activity of a particular place at a particular time." [Grayned.] We have often quoted Justice Holmes' observation that the " 'United States may give up the Post

Office when it sees fit, but while it carries it on the use of the mails is almost as much a part of free speech as the right to use our tongues.' " Our cases have recognized generally that public properties are appropriate fora for exercise of First Amendment rights. While First Amendment rights exercised on public property may be subject to reasonable time, place, and manner restrictions, that is very different from saying that government-controlled property, such as a letter box, does not constitute a public forum. Only where the exercise of First Amendment rights is incompatible with the normal activity occurring on public property have we held that the property is not a public forum. See [e.g., Greer v. Spock; Adderley]. Thus, in answering "[t]he crucial question [whether] the manner of expression is basically incompatible with the normal activity of a particular place at a particular time" [Grayned], I believe that the mere deposit of mailable matter without postage is not "basically incompatible" with the "normal activity" for which a letter box is used, i.e., deposit of mailable matter with proper postage or mail delivery by the Postal Service. On the contrary, the mails and the letter box are specifically used for the communication of information and ideas, and thus surely constitute a public forum appropriate for the exercise of First Amendment rights subject to reasonable time, place, and manner restrictions such as those embodied in § 1725 or in the requirement that postage be affixed to mailable matter to obtain access to the postal system.

The history of the mails as a vital national medium of expression confirms this conclusion. Just as "streets and parks [have] immemorially been held in trust for the use of the public and, time out of mind, have been used for purposes of assembly, communicating thoughts between citizens, and discussing public questions," Hague v. C.I.O., so too the mails from the early days of the Republic have played a crucial role in communication. The Court itself acknowledges the importance of the mails as a forum for communication. [Given] "the historic dependence of the Nation on the Postal Service," it is extraordinary that the Court reaches the conclusion that the letter box, a critical link in the mail system, is not a public forum.

[Moreover, the Court] relies on inapposite cases to reach its result. Greer v. Spock [and Adderley v. Florida] rested on the inherent incompatibility between the rights sought to be exercised and the physical location in which the exercise was to occur. [Lehman] rested in large measure on the captive audience doctrine and in part on the transportation purpose of the city bus system. These cases, therefore, provide no support for the Court's conclusion that a letter box is not a public forum.

B. Having determined that a letter box is not a public forum, the Court inexplicably terminates its analysis. Surely, however, the mere fact that property is not a public forum does not free government to impose unwarranted restrictions on First Amendment rights. [Even] where property does not constitute a public forum, government regulation that is content-neutral must still be reasonable as to time, place, and manner. The restriction in § 1725 could have such an effect on First Amendment rights—and does for Justice Marshall—that it should be struck down. The Court, therefore, cannot avoid analyzing § 1725 as a time, place, and manner restriction.[1]

III. I would conclude, contrary to the Court, that a letter box is a public forum, but, nevertheless, concur in the judgment because I conclude that 18 U.S.C. § 1725 is a reasonable time, place, and manner restriction on appellees' exercise of their First Amendment rights.

Justice WHITE, concurring in the judgment.

There is no doubt that the postal system is a massive, government-operated communications facility open to all forms of written expression protected by the First Amendment. No one questions, however, that the Government, the operator of the system, may impose a fee on those who would use the system, even though the user fee measurably reduces the ability of various persons or organizations to communicate with others. Respondents do not argue that they may use the mail for home delivery free of charge. . . .

No different answer is required in this case because respondents do not insist on free home delivery and desire to use only a part of the system, the mail box. The Government's interest in defraying its operating expenses remains, and it is clear that stuffing the mailbox with unstamped materials is a burden on the system.

This justification would suffice even in those situations where insisting on the fee will totally prevent the putative user from communicating with his intended correspondents, i.e., there would be no adequate alternative means available to reach the intended recipients. For this reason, if for no other, I do not find it appropriate to inquire whether the restriction at issue here is a reasonable time, place or manner regulation. Besides that, however, it is apparent that the validity of user fees does not necessarily depend on satisfying typical time, place or manner requirements.

Equally bootless is the inquiry whether the postal system is a public forum. For all who will pay the fee, it obviously is, and the only question is whether a user fee may be charged, as a general proposition and in the circumstances of this case. Because I am quite sure that the fee is a valid charge, I concur in the judgment.

Justice MARSHALL, dissenting.

[Protecting] the economic viability and efficiency of [the postal] service remains a legitimate and important congressional objective. This case involves a statute defended on that ground, but I believe it is unnecessary for achieving that purpose and inconsistent with the underlying commitment to communication. [The] Court today upholds the statute on the theory that its focus—the letter box situated on residential property—is not a public forum where the First Amendment guarantees access. I take exception to the result, the analysis, and the premise that private persons lose their prerogatives over the letter boxes they own and supply for mail service.

1. Even if the letter box were characterized as purely private property that is being regulated by the Government, rather than property which has become incorporated into the "Postal Service's nationwide system for the receipt and delivery of mail," § 1725 would still be subject to time, place, and manner analysis. See, e.g., Young v. American Mini Theatres, Inc. [Footnote by Justice Brennan.]

First, I disagree with the Court's assumption that if no public forum is involved, the only First Amendment challenges to be considered are whether the regulation is content-based and reasonable. Even if the Postal Service were not a public forum, which [I] do not accept, the statute advanced in its aid is a law challenged as an abridgment of free expression. [The] question, then, is whether this statute burdens any First Amendment rights enjoyed by appellees. If so, it must be determined whether this burden is justified by a significant governmental interest substantially advanced by the statute. See [e.g., Consolidated Edison Co. v. PUC; Grayned].

That appellee civic associations enjoy the First Amendment right of free expression cannot be doubted. [Countervailing] public interests, such as protection against fraud and preservation of privacy, may warrant some limitation on door-to-door solicitation and canvassing. But we have consistently held that any such restrictions, to be valid, must be narrowly drawn " 'in such a manner as not to intrude upon the rights of free speech.' " [Hynes v. Oradell.] Consequently, I cannot agree with the Court's conclusion that we need not ask whether the ban against placing such messages in letter boxes is a restriction on appellees' free expression rights. Once appellees are at the doorstep, only § 1725 restricts them from placing their circulars in the box provided by the resident. [The District Court] concluded that the costs and delays of mail service put the mails out of appellees' reach, and that other alternatives, such as placing their circulars in doorways, are "much less satisfactory." [We] have in the past similarly recognized the burden placed on First Amendment rights when the alternative channels of communication involve more cost, less autonomy, and reduced likelihood of reaching the intended audience. Linmark Associates, Inc. v. Willingboro.

I see no ground to disturb these factual determinations of the trier of fact. And, given these facts, the Postal Service bears a heavy burden to show that its interests are legitimate and substantially served by the restriction of appellees' freedom of expression. [T]he Court finds persuasive the interests asserted by the Postal Service in defense of the statute. Those interests —"protecting mail revenues while at the same time facilitating the secure and efficient delivery of the mails"—are indeed both legitimate and important. But mere assertion of an important legitimate interest does not satisfy the requirement that the challenged restriction specifically and precisely serve that end.

Here, the District Court concluded that the Postal Service "has not shown that failure to enforce the statute as to [appellees] would result in a substantial loss of revenue, or a significant reduction in the government's ability to protect the mails by investigating and prosecuting mail theft, mail

---

1. The Government's interest in ensuring the security of the mails is advanced more directly by [other laws]. To the extent that the security and efficiency problems are attributed to overcrowding in letter boxes, the problem could be resolved simply by requiring larger boxes.

As for protection of mail revenues, it is significant that the District Court found the cost of using the mails prohibitive, given appellees' budgets, and the delays in mail delivery too great to make it useful for appellees' needs. Apparently, appellees' compliance with 18 U.S.C. § 1725 would not increase mail revenues. Although protection of the Postal Service obviously must take the form of national regulation, having broad application, a statute's

fraud, or unauthorized private mail delivery service." [1] In light of this failure of proof, I cannot join the Court's conclusion that the Federal Government may thus curtail appellees' ability to inform community residents about local civic matters. That decision, I fear, threatens a departure from this Court's belief that free expression [must] not yield unnecessarily before such governmental interests as economy or efficiency. Certainly, free expression should not have to yield here, where the intruding statute has seldom been enforced. [T]he statute's asserted purposes easily could be advanced by less intrusive alternatives, such as a nondiscriminatory permit requirement for depositing unstamped circulars in letter boxes.

[Even] apart from the result in this case, I must differ with the Court's use of the public forum concept to avoid application of the First Amendment. Rather than a threshold barrier that must be surmounted before reaching the terrain of the First Amendment, the concept of a public forum has more properly been used to open varied governmental locations to equal public access for free expression, subject to the constraints on time, place or manner necessary to preserve the governmental function. [Given] its pervasive and traditional use as purveyor of written communication, the Postal Service [may] properly be viewed as a public forum. The Court relies on easily distinguishable cases in reaching the contrary conclusion. For the Postal Service's very purpose is to facilitate communication, which surely differentiates it from the military bases, jails, and mass transportation discussed in cases relied on by the Court. [The] inquiry in our public forum cases has instead asked whether "the manner of expression is basically incompatible with the normal activity of a particular place at a particular time." [Grayned.] Assuming for the moment that the letter boxes, as "authorized depositories," are under governmental control and thus part of the governmental enterprise, their purpose is hardly incompatible with appellees' use. For the letter boxes are intended to receive written communication directed to the residents and to protect such materials from the weather or the intruding eyes of would-be burglars.

Reluctance to treat the letter boxes as public forums might stem not from the Postal Service's approval of their form but instead from the fact that their ownership and use remain in the hands of private individuals. Even that hesitation, I should think, would be misguided, for those owners necessarily retain the right to receive information as a counterpart of the right of speakers to speak. [E.g., Lamont v. Postmaster General.] On that basis alone, I would doubt the validity of 18 U.S.C. § 1725, for it deprives residents of the information which civic groups or individuals may wish to deliver to these private receptacles.

I remain troubled by the Court's effort to transform the letter boxes entirely into components of the governmental enterprise despite their private ownership. Under the Court's reasoning, the Postal Service could decline to deliver mail unless the recipients agreed to open their doors to the letter carrier—and then the doorway, or even the room inside could fall within Postal

---

nondiscriminatory terms may not save it where infringement of speech is demonstrated. Murdock v. Pennsylvania. [Footnote by Justice Marshall.]

Service control.[2] Instead of starting with the scope of governmental control, I would adhere to our usual analysis which looks to whether the exercise of a First Amendment right is burdened by the challenged governmental action, and then upholds that action only where it is necessary to advance a substantial and legitimate governmental interest. In my view, the statute criminalizing the placement of hand-delivered civic association notices in letter boxes fails this test. . . .

Justice STEVENS, dissenting.

Justice Marshall has persuaded me that this statute is unconstitutional, but I do not subscribe to all of his reasoning. He is surely correct in concluding that content neutral restrictions on the use of private letter boxes do not automatically comply with the First Amendment simply because such boxes are a part of the Postal Service. Like libraries and schools, once these facilities have come into existence, the Government's regulation of them must comply with the Constitution. I cannot, however, accept the proposition that these private receptacles are the functional equivalent of public fora.

My disagreement with the Court and with Justice Marshall can best be illustrated by looking at this case from the point of view of the owner of the mailbox. The mailbox is private property; it is not a public forum to which the owner must grant access. If the owner does not want to receive any written communications other than stamped mail, he should be permitted to post the equivalent of a "no trespassing" sign on his mailbox. A statute that protects his privacy by prohibiting unsolicited and unwanted deposits on his property would surely be valid. The Court, however, upholds a statute that interferes with the owner's receipt of information that he may want to receive. [The] nationwide criminal statute at issue here deprives millions of homeowners of the legal right to make a simple decision affecting their ability to receive communications from others.

The Government seeks to justify the prohibition on three grounds: avoiding the loss of federal revenues, preventing theft from the mails, and maintaining the efficiency of the Postal Service.[1] In my judgment the first ground is frivolous and the other two, though valid, are insufficient to overcome the presumption that this impediment to communication is invalid.

If a private party—by using volunteer workers or by operating more efficiently—can deliver written communications for less than the cost of postage, the public interest would be well served by transferring that portion of the mail delivery business out of the public domain. I see no reason to prohibit competition simply to prevent any reduction in the size of a subsidized

2. Appellant suggests no First Amendment problem is presented because residents would not erect letter boxes but for the Postal Service, and the First Amendment did not compel the creation of the Service. This argument obviously proves too much, because the First Amendment did not ordain the establishment of schools or libraries, and yet we have held that once established, these public facilities must be managed consistently with the First Amendment. [Footnote by Justice Marshall.]

1. Although the Government also advances the privacy interest of the mailbox owner, those interests would of course be protected by allowing the individual owner to make the choice whether he wanted to receive unstamped mail. [Footnote by Justice Stevens.]

[Margin annotations: "Stevens' Dissent"; "Cannot accept Marshall's argument + mail boxes are public fora."; "(but)"; "Statute deprives homeowners of right to receive communications"]

monopoly. In my opinion, that purpose cannot justify any restriction on the interests in free communication that are protected by the First Amendment.

To the extent that the statute aids in the prevention of theft, that incidental benefit was not a factor that motivated Congress.[2] The District Court [concluded] that the Government had failed to introduce evidence sufficient to justify the interference with First Amendment interests. The Court does not quarrel with any of the District Court's findings of fact, and I would not disturb the conclusion derived from those findings.

Mailboxes cluttered with large quantities of written matter would impede the efficient performance of the mail carrier's duties. [But] as Justice Marshall has noted, the problem is susceptible of a much less drastic solution. [A] simple requirement that over-stuffed boxes be replaced with larger ones should provide the answer to most of the Government's [concern].

2. The Government cites legislative history indicating that the "principal motivation for the statute" was the protection of postal revenues and prevention of overstuffing of mailboxes. The Government later notes that "although Congress' primary purpose in enacting § 1725 was the protection of mail revenues, the statute also plays a role in the investigation of mail theft." Because this justification, unlike the other two, was formulated after the statute was enacted, it is not entitled to the same weight as the purposes that actually motivated Congress. [Footnote by Justice Stevens.]

ACCESS TO INTERNAL COMMUNICATION SYSTEMS

PERRY EDUCATION ASS'N v. PERRY LOCAL EDUCATORS' ASS'N

460 U.S. ——, 103 S.Ct. 948, 74 L.Ed.2d 794 (1983).

[This case, dealing with a claim of equal access to the internal mail distribution system of a public school system, is printed below, addition to 10th Ed., p. 1325; Ind.Rts., p. 945.]

10th ED., p. 1304; IND. RTS., p. 924
Insert after Note 2:

3. *A statutory right of access to the broadcasting media for candidates seeking federal elective office.* Sec. 312(a)(7) of the Communications Act of 1934, as added by the Federal Election Campaign Act of 1971, authorizes the FCC to revoke a broadcaster's license "for willful or repeated failure to allow reasonable access to or to permit purchase of reasonable amounts of time for the use of a broadcasting station by a legally qualified candidate for Federal elective office on behalf of his candidacy." The 6 to 3 decision in CBS, INC. v. FCC, 453 U.S. 367 (1981), found that this provision created a major new right of access—a right that enlarged the political broadcasting responsibilities of licensees. The Court also held that the FCC's interpretation and application of the provision did not violate broadcasters' First Amendment rights.

The controversy originated in October 1979, when the Carter-Mondale Presidential Committee asked each of the three major television networks to sell the Committee a half-hour of early December 1979 air time. The Committee sought to broadcast a documentary on the record of the Carter Administration, to augment President Carter's planned announcement of his candidacy for re-election. All three networks denied the request, relying on their across-the-board rules about political broadcasts: ABC and NBC stated that December 1979 was "too early in the political season"; CBS contended that programming disruption would result if it abandoned its policy of selling only 5-minute spots to candidates. The Committee filed a complaint, and the FCC ruled that the networks' reasons were "deficient" under the FCC's interpretation of the statute. The FCC concluded that the networks had violated the law by failing to provide "reasonable access."

Chief Justice BURGER—who had emphasized "the widest journalistic freedom" for broadcasters when he argued in 1973 (in the CBS v. Democratic National Committee case) that Red Lion did *not* support a First Amendment right of access for editorial advertisements—wrote the majority opinion in the 1981 case. He agreed with the FCC's view that § 312(a)(7) created a major new access right, and he found that this broad reading of the statute did not interfere with the broadcasters' First Amendment rights. He acknowledged that, prior to the enactment of § 312(a)(7) in 1971, candidates' access rights were governed simply by the general "public interest" requirement of the Communications Act. Under this standard, licensees, in order to assure license renewal, had to allocate some time to political issues; but an individual candidate could claim no personal right of access unless his opponent had used the station. But the 1971 provision changed all that, in the majority's view: "By its terms, [the provision] singles out legally qualified candidates for *federal* elective office and grants them a special right of access on an individual basis, violation of which carries the serious consequence of license revocation. The conclusion is inescapable that the statute did more than simply codify the pre-existing public interest standard. [The] legislative history supports the plain meaning of the statute that individual candidates for federal elective office have a right of reasonable access to the use of stations for paid political broadcasts on behalf of their candidacies, without reference to whether an opponent has secured time."

The FCC had developed an elaborate set of standards, "evolved principally on a case-by-case basis and [not] embodied in formalized rules," to implement § 312(a)(7). The Court found that implementation justified. The Chief Justice explained that, under these standards, "once a campaign has begun, [broadcasters] must give reasonable and good faith attention to access requests. [Such] requests must be considered on an individualized basis, and broadcasters are required to tailor their responses to accommodate, as much as reasonably possible, a candidate's stated purposes in seeking air time. [To] justify a negative response, broadcasters must cite a realistic danger of substantial program disruption—perhaps caused by insufficient notice to allow adjustments in the schedule—or of an excessive number of equal time requests [under § 315 of the Act]." Under the Chief Justice's view of the standards, "[i]f broadcasters take the appropriate factors into account and act reasonably and in good faith, their decisions will be entitled to deference even if the Commission's analysis would have differed in the first instance. But if broadcasters adopt 'across-the-board policies' and do not attempt to respond to the individualized situation of a particular candidate, the Commission is not compelled to sustain their denial of access." The FCC had relied on these standards when it ruled that CBS, NBC and ABC had illegally denied the Carter-Mondale Committee's requests.

The networks challenged certain aspects of the standards, but the Court was unsympathetic. Chief Justice Burger rejected the networks' claim that the FCC, by requiring the broadcasters to respond to access requests on an individualized basis, had "attached inordinate significance to candidates' needs" and had unfairly belittled "broadcasters' concerns." Moreover, he upheld the FCC's authority to "independently determine whether a campaign has begun and the obligations imposed by § 312(a)(7) have attached." In sum, the Chief Justice concluded that the FCC had engaged in "a reasoned attempt to effectuate [the statutory] access requirement." In the majority's view, the Commission had not "abused its discretion" in finding that the networks had violated the statute.

Nor had the FCC violated the broadcasters' First Amendment rights. Quoting from Red Lion, the Chief Justice stated: "There is nothing in the First Amendment which prevents the Government from requiring a licensee to share his frequency with others." He elaborated: "Although the broadcasting industry is entitled under the First Amendment to exercise 'the widest journalistic freedom consistent with its public [duties],' CBS, Inc. v. Democratic National Committee, the Court has made clear that: '*it is the right of the viewers and listeners, not the right of the broadcasters which is paramount.*' [The] First Amendment interests of candidates and voters, as well as broadcasters, are implicated by § 312(a)(7). [The provision] makes a significant contribution to freedom of expression by enhancing the ability of candidates to present, and the public to receive, information necessary for the effective operation of the democratic process." The Chief Justice added: "[The networks] are correct that the Court has never approved a *general* right of access to the media. See, e.g., [Tornillo; CBS, Inc. v. Democratic National Committee]. Nor do we do so today. Section 312(a)(7) creates a *limited* right to 'reasonable' access. [Further], § 312(a)(7) does not impair the discretion of broadcasters to present their views on any issue or to carry any particular type of programming." He concluded: "Section 312(a)(7) represents an effort by Congress to assure that an important resource—the airwaves—will be used in the public interest. We hold that the statutory right of access [properly] balances the First Amendment rights of federal candidates, the public, and broadcasters."

Justice WHITE's dissent, joined by Justices Rehnquist and Stevens, strongly disagreed with the Chief Justice's broad reading of the statute and with the Court's endorsement of the FCC's standards and their application. Justice White argued that the majority's approach "conceals the fundamental issue in this case, which is whether Congress intended not only to create a right of reasonable access but also to negate the long-standing statutory policy of deferring to editorial judgments that are not destructive of the goals of the

Act.   In this case, such a policy would require acceptance of network or station decisions on access as long as they are within the range of reasonableness, even if the Commission would have preferred different responses by the networks.   It is demonstrable that Congress did not intend to set aside this traditional policy, and the Commission seriously misconstrued the statute when it assumed that it had been given authority to insist on its own views as to reasonable access even though this entailed rejection of media judgments representing different but nevertheless reasonable reactions to access requests. As this case demonstrates, the result is an administratively created right of access which, in light of the pre-existing statutory policies concerning access, is far broader than Congress could have intended to allow."

Developing that position at length, Justice White claimed that it is "as clear as can be that the regulation of the broadcast media has been and is marked by a clearly defined 'legislative desire to preserve values of private journalism.'   [CBS, Inc. v. Democratic National Committee.]   The corollary legislative policy has been not to recognize [individual] rights of access to the broadcast media.   These policies have been so clear and are so obviously grounded in constitutional considerations that in the absence of unequivocal legislative intent to the contrary, it should not be assumed that § 312(a)(7) was designed to make the kind of substantial inroads in these basic considerations that the Commission has now mandated."   In his view, the legislative history "reveals that Congress sought to codify what it conceived to be the pre-existing duty of the broadcasters to serve the public interest by presenting political broadcasts.   [The history] also negates any suggestion that Congress believed it was creating the extensive, inflexible duty to provide access that the Commission has now fastened upon the broadcasters.   [The] legislative history negates the Commission's conclusion that it was free to so drastically limit the discretion of the broadcasters and to so radically expand its own oversight authority."

Justice White's evaluation of the FCC's application of its standards differed sharply from that of the Chief Justice.   The contrast is particularly well illustrated by Justice White's comment that "the Commission's assertions of deference to editorial judgment are palpably incredible.   [If] the degree of oversight to be exercised by the Commission is to be measured by its work in this case, there will be very little deference paid to the judgment and discretion of the broadcaster."   He charged: "While both the Court and the Commission describe [several] factors considered relevant, such as the number of candidates and disruption in programming, the overarching focus is directed to the perceived needs of the individual candidate."   He called this a "highly skewed approach" and charged the majority with abandoning "the tradition-ally recognized discretion of the broadcaster."   The approach approved by the Court, he insisted, laid the foundation "for the unilateral right of candidates to demand and receive any 'reasonable' amount of time a candidate determines to be necessary.   [The] concomitant Commission involvement is obvious.   There is no basis in the statute for this very broad and unworkable scheme of access."*

---

* Justice STEVENS, who joined Justice White's opinion, also submitted a
brief separate dissent, insisting that
the "reasonable access" issue "must

10th ED., p. 1324; IND. RTS., p. 944
Add at end of footnote 4:

Can sleeping be a form of "symbolic speech"? The issue is considered at great length and with considerable erudition in the various opinions in Community for Creative Non-Violence v. Watt, 703 F.2d 586 (D.C.Cir.1983) (en banc). An extremely divided court upheld the First Amendment rights of the sleepers.

10th ED., p. 1325; IND. RTS., p. 945
Add at end of Chapter 12:

SECTION 4. A CLOSER LOOK AT CONTENT REGULATION AND GOVERNMENT MOTIVE

Introduction. The reference in United States v. O'Brien (above, 10th Ed., p. 1306; Ind.Rts., p. 926) to a "governmental interest [unrelated] to the suppression of free expression" has engendered some important commentary suggesting that the analytical methods of O'Brien are applicable to a wide range of free speech problems, and not just to the question of "symbolic speech." * Under such an approach, a governmental interest that is premised on the effect on recipients of a particular message or class of messages would receive heightened· scrutiny, while limitations of speech that are merely incidental to governmental interests unrelated to a message would be subject to a somewhat more deferential balancing approach. Although this extension of O'Brien is not without its detractors,† aspects of it are nevertheless apparent in the cases that follow. But is it possible to follow this approach without looking closely at legislative or other government motive? After reading the cases that follow, consider what remains of the Court's statement in O'Brien that it would not look at congressional purpose, motive, or intent. (On this aspect of O'Brien, see 10th Ed., p. 244.)

The question of illicit governmental purposes is closely tied to the issue of content regulation. What governmental purposes are in fact illicit? To what extent is discrimination on the basis of the particular subject as much

be answered in the context of an entire political campaign, rather than by focusing upon the licensee's rejection of a single request for access." He argued that the FCC's approach here "creates an impermissible risk that the Commission's evaluation of a given refusal by a licensee will be biased —or will appear to be biased—by the character of the office held by the candidate making the request. [In this case, the 4 to 3 rulings by the FCC in favor of the Carter-Mondale Presidential Committee paralleled the party affiliations of the FCC Commissioners: the majority consisted of the four Democratic Commissioners; the dissenters were the three Republican Commissioners.] Indeed, anyone who listened to the campaign rhetoric that was broadcast during 1980 must wonder how an impartial administrator could conclude that any presidential candidate was denied 'reasonable access' to the electronic media."

* Ely, "Flag Desecration: A Case Study in the Roles of Categorization and Balancing in First Amendment Analysis," 88 Harv.L.Rev. 1482 (1975). See also L.Tribe, American Constitutional Law 580–601 (1978).

† E.g., Redish, "The Content Distinction in First Amendment Analysis," 34 Stan.L.Rev. 113 (1981).

of a First Amendment evil as discrimination on the basis of point of view? **
Content regulation in some form is central to the cases that follow, but what
kind of content regulation is it, and why should it or should it not be subject
to close scrutiny? In reference to the Minneapolis Star and Tribune case,
consider whether discrimination against a particular *format* of speech, or
against speech in general, presents the same dangers as discrimination on
the basis of point of view or subject matter. In this connection, Minneapolis
Star and Tribune should be considered along with the unanswered question
in Metromedia, Inc. v. San Diego (addition to 10th Ed., p. 1262; Ind.
Rts., p. 882) regarding the permissibility of a total ban on all billboards.

[handwritten margin note: Special "use tax" which is disproportionately paid by 5 states largest newspaper Violates 1st Am]

MINNEAPOLIS STAR AND TRIBUNE CO. v. MINNESOTA COMM'R OF REVENUE

460 U.S. —, 103 S.Ct. 1365, 75 L.Ed.2d 295 (1983).

Justice O'CONNOR delivered the opinion of the Court.[1]

This case presents the question of a State's power to impose a special
tax on the press and, by enacting exemptions, to limit its effect to only a few
newspapers.

I. Since 1967, Minnesota has imposed a sales tax on most sales of
goods. [In] general, the tax applies only to retail sales. [As] part of
this general system of taxation and in support of the sales tax, Minnesota
also enacted a tax on the "privilege of using, storing or consuming in Minnesota tangible personal property." This use tax applies to any nonexempt
tangible personal property unless the sales tax was paid on the sales price.
Like the classic use tax, this use tax protects the State's sales tax by eliminating the residents' incentive to travel to States with lower sales taxes to
buy goods rather than buying them in Minnesota.

The appellant, Minneapolis Star and Tribune Company "Star Tribune",
is the publisher of a morning [and] an evening newspaper in Minneapolis.
From 1967 until 1971, it enjoyed an exemption from the sales and use tax
provided by Minnesota for periodic publications. In 1971, however, while
leaving the exemption from the sales tax in place, the legislature amended the
scheme to impose a "use tax" on the cost of paper and ink products consumed
in the production of a publication. Ink and paper used in publications became the only items subject to the use tax that were components of goods to
be sold at retail. In 1974, the legislature again amended the statute, this
time to exempt the first $100,000 worth of ink and paper consumed by a
publication in any calendar year, in effect giving each publication an annual
tax credit of $4,000. Publications remained exempt from the sales tax.

After the enactment of the $100,000 exemption, 11 publishers, pro-
ducing 14 of the 388 paid circulation newspapers in the State, incurred a
tax liability in 1974. Star Tribune was one of the 11, and, of the $893,355
collected, it paid $608,634, or roughly two-thirds of the total revenue raised
by the tax. In 1975, 13 publishers, producing 16 out of 374 paid circula-

---

** On this distinction, see Stone, "Restrictions of Speech Because of Its
Content: The Peculiar Case of Subject-
Matter Restrictions," 46 U.Chi.L.Rev.
81 (1978).

1. Justice BLACKMUN joins this opinion except footnote 12. [Footnote by
the Court.] [Footnote 12, dealing with
tax burdens outside of the First
Amendment context, has been omitted.]

[handwritten margin notes: 1967 Minnesota enacted Sales & use tax but which until 1971, exempted periodic publications | 1971 Amended act to impose use tax on paper and ink | 1974 again amended to exempt 1st of $100k of ink paper costs from use tax | Result: Minneapolis Star biggest paper in state of papers 380 papers | (11-13 publishers) | paid 2/3 of the tax revenues on ink & paper]

tion papers, paid a tax. That year, Star Tribune again bore roughly two-thirds of the total receipts from the use tax on ink and paper.

Star Tribune instituted this action to seek a refund of the use taxes it paid from January 1, 1974 to May 31, 1975. It challenged the imposition of the use tax on ink and paper used in publications as a violation of the guarantees of freedom of the press and equal protection in the First and Fourteenth Amendments. The Minnesota Supreme Court upheld the tax against the federal constitutional challenge. . . .

II. Star Tribune argues that we must strike this tax on the authority of Grosjean v. American Press Co., Inc., 297 U.S. 233 (1936). Although there are similarities, [we] agree with the State that Grosjean is not controlling.

In Grosjean, the State of Louisiana imposed a license tax of 2% of the gross receipts from the sale of advertising on all newspapers with a weekly circulation above 20,000. Out of at least 124 publishers in the State, only 13 were subject to the tax. After noting that the tax was "single in kind" and that keying the tax to circulation curtailed the flow of information, this Court held the tax invalid as an abridgment of the freedom of the press. [All] but one of the large papers subject to the tax had "ganged up" on Senator Huey Long, and a circular distributed by Long and the governor to each member of the state legislature described "lying newspapers" as conducting "a vicious campaign" and the tax as "a tax on lying." [Although] the Court's opinion did not describe this history, it stated, "[The tax] is bad because, in the light of its history and of its present setting, it is seen to be a deliberate and calculated device in the guise of a tax to limit the circulation of information," an explanation that suggests that the motivation of the legislature may have been significant.

Our subsequent cases have not been consistent in their reading of Grosjean on this point. Compare [O'Brien] (stating that legislative purpose was irrelevant in Grosjean) with Houchins v. KQED, Inc., 438 U.S. 1 (1978) (plurality opinion) (suggesting that purpose was relevant in Grosjean). We think that the result in Grosjean may have been attributable in part to the perception on the part of the Court that the state imposed the tax with an intent to penalize a selected group of newspapers. In the case currently before us, however, there is no legislative history and no indication, apart from the structure of the tax itself, of any impermissible or censorial motive on the part of the legislature. We cannot resolve the case by simple citation to Grosjean. Instead, we must analyze the problem anew under the general principles of the First Amendment.

III. Clearly, the First Amendment does not prohibit all regulation of the press. It is beyond dispute that the States and the Federal Government can subject newspapers to generally applicable economic regulations without creating constitutional problems. See, e.g., Citizens Publishing Co. v. United States, 394 U.S. 131 (1969) (antitrust laws); Oklahoma Press Publishing Co. v. Walling, 327 U.S. 186 (1946) (Fair Labor Standards Act). Minnesota, however, has not chosen to apply its general sales and use tax to newspapers. Instead, it has created a special tax that applies only to certain publications protected by the First Amendment. Although the State argues now that the tax on paper and ink is part of the general scheme of taxation, the use tax provision is facially discriminatory, singling out publications for treatment that is [unique] in Minnesota tax law.

Minnesota's treatment of publications differs from that of other enterprises in at least two important respects: it imposes a use tax that does not serve the function of protecting the sales tax, and it taxes an intermediate transaction rather than the ultimate retail sale. A use tax ordinarily serves to complement the sales tax by eliminating the incentive to make major purchases in States with lower sales taxes; it requires the resident who shops out-of-state to pay a use tax equal to the sales tax savings. [As] the regulations state, "The 'use tax' is a compensatory or complementary tax." [Minn.Code of Agency Rules.] Thus, in general, items exempt from the sales tax are not subject to the use tax, for, in the event of a sales tax exemption, there is no "complementary function" for a use tax to serve. But the use tax on ink and paper serves no such complementary function; it applies to all uses, whether or not the taxpayer purchased the ink and paper in-state, and it applies to items exempt from the sales tax.

Further, the ordinary rule in Minnesota [is] to tax only the ultimate, or retail, sale rather than the use of components like ink and paper. [Publishers,] however, are taxed on their purchase of components, even though they will eventually sell their publications at retail.

By creating this special use tax, which [is] without parallel in the State's tax scheme, Minnesota has singled out the press for special treatment. We then must determine whether the First Amendment permits such special taxation. A tax that burdens rights protected by the First Amendment cannot stand unless the burden is necessary to achieve an overriding governmental interest. Any tax that the press must pay, of course, imposes some "burden." But [this] Court has long upheld economic regulation of the press. The cases approving such economic regulation, however, emphasized the general applicability of the challenged regulation to all businesses,[2] suggesting that a regulation that singled out the press might place a heavier burden of justification on the State, and we now conclude that the special problems created by differential treatment do indeed impose such a burden.

There is substantial evidence that differential taxation of the press would have troubled the Framers of the First Amendment.[3] The role of

2. The Court recognized in Oklahoma Press that the FLSA excluded seamen and farm workers. It rejected, however, the publisher's argument that the exclusion of these workers precluded application of the law to the employees of newspapers. The State here argues that Oklahoma Press establishes that the press cannot successfully challenge regulations on the basis of the exemption of other enterprises. We disagree. The exempt enterprises in Oklahoma Press were isolated exceptions and not the rule. Here, everything is exempt from the use tax on ink and paper, except the press. [Footnote by Justice O'Connor.]

3. It is true that our opinions rarely speculate on precisely how the Framers would have analyzed a given regulation of expression. In general, though, we have only limited evidence of exactly how the Framers intended the First Amendment to apply. There are no recorded debates in the Senate or in the States, and the discussion in the House of Representatives was couched in general terms, perhaps in response to Madison's suggestion that the repre-

Handwritten margin notes (top right): 1st Am History / Special Tax Burden on press would have troubled Framers

the press in mobilizing sentiment in favor of independence was critical to the Revolution. When the Constitution was proposed without an explicit guarantee of freedom of the press, the Antifederalists objected. Proponents of the Constitution, relying on the principle of enumerated powers, responded that such a guarantee was unnecessary because the Constitution granted Congress no power to control the press. The remarks of Richard Henry Lee are typical of the rejoinders of the Antifederalists: "I confess I do not see in what cases the congress can, with any pretence of right, make a law to suppress the freedom of the press; though I am not clear, that congress is restrained from laying any duties whatever on printing, and from laying duties particularly heavy on certain pieces printed." [The] concerns voiced by the Antifederalists led to the adoption of the Bill of Rights.

The fears of the Antifederalists were well-founded. A power to tax differentially, as opposed to a power to tax generally, gives a government a powerful weapon against the taxpayer selected. When the State imposes a generally applicable tax, there is little cause for concern. We need not fear that a government will destroy a selected group of taxpayers by burdensome taxation if it must impose the same burden on the rest of its constituency. When the State singles out the press, though, the political constraints that prevent a legislature from passing crippling taxes of general applicability are weakened, and the threat of burdensome taxes becomes acute. That threat can operate as effectively as a censor to check critical comment by the press, undercutting the basic assumption of our political system that the press will often serve as an important restraint on government. "[A]n untrammeled press [is] a vital source of public information," Grosjean, and an informed public is the essence of working democracy.

Handwritten margin notes (right): differential tax as opposed to general tax gives gov powerful weapon / Can act as censor of press

Further, differential treatment, unless justified by some special characteristic of the press, suggests that the goal of the regulation is not unrelated to suppression of expression, and such a goal is presumptively unconstitutional. See, e.g. [Mosely]; cf. Brown v. Hartlage, 456 U.S. 45 (1982) (First Amendment has its "fullest and most urgent" application in the case of regulation of the content of political speech). Differential taxation of the press, then, places such a burden on the interests protected by the First Amendment that we cannot countenance such treatment unless the State asserts a counterbalancing interest of compelling importance that it cannot achieve without differential taxation.[4]

Handwritten margin notes (right): So State must assert an interest of "compelling importance" it cannot achieve another way

---

sentatives not stray from simple acknowledged principles. Consequently, we ordinarily simply apply those general principles, requiring the government to justify any burdens on First Amendment rights by showing that they are necessary to achieve a legitimate overriding governmental interest. But when we do have evidence that a particular law would have offended the Framers, we have not hesitated to invalidate it on that ground alone. Prior restraints, for instance, clearly strike to the core of the Framers' concerns, leading this Court to treat them

as particularly suspect. . . . . [Footnote by Justice O'Connor.]

4. Justice Rehnquist's dissent analyzes this case solely as a problem of equal protection, applying the familiar tiers of scrutiny. We, however, view the problem as one arising directly under the First Amendment, for [the] Framers perceived singling out the press for taxation as a means of abridging the freedom of the press. The appropriate method of analysis thus is to balance the burden implicit in singling out the press against the interest asserted by

IV. The main interest asserted by Minnesota in this case is the raising of revenue. [Standing] alone, however, it cannot justify the special treatment of the press, for an alternative means of achieving the same interest without raising concerns under the First Amendment is clearly available: the State could raise the revenue by taxing businesses generally, avoiding the censorial threat implicit in a tax that singles out the press.

Addressing the concern with differential treatment, Minnesota invites us to look beyond the form of the tax to its substance. The tax is, according to the State, merely a substitute for the sales tax, which, as a generally applicable tax, would be constitutional as applied to the press.[5] There are two fatal flaws in this reasoning. First, the State has offered no explanation of why it chose to use a substitute for the sales tax rather than the sales tax itself. The court below speculated that the State might have been concerned that collection of a tax on such small transactions would be impractical. That suggestion is unpersuasive, for sales of other low-priced goods are not exempt. If the real goal of this tax is to duplicate the sales tax, it is difficult to see why the State did not achieve that goal by the obvious and effective expedient of applying the sales tax.

Further, even assuming that the legislature did have valid reasons for substituting another tax for the sales tax, we are not persuaded that this tax does serve as a substitute. The State asserts that this scheme actually favors the press over other businesses, because the same rate of tax is applied, but, for the press, the rate applies to the cost of components rather than to the sales price. We would be hesitant to fashion a rule that automatically allowed the State to single out the press for a different method of taxation as long as the effective burden was no different from that on other taxpayers or the burden on the press was lighter than that on other businesses. One reason for this reluctance is that the very selection of the press for special treatment threatens the press not only with the current differential treatment, but with the possibility of subsequent differentially more burdensome treatment. Thus, even without actually imposing an extra burden on the press, the government might be able to achieve censorial effects, for "[t]he threat of sanctions may deter [the] exercise of [First Amendment] rights almost as potently as the actual application of sanctions." [NAACP v. Button.][6]

A second reason to avoid the proposed rule is that courts as institutions are poorly equipped to evaluate with precision the relative burdens of various the State. Under a long line of precedent, the regulation can survive only if the governmental interest outweighs the burden and cannot be achieved by means that do not infringe First Amendment rights as significantly. [O'Brien.] [Footnote by Justice O'Connor.]

5. Justice O'Connor relied primarily on Breard v. Alexandria, 341 U.S. 622, (1951), which upheld an ordinance prohibiting door-to-door solicitation even though it restricted magazine sales, to reaffirm that a generally applicable sales tax could constitutionally be applied to newspapers.

6. Justice Rehnquist's dissent deprecates this concern, asserting that there is no threat, because this Court will invalidate any differentially more burdensome tax. That assertion would provide more security if we could be certain that courts will always prove able to identify differentially more burdensome taxes, a question we explore further, infra. [Footnote by Justice O'Connor.]

Rehnquist jumps on this

methods of taxation. The complexities of factual economic proof always present a certain potential for error, and courts have little familiarity with the process of evaluating the relative economic burden of taxes. In sum, the possibility of error inherent in the proposed rule poses too great a threat to concerns at the heart of the First Amendment, and we cannot tolerate that possibility.[7] Minnesota, therefore, has offered no adequate justification for the special treatment of newspapers.[8]

④ *Minn. offers no adequate justification*

V. Minnesota's ink and paper tax violates the First Amendment not only because it singles out the press, but also because it targets a small group of newspapers. The effect of the $100,000 exemption enacted in 1974 is that only a handful of publishers pay any tax at all, and even fewer pay any significant amount of tax. The State explains this exemption as part of a policy favoring an "equitable" tax system, although there are no comparable exemptions for small enterprises outside the press. [Whatever] the motive of the legislature in this case, we think that recognizing a power in the State not only to single out the press but also to tailor the tax so that it singles out a few members of the press presents such a potential for abuse that no interest suggested by Minnesota can justify the scheme. It has asserted no interest other than its desire to have an "equitable" tax system. The current system, it explains, promotes equity because it places the burden on large publications that impose more social costs than do smaller publications and that are more likely to be able to bear the burden of the tax. Even if we were willing to accept the premise that large businesses are more profitable and therefore better able to bear the burden of the tax, the State's commitment to this "equity" is questionable, for the concern has not led the State to grant benefits to small businesses in general. And when the exemption selects such a narrowly defined group to bear the full burden of the tax, the tax begins to resemble more a penalty for a few of the largest newspapers than an attempt to favor struggling smaller enterprises.

Has aspects of a (penalty) for largest newspapers.

looks like a penalty for big paper

VI. We need not and do not impugn the motives of the Minnesota legislature in passing the ink and paper tax. Illicit legislative intent is not the *sine qua non* of a violation of the First Amendment. We have long recognized that even regulations aimed at proper governmental concerns can restrict unduly the exercise of rights protected by the First Amendment.

7. If a State employed the same *method* of taxation but applied a lower *rate* to the press, so that there could be no doubt that the legislature was not singling out the press to bear a more burdensome tax, we would, of course, be in a position to evaluate the relative burdens. And, given the clarity of the relative burdens, as well as the rule that differential methods of taxation are not automatically permissible if less burdensome, a lower tax rate for the press would not raise the threat that the legislature might later impose an extra burden that would escape detection by the courts. Thus, our decision does not, as the dissent suggests, require Minnesota to impose a greater tax burden on publications. [Footnote by Justice O'Connor.]

8. Justice O'Connor suggested that some of Justice Rehnquist's economic conclusions, might, under different hypotheses, lead to a greater rather than lesser economic burden on newspapers. "The dissent's calculations, then, can only be characterized as hypothetical. Taking the chance that [such calculations] are erroneous is a risk that the First Amendment forbids." [Footnote by Justice O'Connor.]

A tax that singles out the press, or that targets individual publications within the press, places a heavy burden on the State to justify its action. Since Minnesota has offered no satisfactory justification for its tax on the use of ink and paper, the tax violates the First Amendment.

[Reversed.]

Justice WHITE, concurring in part and dissenting in part.

This case is not difficult. The exemption for the first $100,000 of paper and ink limits the burden of the Minnesota tax to only a few papers. This feature alone is sufficient reason to invalidate the Minnesota tax.

. . .

Having found fully sufficient grounds for decision, the Court need go no further. The question whether [a] state may impose a use tax on paper and ink that is not targeted on a small group of newspapers could be left for another day.

The Court, however, undertakes the task today. [The] Court concludes that the State has offered no satisfactory explanation for selecting a substitute for a sales tax. If this is so, that could be the end of the matter, and the Minnesota tax would be invalid for a second reason.

The Court nevertheless moves on to opine that the State could not impose such a tax even if "the effective burden was no different from that on other taxpayers or the burden on the press was lighter than that on other businesses." The fear is that the government might use the tax as a threatened sanction to achieve a censorial purpose. As Justice Rehnquist demonstrates, the proposition that the government threatens the First Amendment by favoring the press is most questionable, but for the sake of argument, I let it pass.

Despite having struck down the tax for three separate reasons, the Court is still not finished. "A second reason" to eschew inquiry into the relative burden of taxation is presented. The Court submits that "courts as institutions are poorly equipped to evaluate with precision the relative burdens of various methods of taxation." [Why] this is so is not made clear, and I do not agree that the courts are so incompetent to evaluate the burdens of taxation that we must decline the task in this case.

[Justice White described other areas in which the Court evaluates relative tax burdens.]

There may be cases, I recognize, where the Court cannot confidently ascertain whether a differential method of taxation imposes a greater burden upon the press than a generally applicable tax. In these circumstances, I too may be unwilling to entrust freedom of the press to uncertain economic proof. But, as Justice Rehnquist clearly shows, this is not such a case. Since it is plainly evident that Minneapolis Star is not disadvantaged and is almost certainly benefitted by a use tax vis-à-vis a sales tax, I cannot agree that the First Amendment forbids a state from choosing one method of taxation over another.

Justice REHNQUIST, dissenting.

Rehnquist Dissent [handwritten]

Today we learn from the Court that a State runs afoul of the First Amendment [where] the State structures its taxing system to the advantage of newspapers. This seems very much akin to protecting something so overzealously that in the end it is smothered. While the Court purports to rely on the intent of the "Framers of the First Amendment," I believe it safe to assume that in 1791 "abridge" meant the same thing it means today: to diminish or curtail. Not until the Court's decision in this case, nearly two centuries after adoption of the First Amendment has it been read to prohibit activities which in no way diminish or curtail the freedoms it protects.

I agree with the Court that the First Amendment does not *per se* prevent [Minnesota] from regulating the press even though such regulation imposes an economic burden. I further agree with the Court that application of general sales and use taxes to the press would be sanctioned under this line of cases. Therefore, I also agree with the Court to the extent it holds that any constitutional attack on the Minnesota scheme must be aimed at the classifications used in that taxing scheme. But it is at this point that I part company with my colleagues.

The Court recognizes in several parts of its opinion that [Minnesota] could avoid constitutional problems by imposing on newspapers the 4% sales tax that it imposes on other retailers. Rather than impose such a tax, however, the Minnesota legislature decided to provide newspapers with an exemption from the sales tax and impose a 4% use tax on ink and paper; thus, while both taxes are part of one [system], newspapers are classified differently within that system. The problem the Court finds too difficult to deal with is whether this difference in treatment results in a significant burden on newspapers.

The record reveals that in 1974 the Minneapolis Star & Tribune had an average daily circulation of 489,345 copies. Using the price we were informed of at argument of 25¢ per copy, gross sales revenue for the year would be $38,168,910. The Sunday circulation for 1974 was 640,756; even assuming that it did not sell for more than the daily paper, gross sales revenue for the year would be at least $8,329,828. Thus, total sales revenues in 1974 would be $46,498,738. Had a 4% sales tax been imposed, the Minneapolis Star & Tribune would have been liable for $1,859,950 in 1974. The same "complexities of factual economic proof" can be analyzed for 1975. [Therefore,] had the sales tax been imposed, as the Court agrees would have been permissible, the Minneapolis Star & Tribune's liability for 1974 and 1975 would have been $3,685,092.

The record further indicates that the Minneapolis Star & Tribune paid $608,634 in use taxes in 1974 and $636,113 in 1975—a total liability of $1,244,747. We need no expert testimony from modern day Euclids or Einsteins to determine that the $1,224,747 paid in use taxes is significantly less burdensome than the $3,685,092 that could have been levied by a sales tax. *A fortiori*, the Minnesota taxing scheme which singles out newspapers for "differential treatment" has benefited, not burdened, the "freedom of speech, [and] of the press."

[Right margin handwritten notes:]
Jumps on O'Connor's argument about a tax favoring newspapers runs afoul of 1st Am.

Rehnquist (mischievously?) does economic calculation showing use tax benefits newspaper ($1.2M) over sales tax ($3.6M)

"I don't need Euclids or Einsteins to see that"

Ignoring these calculations, the Court concludes that "differential treatment" alone in Minnesota's sales and use tax scheme requires that the statutes be found "presumptively unconstitutional" and declared invalid "unless the State asserts a counterbalancing interest of compelling importance that it cannot achieve without differential taxation." The "differential treatment" standard that the Court has conjured up is unprecedented and unwarranted. To my knowledge this Court has never subjected governmental action to the most stringent constitutional review solely on the basis of "differential treatment" of particular groups. The case relied on by the Court, [Mosely,] certainly does not stand for this proposition. In Mosely all picketing except "peaceful picketing" was prohibited within a particular public area. Thus, "differential treatment" was not the key to the Court's decision; rather the essential fact was that unless a person was considered a "peaceful picketer" his speech through this form of expression would be totally abridged within the area.

Of course, all governmentally created classifications must have some "rational basis." See [Williamson v. Lee Optical; Railway Express Agency v. New York.] The fact that they have been enacted by a presumptively rational legislature, however, arms them with a presumption of rationality. We have shown the greatest deference to state legislatures in devising their taxing schemes. [Where] the State devises classifications that infringe on the fundamental guaranties protected by the Constitution the Court has demanded more of the State in justifying its action. But there is no *infringement*, and thus the Court has never required more, unless the State's classifications *significantly burden* these specially protected rights. [To] state it in terms of the freedoms at issue here, no First Amendment issue is raised unless First Amendment rights have been infringed; for if there has been no infringement, then there has been no "abridgment" of those guaranties.

Today the Court departs from this rule, refusing to look at the record and determine whether the classifications in the Minnesota use and sales tax statutes significantly burden the First Amendment rights of petitioner and its fellow newspapers. The Court offers as an explanation for this failure the self-reproaching conclusion that "courts as institutions are poorly equipped to evaluate with precision the relative burdens of various methods of taxation." [Considering] the complexity of issues this Court resolves each Term, this admonition as a general rule is difficult to understand. Considering the specifics of this case, this confession of inability is incomprehensible.

Wisely not relying solely on its inability to weigh the burdens of the Minnesota tax scheme, the Court also says that even if the resultant burden on the press is lighter than on others: "[T]he very selection of the press for special treatment threatens the press not only with the current *differential* treatment, but with the possibility of subsequent differentially *more burdensome* treatment." [Surely] the Court does not mean what it seems to say. The Court should be well aware from its discussion of [Grosjean] that this Court is quite capable of dealing with changes in state taxing laws which are intended to penalize newspapers. As Justice Holmes aptly put it, "[T]his Court which so often has defeated the attempt to tax in certain ways can defeat an attempt to discriminate or otherwise go too far without wholly abolishing the power to tax. The power to tax is not the power to destroy while this Court sits." *Panhandle Oil Co.* v. *Knox*, 277 U.S. 218, 223 (1928) (Holmes, J., dissenting). Furthermore, the Court itself intimates that if the State had employed "the same *method* of taxation but applied a lower *rate* to the press, so that there could be no doubt that the legislature was not singling out the press to bear a more burdensome tax" the taxing scheme would be constitutionally permissible. This obviously has the same potential for "the threat of sanctions," because the legislature could at any time raise the taxes to the higher rate. Likewise, the newspapers' absolute exemption from the sales tax, which the Court acknowledges is used by many other States, would be subject to the same attack; the exemption could be taken away.

The State is required to show that its taxing scheme is rational. But in this case that showing can be made easily. The Court states that "[t]he court below speculated that the State might have been concerned that collection of a [sales] tax on such small transactions would be impractical." But the Court finds this argument "unpersuasive," because "sales of other low-priced goods" are subject to the sales tax. I disagree. There must be few such inexpensive items sold in Minnesota in the volume of newspaper sales. [Further,] newspapers are commonly sold in a different way than other goods. The legislature could have concluded that paper boys, corner newsstands, and vending machines provide an unreliable and unsuitable means for collection of a sales tax. In summary, so long as the State can find another way to collect revenue from the newspapers, imposing a sales tax on newspapers would be to no one's advantage; not the newspaper and its distributors who would have to collect the tax, not the State who would have to enforce collection, and not the consumer who would have to pay for the paper in odd amounts. The reasonable alternative Minnesota chose was to impose the use tax on ink and paper.

[The] Court finds in very summary fashion that the exemption newspapers receive for the first $100,000 of ink and paper used also violates the First Amendment because the result is that only a few of the newspapers actually pay a use tax. I cannot agree. As explained by the Minnesota Supreme Court, the exemption is in effect a $4,000 credit which benefits all newspapers. Minneapolis Star & Tribune was benefited to the amount of $16,000 in the two years in question; $4,000 each year for its morning paper and $4,000 each year for its evening paper. Absent any improper motive on the part of the Minnesota legislature in drawing the limits of this exemption, it cannot be construed as violating the First Amendment. The Minnesota Supreme Court specifically found that the exemption was not a "deliberate and calculated device" designed with an illicit purpose. There is nothing in the record which would cast doubt on this conclusion. [There] is no reason to conclude that the State, in drafting the $4,000 credit, acted other than reasonably and rationally to fit its sales and use tax scheme to its own local needs and usages.

To collect from newspapers their fair share of taxes under the sales and use tax scheme and at the same time avoid abridging the freedoms of speech and press, the Court holds today that Minnesota must subject newspapers to millions of additional dollars in sales tax liability. Certainly this is a hollow victory for the newspapers and I seriously doubt the Court's conclusion that this result would have been intended by the "Framers of the First Amendment." *

THE SCOPE OF MINNEAPOLIS STAR

1. *Are newspapers special*? The Court in Minneapolis Star emphasized the dangers involved in singling out newspapers or "the press" for special regulatory treatment. Yet the Court consistently has refused to recognize claims of the press to additional protection beyond that available to anyone who communicates information and opinion. See below, 10th Ed., p. 1501; Ind.Rts., p. 1121. Is the Court's focus on the press therefore superfluous? Or might it suggest that in some areas newspapers *will* receive more protection than other claimants under the First Amendment? If this reading is unwarranted, and there remains nothing constitutionally special about newspapers, does Minneapolis Star suggest instead that certain subjects—criticism of government and politics in a broad sense—will receive special protection?

Assuming that the holding transcends the particular context of newspapers, what does it imply about other areas in which regulatory schemes contain categories directed to activities encompassed by the First Amendment? Is there now a constitutionally significant difference between an ordinance regulating parades, picketing, or demonstrations, as such, and one dealing more broadly with, for example, traffic control or obstruction of sidewalks? Is it permissible for zoning regulations to single out bookstores, newsstands, or billboards for special treatment?

2. *Slippery slopes*. Although couched in different terms, Justice Rehnquist's dissent raises the perennial problem of the use and misuse of "slippery slope" arguments. The same argument appears in numerous guises, including the search for a "stopping point," the fear of "a foot in the door," the question of "Where do you draw the line?", and the wariness of abuse of power. Perhaps the most noteworthy characterization is Justice Stewart's use of an Arabian proverb in his dissent in Pittsburgh Press Co. v. Human Relations Comm'n, 413 U.S. 376 (1973): "The camel's nose is in the tent." But regardless of how phrased, the point is the same—if we permit this seemingly innocuous exercise of a power, we are on a slippery slope leading inevitably to much more dangerous exercises of that same power.

---

* Minnesota Star and Tribune is usefully compared with Washington v. United States, 460 U.S. —— (1983), discussed above, addition to 10th Ed., p. 369. In Washington, the Court, with Justice Rehnquist writing the majority opinion, held that a state tax that placed federal contractors in a separate category did not constitute an impermissibly discriminatory tax on the United States and those with whom it deals because the tax was no greater than a nondiscriminatory tax would have been.

Reactions against the use or overuse of slippery slope arguments also predate Justice Rehnquist's dissent. As far back as Martin v. Hunter's Lessee (10th Ed. and Ind.Rts., p. 36), Justice Story observed that "It is always a doubtful course, to argue against the use or existence of a power, from the possibility of its abuse." In Williams v. Florida, 399 U.S. 78 (1970), Justice White noted that one can get off a slippery slope before reaching the bottom, and in Walz v. Tax Comm'n, 397 U.S. 664 (1969), Justice Harlan's concurrence pointed out that slippery slopes can have constitutional toeholds.

The contrast between the majority and Justice Rehnquist's dissent makes Minneapolis Star an appropriate vehicle for reconsidering under what circumstances, if any, a currently innocuous exercise of power should be precluded for fear that it will lead to a far less innocuous abuse. Is Supreme Court review of every abuse likely? Will such review be timely? If the Court cannot check every abuse, can lower courts serve that function? Can non-judicial bodies be trusted to follow the spirit as well as the letter of constitutional decisions? But does eagerness to decide cases on the basis of where a currently innocuous policy might lead fly in the face of the Court's reluctance to decide anything other than the case before it? Is a slippery slope argument a variant of an advisory opinion, in the sense that the basis for the decision is a hypothetical scenario that has not yet occurred and indeed may never occur? Could we not prevent all abuses of power by granting no power whatsoever?

3. *The role of original intent.* Footnote [3] of Justice O'Connor's majority opinion notes that specific evidence that the Framers would have been offended by a particular law commands that the Court invalidate that law. But is the Court's general reluctance to look at the Framer's intent in First Amendment cases solely a function of the "limited evidence of exactly how the Framers intended the First Amendment to apply"? If the specific views of the Framers, when known, must invalidate a law inconsistent with those views, can equally specific evidence defeat a First Amendment challenge to a law that would *not* have offended the Framers?

PEA v PLEA

Rival teacher Bargaining Unions

PERRY EDUCATION ASS'N v. PERRY LOCAL EDUCATORS' ASS'N

PLEA loses attempt to gain = access to school mailboxes for teachers

460 U.S. —, 103 S.Ct. 948, 74 L.Ed.2d 794 (1983).

Justice WHITE delivered the opinion of the Court.

Perry Education Association is the duly elected exclusive bargaining representative for the teachers of the Metropolitan School District of Perry Township, Indiana. A collective bargaining agreement with the Board of Education provided that Perry Education Association, but no other union, would have access to the interschool mail system and teacher mailboxes in the Perry Township schools. The issue in this case is whether the denial of similar access to the Perry Local Educators' Association, a rival teacher group, violates the First and Fourteenth Amendments.

I. The Metropolitan School District of Perry Township, Indiana, operates a public school system of thirteen separate schools. Each school building contains a set of mailboxes for the teachers. Interschool delivery by school employees permits messages to be delivered rapidly to teachers in the district. The primary function of this internal mail system is to transmit official messages among the teachers and between the teachers and the school administration. In addition, teachers use the system to send personal messages and individual school building principals have allowed delivery of messages from various private organizations.

Prior to 1977, both the Perry Education Association (PEA) and the Perry Local Educators' Association (PLEA) represented teachers in the school district and apparently had equal access to the interschool mail system. In 1977, PLEA challenged PEA's status as *de facto* bargaining representative for the Perry Township teachers by filing an election petition with the Indiana Education Employment Relations Board (Board). PEA won the election and was certified as the exclusive representative, as provided by Indiana law.

The Board permits a school district to provide access to communication facilities to the union selected for the discharge of the exclusive representative duties of representing the bargaining unit and its individual members without having to provide equal access to rival unions. Following the election, PEA and the school district negotiated a labor contract in which the school board gave PEA "access to teachers' mailboxes in which to insert material" and the right to use the interschool mail delivery system to the extent that the school district incurred no extra expense by such use. The labor agreement noted that these access rights were being accorded to PEA "acting as the representative of the teachers" and went on to stipulate that these access rights shall not be granted to any other "school employee organization"—a term of art defined by Indiana law to mean "any organization which has school employees as members and one of whose primary purposes is representing school employees in dealing with their employer."

[The] exclusive access policy applies only to use of the mailboxes and school mail system. PLEA is not prevented from using other school facilities to communicate with teachers. PLEA may post notices on school bulletin boards; may hold meetings on school property after school hours; and may, with approval of the building principals, make announcements on the public address system. Of course, PLEA also may communicate with teachers by word of mouth, telephone, or the United States mail. Moreover, under Indiana law, the preferential access of the bargaining agent may continue only while its status as exclusive representative is insulated from challenge. While a representation contest is in progress, unions must be afforded equal access to such communication facilities.

PLEA [filed] this action [against] PEA and [the] Perry Township School Board. Plaintiffs contended that PEA's preferential access to the internal mail system violates the First Amendment and the Equal Protection Clause of the Fourteenth Amendment. [The District Court ruled for the defendants, but the Seventh Circuit reversed, holding that the preferential access system violated both the Equal Protection Clause and the First Amendment.

III. The primary question presented is whether the First Amendment is violated when a union that has been elected by public school teachers as their exclusive bargaining representative is granted access to certain means of communication, while such access is denied to a rival union. There is no question that constitutional interests are implicated by denying PLEA use of the interschool mail system. "It can hardly be argued that either students or teachers shed their constitutional rights to freedom of speech or expression at the schoolhouse gate." [Tinker.] The First Amendment's guarantee of free speech applies to teacher's mailboxes as surely as it does elsewhere within the school [Tinker] and on sidewalks outside [Mosely.] But this is not to say that the First Amendment requires equivalent access to all parts of a school building in which some form of communicative activity occurs. "Nowhere [have we] suggested that students, teachers, or anyone else has an absolute constitutional right to use all parts of a school building or its immediate environs for . . . unlimited expressive purposes." [Grayned v. Rockford.] The existence of a right of access to public property and the standard by which limitations upon such a right must be evaluated differ depending on the character of the property at issue.

A. In places which by long tradition or by government fiat have been devoted to assembly and debate, the rights of the state to limit expressive activity are sharply circumscribed. At one end of the spectrum are streets and parks which "have immemorially been held in trust for the use of the public, and, time out of mind, have been used for purposes of assembly, communicating thoughts between citizens, and discussing public questions." Hague v. CIO. In these quintessential public forums, the government may not prohibit all communicative activity. For the state to enforce a content-based exclusion it must show that its regulation is necessary to serve a compelling state interest and that it is narrowly drawn to achieve that end. Carey v. Brown. The state may also enforce regulations of the time, place, and manner of expression which are content-neutral, are narrowly tailored to serve a significant government interest, and leave open ample alternative channels of communication. [United States Postal Service v. Council of Greenburgh; Consolidated Edison Co. v. Public Service Comm'n.]

A second category consists of public property which the state has opened for use by the public as a place for expressive activity. The Constitution forbids a state to enforce certain exclusions from a forum generally open to the public even if it was not required to create the forum in the first place. [Widmar v. Vincent.][1] Although a state is not required to indefinitely retain the open character of the facility, as long as it does so it is bound by the same standards as apply in a traditional public forum. Reasonable time, place and manner regulations are permissible, and a content-based prohibition must be narrowly drawn to effectuate a compelling state interest.

---

[1]. A public forum may be created for a limited purpose such as use by certain groups, e.g., Widmar v. Vincent (student groups), or for the discussion of certain subjects, e.g., City of Madison Joint School District v. Wisconsin Public Employment Relations Comm'n, 429 U.S. 167 (1976) (school board business). [Footnote by Justice White.]

Public property which is not by tradition or designation a forum for public communication is governed by different standards. We have recognized that the "First Amendment does not guarantee access to property simply because it is owned or controlled by the government." United States Postal Service v. Greenburgh Civic Ass'n. In addition to time, place, and manner regulations, the state may reserve the forum for its intended purposes, communicative or otherwise, as long as the regulation on speech is reasonable and not an effort to suppress expression merely because public officials oppose the speaker's view. As we have stated on several occasions, "the State, no less than a private owner of property, has power to preserve the property under its control for the use to which it is lawfully dedicated." Id. [Greer; Adderley.]

The school mail facilities at issue here fall within this third category. [Perry] School District's interschool mail system is not a traditional public forum. [On] this point the parties agree. The internal mail system [is] not held open to the general public. It is instead PLEA's position that the school mail facilities have become a "limited public forum" from which it may not be excluded because of the periodic use of the system by private non-school connected groups, and PLEA's own unrestricted access to the system prior to PEA's certification as exclusive representative.

Neither of these arguments is persuasive. The use of the internal school mail by groups not affiliated with the schools is no doubt a relevant consideration. If by policy or by practice the Perry School District has opened its mail system for indiscriminate use by the general public, then PLEA could justifiably argue a public forum has been created. This, however, is not the case. [There] is no indication [that] the school mailboxes and interschool delivery system are open for use by the general public. Permission to use the system to communicate with teachers must be secured from the individual building principal. There is no [evidence] [that] this permission has been granted as a matter of course to all who seek to distribute material. We can only conclude that the schools do allow some outside organizations such as the YMCA, Cub Scouts, and other civic and church organizations to use the facilities. This type of selective access does not transform government property into a public forum. [Greer; Lehman v. Shaker Heights.]

Moreover, even if we assume that by granting access to the Cub Scouts, YMCAs, and parochial schools, the school district has created a "limited" public forum, the constitutional right of access would in any event extend only to other entities of similar character. While the school mail facilities thus might be a forum generally open for use by the Girl Scouts, the local boys' club and other organizations that engage in activities of interest and educational relevance to students, they would not as a consequence be open to an organization such as PLEA, which is concerned with the terms and conditions of teacher employment.

PLEA also points to its ability to use the school mailboxes and delivery system on an equal footing with PEA prior to the collective bargaining agreement signed in 1978. Its argument appears to be that the access policy in effect at that time converted the school mail facilities into a limited public forum generally open for use by employee organizations, and that once this occurred, exclusions of employee organizations thereafter must be judged by the constitutional standard applicable to public forums. The fallacy in the argument is that it is not the forum, but PLEA itself, which has changed. Prior to 1977, there was no exclusive representative for the Perry school district teachers. PEA and PLEA each represented its own members. Therefore the school district's policy of allowing both organizations to use the school mail facilities simply reflected the fact that both unions represented the teachers and had legitimate reasons for use of the system. PLEA's previous access was consistent with the school district's preservation of the facilities for school-related business, and did not constitute creation of a public forum in any broader sense.

Because the school mail system is not a public forum, the School District had no [constitutional obligation to let any organization use the school mail boxes.] In the Court of Appeals' view, however, the access policy adopted by the Perry schools favors a particular viewpoint, that of the PEA, on labor relations, and consequently must be strictly scrutinized regardless of whether a public forum is involved. There is, however, no indication that the school board intended to discourage one viewpoint and advance another. We believe it is more accurate to characterize the access policy as based on the *status* of the respective unions rather than their views. Implicit in the concept of the nonpublic forum is the right to make distinctions in access on the basis of subject matter and speaker identity. These distinctions may be impermissible in a public forum but are inherent and inescapable in the process of limiting a nonpublic forum to activities compatible with the intended purpose of the property. The touchstone for evaluating these distinctions is whether they are reasonable in light of the purpose which the forum at issue serves.[2]

2. [Justice Brennan insists] that the Perry access policy is a forbidden exercise of viewpoint discrimination. [We] disagree. [The] access policy applies not only to PLEA but to all unions other than the recognized bargaining representative, and there is no indication in the record that the policy was motivated by a desire to suppress the PLEA's views. Moreover, under Justice Brennan's analysis, if PLEA and PEA were given access to the mailboxes, it would be equally imperative that any other citizen's group or community organization with a message for school personnel—the chamber of commerce, right-to-work groups, or any other labor union—also be permitted access to the mail system. Justice Brennan's attempt to build a public forum with his own hands is untenable; it would invite schools to close their mail systems to all but school personnel. Although his viewpoint-discrimination thesis might indicate otherwise, Justice Brennan apparently would not forbid the school district

from closing the mail system to all outsiders for the purpose of discussing labor matters while permitting such discussion by administrators and teachers. We agree that the mail service could be restricted to those with teaching and operational responsibility in the schools. But, by the same token—and upon the same principle—the system was properly opened to PEA, when it, pursuant to law, was designated the collective bargaining agent for all teachers in the Perry schools. PEA thereby assumed an official position in the operational structure of the District's schools, and obtained a status that carried with it rights and obligations that no other labor organization could share. Excluding PLEA from the use of the mail service is therefore not viewpoint discrimination barred by the First Amendment. . . . [Footnote by Justice White.] The absence of government hostility towards particular points of view led the Court to reject a claim of unconstitutional content discrimination in Regan v. Taxa-

The differential access provided PEA and PLEA is reasonable because it is wholly consistent with the district's legitimate interest in [preserving the property for the use to which it is lawfully dedicated.] Use of school mail facilities enables PEA to perform effectively its obligations as exclusive representative of *all* Perry Township teachers. Conversely, PLEA does not have any official responsibility in connection with the school district and need not be entitled to the same rights of access to school mailboxes. [Moreover,] exclusion of the rival union may reasonably be considered a means of insuring labor-peace within the schools. The policy "serves to prevent the District's schools from becoming a battlefield for inter-union squabbles." [3]

The Court of Appeals accorded little or no weight to PEA's special responsibilities. In its view these responsibilities, while justifying PEA's access, did not justify denying equal access to PLEA. The Court of Appeals would have been correct if a public forum were involved here. But the internal mail system is not a public forum. As we have already stressed, when government property is not dedicated to open communication the government may—without further justification—restrict use to those who participate in the forum's official business.

Finally, the reasonableness of the limitations on PLEA's access to the school mail system is also supported by the substantial alternative channels that remain open for union-teacher communication to take place. These means range from bulletin boards to meeting facilities to the United States mail. During election periods, PLEA is assured of equal access to all modes of communication. There is no showing here that PLEA's ability to communicate with teachers is seriously impinged by the restricted access to the internal mail system. . . .

(IV.) The Court of Appeals also held that the differential access provided the rival unions constituted impermissible content discrimination in violation of the Equal Protection Clause of the Fourteenth Amendment. We have rejected this contention when cast as a First Amendment argument, and it fares no better in equal protection garb. As we have explained above, PLEA did not have a First Amendment or other right of access to the interschool mail system. The grant of such access to PEA, therefore, does not burden a fundamental right of the PLEA. Thus, the decision to grant such privileges to the PEA need not be tested by the strict scrutiny applied when government action impinges upon a fundamental right protected by the Constitution. See [San Antonio v. Rodriguez.] The school district's policy need only rationally further a legitimate state purpose. That purpose is clearly found in the special responsibilities of an exclusive bargaining representative.

tion With Representation of Washington, 461 U.S. —— (1983), discussed fully below, addition to 10th Ed., p. 1481; Ind.Rts., p. 1101.

3. [This] factor was discounted by the Court of Appeals because there is no showing in the record of past disturbances stemming from PLEA'S past access to the internal mail system or evidence that future disturbance would be likely. We have not required that such proof be present to justify the denial of access to a non-public forum on grounds that the proposed use may disrupt the property's intended function. [Footnote by Justice White.]

The Seventh Circuit and PLEA rely on [Mosley and Carey v. Brown.] In Mosley and Carey, we struck down prohibitions on peaceful picketing in a public forum. In Mosley, the City of Chicago permitted peaceful picketing on the subject of a school's labor-management dispute, but prohibited other picketing in the immediate vicinity of the school. In Carey, the challenged state statute barred all picketing of residences and dwellings except the peaceful picketing of a place of employment involved in a labor dispute. In both cases, we found the distinction between classes of speech violative of the Equal Protection Clause. The key to those decisions, however, was the presence of a public forum. In a public forum, by definition, all parties have a constitutional right of access and the state must demonstrate compelling reasons for restricting access to a single class of speakers, a single viewpoint, or a single subject.

When speakers and subjects are similarly situated, the state may not pick and choose. Conversely on government property that has not been made a public forum, not all speech is equally situated, and the state may draw distinctions which relate to the special purpose for which the property is used. As we have explained above, for a school mail facility, the difference in status between the exclusive bargaining representative and its rival is such a distinction. . . .

[Reversed.]

Justice BRENNAN, with whom Justice MARSHALL, Justice POWELL, and Justice STEVENS join, dissenting.

The Court today holds that an incumbent teachers' union may negotiate a collective bargaining agreement with a school board that grants the incumbent access to teachers' mailboxes and to the interschool mail system and denies such access to a rival union. Because the exclusive access provision in the collective bargaining agreement amounts to viewpoint discrimination that infringes the respondents' First Amendment rights and fails to advance any substantial state interest, I dissent.

I. The Court properly acknowledges that teachers have protected First Amendment rights within the school context. [From] this point of departure the Court veers sharply off course. Based on a finding that the interschool mail system is not a "public forum," the Court states that the respondents have no right of access to the system, and that the school board is free "to make distinctions in access on the basis of subject matter and speaker identity," if the distinctions are "reasonable in light of the purpose which the forum at issue serves." According to the Court, the petitioner's status as the exclusive bargaining representative provides a reasonable basis for the exclusive access policy.

The Court fundamentally misperceives the essence of the respondents' claims. [This] case does not involve an "absolute access" claim. It involves an "equal access" claim. As such it does not turn on whether the internal school mail system is a "public forum." In focusing on the public forum issue, the Court disregards the First Amendment's central proscription against censorship, in the form of viewpoint discrimination, in any forum, public or nonpublic.

A. The First Amendment's prohibition against government discrimination among viewpoints on particular issues falling within the realm of protected speech has been noted extensively in the opinions of this Court. [Nietmotko v. Maryland; Tinker; City of Madison; Mosley.]

There is another line of cases, closely related to those implicating the prohibition against viewpoint discrimination, that have addressed the First Amendment principle of subject matter, or content, neutrality. Generally, the concept of content neutrality prohibits the government from choosing the subjects that are appropriate for public discussion. The content neutrality cases frequently refer to the prohibition against viewpoint discrimination and both concepts have their roots in the First Amendment's bar against censorship. But unlike the viewpoint discrimination concept, which is used to strike down government restrictions on speech by particular speakers, the content neutrality principle is invoked when the government has imposed restrictions on speech related to an entire subject area. The content neutrality principle can be seen as an outgrowth of the core First Amendment prohibition against viewpoint discrimination. [Stone, 46 U.Chi.L.Rev. 81.]

We have invoked the prohibition against content discrimination to invalidate government restrictions on access to public forums. [Carey v. Brown; Mosley.] We also have relied on this prohibition to strike down restrictions on access to a limited public forum. [Widmar.] Finally, we have applied the doctrine of content neutrality to government regulation of protected speech in cases in which no restriction of access to public property was involved. [Consolidated Edison Company v. Public Service Commission; Erznoznik v. City of Jacksonville.]

Admittedly, this Court has not always required content neutrality in restrictions on access to government property. We upheld content-based exclusions in Lehman v. City of Shaker Heights, in Greer v. Spock, and in Jones v. North Carolina Prisoners' Union. All three cases involved an unusual forum, which was found to be nonpublic, and the speech was determined for a variety of reasons to be incompatible with the forum. These cases provide some support for the notion that the government is permitted to exclude certain subjects from discussion in nonpublic forums. They provide no support, however, for the notion that government, once it has opened up government property for discussion of specific subjects, may discriminate among viewpoints on those topics. Although Greer, Lehman, and Jones permitted content-based restrictions, none of the cases involved viewpoint discrimination. All of the restrictions were viewpoint-neutral.

[Once] the government permits discussion of certain subject matter, it may not impose restrictions that discriminate among viewpoints on those subjects whether a nonpublic forum is involved or not. [We] have never held that government may allow discussion of a subject and then discriminate among viewpoints on that particular topic, even if the government for certain reasons may entirely exclude discussion of the subject from the forum. In this context, the greater power does not include the lesser because for First Amendment purposes exercise of the lesser power is more threatening to core values. Viewpoint discrimination is censorship in its purest form and government regulation that discriminates among viewpoints threatens the continued vitality of "free speech."

B. Against this background, it is clear that the Court's approach to this case is flawed. By focusing on whether the interschool mail system is a public forum, the Court disregards the independent First Amendment protection afforded by the prohibition against viewpoint discrimination. This case does not involve a claim of an absolute right of access to the forum to discuss any subject whatever. If it did, public forum analysis might be relevant. This case involves a claim of equal access to discuss a subject that the board has approved for discussion in the forum. In essence, the respondents are not asserting a right of access at all; they are asserting a right to be free from discrimination. The critical inquiry, therefore, is whether the board's grant of exclusive access to the petitioner amounts to prohibited viewpoint discrimination.

II. [The] Court responds to the allegation of viewpoint discrimination by suggesting that there is no indication that the board intended to discriminate and that the exclusive access policy is based on the parties' status rather than on their views. In this case, [the] intent to discriminate can be inferred from the effect of the policy, which is to deny an effective channel of communication to the respondents. In addition, the petitioner's status has nothing to do with whether viewpoint discrimination in fact has occurred. If anything, the petitioner's status is relevant to the question of whether the exclusive access policy can be justified, not to whether the board has discriminated among viewpoints.

Addressing the question of viewpoint discrimination directly, free of the Court's irrelevant public forum analysis, it is clear that the exclusive access policy discriminates on the basis of viewpoint. The Court of Appeals found that "the access policy adopted by the Perry schools, in form a speaker restriction, favors a particular viewpoint on labor relations in the Perry schools . . . .: the teachers inevitably will receive from [the petitioner] self-laudatory descriptions of its activities on their behalf and will be denied the critical perspective offered by [the respondents]."

[On] a practical level, the only reason for the petitioner to seek an exclusive access policy is to deny its rivals access to an effective channel of communication. No other group is explicitly denied access to the mail system. In fact, [many] other groups have been granted access to the system. Apparently, access is denied to the respondents because of the likelihood of their expressing points of view different from the petitioner's on a range of subjects. The very argument the petitioner advances in support of the policy, the need to preserve labor peace, also indicates that the access policy is not viewpoint-neutral.

In short, the exclusive access policy discriminates against the respondents based on their viewpoint. The board has agreed to amplify the speech of the petitioner, while repressing the speech of the respondents based on the respondents' point of view. . . .

III. A. [The] petitioner attempts to justify the exclusive access provision based on its status as the exclusive bargaining representative for the teachers and on the state's interest in efficient communication between collective bargaining representatives and the members of the unit. The petitioner's status and the state's interest in efficient communication are important considerations. They are not sufficient, however, to sustain the exclusive access policy.

As the Court of Appeals pointed out, the exclusive access policy is both "overinclusive and underinclusive" as a means of serving the state's interest in the efficient discharge of the petitioner's legal duties to the teachers. The policy is overinclusive because it does not strictly limit the petitioner's use of the mail system to performance of its special legal duties and underinclusive because the board permits outside organizations with no special duties to the teachers, or to the students, to use the system.

[Putting] aside the difficulties with the fit between this policy and the asserted interests, the Court of Appeals properly pointed out that the policy is invalid "because it furthers no discernible state interest." While the board may have a legitimate interest in granting the petitioner access to the system, it has no legitimate interest in making that access exclusive by denying access to the respondents.* . . .

B. The petitioner also argues, and the Court agrees, that the exclusive access policy is justified by the state's interest in preserving labor peace. As the Court of Appeals found, there is no evidence [that] granting access to the respondents would result in labor instability. In addition, there is no reason to assume that the respondents' messages would be any more likely to cause labor discord when received by members of the majority union than the petitioner's messages would when received by the respondents. Moreover, it is noteworthy that both the petitioner and the respondents had access to the mail system for some time prior to the representation election.

---

* A variant of the "special legal duties" justification for the exclusive access policy is the "official business" justification. [The] government has a legitimate interest in limiting access to a nonpublic forum to those involved in the "official business" of the agency. This interest may justify restrictions based on speaker identity, as for example, when a school board denies access to a classroom to persons other than teachers. Such a speaker identity restriction may have a viewpoint discriminatory effect, but it is justified by the government's interest in clear, definitive classroom instruction.

In this case, an "official business" argument is inadequate to justify the exclusive access policy. [The] exclusive access policy is both overinclusive and underinclusive with respect to an "official business" justification. First, [the] school board neither monitors nor endorses the petitioner's messages. In this light, it is difficult to consider the petitioner an agent of the board. Moreover, in light of the virtually un-

limited scope of a union's collective bargaining duties, it expands the definition of "official business" beyond any clear meaning to suggest that the petitioner's messages are always related to the school system's "official business."

More importantly, however, the only board policy discernible from this record involves a denial of access to one group: the respondents. The board has made no explicit effort to restrict access to those involved in the "offical business" of the schools. In fact, access has been granted to outside groups such as parochial schools, church groups, YMCAs, and Cub Scout units. [The] provision of access to these groups strongly suggests that the denial of access to the respondents was not based on any desire to limit access to the forum to those involved in the "official business" of the schools; instead, it suggests that it was based on hostility to the point of view likely to be expressed by the respondents. . . . [Footnote by Justice Brennan.]

There is no indication that this policy resulted in disruption of the school environment.

Although the state's interest in preserving labor peace in the schools in order to prevent disruption is unquestionably substantial, merely articulating the interest is not enough to sustain the exclusive access policy in this case. There must be some showing that the asserted interest is advanced by the policy. In the absence of such a showing, the exclusive access policy must fall. . . .

A NOTE ON GOVERNMENT SPEECH

Although the majority and the dissent in Perry differ as to the proper characterization of PEA's activities, both agree that granting preferential access to someone clearly performing "official business" would create no significant First Amendment problems. Implicit is the view that government *as speaker* is not constrained by the First Amendment, nor need it provide access to the channels of communication employed by government. This view of the First Amendment as restricting the government only when it plays the role of regulator and not when it itself communicates is an accurate generalization of the current state of the law.[1] Several commentators, however, have maintained that the First Amendment ought to impose some limitations on government speech,[2] at least in those cases in which the nature or extent of governmental communication can be said to distort the political process or the marketplace of ideas.[3] But is it realistic to consider the First Amendment relevant to government speech? Are any of the dangers that prompted the First Amendment present when government is speaking rather than restricting? Are certain types of government speech more dangerous than others? If so, can lines be drawn that would allow some government speech but not others? In connection with these questions, consider the various opinions in Board of Education v. Pico, printed below, addition to 10th Ed., p. 1407; Ind.Rts., p. 1027.

1. See, e.g., Muir v. Alabama Education Television Comm'n, 688 F.2d 1033 (5th Cir. 1982); P.A.M. News Corp. v. Butz, 514 F.2d 272 (D.C.Cir. 1975).

2. Yudof, When Government Speaks: Politics, Law, and Government Expression in America (1983); Kamenshine, "The First Amendment's Implied Political Establishment Clause," 67 Calif. L.Rev. 1104 (1979); Shiffrin, "Government Speech," 27 U.C.L.A.L.Rev. 565 (1980); Ziegler, "Government Speech and the Constitution: The Limits of Official Partisanship," 21 B.C.L.Rev. 578 (1980).

3. The examples most frequently cited relate to active governmental involvement in an issue then before the electorate. In Bonner-Lyons v. School Committee, 480 F.2d 442 (1st Cir. 1973), school authorities were prohibited from using the internal distribution system of the Boston city schools to disseminate to parents notices advertising anti-busing rallies, unless the authorities granted an equal opportunity to pro-busing proponents. Is this outcome consistent with Perry?

Chapter 13

FREEDOM OF EXPRESSION: ADDITIONAL PROBLEMS

10th ED., p. 1373; IND. RTS., p. 993
Insert before Sec. 2B:

[handwritten margin: Overbreadth of statute / Challenge / on its face / fails]

CHILD PORNOGRAPHY:
NOT PROTECTED BY THE FIRST AMENDMENT,
EVEN WHEN NOT "OBSCENE"

[handwritten margin: Unsuccessful attack on N.Y. law prohibiting distribution of material depicting children in sexual conduct even if material not obscene]

In NEW YORK v. FERBER, 458 U.S. —— (1982), the Court unanimously rejected a First Amendment attack on a New York law designed to deal with the problem of child pornography by prohibiting the distribution of material depicting children engaged in sexual conduct without requiring that the material be legally obscene. In reaching that result, Justice WHITE, who wrote the majority opinion, echoed the Chaplinsky approach by "classifying child pornography as a category of material outside the protection of the First Amendment."[1] Ferber, the owner of a Manhattan bookstore specializing in sexually oriented products, was convicted under § 263.15 of the New York Penal Law for selling two films devoted almost exclusively to depicting young boys masturbating. Sec. 263.15 provides: "A person is guilty of promoting a sexual performance by a child when, knowing the character and content thereof, he produces, directs or promotes any performance which includes sexual conduct by a child less than sixteen years of age."[2] The Court found Ferber's conviction constitutional.

[handwritten margin: Ferber convicted for selling films depicting young boys masturbating]
[handwritten margin: law]
[handwritten margin: Conviction affirmed]

Justice White's opinion noted that this case was the Court's "first examination of a statute directed at and limited to depictions of sexual activity in-

1. Although the Court reached a unanimous judgment, only four other Justices (Chief Justice Burger and Justices Powell, Rehnquist and O'Connor) fully supported Justice White's opinion. (Justice O'Connor also submitted a separate concurrence.) Justice Blackmun simply noted his concurrence in the result. Justice Brennan, joined by Justice Marshall, filed an opinion concurring in the judgment. Justice Stevens also submitted a separate opinion concurring in the judgment. (The separate opinions are noted further below.)

2. Another section of the law defines "sexual conduct" as "actual or simulated sexual intercourse, deviate sexual intercourse, sexual bestiality, masturbation, sadomasochistic abuse, or lewd exhibition of the genitals." The law defines the term "promote" as "to procure, manufacture, issue, sell, give, provide, lend, mail, deliver, transfer, transmute, publish, distribute, circulate, disseminate, present, exhibit or advertise, or to offer or agree to do the same."

Ferber was also indicted under a companion provision, which was solely directed at obscenity. He was acquitted of that charge of promoting an obscene sexual performance, but found guilty of violating § 263.15, the child pornography provision, which did not require proof that the films were obscene. (Justice Stevens' concurring opinion noted that Ferber's counsel "conceded at oral argument that a finding that the films are obscene would have been consistent with the Miller definition.")

volving children.[3] We believe our inquiry should begin with the question of whether a State has somewhat more freedom in proscribing works which portray sexual acts or lewd exhibitions of genitalia by children [than in regulating obscenity]." In developing his affirmative answer to that question, Justice White began by noting that Chaplinsky had "excis[ed]" obscenity "from the realm of constitutionally protected expression," and that the Court's later decisions directly addressing obscenity culminated in Miller v. California in 1973. He added: "Over the past decade, we have adhered to the guidelines expressed in Miller, which subsequently [have] been followed in the regulatory schemes of most states." But in his view the Miller obscenity standard did not delineate the extent of state power over child pornography. The portions of Justice White's opinion explaining why states have "greater leeway" over child pornography warrant extensive quotation:

B. The Miller standard, like its predecessors, was an accommodation between the state's interests in protecting the 'sensibilities of unwilling recipients' from exposure to pornographic material and the dangers of censorship inherent in unabashedly content-based laws. Like obscenity statutes, laws directed at the dissemination of child pornography run the risk of suppressing protected expression by allowing the hand of the censor to become unduly heavy. For the following reasons, however, we are persuaded that the States are entitled to greater leeway in the regulation of pornographic depictions of children.

First It is evident beyond the need for elaboration that a state's interest in 'safeguarding the physical and psychological well being of a minor' is 'compelling.' [Globe Newspapers.] Accordingly, we have sustained legislation aimed at protecting the physical and emotional well-being of youth even when the laws have operated in the sensitive area of constitutionally protected rights. [E.g.], In Ginsberg v. New York, we sustained a New York law protecting children from exposure to nonobscene literature. [See also Pacifica.]

"The prevention of sexual exploitation and abuse of children constitutes a government objective of surpassing importance. The legislative findings accompanying passage of the New York laws reflect this concern: 'There has been a proliferation of children as subjects in sexual performances. [The] public policy of the state demands the protection of children from exploitation through sexual performances.' We shall not second-guess this legislative judgment. [Suffice] it to say that virtually all of the States and the United States have passed legislation proscribing the production of or oth-

---

3. Justice White had noted earlier that, "[i]n recent years, the exploitive use of children in the production of pornography has become a serious national problem." The federal government and 47 states had enacted statutes "specifically directed at the production of child pornography." At least half of these did not require "that the materials produced be legally obscene." Moreover, 35 states and Congress had passed legislation pro-

hibiting the distribution of such materials. Twenty of these states prohibited the distribution of material depicting children engaged in sexual conduct without requiring that the material be legally obscene. New York was one of these 20 states. The laws in the other 15 states, as well as the federal law, prohibited the dissemination of such material only if it was obscene.

Handwritten margin notes:

1st Question: whether states have more freedom to suppress material sexual material involving children than they do in regulating obscenity?

Miller Std. did not define state power over child porno.

States have more leeway here because:

① States' compelling interest to safeguard physical & psychological well being of children

Statistics almost all states and U.S. re child porno

We do not second guess this legis. judgment that is harmful to children

State & Fed Laws

erwise combatting 'child pornography.' The legislative judgment, as well as the judgment found in the relevant literature, is that the use of children as subjects of pornographic materials is harmful to the physiological, emotional, and mental health of the child. That judgment, we think, easily passes muster under the First Amendment.

Second. The distribution of photographs and films depicting sexual activity by juveniles is intrinsically related to the sexual abuse of children in at least two ways. First, the materials produced are a permanent record of the children's participation and the harm to the child is exacerbated by their circulation. *Second,* the distribution network for child pornography must be closed if the production of material which requires the sexual exploitation of children is to be effectively controlled. Indeed, there is no serious contention that the legislature was unjustified in believing that it is difficult, if not impossible, to halt the exploitation of children by pursuing only those who produce the the photographs and movies. While the production of pornographic materials is a low-profile, clandestine industry, the need to market the resulting products requires a visible apparatus of distribution. The most expeditious if not the only practical method of law enforcement may be to dry up the market for this material by imposing severe criminal penalties on persons selling, advertising, or otherwise promoting the product. Thirty-five States and Congress have concluded that restraints on the distribution of pornographic materials are required in order to effectively combat the problem, and there is a body of literature and testimony to support these legislative conclusions. Cf. United States v. Darby.

"Respondent does not contend that the State is unjustified in pursuing those who distribute child pornography. Rather, he argues that it is enough for the State to prohibit the distribution of materials that are legally obscene under the Miller test. While some States may find that this approach properly accommodates its interest, it does not follow that the First Amendment prohibits a State from going further. The Miller standard, like all general definitions of what may be banned as obscene, does not reflect the State's particular and more compelling interest in prosecuting those who promote the sexual exploitation of children. Thus, the question under the Miller test of whether a work, taken as a whole, appeals to the prurient interest of the average person bears no connection to the issue of whether a child has been physically or psychologically harmed in the production of the work. Similarly, a sexually explicit depiction need not be 'patently offensive' in order to have required the sexual exploitation of a child for its production. In addition, a work which, taken on the whole, contains serious literary, artistic, political, or scientific value may nevertheless embody the hardest core of child pornography. 'It is irrelevant to the child [who has been abused] whether or not the material . . . has a literary, artistic, political, or social value.' Memorandum of Assemblyman Lasher in Support of § 263.15. We therefore cannot conclude that the Miller standard is a satisfactory solution to the child pornography problem.

Third. The advertising and selling of child pornography provides an economic motive for and is thus an integral part of the production of such materials, an activity illegal throughout the nation. 'It rarely has been sug-

(3) Distribution provides economic motivation for the illegal production of such material

gested that the constitutional freedom for speech and press extends its immunity to speech or writing used as an integral part of conduct in violation of a valid criminal statute.' Giboney v. Empire Storage & Ice Co. We note that were the statutes outlawing the employment of children in these films and photographs fully effective, and the constitutionality of these laws have not been questioned, the First Amendment implications would be no greater than that presented by laws against distribution: enforceable production laws would leave no child pornography to be marketed.

(4) No value in material of this type

Alternatives methods other than use of children

use older, but younger looking, person

"*Fourth,* The value of permitting live performances and photographic reproductions of children engaged in lewd sexual conduct is exceedingly modest, if not de minimis. We consider it unlikely that visual depictions of children performing sexual acts or lewdly exhibiting their genitals would often constitute an important and necessary part of a literary performance or scientific or educational work. As the trial court in this case observed, if it were necessary for literary or artistic value, a person over the statutory age who perhaps looked younger could be utilized. Simulation outside of the prohibition of the statute could provide another alternative. Nor is there any question here of censoring a particular literary theme or portrayal of sexual activity. The First Amendment interest is limited to that of rendering the portrayal somewhat more 'realistic' by utilizing or photographing children.

(5) Consistent w Earlier decisions

"*Fifth.* Recognizing and classifying child pornography as a category of material outside the protection of the First Amendment is not incompatible with our earlier decisions. ' The question whether speech is, or is not protected by the First Amendment often depends on the content of the speech.' [American Mini Theatres (Opinion of Justice Stevens). See also Pacifica (Opinion of Justice Stevens).] It is the content of an utterance that determines whether it is a protected epithet or an unprotected "fighting comment."' [American Mini Theatres.] See [Chaplinsky.] [Thus], it is not rare that a content-based classification of speech has been accepted because it may be appropriately generalized that within the confines of the given classification, the evil to be restricted so overwhelmingly outweighs the expressive interests, if any, at stake, that no process of case-by-case adjudication is required. When a definable class of material, such as that covered by § 263.15, bears so heavily and pervasively on the welfare of children engaged in its production, we think the balance of competing interests is clearly struck and that it is permissible to consider these materials as without the protection of the First Amendment.

Balance of competing interests in favor of considering these materials outside 1st Am

Limits
Conduct must be adequately defined by state law here visual depiction is harm to be combatted

"C. There are, of course, limits on the category of child pornography which, like obscenity, is unprotected by the First Amendment. As with all legislation in this sensitive area, the conduct to be prohibited must be adequately defined by the applicable state law, as written or authoritatively construed. Here the nature of the harm to be combatted requires that the state offense be limited to works that *visually* depict sexual conduct by children below a specified age. The category of 'sexual conduct' proscribed must also be suitably limited and described.

"The test for child pornography is separate from the obscenity standard enunciated in Miller, but may be compared to it for purpose of clarity. The

Miller formulation is adjusted in the following respects: A trier of fact need not find that the material appeals to the prurient interest of the average person; it is not required that sexual conduct portrayed be done so in a patently offensive manner; and the material at issue need not be considered as a whole. We note that the distribution of descriptions or other depictions of sexual conduct, not otherwise obscene, which do not involve live performance or photographic or other visual reproduction of live performances, retains First Amendment protection. As with obscenity laws, criminal responsibility may not be imposed without some element of scienter on the part of the defendant.

'D'   Section 263.15's prohibition incorporates a definition of sexual conduct that comports with the above-stated principles. The forbidden acts to be depicted are listed with sufficient precision and represent the kind of conduct that, if it were the theme of a work, could render it legally obscene: 'actual or simulated sexual intercourse, deviate sexual intercourse, sexual bestiality, masturbation, sadomasochistic abuse, or lewd exhibition of the genitals.' The term 'lewd exhibition of the genitals' is not unknown in this area and, indeed, was given in Miller as an example of a permissible regulation. [We] hold that § 263.15, sufficiently describes a category of material the production and distribution of which is not entitled to First Amendment protection. It is therefore clear that there is nothing unconstitutionally 'underinclusive' about a statute that singles out this category of material for proscription.[4] It also follows that the State is not barred by the First Amendment from prohibiting the distribution of unprotected materials produced outside the State."

After elaborating these central premises, Justice White turned to the claim that the New York law was "unconstitutionally overbroad" because it would forbid the distribution of material with serious literary, scientific or educational value or material which does not threaten the harms sought to be combatted by the State." In rejecting that attack, Justice White relied heavily upon—and elaborated—the "substantial overbreadth" approach of Broadrick v. Oklahoma (a 1973 decision written by Justice White and discussed at length in the Note at 10th Ed., p. 1185; Ind.Rts., p. 805). Ferber had prevailed on the overbreadth ground in New York's highest court. The New York court "recognized that overbreadth scrutiny has been limited with respect to conduct-related regulation [but] did not apply the test enunciated in Broadrick because the challenged statute, in its view, was directed at 'pure speech.'" It accordingly found the law fatally overbroad. But Justice White concluded that the state court was mistaken in holding the law invalid on its face on overbreadth grounds: "[A state court] should not be compelled to

4. "[Erznoznik, relied upon by the highest New York court,] struck down a law against drive-in theaters showing nude scenes if movies could be seen from a public place. Since nudity, without more, is protected expression we proceeded to consider the underinclusiveness of the ordinance. The Jacksonville ordinance impermissibly singled out movies with nudity for special treatment while failing to regulate other protected speech which created the same alleged risk to traffic. Today, we hold that child pornography as defined in § 263.15 is unprotected speech subject to content-based regulation. Hence, it cannot be underinclusive or unconstitutional for a State to do precisely that." [Footnote by Justice White.]

entertain an overbreadth attack when not required to do so by the Constitution." After reviewing the "substantial overbreadth" approach of Broadrick at length, Justice White commented: "Broadrick was a regulation involving restrictions on political campaign activity, an area not considered 'pure speech,' and thus it was unnecessary to consider the proper overbreadth test when a law arguably reaches traditional forms of expression such as books and films. [This case], which poses the question squarely, convinces us that the rationale of Broadrick is sound and should be applied in the present context involving the harmful employment of children to make sexually explicit materials for distribution."

Justice White explained: "The premise that a law should not be invalidated for overbreadth unless it reaches a substantial number of impermissible applications is hardly novel. [While] a sweeping statute, or one incapable of limitation, has the potential to repeatedly chill the exercise of expressive activity by many individuals, the extent of deterrence of protected speech can be expected to decrease with the declining reach of the regulation. This observation appears equally applicable to the publication of books and films as it is to activities, such as picketing or participation in election campaigns, which have previously been categorized as involving conduct plus speech. We see no appreciable difference between the position of a publisher or bookseller in doubt as to the reach of New York's child pornography law and the situation faced by the Oklahoma state employees [in Broadrick] with respect to that state's restriction on partisan political activity." Although "the penalty to be imposed is relevant in determining whether demonstratable overbreadth is substantial, [we] hold that the fact that a criminal prohibition is involved does not obviate the need for the inquiry or a priori warrant a finding of substantial overbreadth."

Applying these principles here, Justice White found § 263.15 "not substantially overbroad": "We consider this the paradigmatic case of a state statute whose legitimate reach dwarfs its arguably impermissible applications. New York, as we have held, may constitutionally prohibit dissemination of material specified in [the law]. While the reach of the statute is directed at the hard core of child pornography, the [highest New York court] was understandably concerned that some protected expression, ranging from medical textbooks to pictorials in National Geographic, would fall prey to the statute. How often, if ever, it may be necessary to employ children to engage in conduct clearly within the reach of the [law] in order to produce educational, medical or artistic works cannot be known with certainty. Yet we seriously doubt [that] these arguably impermissible applications of the statute amount to more than a tiny fraction of the materials within the statute's reach. [Under] these circumstances, § 263.15 is 'not substantially overbroad and whatever overbreadth exists should be cured through case-by-case analysis of the fact situations to which its sanctions, assertedly, may not be applied.' Broadrick v. Oklahoma." Justice White accordingly concluded: "Because § 263.15 is not substantially overbroad, it is unnecessary to consider its application to material that does not depict sexual conduct of a type that New York may restrict consistent with the First Amendment. As applied to Paul Ferber

As Applied Law does not violate 1st Am.

and to others who distribute similar material, the statute does not violate the First Amendment." [5]

Brennan + Marshall Concurr

Justice BRENNAN, joined by Justice Marshall, submitted an opinion concurring in the judgment. He stated that he agreed "with much of what is said in the Court's opinion" and that he had long held the view that "the State has a special interest in protecting the well-being of its youth." That "special and compelling interest, and the particular vulnerability of children," afforded the State leeway to regulate pornographic material harmful to children "even though the State does not have such leeway when it seeks only to protect consenting adults from exposure to such material." He also agreed with the rejection of the overbreadth attack because the "tiny fraction" of arguably protected serious material that could conceivably fall within the statute was insufficient to strike the law on overbreadth grounds even under his dissenting view in Broadrick.

but Brennan qualifies by saying law's application to children's activity depiction that do have serious value would violate 1st Am.

But Justice Brennan then proceeded to add an important qualification. He insisted that application of a law such as New York's to "depictions of children that in themselves do have serious literary, artistic, scientific or medical value, would violate the First Amendment." He explained that "the limited classes of speech, the suppression of which does not raise serious First Amendment concerns, have two attributes": they are "of exceedingly 'slight social value,'" and the state has a compelling interest in their regulation. See [Chaplinsky]." Justice Brennan elaborated: "The First Amendment value of depictions of children that are in themselves serious contributions to art,

5. Justice O'CONNOR, while joining Justice White's opinion, also submitted a separate concurrence. She emphasized that the Court had not held that "New York must except 'material with serious literary, scientific or educational value' from its statute. The Court merely holds that, even if the First Amendment shelters such material, New York's current statute is not sufficiently overbroad to support [Ferber's] facial attack." She went on to suggest that the compelling state interests involved here "might in fact permit New York to ban knowing distribution of works depicting minors engaged in explicit sexual conduct, regardless of the social value of the depictions. For example, a 12-year-old child photographed while masturbating surely suffers the same psychological harm whether the community labels the photograph 'edifying' or 'tasteless.' The audience's appreciation of the depiction is simply irrelevant to New York's asserted interest in protecting children from psychological, emotional, and mental harm." She noted that an "exception for depictions of serious social value [would] actually increase opportunities for the content-based censorship disfavored by the First Amendment."

The New York law sought "to protect minors from abuse without attempting to restrict the expression of ideas by those who might use children as live models."

Justice O'Connor added: "On the other hand, it is quite possible that New York's statute is overbroad because it bans depictions that do not actually threaten the harms identified by the Court. For example, clinical pictures of adolescent sexuality, such as those that might appear in medical textbooks, might not involve the type of sexual exploitation and abuse targeted by New York's statute. Nor might such depictions feed the poisonous 'kiddie porn' market that New York and other States have attempted to regulate. Similarly, pictures of children engaged in rites widely approved by their cultures, such as those that might appear in issues of National Geographic, might not trigger the compelling interests identified by the Court. It is not necessary to address these possibilities further today, however, because this potential overbreadth is not sufficiently substantial to warrant facial invalidation of New York's statute."

literature or science, is, by definition, simply not 'de minimis.' At the same time, the State's interest in suppression of such materials is likely to be far less compelling. For the Court's assumption of harm to the child [lacks] much of its force where the depiction is a serious contribution to art or science. [In] short, it is inconceivable how a depiction of a child that is itself a serious contribution to the world of art or literature or science can be deemed 'material outside the protection of the First Amendment.' "

The longest and most distinctive of the separate opinions came from Justice STEVENS, who concurred only in the judgment. That opinion, too, is worth quoting at some length: "Two propositions seem perfectly clear to me. First, the specific conduct that gave rise to this criminal prosecution is not protected by the Federal Constitution; second, the state statute that respondent violated prohibits some conduct that is protected by the First Amendment. The critical question, then, is whether this respondent, to whom the statute may be applied without violating the Constitution, may challenge the statute on the ground that it conceivably may be applied unconstitutionally to others in situations not before the Court. I agree with the Court's answer to this question but not with its method of analyzing the issue.

"Before addressing that issue, I shall explain why respondent's conviction does not violate the Constitution. The two films that respondent sold contained nothing more than lewd exhibition; there is no claim that the films included any material that had literary, artistic, scientific, or educational value. Respondent was a willing participant in a commercial market that [New York] has a legitimate interest in suppressing. The character of the State's interest in protecting children from sexual abuse justifies the imposition of criminal sanctions against those who profit, directly or indirectly, from the promotion of such films. In this respect my evaluation of this case is different from the opinion I have expressed concerning the imposition of criminal sanctions for the promotion of obscenity in other contexts.[6]

"A holding that respondent may be punished for selling these two films does not require us to conclude that other users of these very films, or that other motion pictures containing similar scenes, are beyond the pale of constitutional protection. Thus, the exhibition of these films before a legislative committee studying a proposed amendment to a state law, or before a group of research scientists studying human behavior, could not, in my opinion, be made a crime. Moreover, it is at least conceivable that a serious work of art, a documentary on behavioral problems, or a medical or psychiatric teaching device, might include a scene from one of these films and, when viewed as a whole in a proper setting, be entitled to constitutional protection. The question whether a specific act of communication is protected by the First Amendment always requires some consideration of both its content and its context.

"The Court's holding that this respondent may not challenge New York's statute as overbroad follows its discussion of the contours of the category of nonobscene child pornography that New York may legitimately prohibit. Having defined that category in an abstract setting, the Court makes the empirical judgment that the arguably impermissible application of the

6. See, e.g., *Smith v. United States* (10th Ed., p. 1369; Ind.Rts., p. 989).

New York statute amounts to only a 'tiny fraction of the materials within the statute's reach.' Even assuming that the Court's empirical analysis is sound,[7] I believe a more conservative approach to the issue would adequately vindicate the State's interest in protecting its children and cause less harm to the federal interest in free expression.

"A hypothetical example will illustrate my concern. Assume that the operator of a New York motion picture theater specializing in the exhibition of foreign feature films is offered a full-length movie containing one scene that is plainly lewd if viewed in isolation but that nevertheless is part of a serious work of art. If the child actor resided abroad, New York's interest in protecting its young from sexual exploitation would be far less compelling than in the case before us. The federal interest in free expression would, however, be just as strong as if an adult actor had been used. There are at least three different ways to deal with the statute's potential application to that sort of case.

"First, at one extreme and as the Court appears to hold, the First Amendment inquiry might be limited to determining whether the offensive scene, viewed in isolation, is lewd. When the constitutional protection is narrowed in this drastic fashion, the Court is probably safe in concluding that only a tiny fraction of the materials covered by the New York statute is protected. And with respect to my hypothetical exhibitor of foreign films, he need have no uncertainty about the permissible application of the statute; for the one lewd scene would deprive the entire film of any constitutional protection.

"Second, at the other extreme, [the] application of this Court's cases requiring that an obscenity determination be based on the artistic value of a production taken as a whole would afford the exhibitor constitutional protection and result in a holding that the statute is invalid because of its overbreadth. Under that approach, the rationale for invalidating the entire statute is premised on the concern that the exhibitor's understanding about its potential reach could cause him to engage in self censorship. This Court's approach today substitutes broad, unambiguous state-imposed censorship for the self censorship that an overbroad statute might produce.

"Third, as an intermediate position, I would refuse to apply overbreadth analysis for reasons unrelated to any prediction concerning the relative number of protected communications that the statute may prohibit. Specifically, I would postpone decision of my hypothetical case until it actually arises. Advocates of a liberal use of overbreadth analysis could object to such postponement on the ground that it creates the risk that the exhibitor's uncertainty

7. "The Court's analysis is directed entirely at the permissibility of the statute's coverage of nonobscene material. Its empirical evidence, however, is drawn substantially from congressional committee reports that ultimately reached the conclusion that a prohibition against *obscene* child pornography—coupled with sufficiently stiff sanctions—is an adequate response to this social problem. The Senate Committee on the Judiciary concluded that 'virtually all of the materials that are normally considered child pornography are obscene under the current standards,' and that '[i]n comparison with this blatant pornography, non-obscene materials that depict children are very few and very inconsequential.' The coverage of the federal statute is limited to obscene material." [Footnote by Justice Stevens.]

may produce self censorship. But that risk obviously interferes less with the interest in free expression than does an abstract, advance ruling that the film is simply unprotected whenever it contains a lewd scene, no matter how brief.

"My reasons for avoiding overbreadth analysis in this case are more qualitative than quantitative. When we follow our traditional practice of adjudicating difficult and novel constitutional questions only in concrete factual situations, the adjudications tend to be crafted with greater wisdom. Hypothetical rulings are inherently treacherous and prone to lead us into unforeseen errors; they are qualitatively less reliable than the products of case-by-case adjudication.

"Moreover, it is probably safe to assume that the category of speech that is covered by the New York statute generally is of a lower quality than most other types of communication. On a number of occasions, I have expressed the view that the First Amendment affords some forms of speech more protection from governmental regulation than other forms of speech.[8] Today the Court accepts this view, putting the category of speech described in the New York statute in its rightful place near the bottom of this hierarchy. Although I disagree with the Court's position that such speech is totally without First Amendment protection, I agree that generally marginal speech does not warrant the extraordinary protection afforded by the overbreadth doctrine. Because I have no difficulty with the statute's application in this case, I concur in the Court's judgment."[9]

10th ED., p. 1392; IND. RTS., p. 1012
Add to footnote 4 (at the end of Bates):

For an elaboration of the application of the requirements of Bates and its progeny in the context of advertising by lawyers, see In the Matter of R——— M. J———, 455 U.S. 191 (1982), where the Court unanimously held unconstitutional a range of Missouri restrictions on lawyer advertising. In the wake of Bates, Missouri had adopted several rules of professional ethics. The rules restricted lawyer advertising to certain categories of information and, in some instances, to certain specified language. Appellant was reprimanded for violating these rules. The Court, in an opinion by Justice Powell (the author of the major dissent in Bates), sustained all of appellant's First Amendment challenges.

For example, Missouri had barred lawyers from deviating from a prescribed list of 23 specific terms describing the areas of practice in which professional services were offered. The State did not claim that appellant's listings were misleading. Justice Powell noted: "The use of the words 'real estate' instead of 'property' could scarcely mislead the public. Similarly, the listing of areas such as 'contracts' or 'securities' [presents] no apparent danger of deception. Indeed, [in] certain respects appellant's listing is more informative than the Missouri list]." He accordingly concluded: "Because the listing published by the appellant has not been shown to

---

8. E.g., Schad; Consolidated Edison; Pacifica; American Mini Theatres.

9. In response to Ferber, Congress and a number of states have enacted or proposed legislation that would conform to the Court's opinion. S.57, currently before the Senate Committee on the Judiciary, would eliminate the requirement found in existing federal law (18 U.S.C. § 2252) that material be obscene in order to be subject to the strictures against child pornography. The bill also provides that in any prosecution for child pornography, "it shall be an affirmative defense that the medium, when taken as a whole, possesses serious literary, artistic, scientific, social, or educational value." Assuming that a defendant is shown to have distributed material depicting sexual activity by a child, is this affirmative defense required by Ferber? If at least this much is required by Ferber, is an affirmative defense sufficient?

be misleading, and because the [state authorities] suggest no substantial interest promoted by the restriction, we conclude that this portion of [the regulation] is an invalid restriction upon speech as applied to appellant's advertisements."

In addition, Missouri restricted the information that could be included in an advertisement to a list of specific categories. The permitted categories did not include information about the jurisdictions in which a lawyer was admitted to practice. Appellant had accurately advertised that he was admitted not only in Missouri but also in Illinois, and that he was a member of the U.S. Supreme Court bar. Justice Powell noted that the State had not asserted any "substantial interest in a rule that prohibits a lawyer from identifying the jurisdictions in which he is licensed to practice. Such information is not misleading on its face." The information about admission in two states rather than one was "factual and highly relevant," "particularly in light of the geography of the region in which appellant practiced." Justice Powell conceded that appellant's listing, "in large boldface type," that he was a member of the U.S. Supreme Court bar was "[s]omewhat more troubling": "The emphasis of this relatively uninformative fact is at least bad taste. Indeed, such a statement could be misleading to the general public unfamiliar with the requirements of admission to the bar of this Court. Yet there is no finding to this effect by the Missouri Supreme Court," and nothing in the record to show that this information was potentially or actually misleading.

Appellant was also charged with violating the rules by mailing cards announcing the opening of his office to a larger audience than the permitted one: "lawyers, clients, former clients, personal friends and relatives." Justice Powell conceded that mailings may be more difficult to supervise than published advertisements. But this was not adequate justification for the ban: "Again we deal with a silent record. There is no indication that an inability to supervise is the reason the State restricts the potential audience of announcement cards. Nor is it clear that an absolute prohibition is the only solution," nor that the total ban resulted from "a failed effort to proceed along [a] less restrictive path." Justice Powell accordingly concluded: "There is no finding that appellant's speech was misleading. Nor can we say that it was inherently misleading, or that restrictions short of an absolute prohibition would not have sufficed to cure any possible deception. We emphasize [that] the States retain the ability to regulate advertising that is inherently misleading or that has proven to be misleading in practice. There may be other substantial state interests as well that will support carefully drawn restrictions. But although the states may regulate commercial speech, [the First Amendment requires] that they do so with care and in a manner no more extensive than reasonably necessary to further substantial interests. The absolute prohibition on appellant's speech, in the absence of a finding that his speech was misleading, does not meet these requirements." *

---

* Note also Justice Powell's more general statements, in earlier passages of his opinion, about the current state of commercial speech doctrine: "Commercial speech doctrine, in the context of advertising for professional services may be summarized generally as follows: Truthful advertising related to lawful activities is entitled to the protections of the First Amendment. But when the particular content or method of the advertising suggests that it is inherently misleading or when experience has proven that in fact such advertising is subject to abuse, the states may impose appropriate restrictions. Misleading advertising may be prohibited entirely. But the states may not place an absolute prohibition on certain types of potentially misleading information, e.g., a listing of areas of practice, if the information also may be presented in a way that is not deceptive. [Although] the potential for deception and confusion is particularly strong in the context of advertising professional services, restrictions upon such advertising may be no broader than reasonably necessary to prevent the deception. Even when a communication is not misleading, the state retains some authority to regulate. But the state must assert a substantial interest and the interference with speech must be in proportion to the interest served. [Central Hudson.] Restrictions must be narrowly drawn, and the state lawfully may regulate only to the extent regulation furthers the state's substantial interest." He added in a footnote: "We recognize, of course, that the generalizations summarized above do not afford precise guidance to the Bar and the courts. They do represent the general principles that may be distilled from our decisions in this developing area of the law. As

10th ED., p. 1406; IND. RTS., p. 1026
Insert after the Central Hudson case (before Sec. 4):

METROMEDIA, INC. v. SAN DIEGO

453 U.S. 490, 101 S.Ct. 2882, 69 L.Ed.2d 800 (1981).

[This case, examining First Amendment objections to a regulation of billboards carrying commercial and noncommercial messages, is printed above, addition to 10th Ed., p. 1262; Ind. Rts., p. 882.]

DEFINING COMMERCIAL SPEECH

In BOLGER v. YOUNGS DRUG PRODUCTS CORP., 463 U.S. —— (1983), the Court had the opportunity not only to apply the analysis in Central Hudson, but also to provide some important clarification on the logically prior issue of what does and does not count as "commercial speech." At issue in Bolger was a First Amendment challenge to a federal statute, 39 U.S.C. § 3001(e)(2), prohibiting the mailing of unsolicited advertisements for contraceptives. Because the degree of First Amendment protection afforded the mailings depended on whether they were characterized as commercial or non-commercial speech, classification of the material was the Court's first task.

Justice MARSHALL's opinion for the Court dealt with the classification of the materials in the context of a "drug store flyer" as well as two informational pamphlets, "Condoms and Human Sexuality" and "Plain Talk about Venereal Disease." One of the informational pamphlets repeatedly referred to Youngs' products by name, and the other emphasized generic descriptions of condoms, a product in which Youngs has a leading market position. Justice Marshall's analysis of whether these materials constituted commercial speech warrants full quotation. "Most of appellee's mailings fall within the core notion of commercial speech—'speech which does "no more than propose a commercial transaction."' [Virginia Pharmacy, quoting Pittsburgh Press.] Youngs' informational pamphlets, however, cannot be characterized merely as proposals to engage in commercial transactions. Their proper classification as commercial or non-commercial speech thus presents a closer question. The mere fact that these pamphlets are conceded to be advertisements clearly does not compel the conclusion that they are commercial speech. [New York Times v. Sullivan.] Similarly, the reference to a specific product does not by itself render the pamphlets commercial speech. Finally, the fact that Youngs has an economic motivation for mailing the pamphlets would clearly be insufficient by itself to turn the materials into commercial speech. [Bigelow.]

"The combination of *all* these characteristics, however, provides strong support for the District Court's conclusion that the informational pamphlets are properly characterized as commercial speech. The mailings constitute

they are applied on a case by case basis [as in this opinion], more specific guidance will be available."

commercial speech notwithstanding the fact that they contain discussions of important public issues such as venereal disease and family planning. [Central Hudson.]   A company has the full panoply of protections available to its direct comments on public issues, so there is no reason for providing similar constitutional protection when such statements are made in the context of commercial transactions.   [We] conclude [that] all of the mailings in this case are entitled to the qualified but nonetheless substantial protection accorded to commercial speech."

Having found the materials to be commercial speech, the Court applied the Central Hudson analysis.   Because the speech was neither misleading nor concerned with unlawful activity, and in fact dealt with "substantial individual and societal interests," it was constitutionally protected.   The Court then had to determine the substantiality of the government's interest. While agreeing that aiding parents' efforts to discuss birth control with their children constituted a substantial interest, Justice Marshall found that the statute provided "only the most limited incremental support for the interest asserted.   We can reasonably assume that parents already exercise substantial control over the disposition of mail once it enters their mailbox."   The Court also found the reach of the statute far more extensive than necessary.   The advertisements were "entirely suitable for adults.   [The] level of discourse reaching a mailbox cannot be limited to that which would be suitable for a sandbox."   Pacifica was distinguished on the grounds that the receipt of mail is "far less intrusive and uncontrollable" than are radio and television broadcasts.

Justice Rehnquist, joined by Justice O'Connor, concurred in the judgment.   He acknowledged the substantial governmental interest in preventing intrusion into the home, but felt that the statute here imposed an unduly large restriction in light of the extent of the intrusion.   Justice Stevens, also concurring in the judgment, took issue with the majority's "virtually complete rejection of offensiveness as a possibly legitimate justification for the suppression of speech."   He also was less sure that this material was properly classified as commercial speech.   But to Justice Stevens the important question was "whether a law regulates communications for their ideas or for their style.   [Regulations] of form and context may strike a constitutionally appropriate balance between the advocate's right to convey a message and the recipient's interest in the quality of his environment.   [The] statute at issue [censors] ideas, not style."   To Justice Stevens a crucial distinction was that this statute dealt only with contraception and not with conception, thus excluding "one advocate from a forum to which adversaries have unlimited access."

10th ED., p. 1407; IND. RTS., p. 1027
Insert before Sec. 4A:

THE FIRST AMENDMENT AT THE WORKPLACE

CONNICK v. MYERS

461 U.S. —, 103 S.Ct. 1684, 75 L.Ed.2d 708 (1983).*

Justice WHITE delivered the opinion of the Court.

In Pickering v. Board of Education, 391 U.S. 563 (1968), we stated that a public employee does not relinquish First Amendment rights to comment on matters of public interest by virtue of government employment. We also recognized that the State's interests as an employer in regulating the speech of its employees "differ significantly from those it possesses in connection with regulation of the speech of the citizenry in general." The problem [was] arriving "at a balance between the interests of the [employee], as a citizen, in commenting upon matters of public concern and the interest of the State, as an employer, in promoting the efficiency of the public services it performs through its employees." . . .

I.   The respondent, Sheila Myers, was employed as an Assistant District Attorney in New Orleans for five and a half years. She served at the pleasure of petitioner Harry Connick, the District Attorney for Orleans Parish. During this period Myers competently performed her responsibilities of trying criminal cases.

In [1980] Myers was informed that she would be transferred to prosecute cases in a different section of the criminal court. Myers was strongly opposed to the proposed transfer[1] and expressed her view to several of her supervisors, including Connick. Despite her objections [Myers] was notified that she was being transferred. Myers again spoke with Dennis Waldron, one of the first assistant district attorneys, expressing her reluctance to accept the transfer.

That night Myers prepared a questionnaire soliciting the views of her fellow staff members concerning office transfer policy, office morale, the need for a grievance committee, the level of confidence in supervisors, and whether employees felt pressured to work in political campaigns. [Myers] [distributed] the questionnaire to 15 assistant district attorneys. Shortly after noon, Dennis Waldron learned that Myers was distributing the survey.

---

* Examination of this case may be postponed to 10th Ed., p. 1479; Ind.Rts., p. 1099, below, especially at footnote 2, for consideration with other cases dealing with restrictions on public employees.

1.   Myers' opposition was at least partially attributable to her concern that a conflict of interest would have been created by the transfer because of her participation in a counseling program for convicted defendants released on probation in the section of the criminal court to which she was to be assigned. [Footnote by Justice White.]

He immediately phoned Connick and informed him that Myers was creating a "mini-insurrection" within the office. Connick returned to the office and told Myers that she was being terminated because of her refusal to accept the transfer. She was also told that her distribution of the questionnaire was considered an act of insubordination. Connick particularly objected to the question which inquired whether employees "had confidence in and would rely on the word" of various superiors in the office, and to a question concerning pressure to work in political campaigns which he felt would be damaging if discovered by the press.

Myers filed suit, [contending] that her employment was wrongfully terminated because she had exercised her constitutionally-protected right of free speech. The District Court agreed. [The] District Court found that although Connick informed Myers that she was being fired because of her refusal to accept a transfer, the facts showed that the questionnaire was the real reason for her termination. The court then proceeded to hold that Myers' questionnaire involved matters of public concern and that the state had not "clearly demonstrated" that the survey "substantially interfered" with the operations of the District Attorney's office. [The] United States Court of Appeals for the Fifth Circuit [affirmed.]

II. For at least 15 years, it has been settled that a state cannot condition public employment on a basis that infringes the employee's constitutionally protected interest in freedom of expression. [Keyishian v. Board of Regents; Pickering; Perry v. Sindermann, 408 U.S. 597 (1972); Branti v. Finkel.] Our task, as we defined it in Pickering, is to seek "a balance between the interests of the [employee], as a citizen, in commenting upon matters of public concern and the interest of the State, as an employer, in promoting the efficiency of the public services it performs through its employees." The District Court [misapplied] [Pickering] and consequently [erred] in striking the balance for respondent.

A. The District Court got off on the wrong foot [by] initially finding that, "[t]aken as a whole, the issues presented in the questionnaire relate to the effective functioning of the District Attorney's Office and are matters of public importance and concern." Connick contends at the outset that no balancing of interests is required in this case because Myers' questionnaire concerned only internal office matters and that such speech is not upon a matter of "public concern," as the term was used in Pickering. Although we do not agree that Myers' communication in this case was wholly without First Amendment protection, there is much force to Connick's submission. The repeated emphasis in Pickering on the right of a public employee "as a citizen, in commenting upon matters of public concern," was not accidental. This language [reflects] both the historical evolvement of the rights of public employees, and the common sense realization that government offices could not function if every employment decision became a constitutional matter.

For most of this century, the unchallenged dogma was that a public employee had no right to object to conditions placed upon the terms of employment—including those which restricted the exercise of constitutional rights. The classic formulation of this position was Justice Holmes, who,

old Holmes view

when sitting on the Supreme Judicial Court of Massachusetts, observed: "A policeman may have a constitutional right to talk politics, but he has no constitutional right to be a policeman." McAuliffe v. Mayor of New Bedford, 155 Mass. 216 (1892). For many years, Holmes' epigram expressed this Court's law.

The Court cast new light on the matter in a series of cases arising from the widespread efforts in the 1950s and early 1960s to require public employees, particularly teachers, to swear oaths of loyalty to the state and reveal the groups with which they associated. [e.g., Wiemann v. Updegraff; Keyishian.]

In [these precedents] in which Pickering is rooted, the invalidated statutes and actions sought to suppress the rights of public employees to participate in public affairs. The issue was whether government employees could be prevented or "chilled" by the fear of discharge from joining political parties and other associations that certain public officials might find "subversive." The explanation for the Constitution's special concern with threats to the right of citizens to participate in political affairs is no mystery. The First Amendment "was fashioned to assure unfettered interchange of ideas for the bringing about of political and social changes desired by the people." [Roth v. United States; New York Times v. Sullivan.] "[S]peech concerning public affairs is more than self-expression; it is the essence of self-government." Garrison v. Louisiana. Accordingly, the Court has frequently reaffirmed that speech on public issues occupies the "highest rung of the heirarchy of First Amendment values," and is entitled to special protection. NAACP v. Claiborne Hardware Co.; Carey v. Brown.

Issue "chilling" effect fear of discharge

[Pickering] followed from this understanding of the First Amendment. In Pickering, the Court held impermissible [the] dismissal of a high school teacher for openly criticizing the Board of Education on its allocation of school funds between athletics and education and its methods of informing taxpayers about the need for additional revenue. Pickering's subject was "a matter of legitimate public concern" upon which "free and open debate is vital to informed decision-making by the electorate." [Pickering,] its antecedents and progeny, lead us to conclude that if Myers' questionnaire cannot be fairly characterized as constituting speech on a matter of public concern, it is unnecessary for us to scrutinize the reasons for her discharge. When employee expression cannot be fairly considered as relating to any matter of political, social, or other concern to the community, government officials should enjoy wide latitude in managing their offices, without intrusive oversight by the judiciary in the name of the First Amendment.

If Meyer's questionnaire not "speech on matter of public concern" then we need not scrutinize reasons for her discharge. but not totally beyond 1st Am protection

[We] do not suggest, however, that Myers' speech, even if not touching upon a matter of public concern, is totally beyond the protection of the First Amendment. [We] in no sense suggest that speech on private matters falls into one of the narrow and well-defined classes of expression which carries so little social value, such as obscenity, that the state can prohibit and punish such expression by all persons in its jurisdiction. For example, an employee's false criticism of his employer on grounds not of public concern may be cause for his discharge but would be entitled to the same protection in a libel action accorded an identical statement made by a man on the street. We hold only that when a public employee speaks not as a citizen upon matters of public concern, but instead as an employee upon matters only of personal interest, absent the most unusual circumstances, a federal court is not the appropriate forum in which to review the wisdom of a personnel decision taken by a public agency allegedly in reaction to the employee's behavior. Our responsibility is to ensure that citizens are not deprived of fundamental rights by virtue of working for the government; this does not require a grant of immunity for employee grievances not afforded by the First Amendment to those who do not work for the state.

Whether an employee's speech addresses a matter of public concern must be determined by the content, form, and context of a given statement, as revealed by the whole record.[2] In this case, with but one exception, the questions posed by Myers to her coworkers do not fall under the rubric of matters of "public concern." We view the questions pertaining to the confidence and trust that Myers' coworkers possess in various supervisors, the level of office morale, and the need for a grievance committee as mere extensions of Myers' dispute over her transfer to another section of the criminal court. [Myers] did not seek to inform the public that the District Attorney's office was not discharging its governmental responsibilities in the investigation and prosecution of criminal cases. Nor did Myers seek to bring to light [wrongdoing] or breach of public trust on the part of Connick and others. Indeed, the questionnaire, if released to the public, would convey no information at all other than the fact that a single employee is upset with the status quo. While discipline and morale in the workplace are related to an agency's efficient performance of its duties, the focus of Myers' questions is not to evaluate the performance of the office but rather to gather ammunition for another round of controversy with her superiors. These questions reflect one employee's dissatisfaction with a transfer and an attempt to turn that displeasure into a cause célèbre.

To presume that all matters which transpire within a government office are of public concern would mean that virtually every remark—and certainly every criticism directed at a public official—would plant the seed of a constitutional case. While as a matter of good judgment, public officials should be receptive to constructive criticism offered by their employees, the First Amendment does not require a public office to be run as a roundtable for employee complaints over internal office affairs.

One question in Myers' questionnaire, however, does touch upon a matter of public concern. Question 11 inquires if assistant district attorneys "ever feel pressured to work in political campaigns on behalf of office supported candidates." We have recently noted that official pressure upon employees to work for political candidates not of the worker's own choice constitutes a coercion of belief in violation of fundamental constitutional rights. Branti v. Finkel; Elrod v. Burns. In addition, there is a demonstrated interest in this country that government service should depend upon meritorious performance rather than political service. Given this history,

---

2. The inquiry into the protected status of speech is one of law, not fact. Thus, we [need not defer] to the views of the District Court. . . . [Footnote by Justice White.]

we believe it apparent that the issue of whether assistant district attorneys are pressured to work in political campaigns is a matter of interest to the community upon which it is essential that public employees be able to speak out freely without fear of retaliatory dismissal.

B. Because one of the questions in Myers' survey touched upon a matter of public concern, and contributed to her discharge we must determine whether Connick was justified in discharging Myers. Here the District Court again erred in imposing an unduly onerous burden on the state to justify Myers' discharge. The District Court viewed the issue of whether Myers' speech was upon a matter of "public concern" as a threshold inquiry, after which it became the government's burden to "clearly demonstrate" that the speech involved "substantially interfered" with official responsibilities. Yet Pickering unmistakably states [that] the state's burden in justifying a particular discharge varies depending upon the nature of the employee's expression. Although such particularized balancing is difficult, the courts must reach the most appropriate possible balance of the competing interests.

C. The Pickering balance requires full consideration of the government's interest in the effective and efficient fulfillment of its responsibilities to the public. [We] agree with the District Court that there is no demonstration here that the questionnaire impeded Myers' ability to perform her responsibilities. The District Court was also correct to recognize that "it is important to the efficient and successful operation of the District Attorney's office for Assistants to maintain close working relationships with their superiors." Connick's judgment [was] that Myers' questionnaire was an act of insubordination which interfered with working relationships. When close working relationships are essential to fulfilling public responsibilities, a wide degree of deference to the employer's judgment is appropriate. Furthermore, we do not see the necessity for an employer to allow events to unfold to the extent that the disruption of the office and the destruction of working relationships is manifest before taking action. We caution that a stronger showing may be necessary if the employee's speech more substantially involved matters of public concern.

[Also] relevant is the manner, time, and place in which the questionnaire was distributed. As noted in Givhan v. Western Line Consolidated School Dist., "Private expression . . . may in some situations bring additional factors to the Pickering calculus. When a government employee personally confronts his immediate superior, the employing agency's institutional efficiency may be threatened not only by the content of the employee's message but also by the manner, time, and place in which it is delivered." Here the questionnaire was prepared, and distributed at the office; the manner of distribution required not only Myers to leave her work but for others to do the same in order that the questionnaire be completed.[3] Although

---

3. The record indicates that some, though not all, of the questionnaires were distributed during lunch. Employee speech which transpires entirely on the employee's own time, and in non- work areas of the office, bring different factors into the Pickering calculus, and might lead to a different conclusion. [Footnote by Justice White.]

some latitude in when official work is performed is to be allowed when professional employees are involved, [the fact] that Myers, unlike Pickering, exercised her rights to speech at the office supports Connick's fears that the functioning of his office was endangered.

Finally, the context in which the dispute arose is also significant. This is not a case where an employee, out of purely academic interest, circulated a questionnaire so as to obtain useful research. Myers acknowledges that it is no coincidence that the questionnaire followed upon the heels of the transfer notice. When employee speech concerning office policy arises from an employment dispute concerning the very application of that policy to the speaker, additional weight must be given to the supervisor's view that the employee has threatened the authority of the employer to run the office.

. . .

III. Myers' questionnaire touched upon matters of public concern in only a most limited sense; her survey, in our view, is most accurately characterized as an employee grievance concerning internal office policy. The limited First Amendment interest involved here does not require that Connick tolerate action which he reasonably believed would disrupt the office, undermine his authority, and destroy close working relationships. Myers' discharge therefore did not offend the First Amendment. We reiterate, however, the caveat we expressed in Pickering: "Because of the enormous variety of fact situations in which critical statements by . . . public employees may be thought by their superiors . . . to furnish grounds for dismissal, we do not deem it either appropriate or feasible to lay down a general standard against which all such statements may be judged."

Our holding today is grounded in our long-standing recognition that the First Amendment's primary aim is the full protection of speech upon issues of public concern, as well as the practical realities involved in the administration of a government office. Although today the balance is struck for the government, this is no defeat for the First Amendment. For it would indeed be a Pyrrhic victory for the great principles of free expression if the Amendment's safeguarding of a public employee's right, as a citizen, to participate in discussions concerning public affairs were confused with the attempt to constitutionalize the employee grievance that we see presented here.

[Reversed.]

Justice BRENNAN, with whom Justice MARSHALL, Justice BLACK-MUN, and Justice STEVENS join, dissenting.

[The] Court concludes that [Myers'] dismissal does not violate the First Amendment [because] the questionnaire addresses matters that [are] not of public concern. It is hornbook law, however, that speech about "the manner in which government is operated or should be operated" is an essential part of the communications necessary for self-governance the protection of which was a central purpose of the First Amendment. Because the questionnaire addressed such matters and its distribution did not adversely affect the operations of the District Attorney's Office or interfere with Myers' working relationship with her fellow employees, I dissent.

I. [The] balancing test articulated in Pickering comes into play only when a public employee's speech implicates the government's interests as an employer. When public employees engage in expression unrelated to their employment while away from the work place, their First Amendment rights are, of course, no different from those of the general public. Thus, whether a public employee's speech addresses a matter of public concern is relevant to the constitutional inquiry only when the statements at issue—by virtue of their content or the context in which they were made—may have an adverse impact on the government's ability to perform its duties efficiently.

The Court's decision today is flawed in three respects. First, the Court distorts the balancing analysis required under Pickering by suggesting that one factor, the context in which a statement is made, is to be weighed *twice*—first in determining whether an employee's speech addresses a matter of public concern and then in deciding whether the statement adversely affected the government's interest as an employer. Second, in concluding that the effect of respondent's personnel policies on employee morale and the work performance of the District Attorney's Office is not a matter of public concern, the Court impermissibly narrows the class of subjects on which public employees may speak out without fear of retaliatory dismissal. Third, the Court misapplies the Pickering balancing test in holding that Myers could constitutionally be dismissed for circulating a questionnaire addressed to at least one subject that *was* "a matter of interest to the community," in the absence of evidence that her conduct disrupted the efficient functioning of the District Attorney's Office.

II. [The] standard announced by the Court suggests that the manner and context in which a statement is made must be weighed on *both* sides of the Pickering balance. It is beyond dispute that how and where a public employee expresses his views are relevant in the second half of the Pickering inquiry—determining whether the employee's speech adversely affects the government's interests as an employer. [But] the fact that a public employee has chosen to express his views in private has nothing whatsoever to do with the first half of the Pickering calculus—whether those views relate to a matter of public concern. [The Court] suggests that there are two classes of speech of public concern: statements "of public import" because of their content, form and context, and statements that, by virtue of their subject matter, are "inherently of public concern." In my view, however, whether a particular statement by a public employee is addressed to a subject of public concern does not depend on where it was said or why. The First Amendment affords special protection to speech that may inform public debate about how our society is to be governed—regardless of whether it actually becomes the subject of a public controversy.

[We] have long recognized that one of the central purposes of the First Amendment's guarantee of freedom of expression is to protect the dissemination of information on the basis of which members of our society may make reasoned decisions about the government. [New York Times v. Sullivan; See A. Mieklejohn, Free Speech and Its Relation to Self-Government (1948).] [Unconstrained] discussion concerning the manner in which the government performs its duties is an essential element of the public discourse necessary to informed self-government. [The] constitutionally protected right to speak out on governmental affairs would be meaningless if it did not extend to statements expressing criticism of governmental officials.

[In] Pickering we held that the First Amendment affords similar protection to critical statements by a public school teacher directed at the Board of Education for whom he worked. In so doing, we recognized that "free and open debate" about the operation of public schools "is vital to informed decision-making by the electorate." We also acknowledged the importance of allowing teachers to speak out on school matters.

Applying these principles I would hold that Myers' questionnaire addressed matters of public concern because it discussed subjects that could reasonably be expected to be of interest to persons seeking to develop informed opinions about the manner in which the Orleans Parish District Attorney, an elected official charged with managing a vital governmental agency, discharges his responsibilities. The questionnaire sought primarily to obtain information about the impact of the recent transfers on morale in the District Attorney's Office. It is beyond doubt that personnel decisions that adversely affect discipline and morale may ultimately impair an agency's efficient performance of its duties. Because I believe the First Amendment protects the right of public employees to discuss such matters so that the public may be better informed about how their elected officials fulfill their responsibilities, I would affirm the District Court's conclusion that the questionnaire related to matters of public importance and concern.

The Court's adoption of a far narrower conception of what subjects are of public concern seems prompted by its fears that a broader view "would mean that virtually every remark—and certainly every criticism directed at a public official—would plant the seed of a constitutional case." Obviously, not every remark directed at a public official by a public employee is protected by the First Amendment*. But deciding whether a particular matter is of public concern is an inquiry that, by its very nature, is a sensitive one for judges charged with interpreting a constitutional provision intended to put "the decision as to what views shall be voiced largely into the hands of each of us. . . ." Cohen v. California.

[The] Court's decision ignores these precepts. Based on its own narrow conception of which matters are of public concern, the Court implicitly determines that information concerning employee morale at an important government office will not inform public debate. To the contrary, the First Amendment protects the dissemination of such information so that the people, not the courts, may evaluate its usefulness. The proper means to ensure that the courts are not swamped with routine employee grievances mis-

---

* Perhaps the simplest example of a statement by a public employee that would not be protected by the First Amendment would be answering "No" to a request that the employee perform a lawful task within the scope of his duties. Although such a refusal is "speech," which implicates First Amendment interests, it is also insubordination, and as such it may serve as the basis for a lawful dismissal. [Footnote by Justice Brennan.]

characterized as First Amendment cases is not to restrict artificially the concept of "public concern," but to require that adequate weight be given to the public's important interests in the efficient performance of governmental functions and in preserving employee discipline and harmony sufficient to achieve that end.

III. Although the Court finds most of Myers' questionnaire unrelated to matters of public interest, it does hold that one question—asking whether Assistants felt pressured to work in political campaigns on behalf of office-supported candidates—addressed a matter of public importance and concern. The Court also recognizes that this determination of public interest must weigh heavily in the balancing of competing interests required by Pickering. Having gone that far however, the Court misapplies the Pickering test and holds—against our previous authorities—that a public employer's mere apprehension that speech will be disruptive justifies suppression of that speech when all the objective evidence suggests that those fears are essentially unfounded. [In] the face of the District Court's finding that the circulation of the questionnaire had no disruptive effect, the Court holds that respondent may be dismissed because petitioner "reasonably believed [the action] would disrupt the office, undermine his authority and destroy close working relationships." Even though the District Court found that the distribution of the questionnaire did not impair Myers' working relationship with her supervisors, the Court bows to petitioner's judgment because "[w]hen close working relationships are essential to fulfilling public responsibilities, a wide degree of deference to the employer's judgment is appropriate."

Such extreme deference to the employer's judgment is not appropriate when public employees voice critical views concerning the operations of the agency for which they work. Although an employer's determination that an employee's statements have undermined essential working relationships must be carefully weighed in the Pickering balance, we must bear in mind that "the threat of dismissal from public employment is . . . . a potent means of inhibiting speech." Pickering. If the employer's judgment is to be controlling, public employees will not speak out when what they have to say is critical of their supervisors. In order to protect public employees' First Amendment right to voice critical views on issues of public importance, the courts must make their own appraisal of the effects of the speech in question. . . .

IV. The Court's decision today inevitably will deter public employees from making critical statements about the manner in which government agencies are operated for fear that doing so will provoke their dismissal. As a result, the public will be deprived of valuable information with which to evaluate the performance of elected officials. Because protecting the dissemination of such information is an essential function of the First Amendment, I dissent.

THE FIRST AMENDMENT IN THE SCHOOL CONTEXT: REMOVAL OF BOOKS FROM SCHOOL LIBRARIES

BOARD OF EDUCATION v. PICO

457 U.S. —, 102 S.Ct. 2799, 73 L.Ed.2d 435 (1982).

Justice BRENNAN announced the judgment of the Court, and delivered an opinion in which Justice MARSHALL and Justice STEVENS joined, and in which Justice BLACKMUN joined except for Part II–A–(1).

The principal question presented is whether the First Amendment imposes limitations upon the exercise by a local school board of its discretion to remove library books from high school and junior high school libraries.

I. Petitioners are the Board of Education of the Island Trees Union Free School District No. 26 in New York, and [the members of the Board]. [The Board operates the District's schools, including a high school and a junior high school. Respondents are five high school students and one junior high school student.] In September 1975, [three Board members] attended a conference sponsored by Parents of New York United (PONYU), a politically conservative organization of parents concerned about education legislation. [At] the conference these [Board members] obtained lists of books described by [one member] as "objectionable" and by [another] as "improper fare for school students." [1] It was later determined that the High School library contained nine of the listed books, and that another listed book was in the Junior High School library.[2] In February 1976, [the] Board gave an "unofficial direction" that the listed books be removed from the library shelves and delivered to the Board's offices, so that Board members could read them. When this directive was carried out, it became publicized, and the Board issued a press release justifying its action. It characterized the removed books as "anti-American, anti-Christian, anti-Semitic, and just plain filthy," and concluded that "It is our duty, our moral obligation, to protect the children in our schools from this moral danger as surely as from physical and medical dangers." A short time later, the Board appointed a "Book Review Committee," consisting of [several parents and members of the school

1. The District Court noted, however, that petitioners "concede that the books are not obscene." [Footnote by Justice Brennan.]

2. The nine books in the High School library were: Slaughter House Five, by Kurt Vonnegut, Jr.; The Naked Ape, by Desmond Morris; Down These Mean Streets, by Piri Thomas; Best Short Stories of Negro Writers, edited by Langston Hughes; Go Ask Alice, of anonymous authorship; Laughing Boy, by Oliver LaFarge; Black Boy, by Richard Wright; A Hero Ain't Nothin' But A Sandwich, by Alice Childress; and Soul On Ice, by Eldridge Cleaver. The book in the Junior High School library was A Reader for Writers, edited by Jerome Archer. Still another listed book, The Fixer, by Bernard Malamud, was found to be included in the curriculum of a twelfth grade literature course. [Footnote by Justice Brennan.]

staff] to recommend [whether] the books should be retained. [The Committee recommended that some (but not all) of the listed books be retained.] The Board substantially rejected the Committee's report later that month, deciding that only one book [Slaughter House Five] should be returned to the High School library without restriction. [The] Board gave no reasons for rejecting the recommendations of the Committee that it had appointed.

Respondents reacted to the Board's decision by bringing the present action under 42 U.S.C. § 1983. They alleged that petitioners had "ordered the removal of the books from school libraries and proscribed their use in the curriculum because particular passages in the books offended their social, political and moral tastes and not because the books, taken as a whole, were lacking in educational value." Respondents claimed that the Board's actions denied them their rights under the First Amendment. [The] District Court granted summary judgment in favor of the petitioners. [A] three judge panel of [the Court of Appeals for the Second Circuit] reversed [and] remanded the action for a trial on respondents' allegations. Each judge on the panel wrote a separate opinion. [Judges Sifton and Newman were in the majority; Judge Mansfield dissented.]

II. We emphasize at the outset the limited nature of the substantive question presented by the case before us. Our precedents have long recognized certain constitutional limits upon the power of the State to control even the curriculum and classroom. For example, Meyer v. Nebraska [1923; 10th Ed., p. 571; Ind.Rts., p. 191] struck down a state law that forbade the teaching of modern foreign languages in public and private schools, and Epperson v. Arkansas [1968; 10th Ed., p. 1564; Ind.Rts., p. 1184] declared unconstitutional a state law that prohibited the teaching of the Darwinian theory of evolution in any state-supported school. But the current action does not require us to re-enter this difficult terrain, which Meyer and Epperson traversed without apparent misgiving. For as this case is presented to us, it does not involve textbooks, or indeed any books that Island Trees students would be required to read. Respondents do not seek in this Court to impose limitations upon their school board's discretion to prescribe the curricula of the Island Trees schools. On the contrary, the only books at issue in this case are library books, books that by their nature are optional rather than required reading. Our adjudication of the present case thus does not intrude into the classroom, or into the compulsory courses taught there. Furthermore, even as to library books, the action before us does not involve the acquisition of books. Respondents have not sought to compel their school board to add to the school library shelves any books that students desire to read. Rather, the only action challenged in this case is the removal from the school libraries of books originally placed there by the school authorities, or without objection from them.

The substantive question before us is still further constrained by the procedural posture of this case. [We can] grant petitioners' request for reinstatement of the summary judgment in their favor only if we determine that "there is no genuine issue as to any material fact," and that petitioners are "entitled to a judgment as a matter of law." Fed.Rule Civ.Proc. 56(c). In making our determination, any doubt as to the existence of a genuine issue of material fact must be resolved against petitioners as the moving party. [In] sum, the issue before us in this case is a narrow one, both substantively and procedurally. It may best be restated as two distinct questions. First, Does the First Amendment impose *any* limitations upon the discretion of petitioners to remove library books from the Island Trees [schools]? Second, If so, do the affidavits and other evidentiary materials before the District Court, construed most favorably to respondents, raise a genuine issue of fact whether petitioners might have exceeded those limitations? . . . .

A. (1) The Court has long recognized that local school boards have broad discretion in the management of school affairs. [E.g., Meyer; Pierce; Epperson; Tinker.] We have also acknowledged that public schools are vitally important [as] vehicles for "inculcating fundamental values necessary to the maintenance of a democratic political system." Ambach v. Norwick [1979; 10th Ed., p. 891; Ind.Rts., p. 511]. We are therefore in full agreement with petitioners that local school boards must be permitted "to establish and apply their curriculum in such a way as to transmit community values," and that "there is a legitimate and substantial community interest in promoting respect for authority and traditional values be they social, moral, or political." At the same time, however, we have necessarily recognized that the discretion of the States and local school boards in matters of education must be exercised in a manner that comports with the transcendent imperatives of the First Amendment. In West Virginia v. Barnette [1943; 10th Ed., p. 1583; Ind.Rts., p. 1203.] we held that under the First Amendment a student in a public school could not be compelled to salute the flag. [See also, e.g., Epperson; Tinker.] In sum, students do not "shed their rights to freedom of speech or expression at the schoolhouse gate" [Tinker] and therefore local school boards must discharge their "important, delicate, and highly discretionary functions" within the limits and constraints of the First Amendment.

The nature of students' First Amendment rights in the context of this case requires further examination. [Barnette] is instructive. There the Court held that students' liberty of conscience could not be infringed in the name of "national unity" or "patriotism." [See also Tinker.] Of course, courts should not "intervene in the resolution of conflicts which arise in the daily operations of school systems" unless "basic constitutional values" are "directly and sharply implicate[d]" in those conflicts. [Epperson.] But we think that the First Amendment rights of students may be directly and sharply implicated by the removal of books from the shelves of a school library. Our precedents have focused "not only on the role of the First Amendment in fostering individual self-expression but also on its role in affording the public access to discussion, debate, and the dissemination of information and ideas." [Bellotti.] And we have recognized that "the State may not, consistently with the spirit of the First Amendment, contract the spectrum of available knowledge." Griswold v. Connecticut. In keeping with this principle, we have held that in a variety of contexts "the Constitution protects the right to receive information and ideas." Stanley v. Georgia. This right is an inherent corollary of the rights of free speech and press that are explicitly guaranteed by the Constitution, in two senses. First, the right to receive ideas follows ineluctably from the sender's First Amendment right to send them.

[More] importantly, the right to receive ideas is a necessary predicate to the recipient's meaningful exercise of his own rights of speech, press, and political freedom. [As] we recognized in Tinker, students too are beneficiaries of this principle. [In] sum, just as access to ideas makes it possible for citizens generally to exercise their rights of free speech and press in a meaningful manner, such access prepares students for active and effective participation in the pluralistic, often contentious society in which they will soon be adult members. Of course all First Amendment rights accorded to students must be construed "in light of the special characteristics of the school environment." [Tinker.] But the special characteristics of the school *library* make that environment especially appropriate for the recognition of the First Amendment rights of students.

A school library, no less than any other public library, is "a place dedicated to quiet, to knowledge, and to beauty." Brown v. Louisiana. [Keyishian] observed that "students must always remain free to inquire, to study and to evaluate, to gain new maturity and understanding." The school library is the principal locus of such freedom. [Petitioners] emphasize the inculcative function of secondary education, and argue that they must be allowed *unfettered* discretion to "transmit community values" through the Island Trees schools. But that sweeping claim overlooks the unique role of the school library. It appears from the record that use of the Island Trees school libraries is completely voluntary on the part of students. Their selection of books from these libraries is entirely a matter of free choice; the libraries afford them an opportunity at self-education and individual enrichment that is wholly optional. Petitioners might well defend their claim of absolute discretion in matters of *curriculum* by reliance upon their duty to inculcate community values. But we think that petitioners' reliance upon that duty is misplaced where, as here, they attempt to extend their claim of absolute discretion beyond the compulsory environment of the classroom, into the school library and the regime of voluntary inquiry that there holds sway.

(2) In rejecting petitioners' claim of absolute discretion to remove books from their school libraries, we do not deny that local school boards have a substantial legitimate role to play in the determination of school library content. We thus must turn to the question of the extent to which the First Amendment places limitations upon the discretion of petitioners to remove books from their libraries. In this inquiry we enjoy the guidance of several precedents. [Barnette] stated that "If there be any fixed star in our constitutional constellation, it is that no official, high or petty, can prescribe what shall be orthodox in politics, nationalism, religion, or other matters of opinion. [If] there are any circumstances which permit an exception, they do not now occur to us." This doctrine has been reaffirmed in later cases involving education. [E.g., Keyishian; Epperson.]

With respect to the present case, the message of these precedents is clear. Petitioners rightly possess significant discretion to determine the content of their school libraries. But that discretion may not be exercised in a narrowly partisan or political manner. If a Democratic school board, motivated by party affiliation, ordered the removal of all books written by or in favor of Republicans, few would doubt that the order violated the constitutional rights of the students denied access to those books. The same conclusion would surely apply if an all-white school board, motivated by racial animus, decided to remove all books authored by blacks or advocating racial equality and integration. Our Constitution does not permit the official suppression of *ideas.* Thus whether petitioners' removal of books from their school libraries denied respondents their First Amendment rights depends upon the motivation behind petitioners' actions. If petitioners *intended* by their removal decision to deny respondents access to ideas with which petitioners disagreed, and if this intent was the decisive factor in petitioners' decision,[3] then petitioners have exercised their discretion in violation of the Constitution. To permit such intentions to control official actions would be to encourage the precise sort of officially prescribed orthodoxy unequivocally condemned in Barnette. On the other hand, respondents implicitly concede that an unconstitutional motivation would *not* be demonstrated if it were shown that petitioners had decided to remove the books at issue because those books were pervasively vulgar. And again, respondents concede that if it were demonstrated that the removal decision was based solely upon the "educational suitability" of the books in question, then their removal would be "perfectly permissible." In other words, in respondents' view such motivations, if decisive of petitioners' actions, would not carry the danger of an official suppression of ideas, and thus would not violate respondents' First Amendment rights.

As noted earlier, nothing in our decision today affects in any way the discretion of a local school board to choose books to *add* to the libraries of their schools. Because we are concerned in this case with the suppression of ideas, our holding today affects only the discretion to *remove* books. In brief, we hold that local school boards may not remove books from school library shelves simply because they dislike the ideas contained in those books and seek by their removal to "prescribe what shall be orthodox in politics, nationalism, religion, or other matters of opinion." [Barnette]. Such purposes stand inescapably condemned by our precedents.

B. We now turn to the remaining question presented by this case: Do the evidentiary materials that were before the District Court, when construed most favorably to respondents, raise a genuine issue of material fact whether petitioners exceeded constitutional limitations in exercising their discretion to remove the books from the school libraries? We conclude that the materials do raise such a question, which forecloses summary judgment in favor of petitioners.

Before the District Court, respondents claimed that petitioners' decision to remove the books "was based upon [their] personal values, morals and tastes." Respondents also claimed that petitioners objected to the books in part because excerpts from them were "anti-American." The accuracy of these claims was partially conceded by petitioners, and petitioners' own affidavits lent further support to respondents' claims. In addition, the record developed in the District Court shows that when petitioners offered their first

---

3. By "decisive factor" we mean a "substantial factor" in the absence of which the opposite decision would have been reached. See Mt. Healthy City Board of Ed. v. Doyle, 429 U.S. 274 (1977). [Footnote by Justice Brennan.]

public explanation for the removal of the books, they relied in part on the assertion that the removed books were "anti-American," and "offensive [to] Americans in general." Furthermore, while the Book Review Committee appointed by petitioners was instructed to make its recommendations based upon criteria that appear on their face to be permissible—the books' "educational suitability," "good taste," "relevance," and "appropriateness to age and grade level"—the Committee's recommendations [were] essentially rejected by petitioners, without any statement of reasons for doing so. Finally, while petitioners originally defended their removal decision with the explanation that "these books contain obscenities, blasphemies, and perversion beyond description," one of the books, A Reader for Writers, was removed even though it contained no such language.

Standing alone, this evidence respecting the substantive motivations behind petitioners' removal decision would not be decisive. This would be a very different case if the record demonstrated that petitioners had employed established, regular, and facially unbiased procedures for the review of controversial materials. But the actual record in the case before us suggests the exact opposite. Petitioners' removal procedures were vigorously challenged below by respondents, and the evidence on this issue sheds further light on the issue of petitioners' motivations.[4] Respondents alleged that in making their removal decision petitioners ignored "the advice of literary experts," the views of "librarians and teachers within the Island Trees School system," the advice of the superintendent of schools, and the guidance of "publications that rate books for junior and senior high school students." Respondents also claimed that petitioners' decision was based solely on the fact that the books were named on the PONYU list and that petitioners "did not undertake an independent review of other books in the [school] libraries." Evidence before the District Court lends support to these claims. [In] sum, respondents' allegations and some of the evidentiary materials presented below do not rule out the possibility that petitioners' removal procedures were highly irregular and ad hoc—the antithesis of those procedures that might tend to allay suspicions regarding petitioners' motivations.

Construing these claims, affidavit statements, and other evidentiary materials in a manner favorable to respondents, we cannot conclude that petitioners were "entitled to a judgment as a matter of law." The evidence plainly does not foreclose the possibility that petitioners' decision to remove the books rested decisively upon disagreement with constitutionally protected ideas in those books, or upon a desire on petitioners' part to impose upon the students [a] political orthodoxy to which petitioners and their constituents adhered. Of course, some of the evidence before the District Court might lead a finder of fact to accept petitioners' claim that their removal decision was based upon constitutionally valid concerns. But that evidence at most

---

4. We have recognized in numerous precedents that when seeking to distinguish activities unprotected by the First Amendment from other, protected activities, the State must employ "sensitive tools" in order to achieve a precision of regulation that avoids the chilling of protected activities. In the case before us, the presence of such sensitive tools in petitioners' decision-making process would naturally indicate a concern on their part for the First Amendment rights of respondents; the absence of such tools might suggest a lack of such concern. [Footnote by Justice Brennan.]

creates a genuine issue of material fact on the critical question of the credibility of petitioners' justifications for their decision: On that issue, it simply cannot be said that there is no genuine issue as to any material fact.

[Affirmed.]

Justice BLACKMUN, concurring in part and concurring in the judgment.

While I agree with much in today's plurality opinion, and while I accept the standard laid down by the plurality to guide proceedings on remand, I write separately because I have a somewhat different perspective on the nature of the First Amendment right involved.

① To my mind, this case presents a particularly complex problem because it involves two competing principles of constitutional stature. On the one hand, [it] seems entirely appropriate that the State use "public schools [to] inculcat[e] fundamental values necessary to the maintenance of a democratic political system." Ambach v. Norwick. On the other hand, [it] is beyond dispute that schools and school boards must operate within the confines of the First Amendment. [See Barnette; Tinker; Keyishian.] In combination with more generally applicable First Amendment rules, most particularly the central proscription of content-based regulations of speech, see [Mosley], [these] cases [yield] a general principle: the State may not suppress exposure to ideas—for the sole *purpose* of suppressing exposure to those ideas—absent sufficiently compelling reasons. [T]his principle necessarily applies in at least a limited way to public education. Surely this is true in an extreme case.

[In] my view, then, the principle involved here is both narrower and more basic than the "right to receive information" identified by the plurality. I do not suggest that the State has any affirmative obligation to provide students with information or ideas, something that may well be associated with a "right to receive." And I do not believe, as the plurality suggests, that the right at issue here is somehow associated with the peculiar nature of the school library; if schools may be used to inculcate ideas, surely libraries may play a role in that process.[1] Instead, I suggest that certain forms of state dis-

1. As a practical matter, however, it is difficult to see the First Amendment right that I believe is at work here playing a role in a school's choice of curriculum. The school's finite resources—as well as the limited number of hours in the day—require that education officials make sensitive choices between subjects to be offered and competing areas of academic emphasis; subjects generally are excluded simply because school officials have chosen to devote their resources to one rather than to another subject. As is explained below, a choice of this nature does not run afoul of the First Amendment. In any event, the Court has recognized that students' First Amendment rights in most cases must give way if they interfere "with the schools' work or [with] the rights of other students to be secure and to be let alone" [Tinker] and such interference will rise to intolerable levels if public participation in the management of the curriculum becomes commonplace. In contrast, library books on a shelf intrude not at all on the daily operation of a school.

I also have some doubt that there is a theoretical distinction between removal of a book and failure to acquire a book. But as Judge Newman observed, there is a profound practical and evidentiary distinction between the two actions: "removal, more than failure to acquire, is likely to suggest that an impermissible political motivation may be present. There are

rather,
discrimination
between ideas
is improper

crimination *between* ideas are improper. In particular, our precedents command the conclusion that the State may not act to deny access to an idea simply because state officials disapprove of that idea for partisan or political reasons.[2]

Certainly, the unique environment of the school places substantial limits on the extent to which official decisions may be restrained by First Amendment values. But that environment also makes it particularly important that *some* limits be imposed. The school is designed to, and inevitably will, inculcate ways of thought and outlooks; if educators intentionally may eliminate all diversity of thought, the school will "strangle the free mind at its source and teach youth to discount important principles of our government as mere platitudes." Barnette. As I see it, then, the question in this case is how to make the delicate accommodation between the limited constitutional restriction that I think is imposed by the First Amendment, and the necessarily broad state authority to regulate education. In starker terms, we must reconcile the schools' "inculcative" function with the First Amendment's bar on "prescriptions of orthodoxy."

II. In my view, we strike a proper balance here by holding that school officials may not remove books or the *purpose* of restricting access to the political ideas or social perspectives discussed in them, when that action is motivated simply by the officials' disapproval of the ideas involved. [The] school board must "be able to show that its action was caused by something more than a mere desire to avoid the discomfort and unpleasantness that always accompany an unpopular viewpoint" [Tinker] and that the board had something in mind in addition to the suppression of partisan or political views it did not share. As I view it, this is a narrow principle. School officials must be able to choose one book over another, without outside interference, when the first book is deemed more relevant to the curriculum, or better written, or when one of a host of other politically neutral reasons is present. [And] even absent space or financial limitations, First Amendment principles would allow a school board to refuse to make a book available to students because it contains offensive language, cf. [Pacifica] or because it is psychologically or intellectually inappropriate for the age group, or even, perhaps, because the ideas it advances are "manifestly inimical to the public welfare." [Pierce.] And, of course, school officials may choose one book over another because they believe that one subject is more important, or is more deserving of emphasis.

what holding should be

what school board may do

[I] do not share Justice Rehnquist's view that the notion of "suppression of ideas" is not a useful analytical concept. [And] I believe that tying the First Amendment right to the *purposeful* suppression of ideas makes the concept more manageable than Justice Rehnquist acknowledges. Most people

many reasons why a book is not acquired, the most obvious being limited resources, but there are few legitimate reasons why a book, once acquired, should be removed from a library not filled to capacity." [Footnote by Justice Blackmun.]

2. In effect, my view presents the obverse of the plurality's analysis: while the plurality focuses on the failure to provide information, I find crucial the State's decision to single out an idea for disapproval and then deny access to it. [Footnote by Justice Blackmun.]

would recognize that refusing to allow discussion of current events in Latin class is a policy designed to "inculcate" Latin, not to suppress ideas. Similarly, removing a learned treatise criticizing American foreign policy from an elementary school library because the students would not understand it is an action unrelated to the *purpose* of suppressing ideas. In my view, however, removing the same treatise because it is "anti-American" raises a far more difficult issue. It is not a sufficient answer to this problem that a State operates a school in its role as "educator," rather than its role as "sovereign," [see Justice Rehnquist's dissent], for the First Amendment has application to all the State's activities. While the State may act as "property owner" when it prevents certain types of expressive activity from taking place on public lands, for example, few would suggest that the State may base such restrictions on the content of the speaker's message, or may take its action for the purpose of suppressing access to the ideas involved. See [Mosley].

[Concededly], a tension exists between the properly inculcative purposes of public education and any limitation on the school board's absolute discretion to choose academic materials. But that tension demonstrates only that the problem here is a difficult one, not that the problem should be resolved by choosing one principle over another. [School] officials may seek to instill certain values "by persuasion and example," [Barnette] or by choice of emphasis. That sort of positive educational action, however, is the converse of an intentional attempt to shield students from certain ideas that officials find politically distasteful. [The] principle involved here may be difficult to apply in an individual case. But on a record as sparse as the one before us, the plurality can hardly be faulted for failing to explore every possible ramification of its decision. And while the absence of a record "underscore[s] the views of those of us who originally felt that the [case] should not be taken," the case is here, and must be decided. Because I believe that the plurality has derived a standard similar to the one compelled by my analysis, I join all but Part IIA(1) of the plurality opinion.

Justice WHITE, concurring in the judgment.

[The Court of Appeals concluded] that there was a material issue of fact that precluded summary judgment sought by petitioners. The unresolved factual issue [is] the reason or reasons underlying the school board's removal of the books. I am not inclined to disagree with the Court of Appeals on such a fact-bound issue and hence concur in the judgment of affirmance. Presumably this will result in a trial and the making of a full record and findings on the critical issues. The Court seems compelled to go further and issue a dissertation on the extent to which the First Amendment limits the discretion of the school board to remove books from the school library. I see no necessity for doing so at this point. [We] should not decide constitutional questions until it is necessary to do so, or at least until there is better reason to address them than are evident here. I therefore concur in the judgment of affirmance.

Chief Justice BURGER, with whom Justice POWELL, Justice REHNQUIST, and Justice O'CONNOR join, dissenting.

[In] an attempt to deal with a problem in an area traditionally left to the states, a plurality of the Court, in a lavish expansion going beyond any prior holding under the First Amendment, expresses its view that a school board's decision concerning what books are to be in the school library is subject to federal court review. Were this to become the law, this Court would come perilously close to becoming a "super censor" of school board library decisions. Stripped to its essentials, the issue comes down to two important propositions: *first*, whether local schools are to be administered by elected school boards, or by federal judges and teenage pupils; and *second* whether the values of morality, good taste, and relevance to education are valid reasons for school board decisions concerning the contents of a school library. In an attempt to place this case within the protection of the First Amendment, the plurality suggests a new "right" that, when shorn of the plurality's rhetoric, allows this Court to impose its own views about what books must be made available to students.

[In this case], no restraints of any kind are placed on the students. They are free to read the books in question, which are available at public libraries and bookstores; they are free to discuss them in the classroom or elsewhere. Despite this, [the] plurality suggest that there is a new First Amendment "entitlement" to have access to particular books in a school library. [This] "right" purportedly follows "ineluctably" from the sender's First Amendment right to freedom of speech and as a "necessary predicate" to the recipient's meaningful exercise of his own rights of speech, press, and political freedom. No such right, however, has previously been recognized. [See also Justice Rehnquist's dissent, below]

(B) Whatever role the government might play as a conduit of information, schools in particular ought not be made a slavish courier of the material of third parties. [If], as we have held, schools may legitimately be used as vehicles for "inculcating fundamental values necessary to the maintenance of a democratic political system," Ambach v. Norwick, school authorities must have broad discretion to fulfill that obligation. [How] are "fundamental values" to be inculcated except by having school boards make content-based decisions about the appropriateness of retaining materials in the school library and curriculum? In order to fulfill its function, an elected school board *must* express its views on the subjects which are taught to its students. In doing so those elected officials express the views of their community; they may err, of course, and the voters may remove them. It is a startling erosion of the very idea of democratic government to have this Court arrogate to itself the power the plurality asserts today.

The plurality concludes that under the Constitution school boards cannot choose to retain or dispense with books if their discretion is exercised in a "narrowly partisan or political manner." The plurality concedes that permissible factors are whether the books are "pervasively vulgar" or educationally unsuitable. "Educational suitability," however, is a standardless phrase. This conclusion will undoubtedly be drawn in many—if not most—instances because of the decisionmaker's content-based judgment that the ideas contained in the book or the idea expressed from the author's method of communication are inappropriate for teenage pupils. The plurality also tells us that a book may be removed from a school library if it is "pervasively vulgar." But why must the vulgarity be "pervasive" to be offensive? Vulgarity might be concentrated in a single poem or a single chapter or a single page, yet still be inappropriate. Or a school board might reasonably conclude that even "random" vulgarity is inappropriate for teenage school students. A school board might also reasonably conclude that the school board's retention of such books gives those volumes an implicit endorsement. Cf. [Pacifica]. Further, there is no guidance whatsoever as to what constitutes "political" factors. This Court has previously recognized that [public education] " 'go[es]' to the heart of representative government.' " Ambach v. Norwick. As such, virtually all educational decisions necessarily involve "political" determinations.

What the plurality views as valid reasons for removing a book at their core involve partisan judgments. Ultimately the federal courts will be the judge of whether the motivation for book removal was "valid" or "reasonable." Undoubtedly the validity of many book removals will ultimately turn on a judge's evaluation of the books. Discretion must be used, and the appropriate body to exercise that discretion is the local elected school board, not judges.[1]

We can all agree that as a matter of *educational policy* students should have wide access to information and ideas. But the people elect school boards, who in turn select administrators, who select the teachers, and these are the individuals best able to determine the substance of that policy. The plurality fails to recognize the fact that local control of education involves democracy in a microcosm. In most public schools in the United States the *parents* have a large voice in running the school. A school board [is] truly "of the people and by the people." [It] could not long exercise unchecked discretion in its choice to acquire or remove books. If the parents disagree with the educational decisions of the school board, they can take steps to remove the board members from office. Finally, even if parents and students cannot convince the school board that book removal is inappropriate, they have alternative sources to the same end. Books may be acquired from book stores, public libraries, or other alternative sources unconnected with the unique environment of the local public schools.

II No amount of "limiting" language could rein in the sweeping "right" the plurality would create. The plurality distinguishes library books from textbooks because library books "by their nature are optional rather than required reading." It is not clear, however, why this distinction requires *greater* scrutiny before "optional" reading materials may be removed. It would appear that required reading and textbooks have a greater likelihood of imposing a " 'pall of orthodoxy' " over the educational process than do op-

1. Indeed, this case is illustrative of how essentially all decisions concerning the retention of school library books will become the responsibility of federal courts. [T]he parties agreed that the school board in this case acted not on religious principles but "on its belief that the nine books removed from the school library and curriculum were irrelevant, vulgar, immoral, and in bad taste, making them educationally unsuitable for the district's junior and senior high school students." Despite this agreement as to motivation, the case is to be remanded for a determination of whether removal was in violation of the standard adopted by the plurality. The school board's error appears to be that they made their own determination rather than relying on experts. [Footnote by Chief Justice Burger.]

tional reading[s]. [The] plurality also limits the new right by finding it applicable only to the *removal* of books once acquired. Yet if the First Amendment commands that certain books cannot be *removed* does it not equally require that the same books be *acquired*? Why does the coincidence of timing become the basis of a constitutional holding? According to the plurality, the evil to be avoided is the "official suppression of ideas." It does not follow that the decision to *remove* a book is less "official suppression" than the decision not to acquire a book desired by someone.[2] Similarly, a decision to eliminate certain material from the curriculum, history for example, would carry an equal—probably greater—prospect of "official suppression." Would the decision be subject to our review?

III. Through use of bits and pieces of prior opinions unrelated to the issue of this case, the plurality demeans our function of constitutional adjudication. Today the plurality suggests that the *Constitution* distinguishes between school libraries and school classrooms, between *removing* unwanted books and *acquiring* books. Even more extreme, the plurality concludes that the *Constitution requires* school boards to justify to its teenage pupils the decision to remove a particular book from a school library. I categorically reject this notion that the Constitution dictates that judges, rather than parents, teachers, and local school boards, must determine how the standards of morality and vulgarity are to be treated in the classroom.

Justice POWELL, dissenting.

Powell
Separate Dissent

The plurality opinion today rejects a basic concept of public school education in our country: that the States and locally elected school boards should have the responsibility for determining the educational policy of the public schools. After today's decision any junior high school student by instituting a suit against a school board or teacher, may invite a judge to overrule an educational decision by the official body designated by the people to operate the schools.

I. [It] is fair to say that no single agency of government at any level is closer to the people whom it serves than the typical school board. I therefore view today's decision with genuine dismay. Whatever the final outcome of this suit and suits like it, the resolution of educational policy decisions through litigation, and the exposure of school board members to liability for such decisions, can be expected to corrode the school board's authority and effectiveness. As is evident from the generality of the plurality's "standard" for judicial review, the decision as to the educational worth of a book is a highly subjective one. Judges rarely are as competent as school authorities to

---

2. The formless nature of the "right" found by the plurality in this case is exemplified by this purported distinction. Presumably a school district could, for any reason, choose not to purchase a book for its library. Once it purchases that book, however, it is "locked in" to retaining it on the school shelf until it can justify a reason for its removal. This anomalous result of "book tenure" was pointed out by the District Court in this case. Under the plurality view, if a school board wants to be assured that it maintains control over the education of its students, every page of every book sought to be acquired must be read before a purchase decision is made. [Footnote by Chief Justice Burger.]

make this decision; nor are judges responsive to the parents and people of the school district.[1]

[The plurality's] new constitutional right ["to receive ideas"] is framed in terms that approach a meaningless generalization. [The] plurality does announce the following standard: A school board's "discretion may not be exercised in a narrowly partisan or political manner." But this is a standardless standard that affords no more than subjective guidance to school boards, their counsel, and to courts that now will be required to decide whether a particular decision was made in a "narrowly partisan or political manner." Even the chancellor's foot standard in ancient equity jurisdiction was never this fuzzy. . . .

II. The plurality's reasoning is marked by contradiction. [Just] this term the Court held [that] the children of illegal aliens must be permitted to attend the public schools. See Plyler v. Doe. [T]he Court noted [for example] that the public schools are "the primary vehicle for transmitting 'the values on which our society rests.'" [Today] the plurality drains much of the content from these apt phrases. A school board's attempt to instill in its students the ideas and values on which a democratic system depends is viewed as an impermissible suppression of other ideas and values on which other systems of government and other societies thrive. Books may not be removed because they are indecent; extoll violence, intolerance and racism; or degrade the dignity of the individual. Human history, not the least of the twentieth century, records the power and political life of these very ideas. But they are not our ideas or values. Although I would leave this educational decision to the duly constituted board, I certainly would not *require* a school board to promote ideas and values repugnant to a democratic society or to teach such values to *children*. In different contexts and in different times, the destruction of written materials has been the symbol of depotism and intolerance. But the removal of nine vulgar or racist books from a high school library by a concerned local school board does not raise this specter. For me, today's decision symbolizes a debilitating encroachment upon the institutions of a free people.*

Justice REHNQUIST, with whom The Chief Justice [BURGER] and Justice POWELL, join, dissenting.

[The] District Court was correct in granting summary judgment. [I] agree fully with the views expressed by The Chief Justice, and concur in his opinion. I disagree with Justice Brennan's opinion because it is largely hypothetical in character, failing to take account of the facts as admitted by the par-

1. The plurality speaks of the need for "sensitive" decisionmaking, pursuant to "regular" procedures. One wonders what indeed does this mean. In this case, for example, the board did not act precipitously. It simply did not agree with the recommendations of a committee it had appointed. Would the plurality require—as a constitutional matter—that the board delegate unreviewable authority to such a committee? [Footnote by Justice Powell.]

* As an appendix to his opinion, Justice Powell reprinted a seven-page summary (compiled by Court of Appeals Judge Mansfield) of "excerpts from the books at issue in this case."

ties pursuant to local rules of the District Court, and because it is analytically unsound and internally inconsistent.[1]

I. A. Justice Brennan's opinion deals far more sparsely with the procedural posture of this case than it does with the constitutional issues. [When] Justice Brennan finally does address the state of the record, he refers to snippets and excerpts of the relevant facts to explain why a grant of summary judgment was improper. But he totally ignores the effect of Rule 9(g) of the local rules of the District Court, under which the parties set forth their version of the disputed facts in this case. Since summary judgment was entered against respondents, they are entitled to have their version of the facts, as embodied in their Rule 9(g) statement, accepted for purposes of our review. Since the parties themselves are presumably the best judges of the extent of the factual dispute between them, however, respondents certainly are not entitled to any more favorable version of the facts than that contained in their own Rule 9(g) statement. Justice Brennan's combing through the record of affidavits, school bulletins, and the like for bits and snatches of dispute is therefore entirely beside the point at this stage of the case.

[Respondents agreed that petitioners] "have not precluded discussion about the themes of the books or the books themselves." Justice Brennan's concern with the "suppression of ideas" thus seems entirely unwarranted on this state of the record, and his creation of constitutional rules to cover such eventualities is entirely gratuitous. [In] the course of his discussion, Justice Brennan states: "[The school board's] discretion may not be exercised in a narrowly partisan or political manner. If a Democratic school board, motivated by party affiliation, ordered the removal of all books written by or in favor of Republicans, few would doubt that the order violated the constitutional rights of the students. [Etc.]."

[I] can cheerfully concede all of this, but as in so many other cases the extreme examples are seldom the ones that arise in the real world of constitutional litigation. In *this case* the facts taken most favorably to respondents suggest that nothing of this sort happened. The nine books removed undoubtedly did contain "ideas," [but] it is apparent that eight of them contained demonstrable amounts of vulgarity and profanity, and the ninth contained nothing that could be considered partisan or political. [R]espondents admitted as much. Petitioners did not, for the reasons stated hereafter, run afoul of the First and Fourteenth Amendments by removing these particular books from the library in the manner in which they did. I would save for another day—feeling quite confident that that day will not arrive—the extreme examples posed in Justice Brennan's opinion.

---

1. I also disagree with Justice White's conclusion that he need not decide the constitutional issue presented by this case. That view seems to me inconsistent with the "rule of four"—"that any case warranting consideration in the opinion of [four Justices] of the Court will be taken and disposed of" on the merits, Ferguson v. Moore-McCormack Lines, 352 U.S. 521, 561 (1957) (Harlan, J., concurring and dissenting)—which we customarily follow in exercising our certiorari jurisdiction. His concurrence, although not couched in such language, is in effect a single vote to dismiss the writ of certiorari as improvidently granted. . . . [Footnote by Justice Rehnquist.]

B. [Had] petitioners been the members of a town council, I suppose all would agree that, absent a good deal more than is present in this record, they could not have prohibited the sale of these books by private booksellers within the municipality. But we have also recognized that the government may act in other capacities than as sovereign, and when it does the First Amendment may speak with a different voice. [E.g., Pickering v. Board of Education (government as employer); Adderley v. Florida (government as property owner).] [With] these differentiated roles of government in mind, it is helpful to assess the role of government as educator, as compared with the role of government as sovereign. When it acts as an educator, at least at the elementary and secondary school level, the government is engaged in inculcating social values and knowledge in relatively impressionable young people. Obviously there are innumerable decisions to be made as to what courses should be taught, what books should be purchased, or what teachers should be employed. In every one of these areas the members of a school board will act on the basis of their own personal or moral values, will attempt to mirror those of the community, or will abdicate the making of such decisions to so-called "experts." [2] In this connection I find myself entirely in agreement with the observation of [a lower federal court] that it is "permissible and appropriate for local boards to make educational decisions based upon their personal, social, political and moral views." In the very course of administering the many-faceted operations of a school district, the mere decision to purchase some books will necessarily preclude the possibility of purchasing others. The decision to teach a particular subject may preclude the possibility of teaching another subject. A decision to replace a teacher because of ineffectiveness may by implication be seen as a disparagement of the subject matter taught. In each of these instances, however, the book or the exposure to the subject matter may be acquired elsewhere. The managers of the school district are not proscribing it as to the citizenry in general, but are simply determining that it will not be included in the curriculum or school library. In short, actions by the government as educator do not raise the same First Amendment concerns as actions by the government as sovereign.

II. [It] is the very existence of a right to receive information, in the junior high school and high school setting, which I find wholly unsupported by our past decisions and inconsistent with the necessarily selective process of elementary and secondary education.

A. The right described by Justice Brennan has never been recognized in the decisions of this Court and is not supported by their rationale. [O]ur past decisions in this area have concerned freedom of speech and expression, not the right of access to particular ideas. [Tinker; Barnette.] But these decisions scarcely control the case before us. [Despite] Justice Brennan's suggestion to the contrary, this Court has never held that the First Amend-

2. There are intimations in Justice Brennan's opinion that if petitioners had only consulted literary experts, librarians, and teachers their decision might better withstand First Amendment attack. These observations seem to me wholly fatuous; surely ideas are no more accessible or no less suppressed if the school board merely ratifies the opinion of some other group rather than following its own opinion. [Footnote by Justice Rehnquist.]

ment grants junior high school and high school students a right of access to certain information in school. It is true that the Court has recognized a limited version of that right in other settings, and Justice Brennan quotes language from [several] such decisions [in order to] demonstrate the viability of the right-to-receive doctrine. But not one of these cases concerned or even purported to discuss elementary or secondary educational institutions.

Nor does the right-to-receive doctrine recognized in our past decisions apply to schools by analogy. Justice Brennan correctly characterizes the right of access to ideas as "an inherent corollary of the rights of free speech and press" which "follows ineluctably from the *sender*'s First Amendment right to send them." But he then fails to recognize the predicate right to speak from which the students' right to receive must follow. It would be ludicrous, of course, to contend that all authors have a constitutional right to have their books placed in [school] libraries. And yet without such a right our prior precedents would not recognize the reciprocal right to receive information. Justice Brennan disregards this inconsistency with our prior cases and fails to explain the constitutional or logical underpinnings of a right to hear ideas in a place where no speaker has the right to express them. Justice Brennan also correctly notes that the reciprocal nature of the right to receive information derives from the fact that it "is a necessary predicate to the *recipient*'s meaningful exercise of his own rights of speech, press, and political freedom." But the denial of access to ideas inhibits one's own acquisition of knowledge only when that denial is relatively complete. If the denied ideas are readily available from the same source in other accessible locations, the benefits to be gained from exposure to those ideas have not been foreclosed by the State. This fact is inherent in the right-to-receive cases relied on by Justice Brennan, every one of which concerned the complete denial of access to the ideas sought. Our past decisions are thus unlike this case where the removed books are readily available to students and non-students alike at the corner bookstore or the public library.

B. There are even greater reasons for rejecting Justice Brennan's analysis, however. [Public schools] fulfill the vital role of "inculcating fundamental values necessary to the maintenance of a democratic political system." [Ambach v. Norwick.] The idea that such students have a right of access, *in the school*, to information other than that thought by their educators to be necessary is contrary to the very nature of an inculcative education. Education consists of the selective presentation and explanation of ideas. The effective acquisition of knowledge depends upon an orderly exposure to relevant information. Nowhere is this more true than in elementary and secondary schools, where, unlike the broad-ranging inquiry available to university students, the courses taught are those thought most relevant to the young students' individual development. Of necessity, elementary and secondary educators must separate the relevant from the irrelevant, the appropriate from the inappropriate. Determining what information *not* to present to the students is often as important as identifying relevant material. This winnowing process necessarily leaves much information to be discovered by students at another time or in another place, and is fundamentally inconsistent with any constitutionally required eclecticism in public education.

Justice Brennan rejects this idea, claiming that it "overlooks the unique role of the school library." But the unique role referred to appears to be one of Justice Brennan's own creation. [In his] paean of praise to [school] libraries as the "environment especially appropriate for the recognition of the First Amendment rights of students," [he] turns to language about *public* libraries from Brown v. Louisiana and to language about universities and colleges from [Keyishian]. Not only is his authority thus transparently thin, but also, and more importantly, his reasoning misapprehends the function of libraries in our public school system. [E]lementary and secondary schools are inculcative in nature. The libraries of such schools serve as supplements to this inculcative role. Unlike university or public libraries, elementary and secondary school libraries are not designed for free-wheeling inquiry; they are tailored, as the public school curriculum is tailored, to the teaching of basic skills and ideas. Thus, Justice Brennan cannot rely upon the nature of school libraries to escape the fact that the First Amendment right to receive information simply has no application to the one public institution which, by its very nature, is a place for the selective conveyance of ideas.

After all else is said, however, the most obvious reason that petitioners' removal of the books did not violate respondents' right to receive information is the ready availability of the books elsewhere. Students are not denied books by their removal from a school library. The books may be borrowed from a public library, read at a university library, purchased at a bookstore, or loaned by a friend. The government as educator does not seek to reach beyond the confines of the school. Indeed, following the removal from the school library of the books at issue in this case, the local public library put all nine books on display for public inspection. Their contents were fully accessible to any inquisitive student.

C. Justice Brennan's own discomfort with the idea that students have a right to receive information from their elementary or secondary schools is demonstrated by the artificial limitations which he places upon the right— limitations which are supported neither by logic nor authority and which are inconsistent with the right itself. The attempt to confine the right to the library is one such limitation. [As] a second limitation, Justice Brennan distinguishes the act of removing a previously acquired book from the act of refusing to acquire the book in the first place. [If] Justice Brennan truly has found a "right to receive ideas," however, this distinction between acquisition and removal makes little sense. The failure of a library to acquire a book denies access to its contents just as effectively as does the removal of the book from the library's shelf.

[The] justification for this limiting distinction is said [to be the] concern in this case with "the suppression of ideas." Whatever may be the analytical usefulness of this appealing sounding phrase, see subpart D, infra, the suppression of ideas surely is not the identical twin of the denial of access to information. Not every official act which denies access to an idea can be characterized as a suppression of the idea. Thus unless the "right to receive information" and the prohibition against "suppression of ideas" are each a kind of mother-hubbard catch phrase for whatever First Amendment doctrines one wishes to cover, they would not appear to be interchangeable.

Justice Brennan's reliance on the "suppression of ideas" to justify his distinction between acquisition and removal of books has additional logical pitfalls. Presumably the distinction is based upon the greater visibility and the greater sense of conscious decision thought to be involved in the removal of a book, as opposed to that involved in the refusal to acquire a book. But if "suppression of ideas" is to be the talisman, one would think that a school board's public announcement of its refusal to acquire certain books would have every bit as much impact on public attention as would an equally publicized decision to remove the books. And yet only the latter action would violate the First Amendment under Justice Brennan's analysis.

The final limitation placed by Justice Brennan upon his newly discovered right is a motive requirement: the First Amendment is violated only "[i]f petitioners *intended* by their removal decision to deny respondents access to ideas with which petitioners disagreed." But bad motives and good motives alike deny access to the books removed. If [there truly is] a constitutional right to receive information, it is difficult to see why the reason for the denial makes any difference. Of course Justice Brennan's view is that intent matters because the First Amendment does not tolerate an officially prescribed orthodoxy. But this reasoning mixes First Amendment apples and oranges. The right to receive information differs from the right to be free from an officially prescribed orthodoxy. Not every educational denial of access to information casts a pall of orthodoxy over the classroom.

It is difficult to tell from Justice Brennan's opinion just what motives he would consider constitutionally impermissible. I had thought that the First Amendment proscribes content-based restrictions on the marketplace of ideas. Justice Brennan concludes, however, that a removal decision based solely upon the "educational suitability" of a book or upon its perceived vulgarity is "'perfectly permissible.'" But such determinations are based as much on the content of the book as determinations that the book espouses pernicious political views. Moreover, Justice Brennan's motive test is difficult to square with his distinction between acquisition and removal. If a school board's removal of books might be motivated by a desire to promote favored political or religious views, there is no reason that its acquisition policy might not also be so motivated. And yet the "pall of orthodoxy" cast by a carefully executed book-acquisition program apparently would not violate the First Amendment under Justice Brennan's view.

D. Intertwined as a basis for Justice Brennan's opinion, along with the "right to receive information," is the statement that "our Constitution does not permit the official suppression of *ideas*." There would be few champions, I suppose, of the idea that our Constitution *does* permit the official suppression of ideas; my difficulty is not with the admittedly appealing catchiness of the phrase, but with my doubt that it is really a useful analytical tool in solving difficult First Amendment problems. Since the phrase appears in the opinion "out of the blue," [it] would appear that the Court for years has managed to decide First Amendment cases without it. I would think that prior cases decided under established First Amendment doctrine afford adequate guides in this area without resorting to a phrase which seeks to express "a complicated process of constitutional adjudication by a deceptive formula."

Kovacs v. Cooper (Frankfurter, J., concurring). A school board which publicly adopts a policy forbidding the criticism of United States foreign policy by any student, any teacher, or any book on the library shelves is indulging in one kind of "suppression of ideas." A school board which adopts a policy that there shall be no discussion of current events in a class for high school sophomores devoted to second-year Latin "suppresses ideas" in quite a different context. A teacher who had a lesson plan consisting of 14 weeks of study of United States history from 1607 to the present time, but who because of a week's illness is forced to forego the most recent 20 years of American history, may "suppress ideas" in still another way.

I think a far more satisfactory basis for addressing these kinds of questions is found in the Court's language in [Tinker], where we noted that "a particular idea—black arm bands worn to exhibit opposition to this Nation's involvement in Vietnam—was singled out for prohibition. Clearly, the prohibition of expression of one particular opinion, at least without evidence that it is necessary to avoid material and substantial interference with school work or discipline, is not constitutionally permissible." In the case before us the petitioners may in one sense be said to have "suppressed" the "ideas" of vulgarity and profanity, but that is hardly an apt description of what was done. They ordered the removal of books containing vulgarity and profanity, but they did not attempt to preclude discussion about the themes of the books or the books themselves. Such a decision [is] sufficiently related to "educational suitability" to pass muster under the First Amendment.

E. The inconsistencies and illogic of the limitations placed by Justice Brennan upon his notion of the right to receive ideas in school are not here emphasized in order to suggest that they should be eliminated. They are emphasized because they illustrate that the right itself is misplaced in the elementary and secondary school setting. Likewise, the criticism of Justice Brennan's newly found prohibition against the "suppression of ideas" is by no means intended to suggest that the Constitution permits the suppression of ideas; it is rather to suggest that such a vague and imprecise phrase, while perhaps wholly consistent with the First Amendment, is simply too diaphanous to assist careful decision of cases such as these.

I think the Court will far better serve the cause of First Amendment jurisprudence by candidly recognizing that the role of government as sovereign is subject to more stringent limitations than is the role of government as employer, property owner, or educator. [With] respect to the education of children in elementary and secondary schools, the school board may properly determine in many cases that a particular book, a particular course, or even a particular area of knowledge is not educationally suitable for inclusion within the body of knowledge which the school seeks to impart. Without more, this is not a condemnation of the book or the course; it is only a determination akin to that referred to by the Court in Village of Euclid v. Ambler Realty Co., 272 U.S. 365 (1926): "A nuisance may be merely a right thing in the wrong place—like a pig in the parlor instead of the barnyard."

III. Accepting as true respondents' assertion that petitioners acted on the basis of their own "personal values, morals, and tastes," I find the actions taken in this case hard to distinguish from the myriad choices made by school boards in the routine supervision of elementary and secondary schools. [In] this case respondents' rights of free speech and expression were not infringed, and by respondents' own admission no ideas were "suppressed." I would leave to another day the harder cases.

⌐ Justice O'CONNOR, dissenting. ⌐

O'Connor Dissents

If the school board can set the curriculum, select teachers, and determine initially what books to purchase for the school library, it surely can decide which books to discontinue or remove from the school library so long as it does not also interfere with the right of students to read the material and to discuss it. As Justice Rehnquist persuasively argues, the plurality's analysis overlooks the fact that in this case the government is acting in its special role as educator. I do not personally agree with the board's action with respect to some of the books in question here, but it is not the function of the courts to make the decisions that have been properly relegated to the elected members of school boards. It is the school board that must determine educational suitability, and it has done so in this case. I therefore join The Chief Justice's dissent.

up to School Board, not us.

10th ED., p. 1417; IND. RTS., p. 1037
Add as footnote to the Note:

For a recent example of a summary rejection of a First Amendment claim in a labor law context, see Longshoremen v. Allied International, Inc., 456 U.S. 212 (1982). The longshoremen's union, protesting the Russian invasion of Afghanistan, refused to unload cargoes shipped from the Soviet Union. The Court found the union's protest to be an illegal secondary boycott under the National Labor Relations Act. The unanimous Court rejected the claim that, because the union boycott "was not a labor dispute with a primary employer but a political dispute with a foreign nation," the Act should be found inapplicable. Justice Powell replied: "The legislative history does not indicate that political disputes should be excluded from the scope of [the Act]." He dispatched the argument that application of the law violated the First Amendment in one brief, final paragraph: "We have consistently rejected the claim that secondary picketing by labor unions in violation of [the Act] is a protected activity under the First Amendment. It would seem even clearer that conduct designed not to communicate but to coerce merits still less consideration under the First Amendment. The labor laws reflect a careful balancing of interests. There are many ways in which a union and its individual members may express their opposition to Russian foreign policy without infringing upon the rights of others."

10th ED., p. 1425; IND. RTS., p. 1045
Insert as Sec. 4D (before Sec. 5):

D. ECONOMIC BOYCOTTS FOR POLITICAL PURPOSES

NAACP v. CLAIBORNE HARDWARE CO., 458 U.S. —— (1982): This case arose from a boycott by black citizens of white merchants in Claiborne County, Mississippi. The boycott, commenced in 1966, sought to persuade white civic and business leaders to comply with a long list of black citizens' demands for equality and racial justice. The boycott was conducted by largely peaceful means, but it included some incidents of violence as well. In a civil action brought by some of the merchants to recover economic losses allegedly caused by the boycott, a state trial court imposed a judgment for more than $1,000,000 on a large group of defendants (including the

NAACP). The Mississippi Supreme Court, although not accepting all of the lower court's reasons, upheld the judgment of liability and remanded for a recomputation of damages.[1] Without dissent,[2] the U. S. Supreme Court reversed, holding "that the nonviolent elements of petitioners' activities are entitled to the protection of the First Amendment" and that, "[w]hile the State legitimately may impose damages for the consequences of violent conduct, it may not award compensation for the consequences of nonviolent, protected activity. Only those losses proximately caused by unlawful conduct may be recovered." The Court remanded the case for further proceedings in accordance with its guidelines.

Justice STEVENS, in his opinion for the Court, summarized his conclusions as follows: "Concerted action is a powerful weapon. History teaches that special dangers are associated with conspiratorial activity. And yet one of the foundations of our society is the right of individuals to combine with other persons in pursuit of a common goal by lawful means. At times the difference between lawful and unlawful collective action may be identified easily by reference to its purpose. In this case, however, petitioners' ultimate objectives were unquestionably legitimate. The charge of illegality—like the claim of constitutional protection—derives from the means employed by the

1. In somewhat fuller detail, the background of the case was as follows: The boycott by black citizens of Port Gibson, Miss., and other areas of Claiborne County began after white elected officials had turned down a long list of demands by black citizens. (The demands included desegregation of public facilities, hiring of black policemen, the end of verbal abuse by the police, and the hiring of more black employees by local stores.) In April 1966, at a local NAACP meeting, several hundred black people voted unanimously to boycott the area's white merchants.

The suit was brought in 1969 by 17 white merchants—many of them civic leaders. In 1973, a state chancellor in equity conducted a lengthy trial. Ultimately, the chancellor held the petitioners liable for all of the respondents' lost earnings during a seven-year period, from 1966 to the end of 1972. The chancellor found all but 18 of the original 148 defendants jointly and severally liable for the entire judgment of $1,250,699 plus interest and costs. The chancellor imposed liability on the basis of three separate conspiracy theories.

The Mississippi Supreme Court rejected two of these conspiracy theories, but upheld the imposition of liability on the basis of the chancellor's common law tort theory—the tort of malicious interference with the plaintiffs' businesses. The highest Mississippi court emphasized that there had been some violence and quoted the lower court finding that "the volition of many black persons was overcome out of sheer fear, and they were forced and compelled against their personal wills to withhold their trade and business intercourse from the complainants." On the basis of this finding, the State Supreme Court concluded that the entire boycott was unlawful: "If any of these factors—force, violence, or threats—is present, then the boycott is illegal regardless of whether it is primary, secondary, economical, political, social or other." Summarily rejecting a First Amendment defense, the court stated: "The agreed use of illegal force, violence, and threats against the peace to achieve a goal makes the present state of facts a conspiracy. We know of no instance [wherein] it has been adjudicated that free speech guaranteed by the First Amendment includes in its protection the right to commit crime." (The Mississippi Supreme Court did find that liability had not been demonstrated in the case of 38 of the defendants and that there had been inadequate proof of some of the damages. It accordingly remanded for further proceedings on the damages issue.)

2. Justice Stevens' opinion of the Court had the support of seven Justices. Justice Rehnquist concurred only in the result. Justice Marshall did not participate in the case.

participants to achieve those goals. The use of speeches, marches, and threats of social ostracism cannot provide the basis for a damage award. But violent conduct is beyond the pale of constitutional protection.

"The taint of violence colored the conduct of some of the petitioners. They, of course, may be held liable for the consequences of their violent deeds. The burden of demonstrating that it colored the entire collective effort, however, is not satisfied by evidence that violence occurred or even that violence contributed to the success of the boycott. A massive and prolonged effort to change the social, political, and economic structure of a local environment cannot be characterized as a violent conspiracy simply by reference to the ephemeral consequences of relatively few violent acts. Such a characterization must be supported by findings that adequately disclose the evidentiary basis for concluding that specific parties agreed to use unlawful means, that carefully identify the impact of such unlawful conduct, and that recognize the importance of avoiding the imposition of punishment for constitutionally protected activity. The burden of demonstrating that fear rather than protected conduct was the dominant force in the movement is heavy. A court must be wary of a claim that the true color of a forest is better revealed by reptiles hidden in the weeds than by the foliage of countless free-standing trees. The findings of [the trial court] are constitutionally insufficient to support the judgment that all petitioners are liable for all losses resulting from the boycott."

In supporting these conclusions, Justice Stevens began by explaining why "the nonviolent elements of petitioners' activities" were entitled to First Amendment protection. He noted that the boycott "took many forms" and that its "acknowledged purpose was to secure compliance by both civic and business leaders with a lengthy list of demands for equality and racial justice. The boycott was supported by speeches and nonviolent picketing. Participants repeatedly encouraged others to join in its cause." He found that each of these elements was "a form of speech or conduct that is ordinarily entitled to protection under the [First Amendment]. The right to associate does not lose all constitutional protection merely because some members of the group may have participated in conduct or advocated doctrine that itself is not protected. [DeJonge v. Oregon.]"

Justice Stevens conceded that the petitioners "did more than assemble peaceably and discuss among themselves their grievances against governmental and business policy." But he insisted that "[o]ther elements of the boycott [also] involved activities ordinarily safeguarded by the First Amendment. [E.g., Thornhill v. Alabama (peaceful picketing).]" Justice Stevens continued: "Speech itself was used to further the aims of the boycott. Nonparticipants repeatedly were urged to join the common cause, both through public address and through personal solicitation. These elements of the boycott involve speech in its most direct form. In addition, [petitioners] sought to persuade others to join the boycott through social pressure and the 'threat' of social ostracism. Speech does not lose its protected character, however, simply because it may embarrass others or coerce them into action. [In sum], the boycott clearly involved constitutionally protected activity. The established elements of speech, assembly, association and petition, 'though not identical, are inseparable.' Thomas v. Collins. Through exercise of these

First Amendment rights, petitioners sought to bring about political, social, and economic change. Through speech, assembly, and petition—rather than through riot or revolution—petitioners sought to change a social order that had consistently treated them as second-class citizens."

True, the "presence of protected activity [did] not end the relevant constitutional inquiry": "Governmental regulation that has an incidental effect on First Amendment freedoms may be justified in certain narrowly defined instances. See United States v. O'Brien. A nonviolent and totally voluntary boycott may have a disruptive effect on local economic conditions. This Court has recognized the strong governmental interest in certain forms of economic regulation, even though such regulation may have an incidental effect on rights of speech and association. See [e.g., Giboney]. The right of business entities to 'associate' to suppress competition may be curtailed. Unfair trade practices may be restricted. Secondary boycotts and picketing by labor unions may be prohibited." But, Justice Stevens added, "[w]hile States have broad power to regulate economic activity, we do not find a comparable right to prohibit peaceful political activity such as that found in the boycott in this case. This Court has recognized that expression on public issues 'has always rested on the highest rung of the hierarchy of First Amendment values.' Carey v. Brown."

Applying these principles, Justice Stevens suggested that the purpose of affecting governmental action was protected by the First Amendment even if there was also an anti-competitive effect: "[A] major purpose of the boycott in this case was to influence governmental action. [The] petitioners certainly foresaw—and directly intended—that the merchants would sustain economic injury as a result of their campaign. [However], the purpose of petitioners' campaign was not to destroy legitimate competition. Petitioners sought to vindicate rights of equality and of freedom that lie at the heart of the Fourteenth Amendment itself. The right of the State to regulate economic activity could not justify a complete prohibition against a nonviolent, politically-motivated boycott designed to force governmental and economic change and to effectuate rights guaranteed by the Constitution itself." [3]

Turning to the specific bases for the Mississippi Supreme Court's imposition of liability here, Justice Stevens conceded that the judgment did not rest "on a theory that state law prohibited a nonviolent, politically-motivated boycott." He added, however: "The fact that such activity is constitutionally protected [imposes] a special obligation on this Court to examine critically the basis on which liability was imposed. In particular, we consider here the effect of our holding that much of petitioners' conduct was constitutionally protected on the ability of the State to impose liability for elements of the boycott that were not so protected." Clearly, there were unprotected aspects of the boycott: "The First Amendment does not protect violence. [There]

---

3. Justice Stevens also quoted with approval a comment by a U.S. Court of Appeals judge in a related proceeding: "[All] of the picketing, speeches, and other communication associated with the boycott were directed to the elimination of racial discrimination in the town. This differentiates this case from a boycott organized for economic ends, for speech to protest racial discrimination is essential political speech lying at the core of the First Amendment."

is no question that acts of violence occurred. No federal rule of law restricts a State from imposing tort liability for business losses that are caused by violence and by threats of violence. When such conduct occurs in the context of a constitutionally protected activity, however, 'precision of regulation' is demanded. NAACP v. Button.[4] Specifically, the presence of activity protected by the First Amendment imposes restraints on the grounds that may give rise to damage liability and on the persons who may be held accountable for those damages."

In articulating these "restraints," Justice Stevens emphasized: "Only those losses proximately caused by unlawful conduct may be recovered. The First Amendment similarly restricts the ability of the State to impose liability on an individual solely because of his association with another. [See Scales; Noto; Healy v. James.] [The] principles announced in Scales, Noto, and Healy are relevant to this case. Civil liability may not be imposed merely because an individual belonged to a group, some members of which committed acts of violence. For liability to be imposed by reason of association alone, it is necessary to establish that the group itself possessed unlawful goals and that the individual held a specific intent to further those illegal aims. 'In this sensitive field, the State may not employ "means that broadly stifle fundamental personal liberties when the end can be more narrowly achieved." Shelton v. Tucker.' Carroll v. Princess Anne."

Under these principles, the Mississippi Supreme Court's award of damages on the view that petitioners were liable for all damages "resulting from the boycott" could not be sustained. The state court's opinion itself demonstrated "that all business losses were not proximately caused by the violence and threats of violence. [To] the extent that the court's judgment rests on the ground that 'many' black citizens were 'intimidated' by 'threats' of 'social ostracism, vilification, and traduction,' it is flatly inconsistent with the First Amendment. The ambiguous findings of the Mississippi Supreme Court are inadequate to assure the 'precision of regulation' demanded by that constitutional provision." Moreover, the record demonstrated that all of the merchants' losses were not proximately caused by violence or threats of violence. The record showed that many boycotters acted voluntarily. "It is indeed inconceivable that a boycott launched by the unanimous vote of several hundred persons succeeded solely through fear and intimidation." The Mississippi Supreme Court had "completely failed to demonstrate that business losses suffered in 1972 [were] proximately caused by the isolated acts of violence found in 1966. It is impossible to conclude that state power has not been exerted to compensate respondents for the direct consequences of nonviolent, constitutionally protected activity."[5]

---

4. "Although this is a civil lawsuit between private parties, the application of state rules of law by the Mississippi state courts in a manner alleged to restrict First Amendment freedoms constitutes 'state action' under the Fourteenth Amendment. New York Times v. Sullivan." [Footnote by Justice Stevens.]

5. Justice Stevens distinguished Milk Wagon Drivers Union v. Meadowmoor Dairies, 312 U.S. 287 (1941), where the Court had held that the presence of violence justified an injunction against both violent and nonviolent activity. In that case, he noted, the violent conduct was "pervasive." Here, by contrast, the Mississippi Supreme Court had "relied on isolated

Moreover, with respect to most of the petitioners, the record failed to show an adequate basis to sustain the judgments against them. For example, mere participation in the local meetings of the NAACP was "an insufficient predicate on which to impose liability." That would "not even constitute 'guilt by association,' since there is no evidence that the association possessed unlawful aims. Rather, liability could only be imposed on a 'guilt *for* association' theory. Neither is permissible under the First Amendment." Similarly, there was no basis for imposing liability on "store watchers"—boycott participants who stood outside of the stores and recorded the names of those not heeding the boycott. True, there was evidence that some "store watchers" engaged in violence or threats of violence. "Unquestionably, these individuals may be held responsible for the injuries that they caused; a judgment tailored to the consequences of their unlawful conduct may be sustained." [6]

10th ED., p. 1438; IND. RTS., p. 1058
Add after Buckley v. Valeo:

CALIFORNIA MEDICAL ASSN. v. FEC, 453 U.S. 182 (1981): Certain provisions of the Federal Election Campaign Act limit the amount an unincorporated association may contribute to a multicandidate political committee. In California Medical Assn. v. FEC, the Court rejected constitutional challenges to these provisions. The central target of the attack was 2 U.S.C. § 441a(a)(1)(C), which prohibits individuals and unincorporated associations from contributing more than $5,000 per calendar year to any multicandidate political committee.[1] This provision was challenged by the California Medical Association (CMA), a not-for-profit unincorporated association of approximately 25,000 California physicians. CMA had formed the California Medical Political Action Committee (CALPAC), a multicandidate politi-

acts of violence during a limited period to uphold respondents' recovery of *all* business losses sustained over a seven-year span. No losses are attributed to the voluntary participation of individuals determined to secure 'justice and equal opportunity.' The court's judgment 'screens reality' and cannot stand."

6. Justice Stevens also found no basis for sustaining the judgments against Charles Evers or, because of his activities, the national NAACP. Charles Evers, the Field Secretary of the NAACP, had helped organize the Claiborne County Branch of the NAACP, at whose meetings the boycott was born. The State claimed, inter alia, that Evers' speeches constituted punishable "incitement." Justice Stevens found that Evers' statements were protected under the First Amendment. His explanation of that conclusion is printed above, with other materials on "incitement" in Sec. 1 of the preceding chapter (as addition to 10th Ed., p. 1183; Ind.Rts., p. 803).

The alleged liability of the NAACP derived solely from the asserted liability of Evers. But that was not adequate: "To impose liability without a finding that the NAACP authorized—either actually or apparently—or ratified unlawful conduct would impermissibly burden the rights of political association that are protected by the First Amendment." Since the chancellor had made no finding that Charles Evers or any other NAACP member "had either actual or apparent authority to commit acts of violence or to threaten violent conduct," his findings were not "adequate" to support the judgment against the NAACP.

1. A related provision of the Act makes it unlawful for political committees to knowingly accept contributions exceeding this limit.

The Act defines a "multicandidate political committee" as a "political committee [which] has received contributions from more than 50 persons, and [has] made contributions to 5 or more candidates for Federal Office."

cal committee within the meaning of the Act. The Federal Election Commission claimed that CMA had violated the Act by making annual contributions to CALPAC in excess of $5,000. CMA's defense relied mainly on the First Amendment and the alleged implications of Buckley v. Valeo.

The Court rejected the First Amendment claim, but could not muster a majority opinion to justify its judgment. Justice Marshall submitted a plurality opinion, joined by Justices Brennan, White and Stevens. Justice Blackmun's concurring opinion, resting on a different analysis, was necessary to achieve the majority result. (The dissent rested on a jurisdictional ground and did not reach the merits.[2])

In disposing of the First Amendment challenge, Justice MARSHALL stated: "Although the $5,000 annual limit [on] the amount that individuals and unincorporated associations may contribute to political committees is, strictly speaking, a contribution limitation [and although Buckley sustained several contribution limitations], appellants seek to bring their challenge [within] the reasoning of Buckley. First, they contend that § 441a (a)(1)(C) is akin to an unconstitutional expenditure limitation because it restricts the ability of CMA to engage in political speech through a political committee, CALPAC. Appellants further contend that even if the challenged provision is viewed as a contribution limitation, it is qualitatively different from the contribution restrictions we upheld in Buckley. Specifically, appellants assert that because the contributions here flow to a political committee, rather than to a candidate, the danger of actual or apparent corruption of the political process recognized by this Court in Buckley as a sufficient justification for contribution restrictions is not present in this case.

"While these contentions have some surface appeal, they are in the end unpersuasive. The type of expenditures that this Court in Buckley considered constitutionally protected were those made *independently* by a candidate, individual or group in order to engage directly in political speech. Nothing in § 441a(a)(1)(C) limits the amount CMA or any of its members may independently expend in order to advocate political views; rather, the statute restrains only the amount that CMA may contribute to CALPAC. Appellants nonetheless insist that CMA's contributions to CALPAC should receive the same constitutional protection as independent expenditures because, according to appellants, this is the manner in which CMA has chosen to engage in political speech.

"We would naturally be hesitant to conclude that CMA's determination to fund CALPAC rather than to engage directly in political advocacy is entirely unprotected by the First Amendment.[3] Nonetheless, the 'speech by

2. Justice Stewart's dissent, joined by Chief Justice Burger and Justices Powell and Rehnquist, argued that "the complex judicial review provisions" of the Act barred exercise of appellate jurisdiction, given the posture of the case. The dissenters accordingly concluded that the appeal should be dismissed "for want of jurisdiction."

3. In Buckley, this Court concluded that the act of contribution involved some limited element of protected speech. [Under the Buckley analysis], CMA's contributions to CALPAC symbolize CMA's general approval of CALPAC's role in the political process. However, this attenuated form of speech does not resemble the direct political advocacy to which this Court in Buckley accorded substantial con-

proxy' that CMA seeks to achieve through its contributions to CALPAC is not the sort of political advocacy that this Court in Buckley found entitled to full First Amendment protection. CALPAC, as a multicandidate political committee, receives contributions from more than 50 persons during a calendar year. Thus, appellants' claim that CALPAC is merely the mouthpiece of CMA is untenable. CALPAC instead is a separate legal entity that receives funds from multiple sources and that engages in independent political advocacy. Of course, CMA would probably not contribute to CALPAC unless it agreed with the views espoused by CALPAC, but this sympathy of interests alone does not convert CALPAC's speech into that of CMA.

"Our decision in Buckley precludes any argument to the contrary. In that case, the limitations on the amount individuals could contribute to candidates and campaign organizations were challenged on the ground that they limited the ability of the contributor to express his political views, albeit through the speech of another. The Court, in dismissing the claim, noted: 'While contributions may result in political expression if spent by a candidate or an association to present views to the voters, the transformation of contributions into political debate *involves speech by someone other than the contributors.*' (Emphasis added). This analysis controls the instant case. If the First Amendment rights of a contributor are not infringed by limitations on the amount he may contribute to a campaign organization which advocates the views and candidacy of a particular candidate, the rights of a contributor are similarly not impaired by limits on the amount he may give to a multicandidate political committee, such as CALPAC, which advocates the views and candidacies of a number of candidates.[4]

"We also disagree with appellants' claim that the contribution restriction challenged here does not further the governmental interest in preventing the actual or apparent corruption of the political process. Congress enacted § 441a(a)(1)(C) in part to prevent circumvention of the very limitations on contributions that this Court upheld in Buckley. Under the Act, individuals and unincorporated associations such as CMA may not contribute more than $1,000 to any single candidate in any calendar year. Moreover, individuals may not make more than $25,000 in aggregate annual political contributions. If appellants' position—that Congress cannot prohibit individuals and unincorporated associations from making unlimited contributions to multicandidate political committees—is accepted, then both these contribution limitations could be easily evaded. Since multicandidate political committees may contribute up to $5,000 per year to any candidate, an individual or association seeking to evade the $1,000 limit on contributions to candidates could do so by channelling funds through a multicandidate political committee. Similar-

---

stitutional protection. [Footnote by Justice Marshall.]

4. "Amicus American Civil Liberties Union suggests that § 441a(a)(1)(C) would violate the First Amendment if construed to limit the amount individuals could jointly expend to express their political views. We need not consider this hypothetical application

of the Act. The case before us involves the constitutionality of § 441a(a)(1)(C) as it applies to contributions to multicandidate political committees. [Contributions] to such committees [are] distinguishable from expenditures made jointly by groups of individuals in order to express common political views." [Footnote by Justice Marshall.]

ly, individuals could evade the $25,000 limit on aggregate annual contributions to candidates if they were allowed to give unlimited sums to multicandidate political committees, since such committees are not limited in the aggregate amount they may contribute in any year.[5] These concerns prompted Congress to enact § 441a(a)(1)(C), and it is clear that this provision is an appropriate means by which Congress could seek to protect the integrity of the contribution restrictions upheld by this Court in Buckley." [6]

Justice BLACKMUN's separate opinion explained why he supported the plurality's result, but could not endorse its reasoning: "[Justice Marshall's approach] appears to rest on the premise that the First Amendment test to be applied to contribution limitations is different from the test applicable to expenditure limitations. I do not agree with that proposition. Although I dissented in part in [Buckley], I am willing to accept as binding the Court's judgment in that case that the contribution limitations challenged there were constitutional. But it does not follow that I must concur in the plurality conclusion today that political contributions are not entitled to full First Amendment protection. It is true that there is language in Buckley that might suggest that conclusion. [At] the same time, however, Buckley states that 'contribution and expenditure limitations both implicate fundamental First Amendment interests,' and that 'governmental "action which may have the effect of curtailing the freedom to associate is subject to the closest scruti-

---

5. "Appellants suggest that their First Amendment concerns would be satisfied if this Court declared § 441a(a)(1)(C) unconstitutional to the extent that it restricts CMA's right to contribute administrative support to CALPAC. [Contributions] for administrative support clearly fall within the sorts of donations limited by § 441a(a)(1)(C). Appellants contend, however, that because these contributions are earmarked for administrative support, they lack any potential for corrupting the political process. We disagree. If unlimited contributions for administrative support are permissible, individuals and groups like CMA could completely dominate the operations and contribution policies of independent political committees such as CALPAC. Moreover, if an individual or association was permitted to fund the entire operation of a political committee, all moneys solicited by that committee could be converted into contributions, the use of which might well be dictated by the committee's main supporter. In this manner political committees would be able to influence the electoral process to an extent disproportionate to their public support and far greater than the individual or group that finances the committee's operations would be able to do acting alone. In so doing, they could corrupt the political process

in a manner that Congress, through its contribution restrictions, has sought to prohibit. We therefore conclude that § 441a(a)(1)(C) applies equally to all forms of contributions specified in § 431(8)(A), and assess appellants' constitutional claims from that perspective." [Footnote by Justice Marshall.]

6. "We also reject appellants' contention that even if § 441a(a)(1)(C) is a valid means by which Congress could seek to prevent circumvention of the other contribution limitations embodied in the Act, it is superfluous and therefore constitutionally defective because other antifraud provisions in the Act adequately serve this end. Because we conclude that the challenged limitation does not restrict the ability of individuals to engage in protected political advocacy, Congress was not required to select the least restrictive means of protecting the integrity of its legislative scheme. Instead, Congress could reasonably have concluded that § 441a(a)(1)(C) was a useful supplement to the other antifraud provisions of the Act. Cf. Buckley v. Valeo (rejecting contention that effective bribery and disclosure statutes eliminated need for contribution limitations)." [Footnote by Justice Marshall.]

ny," ' quoting NAACP v. Alabama. Thus, contribution limitations can be upheld only 'if the State demonstrates a sufficiently important interest and employs means closely drawn to avoid unnecessary abridgment of associational freedoms.' [Buckley.]

"Unlike the plurality, I would apply this 'rigorous standard of review' to the instant case, rather than relying on what I believe to be a mistaken view that contributions are 'not the sort of political advocacy [entitled] to full First Amendment protection.' Respondents claim that § 441a(a)(1)(C) is justified by the governmental interest in preventing apparent or actual political corruption. That this interest is important cannot be doubted. It is a closer question, however, whether the statute is narrowly drawn to advance that interest. Nonetheless, I conclude that contributions to multicandidate political committees may be limited to $5,000 per year as a means of preventing evasion of the limitations on contributions to a candidate or his authorized campaign committee upheld in Buckley. The statute challenged here is thus analogous to the $25,000 limitation on total contributions in a given year that Buckley held to be constitutional.

"I stress, however, that this analysis suggests that a different result would follow if § 441a(a)(1)(C) were applied to contributions to a political committee established for the purpose of making independent expenditures, rather than contributions to candidates. By definition, a multicandidate political committee like CALPAC makes contributions to five or more candidates for federal office. Multicandidate political committees are therefore essentially conduits for contributions to candidates, and as such they pose a perceived threat of actual or potential corruption. In contrast, contributions to a committee that makes only independent expenditures pose no such threat. The Court repeatedly has recognized that '[e]ffective advocacy of both public and private points of view, particularly controversial ones, is undeniably enhanced by group association.' NAACP v. Alabama. By pooling their resources, adherents of an association amplify their own voices. [I] believe that contributions to political committees can be limited only if those contributions implicate the governmental interest in preventing actual or potential corruption, and if the limitation is no broader than necessary to achieve that interest. Because this narrow test is satisfied here, I concur in the result reached [by Justice Marshall on the First Amendment issue]." [7]

---

7. The majority also rejected an equal protection challenge. (On this issue, Justice Blackmun joined Justice Marshall's opinion.) This challenge arose because the Act imposes no limits on contributions by corporations or unions to their segregated political funds. The challengers claimed that such contributions are "directly analogous to an unincorporated association's contributions to a multicandidate political committee." Justice Marshall insisted, however, that the Act did not discriminate between contributions by unincorporated associa-

tions and contributions by corporations and unions: "Appellants' claim of unfair treatment ignores the plain fact that the statute as a whole imposes far *fewer* restrictions on individuals and unincorporated associations than it does on corporations and unions." In his view, the differing restrictions simply reflected the congressional judgment that entities with differing structures and purposes "may require different forms of regulation in order to protect the integrity of the electoral process."

In FEC v. NATIONAL RIGHT TO WORK COMMITTEE, 459 U.S. —— (1982), a unanimous Court upheld and applied the solicitation limitations in § 441(b)(4)(C) of the Federal Election Campaign Act. That provision allows corporations to establish separate funds "to receive and make contributions on behalf of federal candidates," but limits solicitations for funds to stockholders and executive and administrative personnel of the corporation. For a corporation without capital stock, such as the National Right to Work Committee, solicitation is limited to "members." The Committee claimed that this included all those who had responded in some way to their previous solicitations, but the Court, in an opinion by Justice Rehnquist, held that such a construction would be inconsistent with both the language and the purpose of the provision, which was designed to allow corporations without stockholders to solicit on the same basis as those with stockholders.

In holding that this construction of the Act raised no constitutional problems, the Court relied heavily on Buckley v. Valeo in deferring to the Congressional judgment that the limitations on solicitation were necessary to prevent actual or apparent corruption by corporations and labor organizations. And the Court relied as well on California Medical Ass'n for the proposition that different structures or entities might require different forms of regulation.*

———

10th ED., p. 1443; IND. RTS., p. 1063
Add after Bellotti (before Sec. 6):

THE SCRUTINY OF STATE JUSTIFICATIONS FOR REGULATING ELECTIONS IN THE 1980s

1. *Money and local ballot measures.* In CITIZENS AGAINST RENT CONTROL v. BERKELEY, 454 U.S. 290 (1981), the Court invalidated a Berkeley, Calif., ordinance imposing a $250 limit on personal contributions to committees formed to support or oppose ballot measures. A local association, formed to oppose a ballot initiative measure to establish rent control in the city, challenged that restriction. The highest state court, applying strict scrutiny and citing Buckley, upheld the contribution limit. It identified the requisite compelling governmental interest as that of assuring that special interest groups could not "corrupt" the initiative process and thereby cause voter apathy.

Chief Justice BURGER's opinion for the Court found the limit on contributions unconstitutional: "The restraint imposed by the Berkeley Ordinance on rights of association and in turn on individual and collective rights of expression plainly contravenes both the right of association and the speech guarantees of the First Amendment." After stating "that regulation of First

---

* Another First Amendment challenge to provisions of federal campaign regulations reached the Court in Common Cause v. Schmitt, 455 U.S. 129 (1982), but produced no opinions on the merits. Instead, an equally divided Court (with Justice O'Connor not participating) affirmed a lower court invalidation of § 9012(f) of the Presidential Election Campaign Fund Act which, inter alia, imposed spending limits on "unauthorized" political committees seeking to further the election of presidential candidates.

Amendment rights is always subject to exacting judicial review," the Chief Justice emphasized the importance of freedom of association: "To place a spartan limit—or indeed any limit—on individuals wishing to band together to advance their views on a ballot measure, while placing none on individuals acting alone, is clearly a restraint on the right of association."

Although Buckley had sustained limits on contributions in candidate elections (because of the "risk of corruption" rationale), the Chief Justice insisted that "Buckley does not support limitations on contributions to committees formed to favor or oppose *ballot measures*." He pointed out, moreover, that Bellotti had relied on Buckley "to strike down state legislative limits on advocacy relating to ballot measures." He rejected the City's effort to distinguish those cases on the ground that the Berkeley limit was "necessary as a prophylactic measure to make known the identity of supporters and opponents of ballot measures." He found that interest "insubstantial" in this case because the disclosure provisions of the ordinance assured that the identities of contributors would be known. Moreover, there was no evidence in the record that the limit was necessary to preserve voters' confidence in the initiative process.

The Chief Justice also found that the ordinance imposed "a significant restraint on freedom of expression," not only on freedom of association. He noted that, under the ordinance, "an individual may make expenditures without limit but may not contribute beyond the $250 limit when joining with others to advocate common views. The contribution limit thus automatically affects expenditures and limits on expenditures operate as a direct restraint on freedom of expression of a group or committee desiring to engage in political dialogue concerning a ballot measure. [Placing] limits on contributions which in turn limit expenditures plainly impairs freedom of expression." *

The sole dissenter, Justice WHITE, reiterated his dissenting positions in Buckley and Bellotti. He insisted, moreover, that the Berkeley limit was "a

---

* In a concurring statement, Justice REHNQUIST, who had dissented in Bellotti, emphasized that Bellotti did not help the defenders of the Berkeley ordinance because it "was not aimed only at corporations." Justice MARSHALL, concurring only in the judgment, noted that the Court had failed "to indicate whether or not it attaches any constitutional significance to the fact that the Berkeley ordinance seeks to limit *contributions* as opposed to direct *expenditures*," even though, beginning with Buckley, "this Court has *always* drawn a distinction between restrictions on contributions and direct limitations on the amount an individual can expend for his own speech." He accordingly stated: "Because the Court's opinion is silent on the standard of review it is applying to this contributions limitation, I must assume that the Court is follow-

ing our consistent position that this type of governmental action is subjected to less rigorous scrutiny than a direct restriction on expenditures." Justice Marshall joined the result only because the city had failed to disclose "sufficient evidence to justify the conclusion that large contributions to ballot measure committees undermined the 'confidence of the citizenry in government.'" Another separate opinion concurring in the judgment, by Justices BLACKMUN and O'CONNOR, insisted that "exacting scrutiny," a "rigorous standard of review," was appropriate here and concluded "that Berkeley has neither demonstrated a genuine threat to its important governmental interests nor employed means closely drawn to avoid unnecessary abridgment of protected activity."

less encompassing regulation of campaign activity" than those involved in the earlier cases and that the challenged ordinance was "tailored to the odd measurements of Buckley and Bellotti." For example, Berkeley had followed those decisions by regulating "contributions but not expenditures" and by limiting personal but not corporate spending. He commented: "It is for that very reason perhaps that the effectiveness of the ordinance in preserving the integrity of the referendum process is debatable. Even so, the result here illustrates that the Buckley framework is most problematical and strengthens my belief that there is a proper role for carefully drafted limitations on expenditures.

Justice White devoted most of his dissent to arguing that, even under Buckley, "the Berkeley ordinance represents such a negligible intrusion on expression and association that the measure should be upheld." He elaborated: "When the infringement is as slight and ephemeral as it is here, the requisite state interest to justify the regulation need not be so high." He pointed out that the historic purpose of the initiative in California was to prevent "the dominance of special interests" and added: "Perhaps [the City cannot] 'prove' that elections have been or can be unfairly won by special interest groups spending large sums of money, but there is a widespread conviction in legislative halls, as well as among citizens, that the danger is real. I regret that the Court continues to disregard that hazard."

2. *Candidates' promises in election campaigns.* In BROWN v. HARTLAGE, 456 U.S. 45 (1982), the Court examined once again the limited reach of the state interest in preventing "corruption." That decision found a First Amendment violation in the application of Kentucky's Corrupt Practices Act to void an election to local office where the winning candidate had made a campaign statement that he intended to serve at a salary below that "fixed by law." The Act prohibited a candidate from offering material benefits to voters in consideration for their votes, and, conversely, prohibited candidates from accepting payments in consideration for the manner in which they serve their public function. Under the state courts' view of the law, a candidate's promise to serve at a reduced salary was "considered an attempt to buy votes or to bribe the voters."

Justice BRENNAN's opinion for the Court acknowledged that the states have "a legitimate interest in preserving the integrity of their electoral processes," but added: "When a State seeks to restrict directly the offer of ideas by a candidate to the voters, the First Amendment surely requires that the restriction be demonstrably supported not only by a legitimate state interest, but a compelling one, and that the restriction operate without unnecessarily circumscribing protected expression." In exercising strict scrutiny, Justice Brennan noted "three bases upon which the application of the [law] might conceivably be justified: first, as a prohibition on buying votes; second, as facilitating the candidacy of persons lacking independent wealth; and third, as an application of the State's interests and prerogatives with respect to factual misstatements." He found none of these arguments consistent with the First Amendment.

Justice Brennan did not doubt that, as a general rule, "a State may surely prohibit a candidate from buying votes": clearly, "*some* kinds of promises made by a candidate to voters, and *some* kinds of promises elicited by voters from candidates, may be declared illegal without constitutional difficulty." But, he added, "it is equally plain that there are constitutional limits on the State's power to prohibit candidates from making promises in the course of an election campaign." Distinguishing "between those 'private arrangements' that are inconsistent with democratic government and those candidate assurances that promote the representative foundation of our political system" was difficult, to be sure; but this was not a borderline case. The candidate's promise to serve at a reduced salary was "very different in character from the corrupting agreements and solicitations historically recognized as unprotected by the First Amendment." This pledge was "made openly, subject to the comment and criticism of [the candidate's] political opponent and to the scrutiny of the voters." The state courts' effort to analogize the promise to a bribe was accordingly unpersuasive: "there is no *constitutional* basis upon which [the pledge to reduce one's salary] might be equated with a candidate's promise to pay voters for their support from his own pocketbook."

On the corruption issue, Justice Brennan concluded: "[The candidate] did not offer some private payment or donation in exchange for voter support; [his] statement can only be construed as an expression of his intention to exercise public power in a manner that he believed might be acceptable to some class of citizens. If [his] expressed intention had an individualized appeal to some taxpayers who felt themselves the likely beneficiaries of his form of fiscal restraint, that fact is of little constitutional significance. The benefits of most public policy changes accrue not only to the undifferentiated 'public,' but more directly to particular individuals or groups. Like a promise to lower taxes, to increase efficiency in government, or indeed to increase taxes in order to provide some group with a desired public benefit or public service, [this candidate's] promise to reduce his salary cannot be deemed beyond the reach of the First Amendment, or considered as inviting the kind of corrupt arrangement the appearance of which a State may have a compelling interest in avoiding. See Buckley v. Valeo. A State may insist that candidates seeking the approval of the electorate work within the framework of our democratic institutions, and base their appeal on assertions of fitness for office and statements respecting the means by which they intend to further the public welfare. But a candidate's promise to confer some ultimate benefit on the voter, qua taxpayer, citizen, or member of the general public, does not [lie] beyond the pale of First Amendment protection."

Justice Brennan gave much shorter shrift to the other proffered state interests. He noted the State's reliance on "the interest [it] may have in ensuring that the willingness of some persons to serve in public office without remuneration does not make gratuitous service the sine qua non of plausible candidacy." He commented: "The State might legitimately fear that such emphasis on free public service might result in persons of independent wealth but less ability being chosen over those who, though better qualified, could not afford to serve at a reduced salary." But he insisted that, if the law "was designed to further this interest, it chooses a means unacceptable under the First Amendment. In barring certain public statements with respect to this issue, the State ban runs directly contrary to the fundamental premises underlying the First Amendment as the guardian of our democracy. That Amendment embodies our trust in the free exchange of ideas as the means by which the people are to choose between good ideas and bad, and between candidates for political office. The State's fear that voters might make an ill-advised choice does not provide the State with a compelling justification for limiting speech. It is simply not the function of government to 'select which issues are worth discussing or debating' in the course of a political campaign."

Finally, Justice Brennan rejected reliance on "the state interest in protecting the political process from distortions caused by untrue and inaccurate speech." Although he conceded that that interest was "somewhat different from the state interest in protecting individuals from defamatory falsehoods" [see the defamation cases in sec. 2 of this chapter], he insisted that "the principles underlying the First Amendment remain paramount." He observed: "In a political campaign, a candidate's factual blunder is unlikely to escape the notice of, and correction by, the erring candidate's political opponent. The preferred First Amendment remedy of 'more speech, not enforced silence' [Whitney concurrence], thus has special force. Cf. Gertz. There has been no showing in this case that [the candidate] made the disputed statement other than in good faith and without knowledge of its falsity, or that he made the statement with reckless disregard whether it was false or not. Moreover, [he] retracted the statement promptly after discovering that it might have been false. Under these circumstances, nullifying [his] election victory was inconsistent with the atmosphere of robust political debate protected by the First Amendment." All that petitioner had done was to make a promise that he could not keep that he would serve at less than the salary "fixed by law." By voiding his election, the Kentucky courts had imposed absolute liability for the candidate's misstatement. Justice Brennan found that result unacceptable: "The chilling effect of such absolute accountability for factual misstatements in the course of political debate is incompatible with the atmosphere of free discussion contemplated by the First Amendment in the context of political campaigns." †

3. *Ballot access and related issues.* Cases involving claims of ballot access and related electoral issues have traditionally been argued and decided under the "fundamental rights" strand of equal protection analysis. See 10th Ed., p. 934; Ind.Rts., p. 554. More recently, however, the Court has veered away from equal protection in favor of deciding ballot access cases directly on the basis of First Amendment rights to political choice and political association. See especially ANDERSON v. CELEBREZZE, 460 U.S. —— (1983), discussed above, addition to 10th Ed., p. 938; Ind.Rts., p. 558.

† A brief notation by Justice REHN-QUIST, concurring in the result, stated: "Because on different facts I think I would give more weight to the State's interest in preventing corruption in elections, I am unable to join the Court's analogy between such laws and state defamation laws. I think Mills v. Alabama, 384 U.S. 214 (1966) [invalidating a law pro-hibiting press endorsements of candidates on election day], affords ample basis for reaching the result [here], and I see no need to rely on other precedents which do not involve state efforts to regulate the electoral process." Chief Justice BURGER merely noted his concurrence in the judgment.

10th ED., p. 1479; IND. RTS., p. 1099
Add to footnote 2:

In cases such as Pickering and Letter Carriers, the issue was the extent to which an employee's free speech rights *as a citizen* may be restricted because of the demands or nature of public employment. But to what extent does a public employee have free speech rights *as an employee*? Is the dismissal of an employee for what that employee says while on the job subject to First Amendment limitations? In connection with this issue, importantly distinct from the issue in Pickering, see Connick v. Myers, 461 U.S. — (1983), printed above, addition to 10th Ed., p. 1407; Ind.Rts., p. 1027.

10th ED., p. 1481; IND. RTS., p. 1101
Add after Note on "Public Employees" (before "Compelled Disclosure"):

GOVERNMENT BENEFITS OTHER THAN EMPLOYMENT

The principle that governmental benefits may not be conditioned on relinquishing First Amendment rights has not been limited to employment. Thus, in Speiser v. Randall, 357 U.S. 513 (1958), the Court overturned a California requirement that property tax exemptions for veterans would be available only to those who would declare that they did not advocate the forcible overthrow of the government. Rejecting California's claim that it could condition the award of a "privilege" or "bounty," Justice Brennan's opinion for the Court noted that "to deny an exemption to claimants who engage in certain forms of speech is in effect to penalize them for such speech."

In REGAN v. TAXATION WITH REPRESENTATION OF WASHINGTON, 461 U.S. — (1983), a unanimous Court found Speiser clearly distinguishable in a challenge to the Internal Revenue Code's prohibition on lobbying for tax-exempt organizations. Under § 501(c)(3) of the Internal Revenue Code, tax-exempt status is limited to those organizations "no substantial part of the activities of which is carrying on propaganda, or otherwise attempting to influence legislation." Because it engaged in lobbying activities, Taxation With Representation of Washington (TWR) was denied tax-exempt status, the most important aspect of that action being that contributions to TWR would not be deductible by the contributors. TWR filed suit, claiming that § 501(c)(3) violated the First Amendment and the principles of Speiser by conditioning tax-exempt status on refraining from lobbying, an activity protected by the First Amendment.

Justice REHNQUIST's opinion for the Court characterized "[b]oth tax exemptions and tax-deductibility [as] a form of subsidy that is administered through the tax system." But implicit in the Court's decision was an important distinction. In Speiser the exercise of First Amendment activity caused the loss of a benefit otherwise available, a benefit itself unrelated to the First Amendment activity. But here support for the First Amendment activity itself was the very benefit sought. "TWR is certainly correct when it states that we have held that the government may not deny a benefit to a person because he exercises a constitutional right. See Perry v. Sindermann, 408 U.S. 593 (1972). But TWR is just as certainly incorrect when it claims that this case fits the Speiser-Perry model. The Code does not deny TWR the right to receive deductible contributions to support its non-lobbying activity, nor does it deny TWR any independent benefit on account of its intention to lobby. Congress has merely refused to pay for the lobbying out of public monies. [This] aspect of the case is controlled by Cammarano v. United States, 358 U.S. 498 (1959), in which we upheld a Treasury Regulation that denied business expense deductions for lobbying activities. We held that Congress is not required by the First Amendment to subsidize lobbying. [Congress] has not infringed any First Amendment rights or regulated any First Amendment activity. Congress has simply chosen not to pay for TWR's lobbying. We again reject the 'notion that First Amendment rights are somehow not fully realized unless they are subsidized by the State.' "

TWR also presented an equal protection challenge, based on the fact that veterans' organizations are free to lobby without losing their tax-exempt status. TWR argued that strict scrutiny must be applied to a situation, such as this, where Congress chooses to subsidize only the speech of certain organizations. This "content regulation" challenge was rejected by the Court as well. "The case would be different if Congress were to discriminate invidiously in its subsidies in such a way as to 'aim at the suppression of dangerous ideas.' [Cammarano.] But the veterans' organizations [are] entitled to receive tax-deductible contributions regardless of the content of any speech they may use, including lobbying. We find no indication that the statute was intended to suppress any ideas or any demonstration that it has had that effect. The sections of the Internal Revenue Code here at issue do not employ any suspect classification. The distinction between veteran's organizations and other charitable organizations is not like distinctions based on race or national origin." *

Justice BLACKMUN joined the opinion of the Court, but also wrote a separate concurring opinion, joined by Justice Brennan and Justice Marshall. For Justice Blackmun the presence of § 501(c)(4) was crucial to preserving the constitutionality of § 501(c)(3). This latter section allows an organization exempt under § 501(c)(3) to create an affiliated organization under § 501(c)(4). A § 501(c)(4) organization may engage in lobbying without losing its tax-exempt status. But, unlike a § 501(c)(3) organization, contributions to a § 501(c)(4) organization are not deductible from the income of the contributor. Justice Blackmun found that the ability to create a § 501(c)(4) organization to engage in lobbying activities meant that a § 501(c)(3) organization did not have to relinquish its lobbying activities in order to qualify for the tax-exemption. "A § 501(c)(3) organization's

---

* On the relationship between the First Amendment and equal protection, see Chicago Police Dep't v. Mosley, discussed above, 10th Ed., p. 1239; Ind. Rts., p. 859; Perry Education Ass'n v. Perry Local Educators' Ass'n, 460 U.S. —— (1983), printed above, addition to 10th Ed., p. 1325; Ind.Rts., p. 945. Is TWR's claim best characterized in equal protection terms? If a tax deduction or exemption were available to Republicans but not to Democrats, would this be a First Amendment or an equal protection violation? What about a tax exemption available to Baptists and Presbyterians but not to Catholics and Jews? Does it matter which part of the Constitution is used? In this context, note the Court's recent shift from equal protection to First Amendment analysis in ballot access cases. See Anderson v. Celebrezze, 460 U.S. —— (1983), discussed above, 10th Ed., pp. 938 and 1443; Ind.Rts., pp. 558 and 1063.

right to speak is not infringed, because it is free to make known its views on legislation through its § 501(c)(4) affiliate without losing tax benefits for its nonlobbying activities." But if this relationship did not exist, Justice Blackmun would have reached a different concluson. "[A]n attempt to prevent § 501(c)(4) organizations from lobbying explicitly on behalf of their § 501(c)(3) affiliates would perpetuate § 501(c)(3) organizations' inability to make known their views on legislation without incurring the unconstitutional penalty. Such restrictions would extend far beyond Congress' mere refusal to subsidize lobbying [and] would render the statutory scheme unconstitutional."

10th ED., p. 1484; IND. RTS., p. 1104
Add as footnote at end of section B of Buckley v. Valeo:

The Buckley v. Valeo exemption from compelled disclosures for certain minor parties was applied in Brown v. Socialist Workers '74 Campaign Committee (Ohio), 459 U.S. —— (1982). In an opinion by Justice Marshall, the Court held, without dissent on this point, that the Socialist Workers Party in Ohio had made a sufficient showing of a "reasonable probability of threats, harassment, or reprisals" that the Party could not be constitutionally compelled to disclose information concerning campaign contributions. The Court also held, over the dissents of Justices O'Connor, Rehnquist, and Stevens, that the same showing also exempted the Party from compelled disclosure of campaign *disbursements*. The Court reasoned that many disbursements consist of "reimbursements, advances, or wages paid to party members, campaign workers, and supporters, whose activities lie at the very core of the First Amendment." Other disbursements go to those who, whether supporters or not, might be deterred by disclosure from dealing with a party espousing unpopular views. The dissent, written by Justice O'Connor, argued that the balance between governmental interests and the First Amendment interests of the party would be sufficiently different in the case of expenditures that there should be a "separately focused inquiry" into whether disclosure of expenditures, taken alone, would subject the party or recipients of the disbursements to threats, harassment, or reprisals. The dissenters, although agreeing that such a possibility existed for contributors, felt that in this case it did not exist for recipients of expenditures.

10th ED., p. 1520; IND. RTS., p. 1140
Add to footnote 2:

Nebraska Press deals with limitations on the press in order to assure a fair trial, but would limitations on the out-of-court statements of the parties be permissible? What about restrictions imposed upon the attorneys? Jurors? See KPNX Broadcasting Co. v. Arizona Superior Court, 459 U.S. —— (1982) (Rehnquist, J., as Circuit Justice, denying stay).

10th ED., p. 1545; IND. RTS., p. 1165
Add after Richmond Newspapers:

GLOBE NEWSPAPER CO. v. SUPERIOR COURT, 457 U.S. 596 (1982): The Globe Newspaper case explored the bases and implications of Richmond Newspapers. In the 1982 ruling, unlike Richmond Newspapers in 1981, a majority of the Justices managed to agree on an opinion for the Court. The majority concluded that the First Amendment had been violated by a Massachusetts law which had been construed to *require* the exclusion of the press and the general public from the courtroom during the testimony of a minor who had allegedly been a victim of a sex offense. The case arose when the Boston Globe unsuccessfully sought access to a state court trial where the defendant had been charged with the rape of three girls who were minors. In upholding the State's mandatory closure rule, the Massachusetts Supreme Judicial Court had distinguished Richmond Newspapers by emphasizing "at least one notable exception" to the tradition of "openness" in criminal trials: "cases involving sexual assault." The mandatory closure law accordingly operated "in an area of traditional sensitivity to the needs of victims."

Justice BRENNAN, writing for the majority, found the law invalid under the principles of Richmond Newspapers. In his view, Richmond Newspapers "firmly established for the first time that the press and general public have a constitutional right of access to criminal trials," even though no such right was "explicitly mentioned [in] the First Amendment." He added: "The First Amendment [is] broad enough to encompass those rights that, while not unambiguously enumerated in the very terms of the Amendment, are nonetheless necessary to the enjoyment of other First Amendment rights." Protecting "the free discussion of governmental affairs" was a major purpose of the Amendment; offering such protection served "to ensure that the individual citizen can effectively participate in and contribute to our republican system of self-government." A "right of access to *criminal trials*" was properly afforded by the First Amendment [1] because "the criminal trial historically has been open to the press and general public" and because "the right of access to criminal trials plays a particularly significant role in the functioning of the judicial process and the government as a whole." He noted that "the institutional value of the open criminal trial is recognized in both logic and experience."

That constitutional right of access, though not "absolute," was entitled to protection unless the State showed "that the denial [of access] is necessitated by a compelling governmental interest, and is narrowly tailored to serve that interest." [2] Massachusetts' defense of its law could not survive that strict scrutiny. Justice Brennan conceded that the first of the two interests put forth by the state—protecting the physical and psychological well-being of minor victims of sex crimes from further trauma and embarrassment—was "a compelling one." But the closure law was not "a narrowly tailored means of accommodating the State's asserted interest: That interest could be served just as well by requiring the trial court to determine on a case-by-case basis whether the State's legitimate concern for the well-being of the minor victim necessitates closure. Such an approach ensures that the constitutional right of the

1. Justice Brennan devoted only a footnote to rejecting the argument relied upon by the Massachusetts Supreme Judicial Court, that criminal trials have not always been open during the testimony of minors who were sex victims: "Even if appellee is correct in this regard, the argument is unavailing. In Richmond Newspapers, the Court discerned a First Amendment right of access to *criminal trials* based in part on the recognition that as a general matter criminal trials have long been presumptively open. Whether the First Amendment right of access to criminal trials can be restricted in the context of any particular criminal trial, such as a murder trial (the setting for the dispute in Richmond Newspapers) or a rape trial, depends not on the historical openness of that type of criminal trial but rather on the state interests assertedly supporting the restriction."

2. "Of course, limitations on the right of access that resemble 'time, place, and manner' restrictions on protected speech would not be subjected to such strict scrutiny." [Footnote by Justice Brennan.]

press and public to gain access to criminal trials will not be restricted except where necessary to protect the State's interest." [3]

Nor could the closure law be sustained on the basis of the State's second asserted interest—"the encouragement of minor victims of sex crimes to come forward and provide accurate testimony." In rejecting that argument, Justice Brennan stated: "Not only is the claim speculative in empirical terms, but it is also open to serious question as a matter of logic and common sense. Although [the law] bars the press and general public from the courtroom during the testimony of minor sex victims, the press is not denied access to the transcript, court personnel, or any other possible source that could provide an account of the minor victim's testimony. Thus, [the law] cannot prevent the press from publicizing the substance of a minor victim's testimony, as well as his or her identity. If [the State's] interest in encouraging minor victims to come forward depends on keeping such matters secret, [the law] hardly advances that interest in an effective manner. And even if [the law] effectively advanced the State's interest, it is doubtful that the interest would be sufficient to overcome the constitutional attack, for that same interest could be relied on to support an array of mandatory-closure rules designed to encourage victims to come forward: Surely it cannot be suggested that minor victims of sex crimes are the *only* crime victims who, because of publicity, [are] reluctant to come forward and testify. The State's argument based on this interest therefore proves too much, and runs contrary to the very foundation of the right of access recognized in Richmond Newspapers." [4]

Chief Justice BURGER, joined by Justice Rehnquist, were the only members of the Court to dissent on the merits.[5] The Chief Justice disagreed with the majority's "expansive interpretation" of Richmond Newspapers and "its cavalier rejection of the serious interests supporting Massachusetts' mandatory closure rule." He thought the ruling "advance[d] a disturbing para-

---

3. Justice Brennan elaborated the required "case-by-case" approach only briefly: "Among the factors to be weighed [by a trial court seeking to determine whether closure is necessary to protect the welfare of a victim] are the minor victim's age, psychological maturity, and understanding, the nature of the crime, the desires of the victim, and the interests of parents and relatives."

4. In a concluding footnote, Justice Brennan summarized the holding as follows: "We emphasize that our holding is a narrow one: that a rule of mandatory closure respecting the testimony of minor sex victims is constitutionally infirm. In individual cases, and under appropriate circumstances, the First Amendment does not necessarily stand as a bar to the exclusion from the courtroom of the press and general public during the testimony of minor sex-offense victims. But a mandatory rule, requir-

ing no particularized determinations in individual cases, is unconstitutional."

Justice O'CONNOR concurred only in the judgment. She stated that she did not interpret Richmond Newspapers "to shelter every right that is 'necessary to the enjoyment of other First Amendment rights.' Instead, Richmond Newspapers rests upon our long history of open criminal trials and the special value, for both public and accused, of that openness. [Thus] I interpret neither Richmond Newspapers nor [today's decision] to carry any implications outside the context of criminal trials."

5. Justice STEVENS dissented on the ground that the case should have been dismissed for mootness. He charged the majority with rendering an "advisory, hypothetical, and, at best, premature" opinion.

dox": "Although states are permitted, for example, to mandate the closure of all proceedings in order to protect a 17-year-old charged with rape, they are not permitted to require the closing of part of criminal proceedings in order to protect an innocent child who has been raped or otherwise sexually abused." He claimed that Richmond Newspapers had *not* established "a First Amendment right of access to all aspects of all criminal trials under all circumstances." Richmond Newspapers had emphasized the traditional openness of criminal trials in general, but there was "clearly a long history of exclusion of the public from trials involving sexual assaults, particularly those against minors. [It] would misrepresent the historical record to state that there is an 'unbroken, uncontradicted history' of open proceedings in cases involving the sexual abuse of minors"; and such a specific "history of openness" was necessary to invoke Richmond Newspapers.

The Chief Justice also found the majority's "wooden application" of strict scrutiny "inappropriate." He emphasized: "Neither the purpose of the law nor its effect is primarily to deny the press or public access to information; the verbatim transcript is made available to the public and the media and may be used without limit. We therefore need only examine whether the restrictions imposed are reasonable and whether the interests of the [State] override the very limited incidental effects of the law on First Amendment rights." To him, it seemed "beyond doubt, considering the minimal impact of the law on First Amendment rights and the overriding weight of the [State's] interest in protecting child rape victims, that the Massachusetts law is not unconstitutional. [The] law need not be precisely tailored so long as the state's interest overrides the law's impact on First Amendment rights and the restrictions imposed further that interest. Certainly this [law] rationally serves the [State's] overriding interest in protecting the child [from] severe—possibly permanent—psychological damage." Moreover, there was adequate justification for making the law mandatory rather than discretionary: "[V]ictims and their families are entitled to assurance [of] protection. The legislature did not act irrationally in deciding not to leave the closure determination to the idiosyncracies of individual judges subject to the pressures available to the media." He concluded: "Many will find it difficult to reconcile the concern so often expressed for the rights of the accused with the callous indifference exhibited today for children who, having suffered the trauma of rape or other sexual abuse, are denied the modest protection the Massachusetts legislature provided."

Chapter 14

THE CONSTITUTION AND RELIGION

10th ED., p. 1560; IND. RTS., p. 1180
Add to footnote 3:

Senator Helms' efforts to deal with the school prayer issue through jurisdiction-curbing legislation continued into 1982, as noted above, addition to 10th Ed. and Ind. Rts., p. 57. Nothing came of these efforts in the 97th Congress, however, and the drive to enact jurisdiction-curbing prayer legislation may have lost some of its force, at least partly as a result of Administration actions. First, Attorney General Smith (in the letter noted above) cast doubt on the constitutionality of tampering substantially with the Supreme Court's appellate jurisdiction. Second, President Reagan, in May 1982, formally proposed a constitutional amendment providing that "[n]othing in this Constitution shall be construed to prohibit individual or group prayer in public schools or other public institutions. No person shall be required by the United States or by any State to participate in prayer."

Consider the language of the proposed amendment. Note that it deals exclusively with individual or group prayer. In McCollum v. Board of Education (discussed in Zorach and accompanying notes, 10th Ed., p. 1554; Ind.Rts., p. 1174), the Court held that permitting private teachers to come into the public schools during the day to give religious instruction to consenting students violated the Establishment Clause. Would the proposed amendment overturn McCollum? What would be the effect, if any, on Stone v. Graham (discussed below, addition to 10th Ed., p. 1563; Ind.Rts., p. 1183), which held unconstitutional a state statute that required the posting of a copy of the Ten Commandments, purchased with private contributions, on classroom walls? Is that part of Abington v. Schempp that dealt with state sponsorship of devotional Bible reading in the public schools affected by the proposed amendment? In thinking about these questions, bear in mind that the proposed amendment does not by its terms address government involvement with, or sponsorship of, prayer in the public schools. For a comprehensive review of the proposal, see Ackerman, "Legal Analysis of President Reagan's Proposed Constitutional Amendment on School Prayer" (Congressional Research Service, The Library of Congress, June 2, 1982).

Hearings were conducted on the President's proposed amendment in the summer of 1982, but no further action was taken before the 97th Congress adjourned. Reintroduced in the 98th, the proposal has been the subject of intense lobbying by both supporters and opponents. The opponents have principally argued that it is unwise to introduce any kind of organized prayer in the public schools, and that any prayer recitation sanctioned or led by school authorities carries with it a strong if unspoken pressure to participate. In an effort to meet these concerns, and to offer a proposal that he thought could command a majority of the Senate Judiciary Committee, Senator Hatch drafted a compromise amendment. It provides that nothing in the Constitution prohibits "individual or group silent prayer or meditation." Required participation in prayer or government encouragement of "any particular form of prayer or meditation" is prohibited. The Hatch proposal also provides that nothing in the Constitution should be interpreted "to prohibit equal access to the use of public school facilities by all voluntary student groups." Administration opposition to this compromise proposal has delayed the consideration of any school prayer amendments by the Senate Judiciary Committee Constitution Subcomittee, originally scheduled for mid-May 1983. See generally 41 Cong. Quar. Weekly Report 1051–52 (May 28, 1983).

10th ED., p. 1562; IND. RTS., p. 1182
Add to footnote 4:

In Marsh v. Chambers, 463 U.S. —— (1983) (discussed below, addition to 10th Ed., p. 1581; Ind.Rts., p. 1201), the Court distinguished the special context of schools in upholding legislative prayers and chaplains. Justice Brennan, specifically recanting his concurring views in Abington, dissented.

10th ED., p. 1563; IND. RTS., p. 1183

Add as footnote at end of last full paragraph:

In Stone v. Graham, 449 U.S. 39 (1980), the Court held unconstitutional a Kentucky law that required the posting of a copy of the Ten Commandments, purchased with private contributions, on public classroom walls. In sustaining the law, the state trial court had emphasized that the statute's "avowed purpose" was "secular and not religious." The Court, relying in part on its school prayer and Bible reading rulings, reversed summarily, without hearing argument on the merits.

The majority's per curiam opinion concluded that the law had "no secular legislative purpose," even though the statute required that each display of the Ten Commandments have a notation in small print stating: "The secular application of the Ten Commandments is clearly seen in its adoption as the fundamental legal code of Western Civilization and the Common Law of the United States." According to the majority, the preeminent purpose of the posting requirement was "plainly religious," since the Ten Commandments are "undeniably a sacred text in the Jewish and Christian faiths." Even though some of the Commandments address secular matters, "the first part of the Commandments concerns the religious duties of believers." The Court noted that this was not a case "in which the Ten Commandments are integrated into the school curriculum, where the Bible may constitutionally be used in an appropriate study of history, civilization, ethics, comparative religion, or the like. Posting of religious texts on the wall serves no such educational function."

Justice Rehnquist's dissent insisted: "The Court's summary rejection of a secular purpose articulated by the legislature [is] without precedent in Establishment Clause jurisprudence." He added: "The fact that the asserted secular purpose may overlap with what some may see as a religious objective does not render [the law] unconstitutional." In his view, the State was permitted to conclude that "a document with such secular significance should be placed before its students, with an appropriate statement of the document's secular import." And he noted: "The Court's emphasis on the religious nature of the first part of the Ten Commandments is beside the point. The document as a whole has had significant secular impact, and the Constitution does not require that Kentucky students see only an expurgated or redacted version containing only the elements with directly traceable secular effects." Justice Stewart also dissented on the merits; Chief Justice Burger and Justice Blackmun objected to the summary disposition, arguing that the case should have been given plenary consideration.

10th ED., p. 1565; IND. RTS., p. 1185

Add to footnote 4:

An inquiry into legislative motivation constituted a major part of the well-publicized litigation in McLean v. Arkansas Bd. of Education, 529 F.Supp. 1255 (E.D. Ark.1982). At issue was a 1981 Arkansas law requiring that "Public schools within this State shall give balanced treatment to creation-science and to evolution-science." After lengthy proceedings, Judge Overton enjoined enforcement of the law, finding it in violation of the Establishment Clause.

Applying the now-familiar three-part test under the Establishment Clause (see below, 10th Ed., p. 1567; Ind.Rts., p. 1187), Judge Overton concluded that the law had a plainly religious purpose. "The State failed to produce any evidence which would warrant an inference or conclusion that at any point in the process anyone considered the legitimate educational value of the Act. It was simply and purely an effort to introduce the Biblical version of creation into the public school curricula. The only inference which can be drawn [is] that the Act was passed with the specific purpose [of] advancing religion." Additionally, the Act itself, regardless of the motivation for its introduction and passage, was found to be inescapably religious. "The idea of sudden creation from nothing [is] an inherently religious concept." Judge Overton supported this view by concluding that creation science "is simply not science." Because the teaching of creationism could have no effect other than a religious one, and because the discussion of creationism in class would inevitably be a religious discussion, Judge Overton found that the law also failed the "effect" and "entanglement" parts of the Establishment Clause test.

10th ED., p. 1565; IND. RTS., p. 1185
Insert before Note 3:

   2A.   *Do separation of church and state principles justify excluding student religious organizations from public university facilities?*   In WIDMAR v. VINCENT, 454 U.S. 263 (1981) (already noted above, addition to 10th Ed., p. 1287; Ind. Rts., p. 907), the Court held unconstitutional a state university's ban on the use of its facilities by a registered student group planning to conduct religious worship and discussion on campus. The Court noted that the university had made its facilities generally available for the activities of student groups and had thereby created a public forum. The university's exclusionary policy thus violated "the fundamental principle that a state regulation of speech should be content-neutral." [1] In its effort to defend its policy against the Court's First Amendment strict scrutiny, the university contended that it had a "compelling interest" in promoting the separation of church and state mandated by the federal and state constitutions. A lower federal court agreed with that argument: It found the regulation not only justified, but required, by the Establishment Clause. The Supreme Court disagreed.

   In examining the principles of separation of church and state, Justice POWELL's majority opinion turned first to the impact of the Establishment Clause: "We agree that the interest of the University in complying with its constitutional obligations may be characterized as compelling. It does not follow, however, that an 'equal access' policy would be incompatible with this Court's Establishment Clause cases. Those cases hold that a policy will not offend the Establishment Clause if it can pass a three-pronged test [articulated in Lemon v. Kurtzman]." Here, two prongs of the test were clearly met: "an open-forum policy, including nondiscrimination against religious speech, would have [1] a secular purpose [2] and would [2] avoid entanglement with religion."

   The university argued that an open-forum policy would nevertheless violate the third prong of the test, because it would have the "primary effect" of advancing religion. Justice Powell replied: "The University's argument misconceives the nature of this case. The question is not whether the creation of a religious forum would violate the Establishment Clause. [The] question is whether it can now exclude groups because of the content of their speech. In this context we are unpersuaded that the primary effect of the public forum, open to all forms of discourse, would be to advance religion." He conceded that religious groups would probably "benefit from access to University facilities," but emphasized that prior cases had explained that "a religious organization's enjoyment of merely 'incidental' benefits does not violate the prohibition against the 'primary advancement' of religion." [See the financial aid to education cases in the next subsection of this chapter.]

1.   The free speech aspects of this case are considered in the earlier note on the case.

2.   In a footnote at this point, Justice Powell commented: "Because this case involves a forum already made generally available to student groups, it differs from those cases in which this Court has invalidated statutes permitting school facilities to be used for instruction by religious groups, but *not* by others. See, e.g., [McCollum]. In those cases the school may appear to sponsor the views of the speaker."

Justice Powell concluded: "We are satisfied that any religious benefits of an open forum at [the university] would be 'incidental' within the meaning of our cases. Two factors are especially relevant. First, an open forum in a public university does not confer any imprimatur of State approval on religious sects or practices. [Second], the forum is available to a broad class of non-religious as well as religious speakers; there are over 100 recognized student groups at [the university]. The provision of benefits to so broad a spectrum of groups is an important index of secular effect. [At] least in the absence of empirical evidence that religious groups will dominate [the university's] open forum, we [believe] that the advancement of religion would not be the forum's 'primary effect.' "

The university also sought to justify its policy on the ground that Missouri's constitutional provision prohibiting state aid to religion went further than the federal Establishment Clause. Justice Powell rejected that argument as well. He noted that the challengers' "First Amendment rights are entitled to special constitutional solicitude" because "the most exacting scrutiny" is required when a state "undertakes to regulate speech on the basis of its content." He proceeded: "On the other hand, the State interest asserted here—in achieving greater separation of church and State than is already ensured under the Establishment Clause of the Federal Constitution—is limited by the Free Exercise Clause and in this case by the Free Speech Clause as well. In this constitutional context, we are unable to recognize the State's interest as sufficiently 'compelling' to justify content-based discrimination against [the challengers'] religious speech." [3]

Justice WHITE, the sole dissenter, insisted that the university ban was permissible. Although he devoted most of his dissent to free speech and free exercise analyses (as noted earlier), he also commented on the Establishment Clause issue. He argued that the Establishment Clause only *limits* state action; "it does not establish what the State is *required* to do. I have long argued that Establishment Clause limits on state action which incidentally aids religion are not as strict as the Court has held. [In] my view, just as there is room under the Religion Clauses for state policies that may have some beneficial effect on religion, there is also room for state policies that may incidentally burden religion. In other words, I believe the states to be a good deal freer to formulate policies that affect religion in divergent ways than does the majority. The majority's position will inevitably lead to those contradictions and tensions between the Establishment and Free Exercise Clauses warned against by Justice Stewart in Sherbert v. Verner."

10th ED., p. 1566; IND. RTS., p. 1186
Add to footnote 7:

Under the federal-state unemployment tax scheme administered according to the federal standards of the Social Security Act (see Steward Machine Co. v. Davis, 10th Ed., p. 232), religious schools that are unaffiliated with any church are required to pay unemployment insurance taxes. (Church-affiliated schools are exempted by the statute.) A lower federal court held that the coverage provision violated the Establishment Clause. On appeal, the Supreme Court did not reach the

3. Justice STEVENS concurred only in the judgment. His separate opinion, emphasizing free speech analysis, is noted in the earlier addition on this case.

merits of that ruling. Instead, it held that the Tax Injunction Act barred the exercise of federal court jurisdiction. California v. Grace Brethren Church, 457 U.S. 393 (1982), further noted below, addition to 10th Ed., p. 1688; Ind.Rts., p. 1308.

10th ED., p. 1566; IND. RTS., p. 1186
Add to the Notes (before Sec. 1C):

4. *Official preferences among denominations as violations of the Establishment Clause.* In LARSON v. VALENTE, 456 U.S. 228 (1982), the Court invalidated portions of a Minnesota law regulating charitable contributions. The challenge was directed at provisions exempting some, but not all, religious organizations from the law's registration and reporting requirements. The Court found that the exemption scheme discriminated against some religious groups and thus violated the "clearest command of the Establishment Clause": "one religious denomination cannot be officially preferred over another."

In 1961, Minnesota had imposed registration and disclosure requirements on charitable organizations to prevent fraud. The law originally exempted all "religious organizations," but in 1978 the exemption provision was amended to add a "fifty per cent rule"—a rule essentially providing that only those religious organizations receiving more than half of their total contributions from members could claim the exemption. Shortly after the law was amended, the State notified the Unification Church (the "Moonies") that the new fifty per cent rule required the organization to register. Several members of the Church promptly brought this federal action to challenge the constitutionality of the 1978 amendment.

Justice BRENNAN's opinion for the Court sustained the Establishment Clause challenge, insisting that the fifty per cent rule "clearly grants denominational preferences of the sort consistently and firmly deprecated in our precedents."* In the case of a state law granting a denominational preference, Justice Brennan insisted, "[o]ur precedents demand that we treat the

---

* In a footnote at this point, Justice Brennan rejected the claim that the law did not grant denominational preferences at all, but instead was merely "a law based upon secular criteria which may not identically affect all religious organizations." Relying on such decisions as McGowan v. Maryland and the Everson line of cases, the State argued that a law's "disparate impact among religious organizations is constitutionally permissible when such distinctions result from application of secular criteria." Justice Brennan responded: "We reject the argument. [The law] is not simply a facially neutral statute, the provisions of which happen to have a 'disparate impact' upon different religious organizations. On the contrary, [it] makes explicit and deliberate distinctions between different religious organizations. We agree with the Court of Appeals' observation that the provision effectively distinguishes between

'well-established churches' that have 'achieved strong but not total financial support from their members,' on the one hand, and 'churches which are new and lacking in a constituency, or which, as a matter of policy, may favor public solicitation over general reliance on financial support from members,' on the other hand. This fundamental difference between [this law] and the statutes involved in the 'disparate impact' cases cited by [the State] renders those cases wholly inapplicable here."

Contrast Justice WHITE's dissent, joined by Justice Rehnquist: "To say that the rule on its face represents an explicit and deliberate preference for some religious beliefs over others is not credible. [An] intentional preference must be expressed. To find that intention on the face of the provision at issue here seems to me to be patently wrong."

law as suspect and that we apply strict scrutiny in adjudging its constitutionality. The law cannot stand 'unless it is justified by a compelling governmental interest and unless it is closely fitted to further that interest.' "

The Minnesota provision could not survive such intense scrutiny. Justice Brennan was willing to "assume arguendo that the Act generally is addressed to a sufficiently 'compelling' governmental interest"—the "interest in
protecting [Minnesota's] citizens from abusive practices in the solicitation of
funds for charity," an interest that "retains importance when the solicitation
is conducted by a religious organization." But here, the State had failed to
"demonstrate that the challenged fifty per cent rule is closely fitted to further
the interest that it assertedly serves." Justice Brennan found "no substantial
support [in] the record" for any of the "three distinct premises" inherent in
the State's argument: "that members of a religious organization can and will
exercise supervision and control over the organization's solicitation activities
when membership contributions exceed fifty per cent; that membership control, assuming its existence, is an adequate safeguard against abusive solicitations of the public by the organization; and that the need for public disclosure rises in proportion with the *percentage* [rather than the *"absolute
amount"*] of non-member contributions." Accordingly, the State had failed
to show that the fifty per cent rule was "closely fitted" to the furtherance of
a "compelling governmental interest."

In invalidating the law, the lower federal courts had relied heavily on
portions of the three-pronged Establishment Clause test developed in the cases scrutinizing financial assistance to religion. (See, e.g., Note 2, 10th Ed.,
p. 1567; Ind. Rts., p. 1187.) But in Justice Brennan's view that test was "intended to apply to laws affording a uniform benefit to *all* religions, and not
to provisions like [the] fifty per cent rule that discriminate *among* religions."
He nevertheless went on to state: "Although application of the [three-
pronged test] is not necessary to the disposition of the case before us, [it
does] reflect the same concerns that warranted the application of strict scrutiny to [the] fifty per cent rule. [We] view the third of those tests [the criterion requiring that a law "must not foster 'an excessive governmental entanglement with religion' "] as most directly implicated in the present case."
The Minnesota law illustrated one of the dangers against which the "entanglement" barrier was designed to safeguard: "By their 'very nature,' the distinctions drawn [by the Minnesota scheme] 'engender a risk of politicizing
religion'—a risk, indeed, that has already been substantially realized." The
law did not "operate evenhandedly, nor was it designed to do so": "The fifty
per cent rule [effects] the *selective* legislative imposition of burdens and advantages upon particular denominations. The 'risk of politicizing religion'
that inheres in such legislation is obvious, and indeed is confirmed by the
provision's legislative history, [which] demonstrates that the provision was
drafted with the explicit intention of including particular religious denominations and excluding others." For example, an earlier version of the 1978
amendment was eliminated when "the legislators perceived that [it] would
bring a Roman Catholic archdiocese within the Act." Moreover, there was
evidence in the legislative record that some of the lawmakers were eager *not*
to exempt certain other religious organizations from the law. Thus, a state

senator, "who apparently had mixed feelings about the proposed [amendment], stated, 'I'm not sure why we're so hot to regulate the Moonies anyway.'"

Surveying all of the evidence, Justice Brennan found that "the fifty per cent rule's capacity—indeed, its express design—to burden or favor selected religious denominations led the Minnesota legislature to discuss the characteristics of various sects with a view towards 'religious gerrymandering.'" This observation reinforced his conclusion that the "fifty per cent rule sets up precisely the sort of official denominational preference that the Framers of the First Amendment forbade." †

In a dissent joined by Justice Rehnquist, Justice WHITE argued (as noted in footnote *, above) that the fifty per cent rule was not an intentional preference of one denomination over another. He claimed, moreover, that the majority had too readily rejected "the state's submission that a valid secular purpose justifies basing the exemption on the percentage of external funding." He elaborated: "I do not share the Court's view of our omniscience. The state has the same interest in requiring registration by organizations soliciting most of their funds from the public as it would have in requiring any charitable organization to register, including a religious organization, if it wants to solicit funds. And if the state determines that its interest in preventing fraud does not extend to those who do not raise a majority of their funds from the public, its interest in imposing the requirement on others is not thereby reduced in the least. Furthermore, as the state suggests, the legislature thought it made good sense, and the courts, including this one, should not so readily disagree." And he added in summation: "Without an adequate factual basis, the majority concludes that the provision in question deliberately prefers some religious denominations to others. Without an adequate factual basis, it rejects the justifications offered by the state. It reaches its conclusions by applying a legal standard different from that considered by either of the courts below." **

† Justice STEVENS joined Justice Brennan's opinion in a separate notation.

** In another dissent, Justice REHNQUIST, joined by Chief Justice Burger and Justices White and O'Connor, insisted that the challengers lacked Article III standing and charged the majority with rendering "what is at best an advisory constitutional pronouncement." He relied on the fact that, even after the majority's decision, the State remained free to question whether the Unification Church was a bona fide "religious organization" entitled to the exemption. In his view, the challengers had therefore not demonstrated that their injury would in fact be redressed by the invalidation of the fifty per cent provision. He concluded: "Until such time as the requirements of Art. III clearly have been satisfied, this Court should refrain from rendering significant constitutional decisions." (See generally the last chapter of the casebook.)

10th ED., p. 1580; IND. RTS., p. 1200
Insert after Regan (before Note on Higher Education):

———

MUELLER v. ALLEN

463 U.S. —, 103 S.Ct. —, 76 L.Ed.2d — (1983).

Justice REHNQUIST delivered the opinion of the Court.

Minnesota allows taxpayers, in computing their state income tax, to deduct certain expenses incurred in providing for the education of their children. The [Court of Appeals] held that the Establishment Clause of the First and Fourteenth Amendments was not offended by this arrangement. We now affirm.

Minnesota [provides] free elementary and secondary schooling. [820,000] students attended this school system in the most recent school year. During the same year, approximately 91,000 elementary and secondary students attended some 500 privately supported schools located in Minnesota, and about 95% of these students attended schools considering themselves to be sectarian.

Minnesota, by a law originally enacted in 1955, [permits] state taxpayers to claim a deduction from gross income for certain expenses incurred in educating their children. The deduction is limited to actual expenses incurred for the "tuition, textbooks and transportation" of dependents attending elementary or secondary schools. A deduction may not exceed $500 per dependent in grades K through six and $700 per dependent in grades seven through twelve.*

*[The] District Court found that deductible expenses included:

"1. Tuition in the ordinary sense.

2. Tuition to public school students who attend public schools outside their residence school districts.

3. Certain summer school tuition.

4. Tuition charged by a school for slow learner private tutoring services.

5. Tuition for instruction provided by an elementary or secondary school to students who are physically unable to attend classes at such school.

6. Tuition charged by a private tutor or by a school that is not an elementary or secondary school if the instruction is acceptable for credit in an elementary or secondary school.

7. Montessori School tuition for grades K to 12.

8. Tuition for driver eduction when it is part of the school curriculum."

[In] addition, the District Court found that the statutory deduction for "textbooks" included not only "secular textbooks" but also:

"1. Cost of tennis shoes and sweatsuits for physical education.

2. Camera rental fees paid to the school for photography classes.

. . .

5. Costs of home economics materials needed to meet minimum requirements.

6. Costs of special metal or wood needed to meet minimum requirements of shop classes.

7. Costs of supplies needed to meet minimum requirements of art classes.

8. Rental fees paid to the school for musical instruments.

9. Cost of pencils and special notebooks required for class." [Footnote by Justice Rehnquist.]

[Today's] case is no exception to our oft-repeated statement that the Establishment Clause presents especially difficult questions of interpretation and application.

[One] fixed principle in this field is our consistent rejection of the argument that "any program which in some manner aids an institution with a religious affiliation" violates the Establishment Clause. Hunt v. McNair, 413 U.S. 734 (1973). For example, it is now well-established that a state may reimburse parents for expenses incurred in transporting their children to school, [Everson], and that it may loan secular textbooks to all school-children within the state. [Allen.]

Notwithstanding the repeated approval given programs such as those in Allen and Everson, our decisions also have struck down arrangements resembling, in many respects, these forms of assistance. See, e.g., [Lemon; Levitt; Meek v. Pittenger.] [Petitioners] place particular reliance on our decision in [Nyquist,] where we held invalid a New York statute providing public funds for the maintenance and repair of the physical facilities of private schools and granting thinly disguised "tax benefits," actually amounting to tuition grants, to the parents of children attending private schools.

The general nature of our inquiry in this area has been guided, since the decision in [Lemon], by the 'three-part' test laid down in that case.

[Little] time need be spent on the question of whether the Minnesota tax deduction has a secular purpose. Under our prior decisions, governmental assistance programs have consistently survived this inquiry even when they have run afoul of other aspects of the Lemon framework. This reflects, at least in part, our reluctance to attribute unconstitutional motives to the states, particularly when a plausible secular purpose for the state's program may be discerned from the face of the statute.

A state's decision to defray the cost of educational expenses incurred by parents—regardless of the type of schools their children attend—evidences a purpose that is both secular and understandable. An educated populace is essential to the political and economic health of any community, and a state's efforts to assist parents in meeting the rising cost of educational expenses plainly serves this secular purpose of ensuring that the state's citizenry is well-educated. Similarly, Minnesota, like other states, could conclude that there is a strong public interest in assuring the continued financial health of private schools, both sectarian and non-sectarian. By educating a substantial number of students such schools relieve public schools of a correspondingly great burden—to the benefit of all taxpayers. In addition, private schools may serve as a benchmark for public schools. [All] these justifications are [sufficient] to satisfy the secular purpose inquiry of Lemon.

We turn therefore to the more difficult but related question whether the Minnesota statute has 'the primary effect of advancing the sectarian aims of the nonpublic schools." [Regan; Lemon.] In concluding that it does not, we find several features of the Minnesota tax deduction particularly significant. First, an essential feature of Minnesota's arrangement is the fact that § 290.09(22) is only one among many deductions—such as those for medical expenses and charitable contributions—available under the Minnesota tax laws. Our decisions consistently have recognized that traditionally "[l]egislatures have especially broad latitude in creating classifications and distinctions in tax statutes," Regan v. Taxation with Representation, [1983; addition to 10th Ed., p. 1481; Ind.Rts., p. 1101], in part because the "familiarity with local conditions" enjoyed by legislators especially enables them to "achieve an equitable distribution of the tax burden." Madden v. Kentucky, 309 U.S. 83 (1940). Under our prior decisions, the Minnesota legislature's judgment that a deduction for educational expenses fairly equalizes the tax burden of its citizens and encourages desirable expenditures for educational purposes is entitled to substantial deference.

Other characteristics of § 290.09(22) argue equally strongly for the provision's constitutionality. Most importantly, the deduction is available for educational expenses incurred by *all* parents, including those whose children attend public schools and those whose children attend non-sectarian private schools or sectarian private schools. Just as in [Widmar], where we concluded that the state's provision of a forum neutrally "open to a broad class of nonreligious as well as religious speakers" does not "confer any imprimatur of State approval," so here: "the provision of benefits to so broad a spectrum of groups is an important index of secular effect."

In this respect, as well as others, this case is vitally different from the scheme struck down in Nyquist. There, public assistance amounting to tuition grants, was provided only to parents of children in *nonpublic* schools. This fact had considerable bearing on our decision striking down the New York statute at issue; we explicitly distinguished both Allen and Everson on the grounds that "In both cases the class of beneficiaries included *all* schoolchildren, those in public as well as those in private schools." Moreover, we intimated that "public assistance (e.g., scholarships) made available generally without regard to the sectarian-nonsectarian or public-nonpublic nature of the institution benefited," might not offend the Establishment Clause. We think the tax deduction adopted by Minnesota is more similar to this latter type of program than it is to the arrangement struck down in Nyquist. Unlike the assistance at issue in Nyquist, § 290.09(22) permits *all* parents—whether their children attend public school or private—to deduct their childrens' educational expenses. As Widmar and our other decisions indicate, a program [that; neutrally provides state assistance to a broad spectrum of citizens is not readily subject to challenge under the Establishment Clause.

We also agree [that,] by channeling whatever assistance it may provide to parochial schools through individual parents, Minnesota has reduced the Establishment Clause objections to which its action is subject. It is true, of course, that financial assistance provided to parents ultimately has an economic effect comparable to that of aid given directly to the schools attended by their children. It is also true, however, that under Minnesota's arrangement public funds become available only as a result of numerous, private choices of individual parents of school-age children. [It] is noteworthy that all but one of our recent cases [Nyquist] invalidating state aid to parochial schools have involved the direct transmission of assistance from the state to the schools themselves. [Where,] as here, aid to parochial schools is available only as a result of decisions of individual parents no "imprimatur of State approval," Widmar, can be deemed to have been conferred on any particular religion, or on religion generally.

[The] Establishment Clause of course extends beyond prohibition of a state church or payment of state funds to one or more churches. We do not think, however, that its prohibition extends to the type of tax deduction established by Minnesota. The historic purposes of the clause simply do not encompass the sort of attenuated financial benefit, ultimately controlled by the private choices of individual parents, that eventually flows to parochial schools from the neutrally available tax benefit at issue in this case.

Petitioners argue that, notwithstanding [facial neutrality], in application the statute primarily benefits religious institutions. [They] contend that most parents of public school children incur no tuition expenses, and that other expenses deductible under § 290.09(22) are negligible in value; moreover, they claim that 96% of the children in private schools in 1978–1979 attended religiously-affiliated institutions. Because of all this, they reason, the bulk of deductions taken under § 290.09(22) will be claimed by parents of children in sectarian schools.

[We] need not consider these contentions in detail. We would be loath to adopt a rule grounding the constitutionality of a facially neutral law on annual reports reciting the extent to which various classes of private citizens claimed benefits under the law. Such an approach would scarcely provide the certainty that this field stands in need of, nor can we perceive principled standards by which such statistical evidence might be evaluated. Moreover, the fact that private persons fail in a particular year to claim the tax relief to which they are entitled—under a facially neutral statute—should be of little importance in determining the constitutionality of the statute permitting such relief.

Finally, private educational institutions, and parents paying for their children to attend these schools, make special contributions to the areas in which they operate. [If] parents of children in private schools choose to take especial advantage of the relief provided by § 290.09(22), it is no doubt due to the fact that they bear a particularly great financial burden in educating their children. More fundamentally, whatever unequal effect may be attributed to the statutory classification can fairly be regarded as a rough return for the benefits, discussed above, provided to the state and all taxpayers by parents sending their children to parochial schools. In the light of all this, we believe it wiser to decline to engage in the type of empirical inquiry into those persons benefited by state law which petitioners urge.

Thus, we hold that the Minnesota tax deduction for educational expenses satisfies the primary effect inquiry of our Establishment Clause cases.

Turning to the third part of the Lemon inquiry, we have no difficulty in concluding that the Minnesota statute does not "excessively entangle" the state in religion. The only plausible source of the "comprehensive, discriminating, and continuing state surveillance," necessary to run afoul of this standard would lie in the fact that state officials must determine whether particular textbooks qualify for a deduction. In making this decision, state officials must disallow deductions taken from "instructional books and materials used in the teaching of religious tenets, doctrines or worship, the purpose of which is to inculcate such tenets, doctrines or worship." Minn. Stat. § 290.09(22). Making decisions such as this does not differ substantially from making the types of decisions approved in earlier opinions of this Court. [Allen.]

[Affirmed.] *4 Dissent*

Justice MARSHALL, with whom Justice BRENNAN, Justice BLACKMUN and Justice STEVENS join, dissenting.

The Establishment Clause [prohibits] a State from subsidizing religious education, whether it does so directly or indirectly. In my view, this principle of neutrality forbids [any] tax benefit, including the tax deduction at issue here, which subsidizes tuition payments to sectarian schools. I also believe that the Establishment Clause prohibits the tax deductions that Minnesota authorizes for the cost of books and other instructional materials used for sectarian purposes.

I. The majority today does not question the continuing vitality of this Court's decision in Nyquist. That decision established that a State may not support religious education either through direct grants to parochial schools or through financial aid to parents of parochial school students. Nyquist also established that financial aid to parents of students attending parochial schools is no more permissible if it is provided in the form of a tax credit than if provided in the form of cash payments. Notwithstanding these accepted principles, the Court today upholds a statute that provides a tax deduction for the tuition charged by religious schools. The Court concludes that the Minnesota statute is "vitally different" from the New York statute at issue in Nyquist. As demonstrated below, there is no significant difference between the two schemes. The Minnesota tax statute violates the Establishment Clause for precisely the same reason as the statute struck down in Nyquist: it has a direct and immediate effect of advancing religion.

Minnesota statute has direct effect of advancing religion

A. [Like] the law involved in Nyquist, the Minnesota law can be said to serve a secular purpose: promoting pluralism and diversity among the State's public and nonpublic schools. But the Establishment Clause requires more than that legislation have a secular purpose. [As] we recognized in Nyquist, direct government subsidization of parochial school tuition is impermissible because "the effect of the aid is unmistakably to provide desired financial support for nonpublic, sectarian institutions." "[A]id to the educational function of [parochial] schools . . . necessarily results in aid to the sectarian enterprise as a whole" because "[t]he very purpose of those schools is to provide an integrated secular and religious education." Meek v. Pittenger. For this reason, aid to sectarian schools must be restricted to ensure that it may be not used to further the religious mission of those schools.

Indirect assistance in the form of financial aid to parents for tuition payments is [impermissible] because it is not "subject to . . . restrictions" which "'guarantee the separation between secular and religious educational functions and . . . ensure that State financial aid supports only the former.'" [Nyquist, quoting Lemon.] By ensuring that parents will be reimbursed for tuition payments they make, the Minnesota statute requires that taxpayers in general pay for the cost of parochial education and extends a financial "incentive to parents to send their children to sectarian schools." Nyquist. [That] parents receive a reduction of their tax liability, rather than a direct reimbursement, is of no greater significance here than it was in Nyquist. "[F]or purposes of determining whether such aid has the effect of advancing religion," it makes no difference whether the qualifying "parent receives an actual cash payment [or] is allowed to reduce . . . the sum he would otherwise be obliged to pay over to the State." It is equally irrelevant whether a reduction in taxes takes the form of a tax "credit," a tax "modification," or a tax "deduction." What is of controlling significance is not the form but the "substantive impact" of the financial aid. . . .

B.1. [The] majority first attempts to distinguish Nyquist on the ground that Minnesota makes all parents eligible to deduct up to $500 or $700 for each dependent, whereas the New York law allowed a deduction only for parents whose children attended nonpublic schools. Although Minnesota taxpayers who send their children to local public schools may not deduct tuition expenses because they incur none, they may deduct other expenses, such as the cost of gym clothes, pencils, and notebooks, which are shared by all parents of school-age children. This, in the majority's view, distinguishes the Minnesota scheme from the law at issue in Nyquist.

That the Minnesota statute makes some small benefit available to all parents cannot alter the fact that the most substantial benefit provided by the statute is available only to those parents who send their children to schools that charge tuition. It is simply undeniable that the single largest expense that may be deducted under the Minnesota statute is tuition. The statute is little more than a subsidy of tuition masquerading as a subsidy of general educational expenses. The other deductible expenses are *de minimis* in in comparison to tuition expenses.

Contrary to the majority's suggestion, the bulk of the tax benefits afforded by the Minnesota scheme are enjoyed by parents of parochial school children not because parents of public school children fail to claim deductions to which they are entitled, but because the latter are simply *unable* to claim the largest tax deduction that Minnesota authorizes. Fewer than 100 of more than 900,000 school-age children in Minnesota attend public schools that charge a general tuition. Of the total number of taxpayers who are eligible for the tuition deduction, approximately 96% send their children to religious schools. Parents who send their children to free public schools are simply ineligible to obtain the full benefit of the deduction except in the unlikely event that they buy $700 worth of pencils, notebooks, and bus rides for their school-age children. Yet parents who pay at least $700 in tuition to nonpublic, sectarian schools can claim the full deduction even if they incur no other educational expenses.

That this deduction has a primary effect of promoting religion can easily be determined without any resort to the type of "statistical evidence" that the majority fears would lead to constitutional uncertainty. [In] this case, it is undisputed that well over 90% of the children attending tuition-charging schools in Minnesota are enrolled in sectarian schools. History and experience likewise instruct us that any generally available financial assistance for elementary and secondary school tuition expenses mainly will further religious education because the majority of the schools which charge tuition are sectarian. Because Minnesota, like every other State, is committed to providing free public education, tax assistance for tuition payments inevitably redounds to the benefit of nonpublic, sectarian schools and parents who send their children to those schools.

2. The majority also asserts that the Minnesota statute is distinguishable from the statute struck down in Nyquist in another respect: the tax benefit available under Minnesota law is a "genuine tax deduction," whereas the New York law provided a benefit which, while nominally a deduction, also had features of a "tax credit." Under the Minnesota law, the amount of the tax benefit varies directly with the amount of the expenditure. Under the New York law, the amount of deduction was not dependent upon the amount actually paid for tuition but was a predetermined amount which depended on the tax bracket of each taxpayer. The deduction was designed to yield roughly the same amount of tax "forgiveness" for each taxpayer.

This is a distinction without a difference. Our prior decisions have rejected the relevance of the majority's formalistic distinction between tax deductions and the tax benefit at issue in Nyquist. . . .

C. The majority incorrectly asserts that Minnesota's tax deduction for tuition expenses "bears less resemblance to the arrangement struck down in Nyquist than it does to assistance programs upheld in our prior decisions and discussed with approval in Nyquist." One might as well say that a tangerine bears less resemblance to an orange than to an apple. The two cases relied on by the majority, [Allen and Everson] are inapposite today for precisely the same reasons that they were inapposite in Nyquist.

[The] Minnesota tuition tax deduction is not available to *all* parents, but only to parents whose children attend schools that charge tuition, which are comprised almost entirely of sectarian schools. More importantly, the assistance that flows to parochial schools as a result of the tax benefit is not restricted, and cannot be restricted, to the secular functions of those schools. . . .

II. In my view, Minnesota's tax deduction for the cost of textbooks and other instructional materials is also constitutionally infirm. . . .

III. [In] my view, the lines drawn in Nyquist were drawn on a reasoned basis with appropriate regard for the principles of neutrality embodied by the Establishment Clause. I do not believe that the same can be said of the lines drawn by the majority today. For the first time, the Court has upheld financial support for religious schools without any reason at all to assume that the support will be restricted to the secular functions of those schools and will not be used to support religious instruction. This result is flatly at odds with the fundamental principle that a State may provide no financial support whatsoever to promote religion. . . .

ENTANGLEMENT OUTSIDE THE SCHOOLS

LARKIN v. GRENDEL'S DEN, INC.

459 U.S. —, 103 S.Ct. 505, 74 L.Ed.2d 297 (1982).

Chief Justice BURGER delivered the opinion of the Court.

The question presented [is] whether a Massachusetts statute, which vests in the governing bodies of churches and schools the power effectively to veto applications for liquor licenses within a five hundred foot radius of the church or school, violates the Establishment Clause of the First Amendment.

I. A. Appellee operates a restaurant located in the Harvard Square area of Cambridge, Massachusetts. The Holy Cross Armenian Catholic Parish is located adjacent to the restaurant; the back walls of the two buildings are ten feet apart. In 1977, appellee applied to the Cambridge License Commission for approval of an alcoholic beverages license for the restaurant.

Section 16C of Chapter 138 of the Massachusetts General Laws provides: "Premises . . . located within a radius of five hundred feet of a church or school shall not be licensed for the sale of alcoholic beverages if the governing body of such church or school files written objection thereto." [1]

Holy Cross Church objected to appellee's application, expressing concern over "having so many licenses *so* near". The License Commission voted to deny the application, citing only the objection of Holy Cross Church and noting that the church "is within 10 feet of the proposed location."

On appeal, the Massachusetts Alcoholic Beverages Control Commission upheld the License Commission's action. The Beverages Control Commission found that "the church's objection under Section 16C was the only basis on which the [license] was denied."

[Grendel's Den then filed suit in the United States District Court. The District Court's ruling that § 16C violated the Establishment Clause was affirmed by the Court of Appeals for the First Circuit. While these proceedings were in progress, the Massachusetts Supreme Judicial Court,

---

1. Section 16C defines "church" as "a church or synagogue building dedicated to divine worship and in regular use for that purpose, but not a chapel occupying a minor portion of a building primarily devoted to other uses." "School" is defined as "an elementary or secondary school, public or private, giving not less than the minimum instruction and training required by [state law] to children of compulsory school age."

Section 16C originally was enacted in 1954 as an absolute ban on liquor licenses within 500 feet of a church or school. A 1968 amendment modified the absolute prohibition, permitting licenses within the 500-foot radius "if the governing body of such church assents in writing." In 1970, the statute was amended to its present form. [Footnote by Chief Justice Burger.]

in a similar challenge to § 16C, upheld what it characterized as a "veto power."]

B. The Court of Appeals noted that appellee does not contend that § 16C lacks a secular purpose, and turned to the question of "whether the law 'has the *direct* and *immediate* effect of advancing religion' as contrasted with 'only a *remote* and *incidental* effect advantageous to religious institutions.'" [Committee for Public Education v. Nyquist]. The court concluded that § 16C confers a direct and substantial benefit upon religions by "the grant of a veto power over liquor sales in roughly one million square feet . . . of what may be a city's most commercially valuable sites."

The court acknowledged that § 16C "extends its benefit beyond churches to schools," but concluded that the inclusion of schools "does not dilute [the statute's] forbidden religious classification," since § 16C does not "encompass all who are otherwise similarly situated to churches in all respects except dedication to 'divine worship.'" In the view of the Court of Appeals, this "explicit religious discrimination" provided an additional basis for its holding that § 16C violates the Establishment Clause. . . .

II. A. Appellants contend that the State may, without impinging on the Establishment Clause of the First Amendment, enforce what it describes as a "zoning" law in order to shield schools and places of divine worship from the presence nearby of liquor dispensing establishments. It is also contended that a zone of protection around churches and schools is essential to protect diverse centers of spiritual, educational and cultural enrichment. It is to that end that the State has vested in the governing bodies of all schools, public or private, and all churches,[2] the power to prevent the issuance of liquor licenses for any premises within 500 feet of their institutions.

Plainly schools and churches have a valid interest in being insulated from certain kinds of commercial establishments, including those dispensing liquor. Zoning laws have long been employed to this end, and there can be little doubt about the power of a state to regulate the environment in the vicinity of schools, churches, hospitals and the like by exercise of reasonable zoning laws.

[The] zoning function is traditionally a governmental task requiring the "balancing [of] numerous competing considerations," and courts should properly "refrain from reviewing the merits of [such] decisions, absent a showing of arbitrariness or irrationality." Village of Arlington Heights v. Metropolitan Housing Development Corp., 429 U.S. 252 (1977). Given the broad powers of states under the Twenty-First Amendment, judicial deference to the [exercise] of zoning powers by a city council or other legis-

2. Section 16C defines "church" as: "a church or synagogue building dedicated to *divine* worship" (emphasis added). Appellee argues that the statute unconstitutionally differentiates between theistic and nontheistic religions. We need not reach that issue. For purposes of this appeal, we assume [that] the Massachusetts courts would apply the protections of § 16C to "any building primarily used as a place of assembly by a bona fide religious group," and thereby avoid serious constitutional questions that would arise concerning a statute that distinguishes between religions on the basis of commitment to belief in a divinity. [Footnote by Chief Justice Burger.]

lative zoning body is especially appropriate in the area of liquor regulation. See [California v. Larue, 409 U.S. 109 (1972)].

However, § 16C is not simply a legislative exercise of zoning power. As the Massachusetts Supreme Judicial Court concluded, § 16C delegates to private, nongovernmental entities power to veto certain liquor license applications. This is a power ordinarily vested in agencies of government. [We] need not decide whether, or upon what conditions such power may ever be delegated to nongovernmental entities; here, of two classs of institutions to which the legislature has delegated this important decisionmaking power, one is secular, but one is religious. Under these circumstances, the deference normally due a legislative zoning judgment is not merited.[3]

B.   The purposes of the First Amendment guarantees relating to religion were twofold: to foreclose state interference with the practice of religious faiths, and to foreclose the establishment of a state religion familiar in other Eighteenth Century systems. Religion and government, each insulated from the other, could then coexist. Jefferson's idea of a "wall" was a useful figurative illustration to emphasize the concept of separateness. Some limited and incidental entanglement between church and state authority is inevitable in a complex modern society, but the concept of a "wall" of separation is a useful signpost. Here that "wall" is substantially breached by vesting discretionary governmental powers in religious bodies.

This Court has consistently held that a statute must satisfy three criteria to pass muster under the Establishment Clause: First, the statute must have a secular legislative purpose; second, its principal or primary effect must be one that neither advances nor inhibits religion . . .; finally, the statute must not foster "an excessive government entanglement with religion." [Lemon v. Kurtzman, quoting Walz v. Tax Commission.] Independent of the first of those criteria, the statute, by delegating a governmental power to religious institutions, inescapably implicates the Establishment Clause.

The purpose of § 16C, as described by the District Court, is to "protect[] spiritual, cultural, and educational centers from the 'hurly-burly' associated with liquor outlets." There can be little doubt that this embraces valid secular legislative purposes. However, these valid secular objectives can be readily accomplished by other means—either through an absolute legislative ban on liquor outlets within reasonable prescribed distances from churches, schools, hospitals and like institutions,[4] or by ensuring a hearing

---

3.   For similar reasons, the 21st Amendment does not justify § 16C. The 21st Amendment reserves power to states, yet here the State has delegated to churches a power relating to liquor sales. The State may not exercise its power under the 21st Amendment in a way which impinges upon the Establishment Clause of the First Amendment. [Footnote by Chief Justice Burger.] In California v. Larue, the Court relied on the 21st Amendment to uphold restrictions on lewd dancing in

establishments licensed to sell liquor, restrictions that might otherwise be impermissble under the First Amendment. See Schad v. Mt. Ephraim, addition to 10th Ed., p. 1248; Ind.Rts., p. 868. Is this consistent with Chief Justice Burger's statement that the 21st Amendment cannot impinge on the Establishment Clause?

4.   Section 16C, as originally enacted, consisted of an absolute ban on liquor licenses within 500 feet of a church or

for the views of affected institutions at licensing proceedings where, without question, such views would be entitled to substantial weight.[5]

Appellants argue that § 16C has only a remote and incidental effect on the advancement of religion. The highest court in Massachusetts, however, has construed the statute as conferring upon churches a veto power over governmental licensing authority. [The] churches' power under the statute is standardless, calling for no reasons, findings, or reasoned conclusions. That power may therefore be used by churches to promote goals beyond insulating the church from undesirable neighbors; it could be employed for explicitly religious goals, for example, favoring liquor licenses for members of that congregation or adherents of that faith. We can assume that churches would act in good faith in their exercise of the statutory power, yet § 16C does not by its terms require that churches' power be used in a religiously neutral way. "[T]he potential for conflict inheres in the situation," [Levitt]; and appellants have not suggested any "effective means of guaranteeing" that the delegated power "will be used exclusively for secular, neutral, and nonideological purposes." [Nyquist.][6] In addition, the mere appearance of a joint exercise of legislative authority by Church and State provides a significant symbolic benefit to religion in the minds of some by reason of the power conferred. It does not strain our prior holdings to say that the statute can be seen as having a "primary" and "principal" effect of advancing religion.

Turning to the third phase of the inquiry called for by [Lemon], we see that we have not previously had occasion to consider the entanglement implications of a statute vesting significant governmental authority in churches. This statute enmeshes churches in the exercise of substantial governmental powers contrary to our consistent interpretation of the Establishment Clause. "[Under] our system the choice has been made that government is to be entirely excluded from the area of religious instruction *and churches excluded from the affairs of government.* [Lemon.]

[As the] cases make clear, the core rationale underlying the Establishment Clause is preventing "a fusion of governmental and religious functions," [Abington v. Schempp.] The Framers did not set up a system of government in which important, discretionary governmental powers would be delegated to or shared with religious institutions.

Section 16C substitutes the unilateral and absolute power of a church for the reasoned decisionmaking of a public legislative body acting on evidence and guided by standards, on issues with significant economic and political implications. The challenged statute thus enmeshes churches in the pro-

school, and 27 states continue to prohibit liquor outlets within a prescribed distance of various categories of protected institutions, with certain exceptions and variations. The Court does not express an opinion as to the constitutionality of any statute other than that of Massachusetts. [Footnote by Chief Justice Burger.]

5. Eleven states have statutes directing the licensing authority to consider the proximity of the proposed liquor outlet to schools or other institutions in deciding whether to grant a liquor license. [Footnote by Chief Justice Burger.]

6. [An] assumption that the Beverages Control Commission might review the decisionmaking of the churches would present serious entanglement problems. [Footnote by Chief Justice Burger.]

cesses of government and creates the danger of "[p]olitical fragmentation and divisiveness along religious lines," [Lemon.]   Ordinary human experience and a long line of cases teach that few entanglements could be more offensive to the spirit of the Constitution.

[Affirmed.]

Justice REHNQUIST, dissenting.

Dissenting opinions in previous cases have commented that "great" cases, like "hard" cases, make bad law.   Northern Securities Co. v. United States, 193 U.S. at 400–401 (1904) (Holmes, J., dissenting); Nixon v. General Service Administrator, 433 U.S. 425 (1977) (Burger, C. J., dissenting).   Today's opinion suggests that a third class of cases—silly cases—also make bad law.   The Court wrenches from the decision of the Massachusetts Supreme Judicial Court the word "veto," and rests its conclusion on this single term.   The aim of this effort is to prove that a quite sensible Massachusets liquor zoning law is apparently some sort of sinister religious attack on secular government reminiscent of St. Bartholemew's Night.   Being unpersuaded, I dissent.

In its original form, § 16C imposed a flat ban on the grant of an alcoholic beverages license to any establishment located within 500 feet of a church or a school.   [The] majority concedes, as I believe it must, that "an absolute legislative ban on liquor outlets within reasonable prescribed distances from churches, schools, hospitals, and like institutions" would be valid.

Over time, the legislature found that it could meet its goal of protecting people engaged in religious activities from liquor-related disruption with a less absolute prohibition.   Rather than set out elaborate formulae or require an administrative agency to make findings of fact, the legislature settled on the simple expedient of asking churches to object if a proposed liquor outlet would disturb them.   [The] flat ban, which the majority concedes is valid, is more protective of churches and more restrictive of liquor sales than the present § 16C.

The evolving treatment of the grant of liquor licenses to outlets located within 500 feet of a church or a school seems to me to be the sort of legislative refinement that we should encourage, not forbid in the name of the First Amendment.   If a particular church or a particular school located within the 500 foot radius chooses not to object, the state has quite sensibly concluded that there is no reason to prohibit the issuance of the license.   Nothing in the Court's opinion persuades me why the more rigid prohibition would be constitutional, but the more flexible not.

The Court rings in the metaphor of the "wall between church and state," and the "three part test" developed in [Walz] to justify its result.   However, by its frequent reference to the statutory provision as a "veto," the Court indicates a belief that § 16C effectively constitutes churches as third houses of the Massachusetts legislature.   Surely we do not need a three part test to decide whether the grant of actual legislative power to churches is within the proscription of the Establishment Clause of the First and Fourteenth Amendments.   The question in this case is not whether such a statute would be unconstitutional, but whether § 16C is such a statute.   The Court in effect answers this question in the first sentence of its opinion without any discussion or statement of reasons. I do not think the question is so trivial that it may be answered by simply affixing a label to the statutory provision.

Section 16C does not sponsor or subsidize any religious group or activity. It does not encourage, much less compel, anyone to participate in religious activities or to support religious institutions. To say that it "advances" religion is to strain at the meaning of that word.

The Court states that § 16C "advances" religion because there is no guarantee that objections will be made "in a religiously neutral way." It is difficult to understand what the Court means by this. The concededly legitimate purpose of the statute is to protect citizens engaging in religious and educational activities from the incompatible activities of liquor outlets and their patrons. The only way to decide whether these activities are incompatible with one another in the case of a church is to ask whether the activities of liquor outlets and their patrons may interfere with religious activity; this question cannot, in any meaningful sense, be "religiously neutral." In this sense, the flat ban of the original § 16C is no different from the present version. Whether the ban is unconditional or may be invoked only at the behest of a particular church, it is not "religiously neutral" so long as it enables a church to defeat the issuance of a liquor license when a similarly situated bank could not do the same. The state does not, in my opinion, "advance" religion by making provision for those who wish to engage in religious activities, as well as those who wish to engage in educational activities, to be unmolested by activities at a neighboring bar or tavern that have historically been thought incompatible.

The Court is apparently concerned for fear that churches might object to the issuance of a license for "explicitly religious" reasons, such as "favoring liquor licenses for members of that congregation or adherents of that faith." If a church were to seek to advance the interests of its members in this way, there would be an occasion to determine whether it had violated any right of an unsuccessful applicant for a liquor license. But our ability to discern a risk of such abuse does not render § 16C violative of the Establishment Clause.[7] The state can constitutionally protect churches from liquor for the same reasons it can protect them from fire, see Walz, noise, and other harm.

The heavy First Amendment artillery that the Court fires at this sensible and unobjectionable Massachusetts statute is both unnecessary and unavailing.
. . .

In MARSH v. CHAMBERS, 463 U.S. —— (1983), the Court upheld "the Nebraska Legislature's practice of opening each legislative day with a prayer by a chaplain paid by the State." Chief Justice BURGER's majority opinion relied largely on history to sustain the practice despite the fact that the position of chaplain had been held for 16 years by a Presbyterian, that the chaplain is paid at public expense, and that all of the prayers are "in

---

7. The view that unconstitutional abuses should be dealt with only when and if they actually occur is also the theme of Justice Rehnquist's dissent in Minneapolis Star and Tribune Co. v. Min-nesota Comm'n of Revenue, 460 U.S. —— (1983), printed above, with comments on this point, addition to 10th Ed., p. 1325; Ind.Rts., p. 945.

the Judeo-Christian tradition." The majority did not rigidly apply the three-part test now familiar in Establishment Clause cases, but instead looked at the specific features of this practice in light of a long history of acceptance of legislative and other official prayers. "Weighed against the historical background, these factors do not serve to invalidate Nebraska's practice."

The Chief Justice viewed prayer in this context as "unique" in its historical roots. "The opening of legislative and other deliberative public bodies with prayer is deeply embedded in the history and tradition of this country. From colonial times through the founding of the Republic and ever since, the practice of legislative prayer has coexisted with the principles of disestablishment and religious fredom." The Chief Justice also noted the history of a paid chaplain in Congress as far back as the Continental Congress in 1774, the tradition of opening sessions of the Supreme Court and other courts with an invocation, and the long history of opening prayers and paid chaplains in most of the states. Especially in light of the actions of the First Congress, the Chief Justice saw the history as especially important here. "In this context, historical evidence sheds light not only on what the draftsmen intended the Establishment Clause to mean, but also on how they thought that Clause applied to the practice authorized by the First Congress—their actions reveal their intent. [This] unique history leads is to accept the interpretation of the First Amendment draftsmen who saw no real threat to the Establishment Clause arising from a practice of prayer similar to that now challenged. [In] light of the unambiguous and unbroken history of more than 200 years, there can be no doubt that the practice of opening legislative sessions with a prayer has become part of the fabric of our society. To invoke Divine guidance on a public body entrusted with making the laws is not, in these circumstances, an 'establishment' of religion or a step toward establishment; it is simply a tolerable acknowledgment of beliefs widely held among the people of this country."

Justice BRENNAN, joined by Justice Marshall, filed a lengthy dissent, one that is noteworthy because in Abington School Dist. v. Schempp (10th Ed., p. 1563; Ind.Rts., p. 1183), Justice Brennan "came very close to endorsing essentially the result reached by the Court today." In light of this, it is not surprising that Justice Brennan's dissent was very restrained. "The Court today has written a narrow and, on the whole, careful opinion. [The] Court's [limited] rationale should pose little threat to the overall fate of the Establishment Clause. [The] Court makes no pretense of subjecting Nebraska's practice of legislative prayer to any of the formal 'tests' that have traditionally structured our inquiry under the Establishment Clause. That it fails to do so is, in a sense, a good thing, for it simply confirms that the Court is carving out an exception [rather] than reshaping Establishment Clause doctrine to accommodate legislative prayer. [But if] the Court were to judge legislative prayer through the unsentimental eye of our settled doctrine, it would have to strike it down as a clear violation of the Establishment Clause."

Justice STEVENS also dissented, relying on the fact that the particular chaplain was chosen was likely chosen "to reflect the faith of the lawmakers' constituents." Because the designation of the particular chaplain and the content of the prayers given "constitutes the preference of one faith over another," he would have struck down the practice on these grounds alone.

10th ED., p. 1592; IND. RTS., p. 1212
Insert after Sherbert v. Verner:

THOMAS v. REVIEW BD. IND. EMPL. SEC. DIV., 450 U.S. 707 (1981): The Court's 8 to 1 decision relied on Sherbert v. Verner to invalidate Indiana's denial of unemployment compensation to a Jehovah's Witness who had left his factory job because of religious beliefs. Petitioner had originally gone to work in his employer's steel foundry. When the foundry was closed, he was transferred to a department that fabricated turrets for military tanks. Since that job and all other positions to which he could transfer were directly engaged in the production of weapons, he quit, asserting that he could not do such work without violating his religious beliefs. He was denied unemployment compensation under a law barring benefits to "an individual who has voluntarily left his employment without good cause in connection with the work." The highest state court held that, under the statute, a termination motivated by religion is not for "good cause" objectively related to the work and suggested that in any event petitioner's views were more a matter of "personal philosophical choice" than of religious belief.

Chief Justice BURGER's majority opinion stated: "Here, as in Sherbert, the employee was put to a choice between fidelity to religious belief or cessation of work; the coercive impact on Thomas is indistinguishable from Sherbert. [Where] the state conditions receipt of an important benefit upon conduct proscribed by a religious faith, or where it denies such a benefit because of conduct mandated by religious belief, thereby putting substantial pressure on an adherent to modify his behavior and to violate his beliefs, a burden upon religion exists. While the compulsion may be indirect, the infringement upon free exercise is nonetheless substantial." He rejected the argument that Sherbert was inapposite because the employee there left her job because of her employer's action: "In both cases, the termination flowed from the fact that the employment, once acceptable, became religiously objectionable because of changed conditions."

The Chief Justice observed that the State could justify this burden on religion only "by showing that it is the least restrictive means of achieving some compelling state interest." Indiana relied on two interests: avoiding "the burden on the [unemployment] fund resulting if people were permitted to leave jobs for 'personal' reasons"; and preventing "a detailed probing by employers into job applicants' religious beliefs." The Chief Justice found that neither interest was "sufficiently compelling to justify the burden upon Thomas' religious liberty." *

---

* The highest state court had doubted the religious nature of Thomas' objection because he had been willing to work in the steel foundry despite the fact that its products were necessary for the production of tanks. The Chief Justice rebuked the state court, stating: "Courts should not undertake to dissect religious beliefs because the believer admits that he is 'struggling' with his position or because his beliefs are not articulated with the clarity and precision that a more sophisticated person might employ." He also criticized the state court for giving "significant weight" to the fact that a fellow employee of Thomas, another Jehovah's Witness, did not object to

The Court summarily rejected the state court's argument that a grant of benefits to Thomas would violate the Establishment Clause. The Chief Justice conceded that there was, "in a sense, a 'benefit'" to Thomas deriving from his religious beliefs, but added that "this manifests no more than the tension between the two Religion Clauses which the Court resolved in Sherbert." †

Insisting that the decision "adds mud to the already muddied waters of First Amendment jurisprudence," Justice REHNQUIST, the sole dissenter, sharply criticized the majority's failure to resolve the "tension" between the Free Exercise and Establishment Clauses. The ruling simply left the tension "to be resolved on a case-by-case" basis. He insisted that the tension was "largely of this Court's making" and that it "would diminish almost to the vanishing point if the Clauses were properly interpreted." Objecting to the unduly broad reading of the Free Exercise Clause, he urged acceptance of the Braunfeld v. Brown approach and of Justice Harlan's dissent in Sherbert. With respect to the Establishment Clause, he supported Justice Stewart's dissent in Schempp (the Bible reading case in sec. 1 of this chapter). He claimed, moreover, that if the three-part test articulated in Lemon and Nyquist (financial aid to education cases in sec. 1) were applied here, the grant of unemployment benefits to Thomas would "plainly" violate the Establishment Clause. He added: "It is unclear from the Court's opinion whether it has temporarily retreated from its expansive view of the Establishment Clause, or wholly abandoned it. I would welcome the latter." He accordingly concluded: "[M]y difficulty with today's decision is that it reads the Free Exercise Clause too broadly and it fails to squarely acknowledge that such a reading conflicts with many of our Establishment Clause cases. As such, the decision simply exacerbates the 'tension' between the two clauses." **

working on tank turrets. The Chief Justice stated: "Intrafaith differences of that kind are not uncommon among followers of a particular creed, and the judicial process is singularly ill equipped to resolve such differences in relation to the Religion Clauses. One can, of course, imagine an asserted claim so bizarre, so clearly nonreligious in motivation, as not to be entitled to protection under the Free Exercise Clause; but that is not the case here, and the guarantee of free exercise is not limited to beliefs which are shared by all the members of a religious sect. [Courts] are not arbiters of scriptural interpretation."

† A separate notation by Justice BLACKMUN stated that he joined the majority opinion only in its discussion of Free Exercise; with respect to Establishment, he concurred only in the result.

** Justice Rehnquist added in a footnote that, even if Sherbert was correctly decided, this ruling unjustifiably extended Sherbert. He argued that the Sherbert opinion seemed "to suggest by negative implication that where a State makes every 'personal reason' for leaving a job a basis for disqualification from unemployment benefits, the State need not grant an exemption to persons such as Sherbert who do quit for 'personal reasons.'" In Thomas, the highest state court had indeed construed the law "to make every personal subjective reason for leaving a job a basis for disqualification." That made Thomas' case distinguishable from Sherbert's: "Because Thomas left his job for a personal reason, the State of Indiana should not be prohibited from disqualifying him from receiving benefits."

10th ED., p. 1597; IND. RTS., p. 1217
Insert after Yoder (before the Notes):

U. S. v. LEE, 455 U.S. 252 (1982): Lee, a member of the Old Order Amish, employed several other Amish to work on his farm and in his carpentry shop. He objected to paying the social security tax imposed on employers, insisting that payment would violate his religious beliefs. The Court found Yoder distinguishable and rejected Lee's claim to a constitutional exemption.

Chief Justice BURGER's opinion accepted Lee's contention that "both payment and receipt of social security benefits is forbidden by the Amish faith" and conceded that "there is a conflict between the Amish faith and the obligations imposed by the social security system." That acknowledgement, however, was "only the beginning [and] not the end of the inquiry. Not all burdens on religion are unconstitutional. The state may justify a limitation on religious liberty by showing that it is essential to accomplish an overriding governmental interest."

The Chief Justice found that the application of the tax law to Lee survived this strict scrutiny. He noted that "the government's interest in assuring mandatory and continuous participation in and contribution to the social security system is very high" and that "mandatory participation is indispensable to the fiscal vitality of the social security system." He next inquired "whether accommodating the Amish belief will unduly interfere with fulfillment of the governmental interest." He commented: "Religious beliefs can be accommodated, see, e.g., [Thomas; Sherbert], but there is a point at which accommodation would 'radically restrict the operating latitude of the legislature.' Braunfeld." In this instance, unlike "the situation presented in [Yoder], it would be difficult to accommodate the comprehensive social security system with myriad exceptions flowing from a wide variety of religious beliefs." He thought that there was "no principled way [to] distinguish between general taxes and those imposed under the Social Security Act": "If, for example, a religious adherent believes war is a sin, and if a certain percentage of the federal budget can be identified as devoted to war-related activities, such individuals would have a similarly valid claim to be exempt from paying that percentage of the income tax. The tax system could not function if denominations were allowed to challenge [it] because tax payments were spent in a manner that violates their religious belief. Because the broad public interest in maintaining a sound tax system is of such a high order, religious belief in conflict with the payment of taxes affords no basis for resisting the tax."

Chief Justice Burger added: "Congress and the courts have been sensitive to the needs flowing from the Free Exercise Clause, but every person cannot be shielded from all the burdens incident to exercising every aspect of the right to practice religious beliefs." In the Social Security Act, for example, Congress had granted some religious exemptions, but these were only available to self-employed Amish and not, as in this case, employers of others.[1] The statutory exemption reflected the congressional view of the permissible accommodation between the needs of a comprehensive national pro-

1. The Chief Justice added in a foot- the Free Exercise Clause compelled
 note: "We need not decide whether an exemption [for the self-employed];

gram and religious faith. "When followers of a particular sect enter into commercial activity as a matter of choice, the limits they accept on their own conduct as a matter of conscience and faith are not to be superimposed on the statutory schemes which are binding on others in that activity. [The] tax imposed on employers to support the social security system must be uniformly applicable to all, except as Congress provides explicitly otherwise."

In a noteworthy opinion concurring in the judgment, Justice STEVENS disagreed with the Chief Justice's strict scrutiny approach. The majority's constitutional standard, he insisted, "suggests that the Government always bears a heavy burden of justifying the application of neutral general laws to individual conscientious objectors. In my opinion, it is the objector who must shoulder the burden of demonstrating that there is a unique reason for allowing him a special exemption from a valid law of general applicability."

In Justice Stevens' view, the law challenged here would not survive if strict scrutiny were truly applied: "[I]f we confine the analysis to the Government's interest in rejecting the particular claim to an exemption at stake in this case, the constitutional standard as formulated by the Court has not been met." He suggested that it would be relatively simple administratively to extend the statutory exemption to those in Lee's position. Moreover, an enlarged exemption would probably promote federal fiscal policy, "because the nonpayment of these taxes by the Amish would be more than offset by the elimination of their right to collect benefits. In view of the fact that the Amish have demonstrated their capacity to care for their own, the social cost of eliminating [from the social security system] this relatively small group of dedicated believers would be minimal." The Court's rejection of the Amish employer's claim here, he pointed out, rested ultimately on "the risk that a myriad of other claims would be too difficult to process." He thought the Chief Justice had overstated "the magnitude of this risk, because the Amish claim applies only to a small religious community with an established welfare system of its own." [2]

Justice Stevens nevertheless agreed with the Court's conclusion that "the difficulties associated with processing other claims to tax exemption on religious grounds justify a rejection of this claim." He insisted, however that the result should rest on "a different constitutional standard than that the Court purports to apply." He stated the more desirable standard as follows: "[T]here is virtually no room for a 'constitutionally-required exemption' on religious grounds from a valid tax law that is entirely neutral in its general application." [3]

Congress' grant of the exemption was an effort toward accommodation. Nor do we need to decide whether, if Congress [had] intended [the exemption] to reach this case, conflicts with the Establishment Clause would arise."

2. At this point, Justice Stevens added in a footnote: "In my opinion, the principal reason for adopting a strong presumption against such claims is not a matter of administrative convenience. It is the overriding interest in keeping the government [out] of the business of evaluating the relative merits of differing religious claims. The risk that governmental approval of some and disapproval of others will be perceived as favoring one religion over another is an important risk the Establishment Clause was designed to preclude."

3. In an important footnote at this point, Justice Stevens elaborated his approach as follows: "Today's holding

BOB JONES UNIVERSITY v. UNITED STATES, 461 U.S. ——
(1983), produced far more in the way of media attention than it did constitutional law. Bob Jones University, which had previously denied admission
to non-whites, still maintained a policy against interracial marriage or dating
by its students. Goldsboro Christian Schools had a racially discriminatory
admissions policy that limited admissions to whites. Both schools had a
strongly religious orientation. The Court accepted that "the challenged practices of petitioner Bob Jones University were based on a genuine belief that
the Bible forbids interracial dating and marriage." The same assumption of
sincerity was applied to Goldsboro's belief that "[c]ultural or biological mix-
ing of the races [is] a violation of God's command."

At issue was the decision of the Internal Revenue Service to deny tax-
exempt status to both schools on the grounds that their practices of racial discrimination were "contrary to settled public policy," thereby disqualifying the
schools from qualification as "charities." The bulk of Chief Justice BURG-
ER's opinion for the Court was devoted to issues of statutory interpretation
and application. He rejected the claim that the "public policy" standard was
inapplicable here. "[T]here can no longer be any doubt that racial discrimination in education violates deeply and widely accepted views of elementary
justice. [Given] the stress and anguish of the history of efforts to escape
from the shackles of the 'separate but equal' doctrine, [it] cannot be said

is limited to a claim to a tax exemption. I believe, however, that a standard that places an almost insurmountable burden on any individual
who objects to a valid and neutral
law of general applicability on the
ground that the law proscribes (or
prescribes) conduct that his religion
prescribes (or proscribes) better explains most of this Court's holdings
than does the standard articulated by
the Court today. See, e.g., Gillette v.
United States (selective service laws);
Braunfeld v. Brown (Sunday closing
laws); Prince v. Massachusetts (child
labor laws); Jacobson v. Massachusetts (compulsory vaccination laws);
Reynolds v. United States (polygamy
law). The principal exception is Wisconsin v. Yoder, in which the Court
granted the Amish an exemption from
Wisconsin's compulsory school-attend-
ance law by actually applying the
subjective balancing approach it purports to apply today. The Court's attempt to distinguish Yoder is uncon-
vincing because precisely the same religious interest is implicated in both
cases and Wisconsin's interest in requiring its children to attend school
until they reach the age of 16 is surely not inferior to the federal interest
in collecting these social security taxes.

"There is also tension between this
standard and the reasoning in [Thom-
as v. Review Bd.] and Sherbert v.
Verner. Arguably, however, laws intended to provide a benefit to a limited class of otherwise disadvantaged
persons should be judged by a different standard than that appropriate
for the enforcement of neutral laws
of general applicability. A tax exemption entails no cost to the claimant; if tax exemptions were dispensed on religious grounds, every citizen would have an economic motivation to join the favored sects. No
comparable economic motivation could
explain the conduct of the employees
in Sherbert and Thomas. In both of
those cases, changes in work requirements dictated by the employer forced
the employees to surrender jobs that
they would have preferred to retain
rather than accept unemployment
compensation. In each case the treatment of the religious objection to the
new job requirements as though it
were tantamount to a physical impairment that made it impossible for the
employee to continue to work under
changed circumstances could be
viewed as a protection against unequal treatment rather than a grant of
favored treatment for the members of
the religious sect. In all events, the
decision in Thomas was clearly compelled by Sherbert."

that educational institutions that, for whatever reasons, practice racial discrimination, are institutions [that] should be encouraged by having all taxpayers share in their support by way of special tax status. [Whatever] may be the rationale for such private schools' policies, and however sincere the rationale may be, racial discrimination in education is contrary to public policy." The Chief Justice also rejected the argument that the policy of the Internal Revenue Service regarding racially discriminatory institutions had not been authorized by Congress.[4]

Having determined that the denial of tax-exempt status was justified as a matter of statutory interpretation, the Court turned to the claim that the policy could not be applied to religious institutions without violating the Free Exercise Clause.[5] Part of the Court's reason for rejecting the free exercise claim was the impact of compliance on the schools. "Denial of tax benefits will inevitably have a substantial impact on the operation of private religious schools, but will not prevent those schools from observing their religious tenets." But the most significant factor in the result was the Court's application of U. S. v. Lee's standard that "[t]he state may justify a limitation on religious liberty by showing that it is essential to accomplish an overriding governmental interest." The Court had little trouble finding that standard met in this case. "The governmental interest at stake here is compelling. [The] Government has a fundamental, overriding interest in eradicating racial discrimination in education. [That] governmental interest substantially outweighs whatever burden denial of tax benefits places on petitioners' exercise of their religious beliefs. The interests asserted by petitioners cannot be accommodated with that compelling governmental interest [Lee]; and no 'less restrictive means,' [Thomas v. Review Board] are available to achieve the governmental interest."

4. Justice Powell's concurrence and Justice Rehnquist's dissent were directed to the authority of the Internal Revenue Service under the Internal Revenue Code. Both, however, explicitly agreed with the majority regarding the rejection of the First Amendment claim.

5. The Court also rejected the argument that denial of tax-exempt status violated the Establishment Clause by preferring some religions over others. As long as the IRS policy had a secular and neutral basis, the Establishment Clause was not violated "merely because [the regulation] 'happens to coincide or harmonize with the tenets of some or all religions.' McGowan v. Maryland."

Chapter 15

PROPER CONDITIONS FOR CONSTITUTIONAL ADJUDICATION

10th ED., p. 1611; IND. RTS., p. 1231
Add as footnote at end of Note 2:

Lower courts, both state and federal, are clearly bound to follow applicable United States Supreme Court precedent in deciding questions of federal law. But may a lower court at least "consider" whether Supreme Court decisions should be "modified"? If not, what kind of record below will support Supreme Court reconsideration of its own precedent? In Illinois v. Gates, 462 U.S. —— (1983), the Court granted certiorari to decide a particular Fourth Amendment issue, but then requested additional argument on the broader question of a possible "good faith" exception to the exclusionary rule. (On the exclusionary rule, see above, 10th Ed., p. 497; Ind.Rts., p. 117.) The Court then proceeded to render its decision without addressing the "good faith" issue on which it had invited argument. In an extended discussion of the Court's refusal to deal with that issue, Justice Rehnquist's majority opinion concluded that the state had never below "raised or addressed the question of whether the federal exclusionary rule should be modified in any respect, and none of the opinions of the Illinois courts give any indication that the question was considered." Because the factual record in the case was not compiled with those legal questions in mind, the Court determined that there was an inadequate foundation on which to sustain a possible major doctrinal shift.

Justice White, concurring, was unpersuaded by the majority's reasoning in refusing to reach the issue. Noting that the Illinois courts are bound by the Supreme Court's pronouncements regarding the federal exclusionary rule, he saw "little point in requiring a litigant to request a state court to overrule or modify one of this Court's precedents." *Stare decisis* would be undercut by such a practice. "Either the presentation of such issues to the lower courts will be a completely futile gesture or the lower courts are now invited to depart from this Court's decisions whenever they conclude such a modification is in order." To Justice White the proper forum for contesting the issue was the Supreme Court, where the exclusonary rule originated.

The Court's opinion in Gates is usefully contrasted with the following statement from Newport v. Fact Concerts, Inc., 453 U.S. 247, n. 15 (1981). "The Court's exercise of power in these circumstances is no more broad than its notice of plain error not presented by the parties, [its] deciding a question not raised in the lower federal courts, [or] its review of an issue neither decided below nor presented by the parties." The opinion in Newport was written by Justice Blackmun, who joined the majority in Gates.

10th ED., p. 1618; IND. RTS., p. 1238
Add to footnote 1:

For an extensive discussion of parens patriae standing see Snapp & Son v. Puerto Rico, 458 U.S. —— (1982), holding that Puerto Rico had a sufficient "quasi-sovereign" interest to sue Virginia apple growers on a claim that the Virginians had discriminated against Puerto Ricans in favor of foreign laborers.

10th ED., p. 1622; IND. RTS., p. 1242
Insert after Flast v. Cohen (before the notes on modern standing cases):

VALLEY FORGE COLLEGE v. AMERICANS UNITED

454 U.S. 464, 102 S.Ct. 752, 70 L.Ed.2d 700 (1982).

Justice REHNQUIST delivered the opinion of the Court.

I.   [Acting under the Property Clause of the Constitution, Art. IV, § 3, cl. 2, Congress adopted the Federal Property and Administrative Services Act of 1949 to provide for the disposal of surplus federal property. The Act, authorized the Secretary of HEW to dispose of surplus real property for educational purposes by selling or leasing it to nonprofit, tax-exempt educational institutions for consideration that took into account any benefit to the Government from the transferee's use of the property. Pursuant to that statutory authority, HEW conveyed certain property once used as a military hospital to the Valley Forge Christian College (formerly the Northeast Bible College). Although the appraised value of the land was over $500,000, the property was transferred without any financial payment because HEW allowed the College a 100% public benefit allowance. The College, operated by a religious order known as the Assemblies of God, proposed to use the property "to offer systematic training [to] men and women for Christian service as either ministers or laymen."

[This federal court challenge by Americans United for Separation of Church and State claimed that the property transfer violated the Establishment Clause of the First Amendment. The District Court dismissed the case on the ground that the challengers lacked standing as taxpayers under Flast v. Cohen. The Court of Appeals agreed that the challengers could not sue as taxpayers, since this was a challenge to congressional action under the Property Clause, not the taxing and spending powers of Art. I, § 8, that had been involved in Flast. Nevertheless, the majority of the Court of Appeals sustained standing on the ground that the challengers could sue as "citizens" claiming "injury 'in fact' to their shared individuated right to a government that 'shall make no law respecting the establishment of religion.' "] Because of the unusually broad and novel view of standing to litigate a substantive question in the federal courts adopted by the Court of Appeals, we granted certiorari and we now reverse.

II.   [The] judicial power of the United States defined by Art. III is not an unconditioned authority to determine the constitutionality of legislative or executive acts. The power to declare the rights of individuals and to measure the authority of governments "[is] legitimate only in the last resort, and as a necessity in the determination of real, earnest and vital controversy." [As] an incident to the elaboration of this bedrock requirement, this Court has always required that a litigant have "standing" to challenge the action sought to be adjudicated in the lawsuit. The term "standing" subsumes a blend of constitutional requirements and prudential considerations, see Warth v. Seldin. [Warth v. Seldin and the other post-Flast cases discussed in this opinion are noted in the casebook, in the later pages of the section on "standing" in this chapter.] [I]t has not always been clear in the opinions of this Court whether particular features of the "standing" requirement have been required by Art. III ex proprio vigore, or whether they are requirements that the Court itself has erected and which were not compelled by the language of the Constitution.

A recent line of decisions, however, has resolved that ambiguity, at least to the following extent: at an irreducible minimum, Art. III requires the party who invokes the court's authority to "show that he personally has suffered some actual or threatened injury as a result of the putatively illegal conduct of the defendant" and that the injury "fairly can be traced to the challenged action" and "is likely to be redressed by a favorable decision."

The requirement of "actual injury redressable by the court" [Simon] serves several of the "implicit policies embodied in Article III." It tends to assure that the legal questions presented to the court will be resolved, not in the rarified atmosphere of a debating society, but in a concrete factual context conducive to a realistic appreciation of the consequences of judicial action. The "standing" requirement serves other purposes. Because it assures an actual factual setting in which the litigant asserts a claim of injury in fact, a court may decide the case with some confidence that its decision will not pave the way for lawsuits which have some, but not all, of the facts of the case actually decided by the court.

The Art. III aspect of standing also reflects a due regard for the autonomy of those persons likely to be most directly affected by a judicial order. The federal courts have abjured appeals to their authority which would convert the judicial process into "no more than a vehicle for the vindication of the value interests of concerned bystanders." Were the federal courts merely publicly funded forums for the ventilation of public grievances or the refinement of jurisprudential understanding, the concept of "standing" would be quite unnecessary. But the "cases and controversies" language of Art. III forecloses the conversion of courts of the United States into judicial versions of college debating forums. [The] exercise of judicial power, which can so profoundly affect the lives, liberty, and property of those to whom it extends, is therefore restricted to litigants who can show "injury in fact" resulting from the action which they seek to have the Court adjudicate. The exercise of the judicial power also affects relationships between the coequal arms of the national government. The effect is, of course, most vivid when a federal court declares unconstitutional an act of the Legislative or Executive branch. While the exercise of that "ultimate and supreme function" is a formidable means of vindicating individual rights, when employed unwisely or unnecessarily it is also the ultimate threat to the continued effectiveness of the federal courts in performing that role. [Proper] regard for the complex nature of our constitutional structure requires neither that the judicial branch shrink from a confrontation with the other two coequal branches of the federal government, nor that it hospitably accept for adjudication claims of constitutional violation by other branches of government where the claimant has not suffered cognizable injury.

[Beyond] the constitutional requirements, the federal judiciary has also adhered to a set of prudential principles that bear on the question of standing. Thus, this Court has held that "the plaintiff generally must assert his own legal rights and interests, and cannot rest his claim to relief on the legal rights or interests of third parties." Warth v. Seldin. In addition, even when the plaintiff has alleged redressable injury sufficient to meet the requirements of Art. III, the Court has refrained from adjudicating "abstract questions of wide public significance" which amount to "generalized grievances," pervasively shared and most appropriately addressed in the representative branches. Finally, the Court has required that the plaintiff's complaint fall within "the zone of interests to be protected or regulated by the statute or constitutional guarantee in question."

Merely to articulate these principles is to demonstrate their close relationship to the policies reflected in the Art. III requirement of actual or threatened injury amenable to judicial remedy. But neither the counsels of prudence nor the policies implicit in the "case or controversy" requirement should be mistaken for the rigorous Art. III requirements themselves. Satisfaction of the former cannot substitute for a demonstration of " 'distinct and palpable injury' [that] is likely to be redressed if the requested relief is granted." That requirement states a limitation on judicial power, not merely a factor to be balanced in the weighing of so-called "prudential" considerations.

We need not mince words when we say that the concept of "Art. III standing" has not been defined with complete consistency in all of the various cases decided by this Court which have discussed it, nor when we say that this very fact is probably proof that the concept cannot be reduced to a one-sentence or one-paragraph definition. But of one thing we may be sure: Those who do not possess Art. III standing may not litigate as suitors in the courts of the United States.[1] Art. III, which is every bit as important in its circumscription of the judicial power of the United States as in its granting of that power, is not merely a troublesome hurdle to be overcome if possible so as to reach the "merits" of a lawsuit which a party desires to have adjudicated; it is a part of the basic charter promulgated by the framers of the Constitution. . . .

III. The injury alleged by respondents [is] the "depriv[ation] of the fair and constitutional use of [their] tax dollar." As a result, our discussion must begin with Frothingham v. Mellon. [Following] the decision in Frothingham, the Court confirmed that the expenditure of public funds in an allegedly unconstitutional manner is not an injury sufficient to confer standing, even though the plaintiff contributes to the public coffers as a taxpayer. [Doremus v. Board of Education.] [The] Court again visited the problem of taxpayer standing in Flast v. Cohen. [The Flast Court] developed a two-

---

1. The dissent takes us to task for "tend[ing] merely to obfuscate, rather than inform, our understanding of the meaning of rights under the law." Were this Court constituted to operate a national classroom on "the meaning of rights" for the benefit of interested litigants, this criticism would carry weight. The teaching of Art. III, however, is that constitutional adjudication is available only on terms prescribed by the Constitution, among which is the requirement of a plaintiff with standing to sue. The dissent asserts that this requirement "overrides no other provision of the Constitution," but just as surely the Art. III power of the federal courts does not wax and wane in harmony with a litigant's desire for a "hospitable forum." Art. III obligates a federal court to act only when it is assured of the power to do so, that is, when it is called upon to resolve an actual case or controversy. Then, and only then, may it turn its attention to

part test to determine whether the plaintiffs had standing to sue. First, because a taxpayer alleges injury only by virtue of his liability for taxes, the Court held that "a taxpayer will be a proper party to allege the unconstitutionality only of exercises of congressional power under the taxing and spending clause of Art. I, § 8, of the Constitution." Second, the Court required the taxpayer to "show that the challenged enactment exceeds specific constitutional limitations upon the exercise of the taxing and spending power and not simply that the enactment is generally beyond the powers delegated to Congress by Art. I, § 8."

Unlike the plaintiffs in Flast, respondents fail the first prong of the test for taxpayer standing. Their claim is deficient in two respects. First, the source of their complaint is not a congressional action, but a decision by HEW to transfer a parcel of federal property.[2] Flast limited taxpayer standing to challenges directed "only [at] exercises of congressional power." Second, and perhaps redundantly, the property transfer about which respondents complain was not an exercise of authority conferred by the taxing and spending clause of Art. I, § 8. The authorizing legislation [was] an evident exercise of Congress' power under the Property Clause, Art. IV, § 3, cl. 2. [This] is decisive of any claim of taxpayer standing under the Flast precedent.[3] Any doubt that once might have existed concerning the rigor with which the Flast exception to the Frothingham principle ought to be applied should have been erased by this Court's recent decisions in [Richardson and Reservists]. [Respondents], therefore, are plainly without standing to sue as taxpayers. [It] remains to be seen whether respondents have alleged any other basis for standing to bring this suit.

---

other constitutional provisions and presume to provide a forum for the adjudication of rights. [Footnote by Justice Rehnquist.]

2. Respondents do not challenge the constitutionality of the Federal Property and Administrative Services Act itself, but rather a particular Executive branch action arguably authorized by the Act. [Footnote by Justice Rehnquist.]

3. Although not necessary to our decision, we note that any connection between the challenged property transfer and respondents' tax burden is at best speculative and at worst nonexistent. Although public funds were expended to establish the Valley Forge General Hospital, the land was acquired and the facilities constructed thirty years prior to the challenged transfer. Respondents do not challenge this expenditure, and we do not immediately perceive how such a challenge might now be raised. Nor do respondents dispute the government's conclusion that the property has become useless for federal purposes and ought to be disposed of in some productive manner. In fact, respondents' only objection is that the government did not receive adequate consideration for the transfer, because petitioner's use of the property will not confer a public benefit. Assuming arguendo that this proposition is true, an assumption by no means clear, there is no basis for believing that a transfer to a different purchaser would have added to government receipts. As the government argues, "the ultimate purchaser would, in all likelihood, have been another non-profit institution or local school district rather than a purchaser for cash." Moreover, each year of delay in disposing of the property *depleted* the Treasury by the amounts necessary to maintain a facility that had lost its value to the government. Even if respondents had brought their claim within the outer limits of Flast, therefore, they still would have encountered serious difficulty in establishing that they "personally would benefit in a tangible way from the court's intervention." Warth v. Seldin. [Footnote by Justice Rehnquist.]

IV.   Although the Court of Appeals properly doubted respondents' ability to establish standing solely on the basis of their taxpayer status, it considered their allegations of taxpayer injury to be "essentially an assumed role": "Plaintiffs have no reason to expect, nor perhaps do they care about, any personal tax saving that might result should they prevail.   The crux of the interest at stake, the plaintiffs argue, is found in the Establishment Clause, not in the supposed loss of money as such.   As a matter of primary identity, therefore, the plaintiffs are not so much taxpayers as separationists."   In the court's view, respondents had established standing by virtue of an " 'injury in fact' to their shared individuated right to a government that 'shall make no law respecting the establishment of religion.' "   The court distinguished this "injury" from "the question of 'citizen standing' as such."   Although citizens generally could not establish standing simply by claiming an interest in governmental observance of the Constitution, respondents had "set forth instead a particular and concrete injury" to a "personal constitutional right."

In finding that respondents had alleged something more than "the generalized interest of all citizens in constitutional governance" [Reservists], the Court of Appeals relied on factual differences which we do not think amount to legal distinctions.   The court decided that respondents' claim differed from those in [Reservists] and Richardson, which were predicated, respectively, on the Incompatibility and Accounts Clauses, because "it is at the very least arguable that the Establishment Clause creates in each citizen a 'personal constitutional right' to a government that does not establish religion."   The court found it unnecessary to determine whether this "arguable" proposition was correct, since it judged the mere allegation of a legal right sufficient to confer standing.

This reasoning process merely disguises, we think with a rather thin veil, the inconsistency of the court's results with our decisions in [Reservists] and Richardson.   The plaintiffs in those cases plainly asserted a "personal right" to have the government act in accordance with their views of the Constitution;   indeed, we see no barrier to the *assertion* of such claims with respect to any constitutional provision.   But assertion of a right to a particular kind of government conduct, which the government has violated by acting differently, cannot alone satisfy the requirements of Art. III without draining those requirements of meaning.

Nor can Schlesinger and Richardson be distinguished on the ground that the Incompatibility and Accounts Clauses are in some way less "fundamental" than the Establishment Clause.   Each establishes a norm of conduct which the federal government is bound to honor—to no greater or lesser extent than any other inscribed in the Constitution.   To the extent the Court of Appeals relied on a view of standing under which the Art. III burdens diminish as the "importance" of the claim on the merits increases, we reject that notion.   The requirement of standing "focuses on the party seeking to get his complaint before a federal court and not on the issues he wishes to have adjudicated." Flast.   Moreover, we know of no principled basis on which to create a hierarchy of constitutional values or a complementary "sliding scale" of standing which might permit respondents to invoke the judicial power of the United States.[4]

[The] complaint in this case shares a common deficiency with those in [Reservists] and Richardson. Although they claim that the Constitution has been violated, they claim nothing else. They fail to identify any personal injury suffered by the plaintiffs *as a consequence* of the alleged constitutional error, other than the psychological consequence presumably produced by observation of conduct with which one disagrees. That is not an injury sufficient to confer standing under Art. III, even though the disagreement is phrased in constitutional terms. It is evident that respondents are firmly committed to the constitutional principle of separation of church and State, but standing is not measured by the intensity of the litigant's interest or the fervor of his advocacy. "[T]hat concrete adverseness which sharpens the presentation of issues," Baker v. Carr, is the anticipated consequence of proceedings commenced by one who has been injured in fact; it is not a permissible substitute for the showing of injury itself.

In reaching this conclusion, we do not retreat from our earlier holdings that standing may be predicated on noneconomic injury. See [e.g., SCRAP;

4. The dissent is premised on a revisionist reading of our precedents which leads to the conclusion that the Art. III requirement of standing is satisfied by any taxpayer who contends "that the federal government has exceeded the bounds of the law in allocating its largesse." "The concept of taxpayer injury necessarily recognizes the continuing stake of the taxpayer in the disposition of the Treasury to which he has contributed his taxes, and his right to have those funds put to lawful uses." On this novel understanding, the dissent reads cases such as Frothingham and Flast as decisions on the merits of the taxpayers' claims. Frothingham is explained as a holding that a taxpayer ordinarily has no legal right to challenge congressional expenditures. The dissent divines from Flast the holding that a taxpayer *does* have an enforceable right "to challenge a federal bestowal of largesse" for religious purposes. This right extends to "the Government as a whole, regardless of which branch is at work in a particular instance" and regardless of whether the challenged action was an exercise of the spending power.

However appealing this reconstruction of precedent may be, it bears little resemblance to the cases on which it purports to rest. Frothingham and Flast were decisions that plainly turned on *standing*, and just as plainly rejected any notion that the Art. III requirement of direct injury is satisfied by a taxpayer who contends "that the federal government

has exceeded the bounds of the law in allocating its largesse." Moreover, although the dissent's view may lead to a result satisfying to many in this case, it is not evident how its substitution of "legal interest" for "standing" enhances "our understanding of the meaning of rights under law." Logically, the dissent must shoulder the burden of explaining why taxpayers with standing have no "legal interest" in congressional expenditures except when it is possible to allege a violation of the Establishment Clause: yet it does not attempt to do so.

Nor does the dissent's interpretation of standing adequately explain cases such as [Reservists] and Richardson. According to the dissent, the taxpayer plaintiffs in those cases lacked standing, not because they failed to challenge an exercise of the spending power, but because they did not complain of "the distribution of government largesse." And yet if the standing of a taxpayer is established by his "continuing stake . . . in the disposition of the Treasury to which he has contributed his taxes," it would seem to follow that he can assert a right to examine the budget of the CIA, as in Richardson, and a right to argue that members of Congress cannot claim reserve pay from the government, as in [Reservists]. Of course, both claims have been rejected, precisely because Art. III requires a demonstration of redressable injury that is not satisfied by a claim that tax monies have been spent unlawfully. [Footnote by Justice Rehnquist.]

Data Processing]. We simply cannot see that respondents have alleged an *injury of any kind*, economic or otherwise, sufficient to confer standing.[5] Respondents complain of a transfer of property located in Chester County, Pennsylvania. The named plaintiffs reside in Maryland and Virginia; their organizational headquarters are located in Washington, D.C. They learned of the transfer through a news release. Their claim that the government has violated the Establishment Clause does not provide a special license to roam the country in search of governmental wrongdoing and to reveal their discoveries in federal court.[6] The federal courts were simply not constituted as ombudsmen of the general welfare.

V.   The Court of Appeals in this case ignored unambiguous limitations on taxpayer and citizen standing. It appears to have done so out of the conviction that enforcement of the Establishment Clause demands special exceptions from the requirement that a plaintiff allege " 'distinct and palpable injury to himself,' [that] is likely to be redressed if the requested relief is granted." [Warth v. Seldin.] The court derived precedential comfort from [Flast]: "The underlying justification for according standing in Flast it seems, was the implicit recognition that the Establishment Clause does create in every citizen a personal constitutional right, such that any citizen, including taxpayers, may contest under that clause the constitutionality of federal

---

5.   Respondents rely on our statement in [Data Processing] that "[a] person or family may have a spiritual stake in First Amendment values sufficient to give standing to raise issues concerning the Establishment Clause and the Free Exercise Clause. Abington School District v. Schempp." Respondents apparently construe this language to mean that any person asserting an Establishment Clause violation possesses a "spiritual stake" sufficient to confer standing. The language will not bear that weight. First, the language cannot be read apart from the context of its accompanying reference to Abington School District v. Schempp. In Schempp, the Court invalidated laws that required Bible reading in the public schools. Plaintiffs were children who attended the schools in question, and their parents. The Court noted: "It goes without saying that the laws and practices involved here can be challenged only by persons having standing to complain. . . . The parties here are school children and their parents, who are directly affected by the laws and practices against which their complaints are directed. These interests surely suffice to give the parties standing to complain." The Court also drew a comparison with Doremus v. Board of Education, in which the identical substantive issues were raised, but in which the appeal was "dismissed upon the gradua-

tion of the school child involved and because of the appellants' failure to establish standing as taxpayers." The Court's discussion of the standing issue is not extensive, but it is sufficient to show the error in respondents' broad reading of the phrase "spiritual stake." The plaintiffs in Schempp had standing, not because their complaint rested on the Establishment Clause—for as Doremus demonstrated, that is insufficient—but because impressionable schoolchildren were subjected to unwelcome religious exercises or were forced to assume special burdens to avoid them. Respondents have alleged no comparable injury. [Footnote by Justice Rehnquist.]

6.   Respondents also claim standing by reference to the Administrative Procedure Act, which authorizes judicial review at the instance of any person who has been "adversely affected or aggrieved by agency action within the meaning of a relevant statute." Neither the Administrative Procedure Act, nor any other congressional enactment, can lower the threshold requirements of standing under Art. III. Respondents do not allege that the Act creates a legal right, "the invasion of which creates standing," and there is no other basis for arguing that its existence alters the rules of standing otherwise applicable to this case. [Footnote by Justice Rehnquist.]

expenditures." [7] The concurring opinion was even more direct. In its view, "statutes alleged to violate the Establishment Clause may not have an individual impact sufficient to confer standing in the traditional sense." To satisfy "the need for an available plaintiff," and thereby to assure a basis for judicial review, respondents should be granted standing because, "as a practical matter, no one is better suited to bring this lawsuit and thus vindicate the freedoms embodied in the Establishment Clause."

Implicit in the foregoing is the philosophy that the business of the federal courts is correcting constitutional errors, and that "cases and controversies" are at best merely convenient vehicles for doing so and at worst nuisances that may be dispensed with when they become obstacles to that transcendent endeavor. This philosophy has no place in our constitutional scheme. It does not become more palatable when the underlying merits concern the Establishment Clause. "[The] assumption that if respondents have no standing to sue, no one would have standing, is not a reason to find standing." [Schlesinger.] This view would convert standing into a requirement that must be observed only when satisfied. Moreover, we are unwilling to assume that injured parties are nonexistent simply because they have not joined respondents in their suit. The law of averages is not a substitute for standing.

Were we to accept respondents' claim of standing in this case, there would be no principled basis for confining our exception to litigants relying on the Establishment Clause. Ultimately, that exception derives from the idea that the judicial power requires nothing more for its invocation than important issues and able litigants.[8] The existence of injured parties who might not wish to bring suit becomes irrelevant. [W]e are unwilling to countenance such a departure from the limits on judicial power contained in Art. III. . . .

[Reversed.]

7. The majority believed that the only thing which prevented this Court from openly acknowledging this position was the fact that the complaint in Flast had alleged no basis for standing other than the plaintiffs' taxpayer status. [T]his view is simply not in accord with the facts. The Flast plaintiffs and several amici strongly urged the Court to adopt the same view of standing for which respondents argue in this case. The Court plainly chose not to do so. Even if respondents were correct in arguing that the Court in Flast was bound by a "perceived limitation in the pleadings," we are not so bound in this case, and we find no merit in respondents' vision of standing. [Footnote by Justice Rehnquist.]

8. Were we to recognize standing premised on an "injury" consisting solely of an alleged violation of a " 'personal constitutional right' to a government that does not establish religion," a principled consistency would dictate recognition of respondents' standing to challenge execution of every capital sentence on the basis of a personal right to a government that does not impose cruel and unusual punishment, or standing to challenge every affirmative action program on the basis of a personal right to a government that does not deny equal protection of the laws, to choose but two among as many possible examples as there are commands in the Constitution. [Footnote by Justice Rehnquist.]

Justice BRENNAN, with whom Justice MARSHALL and Justice BLACKMUN join, dissenting.

A plaintiff's standing is a jurisdictional matter for Article III courts, and thus a "threshold question" to be resolved before turning attention to more "substantive" issues. But in consequence there is an impulse to decide difficult questions of substantive law obliquely in the course of opinions purporting to do nothing more than determine what the Court labels "standing"; this accounts for the phenomenon of opinions, such as the one today, that tend merely to obfuscate, rather than inform, our understanding of the meaning of rights under the law. The serious by-product of that practice is that the Court disregards its constitutional responsibility when, by failing to acknowledge the protections afforded by the Constitution, it uses "standing to slam the courthouse door against plaintiffs who are entitled to full consideration of their claims on the merits." [1]

The opinion of the Court is a stark example of this unfortunate trend of resolving cases at the "threshold" while obscuring the nature of the underlying rights and interests at stake. The Court waxes eloquent on the blend of prudential and constitutional considerations that combine to create our misguided "standing" jurisprudence. But not one word is said *about the Establishment Clause right that the plaintiff seeks to enforce.* And despite its pat recitation of our standing decisions, the opinion utterly fails, except by the sheerest form of ipse dixit, to explain why this case is unlike [Flast] and is controlled instead by [Frothingham].

I.   There is now much in the way of settled doctrine in our understanding of the injury-in-fact requirement of Article III. At the core is the irreducible minimum that persons seeking judicial relief from an Article III court have "such a personal stake in the outcome of the controversy as to assure that concrete adverseness which sharpens the presentation of issues upon which the court so largely depends." Baker v. Carr. Cases of this Court have identified the two essential components of this "personal stake" requirement. Plaintiff must have sufferd, or be threatened with, some "distinct and palpable injury," Warth v. Seldin. In addition, there must be some causal connection between plaintiff's asserted injury and defendant's challenged action. [Simon; Arlington Heights.] The Constitution requires an Article III court to ascertain that both requirements are met before proceeding to exercise its authority on behalf of any plaintiff, whether the form of relief requested is equitable or monetary.

But the existence of Article III injury "often turns on the nature and source of the claim asserted." Warth v. Seldin.[2] Neither "palpable injury" nor "causation" is a term of unvarying meaning. There is much in the way of "mutual understandings" and "common law traditions" that necessarily guides the definitional inquiry. *In addition,* the Constitution, and by legislation the Congress, may impart a new, and on occasion unique, meaning to the

---

1. Barlow v. Collins (Brennan, J., concurring in the result and dissenting). [Footnote by Justice Brennan.]

2. "Congress may enact statutes creating legal rights, the invasion of which creates standing, even though no injury would exist without the statute." Linda R.S. v. Richard D. The Framers of the Constitution, of course could, and did, exercise the same power. [Footnote by Justice Brennan.]

terms "injury" and "causation" in particular statutory or constitutional contexts. The Court makes a fundamental mistake when it determines that a plaintiff has failed to satisfy the two-pronged "injury-in-fact" test, or indeed any other test of "standing," without first determining whether the Constitution or a statute defines injury, and creates a cause of action for redress of that injury, in precisely the circumstance presented to the Court.

It may of course happen that a person believing himself injured in some obscure manner by government action will be held to have no legal right under the constitutional or statutory provision upon which he relies, and will not be permitted to complain of the invasion of another person's "rights." [3] It is quite another matter to employ the rhetoric of "standing" to deprive a person, whose interest is clearly protected by the law, of the opportunity to prove that his own rights have been violated. It is in precisely that dissembling enterprise that the Court indulges today.

The "case and controversy" limitation of Article III overrides no other provision of the Constitution.[4] To construe that Article to deny standing "to the class for whose sake [a] constitutional protection is given" simply turns the Constitution on its head. Article III was designed to provide a hospitable forum in which persons enjoying rights under the Constitution could assert those rights. How are we to discern whether a particular person is to be afforded a right of action in the courts? The Framers did not, of course, employ the modern vocabulary of standing. But this much is clear: The drafters of the Bill of Rights surely intended that the particular beneficiaries of their legacy should enjoy rights legally enforceable in courts of law. With these observations in mind, I turn to the problem of taxpayer standing in general, and this case in particular.

II.   A.   *Frothingham's reasoning remains obscure.*[5] The principal interpretive difficulty lies in the manner in which Frothingham chose to blend the language of policy with seemingly absolute statements about jurisdiction.

3. Of course, we generally permit persons to press federal suits even when the injury complained of is not obviously within the realm of injuries that a particular statutory or constitutional provision was designed to guard against. We term that circumstance one of "third-party standing." [W]e have only rarely interposed a bar to "third-party standing," particularly when constitutional violations are alleged. Indeed, the only firm exception to this generally permissive attitude toward third-party suits is the restriction on taxpayer suits. [Footnote by Justice Brennan.]

4. When the Constitution makes it clear that a particular person is to be protected from a particular form of government action, then that person has a "right" to be free of that action; when that right is infringed, then there is injury, and a personal stake, within the meaning of Article III. [Footnote by Justice Brennan.]

5. The question apparently remains open whether Frothingham stated a prudential limitation or identified an Article III barrier. It was generally agreed at the time of Flast, and clearly the view of Justice Harlan in dissent, that the rule stated reflected prudential and policy considerations, not constitutional limitations. Perhaps the case is most usefully understood as a "substantive" declaration of the legal rights of a taxpayer with respect to government spending, coupled with a prudential restriction on the taxpayer's ability to raise the claims of third parties. Under any construction, however, Frothingham must give way to a taxpayer's suit brought under the Establishment Clause. [Footnote by Justice Brennan.]

[Frothingham] stressed the indirectness of the taxpayer's injury. But, *as a matter of Article III standing*, if the causal relationship is sufficiently certain, the length of the causal chain is irrelevant. [The] concept of taxpayer injury necessarily recognizes the continuing stake of the taxpayer in the disposition of the Treasury to which he has contributed his taxes, and his right to have those funds put to lawful uses. Until Frothingham there was nothing in our precedents to indicate that this concept [was] inconsistent with the framework of rights and remedies established by the Federal Constitution.

The explanation for the limit on federal taxpayer "standing" imposed by Frothingham must be sought in more substantive realms. The Frothingham rule may be seen as founded solely on the prudential judgment by the Court that precipitate and unnecessary interference in the activities of a coequal branch of government should be avoided. Alternatively, Frothingham may be construed as resting upon an unarticulated, constitutionally established barrier between Congress' power to tax and its power to spend, which barrier makes it analytically impossible to mount an assault on the former through a challenge to the latter. But it is sufficient for present purposes to say that Frothingham held that the federal taxpayer has no continuing legal interest in the affairs of the Treasury analogous to a shareholder's continuing interest in the conduct of a corporation.

Whatever its provenance, the general rule of Frothingham displays sound judgment: Courts must be circumspect in dealing with the taxing power in order to avoid unnecessary intrusion into the functions of the legislative and executive branches. Congress' *purpose* in taxing will not ordinarily affect the validity of the tax. Unless the tax *operates* unconstitutionally, the taxpayer may not object to the use of his funds. Mrs. Frothingham's argument, that the use of tax funds for purposes unauthorized by the Constitution amounted to a violation of due process, did not provide her with the required legal interest because the Due Process Clause of the Fifth Amendment does not protect taxpayers against increases in tax liability. Mrs. Frothingham's claim was thus reduced to an assertion of "the States' interest in their legislative prerogatives," a third-party claim that could properly be barred.[6] But in Flast the Court faced a different sort of constitutional claim, and found itself compelled to retreat from the general assertion in Frothingham that taxpayers have *no* interest in the disposition of their tax payments. To understand why Frothingham's bar necessarily gave way in the face of an Establishment Clause claim, we must examine the right asserted by a taxpayer making such a claim.

6. With respect to the enforcement of constitutional restrictions, we have not been overly elegant in defining the class of persons who may object to particular forms of government action. Only the constitutional minimum of injury-in-fact has been required. [Nevertheless], I do not suggest that the Frothingham limitation on federal taxpayer suits should be abandoned. The barrier it evinces between the taxing power and the spending power, whether it be deemed one of constitutional construction or judicial prudence, reflects fundamental conceptions about the nature of the legislative process, and is, in any event, now firmly embedded in our cases. That barrier is necessarily pierced, however, by an Establishment Clause claim. [Footnote by Justice Brennan.]

B.   In 1947, nine Justices of this Court recognized that the Establishment Clause does impose a very definite restriction on the power to tax. [Everson, in sec. 1A of the preceding chapter.]   In determining whether the law challenged in Everson was one "respecting an establishment of religion," the Court [examined] the historic meaning of the constitutional [provision —the Establishment Clause], "particularly with respect to the imposition of taxes." [It] is clear in the light of this history, that one of the primary purposes of the Establishment Clause was to prevent the use of tax monies for religious purposes. *The taxpayer was the direct and intended beneficiary of the prohibition on financial aid to religion.* [It] seems obvious that all the Justices who participated in Everson would have agreed with Justice Jackson's succinct statement of the question presented: "Is it constitutional to tax this complainant to pay the cost of carrying pupils to Church schools of one specified denomination?" Given this view of the issues, could it fairly be doubted that this taxpayer alleged injury in precisely the form that the Establishment Clause sought to make actionable? [7]

C.   [The] test of standing formulated by the Court in Flast sought to reconcile the developing doctrine of taxpayer "standing" with the Court's historical understanding that the Establishment Clause was intended to prohibit the federal government from using tax funds for the advancement of religion, and thus the constitutional imperative of taxpayer standing in certain cases brought pursuant to the Establishment Clause.   The two-pronged "nexus" test offered by the Court, despite its general language, is best understood as "a determinant of standing of plaintiffs alleging only injury as taxpayers who challenge alleged violations of the Establishment and Free Exercise Clauses of the First Amendment," and not as a general statement of standing principles.   The test explains what forms of governmental action may be attacked by someone alleging *only* taxpayer status, and, without ruling out the possibility that history might reveal another similarly founded provision, explains why an Establishment Clause claim is treated differently from any other assertion that the federal government has exceeded the bounds of the law in allocating its largesse.   Thus, consistent with Doremus, Flast required, as the first prong of its test, that the taxpayer demonstrate a logical connection between his taxpayer status and the type of legislation attacked.   [As] the second prong, consistent with the prohibition of taxpayer claims of the kind advanced in Frothingham, appellants were required to show a connection between their status and the precise nature of the infringement alleged.

---

7.   Justice Jackson, writing for the Court in [Doremus], explored the limitations of taxpayers standing under the Establishment Clause.   [The] Court [in Doremus] had no difficulty distinguishing Everson: "Everson showed a measurable appropriation or disbursement of school-district funds occasioned solely by the activities complained of.   This complaint does not."   The difference between the two cases is relevant to the "standing" of taxpayers generally and most especially to taxpayers asserting claims under the Establishment Clause, for it is clear that even under the Establishment Clause the taxpayer's protection was against the use of his funds and not against the conduct of the government generally.   The distinction between Doremus and Everson may be phrased alternatively: Everson was injured in a manner comprehended by the Establishment Clause, and Doremus was not. [Footnote by Justice Brennan.]

[The] nexus test that the Court "announced" sought to maintain necessary continuity with prior cases, and set forth principles to guide future cases involving taxpayer standing. But Flast did not depart from the principle that no judgment about standing should be made without a fundamental understanding of the rights at issue. The two-part Flast test did not supply the rationale for the Court's decision, but rather its exposition: That rationale was supplied by an understanding of the nature of the restrictions on government power imposed by the Constitution and the intended beneficiaries of those restrictions.

It may be that Congress can tax for almost any reason, or for no reason at all. There is, so far as I have been able to discern, but one constitutionally imposed limit on that authority. Congress cannot use tax money to support a church, or to encourage religion. That is "*the* forbidden exaction." In absolute terms the history of the Establishment Clause of the First Amendment makes this clear. History also makes it clear that the federal taxpayer is a singularly "proper and appropriate party to invoke a federal court's jurisdiction" to challenge a federal bestowal of largesse as a violation of the Establishment Clause. Each, and indeed every, federal taxpayer suffers precisely the injury that the Establishment Clause guards against when the federal government directs that funds be taken from the pocketbooks of the citizenry and placed into the coffers of the ministry.   .   .   .

III.   Blind to history, the Court attempts to distinguish this case from Flast by wrenching snippets of language from our opinions, and by perfunctorily applying that language under color of the first prong of Flast's two-part nexus test. The tortuous distinctions thus produced are specious, at best: at worst, they are pernicious to our constitutional heritage.

First, the Court finds this case different from Flast because here the "source of [plaintiff's] complaint is not a *congressional* action, but a decision by HEW to transfer a parcel of federal property." This attempt at distinction cannot withstand scrutiny. Flast involved a challenge to the actions of [officials] of HEW, in disbursing funds under the Elementary and Secondary Education Act of 1965 to "religious and sectarian" schools. [It] may be that the Court is concerned with the adequacy of respondents' pleading; respondents [unlike the challengers in Flast] have not, in so many words, asked for a declaration that the "Federal Property and Administrative Services Act is unconstitutional and void to the extent that it authorizes HEW's actions." I would not construe their complaint so narrowly. More fundamentally, no clear division can be drawn in this context between actions of the legislative branch and those of the executive branch. [I]t is difficult to conceive of an expenditure for which the last governmental actor, either implementing directly the legislative will, or acting within the scope of legislatively delegated authority, is not an Executive Branch official. The First Amendment binds the Government as a whole, regardless of which branch is at work in a particular instance.

The Court's second purported distinction between this case and Flast is equally unavailing. The majority finds it "decisive" that the [Act] "was an evident exercise of Congress' power under the Property Clause, Art. IV, § 3, cl. 2," while the government action in Flast was taken under Art. I, § 8.

The Court relies on [Richardson and Reservists] to support the distinction between the two clauses, noting that those cases involved alleged deviations from the requirements of Art. I, § 9, cl. 7, and Art. I, § 6, cl. 2, respectively. The standing defect in each case was *not*, however, the failure to allege a violation of the Spending Clause; rather, the taxpayers in those cases had not complained of the distribution of government largesse, and thus failed to meet the essential requirement of taxpayer standing recognized in Doremus.

It can make no constitutional difference in the case before us whether the donation to the defendant here was in the form of a cash grant to build a facility, see Tilton v. Richardson [10th Ed., p. 1580; Ind.Rts., p. 1200], or in the nature of a gift of property including a facility already built. That this is a meaningless distinction is illustrated by Tilton. In that case, taxpayers were afforded standing to object to the fact that the Government had not received adequate assurance that if the property that it financed for use as an educational facility was later converted to religious uses, it would receive full value for the property, as the Constitution requires. The complaint here is precisely that, although the property at issue is actually being used for a sectarian purpose, the government has not received, nor demanded, full value payment. Whether undertaken pursuant to the Property Clause or the Spending Clause, the breach of the Establishment Clause, and the relationship of the taxpayer to that breach, is precisely the same.[8]

IV. Plainly hostile to the Framers' understanding of the Establishment Clause, and Flast's enforcement of that understanding, the Court vents that hostility under the guise of standing, "to slam the courthouse door against plaintiffs who [as the Framers intended] are entitled to full consideration of their [Establishment Clause] claims on the merits." Therefore, I dissent.

Justice STEVENS, dissenting.

In Parts I, II, and III of his dissenting opinion, Justice Brennan demonstrates that respondent taxpayers have standing to mount an Establishment Clause challenge. [For] the Court to hold that plaintiffs' standing depends on whether the Government's transfer was an exercise of its power to spend money, on the one hand, or its power to dispose of tangible property, on the other, is to trivialize the standing doctrine. [T]he plaintiffs' invocation of the Establishment Clause was of decisive importance in resolving the standing issue in [Flast].

[Today] the Court holds, in effect, that the Judiciary has no greater role in enforcing the Establishment Clause than in enforcing other "norm[s] of conduct which the federal government is bound to honor," such as the Accounts Clause [Richardson] and the Incompatibility Clause [Reservists]. Ironically, however, its decision rests on the premise that the difference between a disposition of funds pursuant to the Spending Clause and a disposi-

---

8. The Framers of the First Amendment could not have viewed it as less objectionable to the taxpayer to learn that his tax funds were used by his government to purchase property, construct a church, and deed the property to a religious order, than to find his government providing the funds to a church to undertake its own construction. So far as the Establishment Clause, and the position of the taxpayer are concerned, the situations are interchangeable. . . . . [Footnote by Justice Brennan.]

tion of realty pursuant to the Property Clause is of fundamental jurisprudential significance. With all due respect, I am persuaded that the essential holding of Flast v. Cohen attaches special importance to the Establishment Clause and does not permit the drawing of a tenuous distinction between the Spending Clause and the Property Clause. For this reason, and for the reasons stated in Parts I, II, and III of Justice Brennan's opinion, I would affirm the judgment of the Court of Appeals.

10th ED., p. 1644; IND. RTS., p. 1264
Add after Note 2 following Warth v. Seldin:

3. *Multiple claims for relief.* In view of the focus in Warth on the relationship between the particular plaintiff and the type of relief sought, what type of inquiry is appropriate when a plaintiff claims several different forms of relief? In a case involving the victim of an allegedly unconstitutional police "chokehold," the Court indicated that separate inquiries must be conducted, and on that basis denied standing to claim injunctive relief although it was plain that there was standing to bring an action for damages. LOS ANGELES v. LYONS, 461 U.S. —— (1983), discussed below, addition to 10th Ed., p. 1664; Ind.Rts., p. 1284.

10th ED., p. 1644; IND. RTS., p. 1264
Add to footnote 5:

For a discussion of the modern standing cases (in the course of a reexamination of Flast v. Cohen), see Valley Forge College v. Americans United, 454 U.S. 464 (1982), printed immediately above.

10th ED., p. 1647; IND. RTS., p. 1267
Add after first paragraph of footnote 4:

In two cases decided during the 1982–1983 Term, a unanimous Court found that "special factors counselling hesitation" were present and thus refused to imply private remedies directly from the Constitution. In Chappell v. Wallace, 462 U.S. —— (1983), these factors consisted of the special nature of the military, and its distinct and parallel system of justice, causing the Court, in an opinion written by Chief Justice Burger, to refuse to allow military personnel to sue their superior officers for damages for alleged constitutional violations. And in Bush v. Lucas, 462 U.S. —— (1983), Justice Stevens wrote for the Court in refusing to imply a damages remedy directly from the Constitution for a federal civil service employee who alleged that he had been demoted in retaliation for exercising his First Amendment rights. Relying heavily on the existence of the elaborate federal civil service system, Justice Stevens concluded that deference to Congress in light of this system once again counselled hesitation. "Because [these First Amendment] claims arise out of an employment relationship that is governed by comprehensive procedural and substantive provisions giving meaningful remedies against the United States, we conclude that it would be inappropriate for us to supplement that regulatory scheme with a new judicial remedy."

10th ED., p. 1647; IND. RTS., p. 1267
Add at end of footnote 4:

For a recent revival of Justice Powell's separation of powers objections to the majority's modern tendency to imply private rights of action from congressional acts, see Merrill Lynch, Pierce, Fenner & Smith v. Curran, 456 U.S. 353 (1982).

10th ED., p. 1650; IND. RTS., p. 1270
Add as footnote after first sentence of paragraph:

Note, however, Chief Justice Burger's majority opinion in H. L. v. Matheson, 450 U.S. 398 (1981), refusing to grant standing to a minor to raise an on-the-face overbreadth attack on a state law requiring physicians to notify parents before performing abortions on minors. The appellant sought to challenge the application of the law to *all* unmarried minors, including mature and emancipated ones, even though she was a dependent minor who did not claim that she was mature. The case is noted above (addition to 10th Ed., p. 614; Ind.Rts., p. 234).

10th ED., p. 1655; IND. RTS., p. 1275
Add to the last paragraph of footnote 6:

For a rare reliance on United States v. Johnson—the ban on "collusive" suits —see Justice Blackmun's dissent in Nixon v. Fitzgerald, 457 U.S. 731 (1982) (more fully noted above, addition to 10th Ed., p. 448). The majority decided the merits of the case (and granted the President absolute immunity from civil liability) even though the parties had made an agreement under which Nixon paid $142,000 to Fitzgerald, with only $28,000 "left riding on an outcome favorable to [Fitzgerald], with nothing at all to be paid if [Nixon] prevailed." In dissenting on this issue, Justice Blackmun, joined by Justices Brennan and Marshall, stated: "Surely, had the details of this agreement been known at the time the petition for certiorari came before the Court, certiorari would have been denied. I cannot escape the feeling that this long-undisclosed agreement comes close to being a wager on the outcome of the case, with all of the implications that entails. [The] pertinent question here is not whether the case is moot, but whether this is the *kind* of case or controversy over which we should exercise our power of discretionary review. Cf. United States v. Johnson. Apprised of all developments, I therefore would have dismissed the writ as having been improvidently granted. The Court, it seems to me, brushes by this factor in order to resolve an issue of profound consequence that otherwise would not be here. Lacking support for such a dismissal, however, I join the dissent [on the merits]."

10th ED., p. 1664; IND. RTS., p. 1284
Add after Note 1:

1A. *Los Angeles v. Lyons.* O'Shea v. Littleton and Rizzo v. Goode were relied upon by the Court in LOS ANGELES v. LYONS, 461 U.S. —— (1983), to deny standing in a case challenging the use of "chokeholds" by the Los Angeles Police Department. Justice WHITE's majority opinion found O'Shea and Rizzo controlling in determining that Lyons lacked standing to bring an action for injunctive relief against the Los Angeles Police because "he was [un]likely to suffer future injury from the use of chokeholds by police officers."

Lyons himself had in fact been the victim of the very type of chokehold, imposed during the course of a stop for a motor vehicle violation, that provided the basis for his claim. There was as a result no question but that Lyons had standing to bring an action for damages, in the course of which the constitutionality of the police practices could be adjudicated. But the Court decided that the "case or controversy" requirement of Article III must be satisfied with respect to each separate claim for relief. Thus the fact that the claim for damages satisfied the requirements of Article III with respect to Lyons did not mean that all claims he brought could be adjudicated. "In order to establish an actual controversy [for the purposes of obtaining injunctive relief], Lyons would have had not only to allege that he would have another encounter with the police but also to make the incredible assertion either, (1) that *all* police officers in Los Angeles *always* choke any citizen with whom they happen to have an encounter whether for the purpose of arrest, issuing a citation or for questioning or, (2) that the City ordered or authorized police officers to act in such manner. Although Count V alleged that the City authorized the use of the control holds in situations where deadly force was not threatened, it did not indicate why Lyons might be realistically threatened by police officers who acted within the strictures of the City's policy."

The Court's decision to conduct separate Article III standing inquiries for damage and equitable relief claims brought by the same plaintiff against the same defendant in the same action prompted a lengthy and vigorous dissent by Justice MARSHALL, joined by Justices Brennan, Blackmun, and Stevens. "By fragmenting the standing inquiry and imposing a separate standing hurdle with respect to each form of relief sought, the decision today departs significantly from this Court's traditional conception of the standing requirement and of the remedial powers of the federal courts. We have never required more than that a plaintiff have standing to litigate a claim. Whether he will be entitled to obtain particular forms of relief should he prevail has never been understood to be an issue of standing. In determining whether a plaintiff has standing, we have always focused on his personal stake in the outcome of the controversy, not on the issues sought to be litigated, [Flast], or the [precise nature of the relief sought.]"

10th ED., p. 1673; IND. RTS., p. 1293
Add to footnote 3:

In Anderson v. Celebrezze, 460 U.S. —— (1983), the Court made one of its strongest recent statements concerning "the limited precedential effect to be accorded summary dispositions." In his majority opinion, Justice Stevens went on to state that "[t]he Court of Appeals quite properly concluded that our summary affirmances [were] 'a rather slender reed' on which to rest its decision. We have often recognized that the precedential effect of a summary affirmance extends no further than 'the precise issues presented and necessarily decided by those actions.' A summary disposition affirms only the judgment of the court below, and no more may be read into our action than was necessary to sustain that judgment."

10th ED., p. 1675; IND. RTS., p. 1295
Add to footnote 4:

Note also the divided Court's dismissal of an appeal in Doe v. Delaware, 450 U.S. 382 (1981) (noted above, addition to 10th Ed., p. 635; Ind.Rts., p. 255). The case raised important and controversial questions regarding the constitutionally mandated standards regarding burdens of proof in state proceedings for termination of parental rights. After hearing argument, the majority summarily dismissed the appeal "for want of a properly presented federal question." Justice Brennan's dissent, joined by Justice White, called that disposition "unprecedented and inexplicable." He stated: "The appellate jurisdiction of this Court is not discretionary. Having raised the federal constitutional challenge to the [provision] under which their parental rights were terminated, and having received a final judgment from the highest court of State upholding the statute and affirming the termination order, appellants have a *right* to appellate review." He insisted that Naim v. Naim was distinguishable, claiming that the Court's dismissal of that appeal in 1956 "for want of a properly presented federal question" was "best understood [as] attributable to 'the failure of the parties to bring here all questions relevant to the disposition of the case.'" He added: "In the instant case, there is no such failure." He noted, however, that there had been changes in the factual circumstances and in the applicable state statute since the initial state court proceeding in the case, and accordingly urged that "the proper disposition of this case is to vacate and remand rather than to dismiss for want of a properly presented federal queston." He insisted that this was "not merely to quibble over words," explaining: "To vacate and remand is to recognize that supervening events have made further state court proceedings necessary before this Court can reach the constitutional question; to dismiss is to end the litigation, leaving [the appellants] without any means to vindicate their parental rights." In a separate dissent, Justice Stevens argued that the Court should have decided one of the federal questions—the proper standard of proof in termination cases—and insisted that none of the post-trial changes in circumstances barred adjudication of this issue.

10th ED., p. 1676; IND. RTS., p. 1296
Add to Note b (before Sec. 4B):

Three Justices in HAIG v. AGEE, 453 U.S. 280 (1981), viewed the majority opinion as abandoning the statutory interpretation approach of Kent v. Dulles. Haig v. Agee, like Kent, challenged the State Department's authority to revoke passports in certain cases. But in Agee, in contrast to Kent, the majority found that the challenged regulation was justified by the broad regulatory authority granted to the State Department in the Passport Act of 1926.

The Agee case was brought by a former CIA employee who was engaged in a campaign "to expose CIA officers and agents." His activities abroad had revealed the identities of alleged undercover CIA agents. The State Department revoked his passport, relying on a regulation which authorizes passport revocation where "the Secretary determines that the national's activities abroad are causing or are likely to cause serious damage to the national security or the foreign policy of the United States." The regulation was issued under a broad provision of the 1926 Passport Act authorizing the Secretary to issue passports "under such rules as the President shall designate and prescribe."

Chief Justice BURGER's majority opinion found this statutory grant sufficient to sustain the challenged regulation. He relied primarily on what he considered to be a longstanding "congressional recognition of executive authority to withhold passports on the basis of substantial reasons of national security and foreign policy." The Chief Justice rejected Agee's argument that, on the basis of Kent v. Dulles, "the only way the Executive can establish implicit congressional approval is by proof of longstanding and consistent *enforcement* of the claimed power: that is, by showing that many passports were revoked on national security and foreign policy grounds." Concededly, there was no evidence of any such executive practice. But Chief Justice Burger thought this immaterial. Congressional approval could be inferred, he insisted, because the executive policy was "substantial" and because it had been consistently asserted by the executive branch. (For the Court's rejection of Agee's constitutional challenges, see the additional note on this case above, addition to 10th Ed., p. 1176; Ind. Rts., p. 796.)

Justice BRENNAN's dissent, joined by Justice Marshall, charged that the majority had "departed from the approach set forth in Kent v. Dulles— as well as in a later passport case, Zemel v. Rusk, 381 U.S. 1 (1965)—for determining whether Congress has delegated to the Executive Branch the authority to deny a passport." He asserted that "neither Zemel nor Kent holds that a longstanding Executive *policy* or *construction* is sufficient proof that Congress has implicitly authorized the Secretary's action. The cases hold that an administrative *practice* must be demonstrated; in fact Kent unequivocally states that mere *construction* by the Executive—no matter how longstanding and consistent—is *not* sufficient." He added: "The presence of sensitive constitutional questions in the passport revocation context cautions against applying the normal rule that administrative constructions in cases of statutory construction are to be given great weight.   Only when Congress had maintained its silence in the face of a consistent and substantial pattern of actual passport denials or revocations [can] this Court be sure that Congress is aware of the Secretary's actions and has implicitly approved that exercise of discretion.   [The] point that Kent and Zemel make, and that today's opinion should make, is that the Executive's authority to revoke passports touches an area fraught with important Constitutional rights, and that the Court should therefore 'construe narrowly all delegated powers that curtail or dilute them.' Kent v. Dulles.   [I] suspect that this case is a prime example of the adage that 'bad facts make bad law.'   Philip Agee is hardly a model representative of our Nation.   [But just] as the Constitution protects both popular and unpopular speech, it likewise protects both popular and unpopular travelers. And it is important to remember that this decision applies not only to Philip Agee, whose activities could be perceived as harming the national security, but also to other citizens who may merely disagree with Government foreign policy and express their views.   [I] disagree with the Court's sub silentio overruling of [Kent and Zemel]." *

10th ED., p. 1688; IND. RTS., p. 1308
Add to footnote 12:

By 1982, when Middlesex Cty. Ethics Comm. v. Garden St. Bar Assn., 457 U.S. 423, was decided, the prevailing opinion was able to make the general statement: "The policies underlying Younger are fully applicable to noncriminal judicial proceedings when important state interests are involved. Moore v. Sims ; Huffman v. Pursue, Ltd." In Middlesex, the Court held that "a federal court should abstain from considering a challenge to the constitutionality of disciplinary rules [regarding unethical conduct by attorneys] that are the subject of a pending state disciplinary proceeding within the jurisdiction of the New Jersey Supreme Court." Chief Justice Burger's opinion for the Court stated that "state bar disciplinary hearings within the constitutionally prescribed jurisdiction of the State Supreme Court constitute an ongoing state judicial proceeding," that such proceedings "implicate important state interests," and that there was "an adequate opportunity in the state proceedings to raise [the federal] constitutional challenges." Justice Brennan, concurring in the judgment, noted that he continued "to adhere to [his] view [that] Younger v. Harris is in general inapplicable to civil proceedings." He supported the result here because the "traditional and primary responsibility of state courts for establishing and enforcing standards for members of their bars and the quasi-criminal nature of bar disciplinary proceedings call for exceptional deference by the courts." 1

10th ED., p. 1688; IND. RTS., p. 1308
Insert before Sec. 5:

5. *"Comity" as a barrier to federal court actions for damages.*   In FAIR ASSESSMENT IN REAL ESTATE v. McNARY, 454 U.S. 100 (1981), a sharply divided Court, drawing in part on Younger v. Harris principles, held that "taxpayers are barred by the principle of comity from assert-

---

* In a concurring notation, Justice BLACKMUN acknowledged that the Court was "cutting back somewhat" upon Kent and Zemel. He added: "I would have preferred to have the Court disavow forthrightly the aspects of Zemel and Kent that may suggest that evidence of a longstanding Executive policy or construction in this area is not probative of the issue of congressional authorization. Nonetheless, believing this is what the Court in effect has done, I join its opinion."

1. Justice Marshall, joined by Justices Brennan, Blackmun and Stevens, also submitted a brief statement concurring in the judgment.

ing § 1983 actions against the validity of state tax systems in federal courts." The case involved a § 1983 action for damages brought by taxpayers challenging the allegedly unconstitutional administration of a state property tax system. Justice REHNQUIST's majority opinion perceived two "conflicting lines of authority" bearing on the case. On the one hand, the Tax Injunction Act of 1937 and antecedent decisions of the Court reflected "the fundamental principle of comity between federal courts and state governments that is essential to 'Our Federalism,' particularly in the area of state taxation." That line of authority barred at least federal injunctive and declaratory judgment challenges to state tax laws. On the other hand, federal cases since Monroe v. Pape in 1961 indicated that "comity does not apply where § 1983 is involved." Both lines of authority "cannot govern this case," Justice Rehnquist noted. He chose to go in the direction of federal restraint: in cases such as this, "the principle of comity controls." He explained that "comity" had been relied upon in several modern cases outside the state tax area: "Its fullest articulation was given in the now familiar language of Younger v. Harris. [The] principles of federalism recognized in Younger have not been limited to federal court interference in state criminal proceedings, but have been extended to some state civil actions. Although these modern expressions of comity have been limited in their application to federal cases which seek to enjoin state judicial proceedings, a limitation which we do not abandon here, they illustrate the principles that bar petitioners' suit under § 1983. [P]etitioners' § 1983 action would be no less disruptive of Missouri's tax system than would the historic equitable efforts to enjoin the collection of taxes, efforts which were early held barred by considerations of comity."*

A lengthy opinion by Justice BRENNAN, joined by Justices Marshall, Stevens and O'Connor, strongly disagreed with the majority's approach, even though the dissenters supported the result (but solely on the ground that the petitioners had failed to exhaust state administrative remedies). Justice Brennan emphasized: "I cannot agree that this case, and the jurisdiction of the federal courts over an action for damages brought pursuant to express congressional authority, is to be governed by applying a 'principle of comity' grounded solely on this Court's notion of an appropriate division of responsibility between the federal and state judicial systems. Subject only to constitutional constraints, it is exclusively Congress' responsibility to determine the jurisdiction of the federal courts. Federal courts have historically acted within their

* Contrast the majority's approach in McNary with a decision a few months later in Patsy v. Florida Board of Regents, 457 U.S. 496 (1982). In Patsy, the majority adhered to prior decisions by holding that exhaustion of state administrative remedies is not required as a prerequisite to bringing a § 1983 action. Justice Marshall's majority opinion (with only Justice Powell and Chief Justice Burger dissenting) rejected the argument that the exhaustion requirement should be imposed because "it would further various policies"—i.e., "an exhaustion requirement would lessen the perceived burden that § 1983 actions impose on federal courts; would further the goal of comity and improve federal-state relations; [and] would enable the [state administrative] agency [to] enlighten the federal court's ultimate decision." Justice Marshall replied that "policy considerations alone cannot justify judicially imposed exhaustion unless exhaustion is consistent with congressional intent."

assigned jurisdiction in accordance with established principles respecting the prudent exercise of equitable power.　But this practice lends no credence to the authority which the Court asserts today to renounce jurisdiction over an entire class of damages actions brought pursuant to 42 U.S.C. § 1983.　[Where] Congress has granted the federal courts jurisdiction, we are not free to repudiate that authority.　[The] power to control the jurisdiction of the lower federal courts is assigned by the Constitution to Congress, not to this Court. In its haste to rid the federal courts of a class of cases that it thinks unfit for federal scrutiny, the Court today departs from this fundamental precept. [T]here is absolutely no support, in either the cases of this Court or in Congress' action, for total abdication of federal power in this field."†

10th ED., p. 1712; IND. RTS., p. 1332
Add to footnote 2:

The Court has sustained some deviations from the "one-person one-vote" rule in the context of "property owners only" elections for directors of special purpose governmental units such as water districts. For the most recent example, see Ball v. James, 451 U.S. 355 (1981) (addition to 10th Ed., p. 932; Ind.Rts., p. 552).

10th ED., p. 1713; IND. RTS., p. 1333
Add to Note 2a:

In KARCHER v. DAGGETT, 463 U.S. —— (1983), a 5–4 majority continued to adhere to Kirkpatrick and White in requiring that states, in

† For another reliance on comity and federalism concerns to curtail the federal courts' statutory jurisdiction, see Lehman v. Lycoming Cty. Children's Services, 458 U.S. —— (1982). The majority held that the habeas corpus statute, 28 U.S.C. § 2254, did not confer "jurisdiction on the federal courts to consider collateral challenges to state-court judgments involuntarily terminating parental rights." The statute grants the habeas corpus remedy to persons "in custody pursuant to the judgment of a State court," but Justice Powell's majority opinion concluded that "extending the federal writ to challenges to state child-custody decisions [would] be an unprecedented expansion of the jurisdiction of the lower federal courts." He pointed to "[f]ederalism concerns" as a reason for denying jurisdiction. Justice Blackmun's dissent, joined by Justices Brennan and Marshall, sympathized with the Court's result, but objected to putting it in jurisdictional terms. Justice Blackmun noted that "the literal statutory requisites for the exercise of § 2254 federal habeas corpus jurisdiction are satisfied here" and argued that the Court should have achieved "the same practical result [without] decreeing a complete withdrawal of federal jurisdiction." He supported a "broad district court discretion to withhold the writ in all but the most extraordinary cases" but could not "understand why the

Court's explicit balancing approach yields a strict *jurisdictional* bar." In defense, Justice Powell rejected the dissent's suggestion "that comity and federalism concerns cannot inform a court's construction of a statute in determining a question of jurisdiction over certain kinds of cases. But in [McNary], precisely those concerns led this Court to conclude that § 1983 does not confer jurisdiction on the federal courts to hear suits for tax refunds when state law provides an adequate remedy."

Compare California v. Grace Brethren Church, 457 U.S. 393 (1982) (already noted above, as addition to 10th Ed., p. 1566; Ind.Rts., p. 1186). There, the majority relied on an expansive reading of the Tax Injunction Act, not on "comity" principles, to bar exercise of federal jurisdiction in a declaratory judgment action challenging, under the Religion Clauses of the First Amendment, coverage under the Social Security Act of religious schools unaffiliated with any church. Justice O'Connor's majority opinion concluded that the Tax Injunction Act prohibits federal district courts from issuing declaratory judgments as well as injunctions holding state tax laws unconstitutional. Justice Stevens' dissent, joined by Justice Blackmun, charged the majority with ignoring "the plain meaning of the statute and the limited concerns that gave rise to its enactment."

congressional districting, "come as nearly as practicable to population equality." In the context of a New Jersey apportionment with a maximum variance of approximately 0.7%, the Court, with Justice Brennan writing for the majority, maintained its refusal to acknowledge a *de minimus* exception as long as the state was unable to show why more precise results could not be achieved "using the best available census data." The Court did, however, indicate that certain "consistently applied legislative policies might justify some variance, including, for instance, making districts compact, respecting municipal boundaries, preserving the cores of prior districts, and avoiding contests between incumbent Representatives. [The] State must, however, show with some specificity that a particular objective required the specific deviations in its plan, rather than simply relying on general assertions." Because New Jersey could not make such a showing, even the relatively minor variations were deemed fatal. Justice White, joined by Chief Justice Burger and Justices Powell and Rehnquist, dissented, concluding that if Kirkpatrick and White required overturning an apportionment with so little variance, then it was time that those cases be reconsidered.

10th ED., p. 1714; IND. RTS., p. 1334
Add at end of Note 2b:

The Court continued its more relaxed scrutiny of state legislative apporionment in BROWN v. THOMSON, 463 U.S. —— (1983). Under the Wyoming reapportionment formula, Niobrara County would have been entitled to no representatives, but pursuant to a provision of the state constitution, it was allowed one representative, even though the result, in the case of this county, was a disparity of 60% below the mean. Despite this disparity, however, the Court, with Justice Powell writing for the majority, upheld the apportionment. Relying on Abate and Mahan, Justice Powell determined that the historical adherence to county boundaries in Wyoming justified even a disparity of this magnitude. Moreover, the Court evaluated the disparity marginally, in terms of how the statewide apportionment would be affected if this one county's representative was taken away. Because the grant of a representative to this county was not in itself "a significant cause of the population deviations" that existed in Wyoming apportionment, the Court refused to overturn the apportionment. Justice Brennan, joined by Justices White, Marshall, and Blackmun, dissented, finding the 60% deviation for this county and the 89% maximum deviation for the state as a whole in excess of constitutionally tolerable limits.

10th ED., p. 1716; IND. RTS., p. 1336
Add as footnote at end of Note 3:

In Karcher v. Daggett, 463 U.S. —— (1983), discussed above, addition to 10th Ed., p. 1713; Ind.Rts., p. 1333, Justice Stevens, concurring, and Justice Powell, dissenting, both wrote lengthy opinions urging that purely political gerrymandering should be considered violative of the equal protection clause.

Appendix A

TABLE OF JUSTICES

10th ED. and IND. RTS., p. A–7 (Appendix A)
Add to Table of Justices:

Appointed by President Reagan, Republican from California
(1981– ——)

O'Connor, Sandra Day (1930– ——). Rep. from Ariz. (1981–
——).

* On July 7, 1981, President Reagan announced that he would nominate Sandra Day O'Connor, an appellate court judge from Arizona, to fill the vacancy created by Justice Stewart's retirement. (Justice Stewart had announced on June 18 that he would retire from the Court on July 3, 1981.) Justice O'Connor took the oath of office on Sept. 25, 1981.

Appendix B

THE U.S. CONSTITUTION

10th ED. and IND. RTS., p. B–16
Add to footnote †:

The time for ratification of the proposed 27th Amendment, the Equal Rights Amendment, expired on June 30, 1982. See the Note, "The expiration (and aftermath) of ERA," addition to 10th Ed., p. 885; Ind.Rts., p. 505, above.

†